When should I travel to get the best airfare?
Where do I go for answers to my travel questions?
What's the best and easiest way to plan and book my trip?

frommers.travelocity.com

Frommer's, the travel guide leader, has teamed up with **Travelocity.com**, the leader in online travel, to bring you an in-depth, easy-to-use resource designed to help you plan and book your trip online.

At **frommers.travelocity.com**, you'll find free online updates about your destination from the experts at Frommer's plus the outstanding travel planning and purchasing features of Travelocity.com. Travelocity.com provides reservations capabilities for 95 percent of all airline seats sold, more than 47,000 hotels, and over 50 car rental companies. In addition, Travelocity.com offers more than 2,000 exciting vacation and cruise packages. Travelocity.com puts you in complete control of your travel planning with these and other great features:

> **Expert travel guidance from Frommer's** - over 150 writers reporting from around the world!

> **Best Fare Finder** - an interactive calendar tells you when to travel to get the best airfare

> **Fare Watcher** - we'll track airfare changes to your favorite destinations

> **Dream Maps** - a mapping feature that suggests travel opportunities based on your budget

> **Shop Safe Guarantee** - 24 hours a day / 7 days a week live customer service, and more!

Whether traveling on a tight budget, looking for a quick weekend getaway, or planning the trip of a lifetime, Frommer's guides and Travelocity.com will make your travel dreams a reality. You've bought the book, now book the trip!

Travelocity.com
A Sabre Company

Frommer's®

Other Great Guides for Your Trip:

Frommer's Atlanta

Frommer's Portable Charleston & Savannah

Frommer's USA

Frommer's Unofficial Guide to Atlanta

*Frommer's Unofficial Guide to the Great Smoky &
Blue Ridge Mountains*

*The Civil War Trust's Official Guide to the Civil War
Discovery Trail*

Here's what the critics say about Frommer's:

"Amazingly easy to use. Very portable, very complete."
—*Booklist*

♦

"Complete, concise, and filled with useful information."
—*New York Daily News*

♦

"Hotel information is close to encyclopedic."
—*Des Moines Sunday Register*

♦

"The only mainstream guide to list specific prices. The Walter
Cronkite of guidebooks—with all that implies."
—*Travel & Leisure*

The Carolinas & Georgia

5th Edition

by Darwin Porter
& Danforth Prince

HUNGRY MINDS, INC.
New York, NY • Cleveland, OH • Indianapolis, IN

ABOUT THE AUTHORS

Darwin Porter and **Danforth Prince** are coauthors of a number of best-selling Frommer's guides, notably England, France, the Caribbean, Italy, and Spain. Porter, a bureau chief for *The Miami Herald* at 21, was the author of the first ever Frommer's guide to Germany and has traveled extensively throughout the country ever since. He is joined by Prince, who was formerly of the Paris bureau of the *New York Times*.

PUBLISHED BY:
HUNGRY MINDS, INC.
909 Third Avenue
New York, NY 10022
www.frommers.com

ISBN 0-7645-6286-X
ISSN 1055-5420

Editor: Alexis Flippin
Production Editor: M. Faunette Johnston
Photo Editor: Richard Fox
Design by Michele Laseau
Cartographer: John Decamillis
Production by Hungry Minds Indianapolis Production Services
Front cover: Magnolia Plantation, South Carolina
Back cover: Coast Guard Cottage, Bald Head Island

SPECIAL SALES

For general information on Hungry Minds' products and services please contact our Customer Care department; within the U.S. at 800-762-2974, outside the U.S. at 317-572-3993 or fax 317-572-4002. For sales inquiries and reseller information, including discounts, bulk sales, customized editions, and premium sales, please contact our Customer Care department at 800-434-3422.

Manufactured in the United States of America

5 4 3 2 1

Contents

11   Hilton Head & the Low Country   223

12   Myrtle Beach & the Grand Strand   243

13   Columbia & the Heartland   270

14   The Upstate   283

15   Planning a Trip to Georgia   300

List of Maps

AN INVITATION TO THE READER

There are so many more of you than there are of us that this book can only be informed and enhanced when you share your experiences with us. We welcome your letters. Let us know when we've led you straight and when astray—and let us in on your secret finds, provided that you're willing to have them shared with other readers in future editions. Anticipating your letters, thanks in advance for your contributions. Please send correspondence to:

Frommer's The Carolinas & Georgia, 5th Edition
Hungry Minds, Inc.
909 Third Ave.
New York, NY 10022

AN ADDITIONAL NOTE

Please be advised that travel information is subject to change at any time—and this is especially true of prices. We therefore suggest that you write or call ahead for confirmation when making your travel plans. The authors, editors, and publisher cannot be held responsible for the experiences of readers while traveling. Your safety is important to us, however, so we encourage you to stay alert and be aware of your surroundings. Keep a close eye on cameras, purses, and wallets, all favorite targets of thieves and pickpockets.

WHAT THE SYMBOLS MEAN

❂ Frommer's Favorites

Our favorite places and experiences—outstanding for quality, value, or both.

The following abbreviations are used for credit cards:

AE	American Express	DISC	Discover
CB	Carte Blanche	MC	MasterCard
DC	Diners Club	V	Visa

FIND FROMMER'S ONLINE

www.frommers.com offers up-to-the-minute listings on almost 200 cities around the globe—including the latest bargains and candid, personal articles updated daily by Arthur Frommer himself. No other Web site offers such comprehensive and timely coverage of the world of travel.

The Best of the Carolinas & Georgia

From steep, sloping mountain forests to lush farmlands that evoke the English countryside, the Carolinas and Georgia offer a landscape as diverse and colorful as the personable demeanor of the region's residents.

The tri-state area has aged gracefully with time, leaving in place an amiable drawl and such culinary traditions as hot buttered grits and fresh boiled peanuts, yet it has also managed to rival its Northern competitors in technology and style. Long burdened with a "Scarlett" reputation cluttered with pickup trucks and good ol' boys, these Southern states now boast bright, neon-lighted cities complete with contemporary architecture, high-tech industry, exhilarating sports events, and intricately designed highways—not to mention big-city gridlock.

Still, the Old South lives on, at least in pockets, and some achingly pastoral countryscapes seem to be torn from the pages of such Deep South authors as Tennessee Williams, Eudora Welty, and William Faulkner. But it is in the bosom of the tri-state area, in a setting of old-style graciousness, that the muscular, gleaming New South engine of commerce, industry, and innovation powers on.

Clichés die hard, though, and Hollywood has been reluctant to let go of its love affair with the colorful Old South. Best-selling novels and Academy Award–winning screenplays continue to mine the mystique of a South clad in its own troublesome history. The region has become a major attraction for writers and movie producers lured by superb natural settings, historic ambience, and (in the case of the producers) beneficent right-to-work laws. So many movies have been made in and around Wilmington, North Carolina, that it has been dubbed "Hollywood East"; (the popular TV series "Dawson's Creek" is also filmed on location there).

The South of yore may live on in Hollywood, but the talk today is of the New South, a land characterized less by drawls and "y'alls" and more by a bright, intelligent group of people bringing culture and business to an area that once slept quietly by the cotton gin. These new sons and daughters of the South might invite "y'all to come back" for a second visit; but, they'll suggest that you bring a checkbook to buy their products (such as that set of high-end furniture manufactured in Lenoir) or that you invest in one of the mega pharmaceutical research labs that have set up shop in the Research Triangle of North Carolina.

The Carolinas and Georgia are no longer whistling "Dixie," but standing up and making their voices heard in the world marketplace. The voices reflect the diversity of a population that not so long ago faced considerable challenges regarding racial inequality, challenges that Georgia native son Martin Luther King, Jr., so eloquently called upon the nation to meet. One happy result of the efforts to surmount those challenges in recent years has been the reverse migration of many African-Americans from the North home to the South.

The New South has other voices, including the controversial, but now seriously aging Jesse Helms, the seemingly immortal but likely-to-expire-at-any-minute Strom Thurmond, and, of course, the dignified, soft-spoken peanut farmer from Plains who became president of the United States and is now an agent of world peace.

Visitors won't be alone in reveling in all that the New South has to offer: The Carolinas and Georgia are becoming major destinations for travelers. In the year 2000 alone, Atlanta hosted the Super Bowl, the PGA Tour Championship, and the Major League Baseball All-Star Game, and Charleston and Savannah were ranked third and sixth, respectively, as top cities in the country in *Condé Nast Traveler*'s Readers' Choice Awards 2000. From the Smoky Mountains to the sun-kissed Atlantic coastline, from the windswept dunes of Kitty Hawk all the way to Georgia's Suwannee River country and the Okefenokee Swamp, the tri-state area is attracting visitors by the millions.

Taken as a whole, the North Carolina/South Carolina/Georgia tri-state area is like a country unto itself. It's wildly diverse and packed with places to see and things to do. We've traveled the back roads of the Carolinas and Georgia since we were kids, exploring the Old South and the New South. That's why we feel qualified to bring you our suggestions of the best, with the understanding, of course, that there's always plenty of room for disagreement. Here are our picks for the cream of the crop.

1 The Best Scenic Drives

- **The Outer Banks** (North Carolina): If you can get past the overly crowded high-ways in summer and the tawdry development, prepare yourself for one of the strangest and most beautiful natural geographical areas in North America. To explore this thin slip of land, drive N.C. 12, beginning at Corolla in the north and ending at the Ocracoke lighthouse in the south. Along the way, you'll pass the shifting shoals of Oregon Inlet, Pea Island National Wildlife Refuge, and pristine stretches of beach along the Cape Hatteras National Seashore. Highlight of the tour: Ocracoke Island. See chapter 4.
- **The Blue Ridge Parkway** (North Carolina): This is the single most dramatic drive in the tri-state area and one of the grandest drives in the world. Beginning in Virginia, the parkway winds and twists along mountain crests for some 470 miles. It passes through most of western North Carolina before halting at Great Smoky Mountains National Park near the Tennessee border. See chapter 7.
- **The Grand Strand** (South Carolina): Although woefully overbuilt in part, the Grand Strand is one of nature's spectacular achievements—if you can concentrate on nature instead of on what people have done to it. Beginning at the North Carolina border, the strand stretches for some 60 miles south to Georgetown; Myrtle Beach, with its wall-to-wall development, is at its center. Along the way, you'll find a nice stretch of beachfront, plus dozens of other attractions, including 80 (count 'em) championship golf courses. See chapter 12.
- **Cherokee Foothills Scenic Highway** (South Carolina): Traversing 130 miles into the heart of the Blue Ridge Mountain foothills, this highway (S.C. 11) arcs from I-85 at Gaffney, near the North Carolina border, almost to the Georgia

border at Lake Hartwell State Park. You'll find 10 state parks and five recreational areas en route. See chapter 14.

- **Chattahoochee National Forest** (Georgia): U.S. Route 76 from Ellijay and past Blairsville to Clayton is one of the most scenic routes in Georgia, dating back to the 1920s and 1930s, when the federal government purchased much of the land here. That act alone helped preserve the fading culture of the southern Appalachians, which you can see today as you slowly make your way through this national forest. See chapter 18.

2 The Best Family Vacations

- **Great Smoky Mountains National Park** (North Carolina): Sixteen peaks of the southern Appalachians soar skyward to approximately 6,000 feet. We're attracted not just by the mountains, but also by the surrounding theme parks and activities, ranging from water parks to valley railroads and offering countless opportunities for fun. See chapter 8.
- **Charleston** (South Carolina): If the tri-state area has a town that's designed for families, it's Charleston. The city has been called an 18th-century etching come to life. You can take boat rides to Fort Sumter, where the Civil War began; explore Magnolia Plantation, with its petting zoo and gardens; and visit several family-oriented nature parks, including one at Palmetto Islands. See chapter 10.
- **Hilton Head** (South Carolina): Much more upscale than Myrtle Beach, Hilton Head is filled with broad beaches. You can enjoy myriad activities, such as biking on the beaches; taking a dolphin-watching cruise; and exploring the 605-acre Sea Pines Forest Preserve, a public wilderness tract with walking trails. All major hotels offer summer activity centers for kids. See chapter 11.
- **The Golden Isles** (Georgia): This string of lush, subtropical barrier islands, located south of Savannah near the Florida border, is designed for family fun and adventure. Summer Waves, a 118-acre water park on Jekyll Island, is just one of the many attractions designed with children in mind. Nature still thrives in this setting, including Cumberland Island National Seashore, a 16- by 3-mile wildlife sanctuary. See chapter 21.

3 The Best Places to Rediscover the Old South

- **Beaufort** (North Carolina): Not to be confused with the town of the same name in South Carolina, Beaufort is North Carolina's third-oldest settlement, dating from 1713. Its 200-year-old houses and narrow streets reflect the old way of life. The town is rich in Carolina tradition that predates the Civil War. See chapter 4.
- **Beaufort** (South Carolina): Straight from the screen in *The Big Chill* and *The Prince of Tides,* Beaufort is like a sleepy dream of long ago. Established in 1710, it grew fat from Sea Island cotton. Wealthy owners built lavish antebellum houses, which still stand today, luring visitors with their faded charm. See chapter 11.
- **Georgetown** (South Carolina): A town with surprisingly well-preserved pre-Revolutionary War houses and churches, Georgetown invites you to enter a time capsule. In this small enclave of some 11,000 people, more than 50 historic homes still stand, dating back as far as 1737. See chapter 12.
- **Washington** (Georgia): Washington was the hometown of flamboyant Brig. Gen. Robert Toombs, secretary of state of the Confederacy. It's one of the few communities in Georgia that Gen. William Tecumseh Sherman didn't burn on his

infamous March to the Sea. The town is filled with carefully preserved houses that remain from the *Gone With the Wind* era. See chapter 17.

- **Savannah** (Georgia): Because General Sherman was talked out of burning it, he gave the city to President Lincoln as a Christmas present instead. No city in all the South has Savannah's peculiar charm. Its very name suggests Spanish moss, hoop skirts, mint juleps on the veranda, *Midnight in the Garden of Good and Evil,* and antebellum architecture. See chapter 20.

4 The Best Small Towns

- **Edenton** (North Carolina): Edenton is the quintessential small port town along the Outer Banks. If colonial-style clapboard is your thing, this is the place to see it. You can wander past well-tended gardens on streets shaded by magnolia and pecan trees. Edenton has been here since 1722, and the National Register of Historic Places long ago gave the town its blessing. See chapter 4.
- **Asheville** (North Carolina): The city might object to such a classification, but it's the "small town" of cities. One of the most desirable places to live in America, Asheville has attracted everybody from the Vanderbilts to the tragic feuding couple F. Scott and Zelda Fitzgerald. With its well-tended blocks and broad, tidy streets, it's the most stylish town of its size in the tri-state area, and locals are determined to keep it that way. See chapter 7.
- **Pendleton** (South Carolina): The entire town is listed on the National Register of Historic Places, having one of the largest landmark town centers in the country. Approximately 50 buildings are worth seeing, and many are open to the public and shoppers. See chapter 14.
- **Thomasville** (Georgia): The plantation era never died here, and life still moves at a leisurely pace along Thomasville's shady, tree-lined streets. Over the years, the town's aristocratic elegance has attracted the wintering wealthy, including the Rockefellers and Goodriches. Jacqueline Kennedy fled here to recover from the assassination of her husband. See chapter 19.
- **Macon** (Georgia): In the heart of the state, this sleepy town has a historic core of approximately 50 buildings listed on the National Register of Historic Places. Nearly 600 other structures here have been cited for their architectural significance. Macon long ago decided to let Atlanta race hysterically toward the millennium; it prefers to wander slowly along, content in its appealing charm. See chapter 19.

5 The Best Festivals & Events

- **Old Salem Christmas and Candle Teas** (Winston-Salem, North Carolina): During the first 2 weeks of December, Yuletide is re-created as it was celebrated 200 years ago in Old Salem. Although many Southern towns have similar festivals, this one is the most atmospheric and moving. The taste of a Moravian sugar cake, like Proust's madeleine, evokes yuletides of yore. See chapter 5.
- **Spoleto Festival** (Charleston, South Carolina): This internationally acclaimed cultural event, held in late May or early June, celebrates the arts with diverse performances of jazz, dance, theater, opera, chamber music, and much more. See chapter 10.
- **Atlanta Dogwood Festival:** A week of art shows, open-house tours, concerts, children's activities, food booths, and Earth Day celebrations culminates in Piedmont Park on a weekend night in the middle of April. See chapter 15.

- **Masters Golf Tournament** (Augusta, Georgia): Held during the first weekend in April, this world-class event attracts the world's greatest golfers. Hotel rooms are sold out for miles around. See chapter 17.
- **St. Patrick's Day Celebration on the River** (Savannah, Georgia): On St. Patrick's Day weekend, the Savannah River flows green—and so does the beer, in one of the largest celebrations honoring this saint in the South. The festivities here compete with those in Boston and New York. See chapter 20.

6 The Best Offbeat Travel Experiences

- **White-water Rafting** (in Great Smoky Mountains National Park, North Carolina): Starting at Waterville Power Plant, a 5-mile stretch of Pigeon River offers 10 rapids and some of the most challenging white-water rafting in the South. The trip is definitely an adrenaline rush and demands good teamwork, conditioning, and experience. See chapter 8.
- **Shooting the Hooch** (rafting the Chattahoochee River in North Atlanta): This has been a favorite pastime of Atlantans since Gen. William T. Sherman washed the 2-month-old dirt off his body in the river before setting out to burn down Atlanta. The refreshing trip, from Johnson Ferry to Powers Island, covers 6.3 miles and takes about 3 hours. It's a good way to cool off. See chapter 16.
- **Canoeing the Savannah National Wildlife Refuge** (outside Savannah, Georgia): Only a 10-minute drive from the heart of Savannah, this wildlife refuge is like another world, one populated by such creatures as alligators and bald eagles. Canoeists float along tidal creeks, which are actually fingers of the Savannah River. The site of rice plantations during the 1800s, the refuge has returned to the wild, just the way the local feral hogs like it. See chapter 20.
- **Journeying to Sapelo Island** (Georgia): Visiting this island, which is the site of the R.J. Reynolds State Wildlife Refuge, is like watching a black-and-white *National Geographic* movie from the 1930s. Sapelo Island (reachable from Darien) encompasses 8,240 acres of undeveloped barrier island. It has often been the retreat of the rich and/or famous, including President Jimmy Carter and Charles Lindbergh. It has marsh and beach walks galore. See chapter 21.
- **Camping in Stephen C. Foster State Park** (on the western edge of the Okefenokee Swamp): Anyone who's ever heard Foster's song about the old folks at home along the Suwannee River may be tempted to camp in this 80-acre park near the Florida border. The sprawling forest of gum and cypress trees is one of the thickest stands of vegetation in the Southeast. Its murky waters are alive with a wide array of wildlife, including 55 species of reptiles. See chapter 21.

7 The Best Day Hikes

- **Great Smoky Mountains National Park** (North Carolina): With more than 800 miles of trails, this park has hiking opportunities like no other place in the South. Of the countless possibilities, our favorite trails are Indian Creek Falls Trail (easy); Laurel Falls Trail, the most popular waterfall trail in the park (also easy); and Abrams Falls Trail, a distance of 2 miles (easy to moderate). See chapter 8.
- **The Appalachian Trail, Great Smoky Mountains National Park** (North Carolina): The most famous hiking trail in America, the "A.T." has 68 of its 2,100 miles situated in this park. The trail follows the Smokies' ridgeline from

west to east for almost the entire length of the park, with a strenuous grading. The elevation gained is 980 feet. If you want only a preview of this splendor, try the most popular section, which runs from Newfound Gap to Charlies Bunion. See chapter 8.

- **Sea Pines Forest Preserve** (Sea Pines Plantation, Hilton Head, South Carolina): Sea Pines is one of the leading nature preserves in the South, a 605-acre public wilderness with marked walking trails. All trails lead to public picnic areas in the center of the forest. Alligators roam freely in the lagoons and on the sides of streams. More than 350 species of native American birds have been sighted in the preserve during the past decade. See chapter 11.

- **The Appalachian Trail, Springer Mountain** (Georgia): Hikers—if they make it to the end of this exhausting 2,100-mile trail at Mount Katahdin, Maine—are known as "2,000 Milers." They gather here in April to begin the hike, arriving in Maine after Labor Day. You don't have to be so dedicated, however. The trail runs across Georgia for only 79 miles, and you can get the idea by taking only a fraction of this hike, cutting across some of the South's most rugged mountains. See chapter 18.

- **Cumberland Island** (Georgia): The best place for a day hike along the barrier islands is Cumberland Island, which you reach 7 miles northeast of the port of St. Mary's. Since 1972, the island has been a National Seashore. In an area 16 miles long and 3 miles wide, you can enter a maritime forest—a world of salt marshes and sand dunes teeming with animal life, including alligators and white-tailed deer. See chapter 21.

8 The Best Golf Courses

- **Pinehurst Hotel and Country Club** (Carolina Vista, Pinehurst, North Carolina): This is the only course in the South that has seven signature holes. The original architect was the now-legendary Donald Ross. All the great names in golf—including Nelson, Jones, and Hogan—have played this course. In all, there are 126 holes of golf, with modern holes designed by Tom Fazio and Rees Jones. See chapter 6.

- **Pine Needles Resort** (Southern Pines, North Carolina): This 1927 Donald Ross masterpiece is a challenging par-71 course, attracting golfers of various skills. The course plays to 6,708 yards from the championship tees and has been immaculately restored to its original splendor. See chapter 6.

- **Palmetto Dunes Resort** (Hilton Head, South Carolina): This course, designed by George Fazio, is an 18-hole, 6,534-yard, par-70 course named by *Golf Digest* as one of the "75 Best American Resort Courses." It has been cited for its combined "length and keen accuracy." See chapter 11.

- **Old South Golf Links** (Bluffton, South Carolina): This 18-hole, 6,772-yard, par-72 course has been recognized as one of the "Top 10 Public Courses" by *Golf Digest*. It has panoramic views and a natural setting that ranges from an oak forest to tidal salt marshes. See chapter 11.

- **Sea Island Golf Club** (St. Simons Island, Georgia): Owned by The Cloister, the most exclusive resort in the South, this widely acclaimed golf course lies at the end of the Avenue of Oaks, the site of a former plantation. Opened in 1927, the club consists of several courses, such as the 18-hole Ocean Forest (7,011 yards, par 72). It has been compared favorably to such golfing meccas as St. Andrews in Scotland and Pebble Beach in California. See chapter 21.

9 The Best Beaches

- **Wrightsville Beach** (6 miles east of Wilmington, North Carolina): It's the widest beach on the Cape Fear coast: Wrightsville's beige sands stretch for a mile along the oceanfront, set against a backdrop of thick vegetation. See chapter 4.
- **The Outer Banks** (North Carolina): Some 70 miles of relatively unspoiled beaches begin at Whalebone Junction in South Nags Head and stretch all the way to Ocracoke Island in the south. The only problem is that the favorite beach you discover one day may be gone with the wind tomorrow, as ferocious tides, strong currents, and fickle winds constantly alter the most dramatic of all beaches along the Eastern Seaboard. See chapter 4.
- **Hilton Head** (South Carolina): *Travel & Leisure* has hailed these beaches as being among the most beautiful in the world, and we concur. The resort-studded island offers 12 miles of white-sand beaches; still others front the Calobogue and Port Royal sounds. The sand is extremely firm, providing a good surface for biking and many beach games. It's also ideal for walking and jogging—against a backdrop of natural dunes, live oaks, palmettos, and tall Carolina pines. See chapter 11.
- **Myrtle Beach** (South Carolina): This is the most popular sand strip along the Eastern Seaboard, attracting 12 million visitors a year—more than the state of Hawaii. Sure, it's overdeveloped and maddeningly crowded, but what draws visitors to Myrtle Beach are 10 miles of sand, mostly hard-packed and the color of brown sugar. Myrtle Beach actually is only one section of the Grand Strand, a 60-mile string of beaches that include these popular ones: Little River, Cherry Grove, Crescent Beach, Ocean Drive, Atlantic Beach, Surfside Beach, Garden City, Murrells Inlet, Litchfield Beach, and Pawleys Island. Myrtle Beach State Park has 350 campsites for the best camping along the Strand. See chapter 12.

10 The Best Fishing

- **The Outer Banks** (North Carolina): With both offshore and pier fishing, the Outer Banks is where more than half the state's saltwater-sportsfishing records have been made (and broken). The size of the fish and the diversity of species have put these barrier islands on the map as being one of the hottest fishing spots in the world. The Gulf Stream is just 12 miles offshore—the closest that this fish-filled current comes to land this side of Florida. See chapter 4.
- **Great Smoky Mountains National Park** (North Carolina): For mountain fishing, nothing can compete with the 700 miles of streams in this park, which offers some of the finest fly-fishing in America. Fishing is permitted from sunrise to sunset year-round, although you must obtain a license from the state. The most popular catches are rainbow and brown trout. Not all fishing is in natural streams. At Fontana Lake, for example, anglers hook both smallmouth and large-mouth bass, among other species. See chapter 8.
- **Hilton Head** (South Carolina): One of your best bets for deep-sea fishing is right here. Record catches of amberjack, barracuda, shark, king mackerel, and other species have been recorded. Ocean-bottom fishing is also possible at an artificial reef 12 miles offshore. See chapter 11.
- **Grand Strand** (South Carolina): Because of the warming temperatures of the Gulf Stream, fishing is possible here from early spring until Christmas. Pier fishing is the most popular activity, and various piers are strung along this coast. All resorts can arrange charters for half- or full-day fishing in the Gulf Stream itself. See chapter 12.

11 The Best Luxury Hotels & Resorts

- **Grove Park Inn Resort** (Asheville, North Carolina; ☎ 800/438-5800 or 828/252-2711): The premier resort of the state has sheltered everybody from Thomas Edison to F. Scott Fitzgerald, and the big names still check in. The hotel is continually upgraded, and it is said to be just as grand as it was on the day it opened in 1913. A $14-million full-service spa was set to open in January 2001. An array of activities and facilities, ranging from children's programs to golf, await today's guests. See chapter 7.
- **Sea Pines Plantation** (Hilton Head, South Carolina; ☎ 800/SEA-PINES or 843/785-3333): This is the oldest and most famous of the island's resort developments. Set on 4,500 thickly wooded acres, with a total of three golf courses, Sea Pines competes for the summer beach traffic as few resorts in the Caribbean ever could. Its focal point is Harbour Town, which is built around one of the most charming marinas in the Carolinas. Luxurious homes and villas open onto the ocean or golf courses. See chapter 11.
- **Ritz-Carlton Buckhead** (Atlanta, Georgia; ☎ 800/241-3333 or 404/237-2700): Often a discreet rendezvous for visiting celebrities, this hotel is the epitome of plushness and luxury. General Sherman wouldn't have burned it; he would have checked in and called for room service. European style and flair set the grace notes, evoked by Regency and Georgian antiques, white marble floors, and French-crystal chandeliers. Exquisitely decorated bedrooms and one of Atlanta's premier deluxe restaurants add much allure—and about a dozen martinis are available on the drink menu. See chapter 16.
- **The Gastonian** (Savannah, Georgia; ☎ 800/322-6603 or 912/232-2869): Two 19th-century stone town houses have been turned into a gem of a hotel. Empire furnishings, Persian rugs, working fireplaces, brass headboards, and canopied beds adorn the lushly decorated bedrooms. Antiques, Oriental rugs, fresh flowers in profusion, glowing fires, and even classical music create a welcoming, cozy ambience. Staying at The Gastonian is like living in a wealthy friend's private mansion. See chapter 20.
- **The Cloister** (Sea Island, Georgia; ☎ 800/732-4752 or 912/638-3611): This hotel has been called the grande dame of all resorts in the South. A clubby place, The Cloister means formal dinners by night, outdoor activities by day that range from the best tennis in Georgia to riding, fishing, and swimming (at the beach or in two inviting pools). It's a class act. See chapter 21.

12 The Best Moderately Priced Hotels

- **Cedar Crest Inn** (Asheville, North Carolina; ☎ 800/252-0310 or 828/252-1389): The city is famed for its B&Bs—the finest in North Carolina—and this one rates at the top. A Queen Anne–style mansion built in 1894, Cedar Crest Inn is rich in Victorian trappings, including a captain's walk, projecting turrets, and various architectural follies. The bedrooms are first-class; each one has unique decor, and many have canopied ceilings. See chapter 7.
- **Barksdale House Inn** (Charleston, South Carolina; ☎ 803/577-4800): Constructed as an inn in 1778, near the City Market, this is one of the best B&Bs in high-priced Charleston. The bedrooms often contain four-poster beds and working fireplaces, and about half a dozen have whirlpool tubs. You can have tea or sherry on the back porch in the evening. See chapter 10.
- **Liberty Hall Inn** (Pendleton, South Carolina; ☎ 800/643-7944 or 864/646-7500): Once a summer home, Liberty Hall has grown into the classic

Southern inn of the Upstate. Often filled with antiques hunters because of all the shops in town, the inn is a traditional world of high ceilings, heart-pine floors, antique furnishings, and ceiling fans. The gracious life holds forth until the mad rush for dinner, which features down-home delicacies such as sweet-potato-crusted bobwhite quail. See chapter 14.

- **Beverly Hills Inn** (Atlanta, Georgia; ☎ **800/331-8520** or 404/233-8520): A British owner operates this 1920s California-style building with considerable aplomb. Situated on a tree-lined residential street, the inn welcomes guests with cheerfully decorated bedrooms, replete with floral fabrics and billowing curtains. The inn, which resembles an elegant private home, ranks among the top two or three B&Bs in all of Atlanta. See chapter 16.
- **17 Hundred 90** (Savannah, Georgia; ☎ **800/487-1790** or 912/236-7122): Like a house in 18th-century New England, this is the oldest inn in Savannah. It's even said to be haunted. The bedrooms are small but charming, and the colonial trappings of this place have won many a devotee, some of whom wouldn't stay anywhere else when they visit Savannah. See chapter 20.

13 The Best Budget Hotels

- **Governor Eden** (Edenton, North Carolina; ☎ **252/482-2072**): Located in one of the most historic towns along North Carolina's Outer Banks, this charmer is one of the better B&Bs in the area, close to the historic core. Built in 1906 in the neoclassical style, with large white columns and a wraparound veranda, it is the epitome of Southern antebellum style. See chapter 4.
- **Old Reynolds Mansion Bed & Breakfast** (Asheville, North Carolina; ☎ **828/254-0496**): This antebellum brick house, one of the few left in Asheville, was rescued from the bulldozer and is now a three-story inn. Listed on the National Register of Historic Places, the B&B offers the most inviting budget-priced rooms in the city. See chapter 7.
- **The Greenleaf Inn** (Camden, South Carolina; ☎ **800/437-5874**): Situated in the heart of historic Camden, the Greenleaf is the coziest and most comfortable choice in town. A part of the inn dates from 1805, and it's filled with Victorian furnishings. It's also one of the finest dining choices in Camden, even if you're not a guest. See chapter 13.
- **Buckhead Bed & Breafast Inn** (Atlanta, Georgia; ☎ **888/224-8797**): You can live inexpensively, even in tony, upmarket Buckhead, at this building with columns and wide porches. Sleep in a four-poster bed in rooms named after local trees such as the holly or oak; the peachtree room is particularly fine. See chapter 16.
- **Plains Bed and Breakfast Inn** (Plains, Georgia; ☎ **912/824-7252**): In Jimmy Carter's hometown, this is a stylish B&B built by a Baptist preacher in 1910. It's just two doors away from a service station where the former president's brother, Billy, often held press conferences. Miss Lillian and her husband were said to have "conceived" the future president in one of the tasteful and comfortably furnished upstairs bedrooms. See chapter 19.

14 The Best Camping

- **Great Smoky Mountains National Park** (North Carolina): The best camping in the South is available at this most-visited of all national parks, which offers 10 campgrounds, each with picnic tables, fire grills, cold running water, and flush toilets. Showers and electrical hookups, however, are missing, as you truly return to nature in this setting. Of the 10 campgrounds, our favorites are Cades Cove, Elkmont, and Smokemont. See chapter 8.

- **Myrtle Beach State Park** (South Carolina): This park offers 312 acres of pinewoods and one of the best sandy beaches along the Grand Strand. The park is equipped with toilets, pavilions, and picnic tables. Swimming is good almost anywhere along the ocean. See chapter 12.
- **Family Campground at Stone Mountain Park** (16 miles east of Atlanta, Georgia): The approximately 400 wooded sites here offer facilities for tents and RVs, with full hookups, showers, laundry, swimming, boating, hiking, and fishing. Stone Mountain itself has 3,200 acres of lakes and wooded parkland to explore. See chapter 16.
- **Vogel State Park** (northern Georgia): One of the state's most-frequented parks, this ideal campers' venue sprawls across 240 acres and is laced with nature trails. Campsites are available with power and water hookups, hot showers, and laundry facilities. Vogel, at an elevation of 2,500 feet, is one of the coolest places to be in humid Georgia in July and August. See chapter 18.

15 The Best Restaurants

- **Horizons Restaurant** (in the Grove Park Inn Resort, Asheville, North Carolina; ☎ 828/252-2711): This is the most formal restaurant in western North Carolina, as befits its location in the city's grandest resort. Horizons is consistently rated among the top restaurants in the nation. Patrons are served an excellent array of continental dishes—including brook trout, bouillabaisse, and medallions of venison—prepared from the freshest ingredients on the market. See chapter 7.
- **Anson** (Charleston, South Carolina; ☎ 803/577-0551): Hip, stylish, and upscale, this is one of the favorite dining rooms among discriminating Charlestonians, who flock here for Low Country dishes with an original, modern twist. Anson compares with top-notch restaurants in New York and San Francisco, and offers the best service in the city. Try the fried cornmeal oysters with potato cakes or the cashew-crusted grouper with champagne sauce. See chapter 10.
- **Charlie's L'Etoile Verte** (Hilton Head, South Carolina; ☎ 843/785-9277): Like a whimsical Parisian bistro, this elegant yet unpretentious establishment packs them in every night in an area that has more restaurants than customers. Even President Clinton has dined here. The reason is the food. The cuisine borrows freely from almost everywhere. Our favorite dish is grilled quail with shiitake mushrooms and merlot sauce. See chapter 11.
- **Pano & Paul's** (Atlanta, Georgia; ☎ 404/261-3662): Its place already secure in the dining hall of fame, this Buckhead eatery combines the best of continental selections with American produce, and the results have won it a following not only in Atlanta, but also throughout the Southeast. Patrons receive impeccable service while dining in a setting of Victorian opulence. The broiled dry-aged sirloin steak and the roast double beef fillet are the best in town. See chapter 16.
- **Lady and Sons** (Savannah, Georgia; ☎ 912/233-2600): Launched with $200 in 1989, this restaurant has become one of the finest in eastern Georgia, turning out a Southern cuisine of taste and refinement. Their buffets are reason enough to visit. And wait until you try Paula Deen's chicken potpie. See chapter 20.

For Foreign Visitors 2

This chapter provides some specifics on getting to the United States as economically and effortlessly as possible, plus it gives helpful information on how things are done in the Southeast, from mailing a postcard to making a long-distance telephone call. For more information, see the "Planning a Trip" chapters for each state: chapter 3 for North Carolina, chapter 9 for South Carolina, and chapter 15 for Georgia.

1 Preparing for Your Trip

If you're going to Atlanta, contact the **Atlanta Convention & Visitors Bureau (ACVB),** 233 Peachtree St. NE, Suite 100, Atlanta, GA 30303 (☎ **404/222-6688** or 404/521-6600; www.atlanta.com), and ask for the *International Visitors Guide* for foreign tourists, which is available in five languages (2–3 weeks delivery).

ENTRY REQUIREMENTS
DOCUMENT REQUIREMENTS   Canadian citizens may enter the United States without passports or visas; they need only proof of residence.

British subjects and citizens of New Zealand, Japan, and most Western European countries traveling on valid passports may not need a visa for less than 90 days of holiday or business travel to the United States, providing that they hold a round-trip or return ticket and enter the country on an airline or cruise line that is participating in the visa-waiver program. Holding the ticket provides an exemption from a visa.

Citizens of these visa-exempt countries who first enter the United States may go on to visit Mexico, Canada, Bermuda, and/or the Caribbean islands and then reenter the United States by any mode of transportation without a visa. Further information is available from any U.S. embassy or consulate.

Citizens of countries other than those stipulated in the preceding paragraphs, including citizens of Australia, must have two documents: (1) a valid passport with an expiration date at least 6 months later than the scheduled end of their visit to the United States, and (2) a tourist visa, available without charge from the nearest U.S. consulate. To obtain a visa, the traveler must submit a completed application form (either in person or by mail) with a 1½-inch square (37mm square) photo and must demonstrate binding ties to a residence abroad. Usually, you can obtain a visa at once or within 24 hours, but it may take longer during the summer rush (June to August). If you cannot go in person, contact the nearest U.S. embassy or consulate for directions on applying by mail. Your travel agent or airline office may also be able to provide visa applications and instructions. The U.S. embassy or consulate that issues your visa will determine whether you will be issued a multiple- or single-entry visa and will advise you of any restrictions regarding the length of your stay.

MEDICAL REQUIREMENTS   No inoculations are needed to enter the United States unless you're coming from, or have stopped over in, areas that are known to be suffering from epidemics such as cholera or yellow fever.

If you have a disease that requires treatment with medications containing narcotics or drugs requiring a syringe, carry a valid, signed prescription from your physician to allay any suspicions that you're smuggling drugs.

CUSTOMS REQUIREMENTS   Every visitor who is 21 or older may bring in the following items free of duty: 1 liter of wine or hard liquor, 200 cigarettes *or* 50 cigars (but no cigars from Cuba) *or* 2 pounds of smoking tobacco, and $400 worth of gifts. An additional 100 cigars are allowed under your gift exemption. These exemptions are offered to travelers who spend at least 72 hours in the United States and who have not claimed them within the preceding 6 months. It's forbidden to bring into the country foodstuffs (particularly cheese, fruit, cooked meats, and canned goods) or plants (vegetables, seeds, tropical plants, and so on). Foreign tourists may bring in or take out up to $10,000 in U.S. or foreign currency with no formalities; larger sums must be declared to Customs upon entering or leaving the country.

INSURANCE

The United States has no national health-care system. Because the cost of medical care is extremely high, we strongly advise that every traveler secure health-insurance coverage before setting out. You may want to take out a comprehensive travel policy that covers (for a relatively low premium) sickness or injury costs (medical, surgical, and hospital); loss or theft of your baggage; trip-cancellation costs; guarantee of bail, in case you're arrested; and costs associated with accidents, repatriation, or death.

Packages such as "Europ Assistance Worldwide Services" in Europe are sold by automobile clubs and travel agencies at attractive rates. **Travel Assistance International (TAI)** (☎ **800/821-2828** or 202/331-1609) is the agent for Europ Assistance Worldwide Services, Inc., so holders of this company's policies can contact TAI for assistance while they are in the United States.

Canadians should check with their provincial-health-scheme offices or call **Health-Canada** (☎ **613/783-4400;** www.gov.on.ca/health) to find out the extent of their coverage, as well as what documentation and receipts they must take home in case they are treated in the United States.

British travelers might try **Columbus Travel Insurance, Ltd.** (☎ **020/7375-0011;** www.columbusdirect.net); or, for students, **Campus Travel** (☎ **0870/240-1010;** www.usitcampus.co.uk).

MONEY

CURRENCY & EXCHANGE   The U.S. monetary system has a decimal base. One American **dollar** ($1) = 100 **cents** (100¢).

Dollar bills commonly come in $1 (a "buck"), $5, $10, and $20 denominations. There are also $2 bills (seldom encountered), $50 bills, and $100 bills. The latter two denominations are usually not welcome as payment for small purchases and are not accepted in taxis or at subway ticket booths.

There are six denominations of coins: 1¢ (one cent, or a "penny"), 5¢ (five cents, or a "nickel"), 10¢ (ten cents, or a "dime"), 25¢ (twenty-five cents, or a "quarter"), and two rare coins: 50¢ (fifty cents, or a "half dollar") and the $1 piece (the small Susan B. Anthony coin).

Note: The "foreign-exchange bureaus" that are so common in Europe are rare even at airports in the United States and nonexistent outside major cities. Try to avoid having to change foreign money or traveler's checks that are not denominated in U.S. dollars at small-town banks or even at branch banks in big cities. In fact, leave any currency other than U.S. dollars at home; it may prove to be more of a nuisance to you than it's worth.

ATMs   It's getting easier all the time to use your ATM card to access your bank account from home while you're on the road. Check with your bank at home to be sure your ATM card and password will work in U.S. ATMs.

TRAVELER'S CHECKS   Some people prefer to carry traveler's checks for that extra security. Traveler's checks denominated in U.S. dollars are readily accepted at most hotels, motels, restaurants, and large stores. But the best place to change traveler's checks is at a bank in a large city or town. Do not bring traveler's checks that are denominated in other currencies.

CREDIT & CHARGE CARDS   The method of payment most widely used is credit and charge cards, including Visa (BarclayCard in Britain), MasterCard (EuroCard in Europe, Access in Britain, Chargex in Canada), American Express, Diners Club, Discover, and Carte Blanche. You can save yourself trouble by using so-called "plastic money" rather than cash or traveler's checks in most hotels, motels, restaurants, and retail stores. (A growing number of food and liquor stores now accept credit/charge cards.) You must have a credit or charge card to rent a car. You can also use the card as proof of identity (it often carries more weight than a passport) or as a "cash card," enabling you to draw money from banks and ATMs that accept it.

SAFETY

GENERAL   Although tourist areas are generally safe, crime exists everywhere, and U.S. urban areas tend to be less safe than those in Western Europe or Japan. Visitors should always stay alert. This is particularly true of large U.S. cities, especially Atlanta. Parts of Savannah, Charleston, and Charlotte can be unsafe at night. It is wise to ask the city or area's tourist office if you're in doubt about which neighborhoods are safe. Avoid deserted areas at night. Don't go into any city park at night unless there's an event that attracts crowds. Generally speaking, you can feel safe in areas where there are many people and many open establishments.

Remember also that hotels are open to the public, and in a large hotel, security may not be able to screen everyone who enters. Always lock your room door. Don't assume that once you're inside your hotel, you are automatically safe and no longer need to be aware of your surroundings.

Georgia and the Carolinas are among the safest places in the Southeast, especially in the small towns and villages. Resort areas such as Myrtle Beach attract more crime, of course. But on a per-capita basis, Georgia and the Carolinas have far less crime than does Florida, to the south.

DRIVING   Safety while driving is particularly important. Question your rental agency about personal safety, or ask for a brochure of traveler-safety tips when you pick up your car. Obtain from the agency written directions or a map with the route marked in red, showing you how to get to your destination. If possible, arrive and depart during daylight hours.

If you drive off a highway into a doubtful neighborhood, leave the area as quickly as possible. If you have an accident, even on the highway, stay in your car with the doors locked until you assess the situation or until the police arrive. If you are bumped from behind on the street, or if you are involved in a minor accident with no injuries and the situation appears to be suspicious, motion to the other driver to follow you to a police station or a lighted area where there are people and telephones. *Never* get out of your car in such a situation.

If you see someone on the road who indicates a need for help, *don't stop*. Take note of the location, drive on to a well-lighted area, and telephone the police by dialing ☎ **911.**

Park in well-lighted, well-traveled areas, if possible. Always keep your car doors locked, whether the car is attended or unattended. Look around before you get out of your car, and never leave any packages or valuables in sight. If someone attempts to rob you or steal your car, do *not* try to resist the thief or carjacker; report the incident to the police department immediately.

Also, make sure that you have enough gasoline in your tank to reach your intended destination, so that you're not forced to look for a service station in an unfamiliar and possibly unsafe neighborhood, especially at night.

2 Getting to the U.S.

Atlanta serves as the gateway to the South for most passengers from overseas. From there, connections can be made to destinations in the Carolinas, including such cities as Charleston and Charlotte.

British Airways (☎ **800/AIRWAYS** in the U.S. or 0345/222-111 in the U.K.; www.british-airways.com) flies nonstop every day from London's Gatwick airport to Atlanta (trip time: 7½ hours). Flights depart London daily at 9:45am, arriving in Atlanta at 2:30pm (local time). The BA flight returns from Atlanta every evening at 5:30pm (Atlanta time), arriving at Gatwick at 6:25am (Greenwich Mean Time). Citizens of Ireland can make this connection to Atlanta by flying to London.

Flying to Atlanta from 23 European cities, **Delta Air Lines** (☎ **800/221-1212;** www.delta.com) offers daily nonstop flights to Atlanta from Barcelona, Frankfurt, London, Madrid, Manchester, Munich, Paris, Shannon, and Zurich.

KLM (☎ **800/447-4747** in the U.S. or 020/4747-747 in Amsterdam; www.klm.nl) has direct service 4 days a week from Amsterdam.

For passengers flying from Australia or New Zealand, either BA or **Qantas** (☎ **800/227-4500**) goes from Sydney to London in 24 hours, where a connecting flight on BA can be made into Atlanta (see the British Airways paragraph earlier in this section).

Air Canada (☎ **888/422-7533;** www.aircanada.ca) has four nonstop flights a day from Toronto to Atlanta (flight time: 2¼ hours). Air Canada also has one nonstop flight from Montréal to Atlanta (flight time: 2½ hours). Most passengers from Vancouver go first to Toronto or Montréal to make these connections. In some rare instances, passengers from Vancouver can be routed via Chicago into Atlanta.

Travelers from overseas can take advantage of the **APEX (advance-purchase excursion)** fares offered by all the major international carriers.

The visitor arriving by air, no matter what his or her port of entry, should cultivate patience and resignation before setting foot on U.S. soil. Getting through Immigration Control may take as long as 2 hours on some days, especially during summer weekends. Add the time that it takes to clear Customs, and you'll see that you should make very generous allowance for delays in planning connections between international and domestic flights—an average of 2 to 3 hours, at least.

By contrast, travelers arriving by car or by rail from Canada will find the border-crossing formalities to be streamlined practically to the vanishing point. Air travelers from Canada, Bermuda, and some places in the Caribbean can sometimes go through Customs and Immigration much more quickly at the point of departure.

3 Getting Around the U.S.

BY PLANE   **Delta Air Lines** (☎ **800/221-1212**) offers a discounted "Discover America" airfare that allows unlimited travel within the continental United States. *You must make the purchase outside the United States prior to arrival.* Tickets are available in 3 to 10 segments, ranging in price from $399 to $2,087. You must use the first coupon within 60 days of entering the United States, and you must use the final coupon within 60 days of activating the first coupon. No minimum stay is required, and you don't have to fly to the United States on Delta to purchase one of these tickets. At press time, customers were required to buy tickets by March 2001, but the offer may be extended; call a Delta representative or your travel agent for up-to-the-minute information.

Other airlines offering a similar air pass include American Airlines, Continental, Northwest, TWA, and United. Packaged under the name **Visit USA,** this pass is sold only through airline and travel agents outside the United States. Usually, you must also purchase an inbound international flight from some foreign country, including Canada. The price of each leg of this all-encompassing ticket can vary widely. Regardless of the individual parameters, this system is the best, easiest, and fastest way to see large stretches of the United States, including the Southeast, at a reasonable price. You should obtain information well in advance from your travel agent or from the office of the airline concerned, because the conditions attached to these discount tickets can be changed without notice.

BY CAR   The United States is a car culture—that's for sure—and the most cost-effective, convenient, and comfortable way to travel through the country is to drive. The interstate highway system—high-speed, limited-access roadways—connects cities and towns all over the country, and there's also an extensive network of federal, state, and local highways and roads. Travel by car gives visitors the freedom to make—and alter—their itineraries to suit their own needs and interests. Driving also offers the possibility of visiting some off-the-beaten-path locations that cannot be reached easily by public transportation.

Another convenience of traveling by car is the easy access to inexpensive motels at interstate-highway off ramps. Such motels are almost always cheaper than hotels and motels in downtown areas. Remember that almost none of the smaller American cities offers any kind of comprehensive local in-city transportation system. This is especially true in the South.

The American Automobile Association (AAA) can provide you with an **International Driving Permit** that validates your foreign license. You may be able to join the AAA even if you're not a member of a reciprocal club. To inquire, call ☎ **800/ AAA-HELP.** In addition, some automobile rental agencies provide these services.

BY TRAIN   Long-distance trains in the United States are operated by **Amtrak** (☎ **800/872-7245;** www.amtrak.com), the national passenger rail-service corporation. International travelers can buy a 15- or 30-day **USA Rail Pass.** In 2000, off-peak fares (Sept. 5–May31) for 15 days of unlimited travel nationwide were $295 for adults and $147.50 for children; for 30 days of unlimited travel around the U.S., $385 for adults and $192.50 for children. International and domestic visitors can buy a **North America Railpass,** which is good for 30 days of unlimited travel on Amtrak. The pass is available through many foreign travel agents and at any staffed Amtrak office, but must include travel in both North America and Canada. Prices in 2000 were $459 for off-peak travel and $656 for peak travel (June 1–Oct. 15). Reservations are generally required and should be made for each part of your trip as early as possible. Amtrak also offers an **Air/Rail Travel Plan** that allows you to travel both by train and plane; for information, call ☎ **800/321-8684.**

Visitors should be aware of the limitations of long-distance rail travel in the United States. With a few notable exceptions (such as the Northeast Corridor line between Boston and Washington, D.C.), service is rarely up to European standards. Delays are common, routes are limited and often infrequently served, and fares are rarely significantly lower than discount airfares. Long-distance train travel should be approached with caution.

BY BUS   Generally, the cheapest way to travel in the United States—especially for short hops between cities—is by bus. **Greyhound** (☎ **800/231-2222;** www. greyhound.com), the sole nationwide bus line, offers an **Ameripass** for unlimited travel anywhere in the continental United States. In 2000, an adult 7-day pass cost $209; a 15-day pass, $319; a 30-day pass, $429; and a 60-day pass, $599. Children, students, and seniors receive discounted fares. Reductions are offered for round-trip purchases and, in some cases, for tickets purchased more than 3 weeks in advance. Bus travel in the United States can be both slow and uncomfortable, however, so this option is not for everyone.

Fast Facts: For the Foreign Traveler

Accommodations   It's always a good idea to make hotel reservations as soon as you know the dates of your travel. To make a reservation, you'll usually need to leave a deposit of one night's payment. Some of the major hotels listed in this book maintain overseas reservation networks and can be booked either directly or through travel agents.

In the United States, major downtown hotels, which cater primarily to business travelers, commonly offer weekend discounts of as much as 50 percent to entice vacationers to fill the empty hotel rooms. Resorts and hotels near tourist attractions tend to have higher rates on weekends.

Automobile Organizations   Auto clubs can supply maps, suggested routes, guidebooks, accident and bail-bond insurance, and emergency road service. The major auto club in the United States, with 983 offices nationwide, is the **American Automobile Association (AAA),** 1000 AAA Dr., Heathrow, FL 32746-5063 (☎ **800/AAA-HELP**). Membership costs $45 to $55, but some foreign auto clubs have reciprocal arrangements with AAA, and members enjoy its services at no charge. If you belong to an auto club in your home country, inquire about AAA reciprocity before you leave. AAA can provide you an **International Driving Permit** that validates your foreign license. In addition, some automobile rental agencies now provide these services, so you should inquire about their availability when you rent your car.

Automobile Rentals   To rent a car, you need a major credit or charge card and a valid driver's license. Sometimes, a passport or an international driver's license is also required if your driver's license is in a language other than English. You usually need to be at least 25 years of age, although some companies do rent to younger people (they may add a daily surcharge). Be sure to return your car with the same amount of gasoline that you started out with, because rental companies charge excessive prices for gas. Keep in mind that a separate motorcycle driver's license is required in most states.

Business Hours   The following are general open hours; specific establishments may vary. **Banks:** Monday to Friday from 9am to 3pm (some are also open on Saturday from 9am to noon). You usually have 24-hour access to the automated-teller machines (ATMs) at most banks and other outlets. **Offices:** Monday to Friday from 9am to 5pm. **Stores:** Monday to Saturday from 10am to 6pm, and some also on Sunday from noon to 5pm. Malls usually stay open until 9pm Monday to Saturday, and department stores are usually open until 9pm at least 1 day a week.

Climate   See "When to Go" in chapter 3 for North Carolina, chapter 9 for South Carolina, and chapter 15 for Georgia.

Currency   See the "Money" section of "Preparing for Your Trip," earlier in this chapter.

Currency Exchange   You'll find currency-exchange services in major airports that have international service. Elsewhere, these services may be quite difficult to come by, although some major hotels will exchange currency if you're a registered guest.

Drinking Laws   You must be at least 21 to consume alcoholic beverages.

Electricity   The United States uses 110 to 120 volts AC, 60 cycles, compared with 220 to 240 volts AC, 50 cycles, in most of Europe. In addition to a 110-volt transformer, small appliances of non-American manufacture, such as hair dryers and shavers, require a plug adapter with two flat parallel pins.

Embassies & Consulates   All embassies are located in Washington, D.C.; some consulates are located in major U.S. cities; and most nations have a mission to the United Nations in New York City.

Listed here are the embassies and some consulates of the major English-speaking countries. Travelers from other countries can obtain telephone numbers for their embassies and consulates by calling the "information" number for Washington, D.C. (☎ 202/555-1212).

The embassy of **Australia** is at 1601 Massachusetts Ave. NW, Washington, DC 20036 (☎ 202/797-3000). There are Australian consulates in Chicago, Honolulu, Houston, Los Angeles, New York, and San Francisco. www.austemb.org.

The embassy of **Canada** is at 501 Pennsylvania Ave. NW, Washington, DC 20001 (☎ 202/682-1740). There's a Canadian consulate in Atlanta at 1175 Peachtree St., Atlanta, GA 30361 (☎ 404/532-2000); other Canadian consulates are in Buffalo (N.Y.), Detroit, Los Angeles, New York, and Seattle. www.canadianembassy.org.

The embassy of the **Republic of Ireland** is at 2234 Massachusetts Ave. NW, Washington, DC 20008 (☎ 202/462-3939). There are Irish consulates in Boston, Chicago, New York, and San Francisco. www.irelandemb.org.

The embassy of **New Zealand** is at 37 Observatory Circle NW, Washington, DC 20008 (☎ 202/328-4800). The only New Zealand consulate in the United States is in Los Angeles.www.nzemb.org.

The embassy of the **United Kingdom** is at 3100 Massachusetts Ave. NW, Washington, DC 20008 (☎ 202/588-6500). There's a British consulate in

Atlanta at 245 Peachtree Center Ave., Marquis One Tower, Suite 2700, Atlanta, GA 30303 (☎ **404/524-5856**); other British consulates are in Chicago, Houston, Los Angeles, Miami, and New York. www.britainusa.cm.

The embassy for **South Africa** is at 3051 Massachusetts Ave., NW, Washington, DC 2008 (☎ **202/966-1650**).

Other countries that have consulates in Atlanta include **France,** at 285 Peachtree Center Ave., Suite 2800, Atlanta, GA 30303 (☎ **404/495-1660**); **Germany,** at Marquis Two Tower, Suite 901, 285 Peachtree Center Ave. NE, Atlanta, GA 30303-1221 (☎ **404/659-4760**); and **Japan,** Suite 2000, 100 Colony Sq. at 1175 Peachtree St. NE, Atlanta, GA 30361 (☎ **404/892-2700**). For complete information, contact the Atlanta Chamber of Commerce, International Department, P.O. Box 1740, Atlanta, GA 30301 (☎ **404/586-8470**).

Emergencies   Dial ☎ **911** to report a fire, call the police, or get an ambulance. This is a nationwide toll-free call (no coins are required at a public telephone).

If theft or an accident has left you stranded, check the local telephone directory to find an office of the **Traveler's Aid Society,** a nationwide, not-for-profit social-service organization that is geared to helping travelers in distress. If you're in trouble, seek it out.

In Atlanta, the **Georgia Council for International Visitors,** 34 Peachtree ST., suite 1200, Atlanta, GA 30303 (☎ **404/832-5560**), can provide a wide variety of help to foreign visitors in more than 42 languages.

Gasoline (Petrol)   One U.S. gallon equals 3.8 liters, whereas 1.2 U.S. gallons equals 1 Imperial gallon. You'll notice that several variously named grades (and price levels) of gasoline are available at most gas stations. The unleaded fuels with the highest octane rating are the most expensive; most rental cars take the least expensive "regular" unleaded. Leaded gas is the least expensive, but only older cars can take it anymore, so check if you're not sure. Often, the price is lower if you pay in cash instead of by credit card. Many gas stations offer lower-priced self-service gas pumps; some gas stations, particularly at night, are all self-service.

Holidays   On the following legal national holidays, banks, government offices, post offices, and many stores, restaurants, and museums are closed: January 1 (New Year's Day), the third Monday in January (Martin Luther King, Jr., Day), the third Monday in February (Presidents' Day), the last Monday in May (Memorial Day), July 4 (Independence Day), the first Monday after the first Sunday in September (Labor Day), the second Monday in October (Columbus Day), November 11 (Veterans Day), the fourth Thursday in November (Thanksgiving Day), and December 25 (Christmas). The Tuesday following the first Monday in November is Election Day and is a legal holiday in presidential-election years.

Legal Aid   The foreign visitor will rarely become involved with the American legal system. If you are stopped for a minor infraction (such as speeding on the highway), never attempt to pay the fine directly to the police officer; you may wind up being accused of the much more serious charge of attempted bribery. Pay fines by mail. (You can also pay them directly into the hands of the clerk of the court.) If you're accused of a more serious offense, it's wise to say and do nothing before consulting a lawyer. Under U.S. law, an arrested person is allowed one telephone call to a party of his or her choice. Call your embassy or consulate.

Mail   If you want to receive mail during your vacation, and you aren't sure what your address will be, your mail can be sent in your name, c/o **General Delivery**

(Poste Restante), to the main post office of the city or region where you expect to be. The addressee must pick up mail in person and produce proof of identity (driver's license, credit or charge card, passport, and so on).

Domestic **postage rates** are 20¢ for a postcard and 34¢ for a letter. For overseas mail, a first-class letter (up to half an ounce) is 80¢ (60¢ to Canada and Mexico); a first-class postcard costs 70¢ (50¢ to Canada and Mexico); and a preprinted postal aerogramme costs 70¢.

Generally located at busy intersections, **mailboxes** are blue, with a blue eagle logo and the designation U.S. POSTAL SERVICE. If your mail is addressed to a U.S. destination, don't forget to add the five- (or nine-) digit **postal code,** or ZIP (Zone Improvement Plan) Code, after the two-letter abbreviation of the state (GA for Georgia, NC for North Carolina, SC for South Carolina, and so on).

Measures   The traditional American system of measures is still used in the United States, although many products now carry both U.S. and metric measures. In general, 1 foot equals about 30.48 centimeters; 1 mile about 1.609 kilometers. A pint equals .47 liter, and 1 quart (2 pints) .94 liter, 1 gallon (4 quarts) 3.79 liters. An ounce equals 28.35 grams, and 1 pound (16 ounces) equals .45 kilograms.

Temperature is measured in degrees Fahrenheit: 0° Celsius equals 32° Fahrenheit.

Medical Emergencies   To call an ambulance, dial ☎ **911** from any phone. No coins are needed.

Newspapers & Magazines   National newspapers include the *New York Times, USA Today,* and the *Wall Street Journal.* National news weeklies include *Newsweek, Time,* and *U.S. News & World Report.* In large cities, most newsstands offer a small selection of the most popular foreign periodicals and newspapers, such as *The Economist, Le Monde,* and *Der Spiegel.* For information on leading state newspapers, see the "Fast Facts" sections for each state in chapters 3, 9, and 15.

Radio & Television   Audiovisual media, with four coast-to-coast networks (ABC, CBS, NBC, and Fox), plus the Public Broadcasting System (PBS) and Cable News Network (CNN), play a major part in American life. In big cities, viewers have a choice of about a dozen channels (including the UHF channels), most of them transmitting 24 hours a day, not counting the pay-TV channels that show recent movies or sports events. All options are usually indicated on your hotel TV set.

You'll also find a wide choice of local radio stations, both AM and FM. Stations broadcast particular kinds of talk shows and/or music (classical, country, jazz, pop, or gospel, for example), punctuated by news broadcasts and frequent commercials. You'll usually find the affiliates of the National Public Radio system at the bottom of the radio dial, broadcasting in-depth news programs as well as talk shows and other eclectic programming. In smaller towns and communities, local radio and TV stations have a more limited broadcast range.

Safety   See the "Safety" section of "Preparing for Your Trip," earlier in this chapter.

Taxes   The United States has no VAT (value-added tax) or other indirect tax at the national level. Every state, and each county and city in it, is allowed to levy its own local nonrefundable tax on purchases (including hotels, restaurant checks, airline tickets, and so on) and services. Taxes are already included in the price of certain services, such as public transportation, cab fares, telephone calls, and gasoline. The amount of sales tax varies from about 4% to 12%, depending on the state and city, so when you're making major purchases (such as photographic equipment, clothing, or stereo components), it can be a significant part of the cost.

The state sales tax is 6% in Georgia, 6% in North Carolina, and 5% in South Carolina.

Telephone, Telegraph, Telex & Fax   The telephone system in the United States is run by private corporations, so rates, especially for long-distance service and operator-assisted calls, can vary widely—even on calls made from public telephones. Local calls in the BellSouth area of Georgia, South Carolina, and North Carolina cost 35¢.

Generally, hotel surcharges on long-distance and local calls are astronomical. You're usually better off calling collect, using a telephone charge card, or using **public pay telephones,** which you'll find clearly marked in most public buildings and private establishments as well as on the street. Outside metropolitan areas, public telephones are more difficult to find. Stores and gas stations are your best bet.

Most **long-distance and international calls** can be dialed directly from any phone. (Stock up on quarters and dimes if you're calling from a pay phone, or use a telephone charge card.) For calls to Canada and other parts of the United States, dial 1, followed by the area code and the seven-digit number. For international calls, dial 011, followed by the country code (such as 61 for Australia, 353 for the Republic of Ireland, 64 for New Zealand, and 44 for the United Kingdom), the city code (for example, 020 for London and 0121 for Birmingham), and the telephone number of the person you want to call.

All calls to area codes 800 and 888 are toll-free. Calls to numbers in area codes 700 and 900 (chat lines, bulletin boards, "dating" services, and so on) can be very expensive, however. These calls usually carry a charge of 95¢ to $3 or more per minute, and they sometimes have minimum charges that can run as high as $15 or more.

For **reversed-charge (collect) calls** and for **person-to-person calls,** dial 0 (zero, *not* the letter "O"), followed by the area code and number you want. An operator will then come on the line, and you should specify that you are calling collect, person-to-person, or both. If your operator-assisted call is international, ask for the overseas operator.

For **local directory assistance** ("information"), dial **411;** for **long-distance information,** dial 1, followed by the appropriate area code and 555-1212.

Like the telephone system, **telegraph** and **telex** services are provided by private corporations such as ITT, MCI, and above all, Western Union. You can take your telegram to the nearest Western Union office (there are hundreds across the country) or dictate it over the phone (toll-free call: ☎ **800/325-6000**). You can also telegraph money (using a major credit or charge card), or have it telegraphed to you, very quickly over the Western Union system. (This service can be very expensive, however. The service charge can run as high as 15% to 25% of the amount sent.) If you find yourself out of money, a wire service provided by American Express can help you tap willing friends and family for emergency funds. Through **MONEYGRAM,** 7501 W. Mansfield, Lakewood, CO 80235 (☎ **800/926-9400**), money can be sent around the world in 12 to 24 minutes.

Many hotels have **fax** machines available for guest use (be sure to ask about the charge to use it), and many hotel rooms are even wired for guests' fax machines. Almost all shops that make photocopies offer fax services as well.

Telephone Directory   There are two kinds of telephone directories. The general directory is the so-called **White Pages,** in which private and business subscribers are listed in alphabetical order. The inside front cover lists the emergency numbers for police, fire, and ambulance, and other vital numbers (the Coast Guard, poison-control center, crime-victims' hot line, and so on). The first few pages are devoted to community-service numbers, as well as a guide to long-distance and international calling, complete with country codes and area codes.

The second directory, printed on yellow paper (hence its name, **Yellow Pages**), lists all local services, businesses, and industries by type of activity, with an index at the back. The listings include automobile repairs by make of car, drugstores (pharmacies) by geographical location, restaurants by type of cuisine and geographical location, bookstores by special subject and/or language, places of worship by religious denomination, and other information that the tourist might otherwise not readily find. The Yellow Pages often includes city plans or detailed area maps, as well as ZIP Codes and public-transportation routes.

Time   The United States is divided into six time zones. From east to west, these zones are eastern standard time (EST), central standard time (CST), mountain standard time (MST), Pacific standard time (PST), Alaska standard time (AST), and Hawaii standard time (HST). Always keep the changing time zones in mind if you are traveling (or even telephoning) over long distances in the United States. Noon in New York City (EST), for example, is 11am in Chicago (CST), 10am in Phoenix (MST), 9am in Los Angeles (PST), 8am in Anchorage (AST), and 7am in Honolulu (HST).

Georgia and the Carolinas observe Eastern Standard Time. **Daylight saving time** is in effect from the first Sunday in April through the last Saturday in October (actually, the change is made at 2am on Sunday), except in Arizona, Hawaii, part of Indiana, and Puerto Rico. Daylight saving time moves the clock 1 hour ahead of standard time. (Americans use the adage "spring ahead, fall back" to remember which way to change their clocks and watches.)

Tipping   This is part of the American way of life, on the principle that you must expect to pay for any service that you get. (Many service personnel receive little direct salary and must depend on tips for their income.) Service charges are not included in restaurant checks or hotel bills. Here are some rules of thumb:

In **hotels,** tip bellhops $1 per piece of luggage, and tip the chamber staff $1 per day. Tip the doorman or concierge only if he or she provides some specific service, such as calling a cab for you or obtaining difficult-to-get theater tickets.

In **restaurants, bars, and nightclubs,** tip the service staff 15% of the check; tip bartenders 10% to 15%; tip checkroom attendants $1 per garment; and tip valet-parking attendants $1 per vehicle. Tip the doorman only if he provides some specific service, such as calling a cab for you. Tipping is not expected in cafeterias and fast-food restaurants.

Tip **cab drivers** 15% of the fare.

As for **other service personnel,** tip porters at airports or railroad stations $1 per piece of luggage, and tip hairdressers and barbers 15% to 20%.

You are not expected to tip gas-station attendants or ushers in cinemas or theaters.

3

Planning a Trip to North Carolina

In the pages that follow, we've compiled everything that you need to know to handle the practical details on planning your trip: airlines, a calendar of events, visitor information, and more.

1 The Regions in Brief

THE HIGH COUNTRY The **Blue Ridge Parkway** seems to touch the sky as it traces the jutting peaks and rising plateaus of the North Carolina mountains. Set in the splendor of these hills are the mountain folk, who strive to retain their lifestyle despite the headaches and traffic caused by tourists taking in the sights along the parkway.

The peak time for entering the parkway is May through October, when hotel accommodations are plentiful and visitor facilities are open. Fall is when the landscape is at its best. The natural foliage of the mountain evergreens is magically enhanced by a brisk palette of reds, yellows, oranges, and golds. Although winter rates are appealing, cold-weather conditions may make roads inaccessible. As though the mountains were not inspiring enough, North Carolina also offers other sites filled with natural splendor.

You can create your own script for this 470-mile drive—called the "Most Scenic Highway in America"—by entering at the southern end of Shenandoah National Park near the Virginia border. The slow drive that follows the road's sharp curves and narrow straightaways is full of serendipitous discoveries, from fresh-grown apples sold at stands along the roadside to rustic "junk" stores.

The rolling pasturelands of the Blue Ridge's northern access lie in Allegheny and Ashe counties, picture-perfect with grazing cows and lichen-covered split-rail fences. As you approach Watauga, Avery, and Mitchell counties, the mountains seem to rise like images in a fast-paced video game. **Grandfather Mountain** is the site of a staggering engineering feat: a roadway that swings treacherously 1,243 feet around the curve of craggy mountain. With down-home eateries, inns, panoramic views of misty blue mountains, and hiking trails spread along the length of the parkway, plus the highest peak in the eastern United States at **Mount Mitchell State Park** (6,684 feet), you'll be amazed by the sights you'll see along the road, in spite of the traffic.

There are ways to avoid crowds and traffic even during the peak season. Park rangers suggest that you drive the parkway Monday

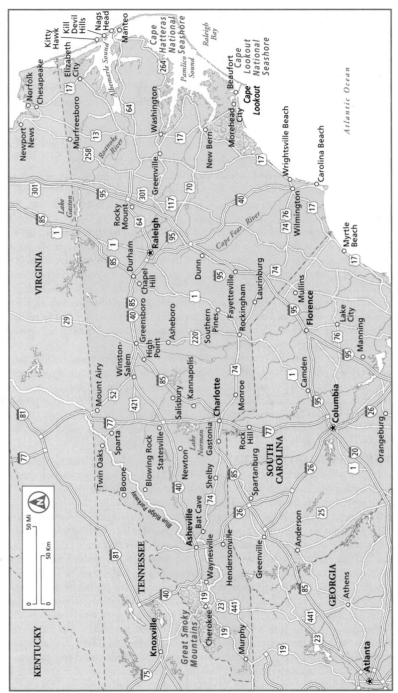

through Friday, when the roads are less congested. Avoid Sunday afternoon altogether, and be adventurous: Go off the beaten track. Numerous side roads run parallel to the parkway or branch off from it. Visitor centers furnish detailed maps, but rangers recommend that you get specific instructions before venturing out onto one of these roads.

Plan on spending at least 2 days in the **Cherokee** area. Although the town is a little touristy, a smattering of intimate hideaways is concealed along the back roads of Great Smoky Mountains National Park near Cherokee.

Set just off the Blue Ridge Parkway, about 40 miles east of Cherokee, is **Asheville,** a stunning small city worthy of a 3-day stay, with attractions such as the Biltmore Estate, the Thomas Wolfe Memorial, and the Folk Art Center.

THE PIEDMONT   After you visit the mountains, head east to **Winston-Salem,** our favorite Piedmont City. The former seat of the powerful Reynolds tobacco fortune, Winston-Salem is also home to Old Salem, a restored 18th- and 19th-century village settled by German-speaking Moravians, and Wake Forest University.

Another component of the Piedmont is the **Raleigh/Durham/Chapel Hill area,** often referred to as the Research Triangle. This area has attracted all sorts of high-tech industry to the state—no wonder, because three of the premier universities in the South (Duke, the University of North Carolina, and North Carolina State) are located here, within a stone's throw of one another. The proximity of Duke to Carolina has given rise to perhaps the greatest rivalry in college-basketball history—although State's consistently competitive hoops program can never be counted out of the equation. Chapel Hill is the charming college town, Durham the up-and-coming hot spot, and Raleigh the bustling state capital.

The largest city in the Piedmont is **Charlotte.** Surprisingly cosmopolitan and set amid rolling hills, this fast-paced city rivals Orlando or Birmingham and dismisses the down-home label. It's a major banking center and transportation hub, and its diversified manufacturing capabilities include machinery, textiles, metals, and food products. Charlotte has also been transformed into a big-time sports town: The state's first pro football team, the Carolina Panthers, and the NBA's Charlotte Hornets have quickly become hot tickets.

THE COAST/THE OUTER BANKS   A trip through North Carolina wouldn't be complete without sticking your toes in the brisk Atlantic. The largest city on the coast is **Wilmington,** although much of North Carolina's shoreline remains much less developed than the frenetic scene along South Carolina's beaches. In spite of the slow-poke summer traffic, **Nags Head** especially has a little something for every family member, from a rustic fishing pier to nearby video arcades. It also offers some of the finest seafood restaurants on the East Coast, many in modest settings. Local specialties include Hatteras-style clam chowder, crab cakes, and deep-fried hush puppies. Surprisingly, Nags Head lacks one thing that most of its rival resorts do have: high-rise condos. Instead, towering overhead is Jockey's Ridge, a giant sand dune that forms the tallest *medano* (large, isolated hill of sand) in the East. Climb to the top of the mile-long, 4,000-foot-wide dune for outstanding views of the ocean and sound.

Another wonderful spot is **Ocracoke Island,** a 45-minute ride across the waters of Pamlico Sound. A free ferry departs Hatteras village every 30 minutes, beginning daily at 5am. Disembarking at the north-end ferry visitor station, head for the town of Ocracoke while enjoying the expanses of wild dunes and forests of cedar and pine. The beaches leading into the town of Ocracoke are some of the best on the East Coast.

Much of the island is a National Seashore area where large development is prohibited. While this is a place where you still can go into the post office barefooted to check your mail, it's not the sleepy little backwater it was even 10 years ago. The town of Ocracoke has ceded to the demands of tourism, building several multi-story hotels around Silver Lake, restaurants, and shops selling the requisite beach hammocks, taffy, T-shirts, and souvenirs. Visit in the fall, when you'll see the island at its best, a real North Carolina charmer.

2 Visitor Information & Money

VISITOR INFORMATION

For specific information, contact the **North Carolina Division of Tourism, Film and Sports Development,** 430 N. Salisbury St., Raleigh, NC 27611 (☎ **800/VISIT-NC** or 919/733-4171; www.visitnc.com). Excellent visitor centers located at the state borders on most major highways can also furnish detailed tourist information.

MONEY

In addition to checking the details in this section, foreign visitors should see "Preparing for Your Trip" in chapter 2.

It's getting easier all the time to access your bank account while you're on the road. You won't have any problem finding ATMs all over the state that are connected to the major national networks. For specific locations of **Cirrus** machines, call ☎ **800/ 424-7787;** for the **PLUS** network, dial ☎ **800/843-7587.**

American Express offices are open Monday to Friday from 8:30am to 5pm. See "Fast Facts: North Carolina," later in this chapter for office locations.

If you run out of funds on the road, you can have a friend or relative advance you some money through a service sponsored by American Express. **MONEYGRAM,** 7501 W. Mansfield, Lakewood, CO 80235 (☎ **800/926-9400**), allows you to transfer

What Things Cost in Asheville	U.S. $
Taxi from the airport to downtown	22.00
Local phone call	.35
Double room at the Richmond Inn Resort (expensive)	295.00
Double room at the Cedar Crest Inn (moderate)	135.00
Double room at the Old Reynolds Mansion Bed & Breakfast (inexpensive)	85.00
Lunch for one at the Mountain Smoke House (moderate)	16.00
Lunch for one at Vicenzo's	12.00
Dinner for one, without wine, at the Horizons Restaurant (expensive)	63.00
Dinner for one, without wine, at the Blue Ridge Dining Room (moderate)	35.00
Dinner for one, without wine, at the Charlotte St. Grill	20.00
Bottle of beer	3.50–5.00
Coca-Cola	.80
Roll of 35mm 200-speed film, 36 exposures	4.95
Movie ticket	6.50
Ticket to the Asheville Symphony	20.00
Adult admission to the Biltmore Estate	32.00

funds from one person to another in less than 10 minutes from thousands of locations. An American Express phone representative will give you the names of four or five offices nearby. The service charge is $21.60 for the first $300 sent, with a sliding scale after that.

3 When to Go

For the most part, North Carolina's climate is moderate, with average winter temperatures in the 60s along the southern coast and in the low 40s inland. Summer temperatures can rise to the high 90s in the state's interior, accompanied by some serious humidity. If you're in the mountains or on the shore, temperatures can be cooled by breezes to the mid-60s or high 70s.

So if you're thinking about a summer vacation in North Carolina, we don't advise heading for the Piedmont, where all that miserable heat and humidity hangs heavy. But you can escape to Boone, which has an average temperature of 69°. It's warm enough during the day to swim or hike, but you'll want a light blanket to sleep under at night. The Outer Banks is another great destination in summer; bring your beach gear, and enjoy the breezes.

Raleigh Average Temperatures & Rainfall

	Jan	Feb	Mar	Apr	May	June	July	Aug	Sept	Oct	Nov	Dec
High (°F)	50	52	61	72	78	85	88	87	81	71	61	52
Low (°F)	29	30	37	46	55	62	67	66	60	47	38	31
Rain (in.)	3.5	3.7	3.8	2.6	3.9	3.7	4.0	4.0	3.2	2.9	3.0	3.2

Asheville Average Temperatures & Rainfall

	Jan	Feb	Mar	Apr	May	June	July	Aug	Sept	Oct	Nov	Dec
High (°F)	49	51	57	68	76	83	85	84	79	69	57	50
Low (°F)	30	30	36	44	52	60	64	63	57	46	36	30
Rain (in.)	3.2	3.0	3.7	3.2	2.9	3.5	4.3	3.6	2.8	2.5	2.2	2.9

In late September or early October, fall colors are brilliant here. During this time, thousands of monarch butterflies cluster in the mountains near Asheville, around Wagon Road Gap on the Blue Ridge Parkway, as part of their annual migration to South America. Don't miss it! (But be prepared for incredible crowds in Asheville and along the parkway.)

Spring is also a spectacular time to visit. In March and April, the state bursts into bloom, with azaleas in vibrant hues everywhere, rhododendrons in the mountains, and the more delicate pink-and-white dogwood blossoms in the woodlands.

North Carolina Calendar of Events

January

- **Black American Arts Festival,** Greensboro. Many cultural and artistic events highlight the achievements of the state's African-American population. Call ☎ **336/373-7523.** Early January to late March.

February

- **Home and Garden Show,** Raleigh. You can find everything from roses to garden fountains to furniture in this vast display, which attracts serious gardeners from all over the South. Call ☎ **919/831-6011.** Mid-February.

- **Edge of the World Snowboard Series,** at Hawksnest Golf & Ski Resort, Seven Devils. This snowboard competition brings visitors from all over to try their skill in four divisions and two disciplines (Freestyle and Boardercross). The event is followed by an awards ceremony with lots of food and musical entertainment. Call ☎ **888/429-5763;** www.hawksnest-resort.com. February 20.
- **NC International Jazz Festival,** Durham. Internationally renowned jazz musicians are featured at various locations throughout the city. Call ☎ **919/ 687-0288** or 800/446-8604; www.durham-nc.com. Late Februrary to early March.

March

○ **Annual Star Fiddlers Convention,** Biscoe. This memorable event features performances by virtuoso bluegrass fiddlers from all over the South. Call ☎ **910/ 428-2972.** First weekend in March.

April

- **Festival of Flowers,** Biltmore Estate, Asheville. The festival celebrates a century of elegance at the Biltmore Estate. The gardens are brilliant with color for your viewing. Call ☎ **800/543-2961;** www.biltmore.com. April 1 to 30.
- **North Carolina Azalea Festival,** Wilmington. A parade, entertainment, and home and garden tours are all included in this annual festival. Call ☎ **910/ 763-0905.** April 5 to 8.
- **Spring Historic Homes and Gardens Tour,** New Bern. Tour Tryon Palace and other area homes, gardens, and historic sites. Call ☎ **252/633-6448.** First weekend in April.
- **Stoneybrook Steeplechase,** Southern Pines. This event features horse races and tailgate parties. Call ☎ **800/847-1862.** Mid-April.
- **Spring Garden Tour,** Winston-Salem. Each spring in historic Old Salem, people gather from everywhere to celebrate spring with a tour of the city's 18th-century gardens. Call ☎ **888/653-7253;** www.oldsalem.org. Mid-April.
- **Easter Sunrise Service,** Winston-Salem. Thousands of people come to see this Moravian religious service in "God's Acres," the cemetery where the early settlers are buried. Call ☎ **336/722-6171.** Easter Sunday.
- **Springfest,** Charlotte. Live bands provide entertainment while folks stroll through the streets of downtown, buying snacks from food vendors and checking out the arts and crafts. Call ☎ **704/552-6500.** Three days in late April.
- **Greater Greensboro Chrysler Classic,** Greensboro. Some 275,000 fans come to the galleries of Forest Oaks Country Club to watch the pros compete for the $1.5 million purse of this nationally televised tournament, one of the richest on the PGA tour. Call ☎ **800-999-5446** or 336/379-1570; www.ggcc.com. April 23–29.

May

- **DoubleTake Documentary Film Festival,** the Carolina Theatre, Durham. Largest festival of its kind in North America, the event has been hailed for its creative programming and exhibition of films rarely seen on screen. Call ☎ **919/660-3699;** www-cds.aas.duke.edu/filmfestival/. Early May.
- **Duke Children's Classic,** Durham. Celebrity golf tournament to benefit Duke Children's Hospital & Health Center at Duke University Medical Center. Official stop on the Celebrity Players Tour. Call ☎ **919/667-2571.** May 19 to 21.
- ○ **Ole Time Fiddlers & Bluegrass Festival,** Union Grove. Traditional musicians and the fans who love bluegrass make a yearly pilgrimage to what may be the

most renowned fiddling competition in the country. PBS made an award-winning documentary on the festival. Call ☎ **704/539-4417.** Memorial Day weekend.

- **Coca-Cola 600,** Charlotte. This action-packed race, which is part of the NASCAR Winston Cup Series, takes place at Lowe's Motor Speedway. Enjoy the Food Lion Speed Street, three days of race-related festivities on Tryon Street in Charlotte; 370,000 people showed up in 2000. Call ☎ **704/455-6814;** www. 600festival.com. May 27.

June

- ✪ **American Dance Festival,** Durham. Considered to be the largest and most prestigious modern-dance event in the world, the festival has been held on the Duke University campus since 1978. Call ☎ **919/684-6402;** www. americandancefestival.org. Early June through late July.

- ✪ **The Lost Colony,** Roanoke Island. Paul Green's moving drama is presented in the Waterside Theater Monday through Saturday at 8:30pm. It's the country's oldest outdoor drama, running since 1937. All seats are reserved; contact the Waterside Theater (☎ **800/488-5012** or 252/473-3414) for Visa or Master-Card bookings. Tickets cost $16 for adults; $15 for senior citizens, military personnel, and people who have disabilities; and $8 for children 11 and under. Early June to late August.

- **Crosby Celebrity Golf Tournament,** Winston-Salem. This annual event is held at Bermuda Run and attracts many celebrities. Call ☎ **336/519-7500.** Mid-June.

- **Hillsborough Hog Day,** Hillsborough. Featured attractions include barbecue, potbellied-pig contests, entertainment, crafts, and a vintage car show. Call ☎ **919/732-7741.** Mid-June.

- ✪ **National Hollerin' Contest,** Spivey's Corner. Immortalized by a visit from Charles Kuralt at its 1969 inaugural, this event celebrates hollerin' as a traditional form of communication. Drawing visitors from all over the country, the contest swells Spivey's Corner's usual population of 49. Call ☎ **910/567-2156.** Third Saturday in June.

July

- **Shindig-on-the-Green,** Asheville. At the City Country Plaza (College and Spruce streets), you'll find mountain musicians and dancers having an old-fashioned wingding. The event is free and lots of fun. Every Saturday night from early July through August (except for the first Saturday in August).

- ✪ **Grandfather Mountain Highland Games and Gathering of the Scottish Clans,** Linville. The event is complete with Scottish dance, music, and athletic competitions. Call ☎ **828/733-1333.** Early July.

- **Festival of the Arts,** Brevard. This weeklong festival features a children's exhibit, creative and performing arts, and food in venues throughout the city. Call ☎ **828/884-2787.** Second week in July.

- **Coon Dog Day,** Saluda. For more than 30 years, coon hunters and nature lovers have gathered for dog trials, arts and craft shows, a parade, food, and a treeing contest. It's truly folkloric Carolina. Call ☎ **828/749-2581.** Saturday following the Fourth of July.

- **Folkmoot USA (North Carolina International Folk Festival),** Waynesville and Maggie Valley. Folkmoot USA provides international music and dance, plus good old-fashioned North Carolina mountain music. Call ☎ **877/365-5872** or 828/452-2997; www.folkmoot.com. Late July.

- **National Black Theatre Festival,** Winston-Salem. This festival includes performances, workshops, and seminars at various theaters around the city, produced and hosted by the city's own North Carolina Black Repertory Co. Call ☎ **336/723-72266;** www.nbtf.org. July 30 to August 4. Held biannually in odd years.

August

- **Annual Mountain Dance and Folk Festival,** Asheville. At the Civic Center on Haywood Street, the fiddlers, banjo pickers, dulcimer players, ballad singers, and clog dancers don't call it quits until nobody is interested in one more dance. This is the oldest such festival in the country, and you're encouraged to join in. First weekend in August.
- **Jazz at Brevard.** Begin today and work your way back to the 1950s as you listen to various styles of jazz. Take a blanket and a picnic basket, or enjoy food provided by local restaurants. Call ☎ **828/884-2787.** Mid-August.
- **Herb Day,** Durham. See displays of traditional herb remedies and recipes of the mid-19th century. There are herbs from an on-site garden, herbal crafts, and food available for purchase. Call ☎ **919/477-5498.** Late August.

September

- **North Carolina Apple Festival,** Hendersonville. Bring your favorite apple-pie recipe, and enjoy music, crafts, games, and a cooking contest. Call ☎ **828/697-4557.** Labor Day weekend.
- **Bald Is Beautiful,** Morehead City. Annual festival and convention sponsored by the Bald Headed Men of America, featuring contest for the shiniest head. Call ☎ **919/726-1855.** Second weekend in September.
- **Festival in the Park,** Charlotte. A celebration of regional arts and crafts, with entertainment and good food as added bonuses. Call ☎ **704/338-1060.** Six days in mid-September.
- **Mayberry Days,** Mount Airy. A celebration of "The Andy Griffith Show," with entertainment, a golf tournament, walking tours, and a pig pickin'. Call ☎ **800/286-6193.** Last weekend in September.
- **Vantage Championship Senior Golf Tournament,** Winston-Salem. Arnold Palmer, Lee Trevino, and many other well-known golfers play in this tournament each year. Call ☎ **336/766-2400.** Late September to early October.

October

- **Annual Chrysanthemum Festival,** Tryon. Tryon Palace Historic Sites and Gardens hosts a street festival loaded with food, fun, arts and crafts, and tours. Call ☎ **252/638-5781.** Early October.
- **Folk Festival IV,** Winston-Salem. This Fiddle & Bow music festival is held each year at the Southeastern Center for Contemporary Art (SECCA), 750 Marguerite Dr., Winston-Salem (☎ **336/725-1904**). Enjoy the contest, country cooking, and entertainment. Call ☎ **336/727-1038.** Mid-October.
- **North Carolina State Fair,** Raleigh. This traditional gathering draws crowds from all over. Call ☎ **919/733-2145;** www.ncstatefair.org. Mid-October.

November

- **Festival of Lights,** Tanglewood Park, Winston-Salem. For 9 weeks, more than 750,000 lights are presented in more than five dozen displays. Enjoy storybook themes. Call ☎ **336/778-6300;** www.tanglewoodpark.org. Early November to early January.
- **Christmas at the Biltmore Estate,** Asheville. The Biltmore Estate becomes a winter wonderland long before Christmas. Enjoy Christmas lights, trees,

A Dilly of an Affair

Like most Southerners, North Carolinians love to eat—and they like nothing better than to celebrate food in the company of others. Year-round, the Tarheel State has a busy calendar of down-home events honoring the local bounty. The **N.C. Pickle Festival** (☎ 919/658-3113), a "dilly of an affair," brings hundreds of visitors to the town of Mount Olive in late April. The Mt. Olive Pickle Company, the largest independent pickle company in the U.S., has been making pickles at the corner of Cucumber and Vine since 1926, and half of the 100 million pounds of cucumbers it puts up yearly come from N.C. farms. The festival features such delicacies as Dill Pickle Pizza, live music, and a walking, talking 8-foot pickle. April is also the month when thousands descend on the town of Grifton to celebrate a small bony fish known as the hickory shad. The popularity of the **Grifton Shad Festival** (☎ 252/524-4934) may rest less on the shad—it's considered a delicacy to some, a poor excuse for a meal to others—than on the festival's fun, creative approach: one-third of the events are arts related, and it even features a celebration of the whopper, the Fishy Tales Story-telling Contest. In May the arrival of the intensely flavored member of the onion family called ramp is celebrated at the **Ramp Festival** (☎ 800/334-9036), in Waynesville. Sweet shrimp from local waters are the source of pride at the **Sneads Ferry Shrimp Festival** (☎ 910/328-4722), held the second weekend in August. September, the harvest month, is one big party: Collard greens are the theme at the **N.C. Collard Festival** (☎ 800/537-5564), in Ayden; in Hendersonville, it's apples—and apple pie, applesauce, crafts, and entertainment—at the **N.C. Apple Festival** (☎ 828/697-4557). In the third week in October, head east to Shallotte, on the southern coast, for the **N.C. Oyster Festival** (☎ 910/426-6644), featuring 100 arts and crafts vendors, live music, and mounds of bivalves. Or go west to the nationally acclaimed—and perhaps quintessential North Carolina food fest—the **Lexington Barbecue Festival** (☎ 336/956-1880).

decorations, and music. Call ☎ **800/413-9790** or 704/255-1700; www.biltmore.com. November 7 to January 3.

December

○ **Old Salem Christmas and Candle Teas,** Winston-Salem. A re-creation of Yuletide as it was celebrated 200 years ago in Old Salem. Enjoy making candles, tasting Moravian sugar cakes, and touring the 1788 Gemeinhaus by candlelight. Call ☎ **800/441-5305.** First 2 weeks in December.

• **Holiday Festival,** Raleigh. The city hosts the Holiday Festival at the North Carolina Museum of Art. It's an old-fashioned Yuletide celebration. Call ☎ **919/839-6262,** ext. 2152; www.ncartmuseum.org. December 7.

4 The Active Vacation Planner

North Carolina presents an incredible array of landscapes and recreational offerings. The beaches are outstanding, and they're never as crowded as those on South Carolina's Grand Strand. Broad stretches of white sand offer waves to challenge the most skillful surfer, and quiet, family-oriented seaside resorts can be found on both the Outer Banks and along the southern "Crystal Coast." Fishing, boating, water skiing, sand skiing, and even hang-gliding from gigantic dunes are all part of the fun up and down the coast.

The opposite end of the state holds the Great Smoky Mountains, which offer some of the most spectacular scenery in the Southeast—not to mention ample opportunities for hiking, fly fishing, white-water rafting, and camping. And if your game is golf or tennis, North Carolina's got plenty to keep you entertained.

ACTIVITIES A TO Z

BICYCLING   Miles of back roads and lots of flat terrain (except in the mountains) make North Carolina an ideal venue for bikers.

Those who like biking by the beach can head for the Outer Banks. It's best to begin in Corolla, where a separate bike path parallels N.C. 12 for many miles south.

The gently sloping Piedmont, with its hard-packed surfaces, is also good road-biking country. The tourist office in Winston-Salem can provide maps of the Piedmont's most scenic bike tours through the historic Bethabara and Tanglewood parks. Outside Charlotte, McAlpine Creek Park has a 2-mile trail for bikers. The nearly deserted lanes and sleepy hamlets of Pinehurst and Southern Pines are our favorite spots.

For mountain bikers, the Asheville Convention and Visitors Bureau supplies a list of outfitters that also provide trail maps. Regrettably, the scenic Blue Ridge Parkway has no lanes for bikers, who are forced to ride single-file along the side of the two-lane highway. Helmets and kneepads are required, and white lights and reflectors are necessary to go through some two dozen dark-as-night tunnels. Fog is also a frequent occurrence. There's less traffic to face Monday to Thursday. Any holiday, and the traffic-clogged months of May and October, are the worst times to bike the Blue Ridge.

For bicycle route maps, contact the **North Carolina Department of Transportation's Bicycle Program,** P.O. Box 25201, Raleigh, NC 27611 (☎ **919/733-2804**). Bikers can also write for a free 50-page catalog of **Backroads Bicycle Touring,** 801 Cedar St., Berkeley, CA 94710-1800 (☎ **800/462-2848**), a reliable firm that offers organized bike tours.

BIRDING   The Outer Banks traditionally draws birders, especially those who are interested in seasonal migrations. Cape Lookout National Seashore is the most remote state beach and a nesting area for the piping plover. On Cape Fear, birders head for Sunset Beach. Here, on the west end, they can wade across Mad Inlet at low tide to reach Bird Island, which is Valhalla for all bird watchers. In this isolated place, herons, egrets, osprey, and an array of other beautiful birds come to feed and nest.

CAMPING   Campers can find very good facilities throughout North Carolina, with fees ranging from $12 to $17 per night. RV hookups, however, are available only at selected sites. For detailed information, contact the **Division of Parks and Recreation,** Department of the Environment, Health and Natural Resources, P.O. Box 27687, Raleigh, NC 27611 (☎ **919/733-4181;** www.ils.unc.edu/parkproject/ ncparks.html). The excellent *Official North Carolina Highway Map and Guide to Points of Interest* also has extensive information about national and state parks and forests.

The **Great Smoky Mountains,** named for the smoky blue haze that crowns their tops, run for more than 70 miles, picking up where the Blue Ridge Parkway ends. The 520,000-acre park lies half in North Carolina and half in Tennessee. It shelters bears, deer, wild turkeys, and grouse, among other forms of wildlife. Summer brings an ever-changing kaleidoscope of color from flowering plants. Within the park boundaries are no fewer than 130 native species of trees in 180,000 acres of virgin forest.

Camping is best along the 70 miles of the Appalachian Trail, which follows the ridge that forms the North Carolina–Tennessee border. Be warned, however, that reservations are required between mid-May and October. Contact **National Park Reservation Service,** P.O. Box 1600, Cumberland, MD 21501 (☎ **800/365-2267;** E-mail: reservations@nps.org).

FISHING   From fly-fishing to deep-sea or light-tackle fishing, the **Outer Banks** provide some of the best opportunities for anglers in the United States. You can catch channel bass in the spring; whiting, flounder, and Spanish mackerel during the summer; and small bluefish in autumn. Pompano run from spring until the beginning of winter. Big bluefish are hunted almost year-round. Unless you want to go deep-sea fishing, you won't need a boat along the 300 miles of coastline, studded with jetties and piers; some 25% of all Atlantic piers are in North Carolina. Some piers are better known than others: Nags Head for flounder, bluefish, mullet, and striped bass; and Ocracoke Island for sea mullet, bluefish, and pompano. Pursuers of big amberjack and tarpon head for the piers along the Bogue Banks in the Neuse River region.

The lakes, rivers, and streams of the mountains are the second major venue for fishermen, especially for those who are seeking trout, muskies, catfish, and small- and largemouth bass. The best places for fishing include the Linville River, the Toe River and its tributaries, the Globe section of the Johns River Gorge, and Howard's Creek (north of Boone). Local tourist offices can supply complete details. For trout fanciers, the lakes and streams of the Blue Ridge are ideal. Trout fishermen are also drawn to the Great Smoky Mountains, with hundreds of miles of streams and creeks that are home to smallmouth bass, rock bass, and brown and rainbow trout. (It's illegal to catch brook trout.) Rangers at the visitor centers provide guidelines, and you can buy Don Kirk's *Smoky Mountains Trout Fishing Guide* if you plan to do serious angling there.

Most hardware and general stores supply fishing licenses, which are required for all fishermen age 16 or older. With the license comes a list of rules and state laws, especially regarding fish size.

GOLF   North Carolina is one of the best states for golf in the nation. Southern Pines and the Pinehurst Sandhills (see chapter 6) are called the Golf Capital of the World—with good reason. Some 35 golf courses fill these sandhills, which have attracted most of the greatest names in the sport. The Pinehurst Hotel and Country Club—the only resort with seven signature courses—is legendary. Equally good are the Pine Needles Resort and the Club at Longleaf.

Golfing isn't confined to the Sandhills region, however. Charlotte is mad for the highly publicized Scottish-style Charlotte Golf Links at Charlotte. The Raleigh-Durham area is filled with master courses, including the one at Duke University designed by Robert Trent Jones.

The best course in the mountains is at Asheville's Grove Park Inn. Yet another high-elevation golfing destination lies in the town of Blowing Rock, a summer haven for golf-loving coastal dwellers who prefer golfing in the much cooler environs of the mountains. Good golfing is also possible on the coast. Cape Fear, near Wilmington, has the most courses, including a George Cobb masterpiece with ocean views at Bald Head Island. Consult the regional chapters that follow for further details.

HIKING & BACKPACKING   The best place for hiking and backpacking in the entire state is Great Smoky Mountains National Park, were you'll find approximately 800 miles of trails. The guide *Walks and Hikes* lists more than 60 of these trails (the best ones) and is available at the visitor centers. Another good source for hiking and backpacking information is **The Great Smoky Mountains Natural History Association,** 16 Cherry St., Gatlinburg, TN 37738 (☎ **865/436-0120**). For the best hiking in North Carolina, you can also contact the **Sierra Club,** ᶜ/o Gordon Smith, 3921 Arbor St., Charlotte, NC 28209 (☎ **704/522-9618**), and the **Appalachian Mountain Club,** 5 Joy St., Boston, MA 02108 (☎ **617/523-0636**); www. outdoors.org.

HORSEBACK RIDING   North Carolina's southern mountains, linked by U.S. 64 south of Asheville, were once the home of the Cherokee, who didn't have horses. But the residents nowadays surely do. Dozens upon dozens of trails offer some of the best riding in the state. Trails are cut through both Nantahala National Forest and Pisgah National Forest. If you'd like to drive down from Asheville for an equestrian day, call the best of the stables: either **Pisgah Forest Stables,** U.S. 276 North, Pisgah Forest (☎ **828/883-8258**), or **Earthshine Mountain Lodge,** Golden Road, Lake Toxaway (☎ **828/862-4207**; www.earthshinemtnlodge.com).

HUNTING   Deer hunting is a passionate pastime for many Southerners. The mating habits and short gestation season of deer count for an overwhelming annual explosion of the deer population. If you're a hunting enthusiast, you already understand the conservation and preservation tenets of the sport. For information, contact the North Carolina Department of Environment and Natural Resources, 512 Salisbury St., P.O. Box 27687, Raleigh, NC 27611 (☎ **919/733-4984;** www.enr.state.nc.us).

RAFTING   The best rafting in the state is in Great Smoky Mountains National Park. Indeed, this white-water country along the Nantahala River offers some of the best rafting in the United States. If you don't know how to practice the sport, you can learn at the **Nantahala Outdoor Center,** U.S. 19/74 (☎ **800/232-7238;** www.noc.com), located 13 miles west of Bryson City, Tennessee. It offers 1- to 7-day-courses. The best outfit to call if you already know how to raft is **Rafting in the Smokies** (☎ **800/776-7328**), which rafts both the Pigeon and Nantahala rivers.

SKIING   For the best skiing in the tri-state area, head for the High Country of North Carolina, where the mountains range from 4,000 to 5,500 feet. Appalachian Ski Mountain, Ski Beech, Hawksnest Golf and Ski Resort, and Sugar Mountain Resort offer snow-laden slopes for both beginners and advanced skiers. The major resorts are close together, and you can easily resort-hop until you find the winter conditions that are suitable for you. Beginners should try the easier slopes of Sugar Mountain. Ski Beech is the highest ski area in eastern North America; the vertical drop is only 830 feet, but it's straight down, so it's only for daredevils. Hawksnest has two short beginner runs, and Appalachian Ski Mountain attracts the family trade and beginners. All ski areas are open for night runs. For more information about skiing the North Carolina mountains, get in touch with **High Country Host,** 1700 Blowing Rock Rd., Boone, NC 28607 (☎ **828/264-1299;** www.highcountryhost.com).

TENNIS   The Piedmont has the greatest number of public courts, including 20 in the Winston-Salem area alone. All the cities, big and small, in North Carolina have courts, as do all the major resorts. Most courts in the High Country are outdoors, so you'll want to restrict your playing to spring through autumn. True tennis buffs find the winds to be just too windy along the Outer Banks, and games there are often restricted to indoor courts.

5 Tips for Travelers with Special Needs

FOR TRAVELERS WITH DISABILITIES   Many hotels and restaurants in North Carolina now provide easy access, and some display the international wheelchair symbol in their brochures. It's always a good idea to call before you book to find out just what the situation is.

Many agencies provide advance data to help you plan your trip. One such agency is **Travel Information Service,** Industrial Rehab Program, 1200 W. Tabor Rd., Philadelphia, PA 19141 (☎ **215/456-9603** or 215/456-9602 for TTY). Another agency is **Mobility International USA,** P.O. Box 10767, Eugene, OR 97440 (☎ **503/343-1284**). It answers questions on various destinations and also offers discounts on videos, publications, and programs that it sponsors. For a free copy of *Air Transportation of Handicapped Persons,* published by the U.S. Department of Transportation, write for Free Advisory Circular No. AC12032, Distribution Unit, U.S. Department of Transportation, Publications Division, M-4332, Washington, DC 20590.

Amtrak, with 24 hours' notice, will provide porter service, special seating, and a substantial discount (☎ **800/USA-RAIL**).

FOR GAY & LESBIAN TRAVELERS   In **Charlotte,** the Gay Visitor Information Line (☎ **704/535-6277**) is open daily from 6:30 to 10:30pm. Throughout the rest of the day, information on gay resources can be directed to the helpful staff at **White Rabbit Books & Things,** 834 Central Ave., Charlotte, NC 28204 (☎ **704/ 377-4067;** www.whiterabbitbooks.com).

Raleigh offers the Gay and Lesbian Helpline (☎ **919/821-0055**). An equally helpful source of information about gay and lesbian issues is **White Rabbit Books & Things,** 309 W. Martin St., Raleigh, NC 27601 (☎ **919/856-1429;** www. whiterabbitbooks.com).

In **Greensboro,** the White Rabbit branch is the chain's flagship, situated at 1833 Spring Garden St., Greensboro, NC 27403 (☎ **336/272-7604**). Open Monday to Saturday 10am to 9pm, Sunday noon to 8pm. It serves as a de-facto clearinghouse for gay-related data and resources.

Men can order *Spartacus,* the international gay guide ($32.95), or *Odysseus 2001, The International Gay Travel Planner,* a guide to international gay accommodations ($29.95). Both lesbians and gay men might want to pick up a copy of *Gay Travel A to Z* ($19.95), which specializes in general information, as well as listings of bars, hotels, restaurants, and places of interest for gay travelers throughout the world. These books and others are available from **Giovanni's Room,** 1145 Pine St., Philadelphia, PA 19107 (☎ **215/923-2960;** E-mail:giothilt@ntex.com), and from most other gay and lesbian bookstores.

Our World, 1104 N. Nova Rd., Suite 251, Daytona Beach, FL 32117 (☎ **904/ 441-5367**), is a magazine devoted to options and bargains for gay and lesbian travel worldwide. It costs $49 for 10 issues. *Out and About,* 657 Harrison St., San Francisco, CA 94107 (☎ **415/486-2591**); P.O. Box 69217, West Hollyood, CA 90069 (☎ **310/859-2774;** www.outandabout.com), has been hailed for its "straight" reporting about gay travel. The publication profiles the best gay or gay-friendly hotels, gyms, clubs, and other places, covering destinations throughout the world. Its cost is $49 a year for 10 information-packed issues. It targets the more upscale gay male traveler and has been praised by everybody from *Travel & Leisure* to the *New York Times.* Both these publications are also available at most gay and lesbian bookstores.

International Gay & Lesbian Travel Association (IGTA), 4331 N. Federal, Suite 304, Fort Lauderdale, FL 33308 (☎ **800/448-8550** for voice mailbox, or 954/776-2626; www.iglta.org), encourages gay and lesbian travel worldwide. With about 1,200 member agencies, it specializes in networking, providing the information that travelers need to link up with the appropriate gay-friendly service organization or tour specialists. It offers quarterly newsletters, marketing mailings, and a membership directory that's updated four times a year. Travel agents who are IGTA members are tied into this organization's vast information resources.

FOR SENIORS   Nearly all major U.S. hotel and motel chains now offer a senior-citizen discount, so ask for the reduction *when you make the reservation;* there may be restrictions during peak days. Then be sure to carry proof of your age (driver's license, passport, and so on) when you check in. Among the chains that offer the best discounts are **Marriott Hotels** (☎ 800/228-9290) for those 62 and older and **La Quinta Inns** (☎ 800/531-5900) for ages 55 and older.

You can save sightseeing dollars if you're 62 or older by picking up a **Golden Age Passport** from any federally operated park, recreation area, or monument.

Elderhostel, 75 Federal St., Boston, MA 02110 (☎ 617/426-7788; www. elderhostel.org), provides stimulating vacations at moderate prices for those over 55, with a balanced mix of learning, field trips, and free time for sightseeing.

If you fancy organized tours, **Saga International Holidays,** 222 Berkeley St., Boston, MA 02116 (☎ 800/343-0273), arranges tours for travelers over 50.

Two senior-citizen organizations also offer a wide variety of travel benefits: the **American Association of Retired Persons (AARP),** 601 E St. NW, Washington, DC 20049 (☎ 202/434-AARP), and the **National Council of Senior Citizens,** 8403 Colesville Rd., Suite 1200, Silver Spring, MD 20910 (☎ 301/578-8800).

6 Getting There

BY PLANE   Delta Air Lines (☎ 800/221-1212; www.delta.com) and **US Airways** (☎ 800/428-4322; www.usairways.com) serve the largest number of North Carolina destinations from out of state, although not all flights are direct. **American Airlines** (☎ 800/433-7300; www.aa.com), **Continental Airlines** (☎ 800/525-0280; www.flycontinental.com), and **United Airlines** (☎ 800/241-6522; www.ual.com) also have direct flights to many North Carolina cities.

An airline that flies to more destinations throughout the Deep South than any other is **Midway Airlines** (☎ 800/327-2008), which defines Raleigh as the hub from which routes to about 20 other cities throughout Georgia and the Carolinas originate. Access into Raleigh is convenient through many other (larger) airlines, but if you want your entire flight aboard the same airline, Midway flies into Raleigh from Boston, Hartford, New York (LaGuardia, Newark), and Orange County's Stewart Newburgh, Indianapolis, Columbus, Rochester, Buffalo, New Orleans, and cities throughout Florida. From Raleigh, flights aboard 98-passenger Fokker 100s continue on to points in the Carolinas and Georgia that include Wilmington, Myrtle Beach, Atlanta, Columbia, New Bern, Greenville, and Spartanburg. The most economical tickets are those where you spend at least one Saturday night away from your point of origin, and where tickets are ordered and paid for at least a week or two in advance of your intended departure date.

Although good regional airports exist, the Raleigh-Durham and Charlotte airports are the major hubs, offering connecting flights to most major U.S. destinations.

BY CAR   From Virginia and South Carolina, you can enter North Carolina on either I-95 or I-85. I-27 and I-77 also lead in from South Carolina. The main Tennessee entry is I-40. All major border points have helpful welcome centers, some with cookout facilities and playground equipment in a parklike setting.

BY TRAIN   North Carolina is on **Amtrak's** New York–Miami and New York–Tampa runs, with stops in Raleigh, Hamlet, Southern Pines, Rocky Mount, and Fayetteville. The New York–Washington–New Orleans route of the *Southern Crescent* stops in Greensboro, High Point, Salisbury, Charlotte, and Gastonia. Be sure to check for excursion fares or seasonal specials. For reservations and fare information, call ☎ **800/USA-RAIL.** You can ask about the money-saving **All Aboard America** regional fares or any other current fare specials. Amtrak also offers attractive rail/drive vacation packages in the Carolinas and Georgia.

BY BUS   Greyhound/Trailways (☎ **800/231-2222**) has good direct service to major cities in North Carolina, with connections to almost any destination. An advance purchase is the best way to get the best fare. Special fares and programs are offered for purchases ranging from 3 days in advance to 30 days in advance, the latter offering substantial savings from normal fares. Call for information and schedules, or contact the Greyhound depot in your area.

PACKAGE TOURS   Tour companies offer package tours that include the Carolinas and Georgia. Most tours include airport transfers, admission to tour attractions, meals, and accommodations. Be sure to ask whether your tour is included under the USOTA consumer-protection guarantee (in case of bankruptcy or insolvency).

Tours in North Carolina are mostly geared to outdoors enthusiasts, but there are touring opportunities for everything from wines to kayaking to those great Southern eats. **Adventures Plus** (☎ **888/338-4844;** www.adventuresplus.com) offers adventure trips for the beginner or intermediate biker/hiker/horseback rider/canoer. Its tour of North Carolina begins on the Blue Ridge Parkway and covers such destinations as Burnsville, Banner Elk, Blowing Rock, and Asheville. The weeklong trips, priced at $1,695 to $2,475 per person, are offered only in September and October.

Barrier Island's Guided Trips (☎ **252/393-6457**) offers day trips to the barrier islands of the Outer Banks of North Carolina. Visit such destinations as Bear Island and Cape Lookout. Day-trip prices range from $45 to $65. Daily equipment rental for outdoors enthusiasts is an additional charge.

Carolina Culture Tours (☎ **888/286-6272**) presents exactly what its name implies. Take day trips or weeklong tours of the vineyards of North Carolina's Piedmont region, arts and craft tours of North Carolina, and tours featuring Southern soul-food delicacies. Trip prices range dramatically, from as little as $95 or less for day trips to weeklong trips for as much as $1,700 per person (double occupancy).

7 Getting Around

BY CAR   North Carolina's 76,000 miles of toll-free, well-maintained highways and some state roads have rest areas with picnic tables and outdoor cooking facilities. Write **Travel and Tourism NC,** Department of Commerce, 430 N. Salisbury St., Raleigh, NC 27611, for the *Official North Carolina Highway Map and Guide to Points of Interest,* which is one of the easiest maps to use; it's also filled with tourist information.

Before leaving home, it's a good idea to join the **American Automobile Association (AAA),** 1000 AAA Dr., Heathrow, FL 32746-5063 (☎ **800/222-4357** or 407/444-7000; fax 407/444-4247). For a very small fee, AAA provides a wide variety of services, including trip planning, accommodation and restaurant directories, and a 24-hour toll-free telephone number set up exclusively to deal with members' road emergencies (☎ **800/AAA-HELP**; www.aaa.com).

The Carolinas Driving Times & Distances

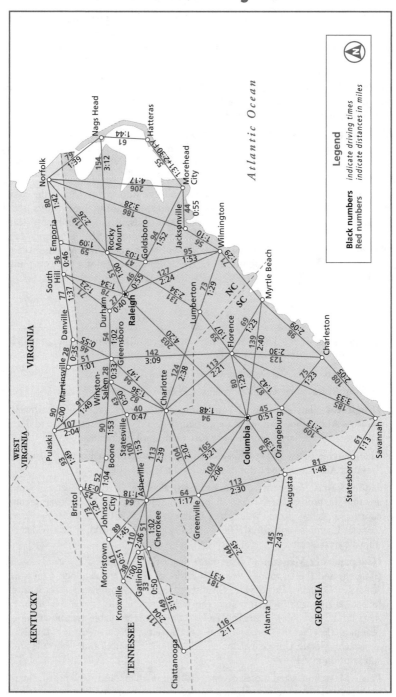

North Carolina has a seat-belt law that requires all front-seat passengers to wear seat belts. The state also has a child-restraint law that requires children 3 years old and younger to be secured in a child safety seat. Children 3 to 6 years old must ride in a safety seat or use a car seat belt.

Leading car-rental firms are represented in North Carolina's major cities and airports. For reservations and rate information, call the following: **Avis** (☎ 800/331-1212), **Budget Car Rental** (☎ 800/472-3325), **Hertz** (☎ 800/654-3001), and **Thrifty Car Rental** (☎ 800/367-2277).

BY PLANE   **US Airways** (☎ **800/428-4322;** www.usairways.com) and **Delta Air Lines** (☎ **800/221-1212;** www.delta.com) have several in-state connecting flights between cities such as Raleigh, Charlotte, Asheville, Wilmington, New Bern, Greensboro, Winston-Salem, Jacksonville, and Fayetteville.

BY FERRY   North Carolina has a system of toll-free auto ferries that ply the coastal sounds and rivers. You can cross Currituck Sound from Currituck to Knotts Island, Hatteras Inlet, and Pamlico River at Bayview, and Neuse River at Minnesott Beach. To get an up-to-date printed ferry schedule, contact the Director, Ferry Division, Room 120, Maritime Building, 113 Arendell St., Morehead City, NC 28557 (☎ **252/726-6446;** fax 252/726-2903; www.dot.state.nc.us/transit/ferry).

Fast Facts: North Carolina

American Express   The main American Express Travel Agency is at 4735 Sharon Rd., Charlotte (☎ **704/364-3373**).

Car Rentals   See "Getting Around" earlier in this chapter.

Driving Rules   See "Getting Around" earlier in this chapter.

Drugstores   The most popular drugstore chains are Eckerd, CVS/Pharmacy, and Rite Aid. Although none of these chains offers 24-hour service, Eckerd does have stores in the larger cities that remain open until midnight.

Emergencies   Dial ☎ **911** for police, medical, and other emergency services. Travelers Aid can also be helpful; check local telephone directories.

Liquor Laws   You must be 21 to order any alcoholic beverage. Beer and wine are sold in grocery stores, but all liquor is sold through local government-controlled package stores, which are commonly called ABC (Alcoholic Beverage Control Commission) stores. The availability of mixed drinks in bars is determined by each county.

Newspapers & Magazines   The state's major dailies are the *News & Observer* (Raleigh) and the *Charlotte Observer* (Charlotte). There are also local papers in Asheville, Durham, Fayetteville, Greensboro, and Winston-Salem. *The State,* a folksy weekly magazine that reflects the Tarheel way of life, is available at most newsstands. *The North Carolina Folklore Journal* is available by subscription (contact the North Carolina Folklore Society, Department of English, Appalachian State University, Boone, NC 28608, for publication schedule and subscription rates).

Pets   Many hotels and motels accept pets for a small fee, and some provide kennel service. This is individually determined by each property. Pets can be taken into car-accessible campgrounds in Great Smoky Mountains National Park, but they are not allowed on the trails in the backcountry.

Police   Call ☎ **911** (no coin required).

Taxes   North Carolina has a 6% sales tax.

Time Zone   North Carolina observes eastern standard time zone and goes on daylight saving time from April to October.

Weather   Phone ☎ **800/932-8437** for an update.

4 Wilmington & the Outer Banks

It's true that they're overcrowded in the summer, but the Outer Banks of North Carolina are unlike anything else along the East Coast. The infamous pirate Blackbeard met his end here, and this also is the place where the Lost Colony mysteriously disappeared. On these shores, Virginia Dare was born, and centuries later, Wilbur and Orville Wright learned to fly. The Outer Banks once enjoyed a dubious reputation as "the graveyard of the Atlantic," and to this day, you'll see the many lighthouses that stood vigil over centuries of shipwrecks. The East Coast's tallest lighthouse is at Cape Hatteras, and the oldest is at Ocracoke Island. Sand dunes tower over the beaches, and you can hop a ferry to explore almost-forgotten islands where the residents (descended from the Elizabethans) say *hoigh toids* instead of *high tides* and call tourists "comers 'n goers."

Both the size of fish and the diversity of species have put the ✪ Outer Banks on the map as being one of the hottest fishing spots in the world. The 2,000-mile Pamlico Sound is a vast estuary providing the breeding grounds for most of the fish caught off the coast, and the Gulf Stream lies just 12 miles offshore—the closest that this fish-laden current comes to land this side of Florida. The water teems with tuna and such trophy fish as blue marlin, white marlin, and sailfish.

As any windsurfer can tell you, the best conditions for sailing on the East Coast are along the Banks—in particular, at a place called Canadian Hole, on Hatteras Island. Constant winds—the same ones that brought the Wright brothers here in the early 1900s—blow across the Outer Banks. There are 800 square miles of accessible water. Wind, water, and temperature conditions are right for ideal sailing from early spring until late autumn.

The southern coast is dominated by the town of Wilmington, which boasts some 200 restored city blocks, forming one of the largest such districts in the National Register of Historic Places. Wilmington is the gateway to the Cape Fear coast, which, in spite of its ominous-sounding name, is filled with azalea gardens and sun-dappled plantation houses.

Base yourself in Nags Head or Duck to explore the northern end of the coast; in historic old Beaufort, Morehead City, or along the string of beaches from Atlantic Beach to Emerald Isle, to visit New Bern and other area attractions; or in Wilmington, to see plantations and gardens, Fort Fisher, and fine beaches.

If you're thinking about camping, you will find campgrounds throughout the region. But you should know in advance that they're flat and sandy, with no shade, and that you'll need tent stakes longer than you'd normally use. Also, no hookups are provided. Sites are available on a first-come, first-served basis, and the maximum stay is 14 days from mid-April to September 10. For private campgrounds in the area, which do have hookups, call the tourist offices listed in the following sections of this chapter.

The traffic to and from the Outer Banks can be maddening in summer. Avoid grid-lock by arriving or leaving on days other than Saturday and Sunday when the weekly rentals begin and end.

1 Wilmington & Cape Fear

123 miles SE of Raleigh

As the chief port of North Carolina, Wilmington is a major retail, trade, and manu-facturing center, but tourism is looming larger than ever in its economy. Known first as New Carthage, and then as New Liverpool, New Town, and Newton, this city was given its present name in 1739 in honor of the earl of Wilmington. Technically, it isn't even on the coast; it's inland a bit, at the junction of the Cape Fear River's northeast and northwest branches. Despite the treacherous shoals that guarded the mouth of Cape Fear when explorers first arrived in 1524, upriver Wilmington developed into an important port for goods shipped to and from Europe during colonial days.

The city's history is evident in the old residential section of town, on the grounds of Orton Plantation, in the excavated foundations of Brunswick Town houses, and in the blockade-runner relics at Fort Fisher. Boasting one of the largest districts listed in the National Register of Historic Places, Wilmington is known for its preservation efforts, which are reflected in the grandeur of its restored antebellum, Victorian, Geor-gian, and Italianate homes.

During both world wars, Wilmington was a major port for naval supplies. Today, the river is busier than ever with industrial shipping. In recent years, a thriving new industry has developed: filmmaking. Ever since 1983, when Dino De Laurentis came here to film *Firestarter*, Wilmington has been a major site for the movie industry, host-ing the production of more than 400 movie features, mini-series, and TV movies. In fact, according to a survey by the International Association of Film Commissioners, Wilmington generated more film revenue than any U.S. city except Los Angeles and New York—giving rise to its nickname "Hollywood East." Among the films made in Wilmington are *Forrest Gump, I Know What You Did Last Summer, Sleeping with the Enemy*, and *Billy Bathgate;* the popular TV series "Dawson's Creek" is filmed on loca-tion here.

ESSENTIALS

GETTING THERE   You can reach Wilmington via I-40, U.S. 117, and U.S. 421 from the northwest, U.S. 74/76 from the west, and U.S. 17 from the northeast and south.

Wilmington's International Airport, 1740 Airport Blvd. (☎ **910/341-4125**), lies half a mile from the center of town. Taxis meet arriving planes. The airport is host to the following major and commuter airlines: **US Airways** (☎ **800/428-4322;** www.usairways.com); **Midway Airline** (☎ **800/446-4392**), and **A.S.A. Delta Connection to Atlanta** (☎ **800/282-3424;** www.delta.com).

VISITOR INFORMATION   The **Cape Fear Coast Convention and Visitors Bureau,** 24 N. 3rd St., Wilmington, NC 28401 (☎ **800/222-4757** or 910/ 341-4030; www.cape-fear.nc.us), offers free brochures on the many attractions and accommodations of the Cape Fear Coast. The efficient staff can provide a self-guided walking-tour map of historic Wilmington and background details on other area attractions. The center is open Monday to Friday from 8:30am to 5pm, on Saturday from 9am to 4pm, and on Sunday from 1 to 4pm.

SPECIAL EVENTS   The **North Carolina Azalea Festival,** held in early April, is the city's most-frequented event. City gardens burst into bloom, and the festivities include garden tours, beauty pageants, and a parade. The dogwoods get almost as much attention as the azaleas. Call ☎ **910/763-0905** for more details.

SEEING THE SIGHTS
IN TOWN

To get an overview of the historic Wilmington waterfront, hop aboard the ✪ *Capt. J. N. Maffitt* (☎ **910/343-1611**), which departs from the foot of Market Street for a 5-mile loop of the Cape Fear River. The 45-minute narrated cruise skirts the busy harbor, passes the Cotton Exchange and the Riverfront Park, and stops at the dock for passengers who want to disembark to tour the battleship USS *North Carolina* (see "Sights Nearby," later in this chapter). The season runs from June to August, with daily departures scheduled at noon and 2:30pm. In May and September, tours depart daily at 3pm. In April and from October to mid-December, tours leave only on Saturday and Sunday at 3pm, if weather permits. The charge is $10, reduced to $5 for children 12 and under.

   Cotton Exchange (☎ **910/343-9896**), an in-town shopping center, is in the old exchange building, which has 2-foot-thick brick walls and hurricane rods. The small shops and restaurants are a delight, and the wrought-iron lanterns and benches add to the setting's charm. It's right on the riverfront, and there's an ample parking deck next door. All shops are open Monday to Saturday 10am to 5:30pm, although some shops are also open Sunday 1 to 4pm.

   In Historic Wilmington—the old residential area bounded roughly by Nun, Princess, Front, and 4th streets—the **Burgwin-Wright House,** 224 Market St. (☎ **910/762-0570**), was constructed in 1771 and used by Cornwallis as his headquarters in 1781. The colonial town house was built over an abandoned city jail. You can tour the interior Tuesday to Saturday from 10am to 4pm. Adults pay $3; children 12 and under are charged $1.

Arlie Gardens. U.S. 76. ☎ **910/763-9991.** Admission $8 adults, or $2 children under 12. Friday to Sunday 9am to 5pm. Take U.S. 76 toward beach and look for signpost.

Once the plantation home of a wealthy rice planter, Arlie is surrounded by huge lawns, serene lakes, and wooded gardens that hold just about every kind of azalea in existence. The blooms are at their height in the early spring, but even when they're faded, this is a lovely spot.

✪ **Cape Fear Museum.** 814 Market St. ☎ **910/341-4350.** Admission $4 adults; $1 children under 17; students, and senior citizens $3. Tues–Sat 9am–5pm, Sun 2–5pm.

This museum showcases the history, science, and culture of the lower Cape Fear region from prehistoric times until the present. Noteworthy are Civil War artifacts and dioramas of the Battle of Fort Fisher and the Wilmington waterfront circa 1863. Children will be interested in a discovery gallery and various hands-on activities.

The North Carolina Coast

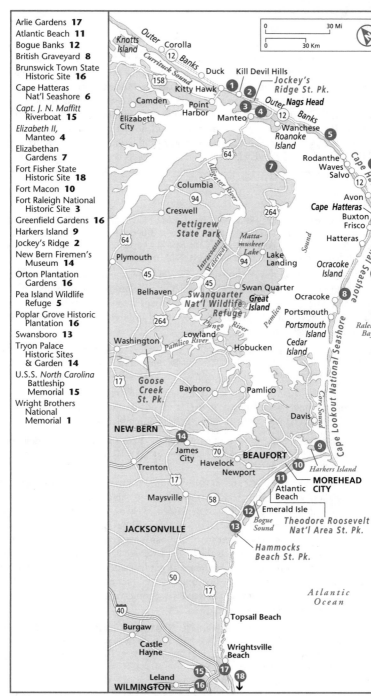

Knotts Island

Corolla

Outer Banks

Currituck Sound

12

Duck

Kill Devil Hills

158

Kitty Hawk

Jockey's
Ridge St. Pk.

Camden

Point
Harbor

Outer Banks

Nags Head

Elizabeth
City

Manteo

12

Wanchese

Roanoke
Island

64

Alligator River

Columbia

Rodanthe

Waves

Salvo

12

94

Avon

Cape Hatteras

Creswell

264

Buxton

Frisco

*Pettigrew
State Park*

Matta-
muskeet
Lake

Hatteras

64

Plymouth

94

Lake
Landing

Sound

Cape Hatteras National Seashore

45

Ocracoke
Island

45

Swan Quarter

Belhaven

*Swanquarter
Nat'l Wildlife
Refuge*

Great
Island

Ocracoke

Pamlico

Portsmouth

264

Intracoastal Waterway

Bungo River

Lowland

*Portsmouth
Island*

*Raleigh
Bay*

Washington

Pamlico River

Hobucken

Cedar
Island

17

*Goose
Creek
St. Pk.*

Bayboro

Pamlico

Cape Lookout National Seashore

Davis

NEW BERN

14

James
City

70

Havelock

BEAUFORT

Core Sound

9

Trenton

Newport

10

Harkers Island

17

11

**MOREHEAD
CITY**

Maysville

58

Atlantic
Beach

JACKSONVILLE

12

Emerald Isle

13

*Bogue
Sound*

*Theodore Roosevelt
Nat'l Area St. Pk.*

*Hammocks
Beach St. Pk.*

50

17

*Atlantic
Ocean*

40

Burgaw

Topsail Beach

Castle
Hayne

Wrightsville
Beach

Leland

15

17

18

WILMINGTON

16

0 .... 30 Mi

0 .... 30 Km

Lights, Camera, Action!

As the movie industry becomes more entrenched in the city, the more the business of making movies draws tourists itching to pay a few bucks to see where films are made. At press time, **Screen Gems Studios,** headed by Frank Capra, Jr., was offering weekend tours of its studio, the largest full-service film lot outside California. Call **On Location Tours & Events** for more information (☎ **910/343-3433**); because this is a *working* studio, and not set up as a tourist attraction, tours may be cancelled because of heavy production schedules. Tours are held on Saturday and Sunday at noon and 2pm; tickets cost $10 per person.

SIGHTS NEARBY

✪ **USS North Carolina Battleship Memorial.** Eagle Island. ☎ **910/251-5797.** Admission $8 adults, $7 seniors, $4 children 6–11. Kids 5 and under free. May 16–Sept 15 daily 8am–8pm. Off-season daily 8am–5pm. On Cape Fear River across from the historic district at junction of Hwy. 17/74/76/421. Easily accessible from I-95 or I-40.

The USS *North Carolina* was commissioned in 1941 and is permanently berthed here as a memorial to the state's World War II dead. You can tour most of the ship, and the Exhibit Hall houses a "through their eyes" exhibit focusing on recollections of the battleship's former crew. The ship is still painted in its 1944–45 camouflage. A visitor center offers a large gift shop and snack bar.

Poplar Grove Historic Plantation. 10200 U.S. 17. ☎ **910/686-9989.** Admission $7 adults, $6 senior citizens, $3 children 6–15. Mon–Sat 9am–5pm, Sun noon–5pm. Take U.S. 17 9 miles northeast of Wilmington.

This restored Greek Revival manor house and estate date from 1850. The outbuildings include a smokehouse, tenant house, and old kitchen. Attractions include demonstrations by a basket weaver, a fabric weaver, and a blacksmith.

✪ **Fort Fisher State Historic Site.** Kure Beach. ☎ **910/458-5538.** Free admission. Apr–Oct, Mon–Sat 9am–5pm, Sun 1–5pm; Nov–Mar, Tues–Sat 10am–4pm, Sun 1–4pm. Follow U.S. 421 south to Kure Beach.

One of the Confederacy's largest and most technically advanced forts, Fort Fisher was the last stronghold of the Confederate Army. Following the defeats at Savannah and Mobile, Confederate Gen. Robert E. Lee depended solely on Fort Fisher for supplies. President Lincoln recognized that to end the war, Fort Fisher would have to be taken. After withstanding two of the heaviest naval bombardments of the Civil War, the fort finally fell to Union forces in what was the largest land–sea battle in U.S. history until World War II. The unconditional Confederate surrender came only 3 months after the fall of Fort Fisher. The visitor center exhibits artifacts of that era, and there's an audio-visual program as well. Costumed tour guides welcome visitors, and living-history events are depicted during the summer.

Orton Plantation Gardens. 9149 Orton Rd. SE. ☎ **910/371-6851.** Admission $8 adults, $7 seniors, $3 children 6–12. Mar–Aug, daily 8am–6pm; Sept–Nov, daily 10am–5pm. Take U.S. 17 across the river and turn onto N.C. 133; the gardens are 18 miles south of Wilmington and 10 miles north of Southport.

The Orton House, dating from 1725, was built by Roger Moore, known as "The King" in this area because of his imperious manner. The house is in the typical Tara style, and although it's a near-perfect example of antebellum architecture, it's privately occupied and can be admired only from the garden paths. Visitors flock to see the gardens, which begin blooming in late winter and reach their height in spring, when camellias, azaleas, pansies, and flowering trees burst into bloom. An occasional alligator drops by to visit.

BEACHES & OUTDOOR PURSUITS

BEACHES   The main summer target is ✪ **Wrightsville Beach,** 6 miles east of Wilmington on U.S. 74/76. The island is separated from the mainland by a small drawbridge. A year-round residence for some 3,200 dwellers, Wrightsville Beach, once known only as "The Banks," is the widest beach on the Cape Fear Coast, stretching for a mile along the oceanfront, its beige sands set against a backdrop of hearty vegetation such as sea oats. The south end isn't ideal for swimming; you'll find better conditions between the rebuilt Johnnie Mercer Pier and Crystal Pier (patrolled by lifeguards in summer).

Another important spot is at **Carolina Beach State Park,** sprawling across 1,770 acres 10 miles north of Wilmington off U.S. 421. This beach, flanked on one bank by the Cape Fear River and on the other by the Intracoastal Waterway, lies at the northern edge of aptly named Pleasure Island. The significance of the park lies not in the beach—in fact, swimming is not allowed—but in the natural flora, including the rare Venus's-flytrap and other insect-eating plants, which abound in the swamp forest. The park has 5 miles of hiking trails. Facilities include toilets, a marina, a picnic area, and a family campground.

At the southern tip of Pleasure Island is the small, family-friendly community of **Kure Beach.** From here, you can see Cape Fear River and the Atlantic Ocean. The white-sand beaches are generally uncrowded, restaurants are informal, and the Kure Beach fishing pier is a magnet for anglers. You can wander through the remains of Fort Fisher (see "Sights Nearby," earlier in this chapter).

FISHING   **Batson's Charter Boats,** Carolina Beach (☎ 910/458-8671), departs from the Carolina Beach Municipal Marina, offering trolling and bottom-fishing charters. The charter boat can accommodate up to six fishers besides the crew. Prices are $330 for 5 hours, $490 for 8 hours, and $620 for 10 hours; rates include rod, reel, and bait.

GOLF   The **Plantation Golf & Racquet Club,** 2368 Country Club Dr., Hampstead (☎ 910/270-2703), is one of the best and most popular courses in the Wilmington area, offering a par-71, 6,401-yard, 18-hole course open daily from 7am to 7pm. It charges greens fees: From Monday to Thursday greens fees are $29 before noon, $22 noon to 2pm, or $20 2 to 7pm. Friday to Sunday greens fees are $35 before noon, $29 noon to 2pm, and $20 noon to 6pm. Clubs can be rented at $20 for 18 holes. Tee-time reservations are requested. Facilities include a clubhouse, restaurant, and pro shop. Professional instruction is available at $25 per half-hour.

The club lies 14½ miles outside Wilmington. Take U.S. 17 north to Hampstead (about 10 miles), and continue on the same route the final 4½ miles.

SCUBA/SNORKELING   The best outfitters are **Aquatic Safaris & Divers Emporium,** 5751 Oleander Dr. (☎ 910/392-4FUN), and **Bottom Time Dive Charters,** 6014 Wrightsville Ave. (☎ 910/397-0181).

TENNIS   **Plantation Golf & Racquet Club** (see "Golf," earlier in this section), has two excellent playing courts open daily from 7am to 7pm. Use costs $3 per player, and reservations are requested. A restaurant and clubhouse with showers and lockers are located on the grounds.

WHERE TO STAY

Cape Fear Coast Convention and Visitors Bureau (see "Essentials," earlier in this chapter) will do more than just send you its *Accommodations Guide.* If you're in the market for an apartment or cottage for a week or more (a dollar-saving approach that's hard to beat), write well in advance, describing just what you have in mind. The bureau will circulate your requirements in a bulletin that goes to area owners and managers, who will then contact you directly.

Campers can check out the **Camelot Campground,** 7415 Market St., Wilmington, NC 28405 (☎ **910/686-7705**), which sits on 43 wooded acres on U.S. 17. Facilities include a pool, recreation room, playground, laundry, and grocery store, and propane gas is available for stoves. Rates range from $20 for tent sites to $28 for full hookups.

Coast Line Inn. 503 Nutt St., Wilmington, NC 28401. ☎ **910/763-2800.** Fax 910/ 763-2785. www.coastline-inn.com. 50 units. A/C TV TEL. Mon–Thurs $89, Fri–Sun $109. Rates include continental breakfast. AE, DC, DISC, MC, V.

Next door to the Coast Line Convention Center, this inn was designed to complement the restored historic rail depot that it's named for. The adjacent full-service restaurant actually occupies one of the original railroad buildings, and has a popular bar and periodic live entertainment. The inn's rooms all have good views of the Cape Fear River. Some units, such as the River's Edge Lounge, afford two river views.

۞ Graystone Inn. 100 S. 3rd St., Wilmington, NC 28401. ☎ **910/763-2000.** Fax 910/ 763-5555. www.graystoneinn.com. E-mail: reservations@graystoneinn.com. 6 units. A/C TV TEL. $159 double; $249–$329 suite. Rates include full breakfast. AE, CB, DC, DISC, MC, V. Free parking. Children under 12 not allowed.

In many ways, this is the grandest of Wilmington's B&B inns. A neoclassical stone mansion from 1905, it offers 12- to 14-foot ceilings and Victorian-period furnishings. It has a large three-story portico and a grand staircase made of hand-carved red oak. A formal dining room, where breakfast is served, the original drawing room and music room, and a library lined with old volumes take you back in time. All the handsomely furnished accommodations are on the third floor. Although all units have a private bath, only the suites have TVs and phones. Guests can watch TV in the library on the main floor. Room service is available.

۞ Inn at St. Thomas Court. 101 S. 2nd St., Wilmington, NC 28401. ☎ **800/525-0909** or 910/343-1800. Fax 910/251-1149. www.innatstthomascourt.com. E-mail: innatstthomascourt@ cs.com. 40 suites. A/C TV TEL. $145 suite for 2; $235 2-bedroom suite for 4; $160 special-occasion suite for 2; $179–$299 luxury suites. Rates include continental breakfast. AE, CB, DC, DISC, MC, V. Free parking.

This renovated 1906 commercial building is rightly regarded as being the premier inn of Wilmington; actually, it's a glorified B&B in which all the rooms are suites. Accommodations on the second and third floors have balconies, and some suites contain kitchenettes, wet bars, and washer/dryers. The two-bedroom suites sleep four guests comfortably, and the special-occasion suite (ideal for a honeymoon) has a fireplace, whirlpool bath, CD player, and TV/VCR. All rooms have either queen- or king-size beds. A small library is near the front desk, and an intimate on-site pub offers beer and wine daily from 2pm to 2am. About a dozen restaurants lie within safe walking distance. The owners recently purchased an antebellum (ca. 1840s) home and restored it to contain an additional six luxury suites, each with a whirlpool, wet bar, mini-bar, and antique reproduction furniture.

۞ The Verandas. 202 Nun St., Wilmington, NC 28401. ☎ **910/251-2212**. www. verandas.com. 8 units. A/C TV TEL. $139–$190 double. AE, DC, DISC, MC, V.

Wilmington

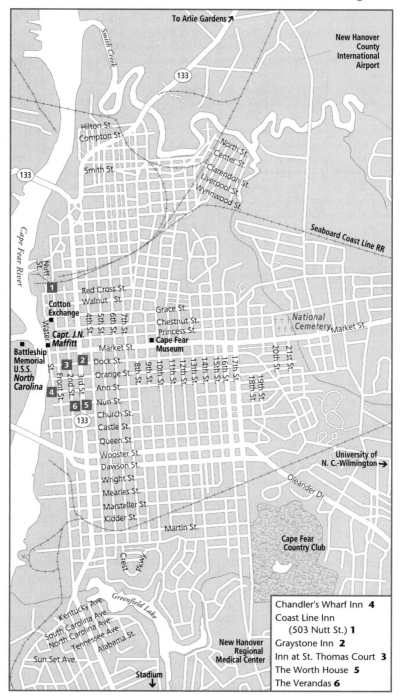

To Arlie Gardens ↗

New Hanover County International Airport

133

Smith Creek

Hilton St.
Compton St.

North St.
Center St.
Clarendon St.
Liverpool St.
Wynnwood St.

Smith St.

133

Seaboard Coast Line RR

Cape Fear River

Nutt St.

1

Cotton Exchange

Red Cross St.
Walnut St.

Water St.

Capt. J.N. Maffitt

■ Battleship Memorial U.S.S. *North Carolina*

4th St.
5th St.
6th St.
7th St.

Grace St.
Chestnut St.
Princess St.

■ Cape Fear Museum

† † † *National Cemetery* Market St.

Market St.

3 **2** Dock St.

Orange St.

8th St.
9th St.
10th St.
11th St.
12th St.
13th St.
14th St.
15th St.
16th St.
17th St.
18th St.
19th St.
20th St.
21st St.

4

Ann St.

Nun St.

3rd St.
2nd St.
Front St.

6 **5**

Church St.

133

Castle St.

Queen St.

Wooster St.

Dawson St.

University of N. C.-Wilmington →

Wright St.

Mearies St.

Oleander Dr.

Marsteller St.

Kidder St.

Martin St.

Cape Fear Country Club

Crest Pkwy

Greenfield Lake

Kentucky Ave.
South Carolina Ave.
North Carolina Ave.
Tennessee Ave.
Alabama St.

Sun Set Ave.

New Hanover Regional Medical Center

Stadium ↓

Chandler's Wharf Inn **4**
Coast Line Inn
  (503 Nutt St.) **1**
Graystone Inn **2**
Inn at St. Thomas Court **3**
The Worth House **5**
The Verandas **6**

47

One of the most appealing and fairly priced B&Bs in Wilmington is a stately, white-sided mansion that, with eight units, is one of the largest owner-occupied guesthouses in town. It was built in 1853 by a local merchant, then transformed into a convent in the 1860s. A century later, the then-dilapidated building was the site of Wilmington's most popular whorehouse before a devastating fire in 1992 reduced its back side to a smoldering ruin. Three years later, former Washington, D.C. residents Dennis Madsen and Charles Pennington embarked on a radical restoration. After rebuilding it from its studs, with the addition of modern infrastructures and lots of English and American antiques, it has blossomed into an utterly charming, and very personalized, inn. Each unit is a corner room flooded with sunlight and includes a VCR, marble-sheathed bathroom, oversized oval tub, and soundproofing. The second-floor rooms are more grand than those on the third floor, which are deliberately cozier and less formal. Throughout the inn, the presence of pets and children under 12 is discouraged. A complimentary wine bar appears every afternoon between 5:30 and 6pm. Breakfasts are elaborate affairs featuring dishes that include croissants with smoked salmon and cream cheese dipped in egg custard and dill and then fried in a way that resembles French toast. If you opt for an overnight here, you'll be in good company—many of the actors working on films in Wilmington like to stay here, as do many business travelers to Washington.

The Worth House. 412 S. 3rd St., Wilmington, NC 28401. ☎ **800/340-8559** or 910/762-8562. Fax 910/763-2173. www.worthhouse.com. 7 units. TEL. $110–$125 double. Each additional person $25. Rates include full breakfast. AE, DISC, MC, V. Free parking.

This 1893 Victorian three-story B&B is a real escape from the modern world. The decorative motif matches the Victorian design of the structure, with the rooms being furnished in 19th-century antiques. One unit, dubbed the Louisiana Room, breaks the mold with an all-French design, bathed in blue and yellow in a style that evokes a New Orleans B&B. Breakfast is served each morning in one of three places: in the main dining room, on the third-floor balcony, or in your room. Some accommodations are equipped with dining nooks. The house is completely no smoking, and children under 8 are not admitted. A TV is provided in the sitting room, and the house has central air-conditioning.

STAYING ON THE BEACH NEARBY

Blockade Runner Resort Hotel & Conference Center. 275 Waynick Blvd. (P.O. Box 555), Wrightsville Beach, NC 28480. ☎ **800/541-1161** or 910/256-2251. Fax 910/256-2251. www.blockade-runner.com. 150 units. A/C TV TEL. Mid-June to mid-Sept, $195–$316 double; off-season, $105–$289 double. Children under 12 stay free in parents' room. AE, CB, DC, DISC, MC, V.

In the middle of Wrightsville Beach, opening onto views of the ocean and Wrightsville Sound, this seven-story hotel is far superior to the lackluster string of motels along Lumina Avenue, north and south. Bedrooms are comfortably and attractively furnished, and often have private patios.

Dining/Diversions: Normally, a hurricane is a bad occurrence, but the Ocean Terrace Restaurant seems to have rebounded from recent hurricanes to become better than ever, luring the former sous-chef of the Harvard Club in Manhattan, Thomas Sullivan. The SeaEscape beach bar offers drinks in a poolside setting, complete with beach volleyball and a new beachfront dining patio.

Amenities: Concierge, room service, bicycle and sailboat rentals. Staff can arrange for a golf outing nearby, and the hotel offers sunset and nature cruises.

WHERE TO DINE

As is true of so many coastal towns, Wilmington's best dining spots are at the beaches or on its fringes, and you'll find more seafood spots (most of them excellent) than you'll have time to sample.

Sooner or later, you're bound to hear the name ✪ **Calabash,** especially if you love seafood. This tiny town of 150 residents, 35 miles south of Wilmington on U.S. 17, is renowned for its bounty of seafood restaurants—about 30 of them within one square mile, vying with one another to serve the biggest and best platter of seafood at the lowest price. Calabash restaurants use family recipes handed down from generation to generation; in one recent year, 1½ million people were served some 668,000 pounds of flounder and 378,000 pounds of shrimp, to say nothing of tons of oysters, scallops, and other fish. Recommendations for specific restaurants? You won't need them; according to locals, you can't miss no matter which one you choose.

MODERATE

Caffè Phoenix. 9 S. Front St. ☎ **910/343-1395.** Main courses $6–$8 at lunch (including soup or salad), $10–$25 at dinner. AE, DC, DISC, MC, V. Mon–Sat 11:30am–10:30pm (with light fare served 3–5pm), Sun 11am–10pm. CONTINENTAL.

This cafe, one block from the water in the center of town, is easily the best bistro in Wilmington. In a renovated and transformed former dry-goods store, it has a light, open, and airy decor, with lots of plants. Luncheon choices include homemade soups, freshly prepared salads, pasta, and sandwiches. Dinner becomes more elaborate, including spinach with prosciutto or chicken piccata. Many Wilmington artists dine here, and the place has a sizable gay following.

Deluxe Restaurant. 114 Market St. ☎ **910/251-0333.** Reservations recommended. Main courses $14–$26. AE, MC, V. Sun–Thurs 5:30–10pm, Fri–Sat 5:30–11pm. Sun brunch 10:30am–2:30pm. NOUVELLE AMERICAN.

Don't underestimate the value of this restaurant's bar as a meeting point for the artistic and the articulate. Lots of musicians and artists are drawn here because of the ambience and the eclectic, vaguely Southwestern decor, which might have been designed by Frank Lloyd Wright on psychedelics. It was established as a coffeehouse in 1995, and expanded into this full-fledged restaurant in 1998. Menu items are imaginative— a welcome change from the catfish and collards that are staples at some of the local competitors. Examples include wasabi tempura shrimp with a cashew dipping sauce; a spectacular salad ("The Deluxe") that pits gorgonzola with pears, roasted chili peppers, pecans, and a shallot and herb vinaigrette. New Zealand rack of lamb is served with couscous or with a Bordeaux-based reduction; and veal scallopine might be offered with goat cheese, roasted peppers, and garlic-flavored spinach. Wines are appropriately eclectic, with origins from around the world.

Elijah's. 2 Ann St., Chandler's Wharf. ☎ **910/343-1448.** Reservations recommended. Lunch main courses $5.95–$8.95; dinner main courses $10.95–$17.95. Daily 11:30am–3pm, Sun–Thurs 5–10pm; Fri–Sat 5–11pm. AMERICAN/SEAFOOD.

This is one of the largest and best-established restaurants along Wilmington's historic riverfront. Elijah's occupies a low-slung, wood-sided building that was originally conceived as a maritime museum. It still contains some of its seafaring memorabilia, which looks striking against the rich paneling that sheathes most of the interior. In the evenings, a wraparound bar with views of the river becomes a convivial nightlife venue. On warm nights, head for the huge waterfront terrace, where a bar is rolled on or off the deck, depending on the weather. Lunches here tend to emphasize sandwiches and simple platters that always include a fine version of crab cakes.

Dinners are more elaborate, with classic and well-prepared dishes that include chicken piccata, soft-shell crabs, shrimp in a Dijon mustard and garlic sauce, and steaks.

✪ **Pilot House.** 2 Ann St., Chandler's Wharf. ☎ **910/343-0200.** Reservations recommended. Lunch $7.95–$11.95; main courses $14.95–$25.95. AE, DC, DISC, MC, V. Sun–Thurs 11:30am–3pm and 5–10pm, Fri–Sat 11:30am–3pm and 5–11pm. LOW COUNTRY/ SEAFOOD.

Located on the Cape Fear River in the historic restored Craig House, the Pilot House serves some of the best seafood dishes in the Wilmington area. Set within a yellow-painted circa-1870 clapboard house immediately adjacent to the Cape Fear River, it was moved to its present site in 1978. This is the Wilmington restaurant that's more attuned to the gourmet allure of Low Country cuisine than any other, offering both classic and nouvelle twists on traditional dishes. More upscale than its neighbor, Elijah's (with which it shares the same owner), the Pilot House seats most of its diners on a sprawling riverfront terrace, with an additional 10 tables in an isolated upstairs garret room that some visitors find romantic and others interpret as an exile to Siberia. Preface your meal with a drink at the cozy nautical-style bar before diving into the specialties, such as shrimp and grits or crunchy catfish, a true Southern delicacy. The seafood platter is the most-ordered dish. One justifiable favorite is the shredded and deep-fried grouper in a sweet-potato crust, accompanied by shrimp in a balsamic vinaigrette sauce. A choice selection of meats is offered, especially prime cuts of beef, and it wouldn't be a Carolina restaurant if it didn't serve pork chops. The Caribbean fudge pie has its fans.

INEXPENSIVE

Circa 1922. 8 North Front St. ☎ **910/762-1922.** Reservations recommended. Tapas $8–$12. Daily 5–10pm. Bar daily 5pm–midnight (2am Fri–Sat). SOUTHERN/INTERNATIONAL.

One of Wilmington's newest restaurants opened in 2000 in a 1920s bank building. Inside you'll find a stately, high-ceilinged interior filled with hardwoods and mirrors, and a menu that consists entirely of tapas, the small-portioned and savory bar food of Spain. The best way to navigate your way through a meal here is to order a medley of the savory dishes to share among your fellow diners. The culinary inspirations range from Asian to Mediterranean; among the tapas selections are a parfait of smoked salmon and caviar, beef tenderloin carpaccio with a tapenade of olives, and various kinds of sushi.

DINING ON THE BEACH NEARBY

Rialto Ristorante. 530 Causeway Dr., Wrightsville Beach. ☎ **910/256-1099.** Reservations recommended. main courses $9.95–$22. MC, V. Daily 5–10:30pm. ITALIAN.

This Italian-American restaurant is the best along Wilmington's Atlantic barrier strip, a culinary landmark surrounded by less worthy, less elaborate eateries. Set in a shopping mall, and filled with plants, painted Italian tiles, and marble, it offers what the owners call "high-end Italian dining in a casual setting." Some aspects are actually more Italian than you might have expected, despite many concessions to American tastes. They use a lot of fresh fish here, including snapper and monkfish. The menu lists 13 preparations of succulent pasta, served in full or half portions; well-prepared veal dishes; and a nicely conceived version of grouper Napoletana, with capers, garlic, white wine, *concasse* of tomatoes, and garlic.

WILMINGTON AFTER DARK

Mickey's. 115 S. Front St. ☎ **910/251-1289.** Cover $4–$8.

This is the only strictly gay men's gathering place in Wilmington. The club features a dance floor, a commodious bar, and a group of locals who seem to have known one another forever. There's also a large fenced-in outdoor patio, which some dancers use to escape from the heat inside. Open nightly from 5pm to 2:30am; no food is served.

The Thalian Hall Theater. 310 Chestnut St. ☎ **910/343-3664.**

If there's a big event being staged in Wilmington, this is likely to be the venue. This restored 1858 theater hosts about 600 events annually. Local theater groups and the symphony also use the theater as their home base for productions. Performances range from live dance to children's dramas performed by local companies. Contact the box office to learn what's happening at the time of your visit. Ticket prices depend on the event. Box-office hours are noon to 5pm Monday to Friday, 2pm to 6pm Saturday and Sunday.

The Water Street Bar & Restaurant. 5 S. Water St. ☎ **910/343-0042.** Cover only on special occasions (prices vary).

Folk, reggae, and the blues are featured here. The club often provides open-mike nights for anyone who thinks that he or she has talent. It's more a pub than a nightclub, and it has a full restaurant. The kitchen is open as long as bands are playing. Live music is featured Thursday to Sunday only. The club opens daily at 11am. Closing times vary according to the day of the week: 9pm Monday to Thursday, until 2am Friday to Sunday.

✪ A SIDE TRIP TO BALD HEAD ISLAND

A 45-minute drive southeast from Wilmington on U.S. 17 South, with a left turn onto N.C. 87, takes you to the little town of Southport, the jumping-off point for the passenger ferry to Bald Head Island. (The terminal is at India Plantation.) You must call ahead to book the ferry (☎ **910/457-5006**). Day-trippers pay $15 for adults and $8 for children 2 to 12; children 1 and under ride free.

Bald Head Island invites nature lovers to visit for much longer than 1 day. There are some 3,000 pristine acres, with 14 miles of sandy beachfront and miles and miles of salt marshes, tidal creeks, and maritime forests. An 18-hole championship golf course and the village of Bald Head Island—with shops, restaurants, private homes, and condominiums—offer other diversions. Activities on the island include swimming (the island has a pool as well as all those miles of beaches), biking, tennis, golf, canoeing, fishing, birding, and just plain beachcombing.

Still, human intrusion is kept to a minimum. No cars are permitted on the island; transportation is provided by golf carts and jitneys. Sea oats, yucca, beach grasses, live oak, red cedar, palmetto, sabal palms, loblolly pines, and a yellow wildflower called galardia thrive here. Such birds as white ibises, great blue herons, snowy egrets, black ducks, mallards, and pintails frequent the island, and a protected population of loggerhead sea turtles nests here.

If you'd like to stay over, private homes, as well as condominiums, are available as rentals. You can also rent either of two historic cottages that were the homes of lighthouse keepers and their families from 1903 to 1958. All units are tastefully furnished, with full kitchens, TVs, and other modern conveniences, and most rates include the use of one of the electric passenger carts. Daily rates are in the $165 to $550 range during the summer months and $99 to $420 in other months. Weekly rates run $899 to $2,990 in summer and $600 to $1,990 off-season. For full details and bookings, contact **Bald Head Island,** P.O. Box 3069, Bald Head Island, NC 28461 (☎ **800/ 234-1666** or 910/457-5000); www.baldheadisland.com.

2 Beaufort

35 miles E of New Bern

North Carolina's third-oldest town, ✪ Beaufort (pronounced *Bo*-fort) dates back to 1713 and still reflects its early history. Along its narrow streets are two 200-year-old houses, and more than a hundred houses are more than a century old. On the last weekend in June, residents open their homes for the annual Old Homes Tour. Beaufort lies on the Taylor Creek waterfront, where a boardwalk with restaurants, shops, and piers offers pleasant strolling.

ESSENTIALS

GETTING THERE   Access is on U.S. 70 just over the Grayden Paul Bridge from Morehead City. From New Bern, take U.S. 70 east.

VISITOR INFORMATION   The **Beaufort Historical Association,** 126 Turner St. (P.O. Box 1709), Beaufort, NC 28516 (☎ 252/728-5225; www.beaufort-nc. com/bha), is open March to November, Monday to Saturday from 9:30am to 5pm; off-season, Monday to Saturday from 10am to 4pm.

EXPLORING THE AREA

The **Beaufort Historic Site,** in the 100 block of Turner Street, includes the 1767 Joseph Bell House; the 1825 Josiah Bell House; the 1796 Carteret County Courthouse; the 1829 county jail; the 1859 apothecary shop and doctor's office; and the 1778 Samuel Leffers House, home of the town's first schoolmaster. Tours are given Monday to Wednesday, Friday and Saturday at 10am, 11:30am, 1pm, and 3pm. Adults pay $6 for the tour; children older than 5 are charged $2. Not included on the tour is the 1732 Rustell House, an art gallery; entry is free of charge.

A block away is the **Old Burying Ground,** dating from 1709 and listed on the National Register of Historic Places. Both self-guided and narrated tours are available. Narrated tours aboard a British double-decker bus are offered on Monday, Wednesday, Friday, and Saturday, June to September, for a $6-per-person fare. Call ☎ 252/ 728-5225 for more information.

From modest beginnings, the **North Carolina Maritime Museum,** 315 Front St. (☎ 252/728-7317), grew into a $2.2-million complex. It has natural- and maritime-history exhibits, ship models, and shell collections, and it offers intriguing field trips and programs for all ages. The Wooden Boat Show is held here the first weekend in May. Admission is free. The museum is open Monday to Friday from 9am to 5pm, Saturday from 10am to 5pm, and Sunday from 1 to 5pm; it's closed on major holidays.

Divers are attracted to this area because of the many wrecks off the coast. If you want to get into this action, contact **Discovery Diving Co.,** 414 Orange St. (☎ 252/ 728-2265), where the staff knows the local waters best. The company offers charter diving tours for prices ranging from $40 to $110 per person, plus use of the company's equipment. Tanks rent for $10, with regulators going for $6 and weights for $4. Masks and fins are priced at $4 each, and extra amenities (such as cameras and computers) cost around $25 extra. Call ahead for equipment reservations. Tours include one dive at a shipwreck site offshore, one farther offshore, and two dives on the reefs closer to shore.

WHERE TO STAY

Beaufort Inn. 101 Ann St., Beaufort, NC 28516. ☎ 252/728-2600. www.beaufort-inn.com. E-mail: beaufortinn@mail.clis.com/beaufort-inn.com. 44 units. A/C TV TEL. June–Sept, $119–$149 double. Off-season, $59–$89 double. Additional person $15. Rates include breakfast. AE, DC, DISC, MC, V.

Katie and Bruce Ethridge have managed to give their Historic District inn a historic feel, even though it's of recent vintage. Rooms are tastefully decorated, with lots of homey touches. Some 15 boat slips are provided for guests who arrive by water, and bicycles are available for rent. A scrumptious hot breakfast is served in the dining area (don't miss Katie's breakfast pie, made of sausages, eggs, and cheese), and several good restaurants are within walking distance.

✪ **Cedars By the Sea.** 305 Front St., Beaufort, NC 28516. ☎ **252/728-7036.** Fax 252/728-1685. www.cedarsinn.com. 14 units. AC/TV. $110–$125 double; $140–$165 suite. Rates include breakfast. AE, DISC, MC, V.

Built in the 1770s and once the home of a shipbuilder, this antiques-filled house overlooking the river is the most intriguing and comfortable historic inn in Beaufort. Four of its suites come with fireplaces. Whirlpools, private patios, and balconies are offered as well, providing modern comforts in gracious surroundings.

✪ **Delamar Inn.** 217 Turner St., Beaufort, NC 28516. ☎ **800/349-5823** or 252/728-4300. www.bbonline.com/nc/delamarinn. 3 units. A/C. Summer, $120 double. Off-season, $88–$106 double. Rates include continental breakfast, and complimentary wines. MC, V. No children under 10.

In 1866, immediately following the Civil War, Jacob Gibbie built this home for his expanding family. In time, the family intermarried with the Delamars, for whom the house is now named. This enlarged saltbox-style cottage is fringed with perennial borders and rosebushes. The decor is homelike and cozy, not at all grandiose. Today, Delamar is one of the finest and best-run B&Bs in Beaufort, recently honored with three diamonds by AAA and two stars by Mobil. Both of the inn's two stories have porches with rockers set out. Each bedroom has a king-size Jenny Lind bed and a private bath with original claw-foot tubs. Only four antiques-furnished bedrooms (each with its own private bath) are offered, so reservations are important in summer.

   Tom and Mabel Steepy are the courteous and helpful hosts, who will provide details about sightseeing in the area. They can also make reservations for ferry connections, advise you about nearby golf, or help you board a charter fishing boat. You can borrow their bicycles, beach chairs, umbrellas, coolers, and beach towels. Soft drinks and cookies will be waiting when you return from exploring.

✪ **Pecan Tree Inn.** 116 Queen St., Beaufort, NC 28516. ☎ **252/728-6733.** www. pecantree.com. E-mail: pecantreeinn@coastalnet.com. 7 units. A/C TEL. $95–$150 double. Rates include continental breakfast. AE, DISC, MC, V.

Named for the two century-old pecan trees that grace the property, the Pecan Tree Inn is housed in a building that was constructed during the mid-1800s. The Victorian porches, turrets, and gingerbread trim that make the house unique were added in 1890. Recent renovations have improved the inn while maintaining its original architectural essence. The rooms and parlor are furnished with a collection of antiques, designed to highlight the use of pine in the construction. Bedrooms feature king, queen, or twin beds; specify which you want when you make reservations. The bridal suite contains a Jacuzzi, and its king-size canopied bed evokes the Southern-plantation ambience. A 5,500-square-foot English garden is in the back, featuring more than 1,000 plants, each with identifying labels to aid the budding botanist. AAA recently honored this inn with three diamonds.

WHERE TO DINE

Clawson's 1905 Restaurant. 429 Front St. ☎ **252/728-2133.** Reservations recommended Fri–Sat nights. Lunch sandwiches and platters $4.25–$10.95; dinner main courses $6.95–$14.95. DISC, MC, V. Daily 11:30am–4:30pm and 4:30–9pm (until 10pm Fri–Sat). AMERICAN.

One of downtown Beaufort's most consistently popular restaurants was built in—you guessed it—1905 by a Swedish immigrant who needed a lot of warehousing space for his growing business. The rough-hewn plank, timber, and brick building has been pierced with skylights and gentrified, with every cranny of its labyrinthine interior jam-packed with nostalgia, diners, and drinkers. If you have to wait at the bar for a table, view the experience as a cultural insight into the New South as you rub elbows with boat owners, local hell-raisers, and golf-playing retirees. Lunches are a lot simpler than dinners, consisting of grilled tuna or mahimahi, fried scallops, salads, and over-stuffed sandwiches. Dinners feature larger portions and lots of combination platters piled high with ribs and shrimp, steak and shrimp, pork, and chicken.

Loughry's Landing. 510 Front St. ☎ **252/728-7541.** Main courses $9.95–$32.95. MC, V. Daily 11:30am–2:30pm and 5–9:30pm. Closed Jan–Feb. SEAFOOD.

On the boardwalk, overlooking the waterfront, this is the best dining choice in town if you're craving fresh local seafood. The nautical decor is bright and contemporary, with evening dining by candlelight; outdoor dining is available, too, weather permitting. Aside from seafood, the large menu offers prime steaks and very tasty Southern fried chicken. There's a freshly prepared salad bar, and breads are home-baked, including the local favorites: Southern-style biscuits and the inevitable cornbread. Service is efficient. Wine and beer are served. There are setups for mixed drinks (BYOB). In summer, there's live music on weekends.

The Spouter Inn. 218 Front St. ☎ **252/728-5190.** Reservations recommended for dinner. Main courses $14–$23. MC, V. Daily 11:30am–2:30pm and 5:30–9pm. SEAFOOD.

Waterfront dining and fresh seafood keep this place humming. The atmosphere is casual, even though the tables are lit by candles in the evening. Popular with both locals and visitors, the restaurant offers lunches with pastas, salads, chowders, and sandwiches. In the evening, more elaborate meals are served, depending largely on the availability of fresh seafood. Continental dishes—rare in this region—are also featured. For dessert, key lime cheesecake or rum cake may appear on the menu.

A SIDE TRIP TO HARKERS ISLAND

If you're a boat owner, you can tie up across the sound from Beaufort at **Calico Jack's Marina** (☎ 252/728-3575) on Harkers Island. If you don't have a boat, a **Park Service Ferry** (☎ 800/BYFERRY) leaves from Calico Jack's for the 35-minute trip to Cape Lookout. The ferry runs between April and December, and the fare is $10 for adults and $6 for children 6 and under. A jitney service between Cape Point and the lighthouse moves visitors from one spot to another. Bring a picnic, insect repellent, and your own water supply. The island's atmosphere is ideal for those who like sailboats, lots of sun, and miles of sandy beaches. It's also a good venue for fishing and beachcombing. The unique diamond-patterned lighthouse has stood here since 1859.

Calico Jack's also takes visitors on four-wheel-drive tours of the island, highlighting its history and pointing out the best spots for shelling. Cost of a 2-hour tour is $10 for adults and $6 for children under age 17. Weather permitting, tours depart daily at 10am, noon, and 2pm.

3 Morehead City

147 miles SE of Raleigh; 3 miles W of Beaufort; 45 miles SE of New Bern; 87 miles NE of Wilmington

This has been an important port for oceangoing vessels since 1857 and is the world's largest tobacco-export terminal. Across the Intracoastal Waterway from Beaufort, and the gateway to the Atlantic Beach area (see "The Bogue Banks," later in this chapter), it attracts many fishers. Both onshore and offshore fishing trips are offered here, and tournaments are held throughout the year. The biggest event is the Big Rock Blue Marlin Tournament (☎ 252/247-3575), staged over 6 days, beginning the second Monday in June. The contest features cash awards.

ESSENTIALS

GETTING THERE   By Plane   The closest commuter-flight connection is the airport at New Bern (See section 4, "New Bern").

By Train   The nearest **Amtrak** stop is at Raleigh on the New York-to-Miami or New York-to-Tampa run. Call ☎ 800/USA-RAIL for schedules and fares.

By Bus   Greyhound/Trailways (☎ 252/726-3029) serves Morehead City. The terminal is at 105 N. 13th St. (☎ 252/726-3029). You can get a taxi here if you're heading for a hotel at Atlantic Beach.

By Car   Morehead City is about a 45-minute drive on U.S. 70 East from New Bern.

VISITOR INFORMATION   For sightseeing and accommodation information, contact the **Carteret County Tourism Bureau,** 3409 Arendell St., P.O. Box 1406, Morehead City, NC 28557 (☎ **800/SUNNYNC** or 252/726-8148; www.sunnync. com). Hours are Monday to Friday from 9am to 5pm, Saturday and Sunday 10am to 5pm.

OUTDOOR PURSUITS

Fishing is especially good here—in fact, it's the reason why most visitors come to Morehead City. The Gulf Stream brings in blue marlin, tarpon, amberjack, and other prizes, in addition to inshore fish. Gulf Stream fishing is possible from April through November. The area has about 80 miles of surf and 400 miles of protected waterways.

A near-perfect day or evening on the water can be enjoyed on the *Carolina Princess,* 604 Evans St., Morehead City (☎ **800/682-3456** or 252/726-5479). The *Princess* is a trim vessel that accommodates up to 100 passengers and has a snack bar and sundeck. Full-day deep-sea fishing trips cost $65 for adults, $50 for children 12 and under, or $20 for a passenger who goes along just for the ride and doesn't fish. The boat supplies the rod, reel, bait, and ice.

WHERE TO STAY

Best Western Buccaneer Motor Inn. 2806 Arendell St. (Hwy. 70), Morehead City, NC 28557. ☎ **800/682-4982** or 252/726-3115. Fax 252/726-3864. www.bestwestern.com. E-mail: buccaneer@clis.com. 91 units. A/C TV TEL. May–Sept, Sun–Thurs $65–$88 double, Fri–Sat $85–$115 double. Jan–Mar, $47 double. Children under 18 stay free in parents' room. Rates include continental breakfast. AE, CB, DC, DISC, MC, V.

If you're looking for a family-friendly motel, head for this chain motel. It's not the largest in the area, but it's one of the best. Housekeeping is good. The hotel has been remodeled recently, and its standard rooms are comfortable and rather tasteful; some have whirlpools. Amenities include free coffee, free local phone calls, and a pool. The Anchor Inn Restaurant, with two dining rooms and a lounge, specializes in seafood, Black Angus steaks, prime rib, and homemade desserts.

The Dill House. 1104 Arendell St., Morehead City, NC 28557. ☎ **252/726-4449.** 3 units (none with bath). A/C. Summer $95–$125 double; off-season $40–$60 double. Rates include full breakfast. No credit cards.

This is a winning choice for those wanting to go the B&B route. The two-story establishment was built in 1918 and has kept the style of that era, with antiques, wicker, and Oriental rugs on the hardwood floors. Rooms are comfortable and tasteful, although without TVs or phones. It's in the town center within walking distance of the waterfront.

WHERE TO DINE

✪ **Bistro by the Sea.** 4031 Arendell St. ☎ **253/243-2777.** Reservations recommended. Main courses $6.95–$24.95. AE, DC, MC, V. Tues–Sat 5–10pm. Closed: Jan. ATLANTIC COASTAL.

The town's best restaurant occupies a contemporary, stone-sided building set beside Highway 70, near the Hampton Inn, in a commercial neighborhood west of the waterfront. Inside, you'll find a stylish bar where a trompe l'oeil mural adorns the edges of a ceiling cupola. Within the dignified dining rooms, you'll be offered savory dishes that include peppercorn-encrusted seared tuna; sautéed salmon scampi with lemon-flavored linguine, shrimp, and a julienne of vegetables; prime rib of beef; and pastas that include cappellini in pesto sauce with fresh-roasted vegetables. There's also an assortment of burgers. Your hosts are Tim Coyne and his wife, Libby Eaton, who began their restaurant career in a beachfront shack in the 1980s, and who eventually expanded into the substantial building you'll see today.

Captain Bill's Waterfront Restaurant. 701 Evans St. ☎ **252/726-2166.** Reservations recommended. Lunch main courses $4.95–$18.95; dinner main courses $7.50–$25. AE, DISC, MC, V. Sun–Thurs 11am–9pm, Fri–Sat 11am–10pm. SEAFOOD.

A tradition since the 1940s, this local favorite overlooks the colorful fishing boats on Bogue Sound. With a name like Captain Bill's, the restaurant obviously specializes in seafood, which is very fresh. Locals look forward to the conch stew on Wednesday and Saturday, as well as all-you-can-eat seafood specials on Monday, Wednesday, and Friday. Prices are a bargain. There's also a good selection of non-finny dishes. The Down East lemon pie is justly celebrated. All desserts, sauces, and salad dressings are homemade. There's also a children's menu.

✪ **Mrs. Willis Restaurant.** 3114 Bridge St. ☎ **252/726-3741.** Reservations accepted in summer. Main courses $8.75–$21.95. AE, DC, DISC, MC, V. Sun–Fri 11am–2pm and 5–9pm, Sat 5pm–2am. Closed Christmas week. SOUTHERN.

"Ma Willis" has been a local legend since 1949, when she served up platters of barbecue from a one-room garage with the help of some of her six children. Originally, she cooked barbecue, chicken, and homemade pies for takeout, but in time, business demanded that she open a full-fledged restaurant. The restaurant has remained a local tradition, known for its prime ribs and choice charcoaled steaks. The barbecue is highly recommended, as are the Southern-style vegetables. The place is cozy and rather rustic, with a fireplace, background music, and lots of Southern hospitality. In addition to a good wine list, there's full bar service.

THE BOGUE BANKS

Atlantic Beach is the oldest of the resorts on the 28-mile stretch of barrier island known as the Bogue Banks, which includes the vacation centers directly south, **Pine Knoll Shores, Salter Path, Indian Beach,** and **Emerald Isle.** You may also hear the area referred to as "The Crystal Coast" (also encompassing Morehead City and Beaufort to the north; see listings above). Whatever its moniker, the long, thin island was relatively undeveloped until 1927, when the first bridge was built across Bogue Sound to Morehead City. It's now one of the state's most popular coastal areas, with fishing festivals and tournaments held in early spring and late fall. A south-facing exposure makes the island's weather less volatile and temperatures milder than that found on the northern Outer Banks, making it virtually a year-round resort. When you begin to feel a bit waterlogged, plenty of sightseeing is within easy reach.

At the tip of Bogue Island sits **Fort Macon,** a restored Civil War landmark that's open to the public at no charge. The jetties (designed by Gen. Robert E. Lee), moats, gun emplacements, and dungeons make it worth the trip. The museum displays weapons, tools, and artifacts. The public beach has bathhouses, a snack bar, and lifeguards. Fort Macon lies 2 miles east of Atlantic Beach off N.C. 58, and is open daily from 9am to 5:30pm. Free guided tours of the fort are offered only in summer at 11am, 1pm, and 3pm. The museum is open in summer from 9am to 5pm. For more information, call ☎ 252/726-3775.

For further information about the Bogue Banks or Crystal Coast area, contact the **Carteret County Tourism Bureau** (☎ 800/786-6962; www.sunnync.com).

WHERE TO STAY & DINE

Oceanana Resort Motel. 700 Fort Macon Rd. (P.O. Box 250), Atlantic Beach, NC 28512. ☎ 252/726-4111. Fax 252/726-4113. E-mail: oceanana@ncnets.net. 109 units. A/C TV TEL. July–Sept, $89–$127 double; $187 suite. Rates include breakfast in summer. Off-season, $58–$70 double; $83–$103 suite. MC, V. Closed Nov–Mar.

This motel at Atlantic Beach proper, directly beside the ocean, has a free fishing pier for guests. If you want to turn the day's catch into the evening meal, you'll find grills and a supply of charcoal, starter fluid, and even ketchup and mustard out by the pool, as well as picnic tables nearby. For the small fry, there's a playground, and for vacationers of all ages, the semiweekly watermelon party out by the pool is a festive occasion. A tropical breakfast, spread under an open poolside pavilion, features more than 15 fresh fruits. There's a fast-food grill out by the fishing pier. Every room has a refrigerator, and suites have stoves. You can take portable grills to the lawn area in front of your room (but not on upper-floor decks) and cook dinner right at your door.

Royal Pavillion Resort. Pine Knoll Shores (P.O. Box 790), Atlantic Beach, NC 28512. ☎ 800/533-3700 or 252/726-5188. Fax 252/726-9963. www.rpresort.com. 110 units. A/C TV TEL. June–Sept $110–$135 double; off-season, $100–$120 double. Children 12 and under stay free in parents' room. AE, DISC, MC, V. Go 3 miles west of U.S. 70 on N.C. 58 to Pine Knoll Shores/Salter Path exit.

Once known as the John Yancey Motor Hotel, this rather grandly named hotel was expanded. Its main allure is that it faces 1,000 feet of broad ocean beach on Salter Path Road. Bedrooms are only standard, but they're clean and well maintained. This hotel has a restaurant and lounge, free coffee and doughnuts, two outdoor pools and a pool bar, and golf and tennis privileges at nearby facilities.

WHERE TO DINE

The Crab Shack. Off Hwy. 58. (behind the Methodist Church), Salter Path, NC 28512. ☎ 252/247-3444. Lunch main courses $4.95–$15; dinner main courses $7.50–$18. Open 7 days a week, year-round; hours seasonal. SEAFOOD.

This is everything a Down East seafood "shack" should be: It's a local favorite with an expansive backside view of Bogue Sound and consistently reliable seafood standards. If it's steamed spiced crabs you crave, here's the spot to order up a dozen or two in season. You won't find fancy sauces here: The Crab Shack offers fresh, unadulterated seafood, fried, grilled, or broiled, a solid Hatteras-style clam chowder (broth-based), and state-of-the-art hush puppies. Families love the friendly, casual ambience. The decor may make you wince, and you'll probably have to wait in line for a table, but for good and simple, you can't beat it. Beer and wine are available.

A Real-Life Desert Island

For those who really want to get away from it all, here's an uninhabited barrier island, where the pristine beaches are strewn with little more than snow-white sand dollars and the delicate tracings of bird feet. You can only reach **Bear Island** by private boat or by seasonal ferry—and visitation is limited to how many people can cross on the ferry, so you really can feel as if the island is your own. Bear Island is the island portion of **Hammocks Beach State Park** (Park office: ☎ 910/326-4881), a 3-mile-long barrier island dominated by high sand dunes, a maritime forest, and unspoiled beach. Primitive camping is allowed here year-round—except for 3 nights each month during the summer nesting season of endangered loggerhead sea turtles, who come here under the full moon to lay their eggs. The passenger ferry leaves from Hammocks Beach Road park entrance in Swansboro hourly from Memorial Day through Labor Day, 9:30am to 5:30pm, and on weekends in April and October 9:30am to 4:30pm. Fees are adults $2, children 4–12 $1, and children under 3 free.

SIDE TRIPS TO SWANSBORO & JACKSONVILLE

Along the coast southwest of Morehead City, the historic little waterfront town of **Swansboro,** bordering the White Oak River across from Cape Carteret, is a real charmer, with shops in renovated centuries-old structures. The **Mullet Festival,** held here every October, draws huge crowds from around the Southeast.

Almost due west of Swansboro, **Jacksonville** sits inland, but only a 20-minute drive from choice beaches. The focal point of the city is the adjacent New River Marine Base, on N.C. 24, universally known as **Camp Lejeune** (☎ 910/451-2197). The 110,000-acre reservation is one of the world's most complete amphibious military training centers, and you can obtain a pass to drive through unrestricted parts of the grounds if you present your driver's license and car registration to personnel at the information center (next to the main gate on N.C. 24).

For a true North Carolina coastal seafood experience, drive south of Jacksonville to the little fishing village of **Sneads Ferry,** which is loaded with eateries featuring right-off-the-boat choices steamed, broiled, or fried to perfection. The town hosts the Sneads Ferry Shrimp Festival the second weekend in August.

For more information on the Jacksonville area, call the **Greater Jacksonville/ Onslow Chamber of Commerce,** 1 Marine Blvd. N., P.O. Box 765, Jacksonville, NC 28541-0165 (☎ 910/347-3141). The chamber can also help you with accommodations and places to eat. Hours are Monday to Friday 9am to 5pm.

WHERE TO DINE NEAR SWANSBORO

The T & W Oyster Bar. 2382 Hwy. 58, Swansboro. ☎ 252/393-8838. Main courses $8–$15. DISC, MC, V. Mon–Sat 5–9pm, Sun noon–9pm. SEAFOOD/STEAKS.

Looking like a country roadhouse from the outside, this restaurant has an interior with five dining rooms, two of which have fireplaces. There is a simplicity here bordering on sophistication, and if the place could be transported back to the 1950s, the food would be just the same as it is now. The oysters arrive in the fall—your choice, raw or steamed, plucked from the shells as fast as you can eat them—but the year-round seafood selections are good and fresh, including several versions of crabs, both deviled and in cakes. The classic dish for Carolina sea captains is Mr. T's baked flounder with "taters and onions." Sandwiches are also sold.

4 New Bern

87 miles NE of Wilmington

Less than 50 miles inland, on U.S. 70 and U.S. 17, New Bern is the state's oldest town, lying between the Neuse and Trent rivers, where swimming, boating, and both fresh- and saltwater fishing are favorite pastimes. Its historic district merits a visit, as it's filled with Georgian, Victorian, and classical-revival architecture.

ESSENTIALS

GETTING THERE   From Beaufort, take U.S. 70 west to Morehead City, and continue along the same western route straight into New Bern. From Wilmington, head north on U.S. 17 through Jacksonville and directly into New Bern. From Raleigh, go east along U.S. 70 to New Bern.

The **Craven County Regional Airport,** 1501 Airport Rd., 2 miles outside New Bern (☎ 252/638-8591), is served by **US Airways** (☎ 800/428-4322), with connections from major cities in North Carolina. A taxi from the **Cherry Cab Co.** (☎ 252/447-3101) will take passengers into the city. A taxi to the center of New Bern from the airport costs approximately $8.

VISITOR INFORMATION   The **Craven County Convention and Visitors Bureau,** located at 314 S. Front St. (☎ 252/637-9400; www.visitnewbern.com), is open Monday to Friday from 8:30am to 6pm (8am to 5pm in winter), on Saturday from 10am to 4pm (10am to 5pm in winter), and on Sunday and holidays from 10am to 2pm (11am to 4pm in winter). The **New Bern Historical Society,** at 511 Broad St. (☎ 252/638-8558), is located in the historic 1790 Attmore-Oliver House, which exhibits 18th- and 19th-century furniture and artifacts. Hours are Monday through Saturday, 1 to 4pm, April to mid-December.

SPECIAL EVENTS   In late March, when the azaleas and dogwoods burst into bloom, New Bern sponsors a **Spring Historic Homes and Garden Tour.** About 10 historic homes in town are open to the public, and tours also feature churches. Tickets cost $16 to $19 per person. For information, call the Preservation Foundation (☎ 252/633-6448) or the New Bern Historical Society (see above).

EXPLORING THE AREA

For fresh air, New Berners head for **Croatan National Forest,** southwest of town via U.S. 17 or U.S. 70. This unique coastal forest covers 157,724 acres and is riddled with waterways and estuaries. It's the alligator's northernmost habitat. Many insect-eating plants are here, including the Venus's-flytrap. Look for it on the pocosins, the Native American word for "swamp on a hill." Activities include boating, fishing on the Neuse River, deer hunting, and camping.

In town, more than 180 18th- and 19th-century structures are listed in the National Register of Historic Places. Among the highlights are the following:

✪ **Tryon Palace Historic Sites & Gardens.** 610 Pollock St. ☎ **252/514-4900.** www.tryonpalace.org. Combination ticket $15 adults, $6 children (preschool children free with adult). Guided tours Mon–Sat 9am–4pm, Sun 1–4pm. Closed New Year's Day, Thanksgiving, and Dec 24–26.

This 19-room museum, built from 1767 to 1770 as both the state capitol and the residence of the royal governor, has been authentically restored. Walking through the elegant rooms, it's easy to see why this mansion was once called the most beautiful in America. The main building burned in 1798 and lay in ruins until the restoration in

1952–59. The handsome grounds and gardens surrounding Tyron Palace are designed in 18th-century style.

Two other landmarks in the 13-acre Tryon Palace complex are the **John Wright Stanly House** (1780), a late Georgian-style mansion with townhouse gardens, and the **Stevenson House** (1805), noted for its rare Federal antiques. Crafts shows and historical dramas are mounted, and seasonal guided tours are available.

New Bern Firemen's Museum. 408 Hancock St. ☎ **252/636-4087.** Admission $2 adults, $1 children. Mon–Sat 10am–4:30pm, Sun 1–5pm.

The original firefighting equipment of New Bern, dating back to the early 19th century, is on display here, including an 1884 horse-drawn steamer and leather fire helmets. There's also a Civil War display case.

SHOPPING

Coco & Co. 218 South Front St. ☎ **252/672-5642.**

This is the most cosmopolitan shop in New Bern. Situated in a 19th-century house near the center of town, it devotes half its floor space to stylish women's sportswear. The other, more interesting section, contains European antiques, Indonesian artifacts, English-inspired garden ornaments, and unusual architectural artifacts gleaned from North Carolina farms and homesteads. Long-time New Bern resident Betsy Hathaway is the creative owner of this place, and much of the inventory reflects her own taste.

The Birthplace of Pepsi. 256 Middle St. (corner of Pollack St.). ☎ **252/636-5898.** www. pepsistore.com.

The antique storefront that contains this place once functioned as Caleb Bradham's Pharmacy, the site where the entrepreneur invented the formula for Pepsi Cola in 1898, 13 years after the development of the original formula for Coca-Cola. Today the site functions as a hybrid store/museum, dispensing nostalgia along with 8-ounce glasses of Pepsi from a replica of an old-time soda fountain for 53¢ each. Also on display are some 200 souvenir items, including Frisbees and commemorative T-shirts, each lauding Pepsi and/or its claim on the American soul, in one or another elusive ways. Subsidized by the Pepsi-Cola Bottling Company of New Bern, serving several counties of eastern North Carolina, the site is open Monday to Saturday, 10am to 6pm.

WHERE TO STAY

✪ **Aerie.** 509 Pollock St., New Bern, NC 28562. ☎ **800/849-5553** or 252/636-5553. Fax 252/514-2157. www.aerieinn.com. E-mail: aeriebb@coastalnet.com. 7 units. A/C TV TEL. $89–$99 double. Rates include full breakfast and afternoon refreshments on weekends. Additional person $20 extra. Children 6 and under stay free in parents' room. DISC, MC, V.

A block east of Tryon Palace, within walking distance of several restaurants, this gracious inn is among the top two or three in town. It was fully restored and redecorated in 1985. Built in 1882, it has only two floors. Inside, the rooms are furnished with antiques or reproductions from the 1880s and 1890s. All have private baths and are nicely maintained. Breakfasts are country-style, and afternoon refreshments, served in the tearoom, have become a local tradition.

Harmony House. 215 Pollock St., New Bern, NC 28560. ☎ **252/636-3810.** Fax 252/536-3810. www.harmonyhouseinn.com. 10 units. A/C TV TEL. $100–$135 double; $150 suite. Rates include full breakfast. Additional person $10 extra. AE, DISC, MC, V.

Close to the Aerie—and a worthy competitor in every way—this Greek Revival house from 1850 receives guests on two floors. The furnishings are contemporary, however, not antique, and the attractive, well-maintained accommodations have either a queen-size bed or twin beds. The owner displays her own needlepoint and artwork throughout the house. Guests quickly gravitate to their favorite rockers on the front porch. In the evening, wine is served. The house maintains two suites, which are ideal for families and small traveling groups, consisting of two bedrooms and a living room with a sleeper sofa.

Kings Arms. 212 Pollock St., New Bern, NC 28560. ☎ **800/872-9306** or 252/638-4409. Fax 252/638-2191. 8 units. TV TEL. $100 double; $145 suite. Rates include full breakfast. Additional person $10 extra. Children 6 and under stay free in parents' room at discretion of management. AE, MC, V.

On the same street as the Aerie and Harmony House, the Kings Arms (built in 1848) is comparable in rating and ambience. This Greek Revival–style home is furnished with antiques and period reproductions. Several restaurants are within walking distance.

WHERE TO DINE

Captain Ratty's. 330 S. Front St. ☎ **252/633-2088.** Reservations recommended Fri–Sat nights. Sandwiches and salads $3.95–$7.95; main courses $14.95–$30.95. MC, V. Mon–Thurs 11:30am–10pm, Fri–Sat 11:30am–11pm. AMERICAN/LOW COUNTRY.

One of New Bern's most popular restaurants occupies a circa-1897 brick structure that functioned throughout most local residents' memory as a pharmacy. Its owners, who know virtually everyone in town, define the place as a tavern in the Carolinas style, and print a calendar of events advertising the evenings when oysters, for example, will sell for only 40¢ each. Some kind of live music is presented every Friday and Saturday from 7pm to midnight, and the menu includes such dishes as platters of king crab legs; New York–style strip steak (served with or without shrimp); mussels in a white wine sauce; any of several other kinds of shellfish and fresh fish; and daily specials. It's hardly haute cuisine, but the food is fresh and crowd-pleasing.

The Chelsea: A Restaurant & Publick House. 335 Middle St. ☎ **252/637-5469.** Reservations recommended. Lunch sandwiches and salads $5.50–$6.95; dinner main courses $12.95–$18.95. AE, DISC, MC, V. Mon–Thurs 11am–9pm, Fri–Sat 11am–10pm. AMERICAN/FUSION.

Engaging and popular, this bar and bistro serves simple, well-prepared food that's offered in a brick-lined setting on wooden tables in a turn-of-the-century pharmacy owned by the inventor of Pepsi-Cola, Caleb Bradham. Many customers like to linger at the bar, but for those interested in an actual meal, menu items include such dishes as Black Strap tenderloin of pork (with Dijon mustard and herbs); crab cakes; shrimp Sonoma; Thai-style red curried seafood; and potato-crusted salmon. The food here has more of a cutting edge and modern twist than that found at its nearby competitors. Sandwiches feature "The Chelsea," made from caramelized onions, roasted peppers, mushrooms, sun-dried tomatoes, pesto, and feta cheese.

✪ **Harvey Mansion.** 221 Tryon Palace Dr. ☎ **252/638-3205.** Reservations recommended. Main courses $12–$25.95; fixed-price 2-course meal with salad $14.95. AE, CB, DC, DISC, MC, V. Tues–Sun 6–10pm. CONTINENTAL.

This is New Bern's premier restaurant, and its 1797 building constructed by a shipping merchant is listed on the National Register of Historic Places. Dine in one of six formal dining rooms, or opt for a light casual menu served in the cellar, an especially popular spot with the younger set. Weather permitting, customers dine outside. The mansion lies near the confluence of the Trent and Neuse rivers.

The menu never falls into tedium. Local foodies and summer tourists on the Carolina-coast circuit come here for a range of dishes that include fresh local fish, shrimp, scallops, crab, and lobster. The chef enjoys a deserved reputation for his game dishes, including venison, rabbit, quail, and duck. A delectable specialty may include veal or crab. The rack of lamb is one of the most elegant and expensive items on the menu, and we've found the cuts of Angus beef to be very tender. The bargain is the two-course meal with salad.

Henderson House. 216 Pollock St. ☎ **252/637-4784.** Reservations recommended. Main courses $17.95–$32.50. AE, DISC, MC, V. Tues–Sat 6–10pm. Closed major holidays. CONTINENTAL.

New Bern's second-leading restaurant has a devoted following. First, the setting is intriguing; this 1790 structure is listed on the National Register of Historic Places. In addition, an art gallery is on-site. It's all quite elegant, with crystal chandeliers, linen tablecloths and napkins, antiques, silver place settings, and lush draperies. But it's the food that keeps regulars coming back. First-rate ingredients are used in such dishes as shrimp amandine; roast lamb; roast duck with a zesty plum sauce; and crabmeat Norfolk, chock full of crab. Guests enjoy full bar service, and appetizers and desserts are made fresh daily. No smoking.

5 Cape Hatteras National Seashore

From Whalebone Junction in South Nags Head, Cape Hatteras National Seashore stretches 70 miles south down the Outer Banks barrier islands. The drive along N.C. 12 (about 4½ hours) takes you through a wildlife refuge and pleasant villages, past sandy beaches, and on to Buxton and the Cape Hatteras Lighthouse, the tallest on the coast. Since 1870, the light has been a beacon for ships passing through these treacherous waters, which have claimed more than 1,500 victims by means of foul weather, strong rip currents, and shifting shoals. This is where the ironclad Union gunboat *Monitor* went down during a storm in December 1862.

From the little village of Hatteras, a car ferry crosses to **Ocracoke Island,** where more than 5,000 acres, including 16 miles of beach, are preserved by the National Park Service for recreation. From the southern end of the island, you can take a ferry across the vast, shallow Pamlico Sound to **Cedar Island.**

The National Seashore is best explored on an all-day trip, or on several half-day trips, from a Nags Head base. (See "Nags Head & the Outer Banks," below for our lodging recommendations.) Try to give yourself plenty of time for swimming, fishing, or just walking along the sand and for visiting the newly moved Cape Hatteras Lighthouse. Stop for lunch or shopping, and get to know the local people who call this necklace of sand home. The hardy "Bankers" can recount tales of heroism at sea and tell you about the ghostly light that bobs over Teach's (Blackbeard's) Hole, as well as the wild ponies that have roamed Ocracoke Island for more than 400 years—all told in a lilting accent that some people say harks back to Devon, England, home base of a band of shipwrecked sailors who came ashore here and stayed.

FROM NAGS HEAD TO HATTERAS

Turn left off N.C. 12 about 8 miles south of U.S. 158 to reach **Coquina Beach,** which offers bath shelters, lifeguards (from mid-June to Labor Day), picnic shelters, and beach walks guided by National Park Service naturalists.

Farther south, across Oregon Inlet, **Pea Island Wildlife Refuge** (☎ 252/ 473-1131), on Hatteras Island (the northern part, south of Bonner Bridge), attracts birders from all over the country to see the snow geese in winter and the wading shore and upland birds in summer. Some 265 species of birds winter here. There's a parking area and raised platforms. The wildlife refuge is open daily 9am to 4pm; admission is free.

All along N.C. 12, you'll see places to pull off and park to reach the beaches, which are hidden from view by huge protective sand dunes. *Note:* Don't try to park anywhere else; the sands are very soft, and it's easy to get stuck.

Warning: Whether you're camping or just stopping at beaches where there are no lifeguards, you should always keep in mind that tides and currents along the Outer Banks are *very* strong, and ocean swimming can be dangerous at times.

When you get to Buxton, turn left off N.C. 12 to see the famed **Cape Hatteras Lighthouse** in its new location. The lighthouse was reopened to the public in May 2000 following a massive relocation effort, which moved the lighthouse back 2,900 feet to save it from toppling into the encroaching sea. Its rotating duplex beacon has a 1,000-watt, 250,000-candlepower lamp on each side and is visible for 20 miles.

The village of ✪ **Hatteras** exists now, as it has from the 1700s, as a fishing center, and large commercial and sport fleets operate from its docks and marinas. In the spring and fall, boats bring in catches of sea trout, king and Spanish mackerel, red drum, and striped bass. In summer, most of the action is offshore, where blue marlin and other billfish are in plentiful supply. If you're interested in doing some fishing yourself, the Outer Banks Chamber of Commerce (see "Nags Head & the Outer Banks," later in this chapter) can supply a list of charter boats and fishing information. Even if you don't fish, it's fun to watch the boats come in between 4 and 6pm.

OUTDOOR PURSUITS

Hatteras Island Fishing Pier, Rodanthe (☎ 252/987-2323), stretches 653 feet out into the Atlantic, charging $6 for fishing or $1 for sightseeing. Fishers can rent rod and reel from the bait shop for $7.50 per day, plus a refundable $30 deposit. Live and artificial bait is available, along with the necessary tackle. At the beach end of the pier is a restaurant, plus toilets, a motel, and cottages for rent. The pier is open 24 hours.

Windsurfers flock to the area—and especially to a spot called **Canadian Hole,** so named for its popularity among Canadian windsurfers—and the best place to hook up with this sport is the **Hatteras Island Surf Shop,** N.C. 12, Waves (☎ 919/987-2296), open Monday to Saturday from 10am to 6pm and on Sunday from 11am to 6pm. Surfboards cost $15 per day, and boogie boards rent for $6, kayaks, single $25, double $30. Windsurfing equipment, goes for $35 per half-day or $60 per full day.

SHOPPING

More than 40 art galleries stretch along the Outer Banks, but one of the most appealing is **Sandy Bay Gallery,** Hwy. 12, Hatteras (☎ 252/986-1338). It features a large inventory of gift and craft items, with tastes that include goodly doses of what you might expect to find in Northern California, infused in many cases with seafront Carolina regionalism. Roanoke Island nostalgia runs rampant here, as expressed in pottery, glass, paper, stained glass, metalwork, wood, and canvas.

WHERE TO STAY

Hatteras Marlin Motel. N.C. 12 (P.O. Box 250), Hatteras, NC 27943. ☎ **252/986-2141.** Fax 252/986-2436. 41 units. A/C TV TEL. May 1–Sept 7, $54–$70 double. Off-season, $54–$70 double. $100 suite up to 6 people. Additional person in room $5 extra. Children 6 and under stay free in parents' room. MC, V.

One of the better motels in the area, this isn't the Ritz, but it's a solid, reliable, and serviceable choice. The rooms with kitchenettes are family favorites. The bedrooms are in standard motel style, but are clean and comfortable. Suites contain full kitchens and two bedrooms, and have balconies. Other facilities include a sundeck surrounding the pool and picnic tables, along with barbecue grills available for the use of guests.

WHERE TO DINE

Austin Creek Grill. Hatteras Landing. ☎ **252/986-1511.** Reservations not necessary. Lunch platters, salads, and sandwiches $5.25–$8.50; dinner main courses $16.95–$22.95. AE, DISC, MC, V. Tues–Sun noon–2pm and 5:30–9:30pm. CONTEMPORARY CAROLINA.

Opened in February 2000, this is the newest and hottest restaurant in Hatteras Landing. Situated in a colony of faux-colonial buildings that's adjacent to the piers where cars line up for the ferryboats, it looks like a postmodern interpretation of a turn-of-the-century boathouse, brightly painted in tones of yellow and blue. Views of the sea and the nearby marina are enhanced by its position directly above the water, rising on foundations that were sunk directly into the seabed. Lunches focus on sandwiches, soups, and salads. Dinner items are more elaborate, and include well-prepared spinach salads garnished with Maytag blue cheese, caramelized pecans, and warm bacon vinaigrette; macadamia-coated shrimp with the salsa of the day; crab cakes with tarragon-flavored béarnaise sauce; island seafood cassoulet with sausage and a medley of shellfish; and pan-fried soba noodles with wok-charred shrimp and vegetable sauté and Szechuan-style scallion sauce.

The Channel Bass. N.C. 12, Hatteras. ☎ **252/986-2250.** Reservations accepted only for parties of 15 or more. Main courses $9.95–$26.95. Apr–Nov, daily 5:30–9:30pm. Take N.C. 12 to 12 miles south of lighthouse. SEAFOOD.

The nautical decor comes as no surprise; neither does the seafood menu at this family-owned place. The clam chowder will have you calling for seconds. In fact, all the seafood is fresh and cooked to perfection. The menu is semi à la carte, and portions are so ample that the steamed sampler appetizer (oysters, clams, and shrimp) could well do you as a full meal. Specialties are fresh local fish, fried or broiled, and crab imperial. Everything comes with those tasty cornmeal fritters known as hush puppies.

OCRACOKE ISLAND

From Hatteras, a free car ferry crosses the inlet to ✪ **Ocracoke Island** in 40 minutes; during the peak summer tourist season, however, be prepared to wait in line to board the ferry.

Ocracoke has shown up on maps as far back as the late 1500s, when Sir Walter Raleigh's Roanoke Island party landed here. It's rumored to have been the last headquarters of Blackbeard, who died here. The wily pirate, after years of terrorizing merchant ships along the Atlantic coast, made his peace with the British Crown in 1712 and received a full pardon from the king. Soon thereafter, however, he came out of retirement and resumed preying on ships from the Caribbean to the Virginia capes, working hand in glove with the colonial governor, Charles Eden, and Colonial Secretary Tobias Knight.

In 1718, Lt. Richard Maynard of the British Royal Navy captured Blackbeard's ship and crew in Ocracoke Inlet, killing the pirate in a bloody duel. Maynard then sailed back to Virginia with Blackbeard's head mounted on his prow to let ships along the coast know that the sea lanes were safe once more. Tales persist to this day of treasure stashed away along the coast of North Carolina, but none has ever been found; it's likely that Blackbeard sold his spoils quickly and squandered the proceeds. (See also "Two Cuts to Blackbeard's Neck," in Appendix A: "The Carolinas & Georgia in Depth.")

When Ocracoke Island was isolated from the mainland and few visitors came by boat, as many as 1,000 wild ponies roamed its dunes. Where they came from—shipwrecks, early Spanish explorers, or English settlers—is uncertain. Eventually, as more and more people traveled to and from the island, many ponies were rounded up and shipped to the mainland. The remnants of the herd (about two dozen) now live at the **Ocracoke Pony Pens,** a range 7 miles north of Ocracoke village, where the National Park Service looks after them.

In a quiet little corner of Ocracoke Island, you'll find a bit of England: The **British Graveyard,** where four British seamen were buried after their bodies washed ashore when the HMS *Bedfordshire* was torpedoed by a German submarine in 1942. The graveyard is leased by the British government but is lovingly tended by townspeople.

Ocracoke village has seen some changes since World War II, when the U.S. Navy dredged out Silver Lake Harbor (still called "Cockle Creek" by many natives) and built a base here. They also brought the first public telephones and paved roads. In spite of the invasion of 20th-century improvements and the influx of tourist-oriented businesses, Ocracoke is essentially what it has always been: a fishing village whose manners and speech reflect its 17th-century ancestry.

WHERE TO STAY

The Island Inn. N.C. 12 (P.O. Box 9), Ocracoke Island, NC 27960. ☎ **252/928-4351.** www.ocracokeislandinn.com. 35 units, 4 villas, 1 cottage. A/C TV TEL. $40–$195 double. $750 per week villa or cottage. Additional person in room $5 extra. AE, DISC, MC, V.

This antiques-filled place was once a school and then a lodge, and was even an officers' headquarters before becoming an inn in the 1940s. During World War II, staying here was viewed by some people as being dangerous because of German submarine activity off the coast. The rooms are attractively furnished and inviting, and are our choice on the island. The inn also has the island's only heated swimming pool.

This longstanding favorite is also one of the best places for meals, which are served daily from 7am to 2pm and 5 to 9pm. The cost is $3.95 to $7.95 for breakfast, $5.95 to $8.95 for lunch, and $8.95 to $15.95 for dinner. Specialties are crab cakes, prime rib, and Carolina clam chowder. The seafood platter is enormous. The restaurant—but not the inn—is closed December to February.

WHERE TO DINE

Howard's Pub and Raw Bar Restaurant. Highway 12. ☎ **252/928-4441.** www. howardspub.com. Reservations not necessary. Salads and Sandwiches $5.25–$7.95; main courses $10.95–$15.95. AE, DC, MC, V. Daily 11–2am. SEAFOOD/AMERICAN.

There's more lore associated with this place, and a greater sense of community among its devoted fans, than any other restaurant on Ocracoke island. Set inside an imposing but weather-beaten building that's the first major business you'll see after heading south from the Hatteras Ferry landing, it occupies the site of what flourished briefly in the 1850s as a pub (Howard's) before it sank into the sands of this reputedly haunted island. Inside the mostly wooden interior, you'll find a cheerful staff that's proud of the establishment's self-sufficiency—thanks to their own generators, they've provided sustenance to famished locals even in the aftermath of hurricanes. Menu items focus on burgers, steaks, fresh oysters and shellfish, barbecued ribs, grilled fish fresh from local waters, Maine lobster, and massive amounts of shrimp.

Local ordinances restrict the serving of hard liquor by the glass, so as a means of compensating, Howard's stocks the largest selection of beer—more than 200 kinds—on the Outer Banks. The bar is the single most popular rendezvous point on the island, serving drinks and good cheer every night between 9:30pm and 2am. Every Tuesday, Wednesday, Friday and Saturday, it doubles as a disco, without cover charge.

CEDAR ISLAND

To reach North Carolina's more southerly beaches, take the ferry from Ocracoke to Cedar Island. You'll need to make a reservation for the 2¼-hour trip over the calm, sparkling waters of the Pamlico Sound; take along a picnic lunch, and don't be surprised to see dolphins cavorting alongside the boat. Call within 30 days of departure to reserve space on one of the scheduled sailings. To sail from Cedar Island, call ☎ 252/225-3551; to sail from Ocracoke, call ☎ 252/928-3841. (East of the Mississippi, you can call Cedar Island at ☎ 800/856-0343 or Ocracoke at ☎ 800/345-1665.) *Reservations are not honored if your car is not in the loading zone at least 30 minutes before departure time.* The fare is $10 per car and occupants, $2 per bicycle and rider, and $1 for pedestrians. For a complete list of ferries, schedules, and fares, contact the **Ferry Division,** Department of Transportation, 113 Arendell St., Morehead City, NC 28557 (☎ 252/726-6446).

On the island, you can explore the **Cedar Island National Wildlife Refuge,** a feeding ground for migratory waterfowl. Once you're here, the best way to see the island is on horseback. Horses can be rented at **Outer Banks Riding Stables,** U.S. 70 east (☎ 252/225-1185), open Sunday to Thursday from noon to 5pm and on Friday and Saturday from 9am to 5pm. Reservations are recommended and are essential on Saturday and Sunday. A guide goes out with all rides. Rates are $20 for 45 minutes, $25 for an hour, $45 for 2 hours, and $35 for sunset rides.

WHERE TO STAY & DINE

Driftwood Motel. P.O. Box 630, Hwy. 12 N. Cedar Island, NC 28520 ☎ 252/225-4861. Fax 252/225-1113. www.clis.com/deg/. E-mail: deg@clis.com. 37 units. A/C TV. $60 double. Children under 12 stay free in parents' room. MC, V.

Simple yet cozy, this accommodation is a 3-minute walk from the beach. For the budget-minded traveler, this is a good bet. The lobby is located on the second floor, above the first-floor gift shop, which has items in the expected nautical theme. Rooms are motel-traditional, and the biggest amenity is the price. One unit is equipped for people with disabilities. The motel also maintains a restaurant, serving dinner nightly from 5 to 9pm and lunch on Sunday from 11am to 2pm. The fare is adequate, with enough seafood and continental dishes to satisfy everyone in your party.

6 Nags Head & the Outer Banks

234 miles N of Wilmington

Nags Head is the largest resort in the Outer Banks area. Its odd name, according to local legend, comes from the practice of wily old land pirates who used to hang lanterns from the necks of ponies and parade them along the dunes at night to lure unsuspecting ships onto shoals. When the ships ran aground, the waiting robbers promptly stripped their cargoes. Another theory holds that the town was named for the highest point of the Isles of Scilly, which was the last sight English colonists had of their homeland.

ESSENTIALS

GETTING THERE From Virginia and points north, reach Nags Head via U.S. 158; from Raleigh, via U.S. 64; from Wilmington, via the Cedar Island ferry (see "Cedar Island," earlier in this chapter). N.C. 12 runs the length of the Outer Banks, from Ocracoke to Duck.

The nearest airport to Nags Head is 80 miles northwest in Norfolk, Virginia. The Norfolk airport is served by **American Airlines** (☎ **800/433-7300;** www.aa.com), **Continental Airlines** (☎ **800/525-0280;** www.flycontinental.com), **Delta Air Lines** (☎ **800/221-1212;** www.delta.com), **Trans World Airlines** (☎ **800/221-2000;** www.twa.com), and **US Airways** (☎ **800/428-4322;** www.usairways.com).

VISITOR INFORMATION   Contact the **Outer Banks Visitors Bureau,** 704 S. Highway 64/264, Manteo, NC 27954 (☎ **800/446-6262,** or 252/441-8144; www.outerbanks.org), for information about accommodations and outdoor activities. The bureau is open Monday to Friday from 9am to 5pm.

SPECIAL EVENTS   On Roanoke Island, where it all happened, Paul Green's moving drama ✪ *The Lost Colony* is presented in the Waterside Theater from mid-June to late August, Sunday to Friday at 8:30pm. It's the country's oldest outdoor drama, running since 1937. All seats are reserved. Contact the **Waterside Theater,** 1409 U.S. 64, Manteo, NC 27954 (☎ **800/488-5012** or 252/473-3414; www.thelostcolony. org) for Visa or MasterCard bookings. Tickets cost about $18 for adults, $15 for senior citizens, and $8 for children 11 and under.

EXPLORING THE AREA

However it got its name, Nags Head has been one of North Carolina's most popular beach resorts for more than a century. The town is overcrowded in the summer, roadsides are chockablock with modern motels, restaurants, and water-sports stores, and erosion has taken its toll on the once-grand beaches in recent years. Still, it has a certain barefoot charm, and the many handsome old wooden homes from the late 19th century—known as the "Unpainted Aristocracy"—hearken back to the time when the town was an idyllic seaside retreat.

Needless to say, beach activities and fishing head the list here. Exercise caution when swimming; riptides can be very strong in these parts.

Jockey's Ridge, north of Nags Head, is the highest sand dune on the East Coast. Its smooth, sandy, 138-foot-high slopes are popular with the hang-gliding crowd, and because it's now a state park, it's open to all. Also north of Nags Head is **Kill Devil Hills** (named for a particularly potent rum once shipped from here), where the Wright brothers made that historic first air flight back in 1903.

SIGHTS NEARBY

✪ WRIGHT BROTHERS NATIONAL MEMORIAL

At milepost 8 on U.S. 158 in Kill Devil Hills, the Wright Brothers National Memorial (☎ **252/441-7430**) is open to the public for $2 per person or $4 per car; senior citizens and children 15 and under are admitted free. Both the hangar and Orville and Wilbur's living quarters have been restored, and the visitor center holds a replica of that first airplane. Exhibits tell the story of the two brothers who came here on vacation from their Dayton, Ohio, bicycle business to turn their dream into reality. The memorial is open daily from 9am to 6pm (9am to 5pm in winter). A park ranger gives a tour every hour from 10am to 4pm.

✪ MANTEO & ROANOKE ISLAND

From Whalebone Junction, U.S. 64/264 leads to Roanoke Island and the village of Manteo. Four miles west, you'll reach **Fort Raleigh National Historic Site,** where the fort from 1585 is but a mound of dirt. But the beauty of the landscaped park is reason enough to visit. The **visitor center** (☎ **252/473-5772**) is a first stop; a museum and an audiovisual program acquaint visitors with the park's story. The site is open from June 15 until the end of August, Sunday to Friday from 9am to 7:30pm and on Saturday from 9am to 6pm; off-season, daily from 9am to 5pm.

Most people visit Roanoke Island to see a performance of *The Lost Colony* at the Waterside Theater (see "Special Events" in the "Essentials" section, earlier in this chapter). The nearby **Elizabethan Gardens,** as well as the Tudor-style auxiliary buildings, remind us that this area was the first connection between Elizabethan England and what was to become the United States of America. The sumptuous gardens are open from the second week in March to November 30, charging $5 for adults and $1 for children 12 to 17; children 11 and under are admitted free; senior citizens $4.50. It's open from March 15 to November, daily from 9am to 5pm March 15 to March 31 and November, to 6pm in April and October, to 7pm in May and September, and to 8pm June through August.

Visitors journey to Manteo to see one of North Carolina's newest state historic sites: the new **Roanoke Island Festival Park,** which features the *Elizabeth II* (☎ 252/473-1144), moored across from the renovated waterfront. This 69-foot-long three-masted bark, a composite design of 16th-century ships, was built in 1984 with private funds for the 400th anniversary of the 1584 and 1587 Roanoke voyages. From mid-June to late August, Tuesday to Saturday, living-history interpreters portray colonists and mariners. The site is open April through October, daily from 10am to 6pm, and November through March, Tuesday to Sunday from 10am to 4pm; it's closed on major holidays. Admission is $8 for adults, $8 for senior citizens, and $5 for students.

EDENTON

About 1½ hours away from Nags Head, a later phase of U.S. history is preserved at ✪ Edenton, an atmospheric old town whose streets are lined with homes built by the planters and merchants who settled along the Albemarle Sound. The women of Edenton held their own "tea party" in 1774—one of the first recorded instances of American women taking political action. Take U.S. 64, turn right at N.C. 37, and then turn left when you reach N.C. 32.

Visit the new **Historic Edenton Visitor Center** at 108 N. Broad St. (signs are posted throughout the town; ☎ 252/482-2637), to view a free 14-minute slide show and purchase a historic-district map. The center is open April to October, Monday to Saturday from 9am to 5pm and on Sunday from 1 to 5pm; off-season, Tuesday to Saturday from 10am to 4pm and on Sunday from 1 to 4pm. Guided tours of four historic buildings—the 1767 Chowan County Courthouse, the 1758 Cupola House, the 1800/1827 James Iredell House State Historic Site, and the restored St. Paul's Episcopal Church—can be booked here for $1 to $7 for adults or $1.50 to $3.50 for students under 18. From April to October, tours are Monday to Saturday from 9:30am to 3pm, and on Sunday from 1:30 to 4pm; off-season, Monday to Saturday from 10:30am to 3pm, and on Sunday at 1:30pm.

BEACHES & OUTDOOR PURSUITS

BEACHES   Toilets, showers, bathhouses, and picnic shelters line some 70 miles of beaches here, but much of what we might say about them would be writ in sand. Ferocious tides, strong currents, and fickle, constantly changing winds alter the beach scene from day to day on the Outer Banks. That wide beach you see today may be narrower tomorrow. Water temperatures in summer average in the 70s, sometimes at the low point. Still, on a glorious July day, the cool, clean seawater and fresh salt air riding the constant winds make beachgoing a fine, invigorating experience.

These very conditions can make ocean swimming hazardous during certain periods, however. When seas are dangerous, red flags go up. If you're with children, stick to the beaches along the northern banks that have lifeguard protection. The coterie of northern-bank beaches include those at Kitty Hawk, Kill Devil Hills, and Nags Head, all of which lie along the Beach Road paralleling N.C. 12. Signs direct you to the various small (and too-often-inadequate) parking lots in the vicinity of the dunes.

FISHING **Kitty Hawk Pier,** Kitty Hawk (☎ 252/261-2772), offers the best pier fishing in the area. Adults are charged $6, and children 12 and under, $4. Those who want to come onto the pier just for sightseeing pay $2. Rods and reels are available for $6 per day, plus a returnable $30 deposit. Live and artificial bait, along with tackle, can be purchased from a shop across the pier. A restaurant is open daily from 5am to 9pm. The pier remains open 24 hours a day.

Nags Head Fishing Pier, milepost 12, Beach Road, Nags Head (☎ 252/441-5141); a rival of the Kitty Hawk Pier, has its devotees, who rent rod and reel for $6 per day. The pier itself is open to fishers for $6 for adults and $3 children, and to sightseers for $2. There's a restaurant on the pier, open daily from 7am to 9pm in season (closed at 2pm in winter). From Memorial Day to Labor Day, the pier is open daily 24 hours; off-season, daily 6am to midnight.

GOLF A popular course is **Nags Head Golf Links,** 5615 S. Seachase Dr., Nags Head (☎ 252/441-8073; www.nagsheadgolflinks.com), which boasts an 18-hole, 6,130-yard, par-71 course that's open daily from 7am to 6pm. Greens fees, including the use of a mandatory cart, start at $69. Reservations are required. Professional instruction is available for $45 for 45 minutes or $120 for a series of lessons. Clubs rent for $35. At the clubhouse, you'll find a restaurant and a pro shop.

Ocean Edge Golf Course, Frisco (☎ 252/995-4100), has an 9-hole, par-30 (18 holes, par 60) course, open daily from 7am to 7pm. Tee-time reservations are requested and can be made at the pro shop. Greens fees, including the use of a manda-tory cart, cost $50 for 18 holes, $30 for 9 holes. Club rental is $7.50 per round. Ocean Edge lies 50 miles outside Nags Head. Leave Nags Head on Highway 12 west, going to Whale Bone Junction, where you continue on Highway 12 west through the com-munities of Rodanthe, Salvo, and Buxton into Frisco.

NATURE WALKS **Nags Head Woods Preserve,** Ocean Acres Drive, off U.S. 158, milepost 9.5, is a fine example of a mid-Atlantic maritime forest. The seashore includes 640 acres of protected wetlands, dunes, and hardwood forest, and is a National Natural Landmark.

At **Jockey's Ridge State Park,** milepost 12 on U.S. 158 (☎ 252/441-7430), you'll find the East Coast's highest sand-dune formation. This 400-acre park makes you feel that you're traversing the Sahara, with its self-guided nature trail through sifting sands and blowing winds. Parking is available at the northern rim of the park.

WATER SPORTS **Kitty Hawk Water Sports Center,** Bypass Highway, milepost 16, Nags Head (☎ 252/441-2756), offers water-sports equipment. Windsurfers especially flock here, renting equipment for $20 per hour, $45 per half-day, or $65 for a full day. Wave runners cost $44 to $54 for a full hour. You can also rent kayaks, for $30 to $40 per half-day, for a trip along the waterways. On the premises are toilets and picnic facilities, and the center is open daily from 9am to 6pm.

Windsurfing Hatteras, N.C. 12, Avon (☎ 252/995-5000), rents a wide range of water-sports equipment. Twenty-four-hour kayak rentals range from $25 to $30; bodyboards rent for $6 for 24 hours; new windsurfing gear is available for 24-hour rental at $39 for the board alone or $65 for a full rig. In addition, a 5-hour introduc-tory windsurfing class is offered for $42. More experienced sailors can rent a 15-foot sailboat for 24 hours for $80.

The Lost Colony

Roanoke Island, between the Outer Banks and the mainland, is where Sir Walter Raleigh's colony of more than 100 men, women, and children settled in 1585 in what was to be England's first permanent New World foothold. Virginia Dare—granddaughter of the little band's governor, John White—was born that year, the first child of English parents to be born in America. When White sailed back to England on the ships that brought the settlers, it was his intention to return within the year. Instead, because of political events in England, White wasn't able to get back to Roanoke until 1590. What he found on his return was a mystery. The rude houses that he had helped build were all dismantled, and the entire area was enclosed by a high palisade that he later described as "very fortlike." At the entrance, crude letters on a post from which the bark had been peeled spelled out the word *Croatan*.

Because White didn't find the prearranged distress signal—a cross—and no evidence suggested violence, his conclusion was that those he'd left on Roanoke Island had joined the friendly Croatan tribe. An unhappy chain of circumstances, however, forced him to set sail for England before a search could be made. Despite all sorts of theories about the colony's fate, no link was ever established between the "lost" colonists and the Native Americans. Recent analysis of tree rings has indicated that the colonists may have suffered horrific drought conditions, but no clue has been unearthed revealing exactly what did happen.

The **Fort Raleigh National Historic Site** at Roanoke was named in 1941, and its visitor center tells the colony's story in exhibits and film. Paul Green's symphonic drama *The Lost Colony* brings the events to life in the amphitheater at the edge of Roanoke Sound.

WHERE TO STAY

Although the beaches are lined with cottage rentals, many of them are spoken for on a year-to-year basis, so it's essential to make reservations well in advance. If you'd like to settle down for a week or more, your best bet is to write the **Outer Banks Visitors Bureau** (see "Essentials," earlier in this section). It is also worth noting that a good number of national motel chains, along with numerous independently owned lodges, are dotted along the coastline and can provide adequate accommodations if you're traveling without reservations.

Nags Head, Kill Devil Hills, and Kitty Hawk are so close together that you can choose your accommodations by style and facilities rather than by location. Duck, about 18 miles north of Nags Head, is the site of an exceptional seaside hotel that's well worth the short drive.

Another option is **camping.** For information about private campgrounds in the area, contact the Outer Banks Visitors Bureau (see "Essentials," earlier in this section).

IN DUCK

✪ **Sanderling Inn Resort and Spa.** 1461 Duck Rd., Duck, NC 27949. ☎ **800/ 701-4111** or 252/261-4111. Fax 252/261-1638. www.sanderlinginn.com. E-mail: sndrling@ interpath.com. 88 units. A/C MINIBAR TV TEL. June–Oct, $251–$323 double; $388–$506 suite. Off-season, $171–$232 double; $299–$420 suite. Additional person $30. Rates include continental breakfast. AE, DISC, MC, V. Take N.C. 12 about 5 miles north of Duck.

Composed of a complex of three large, colonial-inspired buildings, with a separate annex containing a restaurant and bar, this inn was established in 1985 in a location 25 miles north of Nags Head. It is one of the most affluent and eco-sensitive pockets of posh in the Outer Banks, and one of the three great resorts of the entire state. Standing at the narrowest point of the archipelago, on a manicured set of lawns close to the 3,400-acre Pine Island National Audubon Sanctuary, it features a postmodern design that emulates an 18th-century plantation house, complete with weathered shingle siding and wraparound verandas. Don't come here expecting a wild and raucous time in the Deep South—the allure is calm, sedate, and soothing, all within a sand-and-sea-colored enclave that contains more Carolina pinewood trim than virtually any other recently built hotel in the country. Accommodations are filled with deep carpets, deep upholsteries, and an almost overwhelming sense of serenity. Public areas contain majestic spiraling staircases, blazing fireplaces, and what's reputed to be $2 million worth of bird and animal sculptures by a locally famous artist named Granger McKay.

Dining/Diversions: The in-house restaurant, the Sanderling, is recommended separately in "Where to Dine," below.

Amenities: A small-scale spa on the premises offers a limited array of health and beauty regimens. Facilities are on-site for kayak tours through nearby marshlands, jet-skiing, canoeing, and windsurfing; both indoor and outdoor pools are on-premises.

IN EDENTON

✪ **Governor Eden.** 304 N. Broad St., Edenton, NC 27932. ☎ **252/482-2072.** Fax 252/482-3613. 4 units. TV. $85 double. Rates include breakfast. AE, MC, V.

Open year-round, this is one of the better little B&Bs in the area. Within an easy walk of the Edenton Historic District, this 1906-vintage building has large white columns and a wraparound veranda in Southern antebellum style. Many antiques are located throughout the inn. A telephone is set aside downstairs for the use of guests. Breakfast is a choice of nutritious selections or a full country spread with all the trimmings.

✪ **The Lords Proprietors'.** 300 N. Broad St., Edenton, NC 27932. ☎ **252/482-3641.** Fax 252/482-2432. www.edentoninn.com. E-mail: stay@edentoninn.com. 16 units. A/C TV TEL. $155–$225 double. Rates include full breakfast. AE, DISC, MC, V.

The premier inn in Edenton, the Lords Proprietors' offers 20 rooms in three buildings. Set on 1½ acres, each of the buildings has a Victorian parlor filled with antiques. Many guests prefer the Pack House, a converted tobacco barn from a mid-19th-century plantation. The green house with white trim houses eight rooms in its two stories; accommodations include a choice of king- or queen-size beds or twins. The White Bond House, a redbrick Victorian building with equally desirable rooms, was built in 1901, and a third building, the Satterfield House, dates from 1801. The latter houses two rooms upstairs and two downstairs. Dinner is homemade, prepared from fresh ingredients, and consists of four courses. Pool privileges are available nearby.

Trestle House Inn at Willow Tree Farm. 632 Soundside Road, Edenton, NC 27932. ☎ **800/645-8466** or 252/482-2282. Fax 252/482-7003. www.edenton.com/trestlehouse. E-mail: thinn@coastalnet.com. 5 units. A/C. $80–$110 double. Additional person $15 per day. Rates include full breakfast. AE, MC, V.

Overlooking a pond and lake fed by the Albemarle Sound, the Trestle House Inn was built in 1972 as a 7-acre retreat, surrounded on three sides by water and on the fourth side by an 88-acre wildlife refuge that's ideal for bikers, birders, canoers, and fishers. Hosts Peter Bogus and Wendy Jewett have maintained the true tradition of the retreat since they became the innkeepers in 1996. The interior is highlighted by massive beams of California redwood and cedar. Before they became part of the Trestle House Inn, the beams were actual train trestles for the Southern Railway Company. The rooms—Osprey, Cormorant, Mallard, Heron, and Egret—are named for the grand birds that can be viewed from the windows of the respective units. Spacious and furnished with antiques, the rooms contain twin beds or two double beds or a queen- or king-size bed. The management can arrange day trips and tours in either Edenton or the Outer Banks. Smoking is not allowed, and pets are not welcome. The inn has a room for guests' use, containing a library, a television and VCR, and a telephone.

In Kill Devil Hills

Days Inn Wilbur & Orville Wright Court. Milepost 8.5, Beach Road, Kill Devil Hills, NC 27948. ☎ **252/441-7331.** Fax 252/441-8080. 54 units (17 with kitchen). $30–$110 double; $55–$160 two-bedroom suite with kitchen; $40–$150 efficiency apartment with kitchen. AE, DC, MC, V.

One of the longest-standing hotels along the Outer Banks began its life as an unpretentious "courtyard colony" (a series of semi-detached oceanfront cottages, in this case built in 1946 when local zoning permitted that kind of construction) that was expanded in the 1960s with the addition of a conventional motel. Today, it offers a wider variety of accommodations than most of its more modern and more conventional-looking competitors. Regardless of the unit you select, you'll register in a cedar-paneled lobby that might remind you of a resort in Bermuda. The most appealing (and most expensive) accommodations are oceanfront units with kitchens, many of which are booked by families with children who check in during midsummer, for at least a week at a time. Be warned that the units within the conventional motel section are relatively uninspired, built of cinderblocks, and not at all luxurious, but their relatively low prices seem to compensate for their lack of glamour. There's no restaurant on the premises, but many dining places are near at hand.

In Manteo

Roanoke Island Inn. 305 Fernando St., PO Box 970, Manteo, NC 27954. ☎ **252/473-5511** or 877/473-5511. Fax 252/473-1019. www.roanokeislandinn.com. 8 units. A/C TV TEL. $98–$148 double. Rates include breakfast. MC, V.

Nestled in one of the most spectacular gardens in town, this inn is a white-sided clapboard house whose core dates to the 1860s. Each of several subsequent generations have added on to the core to create the rambling, graciously appointed colonial-revival home you'll see today. In 1992, a hip and urbanized new generation of family members, headed by John Wilson, added big-city gloss to the place with a sophisticated array of trompe l'oeil murals in an Italian Renaissance theme, adding greatly to the establishment's sense of cutting-edge allure. Bedrooms are stately, even imperial, in their appointments, with glowing hardwoods, louvered or Venetian blinds, and many concessions to the 18th-century aesthetic of the Outer Banks. Breakfast is the only meal served.

✪ **Tranquil House Inn.** Queen Elizabeth St. (P.O. Box 2045), Manteo, NC 27954. ☎ **800/458-7069** or 252/473-1404. Fax 252/473-1526. www.tranquilinn.com. 25 units. A/C TV TEL. Memorial Day–Labor Day, $149 double; $189 suite. Off-season, $89–$109 double; $115–$129 suite. Rates include continental breakfast. AE, DISC, MC, V. Take U.S. 158 south to Whalebone Junction in South Nags Head, then U.S. 64/264 6 miles west to Manteo. The inn is on the harborfront. (Turn right at the first traffic light onto Sir Walter Raleigh St.)

This inn's major competition is the Sanderling Inn Resort at Duck (see "In Duck," earlier in this section), which we actually prefer, but this is our second choice on the

Outer Banks. A weather-beaten three-story structure, this waterfront resort is like one of those old seaboard inns that could have been part of 19th-century Manteo, yet it dates from 1988. Rear porches face the water and boats bob at anchor in the marina, and an entranceway opens onto the charming historic core of Manteo. The entire structure is sheathed with weather-beaten cedar shingles. Guest rooms are spacious and furnished with reproductions of antiques. Each room also has a well-lighted desk and wheelchair access. Wine and cheese are served each evening from 5 to 6pm.

Dining: The hotel's 1587 Restaurant offers not only excellent continental and *cuisine moderne* dishes but also a water view. See "Where to Dine," below.

Amenities: You can use one of the complimentary bikes to tour the Outer Banks.

IN NAGS HEAD

✪ Cahoon's Cottages. 7213 South Virginia Dare Trail, Milepost 16.5, Nags Head, NC 27959. ☎ **252/441-5358.** Fax 252/441-1734. 2 units, 8 cottages, each with its own kitchen and with two, three, or four bedrooms, TV. Summer $375 double per week, $650–$775 cottage per week. Off-season $245–$280 double per week, $525–$695 per week cottage. MC, V.

There's very little that evokes the era of modern tourism in this cluster of simple cottages. Low-slung, weather-beaten, and separated from the surf only by a sand dune held tenuously together with fragile scrubgrasses, these cottages were built in stages between 1948 and 1968, in a postwar kind of unpretentiousness that many jaded travelers find endearing. Modern building codes long ago prevented equivalent structures from being constructed directly on the dunes, so if you opt for a stay here, consider it a retro-charming kind of holiday that hasn't been very prevalent since the early 1960s. Clientele at this place tends to return year after year, and ever since its hardworking owner, Renée Calhoun, was elected twice as the town's mayor, the place has become a lot more visible. (Beginning in 1991, campaigning on an independent ticket, she's credited with a well-orchestrated grassroots rebellion against the until-then almost invincible political machine. Don't pass up a chance to say hello—she might even invite you on a tour of city hall.) Expect no grandeur, because that definitely isn't the style at a place that's awash with sun-bleached wooden porches, *faux*-wooden paneling, and battered but comfy furniture. What you'll get instead is the Outer Banks of long ago, complete with its earthiness, ironies, and wry humor. There's no restaurant on site and very few amenities other than the beach and the sense of extended families and friends checking in for long, lazy sojourns.

✪ First Colony. 6720 S. Virginia Dare Trail, Nags Head, NC 27959. ☎ **252/441-2342.** Fax 252/441-9234. www.firstcolonyinn.com. E-mail: innkeeper@firstcolonyinn.com. 26 units. A/C TV TEL. Mar 30–May 24 and Sept 1–Oct 28 $115–$300 double; Nov 2–Mar 29 $80–$175. Rates include breakfast. AE, DC, DISC, MC, V.

This impressive two-story inn near the ocean was constructed in 1932 and has a wraparound veranda with rocking chairs. It was built without the help of an architect, which might explain why the veranda is almost as big as the interior space itself. Owned by Alan Lawrence and his family, it has received a four-diamond AAA rating, is listed on the National Register of Historic Places, and is the finest inn in the area. The interior is furnished with reproductions of turn-of-the-century items. Some rooms have kitchenettes with refrigerators and microwaves, and units with sitting areas are also available. Grills and picnic tables are on hand for guests' use on the 4½-acre grounds, and a private access leads across the highway to the beach, known for its sea breezes and seemingly endless gentle dunes. A pool is also available on the premises.

WHERE TO DINE
IN DUCK

The Sanderling. In the Sanderling Inn Resort and Spa, 1461 Duck Rd. ☎ **252/261-4111.**
Reservations recommended. Lunch main courses $8–$14; dinner main courses $18–$26.
AE, MC, V. Daily 11:30am–2pm and 5–9:30pm. COASTAL/SEAFOOD.

Although it's the premier dining enclave of the most upscale and exclusive resort in the
Outer Banks, there's something that's refreshingly simple, even spartan-looking about
this place. Much of it derives from its origins in 1879 as a government-funded rescue
station, when lifeguards and mariners set out from here to rescue crew and passengers
from ships foundering on the region's notoriously treacherous shoals. Look for memorabilia that's associated with a heroic rescue 20 years later of the barkentine *Priscilla*
that earned the site national attention. A brass bell from the original rescue station is
prominently displayed. Top-quality ingredients go into the masterful dishes where
sauces or other adornments never overpower the natural flavors. Dinners might
include barbecued pork with a timbale of garlic-laced potatoes; grilled breast of duck
with white beans; and roasted flounder with spinach. Lunches are simpler, featuring
crab cake sandwiches, risotto with seared scallops, and a form of savory pie (The Boat
House gratin) composed of baked scallops, salmon, leeks, and potatoes beneath a
cheese-and-pastry crust. There's a bar on the second floor, accurate to its original role
as a rescue station, whose severe dignity evokes an antique schoolhouse.

IN KILL DEVIL HILLS

Goombay's Grille & Raw Bar. N.C. 12, milepost 7.5. ☎ **252/441-6001.** Reservations not
accepted. Main dishes $4.95–$16.99. DISC, MC, V. Daily 11:30am–10:30pm. Head 1 block
south of the Sea Ranch and look for the mile markers. SEAFOOD.

This is one of the most fun places you'll find on the Outer Banks. The decor is lively,
with Caribbean colors, fish paintings, knotty-pine tongue-and-groove walls, and fans
hanging from the wood ceiling. Adjoining the main dining room is a raw bar, where
you can order snow-crab legs, a pile of crayfish, and spiced steamed shrimp. On the
main menu are Hatteras chowder (a clear, broth-based soup with potatoes, onions, celery, and clams), johnnycakes stuffed with cheese, fried banana peppers served with
spicy fruit chutney, and jalapeño crab balls. The restaurant smokes its own fish. For
lunch, consider the burger boat, a seafood taco, or West Indian curried chicken. If
you're game, try the tender marinated alligator tail as an appetizer.

Quagmire's Oceanfront Bar & Restaurant. 1315 North Virginia Dare Trail, Milepost 7.5.
☎ **252/441-9188.** Reservations not accepted. Lunch platters $3.99–$8.99. Dinner main
courses $8.99–$17.99. DISC, MC, V. Daily 11:30am–10pm. Bar daily 11:30–2am. Closed
Mon–Tues Oct–Apr. SEAFOOD/MEXICAN.

Of the only two oceanfront dining options in Nags Head and Kill Devil Hills, this is
the most consistently popular. It's housed in the old Croatan Inn. Shingle-sided and
sprawling, it was built in stages between 1928 and 1932, before the introduction of
building codes that prohibited construction on fragile dunes close to the sea. The dining rooms and bars, as well as the panoramic crow's nest bar on the second floor, reek
of Jazz Age nostalgia. (Fellow diners include lots of local politicians, as well as sports
luminaries that have included star quarterback Brad Johnson.) Menu items include a
succulent version of crab cakes, a zesty shrimp Diablo, shrimp and crabmeat enchiladas, steaks and burgers, and a selection of very fresh grilled fish, your best bet.

IN MANTEO

Queen Anne's Revenge. Old Wharf Rd. at Wanchese. ☎ **252/473-5466.** Reservations
accepted only for groups of 8 or more. Main courses $12.95–$25. AE, CB, DC, DISC, MC, V.
Daily 5–9pm (closed Tues in winter). SEAFOOD.

The seafood here is so good that locals return time after time and can't wait to tell visitors about the place. Most of the fish is caught in local waters. The captain's platter, a dull overfried dish in many joints, is quite delectable here; it's served with shrimp, the catch of the day, scallops, and crabmeat, along with vegetables and a salad. Your shrimp dinner can be fried or broiled, and both shrimp and crab are sautéed and served over a bed of homemade fettuccine. Surrounded by island pines, the restaurant also has a garden. The decor is elegant, with white linen tablecloths and paintings of seascapes. It's licensed only for beer and wine.

Restaurant 1587. In Tranquil House Inn, Queen Elizabeth St. ☎ **919/473-1404.** Reservations recommended. Main courses $17.95–$23.95. AE, MC, V. Daily 5–9pm. AMERICAN.

This is the best restaurant in Manteo, with fine cuisine, good service, and a nautical flair that makes everyone feel as if he or she has just stepped off one of the expensive boats bobbing at anchor in the nearby marina. Preface your meal with a drink at the convivial bar, where a bar top sheathed in polished copper reflects the faces and voices of many of the town's amicable locals. Good food and service await you here, and the menu is more sophisticated than most in the area. You might start with a grilled portobello mushroom topped with Thai-style sautéed Asian vegetables and pistachios, or else a caramelized onion and pancetta soup with fried spinach. The salads are especially fresh, and main courses are delightful, especially the risotto with shrimp, scallops, artichoke hearts, and bell peppers, or the pan-seared salmon over wild rice accompanied by a sweet and tangy orange barbecue sauce.

IN NAGS HEAD

Fishermen's Wharf. Roanoke Island, N.C. 345, Wanchese. ☎ **252/473-5205.** Main courses $10.95–$19.95; lunch platters $5.50–$10.50. DC, DISC, MC, V. Mon–Sat noon–9pm. SEAFOOD.

At the south end of Roanoke Island, overlooking the harbor, this restaurant serves the freshest seafood around. It also has a connected retail seafood market. Founded in 1974, it started out serving about 50 diners per day; today, that number has grown to about 600. Lunch sandwiches range from fresh local fish filet (try it!) to a crab-cake delight, everything served with coleslaw and hush puppies. Dinners are more elaborate, including a gargantuan seafood platter with just about everything. Other selections include Miss Maude's crab imperial topped with white sauce. Prime rib is featured Monday to Friday, and a selection of pasta dishes is also offered.

Owens' Restaurant. Milepost 16.5, Beach Rd. ☎ **252/441-7309.** Reservations not accepted. Main courses $12.95–$24.95. AE, DISC, MC, V. Sun–Thurs 5–9pm, Fri–Sat 5–10pm. Closed Christmas. SEAFOOD.

This longtime local favorite has been owned and operated by the Owens family for half a century. Its fans claim that it just keeps getting better. The big, homey spot is decorated with nautical relics and artifacts from the olden days. You can order typical coastal fare, and every dish is down-home style. Many entrees have zesty and spicy flavors, including coconut shrimp or Caribbean-style game fish (sautéed with pineapple, banana, onions, and peppers). Fresh yellowfin tuna is served with a teriyaki, ginger, and Caribbean herb marinade. The ribeye is a 14-ounce cut of Angus steak, broiled to your instructions. A children's menu is also offered.

Sam & Omie's. 7228 South Virginia Dare Trail, Milepost 16.5. ☎ **252/441-7366.** Reservations not accepted. Breakfast $3.50–$6.95. Lunch main courses $4.95–$8.95; dinner main courses $9.95–$18.95. DISC, MC, V. Daily 7am–9pm. Closed Thanksgiving–Mar 1. SEAFOOD.

A father-son partnership established this eatery in the 1930s as a spot where fishers could get a rib-sticking breakfast before heading out onto the high seas. Today, it's a deliberately downscale, endlessly raffish place that has attracted most of North Carolina's leading, and most notorious, politicians—as well as locals who like the quintessentially funky Outer Banks vibe. There's a convivial bar area where old salts and young beauties alike mingle, and a series of pinewood banquettes where copious portions of well-prepared seafood are always in demand. Come here for hefty doses of local color, a sense of folksy authenticity, and food items that include marinated tuna steaks served either as a platter or as a sandwich, she-crab soup, fried locally-caught oysters, crab cakes, and burgers. This is an early-to-bed kind of place. The last food order is accepted here at 9pm, and the bar closes shortly thereafter.

The Piedmont 5

Nowhere in the South do old and new come together quite so dramatically as in North Carolina's Piedmont, which lies between the coastal plains and the mountains. The contrast is especially marked in cities such as Winston-Salem, where the mammoth tobacco industry is represented by R.J. Reynolds and where the Stroh Brewery produces millions of barrels of beer each year, while across town, the streets and buildings of Old Salem have been restored to reflect the life of the Moravians who planned the community in 1753.

The landscape here—red-clay hills, tobacco fields, and peach orchards—is as varied as the region's industry and agriculture.

The Piedmont is the home of the vaunted Research Triangle, a multidisciplinary scientific institute founded in 1958 by Duke University in Durham, the University of North Carolina in Chapel Hill, and North Carolina State University in Raleigh. The region boasts a wealth of other educational institutions, including Wake Forest University in Winston-Salem, and Shaw University in Raleigh, founded in 1865 and the oldest historically black university in the South.

The Piedmont is very much the New South, and its residents won't hesitate to brag a bit about the economic miracle that's transformed the area in the past 3 decades. They're especially proud of their bigtime sports scene. (College basketball is practically a religion in these parts.) But the cities of the Piedmont haven't lost their manners, and a leisurely pace of life persists in the midst of all the growth and change. Travelers will see that streets lined with gorgeous homes and blooming dogwoods haven't been lost in the name of progress. And outside the cities, there's a lot waiting to be discovered, including some of the nation's greatest championship golf courses.

1 Raleigh

143 miles NE of Charlotte

State government has been Raleigh's principal business since 1792, when it became North Carolina's capital. Just before the Civil War, the city was the setting of the fiery legislative debate that led to North Carolina's secession from the Union in 1861. Raleigh endured Union occupation by General Sherman in 1865, and during Reconstruction saw the west wing of its imposing Grecian Doric capitol building turned into a rowdy barroom by "carpetbagger" and "scalawag" legislators, its steps permanently nicked from whiskey barrels rolling in and out of the building.

Today, the 5-acre square fronting the capitol is the focal point for a cluster of state office buildings in the heart of the city. From it radiate wide boulevards and tree-shaded residential streets. Downtown Raleigh has been transformed by an attractive pedestrian mall where trees, fountains, and statuary create a shopping oasis. No fewer than six college campuses dot the city's streets, with wide lawns and impressive brick buildings. The oldest, St. Mary's College, was founded in 1842. The big name in town, though, is North Carolina State University, and cheering for the Wolfpack in basketball or football is more than just an idle pastime. New suburbs and gigantic shopping centers dominate the outskirts of Raleigh, characterized by nicely designed homes blending into a landscape that retains much of its original wooded character.

All this, plus the abundance of good accommodations, makes Raleigh a fine base from which to explore the Research Triangle area. Both Chapel Hill and Durham are within easy reach for day trips, and after a day of sightseeing, the capital city offers a good variety of entertainment options, from college bars to supper-club shows.

ESSENTIALS

GETTING THERE   U.S. 64 and U.S. 70 run east and west from Raleigh; U.S. 1 runs north and south, joining I-85, which runs northeast and is joined by I-40 to the west and I-95 to the east. U.S. 401 also runs northeast and southwest. The AAA is represented by the **Carolina Motor Club,** 2301 Blue Ridge Rd., Raleigh, NC 27607 (☎ **919/832-0543;** www.aaa.carolinas.com).

The Raleigh/Durham International Airport is about 15 miles west of Raleigh, just off I-40. Major airlines serving the airport from out-of-state destinations include **Air Tran** (☎ 800/825-8538; www.airtran.com), **American Airlines** (☎ 800/433-7300; www.aa.com), **Continental Airlines** (☎ 800/525-0280; www.flycontinental.com), **Delta Air Lines** (☎ 800/221-1212; www.delta.com), **Midway Airlines** (☎ 800/ 446-4392; www.midwayair.com), **Northwest Airlines** (☎ 800/225-2525; www. nwa.com), **Trans World Airlines** (☎ 800/221-2000; www.twa.com), **United Air-lines** (☎ 800/241-6522; www.ual.com), and **US Airways** (☎ 800/428-4322; www. usairways.com).

Amtrak (☎ **800/USA-RAIL;** www.amtrak.org) provides rail service from New York and Washington, D.C., to the north and from Florida to the south, with one train daily from each direction.

VISITOR INFORMATION   Contact the **Greater Raleigh Convention and Visitors Bureau,** 421 Fayetteville St. Mall, Suite 1505, Raleigh, NC 27601-1755 (☎ **800/849-8499** or 919/834-5900). Hours are Monday to Friday 8:30am to 5pm. **Capital Area Visitor Center,** 301 N. Blount St. (☎ **919/733-3456;** www. visitnc.com), provides information about the state-government complex, local attractions, and historic sites; bus-route brochures are available. The center is open Monday to Friday from 8am to 5pm, on Saturday from 9am to 5pm, and on Sunday from 1 to 5pm.

SPECIAL EVENTS   In mid-February, the **Home and Garden Show** draws serious gardeners from all over the South; call ☎ **919/831-6011** for details. In mid-October, the **North Carolina State Fair;** www.ncstatefair.org also draws crowds from all over with its livestock competitions, culinary bake-offs, and cornpone charm. (The 2000 Fair featured a butter sculpture of the state's agricultural commissioner, Jim Graham.) The fairgrounds are located 5 miles west of town on I-440 and then 1 mile west on N.C. 54. For exact dates, call ☎ **919/733-2145.** In early December, the city hosts an old-fashioned **Holiday Festival** at the North Carolina Museum of Art (☎ **919/ 839-6262;** www.ncartmuseum.org).

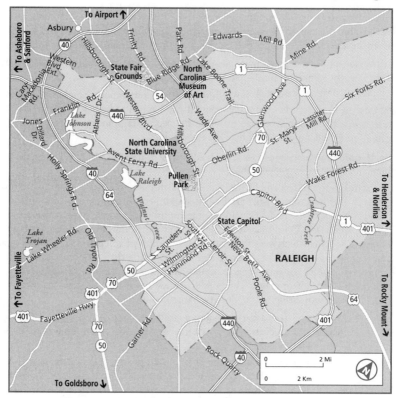

EXPLORING THE CAPITOL & ENVIRONS

For the best possible tour of the capital city, make the **Capital Area Visitor Center** your first stop. The staff starts you off with an orientation film, arms you with brochures, and coordinates walking or driving tours of the area. Most of the attractions listed in this section are within easy walking distance of the state capitol.

⊛ **The State Capitol.** Capitol Sq. ☎ **919/733-4994.** Free admission. Mon–Fri 8am–5pm, Sat 9am–5pm, Sun 1–5pm.

This stately Greek Revival structure (constructed 1833–40) is a national historic landmark. All state business was conducted here until 1888. The building now contains the offices of the governor and lieutenant governor, as well as restored legislative chambers. Beneath the awe-inspiring 97-foot copper dome is a duplicate of Antonio Canova's marble statue of George Washington dressed as a Roman general. The capitol takes about 30 to 45 minutes to tour. Reservations are necessary for guided tours. Call the capitol for additional information and times.

North Carolina Museum of Natural Sciences. Museum Mall. ☎ **919/733-7450.** www.naturalsciences.org. Free admission, but donations accepted. Mon–Sat 9am–5pm, Sun noon–5pm. Closed Thanksgiving and 2 days at Christmas.

Through exhibits and programs for adults and children, North Carolina's oldest museum provides information on the plants and animals of the state and their habitats. Some outstanding displays are the Fossil Lab, where visitors interact with paleontologists working on dinosaur bones; the live habitats of the Mountain to the Sea exhibit; a great whale skeleton collection; and the hands-on Discovery Room. There's even a bird hall and a live snake collection. You'll need at least an hour here.

State Legislative Building. 16 W. Jones St. ☎ **919/733-7928.** Free admission. Mon–Fri 8am–5pm, Sat 9am–5pm, Sun 1–5pm.

Allow about 30 minutes to go through this striking contemporary building, designed by Edward Durrell Stone. But take longer if you happen to be here when the legislature is in session. You'll be able to watch the proceedings and perhaps even spot a young, post-millennium Jesse Helms in the making.

North Carolina Museum of History. 5 E. Edenton St. ☎ **919/715-0200.** Free admission. Tues–Sat 9am–5pm, Sun noon–5pm.

The state's long and colorful history comes alive through innovative exhibits and programs in this new, state-of-the-art facility. It's all here, beginning with the Roanoke Island colonists to the present, including the contributions to the state by women and African Americans. On display until 2003 is the "North Carolina and the Civil War" exhibit. The state, which was initially reluctant to enter what it called "a rich man's war and a poor man's fight," lost more native sons in battle than any other state in the Confederacy. You'll see such items as a captured Union flag and the bloodstained vest of a fallen Confederate major. The Folklife gallery showcases the state's cultural and crafts heritage, exhibiting music, pottery, baskets, and textiles.

North Carolina Museum of Art. 2110 Blue Ridge Rd. ☎ **919/839-6262.** Admission $7 adults $5 seniors and students. Free children under 12. Tues–Thurs 9am–5pm, Fri–Sat 9am–9pm, Sun 11am–7pm.

This museum houses a major collection of European paintings, plus American, 20th-century, ancient, African, Oceanic, and Judaic exhibits. The permanent collection—with works by Raphael, Rubens, van Dyck, Monet, Homer, and Wyeth—is complemented by a program of 12 to 15 special exhibitions annually. Past exhibits include North Carolina in the Spanish War, Health and Healing Experiences, and North Carolina Sports Hall of Fame. There's wheelchair access, and you can plan to have lunch in the **Museum Cafe** (☎ **919/833-3548**), open Tuesday to Friday 11am to 2:30pm, Friday and Saturday 5:30 to 8:30pm, and Sunday 11am to 3pm.

Andrew Johnson's Birthplace (Mordecai Historic Park and Mordecai Plantation House). 1 Mimosa St. ☎ **919/834-4844.** Admission $4 adults, $2 students and children 7–17, free 6 and under. Mon and Wed–Sat 10am–4pm, Sun 1–4pm. Last tour is at 3pm.

One of three North Carolina native sons who became president, Andrew Johnson was born in a small cabin about a block from the capitol building. The 17th president's birthplace has been moved to Mordecai Historic Park and is open to visitors. The restored Mordecai Plantation House contains the original furnishings. Five generations of one of North Carolina's oldest families lived here until 1964. Other historic buildings have also been relocated to the park to create a 19th-century village.

OUTDOOR PURSUITS

Raleigh's **parks** and recreational facilities have won awards. In all, there are 3,904 acres of parkland and 1,332 acres of water. A greenway system covers 1,297 acres, offering hiking and jogging trails that link many of Raleigh's 141 parks.

One of the major recreational centers is **Lake Wheeler,** 6404 Lake Wheeler Rd. (☎ **919/662-5704**), comprising 60 acres of parkland and 600 acres of lake, 5 miles southwest of Raleigh. Activities include sailing, rowing, kayaking, canoeing, and fishing. In summer, open-air concerts are sponsored. Hours are daily 6am to 8pm.

William B. Umstead State Park (☎ **919/571-4170**) is actually two parks, including Crabtree and Reedy Creek. We prefer Crabtree; it has better facilities and a big lake where you can rent boats for $3 and go fishing. It also has a visitor center and picnic tables. Biking and bridle trails riddle the park, as do hiking trails.

The best golf is at the **Cheviot Hills Golf Course,** 6 miles north on U.S. 1 at 7301 Capital Blvd. (☎ **919/876-9920**), an 18-hole championship golf course with Bermuda bent greens. Greens fees range from $16 to $25, and the course is open Monday to Friday from 8am to dusk, on Saturday from 7am to dusk, and on Sunday from noon to dusk. Cart rentals are $10.60 per person.

Raleigh also has about two dozen miles of greenway for **bikers.** For trail maps, call the **Raleigh Parks and Recreation Center** (☎ **919/890-3285**).

Anglers can ask at the visitors bureau for spots in the periphery where the fishing's good. Local bait-and-tackle shops will allow you to purchase a license over the phone, provided that you have a valid MasterCard or Visa. Licenses are sold by the North Carolina Wildlife Commission; call ☎ **919/715-4091** for information.

The best **camping** is at **Raven Rock State Park** (☎ **910/893-4888**) and the **Falls Lake State Recreational Area** (☎ **919/676-1027**). Call for information, which varies seasonally.

Raleigh has at least 75 **tennis** courts in its city parks. For information about one near you, call ☎ **919/733-4181.**

WHERE TO STAY
EXPENSIVE

✪ **Raleigh Marriott Crabtree Valley.** 4500 Marriott Dr. (U.S. 70 W. opposite the Crabtree Valley Mall), Raleigh, NC 27612. ☎ **800/228-9290** or 919/781-7000. Fax 919/781-3059. www.marriott.com. 379 units. A/C TV TEL. $139–$147 double Mon–Fri, $69 double Sat–Sun; $179–$249 suite. Children 17 and under stay free in parents' room. AE, CB, DC, DISC, MC, V. Free parking.

Located 10 minutes northwest of the city center and 7 miles from the airport, this is Raleigh's leading hotel. It lacks some of the charm of the Velvet Cloak Inn (see the listing below) but is professional in every way and caters to a large business clientele. The city's largest hotel, it rises six floors, offering well-furnished guest rooms and large baths. The most luxurious and expensive rooms are on the concierge level. Thoughtful extras such as ironing boards are available, and some accommodations are wheelchair-accessible and no smoking.

Dining/Diversions: A split-level dining room, Scotch Bonnets, decorated with woodwork and stucco, takes a library as its theme and provides competent, if not spectacular, fare. Allies caters more to the family trade, and there's also the Championship Sports Bar.

Amenities: Room service, laundry, spacious outdoor/indoor pool, whirlpool, a rather modest health club, jogging trail, and golf privileges available nearby.

✪ **Velvet Cloak Inn.** 1505 Hillsborough St., Raleigh, NC 27605. ☎ **800/334-4372,** 800/662-8829, or 919/828-0333 in North Carolina. Fax 919/828-2656. 178 units. A/C TV TEL. $117 double Sun–Thurs, $69 double Fri–Sat; $195–$350 suite. Additional person in doubles $10 extra. Children 18 and under stay free in parents' room. AE, CB, DC, DISC, MC, V. Free parking.

Technically, this place might be classified as a motor lodge, but whatever you want to call it, we think that it's the finest accommodation in Raleigh. An 8-minute drive from the city center, this brick New Orleans–style establishment stands between the campuses of St. Mary's College and NCSU. The accommodations, each with a king-size bed or two double beds, are attractive and frequently renovated. The inn's major drawbacks are that windows open onto walkways and that the soundproofing needs to be improved; otherwise, it's all pluses for this property. Extras include complimentary coffee and morning newspapers in the lobby.

Dining/Diversions: Baron's Restaurant and Nightclub provides entertainment. For more elegant dining, there's the Charter Room, which offers a French/American menu. It's often patronized by local politicians.

Amenities: Free airport transportation, an enclosed pool and a tropical garden beloved of Raleigh brides, and health-club privileges right next door.

MODERATE

In addition to the following listings, there's also the newly renovated **Club at Doubletree,** 2815 Capitol Blvd. (☎ **800/222-8733** or 919/872-7666), and a **Courtyard by Marriott,** 1041 Wake Towne Dr. (☎ **800/228-9290** or 919/821-3400).

Brownstone Hotel. 1707 Hillsborough St., Raleigh, NC 27605. ☎ **800/237-0772,** 800/331-7919 in North Carolina, or 919/828-0811. Fax 919/834-0904. www.brownstonehotel. com. 190 units. A/C TV TEL. $89–$110 double; $125–$190 suite. Children 18 and under stay free in parents' room. AE, CB, DC, DISC, MC, V. Free parking.

Though it's been surpassed by other leading hotels in Raleigh, the nine-story Brownstone remains a traditional favorite. It may seem to be a bit dated, even after renovations, but lots of parents visiting their children at adjoining North Carolina State University still favor this place. The upper-floor rooms provide the best views of campus. All accommodations have balconies, and some are equipped with kitchenettes. The hotel also offers a good restaurant, serving food at moderate prices. There's an outdoor pool, and services include laundry and a limousine to the airport. The staff will also provide baby-sitters.

✪ **The Oakwood Inn.** 411 N. Bloodworth St., Raleigh, NC 27604. ☎ **800/267-9712** or 919/832-9712. Fax 919/836-9263. http://members.aol.com/oakwoodbb. E-mail: oakwoodbb@ aol.com. 6 units. A/C TV TEL. $95–$185 double. Rates include full breakfast. AE, DC, DISC, MC, V. Free parking.

Raleigh has no shortage of hotels, motor hotels, and motels, but it has almost no inns. The Oakwood fills the vacuum; it's an inn of charm and character. Built in 1871, the Victorian building lies in the historic district, and guests can stroll to attractions downtown. A wraparound porch evokes the best of Southern architecture in the 19th century, and claw-foot tubs, leaded glass, and mahogany and walnut furniture re-create a long-gone era. It's listed on the National Register of Historic Places. The Oakwood serves the best breakfast in the area.

INEXPENSIVE

Fairfield Inn by Marriott. 2641 Appliance Ct., Raleigh, NC 27604. ☎ **800/228-9290** or 919/856-9800. Fax 919/856-9800. www.marriott.com. 132 units. A/C TV TEL. $69.95 double Sun–Thurs, $65 double Fri–Sat. Children 17 and under stay free in parents' room. Senior discounts available. AE, DC, DISC, MC, V. Free parking.

The Fairfield Inn is just a short drive from downtown. The rooms all have attractive decor and a work area with a desk. Some units are no smoking, and some are accessible for travelers with disabilities. All are good-sized, but those on the third floor are more spacious. There's complimentary coffee in the lobby, and several good restaurants are in the immediate vicinity.

WHERE TO DINE
EXPENSIVE

✪ **Angus Barn.** U.S. 70 W. at Airport Rd. ☎ **919/787-3505.** Reservations recommended. Main courses $17.95–$59.95. AE, DC, MC, V. Mon–Sat 5–11pm, Sun 5–10pm. (Wild Turkey Lounge daily 4–11pm.) Closed major holidays. STEAK.

For 40 years, this has been one of the best places in these parts for charcoal-broiled steak or choice ribs of beef; it also has an excellent selection of fresh seafood. Most dishes are priced at the lower end of the scale (see above). The setting, in a restored 19th-century barn, is rustic, with fireplaces adding a graceful note. The food is superior and can be accompanied by a selection from the impressive Grand Wine Cellar. This place is well worth the drive.

MODERATE

42nd Street Oyster Bar and Seafood Grill. 508 W. Jones St. ☎ **919/831-2811.** Reservations recommended. Lunch $12–$18. Main courses $20–$50. AE, CB, DC, MC, V. Mon–Fri 11am–11pm, Sat 5–11pm, Sun 5–10pm. Closed major holidays. SEAFOOD/GRILL.

Popular among the major politicos (and many who'd like to be), this is the restaurant you'd choose to take the governor to lunch. Lively and buzzing with the latest political gossip, the restaurant has a nautical decor and is housed in a restored 1930s warehouse. The chef doesn't stretch his culinary wings here; people come for the old favorites. Some of these dishes—oysters, prime rib, lobster, pastas, and any steak imaginable—succeed brilliantly, whereas others, depending on the night, are rather uneven. But portions are plentiful, and there's a children's menu. The bar scene is hopping, and live jazz or R&B heats up the atmosphere on Thursday, Friday, and Saturday nights.

Lucky 32. 832 Spring Forest Rd. ☎ **919/876-9932.** Reservations recommended. Main courses $6.25–$17.95. AE, DC, MC, V. Mon–Thurs 11:15am–10:30pm, Fri–Sat 11:15am–11pm, Sun 10am–10pm. AMERICAN.

This extremely modern restaurant offers a wide variety of cuisine in an Art Deco setting. The expansive menu includes pastas, meats, fish, sandwiches, and hamburgers. Appetizers include deep-fried grits with a country-ham cream sauce, crispy salt-and-pepper calamari, and the restaurant's famous mixed-vegetable salad with thick slices of marinated zucchini, onion, pepper, squash, asparagus, and eggplant in a pineapple salsa with riso pasta. The main courses are hearty and not necessarily for vegetarians. If you say "guilt free" while you're ordering, however, the recipe will be converted to conform to the Wake Forest University/Heartwise Dining program. Special fresh fish can be sopped in a delectable pineapple-orange butter, and the roasted pork loin is topped with apple-horseradish and raspberry sauce. Portions are large, so save room for the daily desserts.

INEXPENSIVE

Big Ed's City Market. 220 Wolfe St. ☎ **919/836-9909.** Breakfast $3.75–$6.50; sandwiches $2.50–$5.95; main courses $6.50–$8.50. No credit cards. Mon–Fri 6:30am–2pm, Sat 7am–noon, Thurs–Sat 5–9pm. REGIONAL/AMERICAN.

This is everybody's local favorite, and it serves the best country breakfast in Raleigh. The day starts with eggs, served up with grits, redeye gravy, blackstrap molasses, and hot biscuits. Either at lunch or dinner, you can enjoy such old-time favorites as homemade chicken stew just like Grandma made, barbecued trout (worth a detour), or beef liver with grilled onions. Vegetables are bought fresh at Raleigh's Farmer's Market, and dessert is likely to be homemade fruit cobbler. Dixieland music is presented on nights when dinner is served.

Clyde Cooper's Barbecue. 109 E. Davie St. (1 block east of the mall). ☎ **919/832-7614.** Reservations not accepted. Dinner $4.25–$8. No credit cards. Mon–Sat 10am–6pm. BARBECUE.

Since 1938, this old-timer has been *the* place in Raleigh for barbecue. Even if you think you prefer the Texas stuff, Cooper's will convert you. Prices are reasonable, and portions are generous. The chef slow-cooks only top-grade pork shoulders and hams until they're so tender that they practically melt. They're then mixed with a zesty barbecue sauce good enough to be bottled. For dessert, try the super-moist carrot cake.

Rockford's. 320½ Glennwood Ave. ☎ **919/821-9020.** Main courses $7–$10. AE, CB, DISC, MC, V. Mon–Sat 11:30am–2pm, Sun–Wed 6–10pm, Thurs–Sat 6–10:30pm. CONTINENTAL.

Rockford's big copper bar, hardwood floors, exposed ceilings, and moderate lighting evoke a rustic charm. The menu features everything from the to-die-for house salad (mixed greens, apples, toasted walnuts, and chunky blue cheese in balsamic vinaigrette) to the locally famous ABC sandwich (apples, bacon, and cheddar on French toast). Before your meal, enjoy an aperitif at the bar. Drink specialties include oversized martinis, and there are more than 20 beers and wines. The place is akin to a neighborhood bar and grill. Recorded music ranging from jazz to blues to country to rock will help you digest your meal.

RALEIGH AFTER DARK

The elegantly renovated **Memorial Auditorium,** 1 South St. (☎ **919/831-6011**), is the home of the North Carolina Symphony Orchestra and the North Carolina Theatre. The orchestra gives around 50 performances annually in Raleigh; Gerhardt Zimmermann is music director and conductor. Critics have hailed the North Carolina Theatre as "the best it gets this side of Broadway." It specializes in large-scale Broadway musicals such as *Hello, Dolly,* under the direction of the artistic director, Tony-nominated actor/director Terrence V. Mann. This is the state's only resident professional musical theater. The box office is open Monday to Friday 10am to 5pm.

Berkeley Cafe. 217 W. Martin St. ☎ **919/821-0777.** Cover varies, depending on the band.

This is a blues bar with a back deck. In addition to blues, you're likely to hear everything from folk rock to R&B. Open Tuesday to Wednesday and Friday from 11am to 3pm and 6 to 11pm, and Thursday, plus Saturday and Sunday, 6 to 11pm.

The Brewery. 3009 Hillsborough St. ☎ **919/834-7018.** Cover $4–$10.

It rocks, it rolls, and it dispenses lots of suds to college kids, regardless of the night of the week. The setting is a converted, bench-lined 1940s gas station—indestructible, loud, beer-stained, and manic. But for rock 'n' roll, there's no better place in town. Open Wednesday to Saturday from 9:30pm to 2am, and sometimes (depending on the availability of a band) on other nights as well.

Charlie Goodnight's. 861 W. Morgan St. ☎ **919/828-5233.** Cover $5–$20.

Charlie's is an entertainment complex with a comedy nightclub, its original bar, the New Bar, and two food outlets. The "old bar" has no cover charge and features live bands with rock music. The comedy club features name entertainers, and the New Bar is an upscale dance place with a cover charge. One restaurant offers a Mexican menu; the other is a grill-and-seafood spot. If there's anything big going on in Raleigh, it's probably going on at Charlie's. It's open Tuesday to Saturday from 5:30pm to 2:30am. Shows start at 8:30pm.

2 Durham

23 miles W of Raleigh

In the late 1860s, Washington Duke left the Confederate Army and walked 137 miles back to his farm in Durham, where he took up life again as a tobacco farmer. That first year, he started grinding and packaging the crop to sell in small packets. In 1880, he decided that there was a future in cigarettes—then a new idea—and, along with his three sons, set to work to manufacture them on a small scale. By 1890, the family had formed the American Tobacco Company, and a legendary American manufacturing empire was under way.

Durham, a small village when Duke returned, blossomed into an industrial city, taking its commercial life from the "golden weed." And it still does. From September until the end of December, tobacco warehouses ring with the chants of auctioneers moving from one batch of the cured tobacco to the next, followed by buyers who indicate their bids with nods or hand signals.

Even Duke University, the cultural heart of Durham, owes its life's breath to tobacco. Duke was quiet little Trinity College until national and international prominence came with a Duke family endowment of $40 million in 1924. Along with a change in name, the university gained a new West Campus, complete with massive Gothic structures of stone, flagstone walks, and box hedges. Its medical center is one of the most highly respected in the world.

ESSENTIALS

GETTING THERE   Reached from the east via U.S. 70 and I-40 to N.C. 147, from the north via I-85, from the west via I-40/85 to I-85, and from the south via U.S. 15/501 joining I-40 to N.C. 147. The AAA office in Durham is the **Carolina Motor Club,** 3909 University Dr., Durham, NC 27717 (☎ **919/489-3306**).

For service to Raleigh/Durham International Airport, see "Essentials," under "Raleigh," earlier in this chapter. **Amtrak** (☎ **800/USA-RAIL**) has a station in Durham on Pettegrew Street (☎ **919/872-7245**).

VISITOR INFORMATION   Contact the **Durham Convention & Visitor Bureau,** 101 E. Morgan St., Durham, NC 27701 (☎ **800/446-8604** or 919/ 687-0288; www.dcvb.durham.nc.us/), which can supply local bus-route information.

SPECIAL EVENTS   Running from January to April and September to December, the Duke University **Jazz Festival** showcases big-name jazz musicians at various locations throughout the city. Festival times and dates are usually every 2 weeks during the festival seasons, spring and fall. For more information, contact Duke University's music department at ☎ **919/660-3300**.

EXPLORING THE TOWN & UNIVERSITY

✪ **Duke Homestead State Historic Site.** 2828 Duke Homestead Rd. ☎ **919/ 477-5498.** Free admission. Apr–Oct, Mon–Sat 9am–5pm, Sun 1–5pm; Nov–Mar, Tues–Sat 10am–4pm, Sun 1–4pm. Hours may vary. Take the Guess Rd. Exit 175 from I-85 and drive ½ mile north.

The Duke homestead, where Washington Duke opened his first tobacco factory in a rickety one-room barn, is today a national historic landmark. As a Confederate soldier, Duke learned about the Union soldiers' love of Bright Leaf tobacco, and he returned home to begin the humble enterprise that would one day establish North Carolina as the heart of a worldwide tobacco empire. The homestead has been called a "living museum of tobacco history," and the early farming techniques and manufacturing processes used in the production of tobacco are demonstrated. (Don't mention cancer around here.) A color film, *Carolina Bright,* serves as an orientation to the site.

Museum of Life & Science. 433 Murray Ave. ☎ **919/220-5429.** Admission $8 adults, $5.50 children 3–12, and $7 senior citizens. Labor Day–Memorial Day, Mon–Sat 10am–6pm, Sun noon–6pm; off-season, Mon–Sat 10am–5pm, Sun noon–5pm. Head north of I-85 off Duke St.

This museum is especially designed for children, but no matter what your age, you'll love the interactive, high-tech exhibits on the human body, the weather, geology, and aerospace. One exhibit displays the Apollo 15 lunar landing module, complete with a sample moon rock. Hands-on exhibits are in the Science Arcade and the Scientific Discovery Room. The 70-acre site also holds a farmyard, Loblolly Park, and a mile-long narrow-gauge railroad, charging $1.50 for a ride.

DUKE UNIVERSITY

The campuses of Duke University cover more than 1,000 acres on the west side of the city. The **East Campus,** which was the old Trinity College, features Georgian architecture, and its redbrick and limestone buildings border a half-mile-long grassy mall. An excellent **Museum of Art,** just off West Main Street, holds collections of classical, pre-Columbian, African, medieval, European, American, and Asian art, in addition to changing exhibitions. Admission is free, and it's open Tuesday to Friday from 9am to 5pm, on Saturday from 11am to 2pm, and on Sunday from 2 to 5pm.

The East Campus is pleasant, but it's the **West Campus** (located a short drive away on winding, wooded Campus Drive) that really steals the show. Its Gothic-style buildings and beautifully landscaped grounds are nothing short of breathtaking.

The highlight of this showplace is the ✪ **Duke Chapel,** reminiscent of England's Canterbury Cathedral. The bell tower of the majestic cruciform chapel rises 210 feet and houses a 50-bell carillon that rings out at the end of each workday and on Sunday. A half-million-dollar Flentrop organ with more than 5,000 pipes (said to be one of the finest in the Western hemisphere) is in a special oak gallery, its case 40 feet high. Renowned organists perform public recitals on the first Sunday of each month. The long nave, with its ornate screen and carved-oak choir stalls, is lighted in soft shades of red, blue, green, and yellow from 77 stained-glass windows. Visiting hours are 8am to 5pm daily, and there are interdenominational services every Sunday at 11am.

A visit to the West Campus would not be complete without a peek at **Cameron Indoor Stadium,** since 1935 the home of the Duke Blue Devils basketball team. It's an elegant, intimate place in which to scream your lungs out; indeed, the university's rabid fans take pride in its stature as one of the smallest indoor arenas in the nation.

The university's **Botany Department Greenhouses** are open to the public daily from 10am to 4:30pm. They hold the most diverse collection of plants in the Carolinas in some 13 rooms of plants, both native and rare. Also on the West Campus is the **Duke University Medical Center,** which has gained worldwide fame for its extensive treatment facilities and varied research programs.

To arrange special **guided tours** of the campus and find out more about Duke, call the Admissions Office (☎ **919/684-3214**) Monday to Saturday 9am to 3pm. We recommend a tour of the **Sarah P. Duke Gardens,** 55 lovely acres on the West Campus that draw more than 200,000 visitors each year. In a valley bordered by a pine forest, the gardens feature a lily pond, stone terraces, a rose garden, a native-plant garden, an Asiatic arboretum, a wisteria-draped pergola, and colorful seasonal plantings. The gardens are open every day from 8am until dark—a good place to have picnic lunch or to end a day of campus sightseeing.

THE DURHAM BULLS & THEIR FIELD OF DREAMS

The real name of the game around here is basketball. People take their hoops mighty seriously around here. And fans haven't been disappointed; Coach K's Blue Devils have been one of the most dominant teams in the game throughout the '90s and into the 21st century. But thousands of locals and tourists continue to fill the stands each summer as the **Durham Bulls** play a full season in the Class A Carolina League as an

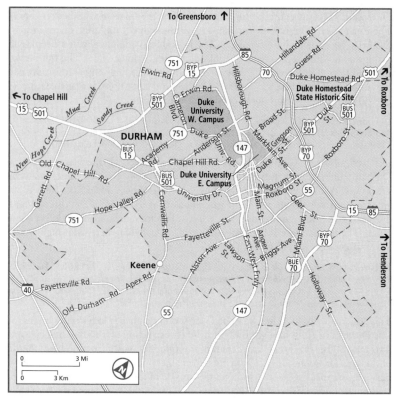

affiliate of the Atlanta Braves. The Bulls shot to fame on the shoulders of Kevin Costner catching for hotshot rookie pitcher Tim Robbins in the 1988 flick *Bull Durham*. But if you're in town for a game, don't expect to see the wonderful old-time ballpark where the film was actually shot. In 1995, the Bulls abandoned the old ballpark for snazzy new digs on Magnum Street, designed by the same architects who conceived Camden Yards in Baltimore. By the way, the famous snorting bull in the movie was a prop that proved such a hit that it's now a Bulls fixture. And there really *was* a Crash Davis on the team in the 1940s. Other famous alums of the Bulls include Joe Morgan, Mark Lemke, Steve Avery, Ryan Klesko, David Justice, Ron Gant, and Rusty Staub. The season usually runs from early April through the first week of September. Unfortunately, tickets are very hard to get. As far in advance as possible, contact the Durham Bulls, P.O. Box 507, Durham, NC 27702 (☎ **919/956-2855**).

WHERE TO STAY

Remember that hotel rates go up during Duke University's graduation ceremonies and for major sporting events.

Arrowhead Inn. 106 Mason Rd., Durham, NC 27712. ☎ **800/528-2207** or 919/ 477-8430. Fax 919/471-9538. www.arrowheadinn.com. E-mail:info@arrowheadinn.com. 10 units. A/C TEL. $98–$150 double, $160–$200 suite, $235 2-room log cabin. Rates include full or continental breakfast. AE, DC, DISC, MC, V.

This circa-1775 inn is one of the most highly honored inns in the area, acknowledged by such publications as *USA Today, Southern Living,* and *Food and Wine.* Your hosts, the Ryans, strive to continue the excellence that they have established at this inn. There's a choice of beautifully furnished rooms furnished with king-, queen-, or twin-size beds. Seven units have fireplaces. The log cabin is complete with a sleeping loft, sitting room with fireplace, and a front porch with rocking chairs. The full breakfast is served from 8 to 9am in the dining room, in the "keeping room," or on the patio; the continental breakfast, left out for the earliest and latest risers, is available from 7:30 to 9:30am. There are hammocks outside for your leisure.

Durham Hilton. 3800 Hillsborough Rd., Durham, NC 27705. ☎ **800/HILTONS** or 919/ 383-8033. Fax 919/383-4287. www.hilton.com. 206 units. A/C TV TEL. $135–$149 double; $199 suite. Special family rates available. AE, CB, DC, DISC, MC, V. Free parking.

Off I-85, about a 10-minute drive from Duke University, the glass-and-concrete Durham Hilton rises six floors. It's a favorite with business travelers but caters to families as well. You're welcomed into a split-level lobby with a sunken bar. The bedrooms are rather festively decorated in rose garden colors. A restaurant serves throughout the day until 10pm to accommodate late arrivals. Facilities include an outdoor pool and sauna. The fitness room is barely adequate; instead of going here, you might want to use your courtesy pass to Gold's Gym.

Hillsborough House. 209 E. Tryon St., Hillsborough, NC 27278. ☎ **800/616-1660** or 919/644-1600. Fax 919/644-1600. www.hillsboroughinn.citysearch.com. 6 units. A/C. $95–$125 double; $200 suite. Rates include continental breakfast. AE, DISC, MC, V. Free parking. Follow I-85 west from Durham 15 miles to Hillsborough Exit 164.

This Italianate-villa-style house, set on 7 acres, offers a bucolic lodging option just outside Durham in Hillsborough. Built in 1790 (construction on this building continued into the 1800s), this house features an 80-foot porch—not uncommon for buildings of this era. The rooms are tastefully furnished and contain either a king- or queen-size bed. The original kitchen was built on the outside of the house (a custom used to prevent kitchen fires from consuming the entire house in the days before the fire engine). Today, it is the property's lone suite, with three rooms behind a brick facade. The inn does not allow smoking, pets, or children under the age of 10. Kirk and Laurie Michel are your gracious hosts.

☉ Washington Duke Inn & Golf Club. 3001 Cameron Blvd., Durham, NC 27706. ☎ **800/443-3853** or 919/490-0999. Fax 919/688-0105. www.washingtondukeinn.com. 171 units. A/C TV TEL. $195–$285 double; $425–$875 suite. AE, CB, DC, DISC, MC, V. Free parking.

On the Duke University campus, about a mile from U.S. 15/501, this is the premier inn of Durham, with an 18-hole golf course. Named for the original tobacco tycoon, it's filled with Duke memorabilia, including Washington Duke's own antique desk. The property is like a castle, with an L-shaped lower wing. Many of the helpful staff members are university students. Although the impressive redbrick mansion is traditional in style, the bedrooms are modern, with big mullioned windows, upholstered chairs, quilted spreads, and either one or two double beds.

   Dining/Diversions: Naturally, someone had to name the bar Bull Durham. The full-service restaurant, Fairview, the most comfortable in town, serves an excellent international cuisine and features piano music.

WHERE TO DINE

Brightleaf Square, a complex of former warehouses built between 1900 and 1904, has a host of restaurants as well as shopping. You can enjoy a stroll and ice cream in the courtyards.

⭘ **Magnolia Grill.** 1002 9th St. ☎ **919/286-3609.** Reservations recommended. Main courses $16.50–$25.95. AE, MC, V. Tues–Thurs 6–9:30pm, Fri–Sat 5–10pm. Closed Sun, Mon, and major holidays. SOUTHERN.

The grandest dining experience in Durham, the Magnolia Grill, with its peach and dark-green interior, delivers old Southern charm with a degree of urban sophistication. The attentive staff brings attractive dishes from the kitchen, which produces a menu with many seafood and beef selections. This restaurant, better described as a bistro, evokes an unexpected coastal feel. Start with the wine list, which features more than 110 bottled varieties, 16 of which are sold by the glass. The menu changes frequently. During one recent visit, we started with the green-tomato soup with crab and country ham, followed by the grilled pork porterhouse with Low Country risotto and crawfish ale. Among the many desserts is a lemon pudding that we found to be a perfect complement to our meal. The restaurant bar opens at 5:30 for predinner drinks.

Nana's. 2514 University Dr. ☎ **919/493-8545.** Reservations recommended. Main courses $16.95–$22. AE, DC, DISC, MC, V. Mon–Sat 5:30–10pm. NEW AMERICAN.

Chef/Owner Scott Howell has presided over this local favorite since 1992, after having worked with David Bouley at his renowned New York restaurant Bouley, cooked in Imola, Italy, at San Domenico's, and sous-chefed at Magnolia Grill (see above). The Asheville native combined his culinary experience with a love for Tarheel regional cooking, and the result is fresh and delicious. The menu changes daily; on one evening, the risotto special contained local sweet corn and coastal white shrimp and was topped off with spinach, Smithfield country ham, and scallions. A house-cured salmon gravlax came with a salad of arugula, Bosc pears, spicy almonds, and green-tomato vinaigrette. The restaurant is known for its special wine dinners, and has won Wine Spectator Magazine's Award of Excellence every year since 1993. Nana's is newly refurbished, and the pleasant ambience is only enhanced by the earth tones and local artists' work on the walls.

DURHAM AFTER DARK
The Down Under Pub. 802 W. Main St. ☎ **919/682-0039.**

Wooden doors open into a chummy pub with a neighborhood feel, where an interesting cross-section of Durhamites meet. Located in the historic downtown area, the Down Under Pub offers a good selection of beers, from European ales and lagers to American microbrews, and more than decent pub food. Play pool, throw darts, or, if you're really parched, belly up to the bar for a beer in yard- or half-yard-size glasses.

George's Garage. 904 W. Main St. ☎ **919/682-0228.**

Named "The Best Club to Be Seen on the Scene" by the local *Spectator,* George's is a restaurant/bar with a lively, energetic bar crowd and very good food, offering such dishes as fire-roasted Black Jack duck and herb chicken and a nightly sushi bar.

3 Chapel Hill

28 miles W of Raleigh; 12 miles SW of Durham

The third point of the Research Triangle area is Chapel Hill, a small city that has managed to hold on to its village atmosphere in spite of the presence of a university that annually enrolls more than 22,000 students. Chapel Hill *is* the University of North Carolina and has been in existence since 1795, when it was the first state university in the country. The 2,000-acre campus holds 125 buildings, ranging from Old East, the oldest state university building in the country (its cornerstone was laid in 1793), to the Morehead Planetarium, which was an astronaut-training center in the early days of the U.S. space program.

Just before the Civil War erupted, the student body was the second-largest in the country, after Yale's. Then the fighting started, and most of UNC's undergraduates and faculty left for the battlefield. The school closed down from 1868 to 1875.

The university has consistently been a leader in American education and a center of liberal intellectualism in a generally conservative state. Sen. Jesse Helms once asked, "Why build a zoo when we can just put up a fence around Chapel Hill?" Was he referring to the town's distinctly liberal bent or to the wild frat parties at the University of North Carolina? At any rate, Chapel Hill (in spite of Helms) has the highest concentrations of Ph.D.s in the United States. By all means, schedule a visit here, ideally in spring, to see the dogwoods and crepe myrtle burst into bloom. At any time, you can wander past the stately pillared houses of Franklin Street and—surprise—find an espresso on virtually every street corner, just as you can in Seattle.

It is estimated that the residents of Chapel Hill purchase more books per capita than anybody else in North Carolina. They also write them. As one local said, "It's no big deal to pick up the Book Review of the *New York Times* and find your neighbor on the cover." Lee Smith, author of 11 novels about the South, lives in the area, as does Allan Gurganus, author of the prize-winning novel *Oldest Living Confederate Widow Speaks Out.*

ESSENTIALS

GETTING THERE   Chapel Hill is reached from the east by I-40 and I-85, from the west by I-85, from the north by N.C. 57, and from the south by N.C. 54.

The nearest airport is in Raleigh.

VISITOR INFORMATION   Information is provided by the **Chapel Hill/Orange County Visitors Bureau,** 105 N. Columbia St., Suite 600 (☎ **919/968-2060;** www.chocvb.org), open Monday to Friday from 9am to 5pm.

EXPLORING ON & OFF CAMPUS

Your best introduction to the university is a free 1-hour **campus tour** that leaves from the Morehead Planetarium (the west entrance) on East Franklin Street. For details, contact the University News Bureau, 210 Pittsboro St. (☎ **919/962-0045**).

With the tour or on your own, look for the **Old Well,** once the only source of drinking water for Chapel Hill. It stands in the center of the campus on Cameron Avenue, in a small templelike enclosure with a dome supported by classic columns. Just east of it is **Old East,** begun in 1793 and the country's oldest state-university building. Across the way stands the "newcomer," **Old West,** built in 1824. **South Main Building** was begun nearby in 1798 and wasn't finished until 1814; in the interim, students lived inside the empty shell in rude huts. At the **Coker Arboretum,** at Cameron Avenue and Raleigh Street, 5 acres are planted with a wide variety of plants. As you walk around the campus, you'll hear popular tunes coming from the 167-foot **Morehead-Patterson Bell Tower,** an Italian Renaissance-style campanile.

Morehead Planetarium, on East Franklin Street (☎ **919/549-6863**), was the first planetarium owned by a university, and it was once used as a NASA training center. The star of the permanent scientific exhibits here is a large orrery, showing the simultaneous action of planets revolving around the sun, moons revolving around planets, and planets rotating on their axes. There's also a stargazing theater with a 68-foot dome. Show times vary considerably, so call for the current schedule. Admission to the planetarium is free; for the show, it's $4 for adults and $3 for senior citizens, students, and children.

UNC has one of the largest athletic programs in the South. The Tarheels field 26 varsity teams and maintain a 24-hour Carolina Hotline number, providing recorded information about all upcoming sporting events to be held on campus. Information is also available from the Smith Center Ticket Office; call ☎ 919/962-2296 Monday to Friday from 8am to 5pm. Carolina basketball is followed passionately all over the state ("If God's not a Tarheel, why did he make the sky Carolina blue?"). Former coach and local icon Dean Smith is practically revered on campus; the Smith Center, named in his honor, is referred to as the Dean Dome. Carolina has a long history of recruiting top players; its famous alums include Michael Jordan and James Worthy.

Off-campus, the **North Carolina Botanical Garden,** on Old Mason Farm Road and U.S. 15/501 Bypass (☎ 919/962-0522), is open mid-March to mid-November, Monday to Friday from 8am to 5pm, Saturday from 10am to 6pm, and Sunday from 1 to 6pm. It boasts 600 acres of nature trails, as well as herb gardens, a collection of carnivorous plants, and native plants in habitat settings. It's the largest natural botanical garden in the Southeast. Admission is free.

OUTDOOR PURSUITS

You'll find several fine golf courses around Chapel Hill. Public ones include the 18-hole **Cedar Grove Golf Course,** 619 McDade Store Rd., Hillsborough (☎ 919/ 732-8397), with greens fees ranging from $12 to $15. Another good course, also an 18-holer, is **Finley Golf Course,** Finley Golf Course Road, Chapel Hill (☎ 919/ 962-2349), with greens fees ranging from $12 to $22.

Orange County has an abundance of parks, gardens, and recreational facilities for visitors, including such activities as boating, fishing, canoeing, camping, biking, and picnicking. For more information, call the following numbers and tell the staff which activities you'd like to pursue: Carrboro Recreation and Parks (☎ 919/968-7703), Chapel Hill Parks and Recreation (☎ 919/968-2784), and Orange County Recreation and Parks (☎ 919/732-8181).

SHOPPING

Many college towns in the South are noted for their quirky character and artistic penchant, however folksy. Chapel Hill is not without its eclectic beat, and you'll discover shops and boutiques that you would expect to find only in big cities. **A Southern Season,** Eastgate Shopping Center, 1800 E. Franklin St. (☎ 919/ 929-7133), is the quintessential Southern gift shop. It's been making gift baskets and gourmet Southern foods since 1975; its most interesting item may be kudzu jelly, made from that green plant (imported from Japan to the South as a way to combat erosion) that has virtually taken over and spread everywhere. The jelly is like a tea jam with a sweet apple flavor and is mostly a tourist novelty that you won't find on many Southern tables. Well-read Chapel Hill has a large book-buying public, and Franklin Street is the site of most bookstores. Open Monday to Saturday 10am to 7pm. The **Avid Reader,** 462 W. Franklin St. (☎ 919/933-9585), and the **Bookshop,** 400 W. Franklin St. (☎ 919/942-5178), have everything from books on Southern gothic to Southern cooking, and all the titles in between. Both are open Monday to Wednesday 11am to 7pm, Friday and Saturday 10am to 8pm, and Sunday 11am to 5pm. Off the beaten path, **World Traveler Books and Maps,** 400 S. Elliott St. (☎ 919/ 933-5111), specializes in travel publications. You can even get your next *Frommer's* guide here. Open Monday to Saturday 10am to 7pm, Sunday 9am to 6pm.

An Artful Getaway

Visitors to the Piedmont area might be surprised to learn that an artists' colony lies tucked away in the woods not far from Chapel Hill. Solitude and open space have attracted artists from all over the United States to this bucolic spot in Chatham County.

The annual **Open Studio Tour,** which takes place the first weekend in December, provides the best opportunity to explore the artists' studios and works. The tour begins with a visit to a gallery displaying the works of more than 42 artists. Next are the actual studios themselves. Decide who you like, grab a map, and venture off into the wilderness that these artists call home. There's no charge for the tour or entry into any of the studios.

If you can't make the Open Studio Tour in December, most of the artists will welcome you any time of year (with an advance appointment). Pottery lovers will especially appreciate the area; potters—who take advantage of the rich local clay—abound. The spiritual **Melody Troncale** (☎ **919/837-2942**) is a ceramic artist who creates jugs typical to this particular area, as well as an eclectic collection of other types of pottery. Much of her work has a Native American influence. Visitors searching for local watercolors should seek out the friendly **Beth Goldston** (☎ **919/708-5153**). Not only is her work delightful, but her newly renovated home/studio also affords a true glimpse into the life of an artist who has settled out in "the middle of nowhere." For more information about the tour and to receive a complete list of artists, call the **Chatham County Arts Council,** ☎ **919/542-0394,** or write P.O. Box 418, Pittsboro, NC 27312.

U.S. routes 15 and 501 link Pittsboro with Chapel Hill and Durham; U.S. 421 connects Greensboro to 64 West, which leads to Pittsboro. Pittsboro is about 45 minutes from both Raleigh and Greensboro; 30 minutes from Durham and an easy 8 miles from Chapel Hill.

—Vanessa Rosen

WHERE TO STAY

Carolina Inn. 211 Pittsboro St., Chapel Hill, NC 27516. ☎ **800/962-8519** or 919/933-2001. Fax 919/962-3400. www.carolinainn.com. 186 units. A/C TV TEL. $159–$169 double; from $244 suite. AE, DC, DISC, MC, V. Valet parking $6, self-parking $3.

Owned and operated by the university, this historic 1924 colonial-style inn is located on campus one block from the center of town. White columns and well-upholstered chairs fill the lobby. The decor is warm and cozy but slightly faded. Rooms vary in size and style, and some are on the bleak side. Yet there's an attractive lounge, plus a moderately priced restaurant and inexpensive cafeteria. Reserve as far in advance as possible at this hostelry, which is an enduring favorite.

Omni Europa. 1 Europa Dr., Chapel Hill, NC 27514. ☎ **919/968-4900.** Fax 919/968-3520. www.sheratonchapelhill.com. E-mail: sheratonchapelhill@sheraton.com. 168 units. A/C TV TEL. $129–$169 double; $189–$219 suite. Children 15 and under stay free in parents' room. AE, DC, DISC, MC, V. Free parking.

This is Chapel Hill's leading hotel, although Fearrington House, on the outskirts (see "Staying Nearby," below), has more character. Parents of university students often stay here. The hotel offers ground-floor rooms with private patios and upper floors with balconies. The decor is tasteful, and the place is well furnished, but it's somewhat unimaginative. Nevertheless, it's the most reliable choice for good, solid comfort. It offers a central location, a pool, gift shop, lighted tennis courts, and golf privileges nearby. The hotel restaurant serves ordinary fare until 10pm. A nearby health club is free to guests.

Siena Hotel. 1505 E. Franklin St., Chapel Hill, NC 27514. ☎ **800/223-7379** or 919/ 929-4000. Fax 919/968-8527. www.sienahotel.com. 80 units. A/C TV TEL. $169 double, $205–$245 suite. Rates include full breakfast. Children 12 and under stay free in parents' room. AE, CB, DC, MC, V. Free parking.

The four-story stucco hotel is designed in Mediterranean style, with the accent on upscale to attract UNC parents. The restaurant enjoys an excellent reputation. There might be a wait to be seated for Sunday brunch here, but the wait is worth it. Other times, the menu is northern Italian. Rooms look European; they're warm and inviting, with remote-control TVs in armoires, upholstered reading chairs, and various bed arrangements. This hotel is also close to Chapel Hill nightlife.

STAYING NEARBY

✪ **Fearrington House Inn.** 2000 Fearrington Village Center (7 min. south of Chapel Hill on U.S. 15/501), Pittsboro, NC 27312. ☎ **919/542-2121.** Fax 919/542-4202. www. fearrington.com. E-mail: fhouse@fearrington.com. 31 units. A/C TV TEL. $175–$350 double. Rates include breakfast and afternoon tea. AE, MC, V.

The Fearrington House will tug at your heart . . . and your purse, but you won't be disappointed. This isn't the kind of place that lends itself to children, so leave the kids at home. Created in 1974 in a planned community of gracious townhouses surrounding a village center, the 60-acre grounds are meticulously kept, with the rose gardens adding a special burst of color. The guest rooms are just as inviting, with lots of little details: silk or dried flowers, antiques mixed with high-quality reproductions, double ottomans, stereos, cable TVs, cathedral ceilings, some seating areas, marble tables, various bed arrangements, and luxuriously appointed baths. Extra amenities at the inn include screened porches, vintage Schwinns ready for your ride around the village, and even fresh flowers in the bathroom.

Dining: The restaurant is in a separate white clapboard building with elegant decor, ranging from sunny French country to Laura Ashley styles. Little alcoves make dining an intimate experience. The food is expertly prepared and served. Anticipate such dishes as sautéed soft-shell crayfish in orange Creole butter or baked striped bass with salmon mousse and citron-infused *fumet* (a concentrated stock). Between courses, you can cleanse your palate with buttermilk sorbet. Another, more traditional restaurant is also available.

WHERE TO DINE

✪ **Crook's Corner.** 610 W. Franklin St. ☎ **919/929-7643.** Reservations recommended Sat–Sun. Main courses $12.95–$21.95. AE, CB, DC, DISC, MC, V. Mon–Sat 5:30–10:30pm, Sun 10:30am–2pm (brunch) and 6–10:30pm. SOUTHERN.

Behind the rather quirky facade of Crook's Corner lurks one of Chapel Hill's superb restaurants. The seasonal menu may include such delights as shrimp and grits with mushrooms, bacon, and scallions; green Tabasco chicken; or mustard-molasses ribs. Among the side dishes are such down-home delicacies as fresh collard greens and hoppin' John (black-eyed peas and rice with scallions, tomato, and Cheddar cheese). Waiters review the "War of Northern Aggression" as they haul out those jalapeño hush puppies along with the oyster and filet mignon scalawags. The wine-by-the-glass list is excellent. The walls of the dining room are a continuously changing exhibition of works by local artists. Seating is limited to 70; there's seating for about 50 more out on the patio in fair weather. You may have to wait for a table, but it's worth it.

Mama Dips Kitchen. 408 W. Rosemary St. ☎ **919/942-5837.** Reservations not accepted. Main courses $6.50–$14.95. Mon–Fri 8am–3pm and 4–10pm; Sat 8am–10pm; Sun 8am–9pm. TRADITIONAL COUNTRY COOKING.

This simple, first-come-first-served place is a great example of how the South likes to live: at the dinner table. Mama Dips' menu serves up succulent fried chicken, zesty beef or pork barbecue, and lip-smacking fried catfish as its tried-and-true specialties, along with a menu so vast that it'll make you wish you had room to eat everything. All the main courses are old-fashioned meat dishes; with them, you can select 2 of 18 different and freshly prepared vegetables every day. Naturally, you get biscuits with everything. The drink of choice, of course, is sweet iced tea. All the vegetables are fresh, and the meat is purchased from the butcher shop down the street. Other good-tasting options include spaghetti, homemade soups, and savory gumbos, along with fresh homemade desserts.

Pyewacket Restaurant. 431 W. Franklin St. ☎ **919/929-0297.** Main courses $8.95–$19.95. AE, DC, DISC, MC, V. Mon–Fri 11:30am–2pm; Mon–Thurs 5:30–9:30pm and Fri–Sat 5:30–10pm; Sun 11:30am–2pm, and 5:30–9pm. SEASONAL AMERICAN.

The most popular eating house in Chapel Hill attracts a crowd of young profession-als who want good food at moderate prices. The decor is a kind of architectural eclec-tic, with cozy dining areas (all smoke-free), ash-paneled walls, and contemporary Italian light fixtures. Smoking is allowed in a separate bar and lounge area. Outside dining on the veranda overlooking Franklin Street is popular during warm weather. The lunch menu includes homemade soups, salads, sandwiches, and freshly made bread. At night, you can try the yummy Southwest crab cakes, made with a tomato cilantro salsa, or sautéed snapper filet with citrus butter. The Indonesian curried shrimp is a delight, served with yogurt and grilled pita bread. All grilled seafood is cooked medium unless otherwise requested. Some vegetarian specials are available.

CHAPEL HILL AFTER DARK

Arts Center, 300-G E. Main St., in Carrboro (☎ **919/929-2787**), presents events Thursday to Sunday for about 50 weeks annually, including regional, national, and international concert tours, plays, and children's programs. Call for information. The box office is open Monday to Friday from 10am to 6pm and on Saturday from noon to 4pm. Ticket costs depend on the event.

　　Cat's Cradle, 300 Main St., in Carrboro (☎ **919/967-9053**). This casual, intimate space is still going strong as *the* venue to see the latest bands—rock 'n' roll, alternative, bluegrass, you name it. The talent is often native-bred, and the scheduling is made with an eye to quality musicianship. Chapel Hill is the hometown of big-time picker James Taylor, after all.

4 Winston-Salem

104 miles W of Raleigh

In 1913, the twin communities of Winston and Salem were incorporated into a sin-gle city. Winston, founded in 1849, contributed an industry-based economy, whereas Salem added the emphasis on education and crafts and the sense of order that its Moravian settlers brought from Pennsylvania in 1766. The union has proved to be happy and productive.

Winston-Salem

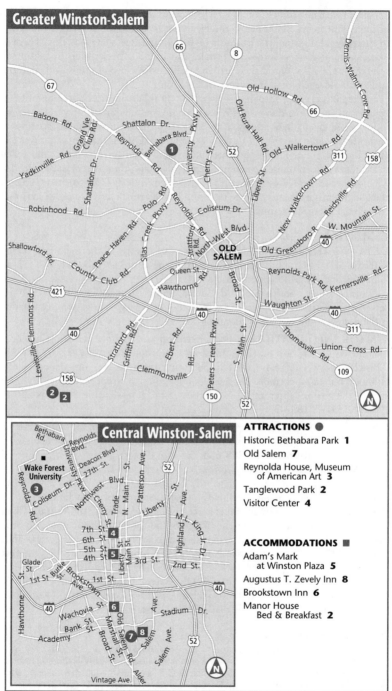

Greater Winston-Salem

66 · 8 · 67 · Dennis-Walnut Cove Rd. · Old Hollow Rd. · 66 · Old Rural Hall Rd. · Old Walkertown Rd. · 311 · 158 · Balsom Rd. · Grand Vie Club Rd. · Shattalon Dr. · Reynolda Rd. · Bethabara Blvd. · University Pkwy · Cherry St. · 52 · Liberty St. · Yadkinville Rd. · Shattalon Dr. · New Walkertown Rd. · Reidsville Rd. · W. Mountain St. · Robinhood Rd. · Polo Rd. · Silas Creek Pkwy · Reynolda Rd. · Coliseum Dr. · Peace Haven Rd. · Stratford Rd. · North-West Blvd. · OLD SALEM · Old Greensboro R · 40 · Shallowford Rd. · Country Club Rd. · 421 · Queen St. · Hawthorne Rd. · Broad St. · Reynolds Park Rd. · Kernersville Rd. · Waughton St. · 40 · 40 · 311 · Lewisville-Clemmons Rd. · 40 · Stratford Rd. · Griffith Rd. · Ebert Rd. · Peters Creek Pkwy · S. Main St. · Thomasville Rd. · Union Cross Rd. · 109 · 158 · Clemmonsville Rd. · 150 · 52 · 2 2 · N

Central Winston-Salem

Bethabara Rd. · Reynolds Blvd. · University · Wake Forest University · 3 · Deacon Blvd. · 27th St. · Reynolda Rd. · Coliseum Dr. · Northwest Blvd. · Cherry St. · Trade St. · N. Main St. · Patterson St. · 52 · Liberty St. · Highland Ave. · M.L. King Jr. Dr. · 7th St. · 4 · 6th St. · 5th St. · 5 · 4th St. · Liberty St. · Main St. · 3rd St. · 2nd St. · Glade St. · Burke St. · Brookstown Ave. · 1st St. · 40 · 40 · Hawthorne Rd. · Wachovia St. · 6 · Stadium Dr. · Bank St. · Academy St. · Old Salem Rd. · Marshall St. · Broad St. · 7 · 8 · Salem Ave. · Alder St. · Salem Ave. · 52 · Vintage Ave. · N

ATTRACTIONS ●
Historic Bethabara Park **1**
Old Salem **7**
Reynolda House, Museum
of American Art **3**
Tanglewood Park **2**
Visitor Center **4**

ACCOMMODATIONS ■
Adam's Mark
at Winston Plaza **5**
Augustus T. Zevely Inn **8**
Brookstown Inn **6**
Manor House
Bed & Breakfast **2**

Salem (the name comes from the Hebrew word *shalom*, meaning *peace*) was the last of three settlements established in the Piedmont by Moravian clergymen and laymen in the early 1750s; the little towns of Bethabara and Bethania came first. The hard-working newcomers were devout people who had fled persecution in Europe and brought to the New World their artisans' skills, a deep love of music and education, and an absolute rejection of violence in any form.

In the 20th century, "progress" encroached on the boundaries of the beautiful old congregational town. But in 1949, an organized restoration effort was begun, and today, more than 30 buildings have been restored, with meticulous attention to authenticity; renovation is still under way on others. Devout the Moravians were, but glum they were not: The bright, cheerful reds and blues and soft greens and yellows in the restored interiors and exteriors replicate the colors they used in those early days. The Moravians' love of good food is also preserved in today's Old Salem, especially at the Old Salem Tavern (see "Where to Dine," below), which serves meals in an authentic colonial Moravian setting.

ESSENTIALS

GETTING THERE   I-40 (the East–West Expressway) is the main approach to Winston-Salem from both east and west; from the north, it's U.S. 311, U.S. 52, and U.S. 158; and from the south, U.S. 52.

Winston-Salem's **Smith Reynolds International Airport** (☎ 336/767-2205) is served by **US Airways Express** (☎ 800/428-4322; www.usairways.com). Charlotte is the nearest airport served by all major carriers.

VISITOR INFORMATION   The **Convention and Visitors Bureau,** Chamber of Commerce, 601 W. 4th St. (P.O. Box 1408), Winston-Salem, NC 27102 (☎ 336/728-4200; www.wscbv.com), can tell you about attractions, accommodations, dining, and local bus transportation. It's open Monday to Friday from 8:30am to 5pm. Also stop by the **visitor center,** 601 N. Cherry St., Suite 100, Winston-Salem, NC 27102 (☎ 800/331-7018 or 336/777-3796).

SPECIAL EVENTS   For a relatively small city, Winston-Salem has quite a calendar of events. In mid-April, the city's 18th-century gardens in Old Salem are open for the **Spring Garden Tour** (call ☎ 888/653-7253 for details). Every year, there's a traditional Moravian **Easter Sunrise Service.** An old-fashioned **Independence Day Celebration** is held each year at Historic Bethabara (call ☎ 336/725-1035 for information). Early September brings the **Chili Championship** to Tanglewood Park (☎ 336/723-4386). Late September and early October usher in the **Vantage Championship Senior Golf Tournament** (☎ 336/766-2400). Mid-October also brings **Folk Festival IV,** a competition complete with country cooking and entertainment (☎ 336/727-1038). Beginning in November and running to January 1 is the **Festival of Lights** in Tanglewood Park (☎ 336/778-6300). And the holiday season wouldn't be complete without the ✪ **Old Salem Christmas and Candle Teas** (☎ 888/653-7253), a re-creation of Yuletide as it was celebrated 200 years ago in Old Salem. (You've got to sample that Moravian sugar cake!)

EXPLORING THE AREA

✪ **Historic Old Salem.** Old Salem Rd. ☎ **888/OLDSALEM** or 336/721-7300. www.oldsalem.org. Combination ticket for Old Salem and Museum of Early Southern Decorative Arts, $20 adults, $11 children 5–16; admission to Old Salem, $15 adults, $8 children; admission to Museum of Early Southern Decorative Arts, $10 adults, $6 children. Mon–Sat 9:30am–5:30pm, Sun 1:30–5pm.

One of the leading attractions of North Carolina, this restoration of a Moravian community demonstrates old-world skills. The **visitor center** has exhibits that trace the Moravians' journey from Europe to America and finally to North Carolina. Costumed hosts and hostesses will show you around, and you'll see craftspeople in Moravian dress practicing the trades of the original settlement.

When Moravian boys reached the age of 14, they moved into the **Single Brothers House**—the half-timbered section was built in 1769, and the brick wing in 1786— where they began a 7-year apprenticeship to a master artisan. Academic studies continued as they learned to be gunsmiths, tailors, potters, and shoemakers. Adolescent girls lived in the **Single Sisters House,** diagonally across the town square, where they learned the domestic arts that they would need when marrying time arrived. Young single women still live in this building; it's a dormitory for Salem College. It is not open for visitation.

Be sure to go into **The Tavern,** built in 1784 to replace an earlier one that burned. George Washington spent 2 nights here in 1791 and commented in his diary on the industriousness of the Moravians. The dining room, sleeping rooms, barns, and grounds are not much different now from when he stopped by; the cooking utensils in the stone-floored kitchen, with its twin fireplaces, are genuine period artifacts.

The **Wachovia Museum** (the Moravians called this region *Wachovia,* after a district in Saxony that had offered refuge to the sect) was once the boys' school. Period musical instruments are displayed here, along with a host of other historical items. You can also visit the **Market-Firehouse** and the **Winkler Bakery,** where breads and cookies are still baked in the big wood-burning ovens. Many homes have distinctive signs hanging outside to identify the shops inside. One of our favorites is the tobacco shop of Matthew Miksch, a yellow, weather-boarded log cottage with a miniature man hanging at the door clutching tobacco leaves and a snuffbox.

Like the historic district of Williamsburg, Virginia, Old Salem still functions as a living community. Many of the restored homes are private residences, and the young people walking the old streets with such familiarity are no doubt students at Salem College, living a 20th-century campus life in an 18th-century setting.

On the square, the **Home Moravian Church,** which dates from 1800, is the center of the denomination in the South. Visitors are always welcome at services; hundreds show up for the Easter Sunrise service, the Christmas Lovefeast (on December 24), and the New Year's Eve Watch Night service. One block north of the square, the graveyard named God's Acre contains more than 4,000 graves, all marked with nearly identical stones. Princes and paupers are shown the same respect. The cemetery is open at the discretion of the church.

The **Museum of Early Southern Decorative Arts** allows you to tour period rooms and galleries, showcasing the furniture, paintings, textiles, ceramics, silver, and other metalwares made and used in the South through 1820. The museum stands at the southern edge of Old Salem.

Historic Bethabara Park. 2147 Bethabara Rd. ☎ **336/924-8191.** Admission $1 adults, 50¢ children 12 and under. Mon–Fri 9:30am–4:30pm, Sat–Sun 1:30–4:30pm. Buildings closed Dec 15–Easter.

On a 130-acre site 3 miles northwest of downtown Winston-Salem is the 1753 locale of the first Moravian settlement in North Carolina. There are two 18th-century homes, a 200-year-old Moravian church, the excavated foundations of the town of Bethabara, a rebuilt French and Indian War fort, nature trails, and picnic tables. A visitor center shows a slide presentation about Bethabara and the beginnings of Winston-Salem.

The Search for Mayberry

Mayberry, the hometown of Sheriff Andy Taylor on *The Andy Griffith Show,* never existed, of course. But its inspiration is said to be **Mount Airy,** lying off U.S. 52 in the Upper Piedmont, to the south of the Virginia/North Carolina border. Andy Griffith was born and raised in this sleepy little town.

The town is an example of television's power to affect tourism. Thousands visit Mount Airy yearly, and the town they see looks very much like the fictional Mayberry of the long-running TV series. Southern oaks border the streets, and "just plain folks" sit out on the verandas, swinging and rocking as though it were still 1902. You expect to see Barney Fife appear at any minute.

Mayberry Days, held the last Thursday, Friday, and Saturday of September, draw visitors from all over the country for traditional "pig-pickin's" cooking and pie-eating contests. Call the Mount Airy Arts Council (☎ **800/286-6193** or 336/786-7998) for information. If you'd like a **walking-tour map** of the town, go to the Mount Airy Chamber of Commerce at 200 N. Main St. (☎ **336/786-6116**), open Monday to Friday from 9am to 5pm.

Mount Airy Visitors Center, 615 N. Main St. (☎ **800/576-0231** or 336/789-4636), is open Monday to Saturday from 9am to 5pm and on Sunday from 11am to 4:30pm. It will guide visitors through the town, pointing out the still-standing birthplace of Andy Griffith and local businesses that were the inspiration for places seen in the TV series, including the replica of the old jail (open Monday to Friday from 9am to 5pm). **Floyd's City Barber Shop (336/786-2346)** is still in operation, and the same barber who used to cut Andy's hair is still in business.

If you'd like to follow in the footsteps of Sheriff Andy, head for the **Snappy Lunch** at 125 N. Main St. (☎ **336/786-4931**) for a pork-chop sandwich. The old-time lunch counter is a virtual showcase for *The Andy Griffith Show.* Andy himself frequented the place as a boy. The proprietor, Charles Dowell, claims to sell about 1,000 pork-chop sandwiches every week. The sandwiches, costing $2.50 each, are consumed at old school desks. The sandwich is a boneless pork chop between steamy bun halves, covered with mustard. It's served Monday to Saturday from 5:45am to 1:45pm.

Reynolda House, Museum of American Art. Reynolda Rd. ☎ **336/725-5325.** Admission: house, $6 adults, $5 seniors, free 21 and under. Gardens, free. House, Tues–Sat 9:30am–4:30pm, Sun 1:30–4:30pm; gardens, daily 7:30am–5pm.

R.J. Reynolds, the tobacco tycoon, built this mansion, which now holds an excellent collection of furnishings and American art. The lake porch has been enclosed to provide an additional 2,000 square feet of space for programs and exhibits. A much-expanded costume collection is also on display.

OUTDOOR PURSUITS

Tanglewood Park, U.S. 158 West in Clemmons (☎ **336/778-6370**), is a year-round recreational facility set on some 1,100 acres. You can enjoy golf on two of *Golf Digest's* top-rated courses, or tennis on one of nine tennis courts, both hard and clay. Stop by the horse stables to ask about trail rides and riding lessons or to arrange a leisurely carriage drive around the park. A nature trail has also been cut through the acreage.

The park has two modern, fully equipped children's playgrounds, plus an Olympic-size pool. It's open daily from 7am to dusk. Admission is $2 per car.

SHOPPING

Winston-Salem offers all types of shopping options, thanks to its dual Southern and Moravian heritage. **Stratford Place,** Stratford Road at Interstate 40 Business (☎ **336/723-2221**), offers a collection of specialty shops and restaurants in one locale. Two shops of interest include the **Craft Gallery** (☎ **336/748-0145**), featuring crafts ranging from pottery to jewelry, and **Gabby's** (☎ **336/727-0005**), carrying stylish women's apparel.

Winston-Salem has a selection of antiques stores, as the neighboring cities do. Those worth a look include **Alice Cunningham Interiors,** 3120 Robinhood Rd. (☎ **336/724-9667**); **Oxford Antiques and Gifts,** 129 S. Stratford Rd. (☎ **336/723-7080**), and **Reynolda Antique Gallery** (☎ **336/748-0741**). All these shops are open Monday to Saturday 10am to 6pm.

If rare and old used books are your forte, we recommend a stop at **Larry Laster Old and Rare Books,** 2416 Maplewood Ave. (☎ **336/724-7544**), a great place to make that rare find. Visits are by appointment only.

For Moravian souvenirs, Old Salem has abundant shopping opportunities. One of the most interesting is the **Moravian Cookie Shop,** 971 Meadowlark Dr. (☎ **800/537-5374**), a company that has been hand-baking cookies since 1938, using the same recipes used by Moravian settlers in the 18th century. Hours are Monday to Friday 7am to 6pm.

Just a 7-mile drive north of Winston-Salem is the town of Germanton, settled in 1790 by German immigrants. It's the home of the **Germanton Art Gallery and Winery,** Highway 8, Germanton (☎ **800/322-2894** or 336/969-6121), where you can find originals and prints by many internationally known artists. The gallery is an authorized dealer for art dealers all over the world. The wines are well worth tasting; the climate of the foothills of the Blue Ridge Mountains provides an ideal setting for the French-American hybrid grape to flourish. Allow yourself time for shopping, and bring a credit card. Open Tuesday to Friday 10am to 6pm.

WHERE TO STAY

✪ **Adam's Mark Winston Plaza.** 425 N. Cherry St., Winston-Salem, NC 27101. ☎ **800/444-2326** or 336/725-3500. Fax 336/721-2240 or 336/728-4025. www.adamsmark.com. 615 units. A/C TV TEL. $109–$159 double; $200–$800 suite. Children 17 and under stay free in parents' room. AE, CB, DC, DISC, MC, V. Parking $6.

The leading hotel of Winston-Salem and one of the state's best, Adam's Mark is located in the heart of the business district and is connected underground to the Benton Convention Center. Consisting of a 17-story and a 9-story building, the complex is like a grand hotel in a major world city. The most expensive rooms are at the luxury-club level on three floors, with a private lounge, complimentary continental breakfast, and concierge. All the bedrooms are tasteful and spacious, however, and many have panoramic views. Some accommodations open onto balconies that overlook the atrium. An indoor pool and spa area are just steps away from the lobby, and the Cherry Street Bar offers an entertainment cafe. Dine in upscale style at Trattoria Carolina, or more casually in the hotel's sports bar, Players.

✪ **Augustus T. Zevely Inn.** 803 S. Main St., Winston-Salem, NC 27101. ☎ **800/928-9299** or 336/748-9299. Fax 336/721-2211. www.winston-salem-inn.com. E-mail: ctheall@dddcompany.com. A/C TEL TV. 12 units. $80–$120 double, $205 suite. Rates include continental breakfast weekdays, full breakfast Sat–Sun. AE, MC, V. Free parking.

This 1844 home of Old Salem physician A.T. Zevely was saved from decay in the 1950s by Old Salem, Inc., a group of citizens who preserve historic Moravian structures, and restored into one of the grandest B&Bs in Old Salem. A first glimpse of the classic 19th-century brick facade evokes the Old Moravian style. Beautifully furnished in Old South style, it's well maintained, snug, and cozy. The inn is centrally located in the historic district, near many sights, shops, and activities, including golfing, tennis, and boating.

Rooms are done in 1800s period style, complete with antique furnishings. Because of its historic relevance and meticulous restoration, children 12 and under are not accepted as guests to the inn. The dining room serves 24 comfortably, and some of the rooms feature fireplaces, refrigerators, and balconies. When you are making reservations, be sure to be specific about which amenities you prefer.

✪ **Brookstown Inn.** 200 Brookstown Ave., Winston-Salem, NC 27101. ☎ **800/845-4262** or 910/725-1120. Fax 336/773-0147. www.brookstowninn.com. E-mail: Brookstowninn@aol. com. 71 units. A/C TV TEL. Sun–Thurs $125–$135 double, $140–$150 suite. Fri–Sat $100–$135 double, $110–$150 suite. Rates include continental breakfast. Children 12 and under stay free in parents' room. AE, DC, MC, V. Free parking. Take the Cherry St. Exit from I-40.

The premier inn of Winston-Salem, the Brookstown is housed in an 1837 cotton mill that supplied material for Confederate uniforms. This jewel of a building offers spacious rooms with two double beds, a chest of drawers, armoire, loveseat, desk, chairs, and tables. Suites have a separate sitting room and garden tub. Silk flowers, quilts, baskets, and wooden decoys adorn the parlor areas, decorated in Wedgwood blue, burgundy, gold, and olive. The inn, listed on the National Register of Historic Places, is conveniently near the Old Salem restoration. Another area of the mill, where its boiler was once located, is the site of one of the popular Darryl's restaurants.

✪ **Manor House Bed & Breakfast.** Tanglewood Park (P.O. Box 1040), Clemmons, NC 27012. ☎ **336/778-6370.** Fax 336/778-6379. www.tanglewoodpark.org. 28 units. $50.50–$119.85 double. Rates include continental breakfast (manor house only). AE, CB, DC, MC, V. Free parking.

In Tanglewood Park, part of the former 1,100-acre estate of William Reynolds (the brother of R.J.), this stately former house lies southwest of Winston-Salem in a landscape of Carolina pines and dogwood. The 1859 home has been restored and adapted for the use of guests. All the rooms are spacious and handsomely furnished, like an English country house. The tasteful decor is in cranberry and hunter green, with louvered wooden blinds and Austrian swag-style draperies. The rooms in the manor house are preferable to the motel's basic accommodations, but if you're watching your budget, staying at the lodge is a fine option. The cost of swimming and fishing nearby is included.

WHERE TO DINE
IN OLD SALEM

✪ **Old Salem Tavern Dining Room.** 736 S. Main St. ☎ **336/748-8585.** Reservations recommended for dinner, and for lunch for parties of 6 or more. Main courses $5.95–$7.95 at lunch, $15.25–$24 at dinner. AE, MC, V. Mon–Sat 11:30am–2pm and 5–9:30pm, Sun 11:30am–2pm. AMERICAN/CONTINENTAL.

Here, as everywhere else in the restored village, authenticity is the keynote. The dining rooms were built in 1816 as an annex to the 1784 Tavern next door, and the simple furnishings and colonial-costumed staff provide an appropriate 18th-century ambience. During the summer months, you can eat in the outdoor arbor, which, like the indoor rooms, is candlelit at night. Favorite dishes include chicken pie (at lunch) and pork tenderloin and smoked filet of beef (dinner only). The pumpkin-and-raisin muffins are a specialty, and for dessert, there's Moravian gingerbread topped with homemade lemon ice cream. The cuisine upholds the Moravian tradition of quality.

IN WINSTON-SALEM

Leon's Café. 924 S. Marshall St. ☎ **336/725-9593.** Reservations recommended. Main courses $13.95–$21.95. AE, MC, V. Daily 6–10pm. Closed holidays. Take the Cherry St. Exit from I-40; it's 1 block west and south of Old Salem. AMERICAN.

In the warehouse district (and hard to find), this little cafe is down a side street close to the Holsum Bakery. Just follow the aroma of bread baking. Continental in style, it attracts savvy locals with flavorful cuisine at a low price. The main courses vary from week to week, depending on the market, but count on finding such dishes as ravioli stuffed with spinach and walnuts and covered in herb-flavored fresh tomato sauce. Some excellent beef and chicken dishes are quite innovative. Service is relaxed but efficient.

Rainbow News & Café. 712 Brookstown Ave. ☎ **336/723-5010.** Main courses $4.95–$8.95 at lunch, $8.95–$16.95 at dinner. AE, DISC, MC, V. Tues–Fri 11am–2:30pm and 5–10pm; Sat 10am–10pm, Sun 10am–9pm. CAFE/AMERICAN.

This old house has been altered to accommodate diners in several rooms, including upstairs. New books are for sale, and two doors away is the secondhand bookstore. This idea is fun and funky, the clientele young and wholesome. At night, the mood is rather romantic. The menu changes daily, but it may include vegetarian selections, sandwiches, salads, Southern gumbo, vegetarian lasagna, red beans and rice, and marinated London broil. The fare is not deluxe, but it's good and filling, and made with fresh ingredients. The restaurant is known for its killer brownies, made with Belgian chocolate and cream cheese. Beer and wine are also served.

✪ **Ryan's.** 719 Coliseum Dr. ☎ **336/724-6132.** Reservations recommended. Main courses $16.95–$36.95. AE, DC, MC, V. Mon–Thurs 5–10pm, Fri–Sat 5–10:30pm. Closed major holidays. Take the Cherry St. Exit from Business I-40. CONTINENTAL.

This restaurant is every bit the equal of Zevely House (recommended below), with which it's often compared. In a wooded setting overlooking a stream, Ryan's is rustic in decor but has a truly sophisticated continental menu. Dishes are executed with a polished technique. Beef dishes are specialties, as are some excellent seafood creations. The homemade soups are exceptional, and there's a good wine list. It's estimated that you could eat here every day of the week and always find something new to surprise and delight you. Valet parking is available.

The Vineyards. 120 Reynolda Village. ☎ **336/748-0269.** Reservations recommended Fri–Sat. Main courses $13–$18 at lunch, $8–$22 at dinner. AE, MC, V. Mon–Sat 5–10pm. Closed major holidays. Take the Silas Creek/Wake Forest U. Exit from I-40 to Reynolda Rd. AMERICAN/CONTINENTAL.

In a setting that evokes the French countryside, this restaurant has an excellent wine list, and in good weather, patio dining is possible. Actual dishes depend on what's best and freshest in any season. One specialty is a pound of pork roasted in a sweet-and-sour sauce for 3 hours. Regional game dishes, such as quail, are on the menu when available. The cooking is American but prepared with a certain continental flair; the chefs have found their own style, and the cuisine has a pure, uncompromising quality. You can spend a wonderful evening at this restaurant.

✪ **Zevely House.** 901 W. 4th St. ☎ **336/725-6666.** Reservations recommended. Main courses $14.95–$28; Sun brunch $6.25–$13.95. AE, DC, MC, V. Tues–Sat 5:30–9:30pm, Sun 11am–2pm (brunch). CONTINENTAL.

Antiques and a fireplace decorate this house, which dates back to 1815. It was constructed by Van Neuman Zevely, a Moravian cabinetmaker, and became the center of his plantation. In 1974, the building was hauled to its present site and authentically restored. This restaurant has steadily improved and truly justifies its star rating. The cuisine is creative and accomplished, the sauces are in harmony, and the wine list is well chosen and reasonable in price. Try the potato cakes with sour cream and caviar, or maybe something simple and grandmotherly—chicken pot pie, for example. A pork tenderloin is perfectly prepared. A mixed grill is often featured, as are venison and beef filet, but pan-fried trout is the signature dish. The pumpkin muffins, Moravian-style, are always a good choice. A fireplace keeps the place snug in winter, although you'll want to retreat to the patio when the weather's fair.

WINSTON-SALEM AFTER DARK

Ziggy's. 43 Baity St. ☎ **336/748-1064.** Cover (sometimes) $5–$15.

Come here for the best live music in Winston-Salem, performed in a battered building that you can find by following the directions in the club's recorded phone message. There's a different event every night of the week, although the schedule changes frequently. The setting is a cramped, once-private house 3 miles north of the town center (near the campus of Wake Forest University) and ringed by the largest deck in town. The club was designed in a way to allow sightlines directly to the stage. Live entertainment may include Elastica and Loud Lucy or Hootie & The Blowfish (before they went platinum). It's open Monday to Saturday from 9pm to 2am.

5 Greensboro

78 miles W of Raleigh; 54 miles W of Durham; 48 miles W of Chapel Hill; 27 miles E of Winston-Salem; and 91 miles NE of Charlotte

Greensboro was settled by freedom-loving Scots-Irish, Germans, and Quakers. The Scots-Irish and Germans fought valiantly in the American Revolution and the War of 1812, but when North Carolina seceded from the Union in 1861, Greensboro became an important Confederate supply depot. Jefferson Davis met here with Union General Johnston to arrange surrender terms after the Southern cause was lost. Today, the thriving city is a leader in higher education and the manufacture of textiles, cigarettes, and electronic equipment, as well as the home of a large insurance industry.

Greensboro, although considered to be one of the most desirable places to live in America for families, is not the first place in the Piedmont that you'd think of visiting. Winston-Salem is far more interesting. But if you're in the area, Greensboro has several attractions that are worthy of attention.

ESSENTIALS

GETTING THERE   By Plane   Planes arrive at Piedmont Triad International Airport, Airport Parkway, off Highway 68 N (☎ **336/665-5666;** www.grboair.org). Greensboro is served by **Air Tran** (☎ 800/247-8726; www.airtran.com), **American Airlines** (☎ 800/433-7300; www.aa.com), **Continental Airlines** (☎ 800/433-7300; www.flycontinental.com), **Delta Air Lines** (☎ 800/221-1212; www.delta.com), **Eastwind Airlines** (☎ 800/644-3592; www.eastwindairlines.com), **Northwest Airlines** (☎ 800/225-2525; www.nwa.com), **United Airlines** (☎ 800/241-6522; www.ual.com), and **US Airways** (☎ 800/428-4322; www.usairways.com).

By Train   **Amtrak** has one northbound and one southbound train through Greensboro daily (☎ **800/USA-RAIL**).

By Bus   The **Greyhound/Trailways** depot is at 501 W. Lee St. (☎ **336/272-8950**).

By Car   Reach Greensboro from the east and southwest via I-85, from the west via U.S. 40, and from the south via U.S. 220. For AAA services, contact the **Carolina Motor Club,** 14-A Oak Branch Dr., Greensboro, NC 27407 (☎ **336/852-0506**).

VISITOR INFORMATION   For tourist information on Greensboro and vicinity, contact the **Greensboro Convention and Visitors Bureau,** 317 South Greene St., Greensboro, NC 27401 (☎ **800/344-2282** or 336/274-2282; www.greensboronc. org). Also ask for information on city bus routes and schedules. Hours Monday to Friday are 8:30am to 5:30pm, Saturday 10am to 5pm, and Sunday 1 to 5pm.

EXPLORING THE AREA

Bargain hunters will want to visit two nearby towns, both of which are overflowing with factory outlet shops. **High Point,** 17 miles south of Greensboro (so named because it was the highest point along the 1853 North Carolina and Midland Railroad from Salem to Fayetteville), is notable for its furniture and hosiery shops. **Burlington,** 21 miles east of Greensboro, is a major textile center, with scores of factory outlets for clothing, fabrics, sheets, towels, blankets, and the like.

IN TOWN

Greensboro Historical Museum. 130 Summit Ave. ☎ **336/373-2043.** Free admission. Tues–Sat 10am–5pm, Sun 2–5pm.

Greensboro was the hometown of O. Henry, the short-story writer known in these parts as William Sidney Porter. Here, you'll find an exhibit illustrating his life and work, plus a fine collection from Dolley Madison's life. Born in Greensboro, Madison was the only native-born North Carolinian to be First Lady. Other exhibits include early modes of transportation, furnishings, pottery, and textiles. An exhibit of note remembers the civil-rights lunch-counter sit-ins at F.W. Woolworth, when, in 1960, four African Americans launched the nation's first major protest against segregation.

SIGHTS NEARBY

Guilford Courthouse National Military Park. 2332 New Garden Rd. ☎ **336/ 288-1776.** Free admission. Visitors' center daily 8:30am–5pm. Closed Christmas Day and New Year's Day. 6 miles northwest of downtown Greensboro on U.S. 220.

This 220-acre park marks one of the closing battles of the Revolution—the Battle of Guilford Courthouse on March 15, 1781. Gen. Nathanael Greene (Greensboro was named for him) led a group of inexperienced troops against British general Lord Cornwallis. Although he was defeated, Greene inflicted severe losses on the British. Cornwallis hotfooted it out of this part of the country and headed for Yorktown, where he surrendered his depleted forces just 7 months later, on October 19. The visitor center has films, brochures, and displays about the historic battle. There are also wayside exhibits along the 2-mile road that connects some of the many monuments.

Alamance Battleground State Historic Site. N.C. 62, Burlington. ☎ **336/227-4785.** Free admission. Visitors center, Apr–Oct, Mon–Sat 9am–5pm, Sun 1–5pm; Nov–Mar, Tues–Sat 10am–4pm, Sun 1–4pm. Take I-85/40 Exit 143 to N.C. 62; then go 6 miles to site.

This is where those upstart farmers marched against Royal Governor Tryon in 1771 to protest corrupt government practices. Ill-trained and poorly equipped, they were soundly defeated—the battle lasted only 2 hours—but the stout-hearted Regulators were among the first Southern colonists to demonstrate their objection to royal rule. The visitor center has an audiovisual presentation. The John Allen House is a restored log dwelling typical of North Carolina backwoods homes at the time of the battle.

Furniture in North Carolina

The town of Hickory is the undisputed king of furniture in North Carolina. Sixty percent of the state's furniture manufacturing industry is located in this town, and people come here from far and wide—if you want the best deals, of course, you must go directly to the source. Hickory has obliged by offering two furniture malls and what is known as the "20-mile stretch"—20 miles of stores and outlets lying end-to-end, stretching from Hickory to Lenoir. The largest of these is the **Catawba Furniture Mall,** 377 Hwy. 70 SW, Hickory (☎ 828/324-9701), which spreads its wares over a total of 335,000 square feet of showroom space. One of the merchants at the mall is an authentic woodwright, who sells his handmade works out of a replica turn-of-the-century woodwright shop. The pieces at this shop have been so popular that custom work has been commissioned by such notables as former president George Bush, Pope John Paul II, and even Willie Nelson. Open Monday to Saturday 10am to 7pm. Another shop of interest is **Nostalgia** (☎ 828/325-4800), with the largest individual showroom of nearly 30,000 square feet, featuring imported, hand-carved Indonesian pieces, made mostly of mahogany and pine. Another outlet worth seeing is the **Hickory Furniture Mart,** 2220 Hwy. 70 SE (☎ 800/462-MART), which describes itself as "20 acres of furniture." It has the look of a typical mall, except there are no Neiman Marcuses here—rather, 85 stores of furniture and more furniture, representing more than 800 manufacturers of high-end furniture.

Both of these latter outlets are open Monday to Saturday 9am to 6pm.

North Carolina Transportation Museum. 411 S. Salisbury Ave., Spencer. ☎ 704/636-2889. Free admission, but donations accepted. Train rides $4–$5 per person. Apr–Oct, Mon–Sat 9am–5pm, Sun 1–5pm. Nov–Mar, Tues–Sat 10am–4pm, Sun 1–4pm. Take Exit 79 off I-85.

About halfway between Greensboro and Charlotte (near historic Salisbury), this museum in the little town of Spencer is a mecca for dyed-in-the-wool railway buffs. The shops were established in 1896 as a major repair facility for the Southern Railway. Opened as a museum in 1983, the Master Mechanics Building is the focal point of the 57-acre site. Visitors are free to wander and inspect the growing collection of transportation memorabilia. Once, during the 1930s, this facility built a locomotive in one day. Staff members are likely to add anecdotes about the shops' history at your first show of enthusiasm. Rail rides are sometimes available, and a large museum shop offers unusual railroad items, ranging from maps to *Orient Express* crystal.

OUTDOOR PURSUITS

Greensboro lives up to the *green* in its name with 110 parks, sprawling over 3,000 acres. On the northwest edge of the city, **Jaycee Park,** off Pisgah Church Road on Forest Lawn Drive adjacent to Country Park (☎ 336/545-5310), is the site of the North Carolina Tennis Hall of Fame, offering facilities for baseball, softball, soccer, football, and tennis, plus a playground beside a lake. The North Carolina Closed Tennis Championship is played here annually on the best of the city's 156 courts.

The previously mentioned **Country Park** (☎ 336/545-5343), adjacent to the Natural Science Center off Lawndale Drive, offers two stocked fishing lakes, pedal boats, three playgrounds, picnic shelters, a softball field, and trails for jogging, hiking, and bicycling.

The **Bryan Park Complex and Lake Townsend,** 27 north on Bryan Park Rd., Browns Summit (☎ **336/375-2222**), boasts two 18-hole championship golf courses, tennis courts, picnic areas, and soccer fields, along with sailing, fishing, and boating at adjacent Lake Townsend.

Golfing is a major pastime in Greensboro, especially in mid-April, when 275,000 fans come to the galleries of Forest Oaks Country Club to watch the pros compete for the $1.5 million purse at the **Greater Greensboro Chrysler Classic** (☎ 800-999-5446 or 336/379-1570; www.ggcc.com). The nationally televised tournament is one of the three oldest, and one of the five richest, PGA tournaments, as well as being North Carolina's only golf tournament on the regular PGA tour.

Most of the major sporting events in town—everything from hockey to college basketball—take place at the **Greensboro Coliseum Complex,** 1921 W. Lee St. Call ☎ **336-373-7474** for a complete list of events. This is the largest and most diversified entertainment, civic, and sports facility in the Southeast, and the home of the Carolina Hurricanes of the National Hockey League.

The best golf is at **Bel Aire Golf Club,** 1518 Pleasant Ridge Rd. at Highway 68, 1½ miles north of Piedmont Triad International Airport (☎ **336/668-2413**). Eighteen holes of golf are set in a scenic, hilly terrain featuring four challenging and heavily wooded lakeside par-3 holes. Other good golf is available at **Bryan Park Complex** (recommended above). Two 18-hole courses here were designed by George Cobb and Rees Jones. The Players course is a championship layout with 84 bunkers and 8 ponds or lakes, and the Champions course was selected in 1990 as one of the nation's best new public courses, with 100 sand and grass bunkers. Six holes border scenic Lake Townsend.

WHERE TO STAY

✪ **Biltmore Greensboro Hotel.** 111 W. Washington St., Greensboro, NC 27401. ☎ **800/332-0303** or 336/2720-3474. Fax 336/275-2523. E-mail: thebiltmore@juno.com. 25 units. A/C TV TEL. $110 double, $125 junior suite. Children under 18 stay free in parents' room. Rates include continental breakfast. AE, CB, DC, DISC, MC, V. Free parking.

Built in 1895, this three-story brick hotel in the center of town is listed on the National Register of Historic Places. One of Greensboro's leading hotels, it's smaller and more intimate than the typical Marriotts and Sheratons that dominate the hotel scene for the business-client dollar. It has been heavily renovated and boasts excellent rooms with hardwood floors, canopied four-poster beds, armoires, remote-control TVs, 18th-century reproduction furniture, and either king-size beds or two doubles or two queen-size beds. A continental breakfast is served in a paneled lobby with a fireplace. Other extras include a small business center.

Hilton Greensboro. 304 North Greene Street, Greensboro, NC 27401. ☎ **800/HILTONS** or 336/379-8000. Fax 336/275-2810. www.hilton.com. 281 units. Sun–Thurs $119, Fri–Sat $89 double. Children under 17 stay free in parents' room. Each additional person $10. Weekend discounts. AE, CB, DC, DISC, MC, V. Parking $6.

Although not as good as it once was, this is the only member of a major chain in the downtown area. Parking is not a problem, because a seven-story garage is available. The hotel shares a building with the Greensboro Athletic Club. The lobby, rising three floors, is impressive, and the health club joined to the hotel is the best in the city. It's got everything: indoor pool, whirlpool, weight machines, and fitness staff. Bedrooms are spacious, with big windows—the best feature, because the decor is lackluster. The rooms offer double or king-size beds and such extras as coffeemakers. The hotel has two bars and a reasonably priced restaurant.

Park Lane Hotel-Four Seasons. 3005 High Point Rd., Greensboro, NC 27403. ☎ **336/ 294-4565.** Fax 336/294-0572. 165 units. $90 double, $155–$250 suite. Extra person in room $10. Children under 16 stay free in parents' room. Rates include continental breakfast. AE, CB, DC, DISC, MC, V. Free parking.

Vastly improved in recent years, this motor hotel on the road to High Point is well run and intimate. Its major competitors are the mammoth Holiday Inn-Four Seasons, rising 17 floors with 524 rooms, and the less glamorous 175-room Howard Johnson Coliseum. All these hotels are crawling with business clients during the week; the pace slows on weekends. We give the nod to Park Lane because it's got better and more personal service than the other giants. Its rooms are comfortably and attractively furnished; some have whirlpools and refrigerators. Suites have wet bars. Some units are especially designed for people with disabilities. Facilities include a heated pool, a sauna, an exercise room, a coin laundry, and nonsmoking rooms. A restaurant serves soups and sandwiches, and a bar is open Monday to Friday from 4:30 to 10pm.

WHERE TO DINE

Cellar Anton's. 1628 Battleground Ave. ☎ **336/273-1386.** Salads and sandwiches $4–$6.50; dinner main courses $8.95–$19.95. AE, MC, V. Mon–Sat 11am–10pm, Sat 4:30–10:30pm. Closed major holidays. INTERNATIONAL.

The loyal local clientele keeps returning—for the food, not the decor. Wholesome cookery at moderate tabs is the deal here. The no-nonsense menu of steak, pasta, and seafood succeeds because the ingredients are fresh and deftly handled. Lunch can be simple fare, such as salad and sandwiches, but at night, the chef reveals more talent. The cooking and homespun charm of the staff left us well fed and smiling.

Gate City Chop House. 106 S. Holden St. ☎ **336/294-9977.** Reservations recommended. Main courses $8–$28. AE, DC, DISC, MC, V. Mon–Fri 11:30am–10pm, Sat 4:30–10:30pm. STEAK/CONTINENTAL.

With a menu especially for the carnivore, the Gate City Chop House takes pride in the number of Black Angus steaks it cooks every night. Five dining areas frame the large salad bar in the center of the restaurant. It's a child-friendly place with a kids' menu. In addition to steaks, the restaurant serves well-prepared chicken and grilled fish, as well as pork chops that would please Andy Griffith. A bar and wine list round out your options.

Southern Lights. 105 N. Smyres Place. ☎ **336/379-9414.** Reservations not accepted. Main courses $10.95–$18.95. Mon–Fri 11:30am–2pm and 5:30–10pm, Sat, Sun 5:30–10pm. AE, MC, V. BISTRO.

This is the best of the city's bistros, a bright and airy place offering freshly prepared food made with choice ingredients. As a budget eatery, it draws a fair share of young people. Enough variety is on the menu to make it appealing for lunch or dinner. Pecan-crusted flounder with mango sauce is likely to appear. You can also check out the blackboard specials. No single dish seems to merit separate praise. If red bean hummus isn't your thing, you can always ask the chef to put a steak on the grill and go heavy on the barbecued onions. After all, this is North Carolina, not Paris, but a culinary surprise nonetheless. You can also order 10 or more wines by the glass—a nice touch, as Hemingway would say.

GREENSBORO AFTER DARK

Music, drama, art, and dance flourish in Greensboro, which is no longer the country town that it once was. At the **Eastern Music Festival,** held over 6 weeks every summer, 300 professional musicians and students from the United States and abroad perform about 40 classical concerts. The visitors' bureau will have complete details.

The Community Theater of Greensboro, 200 N. Davie St. (☎ **336/333-7470**), has been presenting Broadway shows and musicals for nearly half a century. It also offers classical and contemporary drama.

The **Carolina Theatre,** 310 S. Greene St. (☎ **336/333-2600**), opened in 1927 as a venue for vaudeville. Listed on the National Register of Historic Places, it is now a showcase for theater, dance, concerts, and films.

In a lighter vein, the **Barn Dinner Theatre,** 120 Stage Coach Trail (☎ **336/292-2211**), presents Broadway-type plays after a hearty buffet, complete with such dishes as roast top sirloin and baked Alaskan halibut. It is one of the oldest dinner theaters in the country. Dinner and performances take place Wednesday to Sunday from January through November, and 7 days a week in December, from 6 to 10:30pm. Admission costs $25 Wednesday, Thursday, and Sunday, and $34 Friday and Saturday.

The **Comedy Zone,** Holden and Patterson St. (☎ **336/333-1034**), features some of the country's funniest comedians on Friday and Saturday night. It was recently voted Greensboro's best place to go on a date. Admission charges are $8 to $10 per person. One show Friday is at 9pm, with two shows Saturday at 8 and at 10pm.

6 Charlotte

143 miles SW of Raleigh; 91 S of Winston-Salem

In the past decade or so, Charlotte has been sprouting skyscrapers, including the 40-story, trapezoidal steel-and-glass tower of the Bank of America Plaza and the stunning 46-story Hearst Tower, the completion of which was set for 2001. The city has attracted wildly successful professional basketball and football teams—the Charlotte Hornets and the Carolina Panthers, respectively, both of which have become instantly popular in this sports-mad region. Suburban districts have mushroomed, with landscaped housing developments and enormous shopping malls springing up in every direction. This is the New South, built squarely on the foundation of the Old South.

The largest city in the Piedmont, Charlotte was named for George III's wife, Queen Charlotte. Evidently, however, its residents didn't take their royal affiliation too seriously. When Lord Cornwallis occupied the town briefly in 1780, he was so annoyed by patriot activities that he called it a "hornet's nest," a name that has been proudly incorporated into the city seal.

Indeed, more than a year before the Declaration of Independence was signed in Philadelphia, the Mecklenburg Declaration, proclaiming independence from Britain, was signed in Charlotte on May 20, 1775. The Captain James Jack monument (211 W. Trade St.) is a memorial to the man who carried the document on horseback to Philadelphia and the Continental Congress. According to Charlotte's citizens, Thomas Jefferson used their declaration as a model for the one that he wrote.

In 1865, Confederate President Jefferson Davis convened his last full cabinet meeting here. After the Confederacy fell and the local boys came home from war, the city set out on a course that eventually led it to a position of industrial leadership in the South. The Catawba River provided water power for the rapid development of manufacturing plants and textile mills. Today, more than 600 textile plants lie within a 100-mile radius.

For years, the Charlotte region was also the nation's major gold producer. A branch of the U.S. Mint was located here from 1837 to 1913. The exquisite 1835 mint building, designed by William Strickland, is now part of the Mint Museum, which houses one of the southern Atlantic region's major art collections.

Today, the city is booming, and business is just fine, thank you very much. The banking, insurance, and transportation industries keep feeding the economy. With all this growth, a new generation of Charlotteans is champing at the bit for recognition that their city has hit the big time. There's not much here for the casual tourist, but business travelers are certainly coming to town in droves.

ESSENTIALS

GETTING THERE　North–south routes through Charlotte are I-85 and I-77; I-40, a major east–west highway, crosses I-77 some 40 miles to the north. Contact the AAA through the **Carolina Motor Club,** 9433 Pineville-Matthews Road, Suite A, Pineville, NC 28134 (☎ **704/541-7409**).

　　Charlotte-Douglas International Airport (☎ **704/359-4000**) is served by **American Airlines** (☎ 800/433-7300; www.aa.com); **British Airways** (☎ 800/ AIRWAYS; www.british-airways.com); **Air Canada** (☎ 800/776-3000; www. aircanada.ca); **Colgan** (☎ 800/272-5488; www.colganair.com); **Continental Airlines** (☎ 800/525-0280; www.flycontinental.com); **Delta Air Lines, Delta ASA,** and **Delta Comair** (☎ 800/221-1212; www.delta.com); **Northwest Airlines** (☎ 800/225-2525; www.nwa.com); **Trans World Airlines** (☎ 800/221-2000; www.twa.com); **United Airlines** (☎ 800/241-6522; www.ual.com); and **US Airways** and **US Airways Express** (☎ 800/428-4322; www.usairways.com).

　　The daily **Amtrak** (☎ **800/USA-RAIL**) service to Washington, D.C., and Atlanta through Charlotte both depart in the early-morning hours.

VISITOR INFORMATION　Contact the **Charlotte Convention & Visitors Bureau,** 122 E. Stonewall St., Charlotte, NC 28202 (☎ **800/231-4636** or 704/334-2282; www.charlottecvb.org), open Monday to Friday from 8:30am to 5pm, Saturday 9am to 4pm, Sunday 1 to 4pm. **Charlotte Transit** (☎ **704/336-3366**) can furnish local bus routes and schedule information.

SPECIAL EVENTS　In late April, **Springfest** is a three-day festival held in uptown Charlotte. The streets come alive with music and other entertainment, and street vendors dispense a wide variety of foods. In late May, the **Coca-Cola 600** packs 'em in at the Charlotte Motor Speedway (call ☎ **704/455-3200** for details). For six full days in mid-September, the **Festival in the Park** in Freedom Park celebrates regional arts and crafts.

SEEING THE SIGHTS

If you're in Charlotte during April and May, drive north on N.C. 49 to the **University of North Carolina at Charlotte** campus to see the **botanical gardens** (☎ **704/ 547-2364**) in full bloom. The gardens are a wonderland of rhododendrons, azaleas, and native Carolina trees, shrubs, wildflowers, and ferns. A tropical-rain-forest conservatory is in the gardens' McMillan Greenhouse. Open Monday to Saturday 10am to 3pm.

Mint Museum of Art. 2730 Randolph Rd. ☎ **704/337-2000.** Admission $6 adults, $4 students and seniors, free for children 12 and under, free for everyone Tues 5–10pm. Tues 10am–10pm, Wed–Sat 10am–5pm, Sun noon–5pm. Closed Mon and holidays.

With the recently added Dalton Wing, this stately museum displays a fine survey of European and American art, as well as the internationally recognized Delhom Collection of porcelain and pottery. Also featured are pre-Columbian art, contemporary American prints, African objects, vast collections of costumes and antique maps, and gold coins originally minted at the facility. New galleries exhibit studio glass and pottery from North Carolina studios.

Discovery Place Science & Technology Center. 301 N. Tryon St. ☎ **800/935-0553** or 704/372-6261. Admission $6.50 adults, $5 children 6–12, $2.75 children 3–5, free for children 2 and under. Mon–Sat 9am–6pm, Sun 1–6pm.

Charlotte

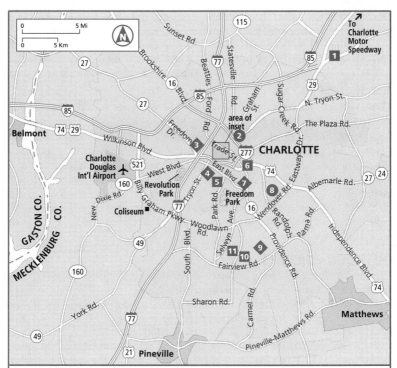

Downtown Charlotte

ACCOMMODATIONS ■
Adam's Mark Hotel **6**
Dunhill **12**
Hyatt Charlotte **11**
The Morehead Inn **5**
Park Hotel **10**
Residence Inn by Marriott **1**

DINING ◆
The Coffee Cup **3**
La Bibliothèque **9**
Lamp Lighter **4**
Mangione's Italian Ristorante **7**

ATTRACTIONS ●
Mint Museum of Art **8**
Discovery Place **2**

Discovery Place is one of the top hands-on science and technology museums in the region. This uptown center features such permanent exhibits as a tropical rain forest and aquarium. There's an OMNIMAX theater, plus a Kelly Space Voyager Planetarium. The static-electricity demonstration, which literally makes your hair stand on end, is a perennial favorite. Temporary exhibits on loan from other science centers keep the place forever changing.

✪ **Wing Haven Gardens & Bird Sanctuary.** 248 Ridgewood Ave. ☎ **704/331-0664.** Free admission. Tues 3–5pm, Wed 10am–noon, Sun 2–5pm.

Since 1927, one of Charlotte's special attractions, created by Elizabeth and Edwin Clarkson, has been a 3-acre enclosed area in the heart of a residential neighborhood. Mrs. Clarkson was known as the city's "bird lady." Some 142 winged species have been sighted in the walled garden, which was once a bare clay field. Birders and garden lovers will have a field day as they browse through the Upper, Lower, Main, Wild, Herb, and Rose gardens. The gardens are at their most splendid in the spring, when birds are returning from their winter migration. A bulletin board tells you which birds are around at the moment.

OUTDOOR PURSUITS

Charlotte is ringed by nature preserves and parks, including the nearly 1,000-acre **McDowell Park and Nature Preserve,** about 12 miles south of the city center on N.C. 49 (☎ **704/588-5224**). Its heart is Lake Wylie, which has a white-sand beach. The preserve has many hiking trails, and paddleboats can be rented on the lake. Swimming isn't allowed, but fishing is. Call for more information.

Even bigger is **Latta Plantation Park,** the largest in the county, at 5225 Sample Rd. in Huntersville (☎ **704/875-1391**), 12 miles northeast of the city center. It's a favorite resting place for waterfowl, and has some 2,500 acres devoted to nature. It also has stables where you can rent horses and ride along some 7 miles of trail. A nature center, playground, and picnic tables are available. Fishing is permitted; swimming is not.

For **bikers,** the best route is between Southpark and uptown Charlotte. If you'd like a route map, write the North Carolina Department of Transportation, P.O. Box 25201, Raleigh, NC 27611.

Because there are so many **fishing** possibilities in the Greater Charlotte area, you may want to obtain a state license from the North Carolina Wildlife Commission; call ☎ **919/733-3391** for more information.

Tennis is available at many places in the area, including several city parks. Among the best are Hornet's Nest, Park Road, and Freedom. The Charlotte Park and Recreation Department (☎ **704/336-3854**) will advise you on which ones are closest to your hotel or motel, assuming that there isn't a court where you're staying. The people of Charlotte, like those in all Piedmont cities, are devoted to golf. The **Visitor Information Center** (☎ **704/334-2282**) has a complete list of courses that are open to the public.

WHERE TO STAY
EXPENSIVE

Adam's Mark Hotel. 555 S. McDowell St., Charlotte, NC 28204. ☎ **800/444-2326** or 704/372-4100. Fax 704/348-4645. www.adamsmark.com. E-mail: bwhelan@adamsmark.co. 613 units. A/C TV TEL. $89–$189 double; $250–$550 suite. Children 18 and under stay free in parents' room. AE, CB, DC, DISC, MC, V. Parking $5.

Less than six blocks from the center of town and only four blocks from the convention center, the 18-story Adam's Mark is a staple of the Charlotte skyline and the hotel scene. We like some of its competitors better, but this place has its fans in the convention crowd. It also has the city's best staff; not only are they efficient, but they're also genuinely courteous and helpful. Dark woods are used in the sleek, spacious lobby, which is a prelude to the spacious, well-maintained bedrooms. Rooms have either one king-size bed or two double beds, and many open onto panoramic cityscapes or offer balconies.

Dining/Diversions: Guests can dine casually and informally in one of the hotel restaurants, although a more formal room offers Italian cuisine with continental flair. This room opens onto views of the pool. For entertainment, waiters serenade the clients. Of the two lounges, one is a tranquil oasis, and the other is hopping with energy, music, and a lot of local young people, especially on weekends.

Amenities: Room service, laundry, free shuttle for shopping trips, two pools, racquetball courts, sauna, fitness room, and whirlpool.

✪ **Hyatt Charlotte.** 5501 Carnegie Blvd. (opposite South Park Mall), Charlotte, NC 28209. ☎ **800/228-9000** or 704/554-1234. Fax 704/554-8319. www.hyatt.com. 266 units. A/C TV TEL. $137–$200 double Sun–Thurs, $99–$120 double Fri–Sat; $380–$659 suite. Children 18 and under stay free in parents' room. AE, CB, DC, DISC, MC, V. Free parking.

In the luxury market, this would be choice no. 2 in Charlotte, outdistanced only by the Park. One of the most stunning choices in western North Carolina, it's 4 miles south of the heart of the city. A seven-story brown brick building accented by greenish glass, it has a four-story atrium and a lobby with a Mexican fountain and an inviting atmosphere. The bedrooms have a decor of inoffensive pastels and well-equipped baths with marble vanity tables. Rooms are also equipped with data ports for laptops and fax machines.

Dining/Diversions: The slant in the more formal restaurant, Scalini's, is northern Italian. You can have a before-dinner drink in the sports bar.

Amenities: Room service (24 hours), laundry/valet service, and free airport transportation. Guests at the health club expend some energy on bikes and at workout stations or enjoy the indoor pool, sauna, and whirlpool.

✪ **The Morehead Inn.** 1122 E. Morehead St., Charlotte, NC 28204. ☎ **888/MOREHEAD** or 704/376-3357 Fax 704/335-1110. www.moreheadinn.com. E-mail:morehead@ charlotte.infi.net. 12 suites. A/C TV TEL $120–$190 double. Rates include breakfast. AE, DC, DISC, MC, V.

This southern estate lies in one of Charlotte's oldest neighborhoods, just minutes from uptown. With its tranquil elegance and fine antiques, it is easily one of the finer inns in western North Carolina. Installed in the historic Dilworth home, the inn is a popular center for local weddings. Its public areas are spacious but offer many cozy nooks, often with intimate fireplaces. Eight private suites are in the main house, and a secluded carriage house across the courtyard offers an additional quartet of suites. The furnishings are tasteful and comfortable. One favorite is "The Romany," a corner room with a queen-size four-poster and a separate office den. "The Mt. Vernon" has a king-size sleigh bed facing an original fireplace, along with a large sunroom.

Dining: Breakfast is the only meal served, but the staff will direct you to many good restaurants nearby for lunch and dinner.

Amenities: Room service limited to crackers, cheese, and fruit; passes to local YMCA.

✪ **Park Hotel.** 2200 Rexford Rd., Charlotte, NC 28211. ☎ **800/334-0331** or 704/364-8220. Fax 704/365-4712. www.theparkhotel.com. 202 units. A/C TV TEL. $165–$220 double; $395–$1,095 suite. Children 17 and under stay free in parents' room. AE, CB, DC, DISC, MC, V. Free parking.

This is Charlotte's four-star hotel. If money is no object, stay here and enjoy the classic styling, with fluted columns and tasteful, luxurious appointments. In Southpark's commercial center, this six-story hostelry attracts those discriminating travelers who want the ultimate in city comfort. The green marble floors are matched by upholstery in Caribbean sea-green colors—an effect that is tasteful and stylish. The bedrooms, the best in town, often have a set of double beds or sometimes a four-poster king-size bed. Commodious bathrooms with marble vanity tables are featured, along with several thoughtful extras, such as irons and ironing boards. Some accommodations contain refrigerators.

Dining/Diversions: The restaurant is elegant; the service, attentive and unobtrusive. A refined and quite sophisticated cuisine is served, and in summer, guests can enjoy piano music Wednesday to Saturday.

Amenities: Room service (24 hours), laundry/valet service, airport transportation, outdoor pool, indoor whirlpool, sauna, and fitness room (with exercise equipment, weight machines, bicycles, and steam room).

MODERATE

Dunhill. 237 N. Tryon St., Charlotte, NC 28202. ☎ **800/354-4141** or 704/332-4141. Fax 704/376-4117. www.dunhillhotel.com. E-mail: choun@bellsouth.net. 60 units. A/C TV TEL. Sun–Thurs $199 double, Fri–Sat $139 double; $179–$299 suite. Children 15 and under stay free in parents' room. AE, CB, DC, DISC, MC, V.

Constructed in 1929, this is one of Charlotte's oldest and most historic hotels. These days, the big names often go elsewhere, but old-timers still prefer the Dunhill's European-style comfort and charm. (The doorman out front often greets returning guests by name.) In the old days, it was called the Mayfair Manor, and some of its most loyal clients still refer to it that way. The artwork in the public areas is by North Carolinian Philip Moose, and a piano player entertains in the stylish lobby. The restored guest rooms have a warm, cozy feeling; they're furnished with handsome reproductions and often with four-poster beds. Monticello's is the hotel restaurant, offering excellent cuisine throughout the day. Health-club privileges can be arranged, and such exercise equipment as a stair machine and treadmill are on-site.

INEXPENSIVE

Residence Inn by Marriott. 8503 N. Tryon Rd., Charlotte, NC 28262. ☎ **800/331-3131** or 704/547-1122. Fax 704/549-1370. www.marriott.com. 91 units. A/C TV TEL. $99–$129 1-bedroom and studio suite; $145 2-bedroom suite. AE, CB, DC, DISC, MC, V. Free parking.

One of the two upscale Marriott facilities in the area, this one is located on the north side of town. Guests enjoy the barbecue and picnic facilities, the swimming pool, and the heated whirlpool. Good restaurants are within easy reach. All the comfortably furnished units have full kitchens, complete with microwave ovens; most have wood-burning fireplaces. Rooms are 50% larger than in most conventional hotels. There's a guest laundry, and each unit has a private entrance with parking just outside. The hotel is wheelchair-accessible, and fitness equipment is available.

WHERE TO DINE

La Bibliothèque. In the Morrison Office Building, 1901 Roxborough Rd. ☎ **704/365-5000.** Reservations required. Jackets preferred for men at dinner. Main courses $7–$11.95 at lunch, $9.95–$23 at dinner. AE, DC, DISC, MC, V. Mon–Fri 11:30am–2:30pm and 5:30–10:30pm, Sat 5:30–10:30pm. FRENCH/INTERNATIONAL.

Relaxation and elegance are virtually guaranteed the moment you step inside this formal dining room, which serves the city's finest French cuisine. The service is formal and efficient, yet friendly and not intimidating. Some of Charlotte's rising young

Finger-Lickin' Down-Home Cooking

Locals are proud of their fancy new restaurants, but sometimes they just want to escape to a roadside dump where—as they say in the South—"all God's children got chicken grease on their fingers." Chris Crowder's place, ✪ **The Coffee Cup,** is where to go. It's in a cinder-block structure across from a garage in an area of truck firms and warehouses. Expect Formica-topped tables, with a bottle of Texas Pete on every one. Vintage soul pours from a jukebox at least 3 decades old. A vivacious mama, Crowder runs the joint and treats her preferred customers very, very familiarly (even calling one of them "Meatball"—a woman, at that!).

When the place opened in the '40s, only whites could dine inside; black customers had to order takeout through a side window (still here, but covered in plywood). Even the toilets once used by black patrons are still outside. "They were good enough for us, and they're good enough for you," Crowder tells her white customers who ask.

In the kitchen, Crowder is called "Alma Fudd" (her nickname) when she starts pan-frying chicken. Locals drive for miles to eat this chicken with their fingers. The menu is not all black soul food. In the '80s, Crowder teamed up with Mary Lou Maynor, a former waitress and a white woman who grew up on a farm in North Carolina. They taught each other the differences between white and black cooking (black cooks in the South traditionally prefer bolder seasonings, for example). "One thing Mary Lou taught me," Crowder says, "was how to make those casseroles you find at so many white church suppers. I still serve my former partner's signature dish: chicken casserole. You white people sure like your casseroles."

The Coffee Cup is at 914 S. Clarkson St. (☎ **704/375-8855**). It's open Monday to Friday from 6am to 3pm and Saturday from 6am to noon. Reservations are recommended. The set breakfast costs $4.35; the set lunch is $5.85. The restaurant doesn't take credit cards but will "gladly accept cash."

professionals take their favored business clients here for dinner. "We're not New York, but we're getting there," one of them said to me. The cooking is worth traveling across the city to sample, and the chef is especially talented in handling seafood from the Carolina coast, although beef and veal dishes are also prepared with flair. Much of the menu depends on the inspiration of the moment. Signature dishes include Dover sole, châteaubriand, and rack of lamb.

Lamp Lighter. 1065 E. Morehead St. ☎ **704/372-5343.** Reservations required. Jacket required for men at dinner. Main courses $17–$45. AE, CB, DC, DISC, MC, V. Mon–Thurs 5:30–10pm, Fri–Sat 5:30–10:30pm, Sun 5:30–9:30pm. FRENCH/CONTINENTAL.

In the 1926 Spanish colonial–style Dilworth house, this is one of Charlotte's three leading restaurants, drawing the business elite during the week and the family trade on Friday and Saturday nights. The restaurant has a tranquil lounge for a before-dinner drink and intimate conversation. Later, you're shown to a beautifully set table in a softly lighted dining nook. The chef's culinary skills are excellent. A trio of meats—tender beef, succulent lamb, and delectable veal—is perfectly satisfying. Maine lobster is also featured, and fresh seafood appears from the Carolina coastal areas. Another specialty, in season, is wild game. Carolina quail is fried in buttermilk and served with cheese grits.

Mangione's Italian Ristorante. 1524 East Blvd. ☎ **704/334-4417.** Reservations required. Main courses $11.99–$18.99. AE, DC, DISC, MC, V. Mon–Sat 5:30–11:30pm. ITALIAN.

Roberto and Anna Maria, your hosts, prepare the city's finest Italian cuisine, much of it inspired by their native island of Sicily. They have brought to Charlotte a love of old-fashioned recipes such as handmade pastas; many of their dishes are almost unknown in the area. They celebrate traditional Sicilian gatherings where the dinner becomes the reason to bring family and friends together. Ingredients are fresh and wisely fashioned into an array of tempting delights. Pasta lovers alone can try the typical lasagna of Sicily—that is, layered with creamy bechamel sauce, sausage, and meat, topped with mozzarella, and baked in the oven until it's a golden brown. The house pasta comes with sun-dried tomatoes and quartered artichoke hearts sautéed with fresh garlic and extra virgin olive oil, finished with a white wine sauce on a bed of linguini. The antipasti is almost worthy of a meal in itself, including prosciutto wrapped in fresh mozzarella made by Roberto, or else a soup of the day influenced by the season, region, or the whims of the chef. Meat and poultry dishes are excellent, including a fresh fish of the day or boneless breast of chicken cacciatore.

CHARLOTTE AFTER DARK

The **Charlotte Symphony Orchestra** (☎ 704/332-6136) season runs from September to April; check local newspapers or call for performance dates. **Opera Carolina** (☎ 704/332-7177) presents performances from October to April, and the **Charlotte Pops** (☎ 704/332-0468) gives outdoor concerts (small fee) in Freedom Park on Sunday evenings in the summer. Classic plays are often performed by **Theatre Charlotte,** 501 Queens Rd. (☎ 704/376-3777), usually Thursday to Sunday. The **Blumenthal Performing Arts Center,** 130 N. Tryon St. (☎ 704/373-1000), is the newest facility to join the performance venues; it features three theaters for various productions, ranging from rock concerts to intimate stage events.

If you're in town and want to catch a live professional basketball or football game, a limited number of single-game tickets are available. For tickets to see the **Charlotte Hornets,** you can buy them direct at the Charlotte Coliseum Box Office (100 Paul Buck Blvd; Mon–Sat, 10am–5pm, Sun 1–5pm) or order them through TicketMaster (**704/522-6500**). For tickets to see the **Carolina Panthers,** visit the Ericsson Stadium Ticket Office (800 S. Mint St., southeast side of the stadium; Mon–Fri, 8:30am–5:30pm) or order through TicketMaster (see above).

Double Door Inn. 218 E. Independence Blvd. ☎ **704/376-1446.** Cover $6–$15 when music is offered.

Some of the blues musicians that appeared here went on to become famous: Willie Dixon, Buddy Guy, and Stevie Ray Vaughn. The setting is a renovated 1920s house on the border of downtown Charlotte and the Elizabeth district, with a likable, battered, absolutely unpretentious ambience. You might catch a zydeco band, if you're lucky. Although the place is open Monday to Friday from 11 to 2am and on Saturday and Sunday from 8pm to 2am, live music is featured only between 10pm and 2am nightly.

Mythos. 6th St. at N. College St. ☎ **704/375-8765.** Cover $4.

This place markets itself as an "alternative/progressive" nightclub and prides itself on an urban hip that's as cool as it is permissive. After you pay your $10-a-year membership fee, plus cover charge, no one will care what you do, as long as it isn't uncool or dangerous. A phone call in advance will tell you what's going on that night: Anything's possible; styles range from techno-rave to "disco-trash" (usually imported direct from counterculture clubs in New York or Los Angeles). There's always a mixture of gays and straights. Sunday-night parties are by far the most overtly gay, featuring drag shows by the best divas of the Southeast. Open 10 to 2am.

Scorpio. 2301 Freedom Dr. ☎ **704/373-9124.** Cover $5.

This popular lesbian and gay nightclub has been going strong for years. Many gays drive for miles—even from across the border in Tennessee—to have a lively night on the town at this bustling joint. Actually, it's several clubs within a club. There's a large dance bar that attracts "same-sexualists" (to use Gore Vidal's term). There's also a country bar called the Queen City Saloon. On certain Friday and Saturday nights, the crowd is so vast here that you'll think everybody in Charlotte has gone gay—at least for the night. The club is open nightly from 9pm to 2am.

Swing 1000. 1000 Central Ave. ☎ **704/334-4443.** Reservations required. Tues–Wed 6–10pm, Thurs 6–11pm, Fri–Sat 6pm–midnight. No cover.

If you want to swing back to the times when stars such as Louis Armstrong were on the radio, Swing 1000 will take you on a journey into nostalgia. This nightclub/restaurant combines a flavorful continental cuisine with retro-style entertainment and dancing to live music. The house band plays '30s and '40s Big Band, featuring songs from Benny Goodman and Glenn Miller, and draws an ardent crowd, mostly in their 20s and 30s. Don't look for campy themes here—the music is delivered with a serious respect for original authenticity. Tuesday (with a D.J.) and Wednesday are dance-lesson nights. The food is much better than you'd expect, and includes such specialties as filet mignon with caramelized red onions and grilled seafood along with pasta dishes to please vegetarians. Prices run from $18 to $35, with a three-course fixed-price meal for $39.99.

6 Southern Pines & the Pinehurst Sandhills

The Sandhills' porous, sandy soil is a reminder that in prehistoric times, this land was under the rolling waters of the Atlantic. This soil provides the ideal drainage that's crucial to the "Golf Capital of the World," for no matter what the rainfall, no puddles accumulate on its rolling golf courses. And with mean temperatures ranging between 44°F and 78°F, the game is played here year-round.

But golf hasn't always been king. When Boston philanthropist James Walker Tufts bought 5,000 acres of land in 1895 for $1 per acre, his plan was to build the little resort village of Pinehurst as a retreat for wealthy Northerners from harsher climes. Recreation then consisted mainly of croquet on the grassy lawns, outdoor concerts, hayrides, and quiet walks through the pines.

Tuft's attention first turned to golf, only recently arrived from Great Britain, when one of his dairy employees complained that guests were "hitting the cows with a little white ball." By 1900, Tufts had enlisted Donald Ross (who had honed his skills at Scotland's St. Andrews) to come to Pinehurst and introduce golf. Ross designed courses here that drew some of the most distinguished golfers in the world: Ben Hogan, Walter Travis, Bobby Jones, Walter Hagen, Patty Berg, Sam Snead, Arnold Palmer, Gary Player, and Jack Nicklaus, to name just a few.

For years, golfing on the superb courses of the Pinehurst Country Club was by invitation only. Even though the golf world's top players still consider Pinehurst to be their own turf, these days you don't have to wait for an invitation—or be a millionaire—to play. Prices are high, but they're not exorbitant compared with those of other luxury resorts around the country. And there are hotels and motels here in almost any price range for experts or duffers who want to play the Pinehurst courses.

In 1973, the first World Open Championship was played in Pinehurst; the event was replaced in 1977 by the Colgate Hall of Fame Classic. In September 1974, President Gerald Ford presided at the opening of the World Golf Hall of Fame, overlooking Ross's famous No. 2 Course (one of the top 10 in the country).

Midland Road (N.C. 2), a highway divided by a stately 6-mile row of pine trees and bordered by sedate homes and lavish gardens, sets the tone for this golf Mecca. From the second green of the Pinehurst No. 2 Golf Course (site of the 1999 U.S. Open) at one end to the little village of Southern Pines at the other, Midland offers an array of both golf courses and lodges. About a third of the area's more than 35 courses are accessible via this road.

Also on Midland Road, you'll pass a rambling white building called **Midland Crafters,** which houses a virtual survey of American crafts, from beanbags to paintings to furniture to pottery to glassware, or almost any handcraft you can conjure up. Over the years, this region has drawn artists, craftspeople, and potters. Scattered around the vicinity in rustic, pine-sheltered workshops, many of the potters welcome visitors, and most are quite happy to have you watch them at their work.

In addition to golf, competitive **tennis** made its mark when the first major tournament, the United North and South Tennis Tournament, hit the courts of the Pinehurst Tennis Club in 1918. That amateur event ran until 1942 and was the proving ground for many nationally ranked players, including the Davis Cup Team of the 1930s. Today, this area enjoys a reputation for some of America's best tennis facilities and programs.

The Sandhills region is also known for its **equestrian competitions.** Most of these events are free to spectators. *Horse Days,* a monthly publication about events that features calendar listings, is available locally at information offices. From late October to May, there are horse trials, shows, or even fox hunts. "Is there really a fox?", we asked a dapper man in a traditional "pink" hunt jacket, knee-high riding boots, and a tall hat, who was sitting straight in the saddle. "Sometimes," he responded.

1 Pinehurst

71 miles SW of Raleigh

Pinehurst, built by Frederick Law Olmsted (the architect/landscaper who planned New York's Central Park), has retained its New England village air, with a town green and shaded residential streets. Year-round greenery is provided by pines (some with needles 15 inches long), stately magnolias, and hollies. Moderate temperatures mean color through all seasons: camellias, azaleas, wisteria, dogwoods, and summer-blooming flowers. Shops, restaurants, hotels, and other business enterprises make this community self-sufficient. Pinehurst offers plenty of recreational facilities for those who aren't interested in chasing after that little white ball: a tennis club with excellent courts; more than 200 miles of riding trails, as well as stables with good mounts for hire; boating on a 200-acre lake; trap and skeet ranges; archery; 9,000 acres of woods to explore via meandering pathways; and, of course, shopping in the boutiques.

But golf is definitely king. If there's a hotel or motel in the area that doesn't arrange play for its guests, we couldn't find it. For a complete list of golf courses, ask the visitor bureau (see "Essentials," below) for its *"Accommodations/Golfing"* brochure.

ESSENTIALS

GETTING THERE   U.S. 1 runs north and south through Southern Pines; N.C. 211 runs east and west; U.S. 15/501 reaches Pinehurst from the north; there's direct area access to I-95, I-85, and I-40. You really need a car to get around this entire area.

Raleigh/Durham is the nearest commercial airport (see "Raleigh," in chapter 5). Moore County has a small private airport with a 5,500-foot runway. An apron extension is planned for 1999. If you are flying in yourself, call for ramp-space reservations (☎ **910/692-3212**). There is a national car-rental desk at the terminal (☎ **910/ 692-4449**), and **Enterprise** will deliver cars from Pinehurst (☎ **910/692-3400**). Call ahead for reservations. **Amtrak** (☎ **800/USA-RAIL**) has one northbound and one southbound train daily through Southern Pines.

VISITOR INFORMATION   We strongly recommend that you write or phone ahead for details on golfing and other sports, sightseeing, accommodations, and dining. Contact the **Pinehurst Area Convention and Visitors Bureau,** P.O. Box

2270, Southern Pines, NC 28388 (☎ **800/346-5362** or 910/692-3330; www. homeofgolf.com).

HITTING THE LINKS

Pinehurst is like a quaint village with the kind of total-golf atmosphere that you find in St. Andrews in Scotland. With its more than 35 superb championship golf courses, some of which are among the highest-rated in the world, the town represents golf's grandest era. Legends were born and nurtured here—names such as Nelson, Zaharias, Jones, Hogan, Snead, and Palmer. Some of the finest golf architects of the 20th century designed courses in the area, Donald Ross, Ellis Maples, and Robert Trent Jones among them.

The courses here are too numerous to recommend. Following are our favorites.

The Club at Longleaf, Pinehurst (☎ **800/889-5323** or 910/692-6100), was called by *Golf Digest* "the most playable course in Pinehurst." It was designed by Dan Maples, architect of the nationally acclaimed Pit Golf Links. The front nine at Longleaf was designed in the Scottish open style, with rolling fairways. Greens fees cost $80, or $90 with cart rental.

Legacy Golf Links, U.S. 15/501 South, Aberdeen (☎ **800/344-8825** or 910/944-8825), is the only golf club in the area to blend the accessibility of a public course with the amenities of a private club. It's also the only public course to receive *Golf Digest*'s four-star rating. Greens fees are $42 per person including cart rental.

The ☼ **Pine Needles Resort,** Southern Pines (☎ **910/692-7111**), is a Donald Ross masterpiece built in 1927, a challenging par-71 course for golfers of all skill levels. The course, playing to 6,708 yards from the championship tees, has been immaculately groomed and restored to its original splendor. Its Bermuda fairways and bent-grass greens are available only to guests staying at the Pine Needles. Greens fees are $150. Package rates are also available in combination with hotel tariffs.

Pinehurst Hotel & Country Club, Carolina Vista at Pinehurst (☎ **800/ ITS-GOLF** or 910/295-6811), is the only resort with seven signature courses. You have to spend at least one night at the hotel to access any of these courses. The original architect was Donald Ross. This is golf in the grandest tradition, and shots played by Hogan, Nelson, and Jones still echo down the fairways. For these 126 holes of golf, the classic designs are by Donald Ross and Ellis Maples; the modern concepts are by Tom Fazio and Rees Jones. Greens fees range from $99 to $300 for 18 holes.

OTHER OUTDOOR PURSUITS

Horseback riders can arrange for mounts by calling the **Pinehurst Stables** (☎ **910/ 295-8456**), where expert instruction is offered to novices and superb mounts are available for experienced riders. The stables also offer carriage rides, which are an especially scenic way to see the village, as well as pony rides for children.

Tennis buffs will find nearly 100 public courts in the area; call ☎ **910/947-2504** for locations, hours, and fees. Most of the resorts have their own court facilities. The Pine Needles Lodge and Golf Club has the only local grass courts, and lighted courts are available in both Southern Pines and Aberdeen.

Bicycling is another major sport. The Pinehurst area has long been regarded as a top-flight training area and proving ground for the U.S., Canadian, and other international cycling teams. Riders of all skill levels can enjoy a variety of mapped courses along peaceful lanes and through country villages. Annual cycling events include the **Tour de Moore,** a grueling 100-mile road race held the last Saturday in April around the perimeter of Moore County. This race draws cyclists from all over the world, who compete for the coveted Pinehurst Cup.

The Links of Pinehurst

North Carolina's Pinehurst/Southern Pines firmly reestablished itself as the "Golf Capital of the World" when the United States Golf Association in 1999 made it the site of the U.S. Open Championship, which marked the second time that the U.S. Open has been played in the Southeast (the first time since 1976).

Nowhere in America do golf past and golf present walk hand in hand as they do in Pinehurst. The area is a museum of golf architecture and a living laboratory of golf design. When the greens of Pinehurst No. 2 were dug up and resurfaced with bent grass in 1987, workers found an old horseshoe buried under the 18th green—a souvenir left by one of the animals that used to drag and shape the putting surface some 80 years ago. When Rees Jones, the famous golf architect, was walking through the woods in 1984, laying out holes for Pinehurst No. 7, he came across several ancient bunkers of a long-abandoned golf course. He ordered the bunkers restored, and they sit today in front of the tee to the fourth hole.

Some holes are nearly a century old, and others have small greens rounded off on the corners—the "upside-down-saucer" effect that Scotsman Donald Ross used so frequently. Some courses have huge greens that require a 7-iron approach if the pin's at the front and a 4-iron if it's in the rear. Still other holes require heroic shots over water or pits of sand, and some have open green entrances that invite the old bump-and-run shot.

The first 18-hole course opened in 1899 and was laid out by Dr. D. LeRoy Culver of New York. Since then, the array of architects has included Ellis and Dan Maples, Tom Fazio, Robert Trent Jones, Peter Tufts, and (one of the latest) Arnold Palmer. And, since a father and son named Nicklaus each won the prestigious North and South Amateur, it's fitting that each has a golf course in the Pinehurst area. Jack, Sr., who won the 1959 North and South, as well as the 1975 Open, completed Pinehurst National in 1989. Jack, Jr., won the 1985 North and South, and completed the Legacy Golf Links in 1991.

Because of the lack of bicycle-rental shops in the area, hotels keep their own stocks to rent to guests who'd like to cycle along the relatively easy terrain. Traffic is generally light, and conditions for cycling are good.

WHERE TO STAY

Although the ✪ Pinehurst Hotel and Country Club is still *the* place to stay in Pinehurst, several other hotels in the village offer luxury on a smaller scale and graciousness on the same level, at somewhat more moderate prices.

Magnolia Inn. 65 Magnolia Rd. (at Chinquapin Rd.; P.O. Box 818), Pinehurst, NC 28370. ☎ **800/526-5562** or 910/295-6900. Fax 910/215-0858. www.themagnoliainn.com. 11 units. A/C TV. $85–$105 per person. Rates include breakfast and dinner. AE, MC, V.

This three-story, white clapboard building is set in the midst of well-landscaped gardens. *Casablanca*-style fans rotate overhead on the front porch, and out back is a little pool. The rooms are sunny and flowery, with double, queen-size, or twin beds. Some of the bathrooms, with their claw-foot tubs, are a little too old-fashioned for comfort. The Olmsted and Page rooms, each of which has a fireplace, are our favorites. There are no in-room phones. A tavern offers your basic pub menu. Breakfast and dinner are served in the dining room. The fare's seasonings (or lack of them) won't frighten away this inn's mostly older patrons.

Pine Crest Inn. Dogwood Rd. (P.O. Box 879), Pinehurst, NC 28370. ☎ **910/295-6121.** Fax 910/295-4880. www.pinecrestinnpinehurst.com. E-mail: frontdesk@pinecrestinnpinehurst. com. 40 units. A/C TV TEL. $132–$149 double. Rates include breakfast and dinner. Golf and sports packages available. AE, CB, DC, DISC, MC, V.

Right in the heart of the village, the Pine Crest Inn has been described by an English visitor as having "all the flavor and courtesies of our countryside inns." It draws people back year after year. Bob Barrett (proprietor since 1961) tells us that approximately 80 percent of his guests are returnees—and small wonder, for the three-story, white-columned building radiates warmth from the moment you enter the lobby, with its comfortable armchairs, fireplace, and bar. Meals in the three dining rooms (with fireplaces and tasteful wallpaper) are of such quality that they draw people from as far away as Raleigh and Charlotte.

✪ **Pinehurst Hotel and Country Club.** Carolina Vista (P.O. Box 4000), Pinehurst, NC 28374. ☎ **800/487-4653** or 910/295-6811. Fax 910/295-8503. www.Pinehurst.com. 270 units, 170 condos. A/C TV TEL. 3-day, 2-night golf packages $638–$675 per person per night double. Rates include breakfast and dinner. AE, CB, DC, DISC, MC, V.

Established in 1901, this is one of the premier golf and tennis resorts in America. Set on 10,000 acres of landscaped grounds, it's a white, four-story clapboard landmark, with porches lined with comfortable rocking chairs. Many people call it by its longtime name, "The Carolina." Here, the art of gracious living is still practiced. The public spaces and guest rooms have undergone extensive renovation. Bright, cheerful colors predominate in the spacious accommodations, which have an air of subdued elegance. In addition, the resort offers recently renovated villas, which are ideal for foursomes or eightsomes; and there's always the cozy Manor Inn for quiet getaways. Some guests prefer a condo by one of the golf courses or facing Lake Pinehurst. The resort also owns the hotel's newly renovated neighbor, the Holly Inn, a charming turn-of-the-century structure that offers deluxe accommodations and an imported Scottish bar. The Spa, a 28,000-square-foot health-club facility, is scheduled to open in spring 2002.

Dining: For the Carolina Dining Room, see "Where to Dine," below.

Amenities: Service by the resort staff is the finest in North Carolina. The major attraction, of course, is the seven 18-hole golf courses, especially the world-famous No. 2. Five courses begin and end at the elegant original clubhouse; courses 6 and 7 have their own clubhouses. Greens fees vary seasonally, and courses 2 and 7 have a surcharge.

The tennis complex has 26 courts (18 clay, 4 lighted for night play). Clinics and individual instruction are available to all guests. There are nine trap and skeet fields (two lighted), as well as croquet and bowling lawns.

To all this, add bicycles, a huge L-shaped pool and deck area, and 200 acres of fishing, boating, and swimming at Lake Pinehurst, and you have a resort with facilities that are second to none.

WHERE TO DINE

✪ **Carolina Dining Room.** In the Pinehurst Resort and Country Club, Carolina Vista. ☎ **910/295-6811.** Reservations required. Jacket required for men at dinner. Fixed price lunch $17.70. Fixed-price 4-course dinner $50. AE, CB, DC, DISC, MC, V. Daily noon–2pm and 6:30–9:30pm (6–9pm in winter). AMERICAN.

The food here is the finest in the area. Only fresh, first-rate ingredients are used, and the dining room itself is worthy of the cuisine, with its series of Murano (Venetian) chandeliers. The menu is extensive, and the service is impeccable. Seafood fresh from

Carolina coastal waters is presented in classic style. Beef so tender that you can cut it with your fork, along with baby veal and succulently flavored chicken (depending on the whim of the chef that evening) also appear on the menu. There may be either a buffet or a four- or five-course set menu. In either case, the price is the same, although surcharges appear if you order costly ingredients such as rack of lamb, lobster, or prime rib. In summer, there's top-flight entertainment, as well as dinner dancing.

Digins Pub. Market Square. ☎ **910/295-3400.** Reservations recommended on weekends. lunch main courses $7–$14; dinner main courses $9–$25. AE, MC, V. Mon–Sat 11:30am–10:30pm; Sun noon–9:30pm. CONTINENTAL.

Across from the Holly Inn, this is the town's leading independent restaurant. Featuring a nautical decor, with natural woods, it also has a pub. Sandwiches and salads are lunch favorites. At night, a selection of seafood, mainly from Carolina coastal waters, is available. Pasta dishes are often overcooked, but the veal is succulent.

Greenhouse Restaurant. Pinehurst Place, 905 Linden Rd. ☎ **910/295-1761.** Lunch $4.95–$6.95. DISC, MC, V. Daily 11:30am–3pm. Closed holidays. AMERICAN.

The Greenhouse is a light, airy place with blond bentwood chairs and lots of hanging plants. The menu has such specialties as crab and other seafood on a toasted English muffin topped with Cheddar-cheese sauce, as well as specialty meatballs and provolone cheese in a zesty tomato sauce on toasted loaf bread. The soups are homemade, as are desserts such as Greenhouse mud pie and strawberry shortcake. There's a wide selection of beer, mixed drinks, and wine by the glass.

Combine lunch with shopping at the stores in this complex. They're open Monday to Saturday from 11am to 3pm and on Sunday from 11am to 4pm. The shops offer a variety of brass, arts and crafts, baskets, sportswear, and candles.

PINEHURST AFTER DARK

Entertainment is mostly available at the golf resorts. Check, though, to see what's going on at **Sandhills Community College,** Airport Road (☎ 910/692-6185), which often stages jazz and other variety shows, with tickets costing from $5 to $15.

SIDE TRIPS IN THE AREA

✪ SEAGROVE & THE POTTERIES   About an hour's drive to the northwest on U.S. 220 is the little town of Seagrove, which has been turning out quality pottery for more than 200 years. This region's red and gray clays were first used by settlers from Staffordshire, England; the first items produced were jugs for transporting whisky. The same art is practiced today just as it was then. Clays are ground and mixed by machines turned by mules, simple designs are fashioned on kick wheels, and glazing is done in wood-burning kilns. Many of the potters work in or behind their homes, with only a small sign outside to identify their trade. If you have difficulty finding them, stop and ask; everybody does, so don't be shy. There are some sales rooms in town, but the real fun is seeing the pottery actually being made.

While you're there, inquire about **Jugtown,** a group of rustic, log-hewn buildings in a grove of pines, where potters demonstrate their art Monday to Saturday. **Friends of the North Carolina Pottery Center** (☎ 336/873-7887) is located at 250 East Avenue. This office displays examples of most of the potters' wares in the area and also serves as an information center, with guide maps available upon request. It's open Monday to Saturday from 10am to 4pm. Admission is $3 or $1 for children under 12.

Of some 40 potters operating in the Seagrove area, one especially has caught our fancy. At **Walton's Pottery and Blue Moon Gallery,** 1387 S. N.C. 705, Seagrove (☎ 336/879-3270), Susan and Don Walton's potter's wheel turns out delicate cutout candleholders, as well as a full line of more-traditional bowls, vases, teapots, and casseroles. The shop is open Monday to Saturday from 10am to 5pm and Sunday 1 to 5pm. The gallery features the work of artists from all over the country.

ASHEBORO & THE ZOO   A few miles north of Seagrove on U.S. 220 is the town of Asheboro, and 6 miles southeast of Asheboro off U.S. 64 and U.S. 220 is the **North Carolina Zoological Park,** Zoo Parkway, Asheboro (☎ **800/488-0444**). The 300-acre Africa region and the 200-acre North America region are the first of seven continental regions planned for the 1,448-acre park, featuring more than 1,000 animals in natural habitats. In this still-developing world-class zoo, gorillas and 200 rare animals such as meerkats inhabit the African Pavilion. Lions, elephants, bears, bison, elk, alligators, chimpanzees, and many other animals dwell in spacious outdoor habitats. A 37-acre African Plains exhibit is the home of a dozen species of antelope, gazelle, and oryx. The R. J. Reynolds Forest Aviary displays 150 exotic birds flying free amid lush tropical trees and plants. There are picnic areas, restaurants, gift shops, and a tram ride. The zoo is open daily from 9am to 5pm from April to October and 9am to 4pm November to March. The park is closed Christmas Day. Adults pay $8; seniors and children 2 to 12, $5; free for children under 2.

MT. GILEAD   West of Pinehurst, just between N.C. 731 and N.C. 73, ✪ **Town Creek Indian Mound,** Rte. 3, Mt. Gilead (☎ **910/439-6802**), gives you a glimpse into the lives of the Native Americans who established a religious, ceremonial, and burial center some 700 years ago on this bluff overlooking the junction of Little River and Town Creek. The remnants—a major temple, the dwelling place of priests, ceremonial grounds, and many, many artifacts—have been excavated and/or reconstructed. There's no admission charge, but donations are suggested. Open Monday to Saturday 9am to 5pm, Sunday 1 to 5pm.

2 Southern Pines

Less than 5 miles to the east, the pleasant village of Southern Pines has its own attractions. It's rare for a building here to be more than two stories tall. Locals readily admit that the main reason to come here is to follow that little white ball, but they are quick to point out that the town has some interesting sights as well.

SEEING THE SIGHTS

The **Campbell House,** a handsome, Georgian former family residence on East Connecticut Avenue, now houses the Arts Council of Moore County, and its galleries display the work of local artists.

   Shaw House, at Southwest Broad Street and Morganton Road (☎ **910/692-2051**), is a stylish antebellum house with unusual carved-cypress mantels. It's the oldest structure in town, dating from the 1770s, and serves as headquarters of the Moore County Historical Association. It's open Wednesday to Sunday from 1 to 4pm, and admission is free. It's closed during the summer, but tours are available. For information on tour times and operators, call the Shaw House.

   On the Fort Bragg-Aberdeen road, 1 mile southeast of Southern Pines, you'll come to **Weymouth Woods-Sandhills Nature Preserve** (☎ **910/692-2167**), a nature spot with foot and bridle paths and about 600 acres of pine-covered "sand ridges." The natural-history museum is open daily from 9am to 6pm; admission is free.

   You'll find a lot of fine horse farms in the Sandhills. Steeplechasers trained here show up regularly at tracks around the country, and trotters and pacers are also trained in the area. The late Del Cameron, renowned three-time winner of the Hambletonian, kept a winter training stable in the Sandhills for more than 30 years.

SPECIAL EVENTS   The **Mid-South Horse Show Association** holds schooling shows every Sunday afternoon from January to April. In early March, there are the **Moore County Hounds Hunter Trials** at Hobby Field, Southern Pines. The **Stoneybrook Steeplechase Races** are held on the second Saturday in April on a farm near Southern Pines, where racehorses are bred and trained the rest of the year by the Michael G. Walsh family. The **Pinehurst Area Convention and Visitors Bureau,** P.O. Box 2270, Southern Pines, NC 28388, can furnish exact dates and full details on all these events, as well as others throughout the year.

Seek out **Downtown Southern Pines,** U.S. 1 in the Broad Street area, for a collection of shops and restaurants in the historic district.

WHERE TO STAY

Hampton Inn Southern Pines. 1675 U.S. 1 N. Southern Pines 28387. ☎ **910/692-9266.** Fax 910/692-9298. www.hamptoninn.com. 126 units. A/C TV TEL. $79 double. Children 17 and under stay free in parents' room. Golf packages available. Rates include continental breakfast. AE, CB, DC, DISC, MC, V.

Hampton Inn is one of the two leading motels in the area, though it's not quite as good as its major competitor, the Holiday Inn (recommended below). Although decorated in standard chain format, it is one of the better-run inns, with styling in the early American mode. Bedrooms are comfortably furnished, making for an inviting family atmosphere. Rates rise during special events, such as NASCAR races, the PGA tournament, and the Stoneybrook Steeplechase races. Facilities include a swimming pool and a coin laundry. Tennis and golf can be arranged, as can entrance to a nearby health club. There is also a restaurant nearby.

Holiday Inn. P.O. Box 1467 on U.S. 1 at Morganton Rd. Southern Pines 28387. ☎ **800/262-5737** or 910/692-8585. Fax 910/692-5213. www.holiday-inn.com. E-mail: holiday@pinehurst.net. 162 units. A/C TV TEL. $84.99 double. Children 17 and under stay free in parents' room. AE, CB, DC, DISC, MC, V.

This is the best motel in the area, attracting a lot of golfers. Although lacking personality, it compensates with good-size rooms, a high level of housekeeping, and personal service. The staff is helpful, providing such extras as free cribs for families who need them. Room service is also available. The fare in the Hennings Restaurant is only ordinary, but the restaurant is conveniently open throughout the day, beginning breakfast at 6:30am for early risers (usually golfers) and serving its last dinner at 9:30pm. Charbroiled steaks are a specialty. Tams Lounge is for music and dancing.

Hyland Hills Resort. U.S. 1 North, Southern Pines, NC 28387. ☎ **800/841-0638** or 910/692-7615. 41 units. A/C TV TEL. $59 double; $62 efficiency. Golf packages available. MC, V.

In an attractive wooded setting, this small resort is nowhere near the match of such better-known places as Mid Pines, but what it has going for it is economy. The efficiencies and rather spacious bedrooms, often with patios, aren't luxurious in any way, but they're comfortable and well maintained, and you can prepare light meals there. It also has a pool. For a $25-to-$36 fee, you can play an 18-hole course right on the grounds.

✪ **Mid Pines Golf Club.** 1010 Midland Rd., Southern Pines, NC 28387. ☎ **800/323-2114** or 910/692-2114. Fax 910/692-4615. www.rossresorts.com. E-mail: info@rossresorts.com. 118 units, 7 cottages, 10 lakeside villas. A/C TV TEL. $100–$140 double; $80 per person cottage or villa. Children 11 and under stay free in parents' room. AE, DC, DISC, MC, V.

Five miles east of Pinehurst, this 1921 hotel retains its old-fashioned comfort and a certain flair. A devoted clientele returns every year, but newcomers are also give a hearty welcome. A Clarion resort, it consists of a graceful three-story, colonial-style main building with wings flanking the entrance. The lobby rotunda is gracious, with twin white staircases. The rooms are decorated with style and taste, although you may prefer one of the golf cottages or villas on the grounds. Some of these accommodations have their own fireplaces. The villas are the most spacious choices; many have kitchens and front porches.

Generous meals are prepared in the formal dining room. In summer, lunch is served on an informal terrace overlooking the fairways of the championship golf course.

Pine Needles. N.C. 2 (1 mile west of U.S. 1) (P.O. Box 88), Southern Pines, NC 28388. ☎ **910/692-7111.** Fax 910/692-5349. www.rossresorts.com. E-mail: info@rossresorts.com. 71 units. A/C TV TEL. $100–$140 per person. Rates include full board. 3-day, 2-night golf packages available. Children 3 and under stay free in parents' room. AE, MC, V.

With all the pine trees in the area, someone had to name a hotel "Pine Needles," and someone did. The resort is the creation of local legend Peggy Kirk Bell, a champion golfer and golf instructor, who opened the resort with her late husband. It has won many a devoted fan over the years. The bedrooms are spread across 10 lodges; returnees often select their favorites. Decidedly informal, the accommodations have rustic styling, often with exposed beams.

Box lunches for picnics are a popular feature, and the hotel offers an array of facilities, including a heated pool, sauna, and whirlpool; lighted tennis courts; an 18-hole golf course (greens fees are $105); a putting green; and a driving range. The adjoining golf course was designed in 1927 by Donald Ross. You can rent bicycles for exploring. There are recreation rooms and a game room. Lawn games, a feature of this area at the turn of the century, still enjoy favor here.

WHERE TO DINE

La Terrace. 270 SW Broad St. ☎ **910/692-5622.** Reservations recommended. Lunch $7.29–$9.50. Main courses $13.50–$25. MC, V. Mon–Fri 11:30am–2pm and 5:30–9pm, Sat 6–9:30pm. CONTINENTAL.

Old-time visitors still show up here looking for Antoine's, but that place is long gone. La Terrace is better than Antoine's ever was, however. It offers flavorful cuisine in a charming setting, both intimate and formal. Local seafood is featured, as is the chef's specialty: stuffed Dover sole. Lamb is also prepared succulently, with just the right time in the oven and just the right seasonings. The service is the finest in town.

The Lob Steer Inn. U.S. 1. ☎ **910/692-3503.** Reservations recommended on weekends. Main courses $12–$35. AE, DC, DISC, MC, V. Daily 5–10:30pm. STEAK/SEAFOOD.

This family favorite is a sure bet for fine dining at a reasonable cost. Tasty preparations of the kind of fare locals like are served, including broiled seafood and prime rib. Guests help themselves at the freshly prepared salad bar and somehow always find room to go to the dessert bar to finish their meal. This is a rather upscale dining choice, despite the casual dress. As a waiter confided, "We're no redneck joint." It's deservedly one of the best and most popular places in the area. Children's plates are offered in a wider variety than usual.

SOUTHERN PINES AFTER DARK

Most area golf resorts offer dancing and occasional evening entertainment. In addition, check the following for current goings-on.

The **Arts Council of Moore County,** P.O. Box 405, Southern Pines, NC 28388 (☎ **910/692-4356**), maintains a cultural calendar at the **Sandhills Little Theater**

(☎ **910/692-3340**) and sponsors other local concert and entertainment groups. It's also the site of periodic travelogues and arts-council shows.

A SIDE TRIP TO CAMERON & SANFORD

The entire little town of **Cameron,** 10 miles north of Southern Pines (off U.S. 1/15/501), has been designated a historic district, with some 19 vintage sites and buildings, including the **Greenwood Inn** (1874). More than 60 antiques dealers have shops here, and an annual antiques street fair is held the first Saturday in May and again in October. Most shops are open Wednesday to Saturday from 10am to 5pm. After a morning of sightseeing and shopping, have lunch at the **Dewberry Deli,** Carthage Street (☎ **910/245-3697**), open Tuesday to Saturday 11am to 4:30pm and on Sunday from 12:30 to 5pm. Located in an old hardware store, this eatery is ideal for a salad or a sandwich.

About 35 miles north of Southern Pines via U.S. 1/15/501 and N.C. 42, North Carolina's frontier days spring to life at the **Alston House,** 324 Alston House Rd., Sanford (☎ **910/947-2051**). It's also known as the "House in the Horseshoe," for the horseshoe bend of the Deep River, which the house overlooks. Built in the late 1770s, the two-story frame house, with its central hall plan, is typical of plantation houses of that era. The bullet holes were made in 1781, when Whigs and Tories battled it out on the grounds. "Miss Ruby" Newton, who takes visitors through the house, will fill you in on other anecdotes about the house and its owners down through the years. The first weekend of August, a Revolutionary War battle is reenacted here, and in early December, there's a cheery open house and candle-lighting celebration. Admission is free, but donations are accepted. From April to October, the house is open Monday to Saturday from 9am to 5pm and on Sunday from 1 to 5pm; November to March, Tuesday to Saturday from 10am to 4pm and on Sunday from 1 to 4pm.

7

Asheville & the High Country

Men and women have made their homes in North Carolina's Blue Ridge Mountains since the first push westward, but nature endures. In late spring, green creeps up the peaks as trees leaf out. In summer, wildflowers make a carpet of colorful blooms. Fall brings vivid reds, yellows, and oranges to give every mountainside a flamelike hue. Wildlife still flourishes; streams are clear; and forests of birch, poplar, beech, hickory, and oak are undisturbed. This is one of those rare places where civilization has been smart enough to protect the natural environment as well as enjoy it.

The largest city in the High Country is handsome Asheville, home of author Thomas Wolfe (*Look Homeward, Angel*) and long a residence of the wealthy and famous. In recent years neighboring Boone, Banner Elk, and Blowing Rock have become important ski centers in the South, especially since the introduction of snowmaking equipment. The best skiing in the area includes Ski Beech, Appalachian Ski Mountain, Hawksnest Golf & Ski Resort, and Sugar Mountain.

1 Enjoying the Great Outdoors in the High Country

Sparkling white winters, fragrant springs, cool summers, and brisk, burnished autumns characterize North Carolina's High Country. Skiing in winter gives way in milder weather to swimming, golfing, fishing, tennis, rafting, horseback riding, backpacking, rock climbing, and rappelling.

The **Blue Ridge Parkway,** a unit of the U.S. National Park System, passes through all five counties of the High Country, offering a vista of natural beauty and rural landscapes (see "The Blue Ridge Parkway," later in this chapter).

Moses Cone Memorial Park, near Blowing Rock on the parkway, has 25 miles of easily graded **hiking** trails. It's also popular for cross-country skiing. The Linville Falls/Linville Gorge area on the parkway has several trails leading to the head of the falls, with views of the cataract and the Linville Gorge Wilderness Area. Moderate trails lead to Grandfather Mountain, and challenging hikes take in part of the fabled Appalachian Trail, stretching from Georgia to Maine. In North Carolina, the trail crosses Roan Mountain, Hump Mountain, and Yellow Mountain, all of which are known for their large expanses of meadows with panoramic views. Trailheads are in Elk Park and at Carver's Gap on Roan.

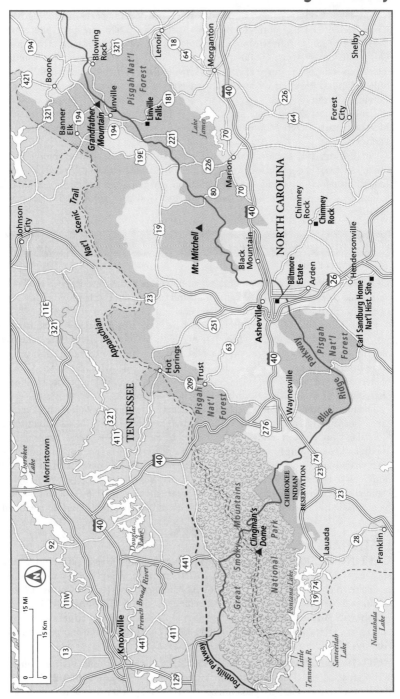

The High Country is also filled with **state and federal parks,** including Moses Cone Memorial Park, north of Blowing Rock. This 3,600-acre park offers bridle paths, hiking trails, trout streams, and two lakes. The other major park is the Linville Gorge Wilderness Area, a 7,600-acre tract set aside to provide a natural environment. The steep walls of the gorge enclose the Linville River, which descends 2,000 feet in only 12 miles. Access is by foot trails via Forest Service Road off U.S. 221 at the Linville Falls exit.

Cross-country **skiing** is the finest in the South. Excellent trails are in Moses Cone Memorial Park, Beech Mountain, and several other locations along the Blue Ridge Parkway.

For **fishing,** area streams and lakes abound in trout, bass, catfish, blue gill, and other varieties. The game fish waters of the Blue Ridge Parkway (Price, Cone, and Doughton parks) are under federal regulation and require a license or permit. The fishing season begins the first Saturday in April and runs through the last day of February.

2 Asheville

241 miles W of Raleigh

✪ Asheville, once just a tiny mountain trading village at the confluence of the French Broad and Swannanoa rivers, has grown up and turned into a year-round resort, complete with architectural gems from several eras and a lively cultural scene.

People who could have lived almost anywhere in the world, including Thomas Edison, often settled in Asheville. Those Jazz Age kids, F. Scott and Zelda Fitzgerald, were among the most famous visitors. Fitzgerald arrived in the summer of 1935, recuperating from a mild case of tuberculosis, and his wife, Zelda, who had suffered a series of nervous breakdowns, was incarcerated at Highland Hospital, a private sanitarium charging $240 a month—an exorbitant fee in those days.

The most famous person associated with Asheville is Thomas Wolfe, whose mother ran a boardinghouse here called "The Old Kentucky Home." It was disguised as "Dixieland" in Wolfe's autobiographical novel, *Look Homeward, Angel.* Fitzgerald and Wolfe had some things in common: TB, an eye for the women, and alcohol. They even shared an editor: the famous Maxwell Perkins. Wolfe's novel (still called "that book" by old-timers in Asheville) was blacklisted here as late as 1949. Although he claimed that "you can't go home again," he eventually did, in 1938. Thousands assembled outside his mother's old boardinghouse to bid him farewell upon his premature death.

ESSENTIALS

GETTING THERE I-40 passes through Asheville from the east and west, I-26 runs southeast (as far as Charleston); U.S. 23/19A runs north and west, and I-240 is a perimeter highway circling the city. For AAA services, contact the **Carolina Motor Club,** 660 Merrimon Ave., Suite A, Asheville, NC 28804 (☎ 828/253-5376).

Asheville Airport (☎ 828/687-9446) is just off I-26. Major airlines serving this airport are **Delta ASA** and **Comair** (☎ 800/221-1212; www.delta.com), and **US Airways** (☎ 800/428-4322; www.usairways.com).

VISITOR INFORMATION The **Asheville Convention and Visitors Bureau,** 151 Haywood St. (P.O. Box 1010), Asheville, NC 28802 (☎ 800/257-1300 or 828/258-6101; www.ashevillechamber.com), is open Monday to Friday from 8:30am to 5:30pm and on Saturday and Sunday from 9am to 5pm. You can also request an

Asheville

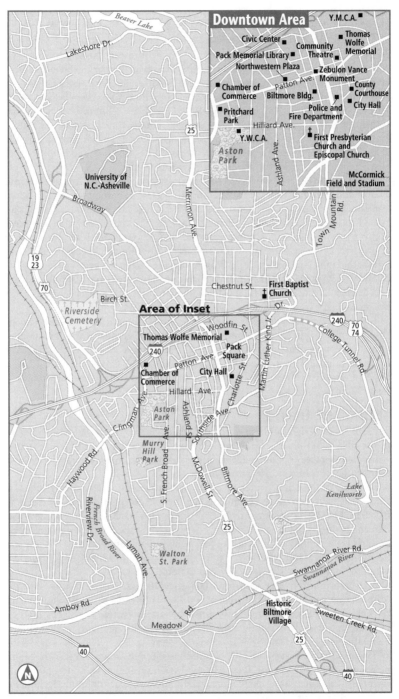

Downtown Area

Y.M.C.A.

Civic Center
Thomas Wolfe Memorial
Community Theatre
Pack Memorial Library
Northwestern Plaza
Zebulon Vance Monument
Chamber of Commerce
Biltmore Bldg.
County Courthouse
City Hall
Pritchard Park
Police and Fire Department
Hilliard Ave.
First Presbyterian Church and Episcopal Church
Y.W.C.A.
Aston Park
McCormick Field and Stadium
Patton Ave.
Ashland Ave.

Beaver Lake
Lakeshore Dr.
25
University of N.C.-Asheville
Broadway
Merrimon Ave.
Town Mountain Rd.
19 23
70
Birch St.
Riverside Cemetery
Chestnut St.
First Baptist Church
240
70 74
College Tunnel Rd.

Area of Inset

Woodfin St.
Thomas Wolfe Memorial
240
Pack Square
Patton Ave.
Chamber of Commerce
City Hall
Hillard Ave.
Aston Park
Ashland St.
Southside Ave.
Charlotte St.
Martin Luther King Jr. Dr.

Clingman Ave.
Murry Hill Park
Haywood Rd.
French Broad River
Riverview Dr.
Lyman Ave.
S. French Broad Ave.
McDowell St.
Biltmore Ave.
Lake Kenilworth
Walton St. Park
25
Swannanoa River Rd.
Swannanoa River
Amboy Rd.
Rd.
Meadow
Historic Biltmore Village
Sweeten Creek Rd.
25
40
40

N

Asheville Visitor Guide from the **Asheville Chamber of Commerce** (☎ 888/ 247-9811; www.ashevillechamber.org).

SPECIAL EVENTS   Special happenings at the **Biltmore Estate** (see "Seeing the Sights," later in this chapter) include a spring Festival of Flowers, September International Exposition, and Christmas at Biltmore—inquire ahead for specific dates.

Special events at the **Folk Art Center** (see "Side Trips from Asheville," later in this chapter) include Fiber Day in May, the World Gee Haw Whimmy Diddle Competition in August, Celebrate Folk Art in September, and Christmas with the Guild in December. In July and October, *Mountain Sweet Talk* is a two-part, two-act play presented by Barbara Freeman and Connie Regan-Blake, who are among this country's best mountain storytellers. Call ahead for dates and times.

If you're here the first weekend of August, you can attend the **Annual Mountain Dance and Folk Festival,** held at the Civic Center on Haywood Street. The fiddlers, banjo pickers, ballad singers, dulcimer players, and clog dancers don't call it quits until nobody is interested in one more dance. This is the oldest such festival in the country, and you're encouraged to join in even if you don't know a "do-si-do" from a "swing-your-partner." Every Saturday night from early July through August (except for the first Saturday in August), there's a **Shindig-on-the-Green** at the City Country Plaza (College and Spruce streets), where you'll find many of the same mountain musicians and dancers having an old-fashioned wingding. It's free, and lots of fun. If sitting on the ground isn't your thing, take along a blanket or chair.

Brevard, 27 miles southwest of Asheville, hosts a music festival from late June through mid-August at the **Brevard Music Center.** Nationally and internationally famous artists perform daily in symphony, chamber-music, band, and choral concerts, as well as musical comedy and opera. Write P.O. Box 312, Brevard, NC 28712, or call ☎ 828/884-2019 for schedules and reservations. Some events are free; others cost from $7 to $40.

SEEING THE SIGHTS

In recent years, a vigorous local effort has been made to preserve and restore remnants of the city's colorful past. *The Asheville Urban Trail* brochure, available free from the Asheville Chamber of Commerce or at the Asheville Visitor Center, is a self-guided tour through the historic downtown district.

Biltmore Village is a cluster of 24 cottages housing boutiques, craft shops, and restaurants. The best of these shops is the **New Morning Gallery,** 7 Boston Way (☎ 828/274-2831); it started in 1972 and today is a 6,000-square-foot showcase of "Art for Living." The New Morning Gallery is one of the South's largest galleries of arts and crafts. It offers a fresh mix of functional and sculptural pottery, fine-art glass, furniture, jewelry, and other handmade objects. It's open Monday to Saturday from 10am to 6pm and on Sunday from noon to 5pm.

Another attraction, the **Montford Historic District,** has more than 200 turn-of-the-century residences. In the downtown area, amid Art Deco buildings, you'll see the **Lexington Park** area, a center for artists and artisans whose workshops are tucked away down a little alleyway, and **Pack Place,** a developing center for a wide variety of cultural activities.

Thomas Wolfe, a native of Asheville, immortalized the town and its citizens in his first novel, *Look Homeward, Angel.* His mother's boardinghouse, at 48 Spruce St., is maintained as a literary shrine. Unfortunately, in the summer of 1998, the house was a victim of arson; it will be closed for repairs until at least 2001. Fortunately, before the fire, the city of Asheville opened a vast exhibit on Wolfe's life. Many of his personal

The Greatest Mansion in the Mountains

George Washington Vanderbilt, a young man of 25 in the late 1880s, came upon the perfect spot in the Blue Ridge for his French Renaissance–style chateau, which was to be built by his friend, architect Richard Morris Hunt.

The great chateau would be called Biltmore. His initial purchase of 125,000 acres outside Asheville has diminished to 8,000. It includes formal and informal gardens designed by the father of landscape architecture in America, Frederick Law Olmsted.

The great house remains the largest private residence in the United States, a National Historic Landmark now owned by Vanderbilt's grandson. Begun in 1890, Biltmore is constructed of tons of Indiana limestone, transported by a special railway spur built specifically to bring the massive amounts of material and supplies to the site. It took hundreds of workers 5 years to complete the house. On Christmas Eve 1895, George Vanderbilt formally opened the doors for the first time to friends and family members.

Like William Randolph Hearst, Vanderbilt journeyed through Europe and the Orient purchasing paintings, porcelains, bronzes, carpets, and antiques, all of which would eventually become part of the collection of 50,000 objects that are still in Biltmore today. Artwork is by Renoir, Sargent, Whistler, Pellegrini, and Boldini, and furniture includes designs by Chippendale and Sheraton.

Fully electric and centrally heated, Biltmore was one of the most technologically advanced structures ever built at the time of its completion. It used some of Thomas Edison's first light bulbs and boasted a fire-alarm system, an electrical call-box system for servants, two elevators, elaborate indoor plumbing for all 34 bedrooms—and a relatively newfangled invention called the telephone.

belongings, such as his typewriter and writing table, were on display in the site's Visitor Center, so they were not destroyed. The exhibit was expanded just after the fire to include a 22-minute video biography and a slide show that depicts the Wolfe house as it was before the devastation. The biography is shown at the beginning of every hour from 9am to 4pm, and the slide show is held from 9:30am to 4:30pm. For information, call, visit, or write the **Visitors Center,** 52 N. Market St., Asheville, NC 28801 (☎ **828/253-8304**). Hours are Monday to Saturday 9am to 5pm; Sunday 1 to 5pm.

Both Wolfe and short-story writer **O. Henry** (William Sydney Porter) are buried in Riverside Cemetery (entrance on Birch Street off Pearson Drive).

Asheville's historic **Homespun Shops** (☎ **828/253-7651**), adjacent to the Grove Park Inn (see "Where to Stay," later in this section), are the home of **Grovewood Gallery** and **Grovewood Studios,** which continue the tradition of craftsmanship begun by Edith Vanderbilt in 1901 as Biltmore Estate Industries. Established as an industrial school to teach boys and girls the traditional skills of wood carving and hand-weaving, the Industries soon became a thriving business, producing home-spun cloth and wood carvings and furniture. The Industries were sold in 1917 to Fred Seely, manager of the Grove Park Inn, who built the present cluster of structures and further developed the woolen cloth into a product known around the world. Cloth production ceased in the early 1980s, but its history is told here at the **North Carolina Homespun Museum.**

The Grovewood Gallery features the work of some of the Southeast's finest crafts-people, including the artists of Grovewood Studios, whose workshops are in the adjoining buildings. The **Estes-Winn Antique Automobile Museum** and the **Grove-wood Café** are also housed here.

The Homespun Shops are open January to March, Monday to Saturday from 9am to 5pm; and April to December, Monday to Saturday from 10am to 6pm and also on Sunday from 1 to 5pm. Admission to the two museums is free. The Homespun Shops are in North Asheville next to the Grove Park Inn, which you reach via Charlotte Street and Macon Avenue. When you are on the grounds of the inn, follow the signs.

As interesting as all the preceding attractions may be, they're dwarfed by the premier attraction in Asheville: the magnificent Biltmore Estate.

Biltmore Estate. 1 N. Pack Sq. (on U.S. 25, 2 blocks north of I-40). ☎ **800/543-2961** or 828/274-6333; www.biltmore.com. House and gardens, $32.00 adults, $24.00 children 10-15. Daily 9am–5pm. Closed Thanksgiving and Christmas Day.

The French Renaissance chateau, built by George W. Vanderbilt, has 250 rooms. There isn't an ordinary spot in the place—not even the kitchen. Vanderbilt gathered furnishings and art treasures from all over the world for this palace (Napoleon's chess set and table from St. Helena are here, for example) and then went further, creating one of the most lavish formal gardens you'll ever see. The garden features more than 200 varieties of azaleas, plus thousands of other plants and shrubs. In addition to the gardens, the estate offers three restaurants, endless gift shops, and tours of the Biltmore Estate Winery.

Two tours are presented. The Behind the Scenes Tour, which provides further access to the house, is available for an additional charge of $11.95 for adults and $9 for children; and the Rooftop Tour, which provides panoramic views, is offered for an additional charge of $11.95 for adults and $9 for children.

OUTDOOR PURSUITS

BICYCLING   The Asheville area is terrific for mountain biking. Bicycle shops and outfitters can provide trail maps and bike rentals. Call the visitors bureau at ☎ **828/258-6101** for a complete list.

FISHING   Best for lake fishing is **Lake Julian,** south of Asheville, which is well stocked with bass and bream. Canoes and picnicking are available. **Lake Powhatan,** on N.C. 191 in the Pisgah National Forest, has a sand beach, swimming, camping, and picnicking in addition to fishing. No boats are available, however. **Lake Lure,** on U.S. 74 about 30 minutes southeast of Asheville, has trout, bass, bream, and water sports; motorboats are available. There's also an abundance of well-stocked rivers and highland streams within easy reach of Asheville. For more information about fishing in the area, call the **Hunter Banks Store (☎ 828/252-3005).**

GOLF   The rolling terrain of the mountains around Asheville presents golfers with hundreds of uncrowded fairways. There are more than 50 golf courses in the state's western region. Our favorite is at the **Grove Park Inn Resort,** 290 Macon Ave. (☎ **828/252-2711**). Open daily throughout the year, the resort's course length depends on the tees, which range from 4,987 yards for teal tees to 6,520 yards for gold tees. The par-71 course is steeped in tradition, having opened in 1899. It was redesigned in 1924 by master golf architect Donald Ross. The oldest operating course in North Carolina, it evokes memories of Harry Vardon, Bobby Jones, and Ben Hogan. Arnold Palmer and Jack Nicklaus are only two of the great golfers who have played here. Tree-lined Bermuda-grass fairways, strategically placed bunkers, and subtle bent-grass greens place an emphasis on accuracy rather than power, making this course ideal for players of all levels. Greens fees are $85.

HIKING   The famous **Appalachian Trail** passes through a large section of Pisgah National Forest and Great Smoky Mountains National Park. The Greater Asheville area is a hiker's paradise, with trails in almost every direction and in every major park. You can purchase the booklet *100 Favorite Trails* at the visitors bureau (☎ 828/258-6101). Otherwise, contact the **U.S. Forestry Service** (☎ 828/253-2352) for trail maps.

HORSEBACK RIDING   Stables in the area offer trail riding with experienced guides. Some stables also offer pack trips in the surrounding mountains. The visitors bureau keeps a complete list; call ☎ **828/258-6101.**

TENNIS   The **Grove Park Inn Resort,** 190 Macon Ave. (☎ 828/252-2711), leads not only in golf but also in tennis. The resort has been ranked as one of the 50 greatest tennis resorts in the U.S. by *Tennis* magazine. It offers six outdoor (four hard, two clay) courts and three indoor courts. Rates per hour range from $20 indoors to $25 outdoors.

WHITEWATER RAFTING   You can choose a raft, kayak, or canoe to ride the whitewater rapids. The rivers of western North Carolina and the Tennessee border offer rapids of Class I–V difficulty. Outfitters offer trips ranging from a half-day to a full weekend. Try the Nolichucky and French Broad rivers to the north or the Nantahala, Ocoee, Chattooga, and Green rivers to the west and south. Call the visitors bureau for more information (☎ 828/258-6101).

SHOPPING

Crafts are so important in the hills of western North Carolina (and in Asheville in particular) that shopping for them is almost like sightseeing. In Asheville, sights and crafts shops are often combined. One of the foremost arts-and-crafts shops is the **Grovewood Gallery** at the **Homespun Shops,** which also enjoys the distinction of being a historical landmark (see "Seeing the Sights," earlier in this chapter).

Asheville is the home of more than 50 galleries exhibiting works by local and national artists, including folk art, Native American art, and antiques. Galleries worth noting include the **Turtle Creek Gallery,** 24 Wall St. (☎ 828/259-9252) and the **Appalachian Craft Center,** 10 N. Spruce St. (☎ 828/253-8499). Hours are Monday to Saturday from 9am to 5pm.

Biltmore Village. Across from main entrance gate of the Biltmore Estate, Swan St. off Biltmore Ave. ☎ **828/274-8788.**

This shopping village is reminiscent of a time capsule. As you walk the cobblestone sidewalk, you feel that you might catch a glimpse of old George Vanderbilt himself. Shops, restaurants, and galleries abound, so allow yourself plenty of time to see everything. One store, the Biltmore Village Co., is quite charming and affordable; it bills itself as a gift shop containing everything—at half-price. Hours are Monday to Friday 9:30am to 6pm, Saturday 10am to 5pm.

Blue Ridge Frame and Gallery. 545 Merriman Ave. ☎ **828/253-3559.**

The name is the best description of this gallery. Specializing in frames and custom framing, the gallery displays the work of folk artists in the Asheville area. Restoration is also among the specialties of this store, which can restore any photo, regardless of age, to near perfection. If you have a portrait that is a family heirloom, you may want to bring it along with you, depending on the length of your stay in Asheville. Hours are Monday to Saturday 9:30am to 6pm.

The Kress Emporium. 19 Patton Ave., Asheville. ☎ **828/281-2252.**

This store serves as a showcase for more than 80 artists and craftspeople in the area. Stained-glass mosaics, lace handwork, fine miniature-furnishing collectibles, silk paintings, frames, and prints are just a few of the things that you will find here. The building that houses the emporium is a reason to visit in its own right; constructed in 1928, it is an architectural landmark designed in neoclassical style. Hours are Monday to Saturday 10am to 6pm.

WHERE TO STAY

For those who've fantasized about staying overnight on the grounds of the Biltmore Estate, the wait is over. At press time, the talk of the town revolved around the 213-room deluxe hotel being constructed on the estate grounds. Scheduled to open in spring 2001, **Inn on Biltmore Estate** features a full-service restaurant, pool, library, carriage rides, and stunning views. Call for more information (☎ **800/624-1575**).

Beaufort House Victorian Bed & Breakfast. 61 N. Liberty St., Asheville, NC 28801. ☎ **800/261-2221** or 828/252-8334. Fax 828/251-2082. www.beauforthouse.com. 11 units. A/C TV TEL $115–$235 double. Rates include full breakfast and afternoon tea. AE, MC, V.

Designed in 1894 by A.L. Melton, a well-known local architect, this landmark Queen Anne confection is among the top two or three B&Bs in Asheville. It lies half a mile from the center of town, in the Grove Park district. The house is operated by Jacqueline and Robert Glasgow, and is listed on the National Register of Historic Places. The individually decorated bedrooms are full of antiques. One accommodation occupies the top floor, and another is in a carriage house with a loft bedroom, kitchenette, private deck, and living room. Three of the four units in the main house have whirlpools. The country breakfast with freshly squeezed juice is a serious reason to stay here. No smoking.

✪ **Cedar Crest Inn.** 674 Biltmore Ave., Asheville, NC 28803. ☎ **800/252-0310** or 828/252-1389. Fax 828/253-7667. www.cedarcrestvictorianinn.com. E-mail: stay@ cedarcrestvictorianinn.com. 11 units. A/C TV TEL $145–$185 double; $145–$235 suite. Rates include breakfast. AE, DC, DISC, MC, V.

A stay here is like entering a time capsule and going back to the Victorian era. This Queen Anne mansion is one of the largest and most opulent residences surviving from Asheville's 1890s boom. The mansion has a captain's walk, projecting turrets, and expansive verandas, and the inside is a fantasy of leaded glass, ornately carved fireplaces, and antique furnishings, with a massive oak staircase. Owners Barbara and Jack McEwan have indulged their romantic and whimsical imaginations in furnishing the guest rooms: All have period antiques and individual decor—a canopied ceiling in the Romeo and Juliet room, a carved walnut bed in another room, and brass bedsteads in a third. Each room has a private baths, and several contain working fireplaces. A cottage with two suites is adjacent to the main house.

Great Smokies Holiday Inn Sunspree Resort. 1 Holiday Inn Dr., Asheville, NC 28805. ☎ **800/HOLIDAY** or 828/254-3211; Fax 828/254-1603. www.holidayinn.com. E-mail: cnuckolls@peppertree.com. 272 units. A/C TV TEL. $29–$49 double; $275–$300 suite. Rates include continental breakfast. AE, DC, DISC, MC, V.

This is Asheville's leading motor hotel, lying directly off I-240, 3 miles from the center of town. Rooms are in a rather bland international style but are clean, comfortable, generous in size, and well maintained, with good tiled baths and adequate space.

Standard double rooms, with either two double beds or a king-size bed, have such extras as refrigerators and coffeemakers. The least expensive suite has a king-size bed with a couch that can be converted to a double bed; middle-range suites contain two bedrooms with two double beds in one and a king-size bed in the other. The most expensive suites offer three bedrooms and a living room, and can easily sleep six. There are a heated pool and sauna, as well as a tennis court and an 18-hole golf course nearby. The restaurant, popular with families, serves typically American fare— perfectly acceptable cuisine; nothing more.

◐ **Grove Park Inn Resort.** 290 Macon Ave., Asheville, NC 28804. ☎ **800/438-5800** or 828/252-2711. Fax 828/252-7053. www.groveparkinn.com. 522 units. A/C TV TEL Summer $200–$275 double; $580 suite. Off-season $150–$175 double, $375 suite. AE, CB, DC, DISC, MC, V.

This resort, built in 1913, is one of the oldest and most famous in the South. Listed on the National Register of Historic Places, it's a favorite year-round destination, providing panoramic views of the city's skyline and the Blue Ridge Mountains, Old World charm, and a long tradition of hospitality. Completely renovated in recent years, it's our favorite choice in the entire western section of North Carolina. And it's getting even better: The resort was scheduled to unveil its new $13 million, 40,000-square-foot full-service spa in January 2001.

The two newer wings reflect the spirit of the original design. Novelist F. Scott Fitzgerald stayed at the hotel while his wife, Zelda, spent her nights in a sanitarium nearby. The hotel offers a romantic-getaway package called The Great Gatsby, although Fitzgerald's stay was hardly romantic. Over the years, the resort has hosted some of the most famous names of the 20th century, including Thomas Edison, Henry Ford, and Harvey Firestone. Presidents Franklin Delano Roosevelt and Woodrow Wilson also slept here.

The inn is built on the side of Sunset Mountain at an elevation of 3,100 feet. Its great-hall lobby is flanked by 14-foot fireplaces; comfortably padded chairs and sofas create a feeling of coziness despite the size of the 120-foot-long room. Twenty-eight of the bedrooms are oversize, containing such amenities as whirlpools.

Dining: Horizons Restaurant, featuring an innovative but classic cuisine, is the finest in the area (see "Where to Dine," later in this chapter). Guests can also dine in the moderately priced Blue Ridge Dining Room, which has a legendary outdoor dining veranda. The Carolina Cafe also overlooks the mountains.

Amenities: Full-service spa, room service, laundry, nine tennis courts, indoor and outdoor swimming pools, sports center, fitness center, racquetball and squash, mountain bikes, 18-hole golf course, aerobics, and saunas.

Haywood Park Hotel. 1 Battery Park Ave., Asheville, NC 28801. ☎ **800/228-2522** or 828/252-2522. Fax 828/253-0481. www.haywoodpark.com. E-mail: hotel@haywoodpark. com. 33 units. A/C TV TEL $165–$325 suite for 2. Rates include continental breakfast. Children 17 and under stay free in parents' room. AE, DC, DISC, MC, V.

In the heart of downtown Asheville, this rather elegant all-suite place is the leading hotel in the city center. The suites are crisp and airy, a blend of luxury—some have Iberian marble baths, recessed closets, oversize tubs, whirlpools, mini-bars, and/or refrigerators—combined with practical details such as computer hookups. All beds are either queen- or king-size. The hotel's deluxe restaurant offers a continental menu specializing in seafood, as well as an extensive wine list. In summer, there's a beer garden. Bicycles are available for rent. Facilities include an exercise room and sauna.

STAYING NEARBY

✪ The Greystone Inn. Greystone Lane, Lake Toxaway, NC 28747. ☎ **800/824-5766** or 828/966-4700. Fax 828/862-5689. www.greystoneinn.com. E-mail: greystone@crtcom.net. 33 units. A/C TV TEL. Sept–Mar, Sun–Thurs $305 double, $510 suite, Fri–Sat $350 double, $550 suite. Apr–Aug $350 double, $550 suite. Rates include breakfast, dinner, champagne, afternoon tea, and sports activities except golf. MC, V.

Henry Ford and John D. Rockefeller once whiled away their summers on the 14 miles of leafy shoreline around Lake Toxaway. Set on a wooded peninsula along the lake, this imposing Swiss Revival mansion, listed on the National Register of Historic Places, was created for Savannah heiress Lucy Armstrong Moltz as a seasonal "cottage." Refurbished in 1985, it welcomes guests with an engaging mix of antique furnishings and modern comforts. Each room has its own character, and many have working fireplaces; all have whirlpools. The stone fireplace is also a focal point in the oak-paneled living room, the library is a tastefully appointed oasis, and the terrace is the ideal setting for before-dinner drinks. For dedicated do-nothings, there are wicker rocking chairs on the glassed-in sun porch overlooking the lake. Complimentary midafternoon tea is served, along with cakes.

Dining: Meals in the Hearthsides dining room (for guests only) feature such gourmet selections as seared Texas antelope and Georgian pecan chicken. Dinner is a six-course affair.

Amenities: Tennis courts, fishing, water skiing, swimming, sailboating, and golf on the property or nearby. Spa-facility treatments and massage therapy are offered to guests for an additional charge.

The Lion and the Rose Bed & Breakfast. 276 Montford Ave., Asheville, NC 28801. ☎ **800/546-6988** or 828/255-7673. Fax 828/285-9810. www.lion-rose.com. E-mail: info@lion-rose.com. 5 units. A/C TV TEL. $145–$245 double; $225 suite. Rates include full breakfast and afternoon tea. AE, DISC, MC, V.

This inn opened in 1987 in a Georgian/Queen Anne–style home in the historic Montford district. The house was built in 1898, during the heyday of Asheville's summer resort boom. Restored to its original grandeur, the inn is run by Lisa and Rice Yordy. Oriental rugs and antiques, some of which are precious family pieces, are used throughout the inn. Sherry (served on the porch) and discreetly placed fresh flowers add grace notes that make this a tranquil retreat—one of the best-run B&Bs in Greater Asheville. Guests dine around the fireplace in cold weather or on the porch in summer. For breakfast, the fresh raspberry crepes with yogurt filling have been justly praised by *Southern Living*. The traditionally styled bedrooms have queen-size beds, and some have a sitting area with a couch. The two-bedroom suite is decorated with white wicker and lace. One bedroom has a queen-size bed, and the other has twin beds; there are also a walk-in shower, TV, and a private balcony.

✪ The Old Reynolds Mansion Bed & Breakfast. 100 Reynolds Heights, Asheville, NC 28804. ☎ **800/709-0496** or 828/254-0496. www.oldreynoldsmansion.com. E-mail: innkeeper@oldreynoldsmansion.com. 10 units; 1 cottage. A/C. $85–$120 double; $135 cottage for 2. Rates include full breakfast. No credit cards. Take U.S. 25 for a 10-minute drive north of the center, past Beaver Lake.

An antebellum brick house—one of the few left in Asheville—this three-story inn, set on 4 acres, dates from 1855, when Col. Daniel Reynolds built it just before the Civil War. It was substantially altered over the years before falling into disrepair. Helen and Fred Faber rescued it from the bulldozer and earned it a position on the National Register of Historic Places. Today, the inn is furnished with antiques, and some of the beautifully decorated bedrooms have fireplaces or 12-foot ceilings and provide panoramic vistas of the mountains. The mansion also has one cottage located on the grounds, with a queen-size bed, a private bath, a living room with fireplace, a kitchen, and a sleeper sofa; it's generally rented to a party of three guests. TV is available only in the cottage. Breakfast can be served by the fireplace on nippy days or on the veranda. A 1930s swimming pool is nestled among the pines.

○ Richmond Hill Inn. 87 Richmond Hill Dr., Asheville, NC 28806. ☎ **828/252-7313.** Fax 828/252-8726. www.richmondhillinn.com. E-mail: info@richmondhillinn.com. 36 units. A/C TV TEL. $155–$315 double; $315–$450 suite. Rates include full breakfast. Children 5 and under stay free in parents' room. AE, MC, V.

Listed on the National Register of Historic Places, this inn was renovated in 1989 and was eventually listed as one of the "Ten Outstanding New Inns in America" by *Inn Review Newsletter.* Constructed in 1889 of granite, slate, and local woods, the house was designed by James Hill, the supervising architect of the U.S. Treasury buildings. The place is Asheville's premier remaining example of Queen Anne–style architecture. The main building is a spacious two-story mansion, painted yellow, with a wraparound porch. The interior is graced by family-heirloom portraits and the house's original oak paneling. Rooms are charming, featuring claw-foot tubs, balconies over-looking a small stream, canopied beds, and fireplaces. The seven rooms on the second floor are preferable to the smaller rooms on the third. Nine cottages containing rooms and suites, all with small porches and rockers, are across the way. Other than the much-larger Grove Park, this is our favorite address in Asheville. The inn also has an excellent restaurant, Gabrielle (named for the former mistress of the house), featuring American contemporary cuisine.

WHERE TO DINE

Blue Ridge Dining Room. In the Grove Park Inn Resort, 290 Macon Ave. ☎ **828/ 252-2711.** Reservations recommended Sat–Sun. Main courses $20–$35; Fri seafood buffet $29.95; Sat prime-rib buffet $28.95; Sun brunch $24.50. AE, DISC, MC, V. Mon–Sat 6:30am–10pm, Sun 6:30–10:30am and 11:30am–10pm. AMERICAN.

This is the moderately priced choice at Asheville's premier resort. The food is not as good as at the Horizon, but the prices are more affordable, and you get excellent quality and generous helpings. The view of the Blue Ridge Mountains alone is worth the trip here. This longtime family favorite is an Asheville tradition, known for its sumptuous international buffet tables laden with many "plantation extras." Omelets and waffles are made to order at breakfast. The Friday-night seafood buffet and Saturday prime-rib dinner are so popular with locals that early reservations are recommended. Sunday brunch is Asheville's best, and it's usually packed.

Charlotte Street Grill and Pub. 157 Charlotte St. ☎ **828/253-5348.** Reservations rec-ommended. Lunch main courses $5.95–$7.95; dinner main courses $11.95–$16.95. Pub lunches $8. Restaurant, Tue–Thurs 11:30am–2pm and 5–9pm, Fri–Sat 5–10pm. Pub, daily 11:30am–2am. AMERICAN.

Downstairs is an authentic-looking English pub, and upstairs is a restaurant with a Victorian decor that offers more intimate dining. The pub keeps the longer hours and is noted for serving one of the best value lunches in Asheville, including freshly made pastas and house salads that are meals in themselves. The food is well prepared and based on fresh ingredients. The mountain trout is an always-reliable choice, as is the succulent seafood steak. Freshly baked breads and homemade desserts attract deserved attention, and there's also an extensive wine list.

○ Horizons Restaurant. In the Grove Park Inn Resort, 290 Macon Ave. ☎ **828/ 252-2711.** Reservations required. Jacket and tie required for men. Dinner $63. AE, DC, DISC, MC, V. Mon–Sat 6–9:30pm. CONTINENTAL.

If the Great Gatsby were alive today, Horizons would surely be his first choice for dining. It certainly would have been the choice of Gatsby's creator, F. Scott Fitzgerald, who was a frequent visitor to the inn some 60 years ago. The most formal, and also the best, restaurant in greater Asheville occupies a prominent position in the city's grandest resort. It's consistently rated among the finest in the nation and has won the AAA Four Diamond Award for seven consecutive years.

Patrons are rewarded with exceptional service and gratifying cuisine. In the formal, ground-level setting in the resort's Sammons Wing, innovative yet classic cuisine is served. Specialties depend on what's fresh at the market on any given day. It may be brook trout, bouillabaisse, or medallions of venison. Dinner includes soup or salad, a main course, dessert, and a nonalcoholic beverage. One food critic declared that the dinner was on a scale that recalled "the scope of Thomas Wolfe's 626-page magnum opus." The wine list is very extensive.

✪ **The Market Place.** 20 Wall St. ☎ **828/252-4162.** Reservations recommended. Main courses $18.95–$26.95. AE, DC, MC, V. Mon–Thurs 6–9pm, Fri–Sat 6–9:30pm. CONTINENTAL.

An upscale casual restaurant with candlelit tables, this establishment has impeccable service. The chef uses extra-fresh ingredients and all herbs and vegetables are grown locally. For all its attributes, the restaurant—although popular with savvy locals—seems to be somehow undervalued and underappreciated, and rarely appears in a guidebook. Yet some of its dishes rival those at the Grove Park Inn. Try, for example, the fresh grilled salmon, the fresh filet mignon, or the duo—a platter of lamb and marinated grilled venison. Many dishes are nouvelle in style and preparation, and the professional staff is knowledgeable about the extensive wine list.

Mountain Smoke House BBQ. 802 Fairview Rd., next door to the River Ridge Market Place. ☎ **828/298-8121.** Reservations required only for groups of 10 or more. Main courses $9–$18; buffet $19. AE, DC, DISC, MC, V. Tues–Sat 11:45am–11pm. SOUTHERN.

This is one of the liveliest places in town and also serves some of the finest Southern dishes, especially barbecue. Situated in a modern upscale building, it's a casual, down-home sort of place with a family atmosphere. The Friday and Saturday night buffet is one of the best values in town, featuring four meat dishes, seven vegetables, and six desserts, plus tea and coffee. You can also order á la carte such local favorites as smoked mountain trout, smokehouse stuffed peppers, smoked salmon, and port barbecue. Vegetarian and children's menus are also offered. The full bar hosts live music on Friday and Saturday, featuring blues or bluegrass.

Vicenzo's. 10 N. Market St. ☎ **828/254-4698.** Reservations suggested but not required. Main courses $10–$26.95. AE, DC, DISC, MC, V. Mon–Fri 11:30am–2pm and Mon–Sat 5:30–11pm, Sun 5:30–9:30pm. NORTHERN ITALIAN.

The premier Italian restaurant in Asheville is in the central part of the historic district. A bustling trattoria with a piano bar, it has eclectic decor with Art Deco overtones. True, chances are that you will have had finer Italian dinners than this in your life, but what you get isn't bad. Try veal chop Milanese with pasta or filet mignon with cream sauce, mussels, and asparagus. Cioppino is filled with goodies, including fresh whitefish, scallops, and shrimp over linguine flavored with a spicy red sauce. The penne pasta with charbroiled chicken, peppers, pepperoni, and spinach is excellent, as are the veal dishes.

ASHEVILLE AFTER DARK

Barley's. 42 Biltmore Ave. ☎ **828/255-0504.**

This pub has a vast array of imported beer, as well as its own microbrewery. There's never a cover charge, although the club is a venue for live entertainment, including jazz, blues, rock, and alternative rock. Pizza, nachos, salads, and soups are offered. Hours are Monday to Thursday 11:30am to midnight and Friday and Saturday 11:30am to 1am.

Be Here Now. 5 Biltmore Ave. ☎ **828/258-2071.** Cover $5–$20.

A smoke-free dance hall, pub, and concert hall, this upscale club features local musicians and performers from around the country. The entertainment, depending on the evening, may range from bluegrass to alternative rock, but there's always a live band. Hours are Monday to Wednesday 1pm to 2am, Thursday and Saturday 1pm to 2am. Live bands go on at 9pm.

Fine Arts Theatre. 36 Biltmore Ave. ☎ **828/232-1536.**

See first-run, art and independent films at this elegant Art Deco/Moderne theater. Beer and wine are also served here. Call for movie titles, times, and ticket prices.

Vincent's Bar. 68B N. Lexington Ave. ☎ **828/259-9119.**

This two-level beer hall and coffeehouse is Asheville's hip address. You reach it through a small side alley. The live entertainment includes everything from poetry slams to heavy metal. The coffeehouse offers an alternative atmosphere for those who don't want to join the bar crowd. There's rarely a cover charge. The food includes cold-cut sandwiches and chicken wings. Hours are Monday to Thursday from noon to midnight, Friday and Saturday from noon to 1am, and Sunday from 3pm to midnight.

SIDE TRIPS FROM ASHEVILLE

About 5 miles east of downtown Asheville, at milepost 382 on the Blue Ridge Parkway, the ✪ **Folk Art Center,** P.O. Box 9545, Asheville, NC 28815 (☎ **828/ 298-7928**), is operated by the Southern Highland Handicraft Guild, a not-for-profit organization of craftspeople in the nine-state southern Appalachian region. The contemporary wood-and-stone structure houses the finest of both traditional and contemporary handcrafts of the region. The **Allanstand Craft Shop,** established in 1895, is one of the oldest craft shops in the country, featuring exhibitions and museum areas. Offered for sale are pottery, ceramics, weavings, jewelry, and handmade quilts, among other merchandise. The center does not charge for admittance but does accept donations. It's open April to December, daily from 9am to 6pm; January to March, daily from 9am to 5pm. The craft shop maintains the same hours.

Chimney Rock Park is 25 miles southeast of Asheville on U.S. 64/74A. The granite monolith rises to a height of 360 feet; you can reach its top by a stairway, a trail, or an elevator. An observation lounge is open daily (weather permitting), and the charge is $10.95 for adults, $5 for children 6 to 15. Trails lead to Needle's Eye, Moonshiner's Cave, and Devil's Head (on the way to Hickory Nut Falls, which is twice the height of Niagara). *The Last of the Mohicans* was filmed here, and costumes and other artifacts from the movie are on display in the observation lounge. Food service is available for $6 or less, and there are picnic facilities. For full details, a free color brochure, and a trail map, contact Chimney Rock Park, P.O. Box 39, Chimney Rock, NC 28720 (☎ **800/277-9611** or 828/625-9611).

Stately **Mount Mitchell,** highest point in the East, is in the state park that bears its name, some 33 miles northeast on the parkway and then 5 miles north on N.C. 128. Mount Mitchell has a museum, a tower, and an observation lodge; camping and picnicking facilities are available in the park.

About 30 miles southeast of Asheville on I-26 is the pastoral little town of Flat Rock, home of the North Carolina State Theater's **Flat Rock Playhouse** (☎ **828/ 693-0731**), which opened in 1952. It hosts the popular Vagabond Players, a troupe launched on Broadway in 1937. The group presents *The World of Carl Sandburg* and *The Rootabaga Stories* annually.

Flat Rock is even more famous as the home of Carl Sandburg, the two-time Pulitzer Prize—winning writer/poet/historian known for his biography of Abraham Lincoln. His **Connemara,** 1928 Little River Rd., just west of I-26 (☎ **828/693-4178**), is open daily from 9am to 5pm, charging an admission of $3 for adults; children 16 and under are admitted free. Now a National Historic Site, the big white farmhouse is administered by the National Park Service, which offers guided formal tours. Sandburg purchased the 240-acre farm in 1945 for $40,000. He called it Connemara, after the mountains of Ireland. Sandburg was quite a reader: The walls of his modest abode are filled with approximately 10,000 volumes of books, bookmarked and dog-eared; in the living room is his collection of walking sticks. The grounds include a goat house occupied by the charming descendants of a prize herd of goats raised by Sandburg's wife. Sandburg died of a stroke in his bedroom here when he was 90.

3 Boone

95 miles NE of Asheville

In the heart of the Blue Ridge Mountains, Boone has long been a favorite vacation destination. During the 1880s, Southerners came here to escape the summer heat. In recent years, Boone has become a ski destination in winter. Daniel Boone traveled through this area on his way to Kentucky in the late 1700s—hence, the town's name.

Boone has been called "the coolest spot in the South," with an average temperature of 68°F in summer. Golf, tennis, swimming, fishing, skiing, and sightseeing are part of the local attractions. The region's rugged terrain lends itself to a variety of high-adventure outdoor sports, from mountain biking and canoeing to whitewater rafting and rock climbing. For summer visitors, there's also the outdoor drama, Kermit Hunter's *Horn in the West,* as well as an Appalachian Summer Festival of concerts, drama, and art exhibits.

ESSENTIALS

GETTING THERE   Boone lies 1 hour from I-77, I-81, and I-40 and is accessible from a trio of major highways, including U.S. 321, U.S. 421, and U.S. 221. N.C. 105 provides access from U.S. 221.

The nearest airport is at Asheville (☎ **828/687-9446**).

VISITOR INFORMATION   The **Boone Area Convention and Visitors Bureau,** 208 Howard St., Boone, NC 28607 (☎ **800/852-9506** or 828/264-2225), is open Monday to Friday from 9am to 5pm. Information is also available at the **High Country Host,** 1700 Blowing Rock Rd. (☎ **828/264-1299**), which is open daily from 9am to 5pm.

SEEING THE SIGHTS

Daniel Boone Native Gardens, Horn in the West Drive, 1 mile east of U.S. 421 (☎ **828/264-6390**), next door to the Daniel Boone Theatre, offers a collection of native North Carolina plants in an informal landscaped design. Weather permitting, the gardens are open daily from May 1 to October 15, and on weekends in October from 9am to 6pm. June 15 to August 15, they remain open until 8pm. Admission is $2 for visitors 16 and older.

Also adjacent to the theater is the **Hickory Ridge Homestead Museum** (☎ **828/ 264-2120**), an 18th-century living-history museum in a re-created log cabin. Traditional craftspeople demonstrate their skills, and there's a homestead store. An apple festival is held on the grounds in late October, and Christmas events are on tap in mid-December. Hours are as follows: May to September, daily 1 to 8pm; October to April, Saturday 10am to 4pm and Sunday 1 to 4:30pm. Admission is $2.

Tweetsie Railroad Theme Park, Blowing Rock Road, halfway between Boone and Banner Elk (☎ **800/526-5740** or 828/264-9061), is not just for the kids; the whole family can enjoy it. An old narrow-gauge train winds along a 3-mile route, suffering mock attacks by "Indians" and "outlaws." There's mountain music and other entertainment, along with restaurants, Western shops, country-fair rides, a petting zoo, and a crafts area. The season lasts from mid-May to November 1, and the park is open daily from 9am to 6pm mid-May to August 30. September 1 to November 1, the park is open Friday to Sunday from 9am to 6pm. The park is also open on Labor Day. Admission is $20 for adults, $14 for children 3 to 12 and seniors over 60. Get your tickets early for the popular "Ghost Train" night rides, part of Tweetsie's Halloween Festival, held on October weekends. An assortment of entertainment and games is available for very young children, for whom the Ghost Train ride is not recommended. Admission is $15 per person, and gates open at 7:30pm.

OUTDOOR PURSUITS

GOLF   The **Boone Golf Club,** U.S. 321/221, Blowing Rock Rd. (☎ **828/264-8760**), an 18-hole, par-71 course designed by Ellis Maples, is 6,400 yards long from its longest tees. It's the standard against which all High Country public courses are measured. Opened in 1958, with its natural routing and electrifying greens, it remains a perennial favorite. Greens fees from June to October are $32 Monday to Thursday, rising to $37 Friday to Sunday. Off-season fees range from $27 to $32. Depending on the weather, the course is open April to November, Monday to Friday from 8am to 7pm and on Saturday and Sunday from 7:30am to 7pm. Professional instruction costs $35 to $40 per hour, and clubs are available for rent at $15 for 18 holes. A pro shop is on-site, and there's a restaurant at the clubhouse.

RAFTING & OTHER SPORTS   **Wahoos,** on U.S. 321 between Boone and the Tweetsie Railroad Theme Park (☎ **800/444-RAFT** or 828/262-5775), is the best all-around center to connect you with year-round outdoor adventures, ranging from whitewater rafting and tubing in summer to cross-country skiing in winter, and including spelunking, fishing, hiking, and snowboarding. Tours are available for all ages. The office is open daily from 8am to 8pm in summer and 9am to 6pm in winter.

Rafting on the Lower Pigeon River costs $20 per person, and participants must be 3 years old for the 1-hour tour. Rafting on the Upper Pigeon River is for those 8 years of age or older; the 1-hour tour costs $35 per person. Nolichucky River rafting is for those 7 years or older, costs $65 to $85 per person, and lasts 5 to 6 hours, including transportation and lunch. Watauga River rafting, for those 3 and older, lasts 2 hours and costs $35 to $42 per person, including lunch and transportation. Canoeing is possible in the New River, with three 5-hour excursions costing $20 per person. Wahoos can also make reservations at local campsites.

SHOPPING

In the tiny town of Valle Crucis, 10 miles west of Boone, **Mast General Store,** Highway 194 (☎ **828/262-0000;** www.mastgeneralstore.com), is arguably the most famous store in Appalachia. Dating from 1883, it is listed on the National Register of Historic Places. Its plank floors are worn to a smooth sheen, and on cold mountain mornings, a potbellied stove is still fired up. From overalls to brogans, red ribbons to calico patterns, the store has a wide assortment of sturdy clothing, shoes, and boots—all the outdoor gear you'll need to become a mountain man or mountain mama. You'll also find old-time salves, wind-up toys, regional music, rock candy, and peanut brittle on sale. Hours are Monday to Saturday 10am to 6pm, Sunday 1 to 6pm. If you don't want to drive out to the hamlet of Valle Crucis, you'll find similar merchandise at the outlet in Boone, **Old Boone Mercantile,** 104 E. King St. (☎ **828/963-6511**). Hours are Monday to Saturday 7am to 6:30pm, Sunday 1 to 6pm.

WHERE TO STAY

Holiday Inn Express. 1855 Blowing Rock Rd., Boone, NC 28607. ☎ **800/HOLIDAY** or 828/264-2451. Fax 828/265-3861. www.holiday-inn.com. E-mail: holidayinn@boone.net. 138 units. A/C TV TEL. $59–$139 double; $150–$249 suite. Rates include continental breakfast. Additional person $8 extra. Children 11 and under stay free in parents' room. AE, CB, DC, DISC, MC, V.

Within 20 minutes of the downhill ski runs, this is the best motel in the Boone area. The rooms are well maintained and exactly what you'd expect from this dependable chain. Facilities include a fitness center and pool. There's no on-site restaurant, although several restaurants and diners are within walking distance.

Lovill House Inn. 404 Old Bristol Rd., Boone, NC 28607. ☎ **800/849-9466** or 828/264-4204. www.lovillhouseinn.com. E-mail: innkeeper@lovillhouseinn.com. 6 units. TV TEL. $145–$210 double. Rates include full breakfast. MC, V. No children under 12.

Dating from 1875, this inn was originally a private home. The house stands on 11 wooded acres. When Lori and Tim Shahen bought it in 1993, the house was in wretched shape, but it's now one of the finest places to stay in the area. Floors and walls are double-insulated, and the bedrooms are tastefully furnished. Quality linens and goose-down comforters are just two of the thoughtful touches. Three of the original brick fireplaces remain. Breakfast is served in a dining room with picture-view windows. In summer, guests gather on a spacious veranda before dinner to meet one another.

WHERE TO DINE

Dan'l Boone Inn. 130 Hardin St. ☎ **828/264-8657.** Reservations accepted only for parties of 15 or more. Breakfast $7.95; lunch/dinner $11.95; children's plates $2.95–$5.95. No credit cards. Breakfast: Sat–Sun 8–11am year-round. Dinner: June–Oct, Mon–Fri 11:30am–9pm, Sat–Sun 11am–9pm; off-season, Mon–Fri 5–8pm, Sat–Sun 11am–9pm. SOUTHERN.

So legendary is this place in this part of North Carolina that many motorists will drive the 5 miles from the parkway to dine here. The inn is one of the oldest buildings in town, with a rustic atmosphere that attracts a huge family trade. But what really brings 'em in is the down-home Southern cooking, served family-style and based on fresh ingredients. That means Southern fried chicken, country-fried steak, and a choice of five vegetables. Lunch or dinner comes with soup or salad, vegetables, a choice of three meats, homemade biscuits, a homemade dessert (usually rich and creamy), and a beverage. Breakfast offers such Southern savories as country ham, grits, and stewed apples. If you come here on New Year's Day, you can participate in the Southern tradition of eating black-eyed peas and collard greens, for good luck in the coming year. The cuisine is in the style of fill-'em up, with heaping platters and bowls of everything. What you get isn't bad, and it's so reasonable that you'll feel the waiter left several items off your bill when it comes time to settle up.

BOONE AFTER DARK

Kermit Hunter's ✪ *Horn in the West* is presented in the Daniel Boone Theatre, 591 Horn in the West Dr., Boone, NC 28607 (☎ **828/264-2120**), every night except Monday from late June through mid-August. The play tells a vivid story of the pioneers' efforts to win freedom during the American Revolution. Performances begin at 8pm, and admission is $12 (half-price for children 12 and under). Tickets can be ordered in advance by mail and will be held at the box office for pickup.

4 Banner Elk

136 miles NW of Charlotte

The village of Banner Elk used to be about the sleepiest place in the High Country until it was discovered by scenery hounds in summer and skiers in winter. Banner Elk is on N.C. 194, enclosed by mountains. In winter, skiers can head for Sugar Mountain or Ski Beech. The town also makes a good center for exploring Grandfather Mountain, just north of Linville, a wealthy enclave where many owners have summer homes.

ESSENTIALS

GETTING THERE   To reach Banner Elk from Asheville, take I-40 east to U.S. 221 north, passing through Marion to Linville. Exit onto N.C. 105 north at Linville until you reach the intersection of N.C. 194 east. Turn left onto N.C. 194 east and proceed for roughly 4 miles into Banner Elk.

VISITOR INFORMATION   The **Avery/Banner Elk Chamber of Commerce,** N.C. 184, High Country Square (P.O. Box 335), Banner Elk, NC 28604 (☎ **800/ 972-2183** or 828/898-5605; www.banner-elk.com), will provide a packet of data about activities in the area to those who write. It's open Monday to Friday from 9am to 5pm.

SPECIAL EVENTS   Kilt-clad Scots from Scotland (as well as all parts of North America) gather here early in July for the annual **Highland Games and Gathering of the Clans.** Bagpipe music, dancing, wrestling, and tossing the caber (a shaft that resembles a telephone pole), as well as the colorful mix of people bent on 2 days of fun, make this a spectacle not to be missed.

GRANDFATHER MOUNTAIN

✪ **Grandfather Mountain,** on U.S. 221 near Linville (☎ **828/733-4337**), a mile off the Blue Ridge Parkway, is the highest peak in the Blue Ridge. You can see as far as 100 miles from the **Mile High Swinging Bridge;** the **Environmental Habitat** is the home of Mildred the Bear and her black-bear friends. In a spacious separate section, you can also view native deer, cougars, and bald and golden eagles (which have been injured and cannot live in the wild on their own). Grandfather Mountain is open daily except Thanksgiving and Christmas from 8am to 5pm in winter, to 6pm in spring and fall, and to 7pm in summer. Admission is $10 for adults, $5 for children 4 to 12.

OUTDOOR PURSUITS

GOLF   The **Hawksnest Golf & Ski Resort,** 1800 Skyland Dr., off N.C. 105 in Seven Devils (☎ **800/822-4295** or 828/963-6561; www.hawksnest-resort.com), is a scenic 18-hole, par-72, 6,200-yard championship course at the cool elevation of 4,200 feet. It's a true mountain course with good putting surfaces. From mid-March to

November, the course is open daily from 7am to 7pm. Including the use of a cart, greens fees are $36 Monday to Friday before 1pm, or $22 after 1pm. On Saturday and Sunday greens fees are $39 before 1pm, or $29 after 1pm. Clubs can be rented for $15 for 18 holes. Reserved tee times are recommended.

Village of Sugar Mountain Golf Course, N.C. 184 (☎ **800/SUGARMT** or 828/ 898-6464), outside Banner Elk, is an 18-hole, par-64 course at the foot of the Sugar Mountain Ski Resort. This executive course offers variety and a par-5 hole designed by Arnold Palmer. It charges $28 for greens fees.

SKIING   The ✪ **Ski Beech Mountain area,** on N.C. 187 at 1007 Beech Mountain Pkwy. (P.O. Box 1118), Beech Mountain, NC 28604 (☎ **800/438-2093** or 828/387-2011), is one of the top ski resorts in the East, and was voted No. 1 in the Southeast by *National Ski Magazine,* competing with slopes in Tennessee, West Virginia, Virginia, and other areas of North Carolina. The Beech Mountain Express is the South's first high-speed quad-chair lift, with a peak elevation of 5,500 feet. There are 14 slopes: five beginner, six intermediate, and three advanced. There's also an 830-foot vertical drop.

The resort is open from Thanksgiving to mid-March. Lift rates are $27 Monday to Friday, going up to $45 on Saturday, Sunday, and holidays. Lifts operate daily from 8:30am to 4:30pm and 6 to 10pm. Ski rental is $12 Monday to Friday and $16 on weekends and holidays. Professional lessons are available for $40 per hour. There's also a nursery, the Land of Oz, which is open during lift hours; the cost is $60 per child for a full day, $45 for a half-day. Snow tubing and ice-skating are also available for $10 each for a 2-hour period. Sessions are held every 2 hours, beginning at noon during the week and 10am on the weekends.

A competing resort, the **Hawksnest Golf & Ski Resort,** 1800 Skyland Dr., Seven Devils, NC 28604 (☎ **800/822-HAWK** or 828/963-6561; www.hawksnest-resort. com), is northeast of Banner Elk and 10 miles south off N.C. 105. It offers 12 slopes—one expert, three advanced, five intermediate, and three beginner—with a peak elevation of 4,819 feet and a 669-foot vertical drop. Lift tickets cost $22 to $35, depending on the time of season and the length of time for which you plan to ski. Ski rentals range from $15. During the December-to-March season, the resort is open Sunday to Thursday from 9am to 10pm, on Friday from 9am to 2am, and on Saturday from 9am to 4:30pm and 6pm to 2am. Professional ski instruction is available for $40 to $60 per half- or full day.

Sugar Mountain, N.C. 194, a mile from N.C. 105 (P.O. Box 369), Banner Elk, NC 28604 (☎ **800/SUGARMT** or 828/898-4521; www.skisugar.com), has 18 slopes—two expert, nine intermediate, and seven beginner—with an elevation of 5,300 feet and a vertical drop of 1,200 feet. The resort is open from mid-November to mid-March. Lifts operate daily from 9am to 4:30pm and 6 to 10pm, with tickets ranging from $16 to $45. Ski rentals range from $6 to $15, depending on the time of day and the type of skis, and professional lessons are also available, at $15 per member of a group or $40 per person hourly. Children 5 to 10 can participate in a Bunny School from 10am to 3pm daily, including lunch, for $50 per student.

WHERE TO STAY

Archer's Mountain Inn. 2489 Beech Mountain Pkwy., Beech Mountain, NC 28604. ☎ **888/827-6155** or 828/898-9004. Fax 828/898-9007. www.archersinn.com. E-mail: tony@archersinn.com. 15 units. TV. $70–$150 double; $125–$200 suite. Rates include full breakfast. Each additional person $10. DISC, MC, V.

Located on Beech Mountain between the towns of Banner Elk and Beech Mountain, this resort is a good choice if you want to sample all the skiing in the area. The inn features 15 rooms in two buildings. Laurel Lodge and the Hawks View both have views of Sugar Mountain and the Grandfather Mountains just outside your window. The rooms in Laurel Lodge are essentially designed for couples; all have fireplaces. Some of the more expensive rooms and suites feature whirlpools. Hawk's View offers more spacious rooms, with efficiency kitchens and fireplaces. These rooms are better equipped for serving a large party. The building has large porches with rockers where the guests can take in views of the mountain range. The inn's restaurant, Jackalope's View, serves international fare prepared by the restaurant's two chefs.

✪ **Banner Elk Inn Bed and Breakfast.** N.C. 407 Main St. E, Banner Elk, NC 28604. ☎ **828/898-6223.** www.bannerelkinn.com. 5 units. $95–$110 double. Rates include full breakfast weekends, continental breakfast weekdays. MC, V.

Beverly Lait is one of the most gracious innkeepers in the High Country. Long an official U. S. embassy host abroad, she launched this B&B in 1990. The handsome, rejuvenated pink house is furnished in a medley of styles and includes antiques and art objects collected during Lait's world travels, as well as art by the hostess herself. The quartet of bedrooms have Victorian double beds or queen-size or twin beds. Two of the units contain private baths; otherwise, baths are shared. Pets are allowed under some circumstances. Smoking is prohibited. Guests meet fellow guests around the fireplace on a nippy afternoon and join one another the following morning for one of the delectable breakfasts that might include sourdough bread fresh from the oven. The inn is about 6 miles from the Blue Ridge Parkway.

The Tufts House Inn. 254 Edgar Tufts Rd. (Rte. 2, Box 25A), Banner Elk, NC 28604. ☎ **828/898-7944.** Fax 828/963-6511. www.highsouth.com/tuftshouse. 4 units. $95–$120 double. AE, CB, DISC, MC, V. No children under 12.

This is hill-country Carolina living at its finest. Set a mile or so from the heart of Banner Elk, this local home, in a pastoral 40-acre setting near the Elk River Resort, was built in 1932 of native wood and stone. Mountain views unfold in many directions. The inn offers four country-style bedrooms. Provincial antiques add grace notes, and guests gather around a warm fire in the best inn tradition. Breakfast is one of the finest served by any B&B in the area. Dean and Nancy Barnett bring a warm and generous spirit to innkeeping, and they are happy to advise guests about outdoor activities in the area, including hiking and biking.

WHERE TO DINE

Morels. 1 Banner St. (off N.C. 184). ☎ **828/898-6866.** Reservations required. Main courses $18–$30. MC, V. Tues–Sun 6–10pm. NEW AMERICAN.

Many local foodies consider this to be the resort's finest dining room, and we concur. Every edible item in the kitchen is homemade, and you can count on cooking with imaginative touches. It's served in a somewhat-cramped dark-green dining room. Standout dishes include roast monkfish with lobster sauce and seasonal vegetables; grilled veal chop with mushrooms and onions; honey and tamari-seared salmon with a sauce made of leeks, cream, and vinegar; and sautéed sweetbreads with a mustard-cream sauce. The restaurant is very popular with skiers in winter.

5 Blowing Rock

90 miles NE of Asheville

One of the oldest resorts in North Carolina, Blowing Rock dates back to the 1800s. Sitting on the Continental Divide at an elevation of 4,000 feet, Blowing Rock is filled with little B&Bs, inns, and galleries. It makes a good base for exploring and offers the state's best skiing (at Appalachian Mountain) in winter.

ESSENTIALS

GETTING THERE   By Car   To reach Blowing Rock from Asheville, head north on the Blue Ridge Parkway or take I-40 east out of Asheville to U.S. 321 north and follow the signs into Blowing Rock. From Boone, take U.S. 321 south directly into Blowing Rock.

VISITOR INFORMATION   The **Blowing Rock Chamber of Commerce,** Main Street (P.O. Box 406), Blowing Rock, NC 28605 (☎ **800/295-7851** or 828/ 295-7851; www.blowingrock.com), is open Monday to Thursday from 9am to 5pm, Friday and Saturday 9am to 5:30pm, dispensing information about the area.

EXPLORING THE AREA

The area's biggest attraction, from which the town takes its name, is ✪ **Blowing Rock** (☎ **828/295-7111**), on U.S. 321, 2 miles south of town. Rising 4,000 feet above John's River Gorge, the mountain has a strong updraft that returns any light object (such as a handkerchief) that's thrown into the void. The observation tower, gazebos, and gardens offer panoramic views of the John's River Gorge and nearby Blue Ridge peaks. You can visit March to April and September daily from 9am to 6pm; April to August daily 8am to 8pm; October daily 8am to 7pm; and in winter daily from 9am to 5pm, weather permitting. Admission is $4 for adults, $1 for children 6 to 11.

Another natural phenomenon at Blowing Rock is **Mystery Hill,** where balls and water run uphill. The pioneer museum is interesting, and you'll get a kick out of the mock grave marked simply HE WAS A REVENOOR—a pile of dirt with boots sticking out one end.

OUTDOOR PURSUITS

HORSEBACK RIDING   Blowing Rock Stables (☎ 828/295-7847) offers rides daily, weather permitting, from 10am to 4:30pm. Both English and Western saddles are used, and there's access to 27 miles of trails. The cost is $30 an hour or $50 for 2 hours. Riders must be 9 years of age or older. Reservations are required. Call for information and directions.

SKIING   The **Appalachian Ski Mountain,** P.O. Box 106, Blowing Rock, NC 28605 (☎ **800/322-2373** or 828/295-7828; www.appskimtn.com), lies 2 miles off U.S. 221/321 between Boone and Blowing Rock near the Blue Ridge Parkway intersection. It offers nine slopes: two beginner, four intermediate, and three advanced. It stands at an elevation of 4,000 feet, with a 365-foot vertical drop. The season runs from the weekend before Thanksgiving to the third weekend in March, when it's open daily from 9am to 4pm and 6 to 10pm. Lift tickets cost $25 for adults Monday to Friday and $35 on weekends and holidays. Children 12 and under are charged $13 and $21, respectively. Ski lessons are available for $35 per hour for private instruction, but cost only $15 per person in a group. Skis can be rented for $15.

SHOPPING

Specializing in rustic handmade furniture, **Appalachian Rustic Furnishings,** 1085 N. Main St. (☎ 828/295-9554), offers one-of-a-kind original furniture. Choose among various styles and accessories in the showroom or place custom orders. Porch swings, chairs, tables, beds, settees, rockers, whatever—it's all here. Hours are Monday to Saturday 10am to 6pm and Sunday noon to 5pm. **Expressions Craft Guild & Gallery,** Main Street (☎ 828/295-7839), is a cooperative gallery featuring handmade contemporary art and crafts from the North Carolina mountains. The location is in the center of Blowing Rock across from the post office. Hours are daily 10am to 6pm.

Orchard at Altapass, milepost 328.4 on the Blue Ridge Parkway, at Spruce Pine on Orchard Road (☎ 828/765-9531), sells apples and peaches from July to November; you pick, or they pick. The orchard offers an array of fresh baked goods, free tours, and even music and tall tales. The proprietors will arrange hay rides for you on Saturday and Sunday. From May to October hours Monday to Saturday are 10am to 6pm or noon to 6pm on. The rest of the year the store is open only on Saturday 10am to 6pm, Sunday noon to 6pm. Finally, **Parkway Craft Center** (☎ 828/295-7938) is at milepost 294 on the Bridge Ride Parkway in the Moses Cone Manor just off Route 221. Here, you'll discover the finest-quality Appalachian Mountain crafts, handmade by members of the Southern Highland Craft Guild. Craft demonstrations are presented on the porch. Open daily 9am to 6pm.

WHERE TO STAY

Crippen's Country Inn (see "Where to Dine," below) also rents bedrooms.

Green Park. P.O. Box 7, Blowing Rock, NC 28605. ☎ **800/852-2462** or 828/295-3141. Fax 828/295-3141. 85 units. TV TEL. $79–$129 double; $119–$149 suite. AE, DISC, MC, V. Take U.S. 321 2 miles southeast of town.

Once upon a time, this 1882 hotel, listed on the National Register of Historic Places, received such guests as John D. Rockefeller, Franklin D. Roosevelt, and Calvin Coolidge. That illustrious list of names might make you think that the place needs refurbishing today, but the old-fashioned and timeworn charm is part of its appeal. The hotel's fans are mostly an older crowd that likes to while away the time in the wicker rocking chairs on the veranda. The sprawling, three-story Victorian inn straddles the Eastern Continental Divide at an elevation of 4,300 feet near John's River Gorge. In these relatively cool climes, there's no air-conditioning, so ceiling fans whirl in the guest rooms. Rooms have one or two queen-size beds and quilted spreads. Both Cajun and Mediterranean specialties are served in the dining room, and facilities include a pool. Golf and tennis are available at a nearby country club.

✪ **Hound Ears Lodge.** Off N.C. 105 S near Boone, P.O. Box 188, Blowing Rock, NC 28605. ☎ **828/963-4321.** Fax 828/963-8030. www.houndears.com. 33 units. A/C TV TEL. $250 double; $289 suite for 2, $600 suite for 4. Rates include breakfast and dinner. AE, MC, V.

If you want high style, this exclusive resort should be your mountain retreat. Its unusual name derives from a nearby rock formation. The setting is panoramic, on 700 acres with an 18-hole golf course. Guest rooms, except for seven in the main clubhouse, are in chalets complete with "Oh, that view!" balconies and pitched roofs. Bedrooms are spacious. The hotel doesn't serve liquor, but guests can bring their own. Facilities include six tennis courts (four clay, two hard), the golf course, small lakes for fishing, and a summer-only heated pool in a grotto. Fishing and skiing are the major pastimes.

WHERE TO DINE

Crippen's Country Inn and Restaurant. 239 Sunset Dr., Blowing Rock, NC 28607. ☎ **828/295-3487.** Fax 828/295-0388. Reservations strongly recommended. Main courses $18–$35. AE, DISC, MC, V. Summer daily 6–9pm. Winter Tues–Sun 6–9pm. AMERICAN.

The restaurant's sophisticated cuisine is one of the reasons why people stay at Crippen's Country Inn. The spacious dining area with circular tables offers a surprising amount of intimacy despite the crowds. The menu changes daily, offering many creative and delectable delights. You may begin with a shrimp brûlée, pan-roasted with blue-spot prawns, or a crispy duck confit with spring rolls and peanut-ginger dressing. The chef's specialties round out the main courses: grilled loin of venison wrapped with applewood-smoked bacon and pan-seared tuna with fried oysters and ham-and-scallions sauce. Reservations are extremely important; the restaurant's closing hours often reflect the number of reservations it receives for the evening. The inn also rents 8 bedrooms, each of which is comfortable and well furnished; prices range from $99 to $120 (double occupancy).

✪ **Riverwood Restaurant.** U.S. 321 just south of the Blue Ridge Parkway. ☎ **828/ 295-4162.** Reservations recommended. Main courses $13.95–$20. DISC, MC, V. Tues–Fri 6–10pm, Sat 5:30–10pm. CONTINENTAL.

One of the most popular restaurants in Blowing Rock, drawing regular patrons from as far away as Raleigh, the Riverwood continues to dazzle diners with inventive creations. Service is on par with the food. A changing menu might start with shrimp sautéed in dill pepperoncini oil with red seedless grapes and feta cheese, served over angel-hair pasta, or fresh portabello mushrooms, garlic, and parsley sautéed in a buttery hazelnut oil and tossed with bow-tie pasta. All main courses are served with a dinner-size house salad, along with rice pilaf, seasonal vegetables, and fresh-baked rolls. Main courses may include Cornish game hen in the chef's sauce and served with wild mushroom aioli or roast half duckling topped with a sun-dried tomato-raspberry glaze. The dill chicken dish draws raves; ask your server about it.

6 The Blue Ridge Parkway

The ✪ **Blue Ridge Parkway** takes up where Virginia's Skyline Drive leaves off at Rockfish Gap, between Charlottesville and Waynesboro. It then continues winding and twisting along the mountain crests for 469 miles, passing through most of western North Carolina before it reaches Great Smoky Mountains National Park near the Tennessee border.

The parkway links the southern end of Shenandoah National Park in Virginia with the eastern entrance of Great Smoky Mountains National Park in North Carolina. When it was begun 60 years ago, the parkway was a great engineering challenge. During the Roosevelt era, it was designed as a federal public-works project to relieve massive unemployment in the region. Its final segment, the Linn Cove Viaduct, was constructed in the 1980s.

The northern section of the parkway skims the crest of the towering Blue Ridge Mountains, with panoramic views of grand valleys on both sides of the road. But when the parkway twists and curls in the more rugged Pisgah and Black mountains to the south, the panoramas become even more dramatic.

Because the mountains are higher in the south—and the temperatures are lower— fall foliage is at its most brilliant here earlier in October than in the northern part. October, in fact, is the peak visiting month, as literally thousands of people come to see the incredible scarlet of sourwoods, orange sassafras, and golden poplars, to name only a few. Traffic moves at a snail's pace in October, and Saturday and Sunday are especially crowded on the parkway. Reservations for lodging and certain attractions in summer and especially in October are essential.

You can detour to Waynesville on October 21 for the best apple festival in the region. On sale are cider, apple butter, and fresh and dried apples. Square dancers perform, and bluegrass bands entertain the crowds. Waynesville lies 7 miles from the parkway at milepost 443.1. For more information, write **Haywood County Apple Festival,** P.O. Box 308, Waynesville, NC 28786 (☎ **828/456-3575**).

Elevations range from 649 to 6,053 feet above sea level. The parkway has frequent exits to nearby towns but no tolls. There are 11 visitor contact stations, nine campgrounds (open May to October only; no reservations) with drinking water and comfort stations, but no shower or utility hookups; restaurants and gas stations; and three lodges, plus one location featuring rustic cabins for overnight stays (reservations recommended). Opening and closing dates for campgrounds and cabins are flexible, so be sure to check in advance. Before you set out, write ahead for maps and detailed information. Contact Superintendent, **Blue Ridge Parkway,** 400 BB&T Building, 1 Pack Sq., Asheville, NC 28801 (☎ **828/298-0358;** www.nps.gov/blueridge).

At many overlooks, you'll see a rifle-and-powderhorn symbol and the word *Trail,* which means that there are marked walking trails through the woods. Some trails take only 10 or 20 minutes and provide a leg-stretching break from the confines of the car; others are longer and steeper and may take an hour or more if you go the entire way.

A few simple rules have been laid down by the National Park Service, which administers the parkway: no commercial vehicles; no swimming in lakes and ponds; no hunting; no pets without a leash; and above all, no fires except in campground or picnic-area fireplaces. Another good rule is to keep your gas tank half-filled at all times; this is no place to be stranded. The speed limit is 45 miles an hour, and they're quite serious about that.

Don't plan to hurry down the Blue Ridge: Take time to amble and drink in the beauty. If you want to drive the entire length of the parkway, allow at least 2 or 3 days. On the first day, drive the Virginia half; then stop for the night at Boone, North Carolina, not far from the state border. The final two legs of the trip—from Boone to Asheville and from there to Fontana Village—can easily be accomplished in another day's drive.

A HOSTEL ALONG THE PARKWAY   The only licensed American Youth Hostel along the Blue Ridge Parkway is about 10 miles southeast of Galax, Virginia, 2 miles north of the North Carolina border and 100 feet off the parkway (milepost 214.5). The hostel building is a faithful copy of an ancient Yorktown house, and adjacent is a 19th-century log cabin. Accommodations are dormitory-style, with a kitchen where hostelers do their own cooking and a common room for relaxing and socializing. A mountain stream flows through the 25 acres on which the hostel sits, and the views are stunning. The overnight fee is $12. Book by contacting **Hostelling International-Blue Ridge Mountains,** 214507 Blue Ridge Pkwy., Galax, VA 24333-3432 (☎ **540/236-4962;** www.hiayh.org). To stay here, however, you must be a member of **Hostelling International/American Youth Hostels,** 733 15th St. NW, Suite 840, Washington, DC 20005 (☎ **202/783-6161**). Full membership is $25 a year for adults or $15 for senior citizens. Temporary membership can be purchased at the hostel for $3 per person daily. There's a separate dormitory for both men and women, with separate communal bathing facilities.

SIGHTS NEAR THE PARKWAY   You can veer off the parkway to see several attractions, including **Linville Falls** and **Linville Gorge Wilderness Area** (☎ 828/765-1045), between Linville and Marion. Parking is available at milepost 316 on the parkway. This is a series of two falls, with an upper level of 12 feet and a lower level of 90 feet. The falls plunge into the 2,000-foot-deep Linville Gorge. A 1-mile round-trip hike takes you to the upper falls; other trails lead to more views. Some of the trails are quite challenging. Open year-round, the falls are free.

The 7,600-acre **Linville Gorge Wilderness Area** is a primitive natural environment, whose access is by foot trails off N.C. 183. You need a permit to enter the area and can obtain one at the district ranger's office (signposted) in Marion.

Another major attraction, **Linville Caverns,** lies about 65 miles north of the Folk Art Center (milepost 382 on the Blue Ridge Parkway), just off U.S. 221 between Linville and Marion (☎ 828/756-4171). The only caverns in North Carolina, these tunnels go 2,000 feet underground. The year-round temperature is 51°F. Admission is $5 for adults, $3 children 5 to 12. The caverns are open March to October, daily from 9am to 5pm; off-season, daily from 9am to 4pm.

8 Great Smoky Mountains National Park

Cloaked in mystery, the Great Smoky Mountains were once known by the Cherokee as *sha-cona-ge,* "land of the blue mist" (or smoke). According to Cherokee legend, people and animals originally lived in the sky above the ocean. When the sky became overcrowded, a water beetle was sent to find land but could not, so it dived to the bottom of the ocean and brought up mud to form the Earth. The Smokies were then formed by a great buzzard whose wings touched the mud, hardening it into a mountain range. Geologists have a counter theory that says this range was actually formed by many upheavals and erosions of the land. Choose the one that appeals to you.

The ✪ **Great Smoky Mountains,** formed hundreds of millions of years ago, are the oldest mountains in the world. They're comprised of peaks that range in elevation from 840 to 6,642 feet. The mountainsides are covered with a wide variety of flora and fauna that have few equals throughout the Temperate Zone.

To preserve the pristine beauty of this environment, Great Smoky Mountains National Park was officially established in June 1934. The area was threatened with destruction by the logging industry. A librarian from St. Louis, Horace Kephart, spearheaded the effort to save the area. He was joined by several prominent citizens from Knoxville. The National Park Service, John D. Rockefeller, and eventually the federal government backed their efforts. The people gave the government the land, making it the first national park to be created in this fashion. In September 1940, Great Smoky Mountains National Park was dedicated by President Franklin D. Roosevelt at the Rockefeller monument at Newfound Gap. The park has become one of the most-frequented national parks in the United States, hosting more than 9 million visitors annually.

The oval park, bisected by the North Carolina–Tennessee border, encompasses more than 520,000 acres of forests, streams, rivers, waterfalls, and hiking trails. These trails pass through valleys, peaks, forests, and overlooks that provide scenic and panoramic views. The park also contains balds—patches of clear land in the midst of the wooded slopes. It's still a mystery why these spots do not support tree growth.

The United Nations has designated the park an International Biosphere Reserve because of its multitude of plants, trees, mammals, birds, and fish. More than 100 species of trees thrive in the park. Growing on some of the relatively drier slopes in the lower to middle

Great Smoky Mountains National Park

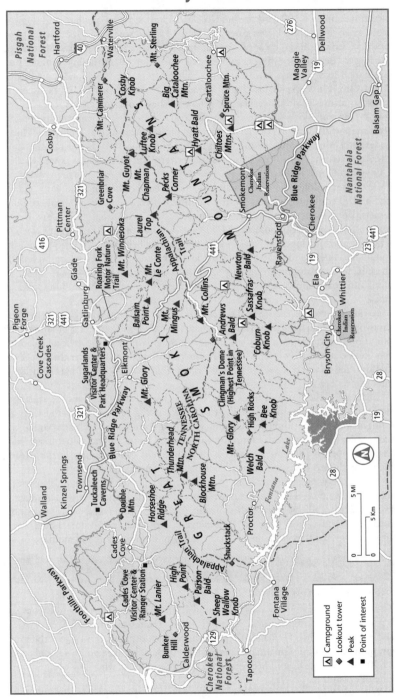

elevations (up to 4,500 feet) are pines, oaks, hickories, yellow poplars, and dogwood trees. Hike the trails at Cades Cove and Laurel Falls to see the species that are typical of this elevation. In several areas, you can find gigantic ancient hemlocks that escaped the loggers' destruction; these hemlocks are located along trails leading from the Roaring Fork Motor Nature Trail to Grotto Falls or from the Newfound Gap Road to Alum Cave Bluffs. At slightly higher elevations are hardwoods typical of those that grow in northern states: beeches and yellow birches. Look for these species at Newfound Gap and along Clingmans Dome Road. The higher elevations (above 4,500 feet) support the kind of evergreens that are typical of areas such as Maine and Quèbec at sea level. Varieties include the Fraser fir and red spruce, which you can find along the Appalachian Trail through most of the eastern half of the park, as well as along Clingmans Dome Road.

Abundant wildflowers offer a kaleidoscope of colors in spring and early summer and a blanket of lush greenery in later summer. Often, nonnative flowers—trilliums, violets, lady's slippers, and jack-in-the-pulpits—have taken over entire areas. Blooming shrubs, numbering more than 1,500 species, are scattered throughout the park. The height of the blooming season is in mid-June, when you'll find rhododendrons, mountain laurels, and azaleas displaying all their beauty. The best places to look for these blooms are among the various balds (such as Gregory, Andrews, and Silers) and along the Cove Hardwoods Nature, the Chimney Tops, and the Noah Bud Ogle Farm trails.

As you ascend the peaks, you'll travel through the blue mists that once were wholly the work of Mother Nature. Unfortunately, they are now composed of almost 70% pollution from factories and cities, and are causing damage to the delicate balance of this area's ecosystem. Pollution has also reduced visibility by 30% over the past several decades. Yet, as you traverse the park, the mists still surround you with a centuries-old aura of mystery.

The park is the home of more than 200 species of birds. The junco, a small gray bird with white outer tailfeathers, patrols the parking lots of Newfound Gap and Clingmans Dome. Although wild turkeys appear throughout the park, you'll most likely view them in the early morning and evening hours around Cades Cove. More than 70 types of fish and 30 varieties of amphibians can be found in the streams, including the red-cheeked salamander, which lives only in the park.

Nearly everyone is interested in the park's wild animals. More than 70 species of mammals live here. The park is known especially for its black bears, which weigh an average 200 to 300 pounds. Other mammals are the white-tailed deer, groundhogs, raccoons, skunks, and bobcats. Park rangers stress that no visitor should try to approach or feed these creatures—for the safety of both humans and animals.

1 Cherokee: Gateway to the Smokies

48 miles SW of Asheville

The Cherokee Nation once claimed around 135,000 square miles of land encompassing sections of South Carolina, North Carolina, Tennessee, Virginia, West Virginia, and Kentucky. When Hernando de Soto, the Spanish explorer, moved into the southern mountains of the Appalachian range in 1540, the Cherokee numbered only about 25,000—a very small number compared with the millions who now occupy former Cherokee land.

When de Soto arrived, he forever changed the way the Cherokee lived. With him on his quest for gold in the name of Spain came misery, disease, and death. Some of de Soto's men killed or enslaved many of the Native Americans, believing that they were holding back information about the location of treasure. It's estimated that during the first 200 years of European occupation, 95% of the Cherokee died of diseases that the foreigners brought with them. The treatment of the Cherokees did not improve in later centuries. When the Cherokees adapted well to the white man's ways and set up a flourishing society, greed and envy eventually culminated, in 1838, in The Trail of Tears. Most of the Cherokee were driven out of the area by military force, and their ancestral lands were taken away.

Today, the Smoky Mountain home of the Cherokee has dwindled to 56,000 acres that make up the Qualla Boundary, also known as the Cherokee Indian Reservation. This land was purchased by a white man, Will Thomas, who gave it to the Cherokee people in the late 1800s. When you visit the reservation, you're entering a sovereign land held in trust specifically for the tribe by the United States government. Known as the Eastern Band of the Cherokee Nation, the Cherokee who still reside here are descendants of the approximately 1,000 Cherokee who hid in these mountains to avoid forced removal to Oklahoma. These people can rightfully claim to be the original inhabitants of the vast Smoky Mountains.

Only a generation ago, the Cherokee language—both the spoken form and the written form—was in danger of becoming extinct. But since the late 1940s, annual increases in tourist-related business and the resultant growth of tribal resources have helped keep it alive. Today, visitors can hear the language spoken at attractions such as the Oconaluftee Indian Village and during the outdoor drama *Unto These Hills.* In Cherokee schools, it's a required subject, and it has also become part of the curriculum of universities such as Western Carolina University in Cullowhee, North Carolina. Tourism is the mainstay of the economy; about 75% of the tribe's revenue is derived from this industry. All business locations within the Qualla Boundary are Native American–owned, but by the authority of the Tribal Council, Native Americans can lease their buildings or businesses to other people. Nearly 30 businesses hold trader's licenses and collect a 6% tribal levy on sales. No other sales tax applies within the boundary, including North Carolina sales tax.

On your visit here, you'll notice several "chiefs" dressed in Western attire. You can have your picture taken with them for a small fee or tip. Many of these "chiefs" have been around for quite a while, priding themselves on having their pictures taken with two or three generations of the same family.

ESSENTIALS

GETTING THERE   From the southern end of the Blue Ridge Parkway and points south, U.S. 441 leads to Cherokee; U.S. 19 runs east and west through the town.

The nearest airport is at Asheville (see "Essentials," in the "Asheville" section of chapter 7).

VISITOR INFORMATION   For more information, contact the **Cherokee Visitor Center,** U.S. 19 (P.O. Box 460), Cherokee, NC 28719 (☎ **800/438-1601** or 828/497-9195), open daily 8am to 5pm.

DISCOVERING CHEROKEE CULTURE

Museum of the Cherokee Indian. U.S. 441 at Drama Rd. ☎ **828/497-3481.** Admission $6 adults, $4 children. Mid-June to Aug Mon–Sat 9am–8pm, Sun 9am–5pm; off-season daily 9am–5pm. Closed major holidays.

The objective of this museum is to "authentically present and preserve thousands of years of Cherokee history and culture." This it does, displaying one of the finest exhibits of Native American artifacts in the United States. In 1997, a $3.5 million renovation was completed, adding features such as an exhibit that includes a digital movie of the creation of the Cherokee Nation. When you enter the building, you begin walking along a timeline, beginning with the Paleolithic era some 10,000 years ago and continuing chronologically to modern times. Also included are lighting special effects, the most impressive of which is a holographic exhibit of the Cherokee. A gift shop is also open in the museum. On the entrance grounds is a 20-foot-tall, hand-carved statue of Sequoyah, the inventor of the Cherokee alphabet. Artifacts that you'll find inside include farming utensils, weapons for hunting and war, clothing, copies of the first photographs taken of the Cherokee people, pottery, baskets, and an art gallery displaying native art and photography.

✪ **Oconaluftee Indian Village.** U.S. 441. ☎ **828/497-2111.** Admission $12 adults, $5 children. Mid-May to Oct, daily 9am–5:30pm.

Operated by the Cherokee Historical Association, this living museum offers a step back in time to the mid-1750s Cherokee way of life. On your tour of the village, you'll see women shaping clay into pottery, arrowheads being chipped, naturally dyed river cane being woven into baskets, and blowguns being demonstrated. Lectures are held at the Ceremonial Grounds, where you'll hear about dances, masks, rattles, feathers, and other facets of Cherokee life, and at the Council House, where presentations are given about Cherokee government, Council House designs, territories, language, and other nonceremonial topics. There's also a mile-long nature trail adjacent to the village. The seven-sided Council House conjures up images of the leaders of seven tribes gathered to thrash out problems or to worship their gods together.

SHOPPING

You'll find many opportunities to take some Cherokee culture home with you. A wide selection of handmade Cherokee products is available, as well as authentic Native American items from other areas. About 16 stores on the Cherokee reservation specialize in crafts, clothing, paintings, or jewelry made by local craftspeople or craftspeople from other tribes. The largest is **Qualla Arts and Crafts** (☎ **828/497-3103**), on U.S. 441 at Drama Road, at the entrance to the *Unto These Hills* arena. Formed in the mid-1940s as a cooperative, Qualla has a current membership of 300 Cherokee, whose items are sold exclusively at the store. It ships products worldwide and is frequently visited by other tribal representatives who are interested in establishing a similar facility on their lands. Whether the craftsperson is a wood carver, pottery maker, finger-weaver, artist, or basket maker, the products show individual artistry and convey a personal link to the makers' ancestors. Hours are daily 9am to 4:30pm.

TROUT FISHING

The major outdoor pursuit on the reservation is **fishing.** Thirty miles of streams are stocked with 400,000 trout annually. Supplemental fish stocks include rainbow, brook, and brown trout, ranging up to trophy size.

Anyone 12 or older needs a tribal permit to fish the Cherokee streams and ponds. No other type of fishing license is accepted on the reservation. The annual season begins the last Saturday of March and ends the last day of February in the following year. Fishing is allowed beginning a half-hour before sunrise and ending a half hour after sunset. The creel limit is 10 trout per day per permit holder. Because of the stocking program, certain sections of the rivers, streams, and ponds are closed on Tuesday and Wednesday. Certain enterprise waters are open only to tribal members.

For complete fishing information, contact **Cherokee Fish and Game Management,** P.O. Box 302, Cherokee, NC 28719, or the visitor center (see "Essentials," earlier in this chapter).

Unto These Hills

Unto These Hills, the most popular outdoor drama in America, is presented each summer at Cherokee. The drama, which has been viewed by some 5 million summer visitors, began in 1950 and has mushroomed since then. It relates the story of the Cherokees from 1540 until The Trail of Tears exodus to Oklahoma in 1838, during which thousands died.

As you watch the first encounter with Hernando de Soto, you'll hear voices echoing off the mountainside—the very mountainside that became a hiding place for Cherokee who were determined to remain in their homeland instead of joining the long march to exile in Oklahoma.

The powerful drama re-creates the inspiration of the great Sequoyah, who created the alphabet that enabled Cherokee to become a written language; the wise leadership of Junaluska; and the sacrifices of Tsali, who gave his life so that a few of his people could remain on their ancestral lands. The emotional impact of this tragic story is supported by a strong musical score.

The 2½-hour show, written by Kermit Hunter, involves 130 performers and technicians. All performances are at the 2,800-seat **Mountainside Theater,** off U.S. 441 (☎ **828/497-2111;** www.untothesehills.com). Traditionally, the drama has a 9-week run. Opening night is around June 15, and the curtain goes down for the last time at August's end. Tickets cost $16 for reserved seating or $14 for general admission; children are charged $6. No shows are presented on Sunday.

WHERE TO STAY

Cherokee has an abundance of motel and hotel rooms offering basic accommodations. In addition to the following listings is the **Holiday Inn-Cherokee,** U.S. 19 S. (☎ **800/HOLIDAY** or 828/497-9181). You'll also find some nifty retro choices that seem to be straight out of a family road trip from the 1940s and 1950s.

Budgetel Inn. U.S. 441 at Acuoni Rd. (P.O. Box 1865), Cherokee, NC 28719. ☎ **800/4-BUDGET** or 828/497-2102. Fax 828/497-5242. www.budgetel.com. 66 units. A/C TV TEL. $45–$85 double; $85–$205 suite. Rates include continental breakfast. AE, DISC, MC, V. Closed mid-Nov to Apr.

Newly built in 1995, this economy choice offers comfortable but decidedly straightforward accommodations. Rooms are basic. Suites contain such amenities as small refrigerators, microwaves, recliners, and sleeper sofas. The rates include in-room coffee and continental breakfast delivered to your door. A swimming pool is on-site. Stay here only for the value.

Hampton Inn. U.S. 19 S. (P.O. Box 1926), Cherokee, NC 28719. ☎ **800/HAMPTON** or 828/497-3115. www.hamptoninn.com. 67 units. A/C TV TEL. $79–$99 double. Rates include continental breakfast. AE, CB, DC, DISC, MC, V.

This place offers simple but perfectly acceptable rooms. Although there's no restaurant on-site, there is a full-service one nearby. An outdoor swimming pool is the most attractive feature here in summer. The motel is located near all major Cherokee attractions, with shopping close by.

Newfound Lodge. 34 U.S. 441, North Cherokee, NC 28719. ☎ **828/497-2746.** Fax 828/497-7136. 72 units. A/C TV TEL. Mar to mid-June $69 double; mid-June to Oct $80 double. AE, DISC, MC, V. Closed Nov–Feb.

Located on the Oconaluftee River, this motel is divided into two sections. One section is set on the mountainside; the other is located across the street and contains balconied rooms overlooking the river. The rooms are spacious; some are decorated in the standard floral motif, whereas others display a more modern geometric design. The bathrooms are rather small. The grounds include a swimming pool, Big Boy restaurant, picnic areas with grills, and a deck that leads down to the rocks below. The motel is centrally located for Cherokee attractions, shopping, and Great Smoky Mountains National Park.

Riverside Motel. U.S. 441 S. at Old Rte. 441 (P.O. Box 58), Cherokee, NC 28719. ☎ **828/ 497-9311.** 24 units. A/C TV TEL. $58–$78 double. AE, DISC, MC, V. Closed Oct–Mar.

Set off the road, this motel offers comfortable, standard rooms overlooking the river. The stone structure seems to fit in well with the environment, not distracting from the beauty of the mountains. A shuttle bus stops here for productions of *Unto These Hills.* The grounds hold a swimming pool and a sheltered picnic area with grills.

WHERE TO DINE

Most restaurants here serve your basic chicken, steak, seafood, and (of course) freshwater fish from local waters. Also, the familiar national chains have long since arrived.

Happy New Restaurant. Aquonia Rd., Saunooke Village. ☎ **828/497-4310.** Lunch main courses $5.75–$7.95, dinner main courses $10.95–$13.95. DISC, MC, V. Tues–Sun 11am–8pm. CHINESE.

Adorned with traditional Chinese artwork, this red-and-gold restaurant offers hearty helpings. The staff makes you feel welcome and is quite attentive throughout the meal. The specialties include battered shrimp lightly fried with a five-spice/salt blend, green peppers, and green onions; and Seven Star around the Moon, which is scallops, chicken, and barbecued pork with broccoli, carrots, snow peas, bamboo shoots, and rice in a brown sauce, with seven fried shrimp surrounding the entire concoction. Although it's not the most original Chinese restaurant, it is consistent and a welcome relief from all the Big Macs.

Peter's Pancakes & Waffles. 34 Hwy. 441. ☎ **828/497-5116.** Breakfast items $1.25–$5.95; lunch $4.50–$7.25. MC, V. Apr–Oct daily 7am–2pm. AMERICAN.

This pancake house offers hearty breakfasts and light lunches featuring sandwiches, soups, and salads. The birdhouse-adorned dining room has tables as well as counter service. Lunch options include reubens, hot ham and cheese, chili dogs, and even PB&J, but the meal to eat here is breakfast. As you walk in the door, the aroma of fresh-cooked waffles and pancakes greets you. Waffles come with fresh fruit on top, and pancakes can be made with pecans. Hearty breakfast platters include the Ranch Hand: country ham, two eggs, two pancakes or biscuits, and grits.

2 The Smokies: Just the Facts

GETTING THERE   Take I-40 from Asheville to U.S. 19; then take U.S. 441 to the park's southern entrance near Cherokee, a distance of 50 miles west.

ACCESS POINTS & ORIENTATION   Although there are several side roads into the park, the best routes are through one of the three main entrances, two of which are located on Newfound Gap Road, U.S. 441, a 33-mile road that stretches north–south through the park. The southern entrance is near Cherokee, North Carolina, whereas the northern entrance is located 33 miles away near Gatlinburg, Tennessee. The third main entrance is on the western side of the park at Townsend,

Tennessee. Other access points are from the campgrounds at the edge of the park. The park is open year-round, and admission is free.

VISITOR CENTERS   At each of the three main entrances are visitor centers for the park. Each center offers information on roads, weather, camping, and backcountry conditions. You'll also find books, maps, and first-aid information.

The **Sugarlands Visitor Center and Park Headquarters** (☎ **865/436-1291** for park headquarters and all three visitor centers) is at the northern entrance, near Gatlinburg, Tennessee. This center is the largest and offers a 10-minute slide show. A natural-history exhibit features stuffed animals (such as a wild boar), and reproductions of journals kept by the first park naturalists are on display.

The smaller **Oconaluftee Visitor Center** is at the southern entrance and offers a few exhibits on what to see and do in the park.

The **Cades Cove Visitor Center,** at the western end of the park on Parson Branch Road about 12 miles southwest of Townsend, Tennessee, is set among a cluster of historic 19th-century farms and buildings.

The visitor centers are open daily from April to October: in April, May, and August to October from 8am to 6pm (9am at the Cades Cove center); June to August, from 8am to 7pm (9am at the Cades Cove center).

FEES, REGULATIONS & PERMITS   Entrance to the park, backcountry permits, and parking permits for people with disabilities (which can be obtained from the visitor centers and ranger stations) are all free.

Park visitors must adhere to quite a few regulations, which help preserve the surroundings and safety of visitors as well as that of the wildlife:

- Alcohol is allowed only in designated picnic and campsite areas and at LeConte Lodge. Open containers in automobiles are illegal.
- No hunting, weapons, or fireworks are allowed, including bows, arrows, and slingshots.
- Fires are allowed only in designated areas, such as established fire rings and fireplaces. No trees can be cut down for firewood, although dead and downed wood may be used. Firewood is sold by concessionaires at the Cades Cove, Elkmont, and Smokemont campgrounds.
- You may camp in designated areas only. To camp overnight in the backcountry, you must obtain a permit from a ranger station, one of the campgrounds, or one of the visitor centers (but not at Cades Cove).
- Motorcycles, bicycles, and mountain bikes are allowed on paved roads and campgrounds. They are not permitted on trails and administrative roads. Helmets are required for motorcyclists. Skateboarding is prohibited in the park.
- Pets are allowed in parking lots, campgrounds that are accessible by motor vehicle, and along paved roads. They are not allowed on the trails, in public buildings, or in the backcountry—with the exception of Seeing-Eye and hearing guide dogs, which are permitted to travel throughout the park.
- It is illegal to pick, damage, destroy, and/or disturb any natural feature of the park. Federal law protects the forests and wildflowers of the Great Smokies.
- Food should never be left out for bears to find. You'll find specially designed trash cans and dumpsters throughout the park for deposit of any food, wrappings, and containers.

SEASONS   With each season come new scenery and several changes in the weather. From late March to June, spring brings great bursts of color from the wildflowers. Flowering shrubs spread across the countryside. This time is known as the wildflower season, although to a lesser degree, summer and fall also produce a panoramic variety. At the higher elevations, mild daytime temperatures around the mid-70s are recorded, although evenings are much cooler, dipping into the mid-40s.

As the season changes over to summer, which lasts from June to August, the lush greenery comes into its full splendor, and the weather gets warm and humid. Although the higher elevations offer milder temperatures, ranging from the low 50s to the mid-60s, the lower ones can bring on days that are in the 90s. Autumn colors first appear at higher elevations when the leaves on the fire cherry tree change to brilliant shades of crimson. Around the beginning of October, elevations above a mile have seen the end of fall, but lower elevations are just coming into their own with brilliant reds, yellows, oranges, purples, and browns. The best time to experience this change is from mid- to late-October. Winter in the park can be very scenic, with snowfalls blanketing the countryside. At higher elevations, the temperature can drop below zero. Throughout the year, one factor remains constant: Weather can change often and rapidly. During the course of a day, you may witness several thunderstorms and breaks of clear, sunshiny skies, while temperatures switch from cool and comfortable to hot and humid. The wettest months are generally March and July.

AVOIDING THE CROWDS   The height of the tourist season lasts from late May until late August. As autumn approaches, the greatest number of visitors come to the park on weekends, with the crowds much more manageable during weekdays. From March to November, the best crowd-avoiding times are the early morning hours. Although the National Park Service tries to keep all roads and trails open and clear in the winter, sometimes that's impossible (especially at the higher elevations), making travel across the park an iffy proposition. Only those who are very well-equipped and skilled in the winter outdoor scene should brave the elements in the park's backcountry during the winter months.

RANGER PROGRAMS   Park rangers provide assistance to visitors at the ranger stations scattered throughout the park, as well as at the visitor centers. Rangers also offer films, short talks, guided nature and history walks, and evening campfire programs, along with slide presentations covering geology, bears, balds, plant life, and early settler life. These programs are posted daily at the visitor centers.

3 Seeing the Park's Highlights

If you have only a couple of days to tour the park, you must start early in the morning to avoid the crowds that increase during the day. When crossing the park on the Newfound Gap Road (U.S. 441), you should allow, at the very least, 1 hour. The speed limit does not rise above 45 miles per hour anywhere in the park. When ascending the mountain slopes, you can rarely go over 25 to 30 miles an hour because of the winding roads. Pack a lunch; the park has no restaurants, but picnic sites abound.

Following are some suggestions for seeing some of the park's most popular sights:

DAY 1   Your best strategy is to visit the sights along the Newfound Gap Road. Begin at the **Oconaluftee Visitor Center,** where you can pick up park information and get details about the weather. Oconaluftee (which means, "by the river") was owned by the Cherokee until settlers acquired the land through treaties. Today, the **Oconaluftee Mountain Farm Museum,** a replica of a pioneer farmstead, operates here in a collection of original log buildings. It features such artifacts as a sorghum molasses mill; a blacksmith shop; a mountain house; a corncrib; and a barn with cows, horses, pigs, geese, and roosters. Park staff, dressed in period costumes, make this a living-history farm from April to October.

Travel about half a mile north on the Newfound Gap Road to the **Mingus Mill,** constructed in 1886 by Dr. John Jacob Mingus, son of this area's first permanent settler. It closed in 1940 and was reopened in 1968 by the park service. This water-powered mill is still in operation, grinding wheat and corn for flour and cornmeal from mid-April to October.

As you travel north, you'll come to a turnoff for **Clingmans Dome,** the highest peak in the park, soaring 6,642 feet and named for Thomas Lanier Clingman, a 19th-century North Carolina senator. After you turn onto this road, you travel 7 miles southwest to a parking lot, where you can walk a steep half-mile to a viewing platform that features one of the park's best views. The platform is generally closed from December to April.

Next comes **Newfound Gap,** which, at 5,048 feet, is the center of the park. A path that the Cherokee traveled was located 2 miles west of the present-day gap. Later, the path was widened and renamed Indian Gap Road. If the sky is clear, you can see for miles around; on other days, you find yourself literally in the clouds. It's best to call ☎ **865/436-1291,** the park's main number, for weather conditions before you set out.

The next point of interest is the **Chimney Tops,** twin peaks that rise close to 2,000 feet. The Cherokee named these peaks *Duniskwalguni* (which means, "forked antlers"), whereas the settlers called them Chimney Tops because of the 30-foot-deep, fluelike cavity located in one of them. If you'd like a closer look, you can hike a 4-mile trail round-trip.

The drive across the park leads you to the **Sugarlands Visitor Center,** where you can stroll through the nature exhibit, view a slide show, or browse through the gift shop. At this point, you can either head into Gatlinburg for the night or go west about 5 miles on Little River Road to **Elkmont Campground.** It's best to make reservations (accepted only from mid-May to October).

DAY 2   Continue your journey west on Little River Road to **Cades Cove,** where you'll find more pioneer structures than at any other location in the park. The best time to go is early in the morning, when you have a better chance of spotting deer grazing in the fields. Plan to spend half a day exploring the many attractions along the 11-mile Cades Cove Loop. Stop at the visitor center for a pamphlet that contains a key to the numbered sights.

Originally called Kate's Cove, after the wife of John Oliver, the cove's first settler, the name evolved over the years into Cades Cove. Founded in 1818, the cove was a thriving, self-supporting community for more than 100 years. Original homesites, such as the log homes of John Oliver, Elijah Oliver, Becky Cable, and Carter Shields, still stand today, giving visitors a glimpse into the lives of the original settlers. The other buildings include smokehouses, cantilevered barns, a blacksmith shop, and corncribs. You'll also find cemeteries with such epitaphs as one from the Civil War that reads BAS SHAW—KILLED BY REBELS. There are three historic churches: **Methodist Church; Missionary Baptist Church;** and the oldest, **Primitive Baptist Church,** built in 1827. Included on the loop is the John P. Cable farm, where you'll find the **1868 Cable Mill** still in operation. Cades Cove offers several nature trails; the short-est in the Cable Mill area consists of a half-mile round-trip.

After you complete the Cades Cove loop, head toward the **Sugarlands Visitor Center** to the Newfound Gap Road to recross the park, this time taking advantage of the numerous pulloff areas dotting the roadside. At most of them, you'll find Quiet Walkways—short paths created for moments of solitude in which visitors can experi-ence nature. Remember to take your camera, because these stops offer a multitude of photo opportunities. Don't be discouraged if a pulloff is full, because another one will appear within a mile.

4 Sports & Outdoor Pursuits

BACKPACKING   Backpacking enthusiasts are required to obtain permits from one of the ranger stations, the Oconaluftee and Sugarlands visitor centers, or the Cades Cove Campground Kiosk before setting out. These permits are used to keep track of visitors for safety reasons, as well as to prevent popular campsites from becoming over-crowded. Campers are allowed to use only designated campsites and shelters. You will be fined if you're caught camping outside one of these sites. A rationing program limits the number of campers at 13 of the 80 campsites and at all 18 of the shelters. It's best to plan your route before visiting the park to determine whether you'll need any of these designated areas. The maximum number of people allowed in a hiking group is eight.

You must obtain shelter and ration (those with electrical and water hookups) camp-site permits in person before departing on any given trail, calling for permits between 8am and 6pm only. Stays are limited to 1 night at shelters and 3 nights at campsites. Tents are not allowed in the shelter areas or along the Appalachian Trail. Shelters are located on the Appalachian Trail and at Laurel Gap, Kephart Prong, Mount LeConte, Rich Mountain, and Scott Gap. Permits for non-ration sites can be obtained upon arrival. For more information, call ☎ **865/936-1231** from 8am to 6pm daily or write **Great Smoky Mountains National Park,** Attn.: Backcountry Office, Gatlinburg, TN 37738.

BIKING   Bicycles are not allowed on the trails, so areas for cyclists are limited. You can ride on roads, but traffic can be very heavy and the inclines quite steep. Try the 11-mile **Cades Cove Loop** from May to mid-October on Saturday mornings before 10am, when it's closed to all automobile traffic. Another possibility is the **Cataloochee Valley.** From April to October, you can rent a bicycle from the **Cades Cove Campground Store** (☎ **865/448-9034**) for $3.25 an hour or $16.25 for a full day. Hours are daily 8:30am to 4:30pm.

BIRDING   With more than 200 species of birds in the park, you should be able to spot a few along your ramblings. The higher elevations support bird life that's typical of parts of northern New England. Also to be seen in the high country along moun-tain crags are falcons, hawks, and ravens. Throughout the park, you may spot grouse and wild turkey, although the latter are quite shy of people.

FISHING   The park contains more than 700 miles of streams suitable for fishing. Fishers must have a valid North Carolina or Tennessee state fishing license, which can be purchased in the gateway towns at sporting-goods stores. In North Carolina, any-one 16 or older must have a license. Trout stamps are not required. Fishing is permit-ted from sunrise to sunset year-round, although the optimum seasons are spring and fall. Popular fishing areas include **Abrams Creek, Big Creek, Fontana Lake,** and **Little River.** The limit is five fish, with the exception of brook trout, which are illegal to possess.

GOLF   One of the best courses in the area is the **Maggie Valley Golf Course,** on U.S. 19 35 miles east of Asheville (☎ **828/926-6013**). A par-72, 6,004-yard course, it offers 18 holes. Greens fees range from $35 to $47.90 but are only $30.90 for 18 holes after 2:30pm and $20.90 after 4pm. Carts are $15.90 per person.

HIKING With more than 800 miles of trails, the park offers visitors of all fitness levels a chance to experience the great outdoors firsthand (see "Nature Trails," below). Before setting out, make sure to check the weather forecast for the duration of your trip, be it a few hours or a few days. If you find yourself caught in a thunderstorm, make sure to avoid all open areas, thereby lessening your chance of being struck by lightning. Carry rain gear, because sudden storms are normal for this area, and leave a copy of your itinerary at one of the ranger stations or visitor centers in case you become lost or injured.

Following are a few of the most popular trails that the park offers:

The **Indian Creek Falls Trail** has an elevation gain of 100 feet and begins at Deep Creek Road near the Deep Creek Campground. The 1-mile flat trail leads to the 60-foot-high Indian Creek Falls. Physical level: easy.

The **Laurel Falls Trail** is the most popular waterfall trail in the park, with an elevation gain of 200 feet. You travel 1¼ miles to the falls from the Laurel Falls parking area, a few miles from the Sugarlands Visitor Center. It's paved and relatively flat. Physical level: easy.

Abrams Falls Trail has an elevation gain of 340 feet. You travel 2½ miles from the Abrams Falls parking lot at the west end of Cades Cove Loop Road to a 20-foot-high waterfall. The trail follows a clear stream and is relatively flat. Physical level: easy to moderate.

Alum Cave Bluffs Trail is deceiving because it starts off easy and grows more difficult. The elevation gain is 2,800 feet, and the distance is 11 miles round-trip. The first 1½ miles takes you to Arch Rock, which contains a tunnel created by erosion. Then the trail becomes steeper and takes you to the 100-foot-high Alum Cave Bluffs. The last leg of the trail is quite steep, and many hikers find it necessary to use trailside cables to maneuver the cliffs. The journey is worth the trouble, because it ends at Mount LeConte, which offers one of the park's best views. Begin at Newfound Gap Road at the Alum Cave Bluffs parking lot, 9 miles south of the Sugarlands Visitor Center. Physical level: moderate.

Charlies Bunion Trail is a 4-mile trek to a 1,000-foot-high cliff where the forest was destroyed by fire in 1925. Part of the Appalachian Trail, it offers an elevation gain of 980 feet and begins at the Newfound Gap Overlook parking lot. Physical level: moderate.

Although the **Boulevard Trail** is the easiest and most popular trail to Mt. LeConte, the 16-mile round-trip categorizes it as strenuous for a lot of people. The elevation gain is 1,545 feet. You must travel the Appalachian Trail from Newfound Gap to reach this trail. Physical level: moderate to strenuous.

Ramsay Cascades Trail has a total elevation gain of 2,375 feet and is 8 miles long round-trip. This trail also leads to Ramsay Cascades, a 100-foot-high waterfall, the park's highest. From Greenbrier Cove, follow the signs to the trailhead. Physical level: strenuous.

The ✪ **Appalachian Trail** is the most famous trail, stretching from Maine to Georgia, and has 68 of its 2,100 miles situated in the park, following the Smokies ridge line from east to west almost the entire length of the park. Access points are Newfound Gap, Clingmans Dome, the end of Tenn. 32 just north of the Big Creek Campground, and the Fontana Dam. The most popular section is from Newfound Gap to Charlies Bunion (see above). Elevation gain is 980 feet. Physical level: strenuous.

HORSEBACK RIDING The park offers some of the state's most panoramic scenery for equestrians. All off-trail and cross-country riding, as well as use of trails designated as foot trails, is prohibited in the park. Horses are restricted from developed campgrounds and picnic areas and on maintained portions of park roadways. Any overnight riders must obtain backcountry permits (see "Backpacking," above). The following five drive-in horse camps offer easy access to designated horse trails: Anthony Creek, Big Creek, Cataloochee, Round Bottom, and Towstring. You can make reservations 30 days in advance with the Backcountry Reservations Office by calling ☎ **865/436-1231.**

If you have your own horse, write for an information packet that describes the park's trails, campsites, and regulations. Contact the Superintendent at Great Smoky Mountains National Park, 107 Park Headquarters Rd., Gatlinburg, TN 37738 (☎ **865/436-1200**).

Horses can be rented for $15 an hour April to October. Ask for details at the individual concessions within the park at **Cades Cove** (☎ **865/448-6286**); **McCarter's Riding Stables,** Newfound Gap Road, near park headquarters (☎ **865/436-5354**); **Smokemont Campground** (☎ **828/497-2373**); and **Smoky Mountains Riding Stables,** U.S. 321 (☎ **865/436-5634**). The park service requires a guide to accompany all rental treks.

NATURE TRAILS   Self-guided nature trails offer even couch potatoes an opportunity to commune with nature. These trails are staked and keyed to pamphlets with descriptions of points of interest along the way. You can obtain a keyed pamphlet from one of the visitor centers or stands at the trailheads. There are about a dozen such trails, ranging in length from a third of a mile to 6 miles. All offer easy walks through peaceful surroundings.

✪ WHITE-WATER RAFTING   Starting at the Waterville Power Plant, a 5-mile stretch of the Pigeon River has 10 rapids and offers some of the most challenging white-water rafting in the South. Water for rafting is released by the Carolina Power & Light Company. **Rafting in the Smokies** rafts both the Pigeon and the Nantahala rivers. A trip on the Pigeon costs $37 per person, but only $27 on the Nantahala. For reservations and details, call the company's central office in Gatlinburg, Tennessee (☎ **865/436-5008**).

WILDLIFE WATCHING   Your chances are best in the spring, summer, and fall. Mammals are the main interest for many park visitors. As in all national parks, native wildlife is protected by federal law. Printed material, available at the visitor center, can provide additional information. For your safety as well as the protection of the wildlife, do *not* tease, harass, feed, or approach any wild animal, and be especially cautious when encountering mothers with their young.

The best-known park mammal is the black bear, which has been known to stop traffic—a situation that park officials try to keep from happening, because bears can become too used to humans. If this happens, bears are relocated to other, less-traveled areas of the park. When bears lose their innate fear of humans, they become more susceptible to poachers. Visitors should heed the rules about bears and the warnings given out by the park authorities.

White-tailed deer used to be hunted by mountain people, but the park has increased their numbers via a policy of protection. The best place to look for deer is around Cades Cove in the early morning and at dusk.

Frequently sighted smaller mammals include cottontail rabbits, squirrels, and woodchucks (groundhogs). Mammals that are seldom seen are raccoons, skunks, opossums, weasels, bobcats, red and gray foxes, mink, and beavers.

The park is the home of at least 23 varieties of snakes. The poisonous ones are timber rattlesnakes and copperheads. If you stay on the trails and away from warm rocky slopes, abandoned buildings, and stone fences, you should have no close encounters. These snakes are not aggressive and generally stay away from areas used by people. Among the nonpoisonous snakes, the most common are the Eastern garter and Northern water snakes. Other varieties include the Northern ringneck, the Eastern king snake, and the Northern black racer.

5 Camping

The park contains 10 campgrounds with picnic tables, fire grills, cold running water, and flush toilets, but they don't have showers or water and electrical hookups (see "Backpacking," above). There are three major campgrounds. **Cades Cove** (161 sites) features a camp store, bike rentals, a disposal station, wood for sale, and naturalist programs held in the small amphitheater. **Elkmont** (220 sites) offers a disposal station, firewood for sale, vending machines, and a telephone. **Smokemont** (140 sites) has a disposal station and firewood for sale.

Reservations (☎ 800/365-CAMP) can't be made more than 8 weeks in advance. The campgrounds are full on weekends beginning in April and daily from July to October. The busiest months are July and October, and you should make reservations at least 4 weeks in advance. Mid-May to October, there's a 7-day maximum stay, and the charge is $17 per day. November to mid-May, with limited sites available, the maximum stay is 14 days, and the charge is also $7 per day. The seven smaller campgrounds, open mid-May to October, are along the boundaries of the park and are slightly cheaper, costing $13 per day.

6 Where to Stay

IN THE PARK

The park's only accommodation, **LeConte Lodge** (☎ 865/429-5704 for reservations), is located on the top of Mount LeConte. The lodge is very back-to-basics: It has no electricity, TV, phone, or indoor plumbing, although there are four flush toilets in outhouses. The only means of access to the lodge is by hiking. The shortest and steepest route is the Alum Çave Bluffs Trail (see "Hiking," above), a 4-mile one-way trip. Lodgings include private bedrooms in cabins with shared living rooms, as well as private cabins. The rates include breakfast, dinner (served family-style), and lunch for those staying more than 1 night. There are seven rooms to rent, costing $76.60 per adult. A two-bedroom lodge costs $400 for up to eight people, plus $26.50 extra per person for meals. Two three-bedroom lodges cost $600 for up to 12 people, plus $26.50 per person for meals. An additional person can stay in any of the lodges at a cost of $50 per person, plus meals. Reservations are difficult to come by if you don't make them in October for the following year. The lodge is open from the last week in March to late November. No credit cards are accepted.

BRYSON CITY

Carriage Inn Resort Motel. U.S. 19 (5 miles east of Bryson City; P.O. Box 1506), Cherokee, NC 28719. ☎ **800/480-2398** or 828/488-2398. Fax 828/488-2398. E-mail: carriageinn@ micworld.com. 25 units. A/C TV TEL. Apr–May and Nov Dec. $38 double. June–Oct $64–$74 double. AE, DISC, MC, V. Closed Jan–Mar.

This is a survivor of the roadside motels that dotted the countryside during the 1940s and 1950s, offering basic but clean and comfortable accommodations. (Think Clark Gable and Claudette Colbert in *It Happened One Night.*) It's a fine choice if you're planning to spend most of your time in the park anyway. All the rooms are ground-level, offering double or king-size beds, cable TV, air-conditioning, and telephones. The rates include free morning coffee. It has an outdoor pool, a small playground, and picnic area; restaurants are nearby.

The Chalet Inn. U.S. 74/441 between Bryson City and Dillsboro (285 Lone Oak Dr., Whittier, NC 28789). ☎ **800/789-8024** or 828/586-0251. www.chaletinn.com. E-mail: paradisefound@chaletinn.com. 6 units. A/C. $87–$115 double; $130–$160 suite. Rates include full breakfast. MC, V. Closed Jan 2–Mar.

On 22 acres of forested mountainsides and ridges with trails, this inn offers the blend of rusticity and traditional comforts of an alpine *Gasthaus*. George and Hanneke Ware own this inn, which offers uniquely decorated rooms with private bathrooms and balconies or porches. Although the rooms have no phones, you have access to cordless phones that you're welcome to use in your room. You can view Doubletop Mountain from the Chalet's Great Room, and if the window is open, you can hear the sounds of the babbling brook that winds its way around the inn. On wintry evenings, you can enjoy one of the books from the inn's library while sitting in front of the fire in the stone fireplace. The grounds include a playground and picnic area, as well as hiking trails. Children are welcome, but from Labor Day until January 1, only children 8 and older are accepted. A whirlpool is available in the Romantic suite.

Folkestone Inn Bed & Breakfast. 101 Folkestone Rd., Bryson City, NC 27813. ☎ **888/812-3385** or 828/488-2730. Fax 828/488-0722. www.folkestone. E-mail: innkeeper@folkestone.com. 10 units. A/C. $78–$108 double. Additional person $12 per night. Rates include full breakfast. AE, DISC, MC, V. Smoking not allowed in building. Children 5 and under not allowed.

Originally a 1920s farmhouse, the Folkestone Inn, which bills itself as a place to escape and explore, has the benefit of location. The structure is framed by a grove of Norway spruce trees, with a mountain stream serving as a boundary with the wilderness. Guests can explore the park and play golf at a nearby course. Asheville and other towns are just an hour's drive away. "Rustic" is the most apt term to describe the rooms, which are furnished with antiques, including the beds (some have queen-size beds). Each unit features its own bathroom with an old-fashioned claw-foot tub. The upstairs rooms have balconies with mountain views; the downstairs rooms have flagstone floors and pressed-tin ceilings. Breakfast is the only meal served, and what you get is a little less uncommon than your standard eggs and bacon; you might see eggs Benedict when you sit down at the table.

✪ **Fryemont Inn.** Fryemont Rd. (P.O. Box 459), Bryson City, NC 28713. ☎ **800/845-4879** or 828/488-2159. www.fryemontinn.com. 44 units. $135 double; $165 suite. Rates include breakfast and dinner. DISC, MC, V. Main lodge closed Nov to mid-Mar.

Listed on the National Register of Historic Places, this inn has been in operation since 1923. Amos Frye, head of a timber empire in the late 1800s, built it of the best chestnut, oak, and maple in the region. The exterior is covered with the bark of huge poplar trees, as sturdy today as when the strips were first cut. Sue and George Brown are the owners of the inn, which the *Atlanta Journal-Constitution* cited as being "a rustic, bark-covered architectural masterpiece." Each of the chestnut-paneled rooms is individually decorated, and some bathrooms contain an old-fashioned pedestal tub. The rooms are large and comfortably furnished, with country touches such as homespun curtains. Units are not air-conditioned, but for the most part, air-conditioning is not needed. The cottage suites, open all year, are housed in a stone structure. Each suite has a loft bedroom overlooking a living area with a fireplace, TV, and wet bar. The suites are no smoking. Meals are served in the dining room in the main lodge, open April 14 through the October 29. The lobby has a TV, two game tables, a fireplace that can burn 8-foot logs, and a library, and porch has rocking chairs. Closely supervised children are allowed in the main lodge, but the cottage suites are for adults only.

Lloyd's on the River. U.S. 19 (P.O. Box 429), Bryson City, NC 28715. ☎ **828/488-3767.** Fax 828/488-9020. www.lloydsontheriver.com. E-mail:lloyds@smnet.net. 21 units. A/C TV. TEL. Mid-Apr to mid-June and mid-Aug to mid-Sept $30–$65 double; mid-June to mid-Aug and mid-Sept to mid-Oct $78–$115 double. AE, DISC, MC, V. Closed Nov to mid-Apr.

This inn offers clean, decent rooms in a relaxed atmosphere, with comfortable furnishings and wood paneling or tasteful wallpaper. No meals are served, although the grounds contain picnic tables along the river and outdoor grills. There is also a swimming pool. With its columned porches accented by hanging plants and rocking chairs, the look is that of an oversize country home—or, as one guest stated, "It's like staying at a B&B without the breakfast." The owner, Bob Starks, offers warm hospitality and can create a personalized trail guide for you.

DILLSBORO

Applegate Inn Bed & Breakfast. 163 Hemlock St. (P.O. Box 1051), Dillsboro, NC 28725. ☎ and fax **828/586-2397.** www.applegatebed-breakfast.com. E-mail: andree@ aplegatedbed-breakfast.com. 11 units. A/C. $70–$100 double; $100–$150 suite. Rates include full country breakfast. AE, CB, DC, DISC, MC, V. Free parking.

Owned by John and Andree Faulk, this inn is situated on a half-acre of land across Scott's Bridge. Although it's just "a footbridge away from the train station," it feels more remote. The inn is family-friendly; its resident animals will amuse the youngsters. Decorating themes include mountain rustic, Victorian, French provincial, and country charm. The apartments include a full kitchen, two bedrooms, and a living area with TVs. Breakfast is hearty, so come with an appetite.

Dillsboro Inn. 146 N. River Rd. (P.O. Box 270), Dillsboro, NC 28725. ☎ **828/586-3898.** www.earthplaza.com/dillsboro. E-mail:dillsboro@earthplaza.com. 5 units. $70–$120 double; $90–$140 suite. Each additional person $20. Rates include full breakfast. AE, MC, V.

Located on the Tuckasegee River, this inn is owned by T.J. Walker, who has maintained the inn's tradition of clean, comfortable accommodations. Rooms and efficiency suites, all with private bathrooms, offer a decor that's a mix of rustic and eclectic. Guests confirm the fact that the inn offers "the most photographed view in Dillsboro."

Olde Towne Inn. 300 Haywood Rd (P.O. Box 485), Dillsboro, NC 28725. ☎ **828/ 586-3461.** 4 units. A/C. Jan–Feb $70 double, $90 suite; Apr–June $75 double, $90 suite; July–Sept and Nov–Dec $80–$85 double, $100 suite; Oct $85 double, $100 suite. Rates include full breakfast. MC, V.

This inn is a restored 1878 home in the heart of Dillsboro. The rooms have a country flair and are tastefully appointed, with antiques and ceiling fans. The inn has been referred to as "a comfortable old home place"—ideally located near shops, restaurants, and the train station. You'll find many guests enjoying the breezes that roll off the mountainside as they rock on the front porch. In the morning, you're greeted by the aroma of a freshly prepared breakfast that's sure to fill you up.

Squire Watkins Inn. U.S. 441 and Haywood Rd. (P.O. Box 430), Dillsboro, NC 28725. ☎ **800/586-2429** or 828/786-5244. 7 units. A/C. $80–$90 double; $70–$100 suite. Rates include full breakfast. No credit cards. No children under 12.

A casual atmosphere set in peaceful surroundings on 3 acres of gardens, this 1880s inn touts itself as "a place to enjoy the sunrise and fireflies, peaches from the garden and eggs from the farm." That's right. Tom and Emma Wertenberger make their guests feel right at home, providing helpful advice on places to go and activities not to miss. They bought this old home in 1983 and restored it. Each morning, you're greeted by freshly baked breads, homemade casseroles, eggs from a farm just down the road, and fresh fruits and juices, all served on sparkling china and silver. The rooms are furnished in period antiques.

FONTANA DAM

Fontana Village Resort. N.C. 28 (P.O. Box 68), Fontana Dam, NC 28733. ☎ **800/ 849-2258** or 828/498-2211. Fax 828/498-2345. www.fontanavillage.com. E-mail: fontana@ fontanavillage.com. 83 units, 130 cottages. A/C TV TEL. $79–$149 double; $89–$209 cottage with kitchenette. AE, DISC, MC, V.

On January 1, 1942, 24 days after the attack on Pearl Harbor, the Tennessee Valley Authority (TVA) got permission to build a dam 480 feet high to produce critically needed hydroelectric energy. This led to the birth of a village to support the workers and their families, including a school, a 50-bed hospital, churches, and space to play. This village has become the largest and most complete resort in the Great Smoky Mountains. Choose a room at the inn, a cottage with a kitchenette, or a campsite. (There are 20 campsites, 10 with hookups. They cost $8 per night without hookup and $20 with hookup.) Although houseboats are available, they're rented only to time-share members.

For dining, the inn's Peppercorn Restaurant serves chicken, steak, and seafood. Amenities include two outdoor pools and one indoor pool, tennis courts, a water slide, a miniature-golf course, and a trout pond. Activities abound for every taste: biking (30 trails), horseback riding, cookouts, square dancing, craft classes, mountain-bike races, and boating. You can even take a tour of the cabin used in the filming of *Nell*, starring Jodie Foster, and learn about moviemaking in a remote location.

MAGGIE VALLEY

Abbey Inn. 6375 Soco Rd. (U.S. 19), Maggie Valley, NC 28751. ☎ **800/545-5853** or 828/ 926-1188. Fax 828/926-2389. www.abbeyinn.com. E-mail: tours@abbeyinn.com. 20 units. TV TEL. Off-season (Apr 1–June 21) $39–$64 double; rest of year $49–$94 double. DISC, MC, V. Closed Nov–Mar.

Reminiscent of the 1950s, this hostelry on the northern slope of Setzer Mountain offers views up to 5 miles away. Mike and Natalie Nelson, owners of the motel, deliver friendly hospitality and advice on what's best to see in the area. The rooms are small, yet reasonably comfortable and appointed with refinished furniture specifically made for the inn. Some accommodations contain kitchenettes with small refrigerators, stoves, and microwaves. All units have bathrooms with oversize showers, ceiling fans, and front porches with great views where you can while away the hours. The 2-acre grounds boast patio swings, a picnic area, grills, and a play area.

✪ **Cataloochee Ranch.** Fie Top Rd., 119 Ranch Dr., Maggie Valley, NC 28751. ☎ **800/ 868-1401** or 828/926-1401. Fax: 828/926-9249. www.cataloochee-ranch.com. 25 units. Apr–Nov $145–$195 double; $195–$385 cabin; $385 house for 4 persons. Rates include breakfast and dinner June–Oct. AE, MC, V. Closed Dec–Mar.

On the border of Great Smoky Mountains National Park, this 1,000-acre ranch offers a wide range of activities. The property includes a main lodge with six double rooms; the Silver Belle, containing the remaining rooms; and seven cabins, each of which is rustic and individual. The cabins contain TVs and small refrigerators. One small house is suitable for four.

Meals are served family-style, and very few people ever leave hungry. The property includes an oversize outdoor hot tub, tennis court, swimming pool, and a trout pond for fishing. There are hiking trails. If you prefer, horseback riding is offered at an additional charge.

The Ketner Inn & Farm. 190 Jonathan Creek Rd., Waynesville, NC 28786. ☎ **828/ 926-1511.** www.bbonline.com/nc/ketner. 5 units. A/C. $70–$80 double. Rates include full breakfast. MC, V.

Set on the mountainside on 27 acres, this B&B is housed in an 1898 farmhouse that has been completely restored by Randall McCrory. Decor highlights include hardwood floors, Victorian and country antiques such as a 7-foot rice-planter bed, and washstands. The rooms were decorated with different themes in mind, including doll, swan, and cat motifs. A hearty turn-of-the-century-style breakfast is served in the dining room. You're welcome to sit on the porches overlooking Jonathan Valley and the rolling hills of the farm or to explore the grounds, where you'll find antique farm equipment, an old barn, a natural spring, and wooded trails.

Maggie Valley Resort and Country Club. 1819 Country Club Rd. (near the intersection of U.S. 19 and U.S. 276), Maggie Valley, NC 28751. ☎ **800/438-3861** or 828/926-1616. Fax 828/926-2906. www.maggievalleyresort.com. E-mail: golf@maggievalleyresort.com. 75 units. A/C TV TEL. Apr–Oct $109–$169 double, $129–$209 villa; Nov–Feb $69–$89 double, $99–$109 villa; Mar $79–$89 double, $109–$169 villa. Golf packages available. AE, DISC, MC, V.

Opening onto panoramic vistas, this resort offers a wide variety of activities to accommodate the whole family. The spacious rooms come with a rather standard decor. The premium ones overlook the front nine holes of the golf course; the villas open onto the back nine. There are four lighted tennis courts, a heated outdoor pool, and an 18-hole championship golf course. Greens fees range from $38 to $53. The facilities also include a lounge and a dining room where you can order steak, seafood, and an array of international dishes. Live entertainment is featured on Friday and Saturday evenings; on Thursday, a country band and cloggers entertain.

7 Where to Dine

Forget the tourist brochures. Some of the worst restaurants in the South are in the towns that cater to the millions of visitors to the Smokies. Fast-food joints are everywhere, and many a cook's idea of a good dinner is a frozen hamburger slapped on a grill. Some good places with country cooking do exist, but they have to be sought out; they can be hard to find. Here's a representative sampling to get you going.

BRYSON CITY

Nantahala Village Restaurant. 9400 Hwy. 19. ☎ **828/488-2826.** Reservations not accepted. Breakfast $3–$6; lunch main courses $4–$9, dinner main courses $5–$17. MC. Daily 7:30am–2pm and 5:30pm. Closed Jan 1–Mar 1. SOUTHERN.

The food at this family-style haven ranges from old-time down-home favorites like mountain trout, fried chicken, and country ham to more electric and lighter varieties that reflect an up-to-date approach to dining. Of the latter, dig into wild forest pasta, sautéed shrimp, and nightly vegetarian specialties. Many guests arrive early to enjoy the sunsets over the Smoky Mountains through the large windows. In cool weather, a fireplace burns brightly. Homemade soups such as corn chowder or lentil and homemade pies and cakes round out the wide variety of meats, poultry, and fish offered as main course selections. As one local habitué informed us, "This place serves portions big enough to satisfy the biggest, hungriest bear."

Relia's Garden. U.S. 19 S. (13 miles southwest of the Nantahala Outdoor Center). ☎ **828/ 488-2175.** Lunch $6–$8; dinner $6–$10. AE,MC, V. Mon–Thurs noon–2pm and 5–9pm; Fri noon–2pm and 5–10pm, Sat noon–2pm and 5–10pm, Sun noon–2pm and 5–9pm. AMERICAN/SOUTHERN.

Part of the Nantahala Outdoor Center, this lodgelike place is worth the trip out of town. Hearty food and a helpful staff make it a family favorite, with a kids' menu and a policy of doggie-bagging. The menu is a bit overfamiliar, but time-tested favorites include rainbow trout and beef kebabs. Everybody likes the baked Cajun catfish. Vegetarian meals are also available. In fair weather, try for a table on the porch.

DILLSBORO

Dillsboro Smokehouse. 267 Haywood St. ☎ **828/586-9556.** Lunch main courses $5–$7, dinner main courses $9.25–$14. AE, DISC, MC, V. Mon–Thurs 11am–9pm, Fri–Sat 11am–10pm, Sun 11am–8pm. Closes an hour earlier Nov–Feb. BARBECUE.

Your best bet in town is hickory-flavored mountain barbecue at this smokehouse, just two blocks down the street from the post office. It's known mainly for the fall-off-the-bones baby back ribs in a peach-flavored sauce. The pork barbecue, served chopped or sliced, has the best flavor, and the smoked brisket of beef is excellent. The chicken, either dark or white meat, can dry out fast when barbecued. Dinners are served with coleslaw, barbecue beans, yams, French fries, and hush puppies (what else?). The restaurant also sells barbecue by the pound to go, in case you've rented a cabin or efficiency nearby.

MAGGIE VALLEY

J. Arthur's Restaurant. 801 Soco Rd. (U.S. 19). ☎ **828/926-1817.** Main courses $9.95–$24. AE, MC, V. Daily 5–9:30pm. AMERICAN/BEEF.

In a classic mountain building, J. Arthur's (which is affiliated with Manero's Restaurant in West Palm Beach, Florida) is oddly named for a Smoky Mountain restaurant. It's a winning choice, however; in fact, it's the best in town. Offering a loft dining area, the restaurant is a family favorite and tailors its menus to diners 12 and under. The kitchen is known for its Gorgonzola cheese salad, which is backed by a choice of prime rib, New York sirloin, broiled filet mignon, and grilled rib-eye. The meat is succulent and very tender (in other words, not the kind that you can purchase in a supermarket). Broiled pork or lamb chops and two fresh seafood dishes are also offered. Southerners really know how to cook pork chops, and this joint doesn't diminish that culinary reputation. Begin with a jumbo shrimp cocktail or French onion soup. The menu is limited but quite choice. You can also order fresh North Carolina rainbow trout, which is delectable.

Maggie's Country Kitchen. 27 Soco Rd. ☎ **828/926-2676.** Reservations not needed. Breakfast $3.49–$7.49; lunch and dinner main courses $4.49–$8.49. MC, V. Daily 7am–10pm. SOUTHERN.

If you're Ma and Pa Kettle with all the kids, this is the best choice for you. A family-style breakfast is served, with bacon, sausage, scrambled eggs, grits or country-style potatoes, along with plenty of home-style gravy, country-cooked apples, homemade biscuits, and all the trimmings. Some 100 hungry diners can crowd in here at any time, and the waitress will not blink an eye if you order pork chops for breakfast—a bit heavy for most appetites, but a preferred way to face the morning around these parts. A homemade soup is featured daily, and you can also order vegetarian dishes. Sandwiches are not the only items offered at lunch; you can order many types of fish including shrimp, catfish, and flounder, along with several heavy meat dishes. Desserts are exceedingly generous in size if you still have room.

Planning a Trip to South Carolina

This chapter tackles the nuts and bolts of your trip to South Carolina. Refer also to chapter 3, "Planning a Trip to North Carolina," and chapter 2, "For Foreign Visitors." Some of the information you need may be discussed in those chapters.

1 The Regions in Brief

SOUTH CAROLINA

THE HEARTLAND   The attraction of these backwater stops is the interaction with the people who live there. A Southern drawl as long as Rhett Butler's coattails prevails here, as do "Yes, ma'am," "No, ma'am," and afternoon naps. You're likely to come upon an old gas station complete with working Pure pumps and ice-cold Coca-Cola in bottles, and you're even more likely to pass a flock of camouflage-clad deer hunters lining a country road with trucks and guns.

A rail and highway hub, **Florence** is simply a convenience off the interstate, with fast-food eateries, clean and inexpensive motels, gas stations, and a midsize mall complete with a cafeteria and restrooms.

A more charming town for a half-day visit is **Darlington,** home of the famed raceway. The small, old-time downtown area features attractive Victorian-style homes and several good restaurants serving home-cooked meals. The Transouth 500, held each Labor Day, and the Stock Car Hall of Fame are ideal for a taste of NASCAR-style racing.

With that small-town feel, South Carolina is a film producer's or vacationer's dream for location and a delight for Northerners seeking a taste of the traditional South. There are courthouses that rival the national Capitol building (on a smaller scale) sitting smack in the middle of Main Street. There are white-picket-fenced homes sporting Victorian woodwork lining two-lane, moss-hung streets. There's a General Hardware store that doubles as a Greyhound bus station. There's a local A&P that has been owned by the same family for more than 50 years. There are a couple of churches where the membership has stayed pretty much the same (with the annual number of births equaling the number of deaths) for who knows how long. There are places such as **Camden** (the home of William F. Buckley, Jr.), which hosts two nationally known horse races: the Camden Classic and the Carolina Classic. **Kingstree** is the home of Nobel Peace Prize winner Dr. Joseph Goldstein. In places such as **Manning** and **Lake City,** the downtown shopping areas are thriving, and a Little Ladies' Bridge Club still meets twice a week.

The towns of South Carolina's heartland are Americana at its best. Cruising all of them, though, may prove to be a bit much, like watching the same movie over and over again. Pick one or two towns and stop over for lunch. If your schedule is limited, and the kids riding in the back seat are screaming for Myrtle Beach, plug in a tape of Fannie Flagg's book *Fried Green Tomatoes*. It'll suffice.

COLUMBIA The state capital, located in the heart of South Carolina, is the home of "The Worst Boiled Peanuts in the World." Cromer's, a state institution for munchies, started here, attracting a loyal following of boiled-peanut eaters with the large banner that adorned the front of its original downtown home on Assembly Street.

Columbia also happens to be the state's largest city, hosting more than 300 factories. In addition, the city is the marketing and distribution center for a large farming area, and it's crawling with college students who attend the University of South Carolina—where Hootie & The Blowfish got their start.

A day's worth of exploring will take you to Ainsley Hall Mansion, President Woodrow Wilson's boyhood home; the State House and Governor's Mansion; the Columbia Museum of Art; and the Town Theatre (1919), one of the oldest theaters in the country. The Riverbanks Park Zoo is an outstanding modern zoo that celebrates Christmas by draping hundreds of twinkling lights throughout the park.

THE UPSTATE The northwestern region of South Carolina lies in the foothills of the Blue Ridge Mountains. Originally it was the place where residents of Charleston fled to escape the summer heat and the mosquitoes. What they discovered was a land of scenic wonders, with mountain peaks, unspoiled forests, waterfalls, and country hamlets. The chief city is **Greenville,** which makes a good base for touring the area, although Greenville is rich in its own attractions. The "second city," **Spartanburg,** is also an ideal base and has several attractions, including Walnut Grove Plantation.

But these cities are not the major reason to visit the Upstate. Escape instead to **Pendleton,** an entire town listed on the National Register of Historic Places. Here, you can visit Ashtabula Plantation, dating from the 1820s and once the most beautiful farm in the Upstate. Parks and battlefields abound, including Cowpens National Battlefield at Chesnee, famous for Daniel Morgan's 1781 defeat of the British. Finally, the Cherokee Foothills Scenic Highway curves for 130 miles through the heart of South Carolina's Blue Ridge foothills.

MYRTLE BEACH & THE GRAND STRAND Like Las Vegas in the desert, Myrtle Beach rises above the Southern coastline in a blaze of neon so bright that you might want to keep your shades handy, even after sunset. This city, a far cry from the historic South, has been transformed into a full-scale, megawatt entertainment mecca. A golfer's paradise, the area now boasts more than 80 championship golf courses designed by such greats as Arnold Palmer, Robert Trent Jones, and Tom Fazio. There are water slides, arcades, giant shopping malls, and a host of children's attractions. Numerous country-music shows are available; in fact, the group Alabama started its career here and has established a huge entertainment complex where famed country artists appear year-round.

If you're hungry for seafood, dining is best at nearby **Murrells Inlet,** a strip along the marsh that's packed with seafood places. You might catch a glimpse of mystery novelist Mickey Spillane, who makes his home here.

South Carolina

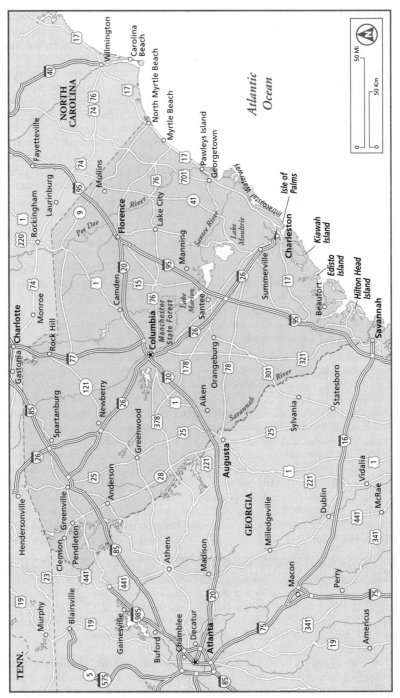

171

CHARLESTON   What can we possibly say about a city so charming that nearly every celebrity who visits ends up driving around town with a real-estate agent? Located on the peninsula between the Cooper and Ashley rivers in southeastern South Carolina, Charleston is the oldest and second-largest city in the state, full of antebellum homes and carefully preserved buildings. Each spring, Charleston hosts the Spoleto Festival, one of the most prestigious performing-arts events in the South.

The Nathaniel Russell House, a National Trust landmark completed in 1808, is especially recommended. A handsome example of Federal architecture set amid formal gardens, the house is recognized as being one of America's most important neoclassical dwellings. One of the finest examples of Colonial architecture in the country is Drayton Hall, an expensive mansion set amid huge oaks draped with Spanish moss. This National Historic Landmark is the only Ashley River plantation house to survive the Civil War intact. Magnolia Plantation, just a few miles down, is also worth visiting for its walking sites and 50-acre garden of camellias and azaleas.

Every day of the week, Charleston's City Market is bustling with craftspeople jammed under the covered breezeways. Sweet-grass basket-weavers hum old spirituals; horse-drawn carriages clop down the street; and thousands of tourists eat, drink, and shop their way along.

A minimum 3-day stay is required if you are to discover Charleston by day and night. Try to include a trip over the Cooper River Bridge to the string of islands that have rebounded from the massive destruction of Hurricane Hugo. Also take time to stop in **Beaufort,** the inspiration for Pat Conroy's novel *The Prince of Tides* (among other best-sellers). The town is full of old-fashioned inns, rustic pubs, and tiny stores along a tailored waterfront park.

HILTON HEAD   Much more commercial than Charleston is Hilton Head Island, home of wealthy Northerners (mostly retired) and vacationers from all parts of the country. With myriad contemporary beachfront restaurants and rows of hotels, time-share villas, and cottages, the island has recently sprouted boutiques and upscale shopping areas. Although the traffic is horrendous (there is only one main thoroughfare both on and off the island), development hasn't obliterated nature on Hilton Head, and you can find solitude at the north end of the beach.

On the positive side, the island has become socially and culturally oriented, playing host to presidents and world leaders and also supporting its own symphony orchestra and ballet company. A yearly golf tournament known as the Heritage Classic and the Family Circle Cup Tennis Championship are played neck to neck at Harbor Town. Sea Pines on Hilton Head is one of the country's premier golf resorts, located on a 605-acre Wildlife Foundation Preserve that's home to birds, squirrels, dolphins, and alligators. Hilton Head has 15 miles of bike paths and 5 miles of pristine beaches.

2 Visitor Information

Before leaving home, write or call ahead for specific information on sports and sightseeing. Contact **South Carolina Division of Tourism,** 1205 Pendleton St. (P.O. Box 71), Columbia, SC 29202 (☎ **803/734-0122;** fax 803/734-0133; www.travelsc. com). It can also furnish *South Carolina: Smiling Faces, Beautiful Places,* a detailed booklet with photos that covers each region of the state.

When you enter South Carolina, look for one of the 10 **travel information centers** located on virtually every major highway near the border with neighboring states. Information sources for specific destinations in the state are listed in the South Carolina chapters that follow. If you have Internet access, a particularly useful resource for travel information is **CityNet** (www.city.net), which provides links organized by location, and then by category, to hundreds of other sites throughout the Internet.

3 When to Go

CLIMATE
Although parts of South Carolina can be very hot and steamy in summer (to say the least), temperatures are never extreme the rest of the year, as shown in the average highs and lows noted in the accompanying charts.

Charleston Average Temperatures & Rainfall

	Jan	Feb	Mar	Apr	May	June	July	Aug	Sept	Oct	Nov	Dec
High (°F)	59	61	68	76	83	87	89	89	85	77	69	61
Low (°F)	40	41	48	56	64	70	74	74	69	49	49	42
Rain (in.)	3.5	3.3	4.3	2.7	4.0	6.4	6.8	7.2	4.7	2.9	2.5	3.2

Columbia Average Temperatures & Rainfall

	Jan	Feb	Mar	Apr	May	June	July	Aug	Sept	Oct	Nov	Dec
High (°F)	56	59	67	77	84	89	91	85	76	68	67	59
Low (°F)	33	35	42	50	59	66	70	69	64	50	41	35
Rain (in.)	4.4	4.1	4.8	3.3	3.7	4.8	5.5	6.1	3.7	3.0	2.9	3.6

South Carolina Calendar of Events

January
- **Low-Country Oyster Festival,** Charleston. Steamed buckets of oysters greet visitors at Boone Hall Plantation. Enjoy live music, oyster-shucking contests, children's events, and various other activities. Contact the Greater Charleston Restaurant Association at ☎ **843/577-4030.** End of January.

February
- **Southeastern Wildlife Exposition,** Charleston. More than 150 of the finest artists and more than 500 exhibitors participate at 13 locations in the downtown area. Enjoy carvings, sculpture, paintings, live-animal exhibits, food, and much more. Call ☎ **843/723-1748;** www.sewe.com for details. Mid-February.

March
- **Festival of Houses and Gardens,** Charleston. For nearly 50 years, people have been enjoying some of Charleston's most historic neighborhoods and private gardens on this tour. Contact the Historic Charleston Foundation, P.O. Box 1120, Charleston, SC 29402 (☎ **848/724-8481**) for details. Mid-March to mid-April.
- **Transsouth 400 and Diamond Hill Plywood 200,** Darlington. These events mark the first of two annual visits to the Darlington Raceway by NASCAR's Winston Cup and Busch Grand National racing series. Tickets for the Saturday Busch Grand National race range from $30 to $35, and tickets for the Sunday Winston Cup race range from $40 to $110. The Sunday crowd can swell in excess of 75,000 fans. Call ☎ **843/395-8499;** www.darlingtonraceway.com for tickets and information. Late March.
- **Carolina Cup,** Camden. The elaborate picnics with silver candelabras and crystal champagne flutes make this annual steeplechase race an event to remember.

Contact the Springdale Race Course at ☎ **803/432-6513** for details. Late March to early April.

☼ **Family Circle Magazine Cup,** Hilton Head Island. This $750,000 tournament brings the best women's tennis players to the island. Call ☎ **843/363-3500** for details. Late March to early April.

• **Flowertown Festival,** Summerville. More than 180 booths of arts and crafts, a road race, a "Youth Fest," and lots of entertainment are set in this historic city surrounded by brilliant azalea and dogwood blossoms. Contact the YMCA at ☎ **843/871-9622** to learn more. Late March to early April.

April

• **Cooper River Bridge Run,** Charleston. Sponsored by the Medical University of South Carolina, this run and walk starts in Mt. Pleasant, goes over the Cooper River, and ends in the center of Charleston. For information, call (☎ **843/ 722-3405.** April 1.

• **MCI Classic,** Hilton Head. This $1.3-million tournament brings an outstanding field of PGA tour professionals to this event each year. The weeklong tournament is held at Harbour Town Golf Links in Sea Pines Plantation. Contact Classic Sports, Inc., 71 Lighthouse Rd., Suite 414, Hilton Head, SC 29928 (☎ **843/671-2448**). Mid-April.

• **World Grits Festival,** St. George. This unique festival is a celebration of that famous Southern staple, grits! For years, contestants have competed in grits-grinding, corn-shelling, grits-eating, and best recipes, as well as traditional festivities. Call ☎ **843/563-7943** to find out more. Mid to late April.

• **Africa Alive,** Rock Hill. Learn about the African heritage by way of storytelling, craft activities, exhibits, and music and dance from the Museum of York County. Call (☎ **803/329-2121** for information; www.yorkcounty.org). Late April.

May

• **American Classic Tea Open House,** Charleston. America's only tea plantation takes you on a free historical tour. Don't forget to buy some great blends when you leave. Contact the Charleston Tea Plantation at ☎ **843/559-0383.** Early May.

• **Issaqueena Festival,** Six Mile. This festival celebrates the legendary Indian maiden who warned a settlers' fort of an impending Indian attack. Enjoy Native American arts, crafts, hot-air-balloon rides, food, fireworks, and more. Contact Six Mile Happenings at ☎ **864/868-2653.** Early May.

• **Spring Fling,** Spartanburg. Live entertainment mixed with arts, crafts, and games make this a popular annual event. Contact Spartanburg Community Events at ☎ **864/596-2020** for details. First weekend in May.

• **Iris Festival,** Sumter. The world-famous Swan Lake Iris Gardens is the setting for this elaborate festival of arts and crafts, food, concerts, garden tours, and a parade. Call ☎ **800/688-4748.** Mid-May.

• **Pontiac Freedom Weekend,** Anderson. This hot-air balloon festival on Memorial Day weekend takes place in Anderson. It is a nonstop four-day extravaganza for the whole family. Featured are 100 hot-air balloons, concerts by well-known entertainment, and lots more at the city's new Sports and Entertainment Center. For more information, call ☎ **864/232-3700.** May 26-29.

☼ **Spoleto Festival U.S.A.,** Charleston. This is the premier cultural event in the tri-state area. This famous international festival—the American counterpart of the equally celebrated one in Spoleto, Italy—showcases world-renowned performers in drama, dance, music, and art in various venues throughout the city. For details and this year's schedule, contact Spoleto Festival U.S.A., P.O. Box 157, Charleston, SC 29402 (☎ 843/722-2764; www.spoletousa.org). Late May through early June.

June

- **Edisto Riverfest,** Walterboro. The main attractions at this festival are guided trips down the blackwater Edisto River. Call ☎ 843/549-5591 for details. Mid-June.

July

- **Lake Murray's July 4th Celebration,** Columbia. Lake Murray plays host to more than 100 boats decorated in red, white, and blue. At night, an elaborate fireworks display is held. Contact the Lake Murray Tourism and Recreation Association at ☎ 803/781-5940. First Saturday in July.
- **Freedom Weekend Aloft,** Greenville. This Fourth of July event features big-name entertainment, amusement rides, a crafts show, daily races of more than 100 hot-air balloons, and a gigantic fireworks finale. It's the nation's largest hot-air balloon Fourth of July event. Contact Freedom Weekend Aloft at ☎ 864/232-3700. First weekend in July.
- **Conway Riverfest,** Conway. You can gather along the banks of the Waccamaw River for a day full of arts and crafts, live entertainment, food, Jell-O jumps, raft races, boat rides, and fireworks. Contact the Conway Area Chamber of Commerce at ☎ 843/248-2273. Early July.

August

- **Shawfest,** Shaw Air Force Base, near Sumter and Cherryvale. This annual event takes the form of a community-appreciation festival. Onlookers are treated to an air show featuring some of the Air Force's top pilots and jets. Call ☎ 803/688-5308 for additional information. Early August.
- **Summerfest,** York. Loads of live entertainment are presented here with four stages, crafts, country food, and a classic car show. Contact the York County Convention and Visitors Bureau at ☎ 800/866-5200. Late August.

September

- **A Taste of Charleston,** Charleston. This annual event offers an afternoon of food, fun, entertainment, and more at the Charleston Civic Center Grand Hall. A selection of Charleston-area restaurants offers their specialties in bite-size portions, so you can sample them all. For more information, call ☎ 843/577-4030. September 1 and 2.
- **Pepsi Southern 500 and Duralube 200,** Darlington. The second of two annual NASCAR Winston Cup and Busch Grand National races held at the Darlington Raceway. Tickets for the Saturday Busch Grand National race range from $30 to $35, and tickets for the Sunday Winston Cup race range from $70 to $110. The Sunday crowd can exceed 75,000 fans. Call ☎ 843/395-8499 for tickets and information. Labor Day weekend.
- **South Carolina's Largest Garage Sale,** Myrtle Beach. One person's trash is another person's treasure, and you're likely to find yours here. Vendors set up shop in a large parking garage to sell clothing, furniture, household goods, and hundreds of other bargains. Contact the Myrtle Beach Parks and Recreation Department at ☎ 843/918-1241. Early September.
- **Scottish Games and Highland Gathering,** Charleston. This gathering of Scottish clans features medieval games, bagpipe performances, Scottish dancing, and

other traditional activities. Call The Scottish Society of Charleston at ☎ 843/556-2417. Mid-September.

- **Candelight Tour of Houses & Gardens,** Charleston. Sponsored by the Preservation Society of Charleston, this annual event provides an intimate look at many of the area's historic homes, gardens, and churches. For more information, call ☎ 843/7222-4630. September 22 to October 28.

October

- **Fall for Greenville,** Greenville. This annual two-day event features more than 40 restaurants and food vendors from around the city presenting a wide variety of their tasty wares. Events include a chili "cook-off," a cooking school, an ice carving, a bartender's mix-off, a waiter's race, and a bike race, along with free entertainment. For more information, call ☎ 864/467-5780. October 6 to 8.
- **Jubilee: Harvest of the Arts,** Rock Hill. Concerts featuring national recording artists, and events such as regional and local talents, are held at this arts festival. Call ☎ 803/328-ARTS. Early October.
- **MOJA Festival,** Charleston. Celebrating the rich African-American heritage in the Charleston area, this festival features lectures, art exhibits, stage performances, historical tours, concerts, and much more. Contact the Charleston Office of Cultural Affairs at ☎ 843/724-7305. Early October.
- **Fall Tour of Homes,** Beaufort. Frank Lloyd Wright's Aldbrass Plantation is only one of the beautiful homes on this tour. The public is invited to get a rare view of this coastal city's most stately residences during a 3-day tour. Call ☎ 843/524-6334; www.beaufortonline.com. Mid-October.
- **Governor's Cup Road Race,** Columbia. This event, more than half a century old, is a half marathon and 8-kilometer race and walk beginning at 8:30am on the State Capitol Grounds. Conducted by the Carolina Marathon Association. For more information, call ☎ 803/929-1996. October 21.

November

- **Treasures By the Sea,** Myrtle Beach. South Carolina's Grand Strand is decorated in a profusion of lights with a nautical theme, including "mermaids," seashells, sea horses, and others. Special events are held throughout the season. Contact the Visitors Bureau, Myrtle Beach Area Chamber of Commerce at ☎ 843/626-7444. November to February.
- **Colonial Cup,** Camden. Every year, this prestigious steeplechase race determines the champion and winner of the NSA's Eclipse award. Tailgating in style is a trademark of this event, with tables covered in linen and patrons dressed in hats and sport coats. Contact the Springdale Race Course at ☎ 803/432-6513; www.carolina-cup.org. Mid-November.
- **Festival of Trees,** Greenville. Professionally decorated trees are displayed in the Hyatt Regency. A Teddy Bear tea, Gingerbread Land, and family brunch are special attractions. Call ☎ 864/255-1659. November 30-December 25.

December

- **Lights Before Christmas,** Columbia. The Riverbanks Zoo becomes a holiday wonderland when thousands of lights are strung around the park. Contact the Riverbanks Zoo at ☎ 803/779-8717. December 1 to 30.
- **Christmas in Charleston,** Charleston. This month-long celebration features home and church tours, Christmas-tree lightings, craft shows, artistry, and a peek at how Old Charleston celebrated the holiday season. For more information on how to participate or to visit, call ☎ 800/868-8118. December 1 to 31.

What Things Cost in Charleston	U.S. $
Taxi from Charleston airport to city center	20.00–25.00
Bus fares (exact change)	.75
Local telephone call	.35
Double room at the John Rutledge House Inn (expensive)	255.00–325.00
One-bedroom suite at the Doubletree Guest Suites (moderate)	99.00–189.00
Double room at the Barksdale House Inn (inexpensive)	109.00
Lunch for one at Magnolias (moderate)	16.00–20.00
Lunch for one at A.W. Shucks (inexpensive)	10.00
Dinner for one, without wine, at Restaurant Million (expensive)	45.00
Dinner for one, without wine, at Carolina's (moderate)	20.00
Dinner for one, without wine, at Hyman's Seafood Co. Restaurant (inexpensive)	16.00
Bottle of beer	2.50
Coca-Cola	.75
Cup of coffee	1.25
Roll of 35mm Kodak film, 36 exposures	7.00
Admission to the Charleston Museum	8.00
Movie ticket	7.00
Ticket to a Charleston Symphony concert	22.00

4 The Active Vacation Planner

BEACHES   The South Carolina coast is the true gem of the state. Along more than 280 miles of seashore are white-sand beaches shaded by palms, stretching from the Grand Strand to the mouth of the Savannah River. Myrtle Beach offers bright lights and a carnival atmosphere, and emphasizes family entertainment. Edisto Beach is a secluded spot. Fripp Island and Hilton Head are luxury resorts.

BIKING   South Carolina's basically flat terrain offers some of the country's best biking areas. The hard-packed sand of the beaches are particularly good for bike riding. Resorts such as Hilton Head have extensive paved bike trails, and many rental outfits operate just off the beaches.

CAMPING   Many of South Carolina's lakes have lakefront campsites. Reservations are not necessary, but you are strongly advised to make reservations for big weekends such as Memorial Day or Labor Day. Campsites are also available in South Carolina's 34 state parks. For more information, contact **South Carolina Department of Parks, Recreation, and Tourism,** P.O. Box 71, Columbia, SC 29202 (☎ **888/887-2757** or 803/734-0159; www.southcarolinaparks.com).

CANOEING   The Broad and Saluda rivers, which flow near Columbia in the center of the state, provide excellent canoeing.

FISHING & HUNTING   Fishing is abundant in South Carolina. On the coast, fish for amberjack, barracuda, shark, king mackerel, and other species. In South Carolina's many lakes and streams, fish for trout, bass, and blue and channel catfish. No license is required for saltwater fishing, but a freshwater license is required. The Upstate is a mecca for waterfowl and wild turkey. The season stretches over fall and winter and sometimes into spring. Hunting on public lands is illegal, but many hunting clubs will allow you to join temporarily if you provide references. For information, write the **South Carolina Department of Natural Resources,** P.O. Box 167, Columbia, SC 29202 (☎ **803/734-3888;** www.dnr.state.sc.us).

GOLF   Some of the best golf in the country is available in South Carolina, at courses such as the one at the fabled Harbor Town at Hilton Head. For information, contact the **South Carolina Department of Parks, Recreation, and Tourism,** P.O. Box 71, Columbia, SC 29202, or call ☎ **888/867-2757** or 803/734-0159; www. southcarolinaparks.com. Ask for the *South Carolina Golf Guide.*

HORSEBACK RIDING   Without question, Aiken County is king of the equine industry in the area. The Carolina Cup and the Colonial Cup steeplechase races are held in Camden each year. For information, contact **Thoroughbred County** at ☎ **803/649-7981,** or write the **Aiken Chamber of Commerce,** 121 Richland Ave., Aiken, SC 19802 (☎ **803/641-1111**).

THE LAKES   South Carolina's rivers feed lakes all over the state, offering boating, fishing, and camping. With 450 miles of shoreline, the lakes are a magnet for commercial development. While lakeside resort communities are booming, 70% of the lakeshore is slated to remain in a natural state. Lakes such as Thurmond, Moultrie, Murray, and Marion are becoming increasingly popular as vacation spots. Many operators and marinas rent boats and watercraft. For information about staying lakeside, contact the **South Carolina Department of Parks, Recreation, and Tourism,** P.O. Box 71, Columbia, SC 29202 or call ☎ **888/887-2757.**

STATE PARKS   Camping, fishing, boating, and extensive hiking are available in South Carolina's many state parks. Cabin accommodations are rented all year in 14 of the parks. All cabins are heated, air-conditioned, and fully equipped with cooking utensils, tableware, and linens. Rates range from $44 to $116 per night or $264 to $770 per week. Cabins can accommodate anywhere from 4 to 12 people. Advance reservations are necessary for summer. For full details, write the **South Carolina State Parks,** 1205 Pendleton St., Columbia, SC 29201 (☎ **803/734-0156**).

WHITE-WATER RAFTING   The Chattanooga River forms part of the lower northeast border with Georgia and is the site of some of the best white-water rafting and canoeing in the United States. **Wildwater Ltd.,** P.O. Box 309, Long Creek, SC 29658 (☎ **800/451-9972**), offers white-water trips along the Chattanooga. Packages including instruction, meals, and lodging are available.

5 Tips for Travelers with Special Needs

The Columbia telephone directory contains a special section of "Community Service Numbers." It's quite comprehensive and includes services for most of these groups.

FOR TRAVELERS WITH DISABILITIES   The State of South Carolina has numerous agencies that assist people with disabilities. For specific information, call the **South Carolina Handicapped Services Information System** (☎ **803/777-5732**). Two other agencies that may prove to be helpful are the **South Carolina Protection & Advocacy System for the Handicapped** (☎ **803/782-0639**) and the **Commission for the Blind** (☎ **803/734-7520**). For more information, see "Tips for Travelers with Special Needs," in chapter 3.

FOR GAY & LESBIAN TRAVELERS   **Gay hot lines** in Charleston fall under the 24-hour crisis-prevention network (☎ **803/744-4357**). Gay hot lines in Columbia are designated as the GLPM hot line (☎ **803/771-7713**).

The most important information center in the state is the **South Carolina Pride Center,** 1108 Woodrow St., Columbia (☎ **803/771-7713**). It's open on Wednesday and Sunday from 1 to 6pm, on Friday from 7 to 11pm, and on Saturday from 1 to 8pm. On the premises are a library, archives, a "gay pride" shop, an inventory of films, and a meeting space. It also functions as a conduit for such other organizations as the **Low Country Gay and Lesbian Alliance** (☎ **843/720-8088**).

For information before you go, refer to "Tips for Travelers with Special Needs," in chapter 3.

FOR SENIORS   Seniors may want to contact the **Retired Senior Volunteer Program** (☎ **803/252-7734**). When you're sightseeing or attending entertainment events, always inquire about discounts for seniors; they're plentiful. Also see "Tips for Travelers with Special Needs," in chapter 3.

FOR FAMILIES   A great vacation idea is to rent a cabin in one of South Carolina's 14 state parks. Rates range from $44 to $116 per night, $264 to $770 per week, and cabins accommodate anywhere from 4 to 12 people. For details on advance reservations and on accommodations at the 34 other state parks, contact **South Carolina State Parks,** 1205 Pendleton St., Columbia, SC 29201 (☎ **803/734-0159**).

6 Getting There

BY PLANE   American Airlines and American Eagle (☎ 800/433-7300), **Continental Airlines** (☎ 800/525-0280), **Delta Air Lines** and **Delta Connection** (☎ 800/221-1212), **United Airlines** and **United Express** (☎ 800/241-6522), and **US Airways** (☎ 800/428-4322) are the major airlines serving South Carolina. **Myrtle Beach** has scheduled air service via Continental, Delta, and US Airways. You can fly into **Charleston** on Continental, Delta, United and United Express, and US Airways. **Columbia** is served by American and American Eagle, Delta and Delta Connection, and US Airways. **Greenville/Spartanburg** is served by Continental, Delta, and US Airways. If you're traveling to **Hilton Head,** you have the option of flying US Airways directly to the island or flying into the Savannah (Georgia) International Airport via Continental or Delta and then driving or taking a limousine to Hilton Head, which is 1 hour away.

BY CAR   Interstate 95 enters South Carolina from the north near Dillon and runs straight through the state to Hardeeville on the Georgia border. The major east–west artery is I-26, running from Charleston northwest through Columbia and on up to Hendersonville, North Carolina. U.S. 17 runs along the coast, and I-85 crosses the northwestern region of the state.

South Carolina furnishes excellent travel information to motorists, and there are well-equipped, efficiently staffed visitor centers at the state border on most major highways. If you have a cellular phone in your car and need help, dial ***HP** for Highway Patrol Assistance.

BY TRAIN   South Carolina is on the **Amtrak** (☎ **800/USA-RAIL**) New York–Miami and New York–Tampa runs, serving Camden, Charleston, Clemson, Columbia, Denmark, Dillon, Florence, Greenville, Kingstree, Spartanburg, and Yemassee. Amtrak also has tour packages that include hotel, breakfast, and historic-site tours in Charleston at bargain rates. Be sure to ask about the money-saving "All Aboard America" regional fares or any other current fare specials. Amtrak also offers attractively priced rail/drive packages in the Carolinas and Georgia.

BY BUS   Greyhound/Trailways (☎ **800/231-2222**) has good direct service to major cities in South Carolina from out of state, with connections to almost any destination. With a 21-day advance purchase, you can get a discounted "Go Anywhere" fare (some day-of-the-week restrictions apply). Call for information and schedules, or contact the Greyhound depot in your area.

PACKAGE TOURS Collette Tours (☎ 401/728-3805 or 800/832-4656; www.collettetours.com) offers an 8-day fly/drive tour, "Charleston/Myrtle Beach Show Tour" that guides you through a day of Charleston's most historic sites, visits a Civil War–era plantation in Georgetown, and ends up in Myrtle Beach for dinner and entertainment at Dixie Stampede, Broadway at the Beach, and Magic on Ice.

Mayflower Tours (☎ 800/365-5359) highlights a tour called "Southern Charms." The 8-day tour originates in Atlanta, the capital of the New South. After a 2-day visit in Atlanta, you travel to Myrtle Beach, the birthplace of beach music and the Shag—the '60s dance that popularized that genre. Myrtle Beach has grown into an entertainment mecca for South Carolina, providing heavy competition for areas such as Nashville and Branson, Missouri. Following Myrtle Beach, you visit the old Southern charm of Charleston, whose sites include Boone Hall Plantation and Fort Sumter, where the first shots of the Civil War were fired. The tour from Charleston makes a brief stop in Beaufort before crossing the Georgia border to visit Savannah, the grand dame of the South and one of the oldest cities in America. Be sure to see the River Street area, along with the historic downtown area, which is virtually as it was when James Oglethorpe designed it in 1733. You spend the last day of the tour traveling back to Atlanta via Macon, site of the Georgia Music Hall of Fame, which has such enshrinees as James Brown, Otis Redding, the Allman Brothers Band, and Little Richard. Prices for the tour start at $950 per person (double occupancy) and include 11 meals and all lodging at reputable hotels along the route. Departures are in March to May and September to December. Ask about special departures to catch the springtime blossoms and the "Christmas in Dixie" jaunts in November and December.

7 Getting Around

BY PLANE Delta Air Lines and **US Airways** (see "Getting There," above) both have flights within South Carolina, although connections are sometimes awkward.

BY CAR South Carolina has a network of exceptionally good roads. Even when you leave the major highways for the state-maintained roadways, driving is easy on wellmaintained roads. AAA services are available through the **Carolina Motor Club** in Charleston (☎ 843/766-2394), Columbia (☎ 803/798-9205), and Spartanburg (☎ 864/583-2766).

In South Carolina, vehicles must use headlights when windshield wipers are in use as a result of inclement weather. Remember that drivers and front-seat passengers must wear seat belts.

Also see "Getting Around," in chapter 3.

Fast Facts: South Carolina

American Express Services in South Carolina are provided through, **B&A Travel Service,** 2001 Greene St., Columbia (☎ 803/256-0547); **Long's Travel Agency,** 33 Office Park Rd., Hilton Head Island (☎ 843/842-4700); and **Woodside World-Wide Travel Service,** 108 W. McBee Ave., Greenville (☎ 864/233-4118).

Area Code   It's 803 for Columbia and environs; 843 for Charleston and the South Carolina coast; and 864 for Greenville, Anderson, Spartanburg and the Upstate area.

Emergencies   Dial ☎ **911** for police, ambulance, paramedics, and the fire department. You can also dial 0 (zero, *not* the letter *O*) and ask the operator to connect you to emergency services. Travelers Aid can also be helpful; check local telephone directories.

Fishing   A **fishing hot line** (☎ **800/ASK-FISH**) gives you an up-to-date fishing report on South Carolina's major lakes, as well as information on fishing regulations. For more information, contact **South Carolina Dept. of Natural Resources,** P.O. Box 167, Columbia, SC 29202 (☎ **803/734-3886** http:// water.dnr.state.sc.us).

Liquor Laws   The minimum drinking age is 21. Some restaurants are licensed to serve only beer and wine, but a great many offer those plus liquor in mini-bottles, which can be added to cocktail mixers. Beer and wine are sold in grocery stores 7 days a week, but all package liquor is offered through local government-controlled stores, commonly called "ABC" (Alcoholic Beverage Control Commission) stores, which are closed on Sundays.

Newspapers and Magazines   The major papers are *The State* (Columbia), the *Greenville News,* and the *Charleston Post and Courier. The Sandlapper* is a local quarterly magazine.

Police   In an emergency, call ☎ **911** (no coin required).

Taxes   South Carolina has a 5% sales tax.

Time Zone   South Carolina is in the Eastern Standard Time zone and goes on daylight saving time in summer.

Weather   Phone ☎ **803/822-8135;** www.nws.noaa.gov for an update.

10 Charleston

In the closing pages of *Gone With the Wind,* Rhett tells Scarlett that he's going back home to Charleston, where he can find "the calm dignity life can have when it's lived by gentle folks, the genial grace of days that are gone. When I lived those days, I didn't realize the slow charm of them." In spite of all the changes and upheavals over the years, Rhett's endorsement of Charleston still holds true.

If the Old South lives all through South Carolina's Low Country, it positively thrives in Charleston. All our romantic notions of antebellum days—stately homes, courtly manners, gracious hospitality, and above all, gentle dignity—are facts of everyday life in this old city, in spite of a few scoundrels here and there, including an impressive roster of pirates, patriots, and presidents.

Notwithstanding a history dotted with earthquakes, hurricanes, fires, and Yankee bombardments, Charleston remains one of the best-preserved cities in America's Old South. It boasts 73 pre-Revolutionary War buildings, 136 from the late 18th century, and more than 600 built before the 1840s. With its cobblestone streets and horse-drawn carriages, Charleston is a place of visual images and sensory pleasures. Jasmine and wisteria fragrances fill the air; the aroma of she-crab soup (a local favorite) wafts from sidewalk cafes; and antebellum architecture graces the historic cityscape. "No wonder they are so full of themselves," said an envious visitor from Columbia, which may be the state capital but doesn't have Charleston's style and grace.

In its annual reader survey, *Condé Nast Traveler* magazine named Charleston the No. 3 city to visit in America, which places it ahead of such perennial favorites as New York, Seattle, and Santa Fe. Visitors are drawn here from all over the world, and it is now quite common to hear German and French spoken on local streets.

Does this city have a modern side? Yes, but it's well hidden. Chic shops abound, as do a few supermodern hotels, but Charleston has no skyscrapers. You don't come to Charleston for anything cutting-edge, though. You come to glimpse an earlier, almost-forgotten era.

Many local families still own and live in the homes that their planter ancestors built. Charlestonians manage to maintain a way of life that in many respects has little to do with wealth. The simplest encounter with Charleston natives seems to be invested with a social air, as though the visitor were a valued guest. Yet there are those who detect a certain snobbishness in Charleston—and truth be told, you'd have to stay a few hundred years to be considered an insider here.

1 Orientation

ARRIVING

BY PLANE   See "Getting There," in chapter 9. **Charleston International Airport** is in North Charleston on I-26, about 12 miles west of the city. Taxi fare into the city runs about $25, and the airport limousine (☎ **843/767-1100**) has a $20 fare. All major car-rental facilities, including Hertz and Avis, are available at the airport. If you're driving, follow the airport-access road to I-26 into the heart of Charleston.

BY CAR   The main north–south coastal route, U.S. 17, passes through Charleston; I-26 runs northwest to southeast, ending in Charleston. Charleston is 120 miles southeast of Columbia via I-26 and 98 miles south of Myrtle Beach via U.S. 17.

BY TRAIN   Amtrak (☎ **800/USA-RAIL**) trains arrive at 4565 Gaynor Ave., North Charleston.

VISITOR INFORMATION

Charleston Convention and Visitors Bureau, 375 Meeting St., Charleston, SC 29402 (☎ **843/853-8000;** www.charlestoncvb.com), just across from the Charleston Museum, provides maps, brochures, tour information, and access to South Carolina Automated Ticketing. The helpful staff will assist you in finding accommodations and planning your stay. Numerous tours depart hourly from the visitors bureau, and rest room facilities, as well as parking, are available. Be sure to allow time to view the 24-minute multi-image presentation "Forever Charleston" and pick up a copy of the visitor's guide. The center is open from April to October, Monday to Friday from 8:30am to 5:30pm and on Saturday and Sunday from 8am to 5pm; and from November to March daily from 8:30am to 5:30pm.

CITY LAYOUT

Charleston's streets are laid out in an easy-to-follow grid pattern. The main north–south thoroughfares are King, Meeting, and East Bay streets. Tradd, Broad, Queen, and Calhoun streets cross the city from east to west. South of Broad Street, East Bay becomes East Battery.

Unlike most cities, Charleston offers a most helpful map, and it's distributed free. Called **"The Map Guide—Charleston,"** it includes the streets of the historic district as well as surrounding areas, and offers tips on shopping, tours, and what to see and do. Maps are available at the **Visitor Reception & Transportation Center,** 375 Meeting St., at John Street (☎ **843/853-8000**).

Neighborhoods in Brief

The Historic District   In 1860, according to one Charlestonian, "South Carolina seceded from the Union, Charleston seceded from South Carolina, and south of Broad Street seceded from Charleston." The city preserves its early years at its southernmost point: the conjunction of the Cooper and Ashley rivers. The White Point Gardens, right in the elbow of the two rivers, provide a sort of gateway into this area, where virtually every home is of historic or architectural interest. Between Broad Street and Murray Boulevard (which runs along the south waterfront), you'll find such sightseeing highlights as St. Michael's Episcopal Church, the Calhoun Mansion, the Edmondston-Alston House, the Old Exchange/Provost Dungeon, the Heyward-Washington House, Catfish Row, and the Nathaniel Russell House.

Downtown   Extending north from Broad Street to Marion Square at the intersection of Calhoun and Meeting streets, this area encloses noteworthy points of interest, good shopping, and a gaggle of historic churches. Just a few of its highlights are the Old City Market, the Dock Street Theatre, Market Hall, the Old Powder Magazine, the Thomas Elfe Workshop, Congregation Beth Elohim, the French Huguenot Church, St. John's Church, and the Unitarian church.

Above Marion Square   The visitor center is located on Meeting Street north of Calhoun. The Charleston Museum is just across the street, and the Aiken-Rhett Mansion, Joseph Manigault Mansion, and Old Citadel are all within easy walking distance in the area bounded by Calhoun Street to the south and Mary Street to the north.

North Charleston   Charleston International Airport is at the point where I-26 and I-526 intersect. This makes North Charleston a Low Country transportation hub. Primarily a residential and industrial community, it lacks the charms of the historic district. It's also the home of the North Charleston Coliseum, the largest indoor entertainment venue in South Carolina.

Mount Pleasant   East of the Cooper River, just minutes from the heart of the historic district, this community is worth a detour. Filled with accommodations, restaurants, and some attractions, it encloses a historic district along the riverfront known as the Old Village, which is on the National Register's list of buildings. Its major attraction is Patriots Point, the world's largest naval and maritime museum; it's also the home of the aircraft carrier *Yorktown.*

Outlying Areas   Within easy reach of the city are Boone Hall Plantation, Fort Moultrie, and the public beaches at Sullivan's Island and Isle of Palms. Head west across the Ashley River Bridge to pay tribute to Charleston's birth at Charles Towne Landing, and visit such highlights as Drayton Hall, Magnolia Gardens, and Middleton Place.

2 Getting Around

BY BUS   City bus fares are 75¢, and service is available from 5:35am to 10pm (until 1am to North Charleston). Between 9:30am and 3:30pm, senior citizens and the handicapped pay 25¢. Exact change is required. For route and schedule information, call ☎ **843/724-7420.**

BY TROLLEY   The **Downtown Area Shuttle (DASH)** is the quickest way to get around the main downtown area daily. The fare is 75¢, and you'll need exact change. A pass that's good for the whole day costs $2. For hours and routes, call ☎ **843/724-7420.**

BY TAXI   Leading taxi companies are **Yellow Cab** (☎ **843/577-6565**) and **Safety Cab** (☎ **843/722-4066**). Each company has its own fare structure. Within the city, however, fares seldom exceed $3 or $4. You must call for a taxi; there are no pickups on the street.

BY CAR   If you're staying in the city proper, park your car and save it for day trips to outlying areas. You'll find **parking facilities** scattered about the city, with some of the most convenient at Hutson Street and Calhoun Street, both of which are near Marion Square; on King Street between Queen and Broad; and on George Street between King and Meeting. If you can't find space on the street to park, the two most centrally located **garages** are on Wentworth Street (☎ **843/724-7383**) and at Concord and Cumberland (☎ **843/724-7387**). Charges are $8 all day.

Leading car-rental companies are **Avis Rent-a-Car** (☎ **800/331-1212** or 843/767-7038), **Budget Car and Truck Rentals** (☎ **800/527-0700;** 843/767-7051 at the airport, 843/760-1410 in North Charleston, or 843/577-5195 downtown), and **Hertz** (☎ **800/654-3131** or 843/767-4552).

Fast Facts: Charleston

American Express   The local American Express office is at 956 Provincial Circle, Mt. Pleasant (☎ **843/881-9339**), open Monday to Friday from 9am to 5pm.

Camera Repair   The best option is **Focal Point,** 4 Apollo Rd. (☎ **843/ 571-3886**), open Monday to Thursday from 9am to 1pm and 2 to 5pm, and on Friday from 9am to noon.

Car Rentals   See "Getting Around," earlier in this chapter.

Climate   See "When to Go," in chapter 9.

Dentist   Consult Orthodontic Associates of Charleston, 86 Rutledge Ave. (☎ **843/723-7242**).

Doctor   For a physician referral or 24-hour emergency-room treatment, contact **Charleston Memorial Hospital,** 326 Calhoun St. (☎ **843/577-0600**). Another option is **Roper Hospital,** 316 Calhoun St. (☎ **843/724-2970**). Contact **Doctor's Care** (☎ **843/556-5585**) for the names of walk-in clinics.

Emergencies   In an emergency, dial ☎ **911.** If the situation isn't life-threatening, call ☎ **843/577-7077** for the fire department, ☎ **843/577-7434** for the police, or ☎ **843/747-1888** for an ambulance.

Eyeglass Repair   Try **LensCrafters,** 7800 Rivers Ave., North Charleston (☎ **843/764-3710**), open Monday to Saturday from 10am to 9pm and on Sunday noon to 6pm.

Hospitals   Local hospitals operating 24-hour emergency rooms include **AMI East Cooper Community Hospital,** 1200 Johnnie Dodds Blvd., Mt. Pleasant (☎ **843/881-0100**); **River Hospital North,** 12750 Spelssegger Dr., North Charleston (☎ **843/744-2110**); **Charleston Memorial Hospital,** 326 Calhoun St. (☎ **843/577-0600**); and **Medical University of South Carolina,** 171 Ashley Ave. (☎ **843/792-2300**). For medical emergencies, call ☎ **911.**

Hot Lines   Crisis Counseling is available at ☎ **800/922-2283** or 843/ 744-HELP. The Poison Control Center is at ☎ **800/922-1117.**

Newspapers & Magazines   *The Post and Courier* is the local daily.

Pharmacies   Try **CVS Drugs,** Wanda Crossing, Mt. Pleasant (☎ **843/ 881-9435**), open Monday to Saturday from 8am to midnight and on Sunday from 10am to 8pm.

Police   Call ☎ **911.** For non-emergency matters, call ☎ **843/577-7434.**

Post Office   The main post office is at 83 Broad St. (☎ **843/577-0688**), open Monday to Friday from 8:30am to 5:30pm and on Saturday from 9:30am to 2pm.

Rest Rooms   These are available throughout the downtown area, including at Broad and Meeting streets, at Queen and Church streets, on Market Street between Meeting and Church streets, and at other clearly marked strategic points in the historic and downtown districts.

Safety　Downtown Charleston is well lighted and patrolled throughout the night to ensure public safety. People can generally walk about downtown at night without fear of violence. Still, after the local trolley system, DASH, closes at 10:30pm, it's wiser to call a taxi than to walk through dark streets.

Taxes　A sales tax of 6% is imposed.

Transit Information　Contact the Charleston Area Convention Visitor Reception & Transportation Center, 375 Meeting St. (☎ **843/853-8000**), for information.

Weather　Call ☎ **843/744-3207** for an update.

3 Accommodations

Charleston has many of the best historic inns in America, even surpassing those of Savannah. Hotels and motels are priced in direct ratio to their proximity to the 789-acre historic district; if prices in the center are too high for your budget, find a place west of the Ashley River, and drive into town for sightseeing. In the last decade, the opening and restoration of inns and hotels in Charleston has been phenomenal, although it's slowing somewhat. Charleston ranks among the top cities of America for hotels of charm and character.

Bed-and-breakfast accommodations range from historic homes to carriage houses to simple cottages, and they're located in virtually every section of the city. For details and reservations, contact **Historic Charleston Bed and Breakfast,** 57 Broad St., Charleston, SC 29401 (☎ **800/743-3583** or 843/722-6606; www.historiccharlestonbedandbreakfast.com). Hours are Monday to Friday 9am to 5pm.

During the Spring Festival of Houses and the Spoleto Festival, rates go up, and owners charge pretty much what the market will bear. Advance reservations are essential at those times.

In a city that has rooms of so many shapes and sizes in the same historic building, classifying hotels by price is difficult. Price often depends on the room itself. Some expensive hotels may in fact have many moderately priced rooms. Moderately priced hotels, on the other hand, may have special rooms that are quite expensive.

When booking a hotel, ask about any package plans that might be available. It pays to ask, because deals come and go; they're most often granted to those who are staying 3 or 4 days.

The down side regarding all these inns of charm and grace is that they are among the most expensive in this tri-state guide. Staying in an inn or B&B in the historic district is one of the reasons to go to Charleston, and can do more to evoke the elegance of the city than almost anything else. Innkeepers and B&B owners know this all too well and charge accordingly, especially in the summer season, although winter reductions are common.

If you simply can't afford a stay at one of these historic inns, you can confine your consumption of Charleston to dining in the old city and sightseeing. For many people, that's a satisfying compromise. During the day, you can soak in the glamour of the city, and at night retire to one of the many clean, comfortable—and yes, utterly dull—chain motels on the outskirts. See the most representative samples with names, phone numbers, and rates under our "inexpensive" category, below.

VERY EXPENSIVE

✪ **Charleston Place Hotel.** 205 Meeting St., Charleston, SC 29401. ☎ **800/611-5545** or 843/722-4900. Fax 843/724-7215. www.charlestonpalacehotel.com. 487 units. A/C TV TEL MINIBAR. $239–$399 double; $500–$1,500 suite. Seasonal packages available. AE, DC, DISC, MC, V. Parking $9.

Charleston Accommodations

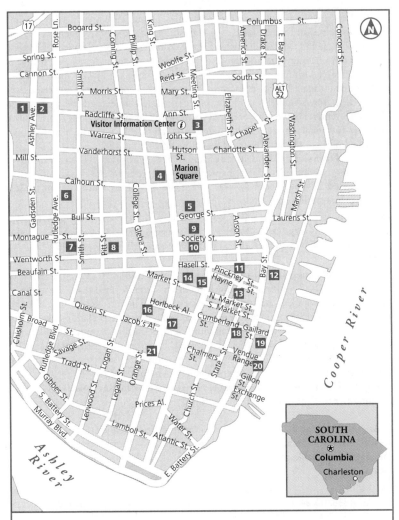

Anchorage Inn **19**
Ansonborough Inn **12**
Ashley Inn **1**
Barksdale House Inn **9**
Battery Carriage House Inn **23**
Best Western King Charles Inn **10**
Cannonboro Inn **2**
Charleston Place Hotel **15**
Doubletree Guest Suites **13**
1837 Bed and Breakfast **8**
Elliott House Inn **17**
Hampton Inn **3**

Indigo Inn/Jasmine House Inn **11**
John Rutledge House Inn **21**
Kings George IV Inn **5**
Lodge Alley Inn **18**
Philip Porcher House **16**
Planters Inn **14**
Rutledge Victorian Inn **6**
Two Meeting Street Inn **22**
Vendue Inn **20**
Wentworth Mansion **7**
Westin Francis Marion Hotel **4**

Charleston's premier hostelry, an Orient Express Property, is an eight-story landmark in the historic district that looks like a postmodern French château. It's big-time, uptown, glossy, and urban—at least, a former visitor, Prince Charles, thought so. Governors and prime ministers from around the world, as well as members of Fortune 500 companies, even visiting celebs such as Mel Gibson, prefer to stay here instead of at one of the more intimate B&Bs. Bedrooms are among the most spacious and handsomely furnished in town—stately, modern, and maintained in state-of-the-art condition. This hotel represents the New South at its most confident, a stylish giant in a district of B&Bs and small converted inns. Acres of Italian marble grace the place, leading to plush bedrooms with decor inspired by colonial Carolina.

Dining/Diversions: The deluxe restaurant, Charleston Grill, is recommended in the "Dining" section later in the chapter. A cafe provides a more casual option.

Amenities: 24-hour room service, baby-sitting, laundry, whirlpool, men's steam bath, aerobics studio, and sundeck.

✪ Planters Inn. Market and Meeting streets, Charleston, SC 29401. ☎ **800/845-7082** or 843/722-2345. Fax 843/577-2125; www.plantersinn.com. E-mail: reservations@ planterinn.com. 62 units. A/C TV TEL. $150–$300 double; $300–$600 suite. AE, DISC, MC, V. Parking $10.

For many years, this distinguished brick-sided inn next to the City Market was left to languish. In 1994, a multimillion-dollar renovation transformed the place into a cozy but tasteful and opulent enclave of colonial charm. The inn has a lobby filled with reproductions of 18th-century furniture and engravings, a staff clad in silk vests, and a parking area with exactly the right amount of spaces for the number of rooms in the hotel. The spacious bedrooms have hardwood floors, marble bathrooms, and 18th-century decor (the work of award-wining decorators). The suites are appealing, outfitted very much like rooms in an upscale private home.

Dining/Diversions: Afternoon tea is served in the lobby, and a well-recommended restaurant, the Peninsula Grill, is described in the "Dining" section later in the chapter.

Amenities: Same-day laundry and dry-cleaning service, concierge, twice-daily maid service, meeting rooms, and modem ports in all accommodations. Baby-sitting and massage are available at an additional charge; a health club and bicycle rentals are located nearby.

Wentworth Mansion. 149 Wentworth St., Charleston, SC 29401. ☎ **888/466-1886** or 843/853-1886. Fax 843/720-5290 www.wentworthmansion.com. E-mail: wentworthmansion@ aol.com. 21 units. A/C MINIBAR TV TEL. $225–$415 double; $395–$695 suite. Rates include breakfast buffet and evening tea. AE, DC, DISC, MC, V. Free parking.

An example of America's Gilded Age, this 1886 Second Empire inn touts such amenities as hand-carved marble fireplaces, Tiffany stained-glass windows, and detailed wood and plasterwork. If it is a grand accommodation that you seek, you've found it. When a cotton merchant built the property in the 1800s, it cost $200,000, an astronomical sum back then. In the mid-1990s a team of local entrepreneurs spent millions renovating it into the smooth and seamless inn you see today. Prior to its reopening in 1998, it had been a rundown office building. The rooms and suites are large enough to have sitting areas. All units have a king-size bed and whirlpool, and most have working gas fireplaces. The mansion rooms and suites also come with a sleeper sofa for extra guests, who are charged an additional $50 per night.

Dining/Diversions: A continental breakfast is served in the inn's sunroom each morning, and guests are invited to relax each evening in the lounge for cordials or spend some quiet time reading in the library. The inn's Circa 1886 Restaurant, one of the grandest in Charleston, is recommended even if you're not a guest of the Wentworth (see "Dining," below).

Amenities: Concierge and turn-down service.

EXPENSIVE

Ansonborough Inn. 21 Hasell St., Charleston, SC 29401. ☎ **800/522-2073** or 843/723-1655. Fax 843/577-6888. www.ansonboroughinn.com. E-mail: info@ansonboroughinn.com. 37 units. A/C TV TEL. Mar–Nov $149–$259 double; off-season $109–$229 double Fri–Sat. Children 11 and under stay free in parents' room. Rates include continental breakfast. AE, DISC, MC, V. Free parking.

This is one of the oddest hotels in the historic district. When they get past the not-very-promising exterior, most visitors really like the unusual configuration of rooms. Set close to the waterfront, the massive building, once a 1900 warehouse, has a lobby that features exposed timbers and a soaring atrium filled with plants. Despite the building's height, it only has three floors, which allows bedrooms to have ceilings of 14 to 16 feet and, in many cases, sleeping lofts. Bedrooms are outfitted with copies of 18th-century furniture and accessories, but the bathrooms are what you'd expect from a motel: molded-fiberglass shower stalls and imitation-marble countertops.

Dining: Breakfast is the only meal served, but many fine dining rooms are located nearby.

Amenities: A panoramic terrace with a hot tub on the rooftop.

Battery Carriage House Inn. 20 S. Battery, Charleston, SC 29401. ☎ **800/775-5575** or 843/727-3100. Fax 843/727-3130. www.charleston-inns.com. E-mail: BCHOCO@aol.com. 11 units. A/C TV TEL. $99–$225 double. Rates include continental breakfast. AE, DISC, MC, V. Free parking. No children under 12.

In one of the largest antebellum neighborhoods of Charleston, this inn offers bedrooms in a carriage house behind the main building. In other words, the owners save the top living accommodation for themselves but have restored the bedrooms out back to a high standard. Recent renovations added four-poster beds and a colonial frill to the not overly large bedrooms. Don't stay here if you want an inn with lots of public space; that, you don't get. But you can enjoy the location, which is a short walk off the Battery—a seafront peninsula where you can easily imagine a flotilla of Yankee ships enforcing the Civil War blockades.

Unfortunately, if you call, you're likely to get only a recorded message until the owners are able to call you back. Despite the inaccessibility of the main house and the difficulty of reaching a staff member, this place provides comfortable and convenient lodging in a desirable neighborhood.

Dining: Breakfast, during nice weather, is served in a carefully landscaped brick courtyard. Afternoon tea and evening wine are also served to guests.

Amenities: Concierge and twice-daily maid service with turn-down service.

Indigo Inn/Jasmine House. 1 Maiden Lane, Charleston, SC 29401. ☎ **800/845-7639** or 843/577-5900. Fax 843/577-0378. http://perl.webmillenia.net/IndigoInn/. E-mail: indigoinn@awod.com. 40 units (Indigo Inn), 10 units (Jasmine House). A/C TV TEL. $159–$225 double in the Indigo Inn, $189–$250 double in the Jasmine House. 10% discounts available in midwinter. Rates include continental breakfast. AE, DISC, MC, V. Free parking.

These are a pair of hotels set across the street from each other, with the same owners and the same reception area in the Indigo Inn. Built as an indigo warehouse in the mid–19th century, and gutted and radically reconstructed, the Indigo Inn (the larger of the two) offers rooms with 18th-century decor and comfortable furnishings. Rooms in the Jasmine House, an 1843 Greek Revival mansion whose exterior is painted buttercup yellow, are much more individualized. Each room has a ceiling of about 14 feet, its own color scheme and theme, crown moldings, whirlpool tubs, and floral-patterned upholsteries. Parking is available only in the lot at the Indigo Inn.

Dining: Both inns serve breakfast on-site for their respective guests.

Amenities: Concierge and some secretarial services.

✪ **John Rutledge House Inn.** 116 Broad St., Charleston, SC 29401. ☎ **800/476-9741** or 843/723-7999. Fax 843/720-2615. www.charminginns.com. E-mail: jrh@charminginns. com. 19 units. A/C TV TEL. $165–$325 double; $290–$374 suite. Rates include continental breakfast. AE, DC, DISC, MC, V. Free parking.

Many of the meetings that culminated in the emergence of the United States as a nation were conducted in this fine 18th-century house, now the most prestigious inn in Charleston. Unfortunately, the inn is near an unsavory neighborhood—which, quite frankly, is the only flaw we can find. It towers over its major rivals, such as the Planters Inn and the Ansonborough Inn, which are also excellent choices. The original builder, John Rutledge, was one of the signers of the Declaration of Independence; he later served as Chief Justice of the U.S. Supreme Court. The inn was built in 1763, with a third story added in the 1850s. Impeccably restored to its Federalist grandeur, it's enhanced with discreetly concealed electronic conveniences.

Dining: Continental breakfast and tea and afternoon sherry are served in a spacious upstairs sitting room, where mementos of the building's history and antique firearms, elaborate moldings, and marble fireplaces help enhance the building's distinguished aura.

Amenities: Concierge, access to a nearby health club, dry cleaning and laundry, massage, and baby-sitting (available at an additional charge).

Kings Courtyard Inn. 198 King St., Charleston, SC 19401. ☎ **800/845-6119** or 843/723-7000. Fax 843/720-2608. www.charminginns.com. E-mail: kci@charminginns.com. 44 units. A/C TV TEL. $150–$210 double. Children 11 and under stay free in parents' room. Off-season 3-day packages available. Rates include breakfast. AE, DC, DISC, MC, V. Parking $5.

The tiny entry to this three-story 1853 inn in the historic district is deceiving, because it opens inside to a brick courtyard with a fountain. A fireplace warms the small lobby, which has a brass chandelier. Besides the main courtyard, two courts offer fine views from the breakfast room. The owners bought the building next door and incorporated 10 more rooms into the existing inn. Your room might be outfitted with a canopy bed, an Oriental rug over a hardwood floor, an armoire, or even a gas fireplace. Some rooms have refrigerators. Rates include evening chocolates and turndown service. A whirlpool is on-site.

Dining: A continental breakfast is included in the rate; a full breakfast is available at an additional charge.

Amenities: Concierge, access to nearby health club, dry cleaning and laundry, massage, and baby-sitting (available at an additional charge).

Lodge Alley Inn. 195 E. Bay St., Charleston, SC 29401. ☎ **800/845-1004** or 843/722-1611. Fax 843/722-1611, ext. 7777. www.lodgealleyinn.com. 95 units. A/C MINIBAR TV TEL. $149–$169 double; $175–$300 suite. Children 12 and under stay free in parents' room. AE, MC, V. Free valet parking.

This sprawling historic property extends from its entrance on the busiest commercial street of the Old Town to a quiet brick-floored courtyard in back. It was once a trio of 19th-century warehouses. Today, it evokes a miniature village in Louisiana, with a central square, a fountain, landscaped shrubs basking in the sunlight, and easy access to the hotel's Cajun restaurant, the French Quarter. Units include conventional and rather standard hotel rooms, suites, and duplex arrangements with sleeping lofts.

Throughout, the decor is American country, with pine floors and lots of colonial accents. Some rooms have fireplaces, and most retain the massive timbers and brick walls of the original warehouses. The staff is usually polite and helpful, but because the hotel hosts many small conventions, they may be preoccupied with the demands of whatever group happens to be checking in or out.

Dining: A full or continental breakfast is available each morning.

Amenities: Room service, conference rooms, dry cleaning and laundry, baby-sitting, access to nearby health club (available at an additional charge).

Philip Porcher House. 19 Archdale St., Charleston 29401. ☎ **843/722-1801.** www. bbonline.com/sc/porcher. E-mail: porcherhhome.com. 1 2 bedroom apt. TV TEL. $200 for 2, $300 for 4. Rates include continental breakfast. No credit cards. Free parking.

Hailed by *Travel and Leisure* as one of the top B&Bs in the South, this beautifully restored 1770 Georgian home stands in the heart of the historic district. Built by a French Huguenot planter, Philip Porcher, the house was renovated in 1997. Handsome Georgian revival oak paneling was installed from the demolished executive offices of the Pennsylvania Railroad in Pittsburgh. The apartment was attractively furnished with period antiques and 18th-century engravings. The one rental unit on the ground floor consists of five rooms, and is rented to only one party (with two bedrooms, the apartment can accommodate up to four guests, ideal for families). Good books and music create a cozy environment. A comfortable sitting room has a working fireplace. One twin-bedded bedroom also has a fireplace. There is one bathroom with an elegant glass shower and double sinks. A screened gallery opens onto a wonderful secret walled garden.

○ Two Meeting Street Inn. 2 Meeting St., Charleston, SC 29401. ☎ **843/723-7322.** 9 units. A/C TV. $159–$290 double. Rates include continental breakfast and afternoon tea. No credit cards. Free parking. No children under 12.

Set in an enviable position near the Battery, this house was built in 1892 as a wedding gift from a prosperous father to his daughter. Inside, the proportions are as lavish and gracious as the Gilded Age could provide. Stained-glass windows, mementos, and paintings were either part of the original decorations or collected by the present owners, the Spell family. Most bedrooms contain four-poster beds, ceiling fans, and (in some cases) access to a network of balconies.

Dining: A continental breakfast with home-baked breads and pastries is available.

Vendue Inn. 19 Vendue Range, Charleston, SC 29401. ☎ **800/845-7900** or 843/577-7970. Fax 843/722-8381. www.charlestonvendueinn.com. E-mail: vendueinnsales@aol.com. 45 units. TV TEL. $135–$189 double; $219–$295 suite. Rates include full Southern breakfast. AE, DISC, MC, V. Parking $8.

This recently expanded, three-story inn manages to convey some of the personalized touches of a B&B. Its public areas—a series of narrow, labyrinthine spaces—are full of antiques and colonial accessories that evoke a cluttered, and slightly cramped, inn in Europe. Bedrooms do not necessarily follow the lobby's European model, however, and appear to be the result of decorative experiments by the owners. Room themes may be based on aspects of Florida, rococo Italy, or 18th-century Charleston. Marble floors and tabletops, wooden sleigh beds, and (in some rooms) wrought-iron canopy beds, while eclectically charming, might be inconsistent with your vision of colonial Charleston. Overflow guests are housed in a historic, brick-fronted annex across the cobblestone-covered street.

Dining: The inn's restaurant is called The Library at Vendue. The chef here offers a menu of local favorites with unusual twists. The other restaurant, The Roof Top Terrace, offers a more informal atmosphere with a panoramic view of the harbor and of the historic district. A complete luncheon and dinner menu of local and American favorites is offered here.

Amenities: Concierge, meeting rooms, and fitness center. Laundry service, dry-cleaning service, and baby-sitting are available for an additional charge. A full health club, massage, and bicycle rentals are available nearby.

Westin Francis Marion Hotel. 387 King St., Charleston, SC 29403. ☎ **888/627-8510** or 843/722-0600. Fax 843/723-4633. www.weston.com. E-mail: westinfmsale@charleston.net. 226 units. A/C TV TEL. $99–$205 double, $189–$319 suite. Children 11 and under stay free in parents' room. AE, CB, DC, DISC, MC, V. Parking $10–$14.

A $14-million award-winning restoration has returned this historic hotel to its original elegance. Although the 12-story structure breaks from the standard Charleston decorative motif and has rooms furnished in traditional European style, it is not devoid of Charleston charm. Rooms feature a king, queen, or double bed, and recently renovated bathrooms are adorned with brass fixtures.

Dining/Diversions: The hotel's restaurant, Elliott's on the Square, features an extensive international and continental menu, serving dinner from 6:30 to 10pm and providing room service for hotel guests until 11pm. The hotel bar begins serving at 10am until 10pm.

Amenities: Modem ports in each room, business services and meeting rooms, concierge, a fitness room, and in-room massage.

MODERATE

Reliable motel accommodations are also available at the **Hampton Inn Historic District,** 345 Meeting St. (☎ **800/HAMPTON** or 843/426-7866), across from the visitor center.

✪ Anchorage Inn. 26 Vendue Range, Charleston, SC 29401. ☎ **800/421-2952** or 843/723-8300. Fax 843/723-9543. www.anchoragencharleston.com. E-mail: anchorage@islc.net. 19 units. A/C TV TEL. $109–$149 double; $169–$210 suite. Rates include continental breakfast and afternoon tea. AE, MC, V. Parking $6.

Other than a heraldic shield out front, few ornaments mark this bulky structure, which was built in the 1840s as a cotton warehouse. The inn boasts the only decorative theme of its type in Charleston: a mock-Tudor interior with lots of dark paneling; references to Olde England; canopied beds with matching tapestries; pastoral or nautical engravings; leaded casement windows; and, in some places, half-timbering. Because bulky buildings are adjacent to the hotel on both sides, the architects designed all but a few rooms with views overlooking the lobby. (Light is indirectly filtered inside through the lobby's overhead skylights—a plus during Charleston's hot summers.) Each room's shape is different from that of its neighbors, and the expensive ones have bona-fide windows overlooking the street outside.

The inn serves continental breakfast and afternoon tea, complete with sherry, wine and cheese, and fruit and crackers. Amenities include a concierge and tour desk.

Ashley Inn. 201 Ashley Ave., Charleston, SC 29403. ☎ **800/581-6658** or 843/723-1848. Fax 843/723-8007. www.charleston-sc-inns.com. 7 units. A/C TV. $110–$185 double. Rates include full breakfast and afternoon tea. AE, DISC, MC, V. Free off-street parking.

Partly because of its pink clapboards and the steep staircases that visitors must climb to reach the public areas, this imposing bed-and-breakfast inn might remind you of an antique house in Bermuda. Built in 1832 on a plot of land that sold at the time for a mere $419, it has a more appealing decor than the Cannonboro Inn, which belongs to the same Michigan-based owners. Breakfast and afternoon tea are served on a wide veranda overlooking a brick-paved driveway whose centerpiece is a formal fountain/goldfish pond evocative of Old Charleston. The public rooms, with their high ceilings and deep colors, are appealing. If you have lots of luggage, know in advance that negotiating this inn's steep and frequent stairs might pose something of a problem. None of the rooms contains a phone.

✪ Barksdale House Inn. 27 George St., Charleston, SC 29401. ☎ **843/577-4800.** Fax 843/853-0482. www.barksdalehouse.com. 14 units. A/C TV TEL. Summer $135–$195 double; off-season $110–$150. Rates include continental breakfast. MC, V. Free parking. No children under 7.

This is a neat, tidy, and well-proportioned Italianate building near the City Market, constructed as an inn in 1778 but altered and enlarged by the Victorians. Behind the inn, guests enjoy a flagstone-covered terrace where a fountain splashes. Bedrooms often contain four-poster beds and working fireplaces, and about half a dozen have whirlpool tubs. Throughout, the furnishings, wallpaper, and fabrics evoke the late 19th century. Sherry and tea are served on the back porch in the evening.

Cannonboro Inn. 184 Ashley Ave., Charleston, SC 29403. ☎ **800/235-8039** or 843/723-8572. Fax 843/723-8007. www.charleston-sc-inns.com. E-mail: cannonboroinn@ aol.com. 8 units. A/C TV. $79–$190 double; $150–$220 suite. Rates include full breakfast and afternoon tea and sherry. AE, DISC, MC, V. Free parking. No children under 10.

This buff-and-beige 1856 house was once the private home of a rice planter. The decor isn't as carefully coordinated or as relentlessly upscale as that of many of its competitors; throughout, it has a sense of folksy informality. Although there's virtually no land around this building, a wide veranda on the side creates a "sit-and-talk-a-while" mood. Each accommodation contains a canopy bed; formal, old-fashioned furniture; and cramped, somewhat dated bathrooms.

Doubletree Guest Suites. 181 Church St., Charleston, SC 29401. ☎ **843/577-2644.** Fax 843/577-2697. www.doubletree.com. 181 units. A/C TV TEL. $99–$189 1-bedroom suite; $200–$285 2-bedroom suite. Rates include buffet breakfast. AE, DC, DISC, MC, V. Parking $14.

A somber, five-story 1991 building adjacent to the historic City Market, the Doubletree (formerly the Hawthorne), offers suites instead of rooms, each outfitted with some type of kitchen facility, from a wet bar, refrigerator, and microwave oven to a fully stocked kitchenette with enough utensils to prepare a simple dinner. The accommodations here tend to receive heavy use, thanks to their appeal to families, tour groups, and business travelers. Breakfast is the only meal served. Amenities include a bar/lounge, a fitness center, a swimming pool, and a coin-operated laundry. Parking is available in the underground parking garage.

1837 Bed & Breakfast. 126 Wentworth St., Charleston, SC 29401. ☎ **843/723-7166.** Fax 843/722-7179. www.1837bb.com. 9 units. A/C TV. $109–$139 double. Rates include full breakfast. AE, MC, V. Free off-street parking.

Built in 1837 by Nicholas Cobia, a cotton planter, this place was restored and decorated by two artists. It's called a "single house" because it's only a single room wide, which makes for some interesting room arrangements. Our favorite room is No. 2 in the Carriage House, which has authentic designs, exposed-brick walls, warm decor, a beamed ceiling, and three windows. All the rooms have refrigerators and separate entrances because of the layout, and all contain canopied poster rice beds. On one of the verandas, you can sit under whirling ceiling fans and enjoy your breakfast (sausage pie or eggs Benedict, and homemade breads) or afternoon tea. The parlor room has cypress wainscoting and a black-marble fireplace; the breakfast room is really part of the kitchen.

Elliott House Inn. 78 Queen St. (between King and Meeting sts.), Charleston, SC 29401. ☎ **800/729-1855** or 843/723-1855. Fax 843/722-1567. www.elliotthouseinn.com. 24 units. A/C TV TEL. $135–$160 double; off-season $94–$105 double. Rates include continental breakfast. AE, DISC, MC, V. Parking $15.

Historians have researched anecdotes about this place going back to the 1600s, but the core of the charming inn that you see today was built as a private home—probably for slaves—in 1861. You get a warm welcome from a very hip staff, and there's lots of colonial inspiration in the decor of the comfortable and carefully maintained rooms. But despite all the grace notes and the landscaping (the flowerbeds are touched up every 2 weeks), the place seems like a raffish, indoor/outdoor motel, which some guests find appealing. The rooms are arranged in a style that you might expect in Key West—off tiers of balconies surrounding a verdant open courtyard. Each room contains a four-poster bed (the one in No. 36 is especially nice) and provides a feeling of living in an upscale cottage. Avoid the units that have ground-level private outdoor terraces, however; they're cramped and claustrophobic, don't have attractive views, and tend to be plagued by mildew problems. Conversation often becomes free and easy beneath the city's largest wisteria arbor, near a bubbling whirlpool designed for as many as 12 occupants at a time.

INEXPENSIVE

To avoid the high costs of the elegant B&Bs and deluxe inns of historic Charleston, try one of the chain motels such as **Days Inn,** 2998 W. Montague Ave., Charleston 29418 (☎ **843/747-4101;** fax: 843/566-0378), near the International Airport. Doubles range from $50 to $72, with an extra person housed for $6. Children under 12 stay free, and cribs are also free. **Lands Inn,** 2545 Savannah Hwy., Charleston 29414 (☎ **843-763-885;** fax 843/556-9536), is another bargain, with doubles costing from $69 to $79, and an $10 extra charged for each additional person. Children under 16 stay free. A final bargain is **Red Roof Inn,** 7480 Northwoods Blvd., Charleston 29406 (☎ **843/572-9100;** fax 843/572-0061), where doubles cost $44 to $57, and $7 charged for each additional person. Those 18 and under are housed free.

Best Western King Charles Inn. 237 Meeting St. (between Wentworth and Society sts.), Charleston, SC 29401. ☎ **800/528-1234** or 843/723-7451. Fax 843/723-2041. 91 units. A/C TV TEL. $99–$199 double. Children 17 and under stay free in parents' room. AE, CB, DC, DISC, MC, V. Free parking.

One block from the historic district's market area, this three-story hotel has rooms that are better than you might expect from a motel and are likely to be discounted off-season. Some rooms have balconies, but the views are limited. Although short on style, the King Charles is a good value and convenient to most everything. Breakfast is served in a colonial-inspired restaurant, and the hotel has a small pool and a helpful staff.

King George IV Inn. 32 George St., Charleston, SC 29401. ☎ **888/723-1667** or 843/723-9339. Fax 843/723-7749. www.kinggeorgeiv.com. E-mail: info@kinggeorgeiv.com. 10 units, 2 with shared bathrooms. A/C TEL TV. $99–$175 double without bathroom. $125–$159 double with bathroom. Rates include continental breakfast. AE, MC, V. Free parking.

This four-story 1790 Federal-style home in the heart of the historic district serves as an example of the way Charleston used to live. Named the Peter Freneau House, it was formerly the residence of a reporter and co-owner of the *Charleston City Gazette*. All rooms have wide-planked hardwood floors, plaster moldings, fireplaces, and 12-foot ceilings, and are furnished with antiques. Beds are either Victorian or four-poster double or queen-size. All guests are allowed access to the three levels of porches on the house. The location is convenient to many downtown Charleston restaurants; tennis

> ## ⊕ Family-Friendly Hotels
>
> **Ansonborough Inn** *(see p. 189)*   This is a good value for families that want to stay in one of the historic inns, as opposed to a cheap motel on the outskirts. Many of the high-ceilinged rooms in this converted warehouse have sleeping lofts.
>
> **Best Western King Charles Inn** *(see p. 194)*   This is one of the best family values in Charleston. Children 17 and under stay free in their parents' room. The location is only a block from the historic district's market area, and there's a small pool.
>
> **Doubletree Guest Suites** *(see p. 193)*   This is a good choice for families that want extra space and a place to prepare meals. Some suites are bilevel, giving families more privacy. The location is adjacent to the City Market.
>
> **Knights Inn** *(see p. 195)*   Suites complete with kitchenettes make this inexpensive place an outstanding value for families. Two pools where you can cool off in the hot, humid weather add to the attraction.

is a 5-minute drive, the beach is 15 minutes away, and some 35 golf courses are nearby. The continental breakfast consists of cereals, breads, muffins, and pastries.

Rutledge Victorian Guest House. 114 Rutledge Ave., Charleston, SC 29401. ☎ **888/ 722-7553** or 843/722-7551. Fax 843/727-0065. www.bbonline.com/sc/rutledge. E-mail: normlyn@prodigy.net. 10 units, 8 with private bathroom. A/C TV TEL. $89–$129 double without private bathroom, $109–$159 double with private bathroom. Rates include continental breakfast. MC, V. Free parking.

This 19th-century structure is a sibling property of the King George IV Inn (described earlier in this section). The Italianate building is kept immaculate; rooms, as well as the inn, are furnished with Victorian antiques and have four-poster, rice, mahogany, or Italian rope beds in double, queen, and twin sizes. The location is just a short trek from many of Charleston's notable restaurants, and activities such as golf and tennis are just minutes away. Most rooms have working fireplaces and private bathrooms. In addition, the Rutledge Victorian Guest House has accommodations at another nearby property, Number Six Ambrose Alley. Specify your room requests and accommodations when you make your reservation; doing so as far in advance as possible is highly recommended.

NORTH CHARLESTON
INEXPENSIVE

Knights Inn. 2355 Aviation Ave., North Charleston, SC 29418. 11 miles NW of Historic District off Interstate 26. ☎ **800/845-1927** or 843/744-4900. Fax 843/745-0668. 242 units. A/C TV TEL. $48 double; $78 suite. Rates include continental breakfast. AE, DC, DISC, MC, V. Free parking.

There aren't many places in the Charleston area where families can rent suites, complete with kitchenettes, that start at $75 a night, but this is one of them. The double rooms, starting at $45 a night, also attract serious budgeteers, and there's more good news: 17 of the standard doubles also contain kitchenettes. Rooms, as you'd expect, are in the standard motel format that you've seen a thousand times, and suites are little more than a small living room and bedroom. A coin laundry and two swimming pools make this place especially popular with families traveling during the hot, humid months.

Ramada Inn. W. Montigue Ave., North Charleston, SC 29418. ☎ **800/272-6232** or 843/744-8281. Fax 843/744-6230. www.ramada.com. 155 units. A/C TV TEL. Mar–Oct, $105 double; off-season, $85 double. $10 each additional person. AE, DC, DISC, MC, V. Free parking. 8 miles NW of Charleston off Interstate 26.

This major competitor of the Holiday Inns is hardly in the same class as the historic inns discussed earlier in this chapter, but it's kind to the frugal vacationer. An outpost for the weary interstate driver, the inn is convenient to the airport and major traffic arteries, and the hotel provides free transportation to and from the airport. Charleston's downtown mass transit system doesn't serve this area, however, so be warned that you'll have to depend on your car. Your buck gets more than you might expect at this well-run chain member. Although you don't get charm, you do get good maintenance and proper service, and a refrigerator and microwave are available upon request. An on-site restaurant serves three meals a day, and other choices (including a Red Lobster) are within walking distance. The hotel also offers a Ramada Live Lounge that features nightly entertainment ranging from country music to karaoke and even comedy specialties.

4 Dining

Foodies from all over the Carolinas and as far away as Georgia flock to Charleston for some of the finest dining in the tri-state area. You get not only the refined cookery of the Low Country, but also an array of French and international specialties. Space does not permit us to preview all the outstanding restaurants of Charleston—much less the merely good ones.

VERY EXPENSIVE

✪ **Circa 1886 Restaurant.** In the Wentworth Mansion, 149 Wentworth St. ☎ **843/ 853-1886.** Reservations required. Main courses $18.50–$38.50. AE, DC, DISC, MC, V. LOW COUNTRY/FRENCH.

Situated in the carriage house of the Wentworth Mansion (see earlier in this chapter), this deluxe restaurant offers grand food and formal service. Begin by taking the invitation of the concierge for a view of Charleston from the cupola, where you can see all the bodies of water surrounding the city. Seating 50, two main rooms are beautifully set, the most idyllic place for a romantic dinner in Charleston. The chef prepares an updated version of Low Country cookery, giving it a light, contemporary touch but still retaining the flavors of the Old South. Menus are rotated seasonally to take advantage of the best and freshest produce. For a first course, try the likes of crab cake soufflé with mango coulis and sweet pepper sauce, or a Southern shrimp spring roll with peanut sauce. For the main course, opt for the lavender poached spiny lobster with artichokes or blackened mahi-mahi with a coconut rice pilaf.

Special attention is paid to the salad courses, as exemplified by a concoction of baby spinach, strawberries, wild mushrooms, and red onion, all flavored with a champagne-and-poppy-seed vinaigrette.

Desserts, ordered at the beginning of the meal, include a unique baked Carolina with orange and raspberry sorbets or pan-fried angel food cake with fresh berries and peach ice cream.

✪ **Louis's Restaurant and Bar.** 200 Meeting St., at the corner of Pinckney Street, in the Bank of American Building. ☎ **843/853-2550.** Reservations required. Main courses $16–$32. AE, DC, DISC, MC, V. Daily 5–10pm. MODERN/LOW COUNTRY.

Renowned Chef Louis Osteen opened this restaurant to rave reviews on March 1, 1998. After learning his craft in the kitchens of the French restaurants of Atlanta and in his own Low Country kitchen on Pawley's Island, Osteen brought his talents to the Charleston Place Hotel in 1989 and opened Louis's Charleston Grill, where he embraced the new culinary movement of American regionalism—with immediate success. His fame grew, and his desire to reach a larger audience gave birth to his current kitchen. The restaurant's decor is by Adam Tihany, known for his designs for New York's Le Cirque 2000. He turned the restaurant into a work of art, with a design that's both efficient and quietly graceful.

The menu changes frequently. But if you've ever dined at the Charleston Grill, you will recognize his signature dishes. Starters, such as McClellanville lump crabmeat with melted butter on avocado blini or Mediterranean mussels steamed in Belgian beer, will whet your appetite absolutely. Main courses range from grouper wrapped in pancetta with gingered carrots and parsnip broth to properly aged and meltingly tender black Angus strip steak with green-peppercorn-and-Calvados sauce. The desserts are best complemented by a glass of port. The wine list is vast—the largest in Charleston.

Louis's list of awards and recognitions reads almost like a resume. He was twice nominated by the James Beard Foundation as the American Express Chef Southeast.

✪ Robert's of Charleston. 182 East Bay St. ☎ **843/577-7565.** Reservations essential. 7-course fixed-price menu, including wine and coffee, $75 per person. 1-seating Thurs–Sat 7:30pm. AE, DC, MC, V. FRENCH.

One of the most unusual restaurants in Charleston, and one of the best and most exclusive, this formal choice is a winner in cuisine, service, and ambience. Chef/owner Robert Dickson has brought a whole new dimension to dining in Charleston. His set menu, which is served in a long, narrow room that evokes an intimate dinner party, is the town's finest.

Guests peruse the menu while listening to music from a pianist. The waiter will explain each course on a menu that is seasonally adjusted. He'll also give you a preview of each wine that you'll be served. Don't be surprised if the chef himself suddenly bursts through the door from the kitchen in the back, singing *Oliver's* "Food, Glorious Food." Each dish we've ever sampled here has been a delight in flavor and texture, ranging from sea scallops mousse in a Maine lobster sauce as an appetizer, to very tender, rosy duck breast in a yellow pepper cream sauce. The garnishes served with the dishes—often ignored in most restaurants—are especially tasty here, including roasted red pepper or hot fried eggplant. Tossed in a homemade vinaigrette, salads are zesty with wild mixed greens and such vegetables as mushrooms and artichokes. For a main course, dig into a chateaubriand with a demi-glaze flavored with mushrooms from the woods, or perhaps steamed salmon. Desserts often include the best and richest chocolate cake in Charleston. It comes with vanilla sauce, strawberries, and almond praline, but perhaps that's gilding the lily.

EXPENSIVE

✪ Anson. 12 Anson St. ☎ **843/577-0551.** Reservations recommended. Main courses $16.95–$26.95. AE, DC, DISC, MC, V. Sun–Thurs 5:30–11pm, Fri–Sat 5:30pm–midnight. LOW COUNTRY/MODERN AMERICAN.

We think it's simply the best. Charlestonians know that they can spot the local society types here; newcomers recognize it as a hip, stylish venue with all the grace notes of a top-notch restaurant in New York or Chicago, but with reminders of Low Country charm. The setting is a century-old, brick-sided ice warehouse. The present owners have added New Orleans–style iron balconies, Corinthian pilasters salvaged from demolished colonial houses, and enough Victorian rococo for anyone's taste. A well-trained staff in long white aprons describes dishes that are inspired by traditions of the coastal Southeast. But this isn't exactly down-home cookery, as you'll see after sampling the fried cornmeal oysters with potato cakes; the lobster, corn, and black-bean quesadillas; the cashew-crusted grouper with champagne sauce; and a perfectly prepared rack of lamb in a crispy Dijon-flavored crust with mint sauce. Our favorite is the crispy flounder, which rival chefs have tried to duplicate but haven't equaled.

✪ **Charleston Grill.** In the Charleston Place Hotel, 224 King St. ☎ **843/577-4522.** Reservations recommended. Main courses $17–$29. AE, DISC, DC, MC, V. Sun–Thurs 6–10pm, Fri–Sat 6–11pm. LOW COUNTRY/FRENCH.

Chef Bob Waggoner, from the Wild Boar in Nashville, has a devoted local following. This is the most ostentatiously formal and pleasing restaurant in Charleston, with superb service, grand food, an impeccably trained staff, and one of the city's best selections of wine. His French cuisine draws rave reviews, earning the restaurant the Mobil Four-Star rating—the only restaurant in South Carolina to have such a distinction. The decor makes absolutely no concessions to Southern folksiness, and the marble-floored, mahogany-sheathed dining room is one of the city's most luxurious. Menu items change with the seasons, and you will be pleasantly surprised by how well Low Country and French cuisine meld. Some absolutely delectable items include chilled summer carrot and sweet cantaloupe soup; Maine lobster tempura served over lemon grits with fried green tomatoes in a yellow tomato and tarragon butter; and, most delightful, McClellanville lump crabmeat cakes with roasted pistachio and a chive sauce. Not to be missed is red deer tenderloin over honey-roasted pears with almonds in a sweet cranberry and orange coulis. For something more down-home, try Okee-chobee catfish with poached crayfish tails over succotash in a Chardonnay-and-thyme-flavored butter sauce.

✪ **Peninsula Grill.** In the Planters Inn, 112 N. Market St. ☎ **843/723-0700.** Reservations required. Main courses $18–$28. AE, DC, DISC, MC, V. Mon–Thurs 5:30–10pm, Fri–Sat 5:30–11pm. CONTINENTAL/INTERNATIONAL.

There's an old Southern saying about "country come to city." This is one case where "city has come to country." The Peninsula Grill, in the historic Planters Inn, has caused quite a stir in the gastronomic world—not just in Charleston, but also around the country. Quaint and quiet, the setting has a 19th-century charm unlike any other restaurant in Charleston. The menu changes frequently. You may start with James Island clams with wild-mushroom bruschetta or roasted-acorn-squash soup. Main courses run the gamut from the succulent chargrilled double pork chops with hoop cheddar grits to the to-die-for, pistachio-crumb-crusted sea bass. The kitchen does a marvelous job of bringing new cuisine to an old city without compromising the delicacies that have made dining in Charleston famous.

MODERATE

The Boathouse on East Bay. 549 E. Bay St. Reservations recommended. Main courses $12.95–$22.95. AE, MC, V. Sun–Thurs 5–10pm, Fri–Sat 5–11pm. SEAFOOD.

Briny delights await you at this bustling restaurant at the corner of Chapel and East Bay. It is a curious blend of family friendliness and two-fisted machismo, appealing to a wide range of denizens from Charleston plus visitors who are just discovering the place. The setting is in a turn-of-the-century warehouse where boats were once repaired. Massive antique timbers on the heavily trussed ceiling remain. On the northern perimeter of the historic core, the restaurant has a raw bar open daily from 4 to midnight. Shellfish platters are the chef's specialty, including the $69 "J Boat," which

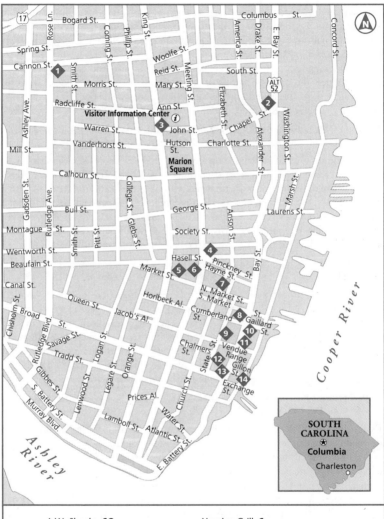

A.W. Shucks **12**

Anson **7**

The Boathouse of East Bay **2**

Carolina's **14**

Charleston Grill **13**

Circa 1886 Restaurant **16**

82 Queen **15**

High Cotton **8**

Hominy Grill **1**

Hyman's Seafood Company Restaurant **6**

Joe Pasta **3**

Louis's Restaurant and Bar **4**

Magnolias **9**

Peninsula Grill **5**

Robert's of Charleston **11**

S.N.O.B. (Slightly North of Broad) **10**

can be shared. On it are some of the city's best oysters, littleneck clams, smoked mussels, king crab legs, and fresh shrimp. Every night four different types of fish, ranging from mahimahi to black grouper, are grilled and served with a range of sauces, from mustard glaze to hoisin ginger.

Familiar Charleston specialties include shrimp and grits and crab cakes with green Tabasco sauce, the latter being one of our favorites. For those who don't want fish, a selection of pasta, beef, and chicken dishes are also served. For dessert, opt for the strawberry cobbler or Key lime pie.

Carolina's. 10 Exchange St. ☎ **843/724-3800.** Reservations recommended. Main courses $8–$32. AE, DISC, DC, MC, V. Mon–Thurs 5:30–11pm, Fri–Sun 5–11pm. AMERICAN.

This restaurant is usually included on any local resident's short list of noteworthy local bistros. An antique warehouse has been transformed into a stylish, minimalist enclave of hip, where old-time dishes are prepared with uptown flair: Carolina quail with goat cheese, salmon with coriander sauce, loin of lamb with jalapeño chutney, the best crab cakes in town, and an almost excessively elaborate version of local grouper cooked in almond-and-black-sesame-seed crust and topped with crabmeat and lemon-butter sauce. As you dine, admire the antique French movie posters on the walls.

82 Queen. 82 Queen St. ☎ **843/723-7591.** Reservations recommended for dinner. Main courses $17–$22. AE, MC, V. Daily 11:30am–3pm and 6–10:30pm. LOW COUNTRY.

In its way, this is probably the most unusual compendium of real estate in Charleston: three 18th- and 19th-century houses clustered around an ancient magnolia tree, with outdoor tables arranged in its shade. Menu items filled with flavor and flair include an award-winning version of she-crab soup laced with sherry, fried Carolina alligator with black-bean sauce and fresh tomato salsa and sour cream, Carolina bouillabaisse; down-home shrimp-and-chicken gumbo with andouille sausage and okra, and melt-in-the-mouth crab cakes with sweet-pepper-and-basil rémoulade sauce.

High Cotton. 199 E. Bay St. ☎ **843/724-3815.** Reservations recommended. Main courses $15–$34. AE, DC, MC, V. SOUTHERN/STEAK.

Established in 1999, this is a blockbuster of a restaurant, catering to an increasingly devoted clientele of locals who prefer its two-fisted drinks in an upscale macho decor, and a tasty cuisine that defines itself as a Southern-style steakhouse. It's also a good choice for nightlife because of its busy and cozy bar. If you decide to stick around for dinner, expect more than steaks. Dig into the buttermilk-fried oysters with arugula in a green goddess dressing, or order the terrine of foie gras. (How did that get on the menu?) Follow with such delights as medallions of venison with glazed carrots in a red wine and juniper sauce. Most diners go for one of the juicy steaks, which are tender and succulent, and served with sauces ranging from bourbon to béarnaise. Most dishes are moderate in price. You can also order items such as roasted squab with a potato and leek hash and a particularly lavish Charleston-style praline soufflé.

Magnolias. 185 E. Bay St. ☎ **843/577-7771.** Reservations recommended. Main courses $14.50–$24.95. AE, DC, MC, V. Sun–Thurs 11:30am–10pm, Fri–Sat 11:30am–11pm. SOUTHERN.

Magnolias manages to elevate the regional, vernacular cuisine of the Deep South to a hip, postmodern art form that's suitable for big-city trendies, but is more likely to draw visiting tourists instead. The city's former Customs House has been revised into a sprawling network of interconnected spaces with heart-pine floors, faux-marble columns, and massive beams. Everybody's favorite lunch here is an open-face veal meatloaf sandwich—which, frankly, we find to be rather dull. But the soups and salads tend to be excellent; try the salad made with field greens, lemon-lingonberry vinaigrette, and crumbled bleu cheese. Down South dinners include everything from Carolina carpetbaggers beef filet with Parmesan-fried oysters, green beans, Madeira and béarnaise sauce, to chicken and dumplings with shiitake mushrooms.

S.N.O.B. (Slightly North of Broad). 192 E. Bay St. ☎ **843/723-3424.** Reservations accepted only for parties of 6 or more. Main courses $10–$22. AE, DC, DISC, MC, V. Mon–Fri 11:30am–3pm and 5:30–11pm, Sat–Sun 5:30–11pm. SOUTHERN.

You'll find an exposed kitchen, a high ceiling crisscrossed with ventilation ducts, and vague references to the South of long ago—including a scattering of wrought iron—in this snazzily rehabbed warehouse. The place promotes itself as being Charleston's culinary maverick, priding itself on updated versions of the vittles that kept the South alive for 300 years, but frankly, the menu seems to be tame compared with the innovations being offered at many of its upscale, Southern-ethnic competitors. After you get past the hype, however, you might actually enjoy the place. Former diners include Timothy ("007") Dalton, Lee Majors, Sly Stallone, and superlawyer Alan Dershowitz. Main courses can be ordered in medium and large sizes—a fact appreciated by dieters. Flounder stuffed with deviled crab, grilled dolphin glazed with pesto on a bed of tomatoes, and grilled tenderloin of beef with green-peppercorn sauce are examples of this place's well-prepared—but not particularly Southern—menu. For dessert, make it the chocolate pecan torte. Together with sibling restaurants, Slightly Up the Creek and Elliott's on the Square, the restaurant has launched a private-label wine, dubbed MSK (for "Maverick Southern Kitchen").

INEXPENSIVE

A. W. Shucks. 70 State St. ☎ **843/723-1151.** Lunch $5–$11. Main courses $13–$20. AE, DC, DISC, MC, V. Sun–Thurs 11:30am–10pm, Fri–Sat 11am–11pm. SEAFOOD.

This is a hearty oyster bar, a sprawling, salty tribute to the pleasures of shellfish and the fishers who gather them. A short walk from the Public Market, in a solid, restored warehouse, the setting is one of rough timbers with a long bar where thousands of crustaceans have been cracked open and consumed, as well as a dining room. The menu highlights oysters and clams on the half-shell, tasty seafood chowders, deviled crab, shrimp Creole, and succulent oysters prepared in at least half a dozen ways. Chicken and beef dishes are also listed on the menu, but they're nothing special. A wide selection of international beers is sold. Absolutely no one cares how you dress; just dig in.

✪ **Hominy Grill.** 207 Rutledge Ave. ☎ **843/937-0930.** Brunch from $10; lunch main courses $4.25–$7.50; dinner main courses $8.50–$15.50. MC, V. Mon–Fri 7:30–11am and 11:30am–2:30pm; Mon–Sat 5:30–10pm, Sat–Sun 9am–2:30pm. LOW COUNTRY.

Owned and operated by Chef Robert Stehling, Hominy Grill features simply and beautifully prepared dishes inspired by the kitchens of the Low Country. Since its opening, it has gained a devoted local following, who come here to feast on such specialties as barbecue chicken sandwich, avocado and wehani rice salad and grilled vegetables, okra and shrimp beignets, and—a brunch favorite—smothered or poached eggs on homemade biscuits with mushroom gravy. At night, try oven-fried chicken with spicy peach gravy (yes, that's right) or grilled breast of duck with eggplant and sautéed greens. Stehling claims that he likes to introduce people to new grains in the place of pasta or potatoes; many of his dishes, including salads, are prepared with grains such as barley and cracked wheat. The menu is well balanced between old- and new-cookery styles. Dropping in for breakfast? Go for the buttermilk biscuits, the

---

ⓘ   Family-Friendly Restaurants

Magnolias *(see p. 200)*   Southern hospitality and charm keep this place buzzing day and night. Lunch is the best time for families and children. An array of soups, appetizers, salads, sandwiches, and pastas is available. But in-the-know local kids go easy on these items, saving room for homemade fare such as the warm cream-cheese brownie with white-chocolate ice cream and chocolate sauce.

Hominy Grill *(see p. 201)*   Locally loved, this grill has been a friendly, homelike family favorite since 1996. Fair prices, good food, and an inviting atmosphere lure visitors to sample an array of Southern specialties at breakfast, lunch, or dinner.

---

meaty bacon, and the home-style fried apples. There's even liver pudding on the menu. A lunch of catfish stew with cornbread is a temptation on a cold, rainy day, and the banana bread is worth writing home about.

Hyman's Seafood Company Restaurant. 215 Meeting St. ☎ **843/723-6000.** Lunch $5–$10; seafood dinners and platters $12–$20. AE, DISC, MC, V. Mon–Fri 11am–11pm, Sat–Sun 7am–11pm. SEAFOOD.

Hyman's was established a century ago and honors old-fashioned traditions. The building sprawls over most of a city block in the heart of Charleston's business district. Inside are at least six dining rooms and a take-away deli loaded with salmon, lox, and smoked herring, all displayed in the style of the great kosher delis of New York City. One sit-down section is devoted to deli-style sandwiches, chicken soup, and salads; another, to a delectably messy choice of fish, shellfish, lobsters, and oysters. We can ignore the endorsement of old-time Sen. Strom Thurmond, but we take more seriously the praise of such big-time foodies as Barbra, Oprah, and Baryshnikov.

Joe Pasta. 428 King St. ☎ **843/965-5252.** Reservations not needed. Sandwiches 95¢ each; all pastas $4.50. DISC, MC, V. Tues–Thurs 11:30am–11pm, Fri–Sat 11:30am–midnight. ITALIAN/PASTA.

Favored by college students and budget-conscious locals, this is a clean, well-organized pasta joint evocative of an Italian trattoria with a full bar and a standard, limited, but still savory menu. Pasta can be ordered with at least four different degrees of doneness, ranging from al dente to mushy. Begin with soup or the house salad or perhaps one of the appetizers such as an antipasti platter or bruschetta—here, garlic bread topped with a tomato and fresh basil salad. Sandwiches range from meatball Parmesan to chicken. But pastas dominate the menu, and the sauces go from pesto to marinara. We're fond of the baked ziti with three cheeses. Finish off with an Italian ice or a piece of cheesecake.

5 Attractions

We always head for the **Battery** (officially, the White Point Gardens) to get into the feel of this city. It's right on the end of the peninsula, facing the Cooper River and the harbor. It has a landscaped park, shaded by palmettos and live oaks, with walkways lined with old monuments and other war relics. The view toward the harbor goes out to Fort Sumter. We like to walk along the seawall on East Battery and Murray Boulevard and slowly absorb the Charleston ambience.

Note that you can visit several of the attractions listed in this section by buying a Passport Ticket for $29. The ticket provides admission to Middleton Place, Drayton

Hall, the Nathaniel Russell House, the Gibbes Museum, and the Edmondston-Alston House.

THE TOP ATTRACTIONS
A NATIONAL MONUMENT

✪ Fort Sumter National Monument. In Charleston Harbor. ☎ **843/883-3123** or 843/ 722-1691. Fort, free; boat trip, $11 adults, $6 children 6–11, children 5 and under free.

It was here that the first shot of the Civil War was fired on April 12, 1861. Confederate forces launched a 34-hour bombardment of the fort. Union forces eventually surrendered, and the Rebels occupied federal ground that became a symbol of Southern resistance. This action, however, led to a declaration of war in Washington. Amazingly, Confederate troops held onto Sumter for nearly 4 years, although it was almost continually bombarded by the Yankees. When evacuation finally came, the fort was nothing but a heap of rubble.

Park rangers today are on hand to answer your questions, and you can explore gun emplacements and visit a small museum filled with artifacts related to the siege. A complete tour of the fort, conducted daily from 9am to 5pm, takes about 2 hours.

Though you can travel to the fort via your own boat, most people take the tour of the fort and harbor offered by **Fort Sumter Tours,** 205 King St., Suite 204 (☎ **843/ 722-1691**). You can board at either of two locations: Charleston's City Marina on Lockwood Boulevard or Mount Pleasant's Patriots Point, the site of the world's largest naval and maritime museum. Sailing times change every month or so, but from March to Labor Day, there generally are three sailings per day from each location, beginning at 9:30 or 10:45am. Winter sailings are more curtailed. Call for details. Each departure point offers ample parking, and the boats that carry you to Fort Sumter are sightseeing yachts built for the purpose; they're clean, safe, and equipped with modern conveniences.

HISTORIC HOMES

✪ Edmondston-Alston House. 21 East Battery. ☎ **843/722-7171.** Admission $7; included in Passport Ticket (see "Attractions," above). Guided tours Tues–Sat 10am–4:30pm, Sun–Mon 1:30–4:30pm.

On High Battery, an elegant section of Charleston, this house (built in 1825 by Charles Edmondston, a Charleston merchant and wharf owner) was one of the earliest constructed in the city in the late Federalist style. Edmondston sold it to Charles Alston, a Low Country rice planter, who modified it in Greek Revival style. The house has remained in the Alston family, which opens the first two floors to visitors. Inside are heirloom furnishings, silver, and paintings. It was here in 1861 that General Beauregard joined the Alston family to watch the bombardment of Fort Sumter. Gen. Robert E. Lee once found refuge here when his hotel uptown caught on fire.

✪ Nathaniel Russell House. 51 Meeting St. ☎ **843/724-8481;** www.historiccharleston. org. Admission $7; included in Passport Ticket (see "Attractions," above). Guided tours Mon–Sat 10am–4:30pm, Sun and holidays 2–4:30pm.

One of America's finest examples of Federal architecture, this 1808 house was completed by Nathaniel Russell, one of Charleston's richest merchants. It is celebrated architecturally for its "free-flying" staircase, spiraling unsupported for three floors. The staircase's elliptical shape is repeated throughout the house. The interiors are ornate with period furnishings, especially the elegant music room with its golden harp and neoclassical-style sofa.

○ **Heyward-Washington House.** 87 Church St. (between Tradd and Elliott sts.).
☎ **843/722-0354.** Admission $8 adults, $4 children 3–12; combination ticket to the
Charleston Museum and Joseph Manigault House, $18. Mon–Sat 10am–5pm, Sun 1–5pm.
Tours leave every half hour until 4:30pm.

In a district of Charleston called Cabbage Row, this 1772 house was built by Daniel
Heyward, called "the rice king," and was the setting for Dubose Heyward's *Porgy.* It
was also the home of Thomas Heyward, Jr., a signer of the Declaration of Independence. President George Washington bedded down here in 1791. Many of the fine
period pieces in the house are the work of Thomas Elfe, one of America's most famous
cabinetmakers. The restored 18th-century kitchen is the only historic kitchen in the
city that is open to the public. It stands behind the main house, along with the
servants' quarters and the garden.

Calhoun Mansion. 16 Meeting St. (between Battery and Lamboll sts.). ☎ **843/722-8205.**
Admission $15 adults, $7 children 6–10. Wed–Sun 10am–4pm. Closed holidays.

This 1876 Victorian showplace is complete with period furnishings (including a few
original pieces); porcelain-and-etched-glass gas chandeliers; ornate plastering; and
cherry, oak, and walnut woodwork. The ballroom's 45-foot-high ceiling has a skylight.
A freestanding spiral staircase is one of the remarkable features of this house. Among
the tales of its many vicissitudes is the rescue of the once-deteriorating house by the
U.S. Navy, which painted it battleship-gray inside and out.

Joseph Manigault House. 350 Meeting St. (at John St.). ☎ **843/722-2996.** Admission
$8 adults, $4 children 3–12; combination ticket to the Heyward-Washington House and
Charleston Museum, $18. Mon–Sat 10am–5pm, Sun 1–5pm.

This 1803 Adams-style residence, a National Historic Landmark, was a wealthy rice
planter's home. The house features a curving central staircase and an outstanding
collection of Charlestonian, American, English, and French period furnishings. It's
located diagonally across from the visitor center.

NEARBY PLANTATIONS

○ **Middleton Place.** Ashley River Rd. ☎ **843/556-6020.** Admission $18 adults, $15 children 6–12, free for children 5 and under. Tour of House, additional $15, children 6–12 $7.
Gardens and stable yards daily 9am–5pm; house Mon 1:30–4:30pm, Tues–Sat 10:30am–
4:30pm. Take U.S. 17 west to S.C. 61 (Ashley River Rd.) 14 miles northwest of Charleston.

This was the home of Henry Middleton, president of the First Continental Congress,
whose son, Arthur, was a signer of the Declaration of Independence. Today, this
National Historic Landmark includes America's oldest landscaped gardens, the Middleton Place House, and the Plantation Stableyards.

The gardens, begun in 1741, reflect the elegant symmetry of European gardens of
that period. Ornamental lakes, terraces, and plantings of camellias, azaleas, magnolias,
and crape myrtle accent the grand design.

The Middleton Place House itself was built in 1755, but in 1865, all but the south
flank was ransacked and burned by Union troops. The house was restored in the 1870s
as a family residence and today houses collections of fine silver, furniture, rare first editions by Catesby and Audubon, and portraits by Benjamin West and Thomas Sully.
In the stable yards, craftspeople demonstrate life on a plantation of yesteryear. There
are also horses, mules, hogs, cows, sheep, and goats.

A plantation lunch is served at the Middleton Place Restaurant, which is a replica
of an original rice mill. *American Way* magazine cited this restaurant as being one of
the top 10 representing American cuisine at its best. Specialties include she-crab soup,
Hoppin' John and ham biscuits, okra gumbo, Sea Island shrimp, and corn pudding.

Charleston Sights

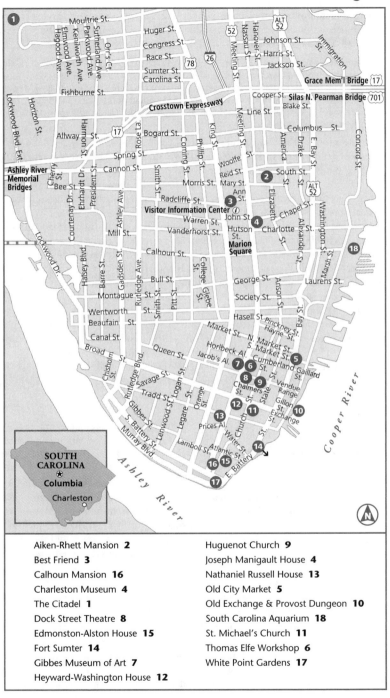

Aiken-Rhett Mansion **2**
Best Friend **3**
Calhoun Mansion **16**
Charleston Museum **4**
The Citadel **1**
Dock Street Theatre **8**
Edmonston-Alston House **15**
Fort Sumter **14**
Gibbes Museum of Art **7**
Heyward-Washington House **12**

Huguenot Church **9**
Joseph Manigault House **4**
Nathaniel Russell House **13**
Old City Market **5**
Old Exchange & Provost Dungeon **10**
South Carolina Aquarium **18**
St. Michael's Church **11**
Thomas Elfe Workshop **6**
White Point Gardens **17**

Service is daily from 11am to 3pm. Dinner is served daily 5 to 9pm, and is likely to include panned quail with ham, sea scallops, or broiled oysters. For dinner reservations, call ☎ **843/556-6020.**

○ **Magnolia Plantation.** S.C. 61. ☎ **800/367-3517** or 843/571-1266. Admission to garden and grounds, $11 adults, $10 seniors, $9 children 13–19, $5 children 6–12. Tour of plantation house is an additional $6 for ages 6 and up; children under 6 not allowed to tour the house. Admission to Audubon Swamp Garden, $5 adults and seniors, $4 children 13–19, $3 children 6–12. Magnolia Plantation and Audubon Swamp Gardens, summer daily 8am– 5:30pm, winter daily 9am–5pm.

Ten generations of the Drayton family have lived here continuously since the 1670s. They haven't had much luck keeping a roof over their heads; the first mansion burned just after the Revolution, and the second was set afire by General Sherman. But you can't call the replacement modern. A simple, pre-Revolutionary house was barged down from Summerville and set on the basement foundations of its unfortunate predecessors.

The house has been filled with museum-quality Early American furniture, appraised to exceed $500,000 in value. An art gallery has been added to the house as well.

The flowery gardens of camellias and azaleas—among the most beautiful in America—reach their peak bloom in March and April but are colorful year-round. You can tour the house, the gardens (including an herb garden, horticultural maze, topiary garden, and biblical garden), a petting zoo, and a waterfowl refuge, or walk or bike through wildlife trails.

Other sights include an antebellum cabin that was restored and furnished, a plantation rice barge on display beside the Ashley River, and a Nature Train that carries guests on a 45-minute ride around the plantation's perimeter.

Low Country wildlife is visible in marsh, woodland, and swamp settings. The **Audubon Swamp Garden,** also on the grounds, is an independently operated 60-acre cypress swamp that offers a close look at other wildlife, such as egrets, alligators, wood ducks, otters, turtles, and herons.

Drayton Hall. Old Ashley River Rd. (S.C. 61). ☎ **843/766-0188.** Admission $8 adults, $6 children 12–18, $4 children 6–11; included in Passport Ticket (see "Attractions," above). Mar–Oct, daily 10am–4pm, with tours on the hour; Nov–Feb, daily 9:30am–3pm. Closed Thanksgiving Day and Dec 25. Take U.S. 17 S. to S.C. 61; it's 9 miles northwest of Charleston.

This is one of the oldest surviving plantations, built in 1738 and owned by the Drayton family until 1974. Framed by majestic live oaks, the Georgian-Palladian house is a property of the National Trust for Historic Preservation. Its hand-carved woodwork and plasterwork represent New World craftsmanship at its finest. Because such modern elements as electricity, plumbing, and central heating have never put in an appearance, the house is much as it was in its early years; in fact, it is displayed unfurnished.

Boone Hall Plantation. Long Point Rd. (U.S. 17/701), Mt. Pleasant. ☎ **843/884-4371.** Admission $12.50 adults, $10 seniors 55 and over, $8 children 6–12. Apr–Labor Day, Mon–Sat 8:30am–6:30pm, Sun 1–5pm; day after Labor Day–Mar, Mon–Sat 9am–5pm, Sun 1–4pm. Take U.S. 17/701 9 miles north of Charleston.

This unique plantation is approached by a famous ○ **Avenue of Oaks,** huge old moss-draped trees planted in 1743 by Capt. Thomas Boone. The first floor of the plantation house is elegantly furnished and open to the public. Outbuildings include the circular smokehouse and slave cabins constructed of bricks made on the plantation. A large grove of pecan trees lies behind the house. Note that Boone Hall is not an original structure, but a replica; diehard history purists may be disappointed in the plantation house, but the grounds are definitely worth seeing.

SPECTACULAR GARDENS

See also the listing for Magnolia Plantation in "Nearby Plantations," earlier in this chapter.

✪ **Cypress Gardens.** U.S. 52, Moncks Corner. ☎ **843/553-0515.** $7 adults, $6 seniors, $2 children 6–16. Daily 9am–5pm. Closed Jan. Take U.S. 52 some 24 miles north of Charleston.

This 163-acre swamp garden was used as a freshwater reserve for Dean Hall, a huge Cooper River rice plantation, and was given to the city in 1963. Today, the giant cypress trees draped with Spanish moss provide an unforgettable setting for flat-bottom boats that glide among their knobby roots. Footpaths in the garden wind through a profusion of azaleas, camellias, daffodils, and other colorful blooms. Visitors share the swamp with alligators, pileated woodpeckers, wood ducks, otters, barred owls, and other abundant species. The gardens are worth a visit at any time of year, but they're at their most colorful in March and April. Closed: Thanksgiving; December 22 to February 21.

MUSEUMS

✪ **Charleston Museum.** 360 Meeting St. ☎ **843/722-2996;** www.charlestonmuseum. com. Admission $8 adults, $4 children 3–12; combination ticket to the Joseph Manigault House and Heyward-Washington House, $18. Mon–Sat 9am–5pm, Sun 1–5pm.

The Charleston Museum, founded in 1773, is the first and oldest museum in America. The collections preserve and interpret the social and natural history of Charleston and the South Carolina coastal region. The full-scale replica of the famed Confederate submarine *Hunley* standing outside the museum is one of the most-photographed subjects in the city. The museum also exhibits the largest silver collection in Charleston; early crafts; historic relics; and the state's only "Discover Me" room, which has hands-on exhibits for children.

Gibbes Museum of Art. 135 Meeting St. ☎ **843/722-2706.** www.gibbes.com. Admission $7 adults, $6 seniors and students and military, $3 children 6–18, children under 6 are free; included in Passport Ticket (see "Attractions," above). Tues–Sat 10am–5pm, Sun 1–5pm. Closed Mondays and holidays.

Established in 1905 by the Carolina Art Association, the Gibbes Museum contains an intriguing collection of prints and drawings from the 18th century to the present. On display are landscapes, genre scenes, panoramic views of Charleston harbor, and portraits of South Carolinians (see *Thomas Middleton* by Benjamin West, *Charles Izard Manigault* by Thomas Sully, or *John C. Calhoun* by Rembrandt Peale). The museum's collection of some 400 miniature portraits ranks as one of the most comprehensive in the country.

The Wallace Exhibit has 10 rooms, 8 replicated from historic American buildings and 2 from classic French styles. Styles range from the plain dining room of a sea captain's house on Martha's Vineyard to the elegant drawing room of Charleston's historic Nathaniel Russell House (see "Historic Homes," earlier in this chapter).

MORE ATTRACTIONS

✪ **Charles Towne Landing.** 1500 Old Towne Rd. (S.C. 171, between U.S. 17 and I-126). ☎ **843/852-4200.** Admission $5 adults, $2.50 seniors and children 6–14, free for those with disabilities. Daily 8:30am–6pm.

This 663-acre park is located on the site of the first 1670 settlement. Underground exhibits show the colony's history, and the park features a re-creation of a small village, a full-scale replica of a 17th-century trading ship, and a tram tour for $1 (or you can rent a bike). Because trade was such an important part of colonial life, a full-scale reproduction of the 17th-century trading vessel *Adventure* is an excellent addition to the site. After touring the ship, you can step into the Settler's Life Area and view a 17th-century crop garden where rice, indigo, and cotton were grown. There's no flashy theme-park atmosphere here: What you see as you walk under huge old oaks, past freshwater lagoons, and through the Animal Forest (with the same species that lived here in 1670) is what those early settlers saw.

Charleston Tea Plantation. 6617 Maybank Hwy. (15 miles S of Charleston on Wadmalaw Island). ☎ **843/559-0383.** May–Oct, first Sat of each month 10am–1pm (tours on the half-hour). Free admission.

This plantation is the only one in America that actually grows tea, sold as American Classic tea. The plantation has been growing tea since 1799, when a French botanist brought the first tea plants to Charleston. Today, the plantation uses a state-of-the-art harvesting machine (designed on-site) that you can see on the free tours offered during the harvest season. Private tours, costing $5 per person, are available for groups of 20 or more; you must make an appointment. Note that inclement weather cancels any tour. Be sure to buy some tea while you're here; you won't find anything fresher in the stores.

Citadel. Moultrie St. and Elmwood Ave. ☎ **843/953-3294.** Free admission. Daily 24 hours for drive-through visits; museum, Sun–Fri 2–5pm, Sat noon–5pm. Closed religious and school holidays.

The all-male (at that time) Citadel was established in 1842 as an arsenal and a refuge for whites in the event of a slave uprising. In 1922, it moved to its present location.

The school received worldwide notoriety in 1995 during the failed attempt of Shannon Faulkner to join the ranks of the cadets. After winning a legal battle to be admitted, she dropped out, citing continual harassment as the cause. Faulkner's ordeal drew fiercely divided opinions. As best-selling author Pat Conroy, a Faulkner supporter, said, "They made sure that everyone in America saw that that college hates women." Conroy's novel *The Lords of Discipline* is based on his 4 years at the school. Since then, four more women have been admitted, two of whom have remained.

The campus of this military college features buildings of Moorish design, with crenellated battlements and sentry towers. It is especially interesting to visit on Friday, when the college is in session and the public is invited to a precision-drill parade on the quadrangle at 3:45pm. For a history of the Citadel, stop at the **Citadel Memorial Archives Museum** (☎ **843/953-6846**).

Old Exchange & Provost Dungeon. 122 E. Bay St. ☎ **843/727-2165.** Admission $6 adults, $5.50 seniors, $3.50 children 7–12. Daily 9am–5pm. Closed Thanksgiving Day, Dec 23–25.

This is a stop that many tourists overlook, but it's one of the three most important colonial buildings in the United States because of its role as a prison during the American Revolution. In 1873, the building became City Hall. You'll find a large collection of antique chairs, supplied by the local Daughters of the American Revolution, each of whom brought a chair here from home in 1921.

Fort Moultrie. 1214 Middle St., on Sullivan's Island. ☎ **843/883-3123.** Admission $4 adults, $2 child under 15 and seniors over 62. Federal Recreation Passports honored. Daily 9am–5pm. Closed Christmas Day. Take S.C. 103 from Mt. Pleasant to Sullivan's Island.

Only a palmetto-log fortification at the time of the American Revolution, the half-completed fort was attacked by a British fleet in 1776. Col. William Moultrie's troops repelled the invasion in one of the first decisive American victories of the Revolution.

> ⭐ **Frommer's Favorite Charleston Experiences**
>
> **Playing Scarlett & Rhett at Boone Hall.** Over in Mount Pleasant, you can pre-tend that you're one of the romantic figures in Margaret Mitchell's *Gone With the Wind* by paying a visit to this 738-acre estate, a cotton plantation settled by Maj. John Boone in 1681. It was used for background shots in the films *Gone With the Wind* and *North and South.*
>
> **Going Back to Colonial Days.** At Charles Towne Landing, you get insight into how colonists lived 300 years ago, when they established the first English settlement in South Carolina. A visit here features hands-on activities. Even the animals that the settlers encountered, from bears to bison, roam about. You can also enjoy 80 acres of gardens by walking or bicycling along the marsh and lagoons.
>
> **A Cuppa at the Charleston Tea Plantation.** Only 15 miles south of Charleston on Wadmalaw Island, this plantation boasts the only tea that's grown in America. Called American Classic, the tea has to be the freshest on the shelves (imported teas can take 9 to 12 months for delivery), and it's the tea served at the White House. But in case George W. and Laura don't invite you for a cup, you can sample it here. Your visit will be an experience that's possible nowhere else in America.

The fort was subsequently enlarged into a five-sided structure with earth-and-timber walls 17 feet high. The British didn't do it in, but an 1804 hurricane ripped it apart. By the War of 1812, it was back and ready for action.

Osceola, the fabled leader of the Seminoles in Florida, was incarcerated at the fort and eventually died here. During the 1830s, Edgar Allen Poe served as a soldier at the fort. He set his famous short story "The Gold Bug" on Sullivan's Island. The fort also played roles in the Civil War, the Mexican War, the Spanish-American War, and even in the two World Wars, but by 1947, it had retired from action.

Southern Carolina Aquarium. 100 Aquarium Wharf. ☎ **843/720-1990.** Admission $14 adults, $12 students 13–17, $7 youth 4–12, children under 3 free. July–Aug daily 9am–7pm, Sept–Oct and May–June daily 10am–5pm; off season daily 10am–5pm.

Visitors can explore Southern aquatic life in an attraction filled with thousands of enchanting creatures and plants in amazing habitats, from five major regions of the Appalachian Watershed. Jutting out into the Charleston Harbor for 2,000 feet, the focal point at this brand-new attraction, which opened in 2000, is a 93,000-square-foot aquarium featuring a two-story Great Ocean Tank Exhibition. Contained within are some 800 animals, including deadly sharks but also sea turtles and stingrays. Every afternoon at 4pm the aquarium offers a dolphin program, where bottle-nosed dolphins can be viewed from an open-air terrace. One of the most offbeat exhibits replicates a blackwater swamp, with atmospheric fog, a spongy floor, and twinkling lights.

ESPECIALLY FOR KIDS

For more than 300 years, Charleston has been the home of pirates, patriots, and presidents. Your child can see firsthand the **Great Hall at the Old Exchange,** where President Washington danced; the **Provost Dungeons,** where South Carolina patriots spent their last days; and touch the last remaining structural evidence of the **Charleston Seawall.** Children will take special delight in **Charles Towne Landing** and **Middleton Place.** At **Fort Sumter,** they can see where the Civil War began. Children will also enjoy **Magnolia Plantation,** with its Audubon Swamp Garden.

Kids and Navy vets will also love the aircraft carrier **USS *Yorktown,*** at Patriots Point, 2 miles east of the Cooper River Bridge. Its World War II, Korean, and Vietnam exploits are documented in exhibits, and general naval history is illustrated through models of ships, planes, and weapons. You can wander through the bridge wheelhouse, flight and hangar decks, chapel, and sick bay, and view the film *The Fighting Lady,* which depicts life aboard the carrier. Also at Patriots Point are the nuclear ship *Savannah,* the world's first nuclear-powered merchant ship; the World War II destroyer *Laffey;* the World War II submarine *Clamagore;* and the cutter *Ingham.* Patriots Point is open daily from 9am to 6pm April to October, until 5pm November to March. Admission is $11 for adults, $10 for seniors over 62 and military personnel in uniform, $5 for kids 6 to 11. Adjacent is the fine 18-hole public Patriots Point Golf Course. For further information, call ☎ 843/884-2727.

Another kid-pleaser, **Best Friend,** adjacent to the visitor center on Ann Street (☎ 843/973-7269), combines a museum and an antique train. The train features a full-size replica of the 1830 locomotive that was the first steam engine in the United States used for regularly scheduled passenger service. The train was constructed from the original plans in 1928 and donated to Charleston in 1993. Hours are Monday to Saturday from 9am to 5pm and on Sunday from 1 to 5pm; admission is free.

6 Organized Tours

BY HORSE & CARRIAGE   The **Charleston Carriage Co.,** 96 N. Market St. (☎ 843/577-0042), offers narrated horse-drawn-carriage tours through the historic district daily from 9am to dusk. There's free shuttle service from the visitor center and downtown hotels. The cost is $17 for adults, $15 for seniors and military personnel, and $8 for children 6 to 12.

BY MULE TEAM   **Palmetto Carriage Tours,** 40 N. Market St., at Guignard Street (☎ 843/723-8145), uses mule teams instead of the usual horse and carriage for its guided tours of Old Charleston. Tours originate at the Big Red Bar behind the Rainbow Market. The cost is $17 for adults, $15 for senior citizens, and $6 for children 6 to 11. Daily 9am to 5pm.

BY BOAT   **Fort Sumter Tours,** 205 Kings St., Suite 204 (☎ 843/722-1691), offers a **Harbor and Fort Sumter Tour** by boat, departing daily from the City Marina and from the Patriots Point Maritime Museum. This is the only tour to stop at Fort Sumter, target of the opening shots of the Civil War. Adults $11, children 6–12 $6. The operator also has an interesting **Charleston Harbor Tour,** with daily departures from Patriots Point. The 2-hour cruise passes the Battery, Charleston Port, Castle Pinckney, Drum Island, Fort Sumter, and the aircraft carrier USS *Yorktown,* and sails under the Cooper River Bridge and on to other sights. $10.50 for adults, children $5.50.

WALKING TOURS   One of the best offbeat walking tours of Charleston is the **Charleston Tea Party Walking Tour** (☎ 843/577-5896). It lasts 2 hours and costs $13 for adults or $6 for children up to age 12. Departing year-round Monday to Saturday at 9:30am (returning at 2pm), tours originate at the Kings Courtyard Inn, 198 Kings St. The tour goes into a lot of nooks and crannies of Charleston, including secret courtyards and gardens. Finally, you get that promised tea.

The embattled city of Charleston during one of the worst phases in its history comes alive again on the **Civil War Walking Tour,** conducted daily at 9am by a guide well versed in the lore of "The War of Northern Aggression." You can stroll down cobblestone streets and listen to firsthand accounts and anecdotes of Charleston during its years of siege by Union troops. Tours depart March to December, Wednesday to Sunday at 9am from the Mills House Hotel Courtyard at 115 Meeting St. Adults pay $15, and children 12 and under go free. Call Jack Thomson at ☎ **843/722-7033** for more information; reservations are appreciated.

Tours of Charleston's 18th-century **architecture** in the original walled city begin at 10am, and tours of 19th-century architecture along Meeting Street and the Battery begin at 2pm. Departures are from in front of the Meeting Street Inn, 173 Meeting St. Tours last 2 hours and are given daily. The cost is $15 (free for children 12 and under). For reservations, call ☎ **843/893-2327.**

7 Beaches & Outdoor Pursuits

BEACHES   Three great beaches are within a 25-minute drive of the center of Charleston.

In the West Islands, **Folly Beach,** which had degenerated into a tawdry Coney Island–type amusement park, is making a comeback following a multimillion-dollar cleanup, but it remains the least-pristine beach in the area. The best bathroom amenities are located here, however. At the western end of the island is the **Folly Beach County Park,** with bathrooms, parking, and shelter from the rain. To get here, take U.S. 17 East to S.C. 171 South to Folly Beach.

In the East Cooper area, both the **Isle of Palms** and **Sullivan's Island** offer miles of public beaches, mostly bordered by beachfront homes. Windsurfing and jet skiing are popular here. Take U.S. 17 East to S.C. 703 (Ben Sawyer Boulevard). South Carolina 703 continues through Sullivan's Island to the Isle of Palms.

Kiawah Island has the area's most pristine beach—far preferable to Folly Beach, to our tastes—and draws a more up-market crowd. The best beachfront is at **Beach-walker County Park,** on the southern end of the island. Get there before noon on weekends; the limited parking is usually gone by then. Canoe rentals are available for use on the Kiawah River, and the park offers not only a boardwalk but also bathrooms, showers, and a changing area. Take U.S. 17 E to S.C. 171 South (Folly Beach Road), turn right onto S.C. 700 SW (Maybank Highway), to Bohicket Road, which turns into Betsy Kerrigan Parkway. Where Betsy Kerrigan Parkway dead-ends, turn left on Kiawah Parkway, which takes you to the island.

For details on the major resorts on Kiawah Island and the Isle of Palms, see "Kiawah Island and the Isle of Palms," later in this chapter.

BIKING   Charleston is basically flat and relatively free of traffic, except on its main arteries at rush hour. Therefore, biking is a popular local pastime and relatively safe. Many of the city parks have biking trails. Your best bet for rentals is **The Bicycle Shoppe,** 280 Meeting St. (☎ **843/722-8168**), which rents bikes for $4 per hour or $15 for a full day. A credit-card imprint is required as a deposit.

BOATING   A true Charlestonian is as much at home on the sea as on land. Sailing local waters is a popular family pastime. One of the best places for rentals is **Wild Dunes Yacht Harbor,** Isle of Palms (☎ **843/886-5100**), where 16-foot boats, big enough for four people, rent for $165 for 4 hours, plus fuel. A larger pontoon boat, big enough for 10, goes for $260 for 4 hours, plus fuel.

DIVING   Several outfitters provide rentals and ocean charters, as well as instruction for neophytes. **Aqua Ventures,** 426 W. Coleman Blvd., Mt. Pleasant (☎ **843/884-1500**), offers diving trips off the local shoreline at a cost of $60 to $80 per person. You can rent both diving and snorkeling equipment. Diving equipment costs $32 or $14 for a regulator. It's open Monday to Saturday from 10am to 6pm.

The Wet Shop, 5121 Rivers Ave. (☎ **843/744-5641**), rents scuba equipment for $45 a day, including two tanks, a regulator, wetsuit, diving knife, and weight belt. It's open July and August, Monday to Saturday from 10am to 6pm.

FISHING   Freshwater fishing charters are available year-round along the Low Country's numerous creeks and inlets. The waterways are filled with flounder, trout, spot-tail, and channel bass. Some of the best striped-bass fishing available in America can be found at nearby Lake Moultrie.

Offshore-fishing charters for reef fishing (where you'll find fish such as cobia, black sea bass, and king mackerel) and for the Gulf Stream (where you fish for sailfish, marlin, wahoo, dolphin, and tuna) are also available. Both types of charters can be arranged at the previously recommended **Wild Dunes Yacht Harbor,** Isle of Palms (☎ **843/886-5100**). A fishing craft holding up to six people rents for $725 for 6 hours, including everything but food and drink. Reservations must be made 24 hours in advance.

Folly Beach Fishing Pier at Folly Beach is a wood pier, 25 feet wide, that extends 1,045 feet into the Atlantic Ocean. Facilities include rest rooms, a tackle shop, and a restaurant. It's handicapped-accessible.

Those who'd like a true Low Country experience might even want to try crabbing or shrimping.

GOLF   Charleston is said to be the home of golf in America. Charlestonians have been playing the game since the 1700s, when the first golf clubs arrived from Scotland. With 17 public and private courses in the city, there's a golf game waiting for every buff.

Wild Dunes Resort, Isle of Palms (☎ **803/886-6000**), offers two championship golf courses designed by Tom Fazio. **The Links** is a 6,722-yard, par-72 layout that takes the player through marshlands, over or into huge sand dunes, through a wooded alley, and into a pair of oceanfront finishing holes once called "the greatest east of Pebble Beach, California." The course opened in 1980 and has been ranked among the 100 greatest courses in the United States by *Golf Digest* and among the top 100 in the world by *Golf Magazine. Golf Digest* has also ranked the Links as the 13th-greatest resort course in America. **The Harbor Course** offers 6,402 yards of Low Country marsh and Intracoastal Waterway views. This par-70 layout is considered to be target golf, challenging players with two holes that play from one island to another across Morgan Creek. Greens fees at these courses can range from $42 to $100, depending on the season. Clubs can be rented at either course for $25 for 18 holes, and professional instruction costs $45 for a 45-minute session. Both courses are open daily from 7am to 6pm year-round.

Your best bet, if you'd like to play at any of the other Charleston-area golf courses, is to contact **Charleston Golf Partners** (☎ **800/774-4444** or 843/847-9770, Monday to Friday from 10am to 6pm). The company represents 15 golf courses, offering packages that range from $89 to $110 per person March to August. Off-season packages range from $69 to $99 per person. Prices include greens fees on one course, a hotel room based on double occupancy, and taxes. Travel professionals here will customize your vacation with golf-course selections and tee times; they can also arrange rental cars and airfares.

HIKING   The most interesting hiking trails begin around Buck Hall in **Francis Marion National Forest** (☎ **843/887-3257**), located some 40 miles north of the center of Charleston via U.S. 52. The site consists of 250,000 acres of swamps, with towering oaks and pines. Also in the national forest, **McClellanville,** reached by U.S. 17/701 north from Charleston, has 15 camping sites (cost: $10 per night), plus a boat ramp and fishing. Other hiking trails are at **Edisto Beach State Park,** State Cabin Road, on Edisto Island (☎ **843/869-2156**).

HORSEBACK RIDING   Our pick is **Seabrook Island Resort,** 1002 Landfall Way, Seabrook Island (☎ **843/768-1000**), although reservations for these guided rides are required 3 or 4 days in advance. The resort has an equestrian center and offers both trail rides and beach rides. The beach ride (for advanced riders only) leaves at 8am daily and costs $70 per person; the trail ride (also for advanced riders) leaves at 10:30am daily, going for $60 per person. For beginners, the "Walking Scenic" ride is offered; it lasts 1 hour and costs $50.

PARASAILING   **Island Water Sports,** South Beach Marina (☎ **843/671-7007**), allows you to soar up to 700 feet. The cost ranges from $45 to $55, depending on the length of line used. It's open April to October only, daily from 11am to 8pm.

TENNIS   Charlestonians have been playing tennis since the early 1800s. The **Charleston Tennis Center,** Farmfield Avenue (west of Charleston on U.S. 17), is your best bet, with 15 well-maintained outdoor courts lighted for night play. The cost is only $2.50 per person per hour of court time. The center is open Monday to Thursday from 8:30am to 10pm, on Friday from 8:30am to 7pm, on Saturday from 9am to 6pm, and on Sunday from 10am to 6pm.

At the **Shadowmoss Plantation Golf & Country Club,** 20 Dunvegan Dr. (☎ **843/556-8251**), nonmembers can play free (as space allows) daily from 7am to 7pm. Call ahead for court times.

WINDSURFING   The temperate waters and wide open spaces make the Low Country a favorite of windsurfers. Windsurfing can be arranged through **McKevlin's Surf Shop,** 1101 Ocean Blvd., Isle of Palms (☎ **843/886-8912**), which rents surfboards for $5 per hour. It's open in summer daily from 10am to 6pm; off-season, call for hours, which are subject to change.

8 Shopping

King Street is lined with many special shops and boutiques. The **Shops at Charleston Place,** 130 Market St., is an upscale complex of top designer-clothing shops (Gucci, Jaeger, Ralph Lauren, and so on), and the lively **State Street Market,** just down from the City Market, is another cluster of shops and restaurants.

ART

African American Art Gallery. 43 John St. ☎ **843/722-8224.**

With some 2,900 square feet of exhibition space, this is the largest African-American art gallery in the South. The original pieces change every 2 months. On permanent display are the works of prominent artists including Dr. Leo Twiggs and historical artist Joe Pinckney. Monday to Saturday: 10am to 6pm.

Lowcountry Artists. 87 Hasell St. ☎ **843/577-9295.**

In a former book bindery, this gallery is operated by eight local artists, who work in oil, watercolor, drawings, collage, woodcuts, and other media. Monday to Saturday: 10am to 5pm, Sunday noon to 5pm.

Waterfront Gallery. 215 E. Bay St. (across from Custom House). ☎ **843/722-1155.**

Facing Waterfront Park, this gallery is the premier choice for the work of South Carolina artists. The works of 21 local artists are presented, with original works beginning at $95. For sale are pieces ranging from sculpture to oils. Monday to Thursday 11am to 6pm, Friday to Saturday 11am to 10pm.

Wells Gallery. 103 Broad St. ☎ **843/853-3233.**

Artists from the Low Country and all over the Southeast are on display at this Charleston gallery. Specializing in Low Country landscapes, the gallery offers works by two of South Carolina's most respected artists: Betty Anglain Smith and Mickey Williams. Prices range from $300 to $12,000. Monday to Saturday 10am to 6pm.

ANTIQUES
George C. Birlant and Co. 191 King St. ☎ **843/722-3842.**

If you're in the market for 18th- and 19th-century English antique furnishings, this is the right place. This Charleston staple prides itself in its Charleston Battery Bench, which is seen (and sat upon) throughout the Battery. The heavy iron sides are cast from the original 1880 mold, and the slats are authentic South Carolina cypress. It's as close to the original as you can get. Monday to Saturday 9am to 5:30pm.

Livingston Antiques. 163 King St. ☎ **843/723-9697.**

For nearly a quarter of a century, discriminating antiques hunters have patronized the showroom of this dealer. Both authentic antiques and fool-the-eye reproductions are sold. If you're interested, the staff will direct you to the shop's 30,000-square-foot warehouse on West Ashley. Monday to Friday 9am to 6pm, Saturday 10am to 4pm.

BOOKS
Atlantic Books. 310 King St. ☎ **843/723-4751.**

Amelia and Gene Woolf offer thousands of good used books at moderate prices, along with a collection of rare books. The store's specialties are books on South Carolina and the Civil War. It also has a goodly collection of the works of Southern authors, along with modern first editions and books on Americana, children's literature, and nautical subjects. Monday to Saturday 10am to 6pm, Sunday 1 to 6pm.

CIVIL WAR ARTIFACTS
Sumter Military Antiques & Museum. 54 Broad St. ☎ **843/577-7766.**

Relics from that "War of Northern Aggression" are sold here. You'll find a collection of authentic artifacts that range from firearms and bullets to Confederate uniforms and artillery shells and bullets. There are some interesting prints, along with a collection of books on the Civil War. Monday to Saturday 10am to 6pm.

CRAFTS & GIFTS
Charleston Crafts. 38 Queen St. ☎ **843/723-2938.**

This is a permanent showcase for Low Country craft artists who work in a variety of media, including metal, glass, paper, clay, wood, and fiber. Handmade jewelry is also sold, along with basketry, leather, traditional crafts, and even homemade soaps. Monday to Saturday 10am to 6pm.

Clown's Bazaar. 56 Broad St. ☎ **843/723-9769.**

Store owner Deanna Wagoner's heart is as big as her smile. Her store is indeed one of a kind—the city's only tax-exempt, self-help crafts organization. Originally, it was in Katmandu, Nepal, founded to help Third World families help themselves. Economic and political circumstances forced the store's relocation to Charleston, but the objective of helping Third World families hasn't changed. The store features handmade carvings, silks, brasses, and pewter from exotic locales such as Africa, Nepal, India, Bangladesh, and the Philippines, as well as wooden toys and books, including some in Gullah, a lost language that is still spoken in some areas of the city. Oh, and if you're looking for clown dolls, Deanna has those, too. Daily 11am to 5pm.

Wired & Fired. 159 E. Bay St. ☎ **843/579-0999.**

This shop is a combination crafts shop and cafe established in the late 1990s. You enter what looks like an artist's studio in disarray, the walls containing shelves filled with unglazed ceramics. Clients buy the unglazed ceramics and apply the decorations themselves. Unglazed ceramics cost from $5 to $30 per object, plus a $3 firing fee. You are also charged $8 for time spent in the studio. Surprisingly, this is also one the most popular spots for a young man to take his girlfriend for the evening. Sunday 1 to 9pm, Monday 11am to 9pm, Tuesday to Thursday 11am to 10pm, Friday to Saturday 11am to midnight.

FASHION
Ben Silver. 149 King St. ☎ **843/577-4556.**

One of the finer men's clothiers in Charleston, this is the best place to get yourself dressed like a member of the city's finest society. The store specializes in blazers and buttons; it has a collection of more than 600 blazer-button designs that are unique in the city. The store features house names and designs only, so don't go looking for Ralph Lauren here. Monday to Saturday 9am to 6pm.

Nancy's. 342 King St. ☎ **843/722-1272.**

On the main street, Nancy's specializes in clothing for the woman who wants to be both active and stylish. Complete outfits in linen, silk, and cotton are sold, along with such accessories as belts and jewelry. Nancy's aims for a "total look." Monday to Saturday 10am to 5:30pm, Sunday 1 to 5pm.

FURNISHINGS
✪ **Historic Charleston Reproductions.** 105 Broad St. ☎ **843/723-8292.**

It's rare that a store with so much to offer could be not-for-profit, but that's the case here. All items are approved by the Historic Charleston Foundation, and all proceeds benefit the restoration of Charleston's historic projects.

Licensed-replica products range from furniture to jewelry. The pride of the store is its home-furnishings collection by Baker Furniture, an esteemed company based in Michigan. What makes this collection unusual is the fact that the pieces are adaptations of real Charleston antiques, made of mahogany, a rich dark wood with an authentic feel that can only be found here.

If one of Charleston's iron designs around town has caught your eye, there's a chance that you'll find a replica of it in the form of jewelry. A collection of china from Mottahedeh is also featured. Monday to Saturday 10am to 5pm.

The store operates shops in several historic houses, and for slightly more than basic souvenirs, see its Francis Edmunds Center Museum Shop at 108 Meeting St. (☎ 843/724-8484). Monday to Saturday 10am to 5pm, Sunday 2 to 5pm.

HAMMOCKS
The Original Pawleys Island Rope Hammock. Hwy. 17, Pawleys Island. ☎ **843/237-9122.**

Looking for a backyard retreat after you return home? This shop may give you some ideas. Handmade quality and durability are the lure, because these hammocks have been made in the same way and in the same location for more than 100 years. Their creator, riverboat Capt. Joshua Ward, thought that the grass mattresses in his shop were too hot, not to mention quite uncomfortable. Because necessity is the mother of invention, he hand-wove the first Original Pawleys Island Rope Hammock. You can choose between cotton and polyester ropes for your personal order. Monday to Friday 9:30am to 6pm, Sunday noon to 5pm.

JEWELRY

Croghan's Jewel Box. 308 King St. ☎ **843/723-3594.**

You'll find gift ideas for any situation, from baby showers to weddings. Estate jewelry and some contemporary pieces are featured. This store also sets diamonds for rings and pendants, and can even secure the diamond for you, with the price depending on the type of stone and grade that you choose. Monday to Saturday 9:30am to 5:30pm.

Dazzles. Charleston Place, 226 King St. ☎ **843/722-5951.**

One-of-a-kind jewelry is sold here, along with the finest collection of handmade 14-karat-gold slide bracelets in town. Some of the jewelry is of heirloom quality. The staff will also help you create jewelry of your own design, including a choice of stones. Daily 10am to 7pm.

Geiss & Sons Jewelers. 116 E. Bay St. ☎ **843/577-4497.**

Jewelry here is custom-designed by Old World–trained craftspeople. This is a direct offshoot of a store opened by the Geiss family in Brazil in 1919. It's an official watch dealer for names such as Rolex, Bertolucci, and Raymond Weil. Repair jobs are given special attention. Monday to Saturday 10am to 5:30pm.

JOGGLING BOARDS

Old Charleston Joggling Board Co. 652 King St. ☎ **843/723-4331.**

Since the early 1830s, joggling boards have been a Charleston tradition. These boards are the creation of Mrs. Benjamin Kinloch Huger, a native who sought a mild form of exercise for her rheumatism. Mrs. Huger's Scottish cousins sent her a model of a joggling board, suggesting that she sit and gently bounce on the board. The fame of the device soon spread, and the board soon turned up in gardens, patios, and porches throughout the Charleston area. After World War II, joggling boards became rare because of the scarcity of timber and the high cost of labor, but the tradition was revived in 1970. The company also produces a joggle bench, a duplicate of the joggling board but only 10 feet long (as opposed to the original 16 feet) and 20 inches from the ground. Monday to Friday 8am to 5pm.

PERFUME

Scents of Charleston. 92 N. Market St. ☎ **843/853-8837.**

Favorite fragrances are found here, and prices (for the most part) are relatively reasonable. The shop evokes a perfumery in Europe. Scents creates its own exclusive brands, and also features classic and popular fragrances. Monday to Friday 10am to 9pm, Saturday to Sunday 9am to 5pm.

SMOKESHOP

The Smoking Lamp. 189 E. Bay St. ☎ **843/577-7339.**

This is Charleston's oldest smokeshop, with the most complete array of tobacco products in the city. You'll find an assortment of pipes, tobacco, cigars, even walking canes and other paraphernalia. Monday to Saturday 10am to 10pm, Sunday 11am to 6pm.

9 Charleston After Dark

THE PERFORMING ARTS

Charleston's major cultural venue is the **Dock Street Theater,** 133 Church St. (☎ 843/965-4032), a 463-seat theater. The original was built in 1736 but burned down in the early 19th century, and the Planters Hotel (not related to the Planters Inn) was constructed around its ruins. In 1936, the theater was rebuilt in a new location. It's the home of the **Charleston State Company,** a local not-for-profit theater group whose season runs from mid-September to May. Dock Street hosts various companies throughout the year, with performances ranging from Shakespeare to *My Fair Lady.* It's most active during the annual ✪ **Spoleto Festival USA** in May and June. The box office is open Monday to Thursday from noon to 5pm, on Friday and Saturday from 10am to 8pm, and on Sunday from 10am to 3pm.

The **Robert Ivey Ballet,** 1910 Savannah Hwy. (☎ 843/556-1343), offers both classical and contemporary dance, as well as children's ballet programs. The group performs at various venues throughout the Charleston area, with general-admission prices of $18 for adults and $13 for children.

Charleston Ballet Theatre, 477 King St. (☎ 843/723-7334), is one of the South's best professional ballet companies. The season begins in late October and continues into April. Admission $15.

Charleston Symphony Orchestra, 14 George St. (☎ 843/723-7528), performs throughout the state, but its main venues are the Gaillard Auditorium and Charleston Southern University. The season runs from September to May.

THE CLUB & MUSIC SCENE

Cumberland's. 26 Cumberland St. ☎ **843/577-9469.** Cover $3–$6.

If your musical tastes run from Delta blues to rock to reggae, this is the place for you. The dominant age group at this bar depends on the act playing. You will find that the generation gap isn't strong here, with college students toasting glasses with midlifers. Greasy chicken wings and lots of suds make this place ever popular. Music is the common bond. Daily 11am to 2am.

Henry's. 54 N. Market St. ☎ **843/723-4363.** Cover $12 for Comedy Show, Fri–Sat 9pm–1am; no cover Sun–Thurs.

One of the best places for jazz in Charleston, this club features a live band on Friday and Saturday. Otherwise, you get taped top-40 music for listening and dancing. If you're a single man or woman with a roving eye, this is one of the hottest pick-up bars in town. It attracts mainly an over-30 crowd. Happy hour, with drink discounts and free appetizers, is Monday to Friday from 4 to 7pm.

Music Farm. 32 Ann St. ☎ **843/722-8904.** Cover $2–$25.

This club is self-described as being "Charleston's premier music venue." It covers nearly every taste in music, from country to rock. You're as likely to hear funkster George Clinton as you are country legend George Jones. The club hosts local and regional bands, as well as national acts. Music is present anywhere from 2 to 6 nights a week from 9am to 2am. Call **843/853-FARM** for schedules and information.

Tommy Condon's Irish Pub. 160 Church St. ☎ **843/577-3818.** No cover.

Located in a restored warehouse in the City Market area, this Irish pub and family restaurant is full of Old Ireland memorabilia. The bartender turns out a leprechaun punch, a glass of real Irish ale, and most definitely Irish coffee. The menu offers Irish food, along with Low Country specials such as shrimp and grits or jambalaya. Happy hour, with reduced drink prices, is Monday to Friday from 5 to 7pm. Live Irish entertainment is presented Wednesday to Sunday from 8:30pm until closing. Pub hours are Sunday to Thursday 11:30am to 10pm, Friday to Saturday 11am to 11pm.

THE BAR SCENE

First Shot Bar. In the Mills House Hotel, 115 Meeting St. ☎ **843/577-2400.** No cover.

Our preferred watering hole is this old standby, where we've seen such visiting celebs as Gerald Ford and Elizabeth Taylor (not together, of course) over the years. The bar is one of the most elegant in Charleston, a comfortable and smooth venue for a drink. If you get hungry, the kitchen will whip you up some shrimp and grits.

The Griffon. 18 Vendue Range. ☎ **843/723-1700.** No cover.

A lot of Scotch and beer is consumed at this popular Irish pub. A full array of home-cooked specials from the old country is served as well, including such pub-grub favorites as steak pies, bangers and mash (English sausage and mashed potatoes), and the inevitable fish and chips. Happy hour is Monday to Friday from 4 to 7pm.

Habana Club. 177 Meeting St. ☎ **843/853-5900.**

With the ambience of a private club, this second-floor house from 1870 is where the Ernest Hemingway of today would head if he were in Charleston. Relax in one of three Gilded Age salons, each evocative of the Reconstruction era of the Old South. The house specializes in exotic cigars and martinis, and serves appetizers, desserts, fruit and cheese plates, and even some miniature beef Wellingtons. When filming *The Patriot,* Mel Gibson made Habana his second home in the city. You pass through a well-stocked tobacco store downstairs to reach the club.

Jack's Tavern. 213 E. Bay St. ☎ **843/720-7788.**

Set in what was built in the 19th century as a warehouse, this neighborhood bar is lined with hand-made bricks and capped with heavy timbers. It receives a wide medley of drinkers, everyone from college students to local dockyard workers, as well as a scattering of travelers from out of town. Appetizers and burgers are the only food served, but at least a dozen beers are on tap. Live music begins at 9:30pm Wednesday to Saturday. The tavern is open Tuesday to Sunday 4pm to 2am.

Mike Calder's Pub. 288 King St. ☎ **843/577-0123.** No cover.

Mike Calder's place is a local favorite, with 15 imported beers on tap from England, Scotland, and Ireland. The bartender makes a mean Bloody Mary.

Vicery's Bar & Grill. 15 Beaufain. ☎ **843/577-5300.** No cover.

This is one of the most popular gathering places in Charleston for the younger crowd, especially students. It's also a good dining choice, with an international menu that includes jerk chicken and gazpacho. But the real secrets of the place's success are its 16-ounce frosted mug of beer for $1 and the convivial atmosphere.

MICROBREWERIES

For some, an evening in a microbrewery is the way to go in Charleston. Our favorites include **Southend Brewery & Smokehouse,** 161 East Bay St. (☎ 843-853-4677), which specializes in wood-fired pizzas, freshly made salads, and barbecue. Of course, all this is washed down with a variety of original microbrews. You might also try **Zebo,** 275 King St. (☎ **843/577-7600**), a brewpub featuring a menu of wood-fired pizza, pasta, and appetizers along with a salad bar. Naturally, the home brew accompanies meals except at the Sunday brunch at 10:30am. This microbrewery rises three stories at the corner of Wentworth Street.

GAY & LESBIAN BARS

The Arcade. 5 Liberty St. ☎ **843/722-5656.** Cover $3–$5.

Set in the heart of historic Charleston, on the premises of what was once a 1930s movie theater, this is the largest and most high-energy dance bar in Charleston. Catering with equal ease to gays and lesbians, it features two to four bars (depending on the night of the week). The atmosphere ranges from quiet and conversational to danceaholic and manic.

Déjà Vu II. 4634 Prulley Ave, N. Charleston. ☎ **843/554-5959.** Cover $3–$5.

Some people say this is the coziest and warmest "ladies' bar" in the Southeast. Rita Taylor, your host, has transformed what used to be a supper club into a cozy enclave with two bars, weekend live entertainment (usually by "all-girl bands"), and a clientele that's almost exclusively gay and 75% lesbian. The ambience is unpretentious and charming, and definitely does not exclude sympathetic patrons of any ilk.

Dudley's. 346 King St. ☎ **843/723-2784.** Cover $1 after 8pm.

It's the coziest, clubbiest, and—in its low-key way—most welcoming gay bar in Charleston. Some regulars compare it with a gay version of "Cheers" because of its wood paneling and bricks, and its amused and bemused sense of blasé permissiveness. Most of the chatting occurs on the street level, where an advance call from nonmembers is considered to be necessary to guarantee admittance. Upstairs is a game room with pool tables and very few places to sit. The cover is charged as a means of ensuring status as a private club.

Patrick's Pub & Grill. 1377 Ashley River Rd. (Hwy. 61). ☎ **843/571-3435.**

If you like your men in leather, chances are you'll find Mr. Right here. A gay pub and grill, right outside Charleston, this is a late-night venue for some of the hottest men in Charleston. Levis take second place to leather.

LATE-NIGHT BITES

Kaminsky's Most Excellent Café. 78 N. Market St. ☎ **843/853-8270.**

Following a night of jazz or blues, this is a good spot to rest your feet and order just the power boost you need to make it through the rest of the evening. The handsome bar offers a wide selection of wines and is ideal for people-watching. Visitors who like New York's SoHo will feel at home here. The desserts are sinful, especially the Italian cream cake and mountain chocolate cake. Daily noon to 1am.

10 A Side Trip to Edisto Island

Isolated, and offering a kind of melancholy beauty, Edisto lies some 45 miles south of Charleston (take U.S. 17 west for 21 miles; then head south along Highway 174 the rest of the way). By the late 18th century, Sea Island cotton made the islanders wealthy, and some plantations from that era still stand.

Today, the island attracts families from Charleston and the Low Country to its white sandy beaches. Water sports include shrimping, surf-casting, deep-sea fishing, and sailing.

Edisto Beach State Park, State Cabin Road, sprawls across 1,255 acres, opening onto 2 miles of beach. There's also a signposted nature trail. Enjoy a picnic lunch under one of the shelters. The park has 75 campsites with full hookups and 28 with no hookups. Campsites cost $20 per night (the price is the same for RV hookups). Five cabins are also available for rent, ranging from $62 to $67 daily. There are two restaurants within walking distance of the campsite, plus a general store nearby.

WHERE TO STAY

Fairfield Ocean Ridge. King Cotton Rd., Edisto Island, SC 29438. ☎ **800/845-8500** or 843/869-2561. www.fairfieldvacations.com. 40 units. A/C MINIBAR TV TEL. $350 1-bedroom villa; $265 2-bedroom villa; $475 2-bedroom deluxe villa. AE, DC, DISC, MC, V.

At the south end of Edisto Beach, this 300-acre resort is a favorite summer rendezvous for Charleston families. Birders flock to the area, as do shellers, and there is plenty of good fishing, along with summer picnics. It's an old-fashioned America-by-the-sea. Golf, jet skiing, parasailing, and tennis are among the other recreational activities. A timeshare resort, Fairfield rents villas and condos ranging from a one-bedroom villa up to a two-bedroom duplex villa with sleeping lofts. Each villa, complete with kitchen, is individually furnished according to the tastes of its owner. Most rooms have VCRs, and fax service is available at the rental office. A restaurant is on the premises, and a continental breakfast is free on Monday only.

WHERE TO DINE

The Old Post Office. Hwy. 174 at Store Creek. ☎ **843/869-2339.** Main courses $17–$22. MC, V. Mon–Sat 6–10pm. SOUTHERN.

This is the most prominent building that you're likely to see as you drive through the forests and fields across Edisto Island. About 5 miles from the beach, the restaurant was once a combination post office and general store, as its weathered clapboards and old-time architecture imply. Partners David Gressette and Philip Bardin, who transformed the premises in 1988, prepare a worthy compendium of Low Country cuisine and serve it in copious portions. Try Island corn and crabmeat chowder, Orangeburg onion sausage with black-bean sauce, scallops and grits with mousseline sauce, fried quail with duck-stock gravy, and "fussed-over" pork chops with hickory-smoked tomato sauce and mousseline.

Sunset Grille. 3701 Docksite Rd. at the Edisto Marina. ☎ **843/869-1010.** Reservations not needed. Main courses $5–$18. MC, V. Mon–Sat 11am–10pm. SEAFOOD.

This is the sibling restaurant to The Old Post Office just recommended, and it is a family favorite. It opens onto Big Bay Creek overlooking the Intracoastal Waterway. The fresh fish and locally caught shellfish are delivered to the restaurant dock daily, and you can request it broiled, grilled, or fried. The lunch and dinner menus have variety, and the freshest of ingredients are used. The brunch on Sunday is the island's best. At lunch an array of fresh salads (including one made with local oysters) is served along with burgers, chicken grills, and a selection of the best-stuffed sandwiches on Edisto. You can also order a big bowl of South Carolina she-crab soup. The menu at night is more elaborate, with a selection of appetizers ranging from a fish stew in a robust tomato and fish stock to fried alligator served with honey mustard. New York strip appears as a main course, as do the delicious Edisto crab cakes. "Bell Boil" is a local favorite, fresh shrimp boiled in seasoned stock and served hot.

11 Kiawah Island & the Isle of Palms

KIAWAH ISLAND

This eco-sensitive private residential and resort community sprawls across 10,000 acres 21 miles south of Charleston. Named for the Kiawah Indians who inhabited the islands in the 17th century, it today consists of two resort villages: East Beach and West Beach. The community fronts a lovely 10-mile stretch of Atlantic beach; magnolias, live oaks, pine forests, and acres of marsh characterize the island.

Kiawah boasts many challenging golf courses, including one designed by Jack Nicklaus at Turtle Point that *Golf Digest* has rated among the top 10 courses in South Carolina. Golf architect Pete Dye designed a 2½ mile oceanfront course to host the 1991 PGA Ryder Cup March. *Tennis* magazine rates Kiawah as one of the nation's top tennis resorts, with its 28 hard-surface or Har-Tru clay courts. Anglers are also attracted to the island, especially in spring and fall.

For more information on golf and the beaches, see "Beaches and Outdoor Pursuits," earlier in this chapter.

Kiawah Island Resort. Kiawah Island (P.O. Box 12357), Charleston, SC 29412. ☎ **800/654-2924** or 843/768-2122. Fax 843/768-9386. www.kiawahislandresort.com. E-mail: reservation@kiawahresort.com. 650 units. A/C TV TEL. $139–$259 double; $139–$1,000 townhouse or villa. AE, DC, DISC, MC, V.

A self-contained community, this complex opened in 1976 at West Beach village. Since then, East Beach village has joined the community. Regular hotel-style rooms are available in four buildings, opening onto the lagoon or the Atlantic. Rooms have one king or two double beds, along with private balconies and combination bathrooms. Villas, with up to four bedrooms, are casually furnished and have complete kitchens and such amenities as washers and dryers.

Dining: Several dining options include the Jasmine Porch and Veranda and Indigo House. Diners have tables facing the lagoon at the Park Cafe. Low Country and international dishes are featured.

THE ISLE OF PALMS

A residential community bordered by the Atlantic Ocean and lying 10 miles north of Charleston, this island, with its salt marshes and wildlife, has been turned into a vacation retreat, but one that is more downscale than Kiawah Island. The attractions of Charleston are close at hand, but the Isle of Palms is also self-contained, with shops, dining, an array of accommodations, and two championship golf courses.

Charlestonians have been flocking to the island for holidays since 1898. The first hotel opened here in 1911. I-26 intersects with I-526 heading directly to the island via the Isle of Palms Connector (SC 517). Seven miles of wide, white sandy beach are the island's main attraction, and sailing and windsurfing are popular. The more adventurous will go crabbing and shrimping in the creeks.

Wild Dunes Resort. Isle of Palms (P.O. Box 20575), Charleston, SC 29413. ☎ **800/845-8880** or 843/886-6000. Fax 843/886-2916. www.wilddunes.com. 312 units. A/C TV TEL. $281–$550 villa or cottage. Golf packages available. AE, MC, V. Free parking.

A bit livelier than Kiawah Island, its major competitor, this complex is set on landscaped ground on the north shore. The 1,600-acre resort has not only two widely acclaimed golf courses, but also an array of other outdoor attractions. Many families settle in here for a long stay, almost never venturing into Charleston. Guests are housed in condos and a series of cottages and villas. Many accommodations have only one bedroom, but others have as many as six. Villas and cottages are built along the shore, close to golf and tennis. Furnishings are tasteful and resortlike, with kitchens, washers and dryers, and spacious bathrooms with dressing areas. Some of the best units have screened-in balconies.

Dining/Diversions: Edgar's Restaurant serves standard American cuisine and regional specialties. The hotel also maintains a lounge, which stays open until 2am.

Amenities: The resort's own private beach stretches over 2½ miles. There are two outstanding golf courses (see "Beaches and Outdoor Pursuits," earlier in this chapter for details), 19 hard-surface tennis courts, and 20 pools in all. You can also enjoy surf-casting, water sports, a racquet club, a yacht harbor on the Intracoastal Waterway, nature trails, and bicycling. Children's programs are available.

Hilton Head & the Low Country

The largest sea island between New Jersey and Florida and one of America's great resort meccas, Hilton Head is surrounded by the Low Country, where much of the romance, beauty, and graciousness of the Old South survives. Broad white-sand beaches are warmed by the Gulf Stream and fringed with palm trees and rolling dunes. Palms mingle with live oaks, dogwood, and pines, and everything is draped in Spanish moss. Graceful sea oats, anchoring the beaches, wave in the wind. The subtropical climate makes all this beauty the ideal setting for golf and for some of the Southeast's finest saltwater fishing. Far more sophisticated and upscale than Myrtle Beach and the Grand Strand, Hilton Head's "plantations" (as most resort areas here call themselves) offer visitors something of the traditional leisurely lifestyle that's always held sway here.

Although it covers only 42 square miles (it's 12 miles long and 5 miles wide at its widest point), Hilton Head feels spacious, thanks to judicious planning from the beginning of its development in 1952. And that's a blessing, because about half a million resort guests visit annually (the permanent population is about 25,000). The broad beaches on its ocean side, sea marshes on the sound, and natural wooded areas of live and water oak, pine, bay, and palmetto trees in between have all been carefully preserved amid commercial explosion. This lovely setting attracts artists, writers, musicians, theater groups, and craftspeople. The only city (of sorts) is Harbour Town, at Sea Pines Plantation, a Mediterranean-style cluster of shops and restaurants.

1 Essentials

GETTING THERE   It's easy to fly into Charleston, rent a car, and drive to Hilton Head (about 65 miles south of Charleston). See chapter 10 for complete details on all the airlines flying into Charleston. If you're driving from other points south or north, just exit off I-95 to reach the island (Exit 28 off I-95 south, Exit 5 off I-95 north). U.S. 278 leads over the bridge to the island. It's 52 miles northeast of Savannah and located directly on the Intracoastal Waterway.

VISITOR INFORMATION   The **Island Visitors Information Center** is on U.S. 278 at S.C. 46 (☎ **888/741-7666** or 843/785-4472; www.islandvisitorcenter.com), just before you cross over from the mainland. It offers a free *Where to Go* booklet, including a visitor map and guide. It's open daily from 9am to 6pm.

The **Hilton Head Visitors and Convention Bureau** (Chamber of Commerce), 1 Chamber Dr. (☎ **843/785-3673;** www.hiltonheadisland.org), offers free maps of the area and will assist you in finding places of interest and outdoor activities. It will not, however, make hotel reservations. It's open Monday to Friday from 8:30am to 5:30pm.

GETTING AROUND   U.S. 278 is the divided highway that runs the length of the island.

Yellow Cab (☎ **843/686-6666**) has flat two-passenger rates determined by zone, with an extra $2 charge for each additional person.

SPECIAL EVENTS   The earliest annual event is **Springfest,** a March festival featuring seafood, live music, stage shows, and tennis and golf tournaments. In early or mid-April, top tennis players congregate for the **Family Circle Magazine Cup Tennis Tournament,** held at the Sea Pines Racquet Club. Outstanding PGA golfers also descend on the island in mid-April for the **MCI Heritage Classic** at the Harbour Town Golf Links. To herald fall, the **Hilton Head Celebrity Golf Tournament** is held on Labor Day weekend at Palmetto Dunes and Sea Pines Plantation.

2 Beaches, Golf, Tennis & Other Outdoor Pursuits

You can have an active vacation here any time of year; Hilton Head's subtropical climate ranges in temperature from the 50s in winter to the mid-80s in summer. And if you've had your fill of historic sights in Savannah or Charleston, don't worry—the attractions on Hilton Head mainly consist of nature preserves, beaches, and other places to play.

The **Coastal Discovery Museum of Hilton Head,** 100 William Hilton Pkwy. (☎ **843/689-6767**), hosts 15 separate walks and guided tours. Tours go along island beaches and explore the salt marshes, stopping at Native American sites and the ruins of old forts or long-gone plantations. Most of the emphasis will be on the ecology of local plants and animals. There are no fees for this service; instead, a donation of $2 is requested. Hours are Monday to Saturday 9am to 5pm, Sunday 10am to 3pm.

BEACHES   *Travel & Leisure* ranked ✪ Hilton Head's beaches as among the most beautiful in the world, and we concur. The sands are extremely firm, providing a sound surface for biking, hiking, jogging, and beach games. In summer, watch for the endangered loggerhead turtles that lumber ashore at night to bury their eggs.

All beaches on Hilton Head are public. Land bordering the beaches, however, is private property. Most beaches are safe, although there's sometimes an undertow at the northern end of the island. Lifeguards are posted only at major beaches, and concessions are available to rent beach chairs, umbrellas, and water-sports equipment.

There are four public entrances to Hilton Head's beaches. The main parking and changing areas are on Folly Field Road, off U.S. 278 (the main highway), and at Coligny Circle, close to the Holiday Inn. Other entrances (signposted) from U.S. 278 lead to Singleton and Bradley beaches.

Most frequently used are **North** and **South Forest Beach,** adjacent to Coligny Circle (enter from Pope Avenue across from Lagoon Road). You'll have to use the parking lot opposite the Holiday Inn, paying a $4 daily fee until after 4pm. The adjacent Beach Park has toilets and a changing area, as well as showers, vending machines, and phones. It's a family favorite.

Of the beaches on the island's north, we prefer **Folly Field Beach.** Toilets, changing facilities, and parking are available.

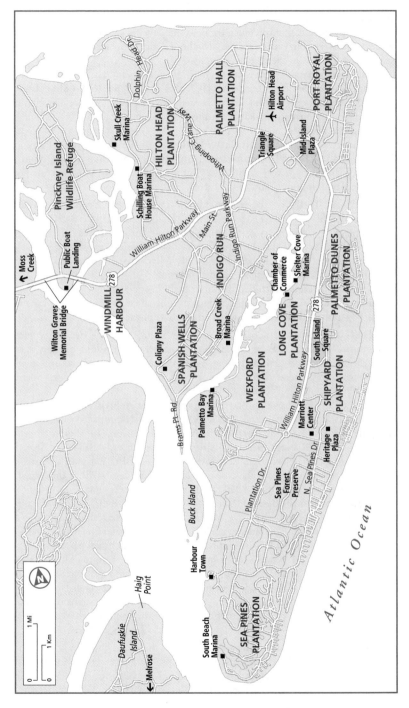

Dolphin Head Dr

Skull Creek Marina

HILTON HEAD PLANTATION

PALMETTO HALL PLANTATION

Hilton Head Airport

PORT ROYAL PLANTATION

Whooping Crane Way

Triangle Square

Mid-Island Plaza

Schilling Boat House Marina

Pinckney Island Wildlife Refuge

Moss Creek

Public Boat Landing

William Hilton Parkway

Main St.

Indigo Run Parkway

INDIGO RUN

Chamber of Commerce

Shelter Cove Marina

PALMETTO DUNES PLANTATION

Wilton Graves Memorial Bridge

WINDMILL HARBOUR

278

SPANISH WELLS PLANTATION

Coligny Plaza

Broad Creek Marina

LONG COVE PLANTATION

278

South Island Square

Brams Pt. Rd.

Palmetto Bay Marina

WEXFORD PLANTATION

William Hilton Parkway

Marriott Center

SHIPYARD PLANTATION

Heritage Plaza

Plantation Dr.

Sea Pines Forest Preserve

N. Sea Pines Dr.

Buck Island

Haig Point

1 Mi

1 Km

Harbour Town

Daufuskie Island

Melrose

South Beach Marina

SEA PINES PLANTATION

Atlantic Ocean

BIKING   Enjoy Hilton Head's 25 miles of bicycle paths, but stay off U.S. 278, the main artery, which has far too much traffic. Some beaches are firm enough to support wheels, and every year, cyclists seem to delight in dodging the waves or racing the fast-swimming dolphins in the nearby water.

Most hotels and resorts rent bikes to guests. If yours doesn't, try **Hilton Head Bicycle Company,** off Sea Pines Circle at 11B Archer Dr. (☎ **843/686-6888**). The cost is $12 per day, but only $18 for 3 days. Baskets, child carriers, locks, and headgear are supplied, and the inventory includes cruisers, BMXs, mountain bikes, and tandems. Hours are daily 9am to 5pm.

Another rental place is **South Beach Cycles,** South Beach Marina Village in Sea Pines (☎ **843/671-2453**), offering beach cruisers, tandems, child carriers, and bikes for kids. There's free delivery islandwide. Cost is $8 per half-day, $12 for a full day, or $19 for 3 days. Hours are 9am to 6pm daily.

CRUISES & TOURS   To explore Hilton Head's waters, contact **Adventure Cruises, Inc.,** Shelter Cove Harbour, Suite G, Harbourside III (☎ **843/785-4558**). Outings include a nature cruise to Daufuskie Island (made famous by Pat Conroy's book *The Water Is Wide* and the film *Conrack*), with a guided safari on a jungle bus. The cost is adults $15 and children $7.50 round-trip. Departures are daily at 12:15pm, with a return to Hilton Head at 4:45pm.

Other popular cruises include a 1½-hour dolphin-watch cruise, which costs adults $16 and children $6. A 3-hour sunset dinner cruise aboard the vessel *Adventure* costs adults $34 and children $17, including an all-you-can-eat buffet.

FISHING   No license is needed for saltwater fishing, although freshwater licenses are required for the island's lakes and ponds. The season for fishing offshore is from April through October. Inland fishing is good between September and December. Crabbing is also popular; crabs are easy to catch in low water from docks, boats, or right off a bank.

Off ✪ Hilton Head, you can go deep-sea fishing for amberjack, barracuda, shark, and king mackerel. Many rentals are available; we've recommended only those that have the best track records. Foremost is **A Fishin' Mission,** 145 Squire Pope Rd. (☎ **843/785-9177**), captained by Charles Getsinger aboard his 34-foot *Sportsfish.* Ice, bait, and tackle are included. Reservations are needed 1 to 2 days in advance. The craft carries up to six people. The cost is $325 for a half-day, $475 for three-quarters of a day, $630 for a full day, or $250 for an evening trip (6 to 9pm).

Harbour Town Yacht Basin, Harbour Town Marina (☎ **843/671-2704**), has four boats of various sizes and prices. *The Manatee,* a 40-foot vessel, can carry a group of 8 to 15. The rates, set for 6 passengers, are $375 for 4 hours, $565 for 6 hours, and $750 for 8 hours. A charge of $15 per hour is added for each additional passenger.

The Hero and *The Echo* are 32-foot ships. Their rates for a group of 6 are $340 for 4 hours, $510 for 6 hours, and $680 for 8 hours. A smaller 3-passenger inshore boat is priced at $250 for 4 hours, $375 for 6 hours, and $500 for 8 hours.

A cheaper way to go deep-sea fishing—only $40 per person—is aboard *The Drifter* (☎ **843/671-3060**), a party boat that departs from the South Beach Marina Village. Ocean-bottom fishing is possible at an artificial reef 12 miles offshore.

✪ **GOLF**   With 22 challenging golf courses on the island and an additional nine within a 30-minute drive, this is heaven for both professional and novice golfers. Some of golf's most celebrated architects—including George and Tom Fazio, Robert Trent Jones, Pete Dye, and Jack Nicklaus—have designed championship courses on the island. Wide, scenic fairways and rolling greens have earned Hilton Head the reputation of being the resort with the most courses on the "World's Best" list.

Many of Hilton Head's championship courses are open to the public, including the **George Fazio Course** at ☯ Palmetto Dunes Resort (☎ **843/785-1130**), an 18-hole, 6,534-yard, par-70 course that *Golf Digest* ranked in the top 50 of its "75 Best American Resort Courses." The course has been cited for its combined length and keen accuracy. The cost is $90 for 18 holes, and hours are daily from 6:30am to 6:30pm.

☯ **Old South Golf Links,** 50 Buckingham Plantation Dr., Bluffton (☎ **800/ 257-8997** or 843/785-5353), is an 18-hole, 6,772-yard, par-72 course, open daily from 7:30am to 7pm. It's recognized as one of the "Top 10 New Public Courses" by *Golf Digest,* which cites its panoramic views and setting ranging from an oak forest to tidal salt marshes. Greens fees range from $62 to $75. The course lies on Highway 278, 1 mile before the bridge leading to Hilton Head.

Hilton Head National, Highway 278 (☎ **843/842-5900**), is a Gary Player Signature Golf Course, including a full-service pro shop and a grill and driving range. It's an 18-hole, 6,779-yard, par-72 course with gorgeous scenery that evokes Scotland. Greens fees range from $50 to $64, and hours are daily 7:45am to 6:30pm. A regulation 9-hole course was added in 1999. Greens fees on this course are $34.

Island West Golf Club, Highway 278 (☎ **843/689-6660**), was nominated in 1992 by *Golf Digest* as the best new course of the year. With its backdrop of oaks, elevated tees, and rolling fairways, it's a challenging but playable 18-hole, 6,803-yard, par-72 course. Greens fees range from $40 to $56, and hours are from 7am to 6pm daily.

Robert Trent Jones Course at the Palmetto Dunes Resort (☎ **843/785-1138**) is an 18-hole, 6,710-yard, par-72 course with a winding lagoon system that comes into play on 11 holes. The greens fees are $90 to $130 for 18 holes, and hours are daily from 7am to 6pm.

KAYAK TOURS   Eco-Kayak Tours, Palmetto Bay Marina (☎ **843/785-7131**), operates guided tours in Broad Creek. About four to five trips are offered each day; the cost is $30 to $50 per person, and anyone age 7 to 82 is welcome to participate. The Eco-Explorer outing begins at 8:30am; the excursion lasts 1½ hours and costs $20 for adults and $18 for children under 12. The tour explores the South Carolina Low Country environment, and you'll see local wildlife along the way.

Outside Hilton Head, the **Plaza at Shelter Cove** (☎ **843/686-6996**) and **South Beach Marina Village** (☎ **843/671-2643**) allow you to tour Low Country waterways by kayak. A 2-hour Dolphin Nature Tour costs $35 (half price for children under 12). The tour takes you through the salt-marsh creeks of the Calibogue Sound or Pinckney Island Wildlife Refuge. The trip begins with brief instructions on how to control your boat. The Off-Island Day Excursion, at $60 per person, for 6 hours, or $48 for 4 hours, takes you along the Carolina barrier islands and the surrounding marshlands. These trips last 6 to 8 hours and include lunch.

HORSEBACK RIDING   Riding through beautiful maritime forests and nature preserves is reason enough to visit Hilton Head. We like **Lawton Fields Stables,** 190 Greenwood Dr., Sea Pines (☎ **843/671-2586**), offering rides for both adults and kids (kids ride ponies) through the Sea Pines Forest Preserve. The cost is $30 per person for a ride that lasts somewhat longer than an hour. Reservations are necessary.

JOGGING   Our favorite place for jogging is Harbour Town at Sea Pines. Go for a run through the town just as the sun is going down. Later, you can explore the marina and have a refreshing drink at one of the many outdoor cafes. In addition, the island offers lots of paved paths and trails that cut through scenic areas. Jogging along U.S. 278, the main artery, can be dangerous because of heavy traffic, however.

NATURE PRESERVES   The **Audubon-Newhall Preserve,** Palmetto Bay Road
(☎ 843/689-2989), is a 50-acre preserve on the south end of the island. Here, you
can walk along marked trails to observe wildlife in its native habitat. Guided tours are
available when plants are blooming. Except for public toilets, there are no amenities.
The preserve is open from sunrise to sunset; admission is free.

The second-leading preserve is also on the south end of the island. ✪ **Sea Pines Forest Preserve,** Sea Pines Plantation (☎ 843/671-6486), is a 605-acre public wilderness
with marked walking trails. Nearly all the birds and animals known to live on Hilton
Head can be seen here. (Yes, there are alligators, but there are also less fearsome creatures,
such as egrets, herons, osprey, and white-tailed deer.) All trails lead to public picnic areas
in the center of the forest. The preserve is open from sunrise to sunset year-round, except
during the Heritage Golf Classic in early April. Maps and toilets are available.

PARASAILING   **Para-Sail Hilton Head,** Harbour Town (☎ 843/671-4386),
takes you in a Sea Rocket powerboat for parasailing daily from 8am to 6:15pm. The
cost is $45 per person for 400 feet of line or $55 for 700 feet of line, and reservations
are necessary. Catamaran rides for up to six passengers are also featured, and sailing
lessons are offered.

SAILING   *Pauhana* and *Flying Circus,* Palmetto Bay Marina (☎ 843/686-2582),
are two charter sailboats on Hilton Head piloted by Capt. Jeanne Zailckas. You can
pack a picnic lunch and bring your cooler aboard for a 2-hour trip—in the morning
or afternoon, or at sunset. The cost is $20 for adults and $15 for children. *Flying
Circus* offers private 2-hour trips for up to 6 people, costing $150.

Harbour Town Yacht Basin (☎ 843/363-2628), offers both rentals and charters
for sailing. Rental prices range from $175 to $389 for 3 to 8 hours. Charters range
from $110 to $135 for 2 hours. Dolphin, sunset, and evening cruises are available.
Reservations are suggested.

✪ **TENNIS**   *Tennis* magazine ranked Hilton Head among its "50 Greatest U.S.
Tennis Resorts." No other domestic destination can boast such a concentration of tennis facilities: more than 300 courts that are ideal for beginners, intermediate, and
advanced players. The island has 19 tennis clubs, 7 of which are open to the public. A
wide variety of tennis clinics and daily lessons are available.

Sea Pines Racquet Club, Sea Pines Plantation (☎ 843/363-4495), has been
ranked by *Tennis* magazine as a top-50 resort and was selected by the *Robb Report* as
the best tennis resort in the United States. The club has been the site of more nationally televised tennis events than any other location, and it's the home of The Family
Circle Magazine Cup Women's Tennis Championships. Two hours of tennis is complimentary for guests of the hotel; otherwise, there's a $20-per-hour charge. The club
has 25 clay and 5 hard courts (hard courts are lighted for night play).

Port Royal Racquet Club, Port Royal Plantation (☎ 843/686-8803), offers
10 clay and 4 hard courts, plus 2 natural-grass courts. Night games are possible on all
courts. Charges range from $18 to $20 per hour, and reservations should be made a
day in advance. Clinics are $18 per hour.

Hilton Head Island Beach and Tennis Resort, 40 Folly Field Rd. (☎ 843/
842-4402), features a dozen lighted hard courts, costing only $15 per hour.

Palmetto Dunes Tennis Center, Palmetto Dunes Resort (☎ 843/785-1152), has
19 clay, 2 hard, and 4 artificial-grass courts (some lighted for night play). Hotel guests
pay $20 per hour; otherwise, the charge is $25 per hour.

WINDSURFING   Hilton Head is not recommended as a windsurfing destination.
Finding a place to windsurf is quite difficult, and one windsurfer warns that catching
a tailwind at the public beaches at the airport and the Holiday Inn could land you at

Hilton Head's Wonderful Wildlife

Hilton Head has preserved more of its wildlife than almost any other resort destination on the East Coast.

Hilton Head Island's alligators are a prosperous lot, and in fact, the South Carolina Department of Wildlife and Marine Resources uses the island as a resource for repopulating state parks and preserves in which alligators' numbers have greatly diminished. The creatures represent no danger if you stay at a respectful distance. (Strange as it may seem, some unsuspecting tourists, thinking that the dead-still alligators are props left over from Disney, often approach the reptiles and hit them or kick at them—obviously, not a very good idea.)

Many of the large water birds that regularly grace the pages of nature magazines are natives of the island. The island's Audubon Society reports around 200 species of birds every year in its annual bird count, and more than 350 species have been sighted on the island during the past decade. The snowy egret, the large blue heron, and the osprey are among the most noticeable. Here, too, you may see the white ibis, with its strange beak that curves down, plus the smaller cattle egret, which first arrived on Hilton Head Island in 1954 from a South American habitat. They follow the island's cows, horses, and tractors to snatch grasshoppers and other insects.

A big part of the native story includes deer, bobcat, loggerhead turtles, otter, mink, and even a few wild boars. The bobcats are difficult to see, lurking in the deepest recesses of the forest preserves and in the undeveloped parts of the island. The deer, however, are easier to encounter. One of the best places to watch these timid creatures is Sea Pines Plantation, on the southern end of the island. With foresight, the planners of this plantation set aside areas for deer habitat back in the 1950s, when the island master plan was conceived.

The loggerhead turtle, an endangered species, nests extensively along Hilton Head's 12 miles of wide, sandy beaches. Because the turtles choose the darkest hours of the night to crawl ashore and bury eggs in the soft sand, few visitors meet these 200-pound giants.

Ever-present is the bottle-nosed dolphin, usually called a porpoise by those who are not familiar with the island's sea life. Hilton Head Plantation and Port Royal Plantation adjacent to Port Royal Sound are good places to meet up with the playful dolphins, as are Palmetto Dunes, Forest Beach, and all other ocean-front locations. In the summer, dolphins are inclined to feed on small fish and sea creatures very close to shore. Island beaches are popular with bikers, and this often offers a real point of interest for curious dolphins, who sometimes seem to swim along with the riders. Several excursion boats offer tours that provide an opportunity for fellowship with dolphins. Shrimp boats are a guaranteed point of congregation for the hungry guys.

The Sea Pines Forest Preserve, the Audubon-Newhall Preserve, and the Pinckney Island Wildlife Preserve, just off the island between the bridges, are of interest to nature lovers. The **Costal Discovery Museum of Hilton Head** hosts several guided nature tours; call ☎ **843/689-6767.** Tours conducted Tuesday to Thursday, cost $10 for adults and $5 for children.

the bombing range on Parris Island, the Marine Corps' basic-training facility. Your resort may have equipment for rent, although what's usually available has been described as antiquated.

SHOPPING

Hilton Head is browsing heaven, with more than 30 shopping centers spread around the island. Chief shopping sites include **Pinelawn Mall** (Matthews Drive and U.S. 278), with more than 30 shops and half a dozen restaurants; and **Coligny Plaza** (Coligny Circle), with more than 60 shops, a movie theater, food stands, and several good restaurants. We've found some of the best bargains in the South at **Low Country Factory Outlet Village** (☎ 843/837-4339), on Highway 278 at the gateway to Hilton Head. The outlet has more than 45 factory stores, including Ralph Lauren, Brooks Brothers, and J. Crew. The hours of most shops are Monday to Saturday from 10am to 9pm and Sunday from 11am to 6pm.

3 Where to Stay

Hilton Head has some of the finest hotel properties in the Deep South, and prices are high—unless you book into one of the motels run by national chains. Most facilities offer discount rates from November to March, and golf and tennis packages are available.

The most comprehensive central reservations service on the island, **The Vacation Company,** P.O. Box 5312, Hilton Head Island, SC 29938 (☎ **800/845-7018** in the United States and Canada; www.hiltonheadcentral.com), can book you into any hotel room or villa on the island at no charge. It's open Monday to Saturday from 9am to 5pm.

Another option is renting a private home, villa, or condo. Families might consider a villa rental if it fits into their budget. For up-to-date availability, rates, and bookings, contact **Island Rentals and Real Estate,** P.O. Box 5915, Hilton Head Island, SC 29938 (☎ **800/845-6134** or 843/785-3813). The toll-free number is in operation 24 hours, but office hours are Monday to Friday from 8:30am to 6pm, Saturday 8:30 to 11:30am and 2 to 5pm.

VERY EXPENSIVE

Hyatt Regency Hilton Head. In Palmetto Dunes Plantation (P.O. Box 6167), Hilton Head Island, SC 29938. ☎ **800/55-HYATT** or 843/785-1234. Fax 843/842-4695. www.hyatthiltonhead.com. E-mail: Hyattresort@hargray.com. 505 units. A/C TV TEL. $195–$275 double; $400–$850 suite. AE, DC, DISC, MC, V. Parking $8.

Lacking the pizzazz of the Westin (recommended below), this is the largest hotel on the island, set on two landscaped acres surrounded by the much-more-massive acreage of Palmetto Dunes Plantation. The 10-story tower virtually dominates everything around it. Bedrooms are smaller and less opulent than you might expect of such a well-rated hotel, but their unremarkable decor is offset by balconies looking out over the gardens or the water.

Dining/Diversions: Hemingway's is one of the island's best restaurants (see "Where to Dine," later in this chapter). A cabaret-style dining and drinking club offers diversion. Sunday brunch is an island event.

Amenities: Room service, baby-sitting, laundry, Camp Hyatt for children, outdoor pool and whirlpool, three 18-hole golf courses, 25 tennis courts, sailboats, and health club (with saunas, whirlpool, indoor pool, and exercise room).

✪ **Main Street Inn.** 2200 Main St., Hilton Head Island, SC 29926. ☎ **800/471-3001** or 843/681-3001. Fax 843/681-5541. www.mainstreetinn.com. 33 units. A/C TV TEL. $185–$275 double. $35 surcharge for 3rd occupant of double room. Rates include breakfast and afternoon tea. AE, DC, MC, V. Free parking.

Don't expect cozy Americana from this small, luxurious inn, as it's grander and more European in its motifs than its name would imply. Designed like a small-scale villa that you might expect to see in the south of France, it was built in 1996 in a format that combines design elements from both New Orleans and Charleston, including cast-iron balustrades and a formal semi-tropical garden where guests are encouraged to indulge in afternoon tea. Inside, you'll find artfully clipped topiary, French provincial furnishings, and accommodations that are more luxurious, and more richly appointed, than any other hotel in Hilton Head. Color schemes throughout make ample use of golds, mauves, and taupes; floors are crafted from slabs of either stone or heart pine; fabrics are richly textured; and plumbing and bathroom fixtures are aggressively upscale. Overall, despite a location that requires a drive to the nearest beach, the hotel provides a luxe alternative to the less personalized megahotels that lie nearby. No children under 12 are admitted into this very adult property. AAA, incidentally, awarded it a much-coveted four-star rating.

Dining: No meals are served here, other than breakfast and afternoon tea.

Amenities: A garden overlooks one of the putting greens of the Bear Creek golf course. There's a 4-foot-deep lap pool in the garden, a whirlpool, and a staff that can arrange access to virtually every outdoor activity available in Hilton Head. There's also a small-scale spa on the premises, offering a limited array of massage, health, and beauty treatments.

✪ **Westin Resort.** Two Grasslawn Ave., Hilton Head Island, SC 29928. ☎ **800/ WWESTIN-1** or 843/681-4000. Fax 843/681-1087. www.westin.com. E-mail: tood.aaronson@ westin.com. 412 units. A/C MINIBAR TV TEL. $195–$395 double; $500–$8600 suite. Children 17 and under stay free in parents' room; children 4 and under eat free. Special promotions offered. AE, CB, DC, DISC, MC, V.

Set near the isolated northern end of Hilton Head Island on 24 landscaped acres, this is the most opulent European-style hotel in town. Its Disneyesque design, including cupolas and postmodern ornamentation that looks vaguely Moorish, evokes fanciful Palm Beach hotels. If there's a drawback, it's the stiff formality. Adults accompanied by a gaggle of children and bathers in swimsuits will not necessarily feel comfortable in the reverently hushed corridors. The bedrooms, most of which have ocean views, are outfitted in Low Country plantation style, with touches of Asian art thrown in for additional glamour.

Dining/Diversions: The Barony (see "Where to Dine," later in this chapter) is the best place for food. Poolside dining is available, and there's also a seafood buffet restaurant. A lounge is in the lobby.

Amenities: Room service, baby-sitting, laundry, health club, three top-notch golf courses, Palm Beach–style racquet club with 16 tennis courts, and palm-flanked swimming pool (with immediate access to a white-sand beach).

EXPENSIVE

Disney Hilton Head Island Resort. 22 Harbourside Lane, Hilton Head Island, SC 29928. ☎ **800/453-4911** or 843/341-4100. Fax 843/341-4130. www.dvcresorts.com. 31 studios, 88 villas. A/C TV TEL. $105–$255 studio; $140–$330 1-bedroom villa; $160–$395 2-bedroom villa; $305–$675 3-bedroom villa. AE, MC, V.

This family-conscious resort is on a 15-acre island that rises above Hilton Head's widest estuary, Broad Creek. When it opened in 1996, it was the only U.S.-based Disney resort outside Florida and California. About 20 woodsy-looking buildings are arranged into a compound. Expect lots of pine trees and fallen pine needles, garlands of Spanish moss, plenty of families with children, and an ambience that's several notches less intense than that of hotels in Disney theme parks. Part of the fun, if you like this sort of thing in concentrated doses, are the many summer-camp-style activities. Public areas have outdoorsy colors (forest green and cranberry), stuffed game fish, and varnished pine. References are made to Shadow the Dog (a fictitious Golden Retriever that is the resort's mascot) and Mathilda (a maternal figure who conducts cooking lessons for children as part of the resort's planned activities). All accommodations contain mini-kitchens, suitable for feeding sandwiches and macaroni to the kids but hardly the kind of thing that a gourmet chef would enjoy, and wooden furniture that's consistent with the resort's vacation-home-in-the-forest theme.

Dining/Diversions: For elaborate restaurants and bars, look elsewhere. Tide Me Over is a walk-up window serving Carolina cookery for breakfast and lunch. Those who don't cook their meals in-house can trek a short distance to the dozen or so eateries and bars in the nearby marina complex at Shelter Harbour.

Amenities: Children's activities usually last 90 to 120 minutes, giving parents a chance to be alone for a while. Programs include eco-tours with Disneyesque themes, arts and crafts, boat trips to look for dolphins, canoeing lessons, weenie roasts, marshmallow roasts with campfire songs, and "unbirthday" celebrations for any adult or child who doesn't happen to be celebrating a birthday that day. Baby-sitting can be arranged for an extra fee.

On the property is a swimming pool with a giant water slide. The beach club (about a mile distant) includes direct access to the sands of Palmetto Cove, a second swimming pool, water sports, and a lunch-only snack bar. A shuttle bus makes frequent connections between the beach club and hotel daily between 8:30am and 5pm. One of Hilton Head's most beautiful fishing piers allows easy access to whatever bites underwater. A deli and general store sell provisions.

Hilton Head Crowne Plaza Resort. 130 Shipyard Dr., Shipyard Plantation, Hilton Head Island, SC 29928. ☎ **800/465-4329** or 843/842-2400. Fax 843/785-8463. www. crowneplaza.com. 340 units. A/C MINIBAR TV TEL. $179–$207 double; $320–$520 suite. AE, DC, DISC, MC, V.

Tucked away within the Shipyard Plantation, and designed as the centerpiece of that plantation's 800 acres, this five-story inn gives its major competitor, Westin Resort, stiff competition. It underwent a $10 million renovation in 1993 and today has the island's most dignified lobby: a mahogany-sheathed postmodern interpretation of Chippendale decor. The golf course associated with the place has been praised by the National Audubon Society for its respect for local wildlife. Bedrooms are nothing out of the ordinary, yet the sheer beauty of the landscaping, the attentive service, the omnipresent nautical theme, and the well-trained staff (dressed in nautically inspired uniforms) can go a long way toward making your stay memorable.

Dining: On the premises are three restaurants. The most glamorous is Portz, off the establishment's main lobby. A good middle-bracket choice is Brella's, serving both lunch and dinner, and the premier bar, Signals Lounge, is the site of live music.

Amenities: Room service; valet laundry and dry-cleaning service; meeting and conference rooms; concierge; car rental; leisure-activities desk; health club with sauna and whirlpool; outdoor covered pavilion; and indoor, outdoor, and children's pools. Golf and tennis can be arranged.

⭕ **Hilton Oceanfront Resort.** 23 Ocean Lane (P.O. Box 6165), Hilton Head Island, SC 29938. ☎ **800/345-8001** or 843/842-8000. Fax 843/341-8037. www.hilton.com. E-mail: hiltonhh@hargray.com. 324 units (with kitchenette). A/C TV TEL. $190–$259 double; $350–$450 suite. AE, CB, DC, DISC, MC, V.

This award-winning property isn't the most imposing on the island. Many visitors, however, prefer the Hilton because of its hideaway position: tucked in at the end of the main road through Palmetto Dunes. The low-rise design features hallways that open to sea breezes at either end. The bedrooms are some of the largest on the island, and balconies angling out toward the beach allow sea views from every accommodation.

Dining/Diversions: Mostly Seafood is the resort's premier restaurant, although cafes and bars—and even a Pizza Hut on the grounds—serve less-expensive fare.

Amenities: Room service, baby-sitting, laundry, children's vacation program (like a summer camp and the best on the island), modest health club, whirlpool, sauna, two outdoor pools, and expansive sandy beach.

MODERATE

Holiday Inn Oceanfront. (P.O. Box 5728), 1 S. Forest Beach Dr., Hilton Head Island, SC 29938. ☎ **800/HOLIDAY** or 843/785-5126. Fax 843/785-6678. www.holiday-inn.com. 202 units. A/C TV TEL. $79–$209 double; $250 suite. AE, CB, DC, DISC, MC, V. Parking $2.

The island's leading motor hotel, across from Coligny Plaza, this five-story high-rise opens onto a quiet stretch of beach on the southern side of the island, near Shipyard Plantation. It's better than ever after a 1995 renovation. The rooms are spacious and well furnished, decorated in tropical pastels, but the balconies are generally too small for use. The upper floors have the views, so you should try for accommodations there. In summer, planned children's activities are offered. No-smoking and handicapped-accessible rooms are available.

Radisson Suite Resort. 12 Park Lane (in Central Park), Hilton Head Island, SC 29938. ☎ **800/333-3333** or 843/686-5700. Fax 843/686-3952. www.radisson.com. 156 units. A/C TV TEL. Apr–Sept $139–$149 suite; Oct–Mar $89–$99 suite. Rates include continental breakfast. AE, DC, DISC, MC, V.

Set on the eastern edge of Hilton Head's main traffic artery, midway between the Palmetto Dunes and Shipyard plantations, this is a three-story complex of functionally furnished but comfortable one-bedroom suites. The setting is wooded and parklike, and both cost-conscious families and business travelers on extended stays appreciate the simple cooking facilities in each accommodation. Each unit has an icemaker, microwave, and coffeemaker. Limited resort facilities are on-site, including a swimming pool, a hot tub, and a cluster of lighted tennis courts.

South Beach Marina Inn. 232 S. Sea Pines Dr., (in Sea Pines Plantation), Hilton Head Island, SC 29938. ☎ **843/671-6498.** www.southbeachvillage.com. 17 units. A/C TV TEL. $109–$159 1-bedroom apt; $169–$210 2-bedroom apt. AE, DISC, MC, V.

Of the dozens of available accommodations in Sea Pines Plantation, this 1986 clapboard-sided complex of marina-front buildings is the only place offering traditional hotel-style rooms by the night. With lots of charm, despite its aggressive theme, the inn meanders over a labyrinth of catwalks and stairways above a complex of shops, souvenir kiosks, and restaurants. Each unit is cozily outfitted with country-style braided rugs, pinewood floors, and homespun-charm decor celebrating rural 19th-century America. All units include a kitchenette.

INEXPENSIVE

Fairfield Inn and Suites by Marriott. 9 Marina Side Dr., Hilton Head Island, SC 29938. ☎ **800/228-2800** or 843/842-4800. Fax 843/842-4800. www.marriott.com. 119 units. A/C TV TEL. $69–$79 double; $105 suite. Rates include continental breakfast. Children 17 and under stay free in parents' room. Senior discounts available. AE, DC, DISC, MC, V.

This three-story motel in Shelter Cove has all the features of Marriott's budget chain, including complimentary coffee in the lobby, no-smoking rooms, and same-day dry cleaning. The inn provides easy access to the beach, golf, tennis, marinas, and shopping. The rooms are wheelchair-accessible and, although they're unremarkable, they are a good value for expensive Hilton Head. Families save extra money by using one of the grills outside for a home-style barbecue, to be enjoyed at one of the picnic tables. In addition, a heated pool is provided.

Hampton Inn. 1 Airport Rd., Hilton Head Island, SC 29926. ☎ **800/HAMPTON** or 843/681-7900. Fax 843/681-4330. www.hampton-inn.com. 124 units (12 with kitchen units). A/C TV TEL. $69–$79 double. Children under 18 stay free in parents' room. Rates include continental breakfast. AE, CB, DC, DISC, MC, V.

Although slightly edged out by its major competitor, the Fairfield Inn by Marriott, this is the second-most-sought-after motel on Hilton Head, especially by families and business travelers. It's 5 miles from the bridge and the closest motel to the airport. Rooms in pastel pinks and greens are quite comfortable and well maintained. Some units have refrigerators. Local calls are free, and no-smoking rooms are available. A health spa features an outdoor pool, whirlpool, and exercise equipment. A coin laundry is on-site, and tennis and golf can be arranged. Bicycles can also be rented.

Quality Inn & Suites. Highway 278, 200 Museum St., Hilton Head Island, SC 29926. ☎ **843/342-7253.** Fax 843/681-3655. www.qualityinnandsuites.com. 138 units. A/C TV TEL. $68–$78 double. AE, DC, DISC, MC, V.

Neck and neck with the Red Roof Inn, this motel attracts families watching their budgets. It's acceptable and clean in every way. Part of the Shoney empire, it offers basic bedrooms with streamlined modern furnishings. Some accommodations are reserved for nonsmokers and people with disabilities. Rooms have king-size or double beds and cable TVs. A large outdoor pool is on-site, and a Chinese restaurant is right next door. The restaurant serves breakfast, lunch, and dinner, and meals can be charged to your room. Golf and tennis can be arranged nearby.

Red Roof Inn. 5 Regency Pkwy. (off U.S. 278 between Palmetto Dunes and Shipyard Plantation), Hilton Head Island, SC 29938. ☎ **800/843-7663** or 843/686-6808. Fax 843/842-3352. www.redroof.com. 112 units. A/C TEL TV. $59.99–$79.99 double; $129 suite. Rates include coffee and USA Today. AE, DC, DISC, MC, V.

Popular with families, this chain hotel is the island's budget special. Its rooms are basic motel-style, with king-size or double beds, but they're well maintained. Local calls are free, and Showtime is on the cable TVs. There's an outdoor pool, and public beaches and sports facilities are close at hand. The hotel is wheelchair-accessible.

VILLA RENTALS

Palmetto Dunes Resort. (P.O. Box 5606) Palmetto Dunes, Hilton Head Island, SC 29938. ☎ **800/845-6130** or 843/785-1161. Fax 843/842-4482. www.palmettodunesresort.com. 500 units. A/C TV TEL. $70–$155 double; $105–$225 villas and condos. Golf and honeymoon packages available. 2-night minimum stay. 50% deposit for reservations. AE, DC, DISC, MC, V.

This relaxed and informal enclave of privately owned villas is set within the sprawling 1,800-acre complex of Palmetto Dunes Plantation, 7 miles south of the bridge. Accommodations range all the way from rather standard hotel rooms, booked mostly by groups, to four-bedroom villas, each of the latter furnished in the owner's personal taste. This is the place for longer stays, ideal for families that want a home away from home when they're traveling. Villas are fully equipped and receive housekeeping service; they're located on the ocean, fairways, or lagoons. Each villa comes with a full kitchen, washer and dryer, living room and dining area, and balcony or patio.

Facilities include a tennis center with 25 courts, 5 golf courses, 3 miles of beach, 20 restaurants, a 10-mile lagoon ideal for canoeing, a playground, and a 200-slip marina.

✪ **Sea Pines Plantation.** Sea Pines (P.O. Box 7000), Hilton Head Island, SC 29938. ☎ **800/SEA-PINES** or 843/785-3333. Fax 843/842-1475. www.seapines.com. 400 units (with kitchenette or kitchen). A/C TV TEL. Year-round $139–$235 1-bedroom villa; $157–$279 2-bedroom villa; $189–$319 3-bedroom villa. Rates are daily, based on 2-night stay. AE, DC, DISC, MC, V.

Since 1955, this has been one of the leading condo developments in America, sprawling across 5,500 acres at the southernmost tip of the island. Don't come to Sea Pines looking for a quick overnight accommodation. The entire place encourages stays of at least a week. Lodgings vary—everything from one- to four-bedroom villas to opulent private homes that are available when the owners are away. The clientele here includes hordes of golfers, because Sea Pines is the home of the MCI Classic, a major stop on the PGA tour. If you're not a Sea Pines guest, you can eat, shop, or enjoy some aspects of its nightlife, but there's a $5 entrance fee. For full details on this varied resort/residential complex, write for a free *Sea Pines Vacation* brochure.

4 Where to Dine

VERY EXPENSIVE

The Barony. In the Westin Resort, 2 Grass Lawn Ave. ☎ **843/681-4000.** Reservations recommended. Main courses $25–$35. AE, DC, DISC, MC, V. Tues–Sat 5:30–10pm. INTERNATIONAL.

The Barony, quick to promote itself as the only AAA four-star restaurant on Hilton Head Island, didn't shy away from installing decor that's a hybrid between a stage set in Old Vienna and a brick-lined, two-fisted steakhouse. The lighting is suitably dim; the drinks are appropriately stiff; and as you dine in your plushly upholstered alcove, you can stare at what might be the largest wrought-iron chandelier in the state. The place caters to a resortgoing crowd of casual diners. Everything is well prepared and in copious portions, although the chef doesn't experiment or stray far from a limited selection of tried-and-true steak-and-lobster fare. Your meal might include New York strip steak, tenderloin of pork with purée of mangos, lobster thermidor, or fresh Atlantic swordfish with pistachios.

✪ **Hemingway's.** In the Hyatt Regency Hilton Head, Palmetto Dunes Resort. ☎ **843/785-1234.** Reservations recommended. Main courses $22–$32. AE, DC, DISC, MC, V. Daily 5–11pm. SEAFOOD/INTERNATIONAL.

This is the most upscale and charming hotel restaurant on the island. The dining experience here offers competent but unpretentious service and a nautical decor that includes a view of an exposed kitchen. The most worthwhile aspect of the menu is fresh fish cooked to perfection. Other choices include filet mignon, bullfighter-style paella, and very appealing charcoal-grilled poultry with lemon-thyme sauce. Your meal might be preceded by a frothy, rum-based tropical concoction flavored with coconut, banana, pineapple, and grenadine.

EXPENSIVE

Alexander's. 76 Queen's Folly, Palmetto Dunes. ☎ **843/785-4999.** Reservations recommended. Main courses $17.50–$24.95. AE, DC, MC, V. Daily 5–10pm. INTERNATIONAL.

One of the most visible independent restaurants (i.e., not associated with a hotel) on Hilton Head lies in a gray-stained, wood-sided building just inside the main entrance into Palmetto Dunes. You'll find a decor that includes Oriental carpets, big-windowed views over the salt marshes, wicker furniture, and an incongruous—some say startling—collection of vintage Harley-Davidson motorcycles, none with more than 1,000 miles on them, dating from 1946, 1948, 1966, and 1993, respectively. Each is artfully displayed as a work of sculpture and as a catalyst to dialogues. Powerful flavors and a forthright approach to food are the rules of the kitchen. The chefs don't allow a lot of innovation on their menu—you've had all these dishes before—but fine ingredients are used, and each dish is prepared with discretion and restraint. Try the oysters Savannah or the bacon-wrapped shrimp and most definitely a bowl of Low Country seafood chowder. Guaranteed to set you salivating are the seafood pasta and the grilled Chilean sea bass in an herb vinaigrette. Steaks, duck, lamb, and pork—all in familiar versions—round out the menu.

✪ **Charlie's L'Etoile Verte.** 1000 Plantation Center. ☎ **843/785-9277.** Reservations required. Lunch $9–$14; main courses $19–$28. AE, DISC, MC, V. Tues–Sat 11:30am–2pm and 6–9pm. INTERNATIONAL.

Outfitted like a tongue-in-cheek version of a Parisian bistro, our favorite restaurant on Hilton Head Island was also a favorite with former President Clinton during one of his island conferences. The atmosphere is unpretentious but elegant, and it bursts with energy in an otherwise-sleepy shopping center. The service is attentive, polite, and infused with an appealingly hip mixture of old- and new-world courtesy. The kitchen has a narrow opening that allows guests to peep inside at the controlled hysteria. Begin with shrimp-stuffed ravioli, and move on to grilled tuna with a jalapeño beurre blanc (white butter) sauce, grilled quail with shiitake mushrooms and a Merlot sauce, or veal chops in peppercorn sauce. End this rare dining experience with biscotti or a "sailor's trifle." The wine list is impressive.

MODERATE

Stellini Italian Restaurant. 302 Moss Creek Village. ☎ 843/837-7000. Dinner main courses $11.95–$21.95. AE, DC, MC, V. Lunch: Mon–Fri 11:30am–2pm. Dinner Mon–Sat 5–till. Closed Sun. ITALIAN.

If you're looking for good, traditional Northern Italian food, visit this offshoot of the original Stellini Italian Restaurant (located at 15 Pope Avenue). You'll dine in a burgundy-colored room with a mural of the Italian wine country. Try the specialty of the house, chicken pancetta: chicken, broccoli, and pancetta ham sauteed in a light cream sauce, served over cappellini. Or go for the hearty veal chop stuffed with prosciutto and mozzarella. The restaurant, situated in the former home of Cattails Restaurant, has a rather inconvenient location: in a shopping center that's 17 miles north of the southern tip of the resort.

Café Europa. Harbour Town, Sea Pines Plantation. ☎ **843/671-3399.** Reservations recommended for dinner. Lunch $10–$12; main courses $17–$23,. AE, DC, MC, V. Daily 11am–2:30pm and 5:30–10pm. CONTINENTAL/SEAFOOD.

This fine European restaurant is at the base of the much-photographed Harbour Town Lighthouse, opening onto a panoramic view of Calibogue Sound and Daufuskie Island. In an informal, cheerful atmosphere, you can order fish that's poached, grilled, baked, or even fried. Baked Shrimp Daufuskie was inspired by local catches; it's stuffed with crab, green peppers, and onions. Grilled grouper is offered with a sauté of tomato, cucumber, dill, and white wine. Specialty dishes include a country-style chicken recipe from Charleston, with honey, fresh cream, and pecans. Tournedos au poivre is flambéed with brandy and simmered in a robust green-peppercorn sauce. The omelets, 14 in all, are perfectly prepared at breakfast (beginning at 10am) and are the island's finest. The bartender's Bloody Mary won an award as the island's best in a *Hilton Head News* contest.

Heritage Grill. In the Harbour Town Golf Links Clubhouse, Sea Pines. ☎ **843/363-4080.** Reservations recommended for dinner only. Lunch sandwiches and platters $7.95–$9.50; dinner main courses $18.50–$29.95. AE, DC, MC, V. Daily 11am–3pm; Wed–Sun 6–10pm. AMERICAN.

For years, this woodsy-looking refuge of golfers and their guests was open only to members of the nearby golf club. Several years ago, however, it opened to the public at large, a fact that's still not widely publicized in Hilton Head, and which sometimes seems to catch some local residents by surprise. Looking something like a postmodern version of a French château, this small-scale affair has views over the 9th hole and room for only about 50 diners at a time. Inside it's sporty-looking and relatively informal during the day, when most of the menu is devoted to thick-stuffed deli-style sandwiches and salads named in honor of golf stars who triumphed on the nearby golf course. Dinners are more formal and more elaborate, with good-tasting dishes such as local shrimp sautéed with ginger, Vidalia onions, and collard greens; roasted rack of American lamb with white beans, spinach and rosemary; very fresh fish prepared any way you want; and an array of thick-cut slabs of meat that include beef, lamb, veal, and chicken.

Hudson's Seafood House on the Docks. 1 Hudson Rd. (Go to Skull Creek just off Square Pope Rd. signposted from U.S. 278). ☎ **843/681-2772.** Reservations not accepted. Main courses $13–$20. AE, DC, MC, V. Daily 11am–2:30pm and 5:30–10pm. SEAFOOD.

Built as a seafood-processing factory in 1912, this restaurant still processes fish, clams, and oysters for local distribution, so you know that everything is fresh. If you're seated in the north dining room, you'll be eating in the original oyster factory. We strongly recommend the crab cakes, steamed shrimp, and the especially appealing blackened catch of the day. Local oysters (seasonal) are also a specialty, breaded and deep-fried. Before and after dinner, stroll on the docks past shrimp boats, and enjoy the view of the mainland and nearby Parris Island. Sunsets here are panoramic. Lunch is served in the Oyster Bar.

Mostly Seafood. In the Hilton Head Island Hilton Resort, Palmetto Dunes Plantation. ☎ **843/842-8000.** Reservations recommended. Main courses $14.95–$27. AE, DC, DISC, MC, V. Daily 5:30–10pm. SEAFOOD/AMERICAN.

The most elegant and innovative restaurant in the Hilton resort, it's noted for the way its chefs make imaginative dishes out of fresh seafood. Something about the decor— backlighting and glass-backed murals in designs of sea-green and blue—creates the illusion that you're floating in a boat. Menu items include fresh grouper, snapper, swordfish, flounder, salmon, trout, halibut, and pompano, prepared in any of seven ways. Dishes that consistently draw applause are corn-crusted fillet of salmon with essence of hickory-smoked veal bacon and peach relish; and "fish in the bag," prepared with fresh grouper, scallops, and shrimp, laced with a dill-flavored cream sauce and baked in a brown paper bag.

✪ Neno's (Neno Il Toscano). 105 Festival Center, Rte. 278. ☎ **843/342-2400.** Reservations recommended. Main courses $8.95–$11.95 at lunch, $13.95–$23.95 at dinner. AE, MC, V. Mon–Fri 11:30am–2pm; Mon–Sat 6–10:30pm. ITALIAN.

One of the best restaurants on Hilton Head is incongruously tucked behind the big windows of what was originally conceived as a shop, inside a busy shopping mall, near a Wal-Mart store. Behind the white translucent curtains you'll find the airy, breezy kind of Italian restaurant you might have expected on southern Italy's Costa Smeralda. Amid mahogany and granite trim, and a mostly cream-colored decor, you can enjoy a rich inventory of summery dishes, with a menu that's enhanced by at least a dozen daily specials every day. Examples include thin-sliced veal served either with smoked prosciutto or with brandy, sausages, and mushrooms; charbroiled tuna on a bed of baked onions and herbs; and savory portobello mushrooms with goat cheese. Extensively promoted by the Food Network, this is the kind of place where well-heeled local residents come with friends and family to dine.

Santa Fe Café. 700 Plantation Center. ☎ 843/785-3838. Reservations recommended. Main courses $4.95–$7.95 at lunch, $14–$25 at dinner. AE, DISC, MC, V. Mon–Fri noon–2pm and daily 6–10pm. MEXICAN.

The best, most stylish Mexican restaurant on Hilton Head, it has rustic, Southwestern-inspired decor and cuisine that infuses traditional recipes with nouvelle flair. Menu items are often presented in colors as bright as the Painted Desert. Dishes might include tequila shrimp, herb-roasted chicken with jalapeño cornbread stuffing and mashed potatoes laced with red chiles, grilled tenderloin of pork with smoked habañero sauce and sweet-potato fries, and worthy burritos and chimichangas. The chiles rellenos are exceptional, stuffed with California goat cheese and sun-dried tomatoes. The quesadilla is one of the most beautifully presented dishes of any restaurant in town.

INEXPENSIVE

The Crazy Crab North. U.S. 278 at Jarvis Creek. ☎ **803/681-5021.** Reservations not accepted. Lunch $6–$15, main courses $11.95–$22.95. AE, DC, DISC, MC, V. Daily 11:30am–10pm. SEAFOOD.

This is a branch of the chain that's most likely to be patronized by locals. In a modern, low-slung building near the bridge that connects the island with the South Carolina mainland, it serves baked, broiled, or fried versions of stuffed flounder; seafood kebabs; oysters; the catch of the day; and any combination thereof. She-crab soup and New England–style clam chowder are prepared fresh daily; children's menus are available; and desserts are a high point for chocoholics.

Hofbrauhaus. In the Pope Avenue Mall. ☎ **843/785-3663.** Reservations recommended. Early-bird dinner (5–6:30pm only) $12.50; main courses $14–$21. AE, MC, V. Daily 5–10pm. GERMAN.

A sanitized German beer hall, this family favorite serves locals and visitors such national specialties as grilled bratwurst and smoked Westphalian ham, along with Wiener schnitzel and sauerbraten. One specialty that we like to order is roast duckling with spaetzle, red cabbage, and orange sauce. Note the stein and mug collection as you're deciding which of the large variety of German beers to order. A children's menu is available.

Taste of Thailand. Plantation Center, 807 William Hilton Parkway. ☎ **843/341-6500.** Reservations recommended. Main courses $5–$8 at lunch, $12–$17 at dinner. AE, DC, MC, V. Tues–Fri 11:30am–2pm and 5–11pm. THAI.

Although this place is surpassed by its more glamorous neighbors, Charlie's and the Santa Fe Café, it does a bustling business with cost-conscious diners who appreciate the emphasis on exotic curries, lemongrass, and coconuts. Among scattered examples of Thai woodcarvings and handicrafts, you can enjoy a choice but limited menu offering beef, pork, chicken, shrimp, mussels, or tofu in a choice of different flavors. One of our favorites is chicken with stir-fried vegetables, Thai basil, and oyster sauce. The hottest dish is the green curry, but equally delectable is the curry with roasted peanuts and red chiles flavored with cumin seeds. Cold Thai spring rolls appear as an appetizer. A hot and sour soup is always on the menu, as is a spicy squid salad.

5 Hilton Head After Dark

Hilton Head doesn't have Myrtle Beach's nightlife, but enough is here, centered mainly in hotels and resorts. Casual dress (but not swimming attire) is acceptable in most clubs.

Cultural interest focuses on the **Hilton Head Playhouse,** in the Self Family Arts Center, 14 Shelter Cove Lane (☎ **843/842-ARTS**), which enjoys one of the best theatrical reputations in the Southeast. Hilton Head Playhouse Productions and other groups are sponsored at two venues. The Elizabeth Wallace Theater, a 350-seat, state-of-the-art theater, was added to the multiplex in 1996. The older Dunnagan's Alley Theater is located in a renovated warehouse. A wide range of musicals, contemporary comedies, and classic dramas is presented. Show times are 8pm Tuesday to Saturday, with a Sunday matinee at 2pm. Adult ticket prices range from $45 for a musical to $20 for a play. Children 16 and under are charged $8 to $15.

Quarterdeck. Harbour Town, Sea Pines Plantation. ☎ **843/671-2222.**

Our favorite waterfront lounge is the best place on the island to watch sunsets, but you can visit at any time during the afternoon and in the evening until 2am. Try to go early and grab one of the outdoor rocking chairs to prepare yourself for nature's light show. There's dancing every night to beach music and top-40 hits. Daily 9am to 10pm.

Remy's. 28 Arrow Rd. ☎ **843/842-3800.**

Got the munchies? At Remy's, you can devour buckets of oysters or shrimp, served with the inevitable fries. The setting is rustic and raffish, and live music is provided. Daily 11am to 4am.

The Salty Dog Cafe. South Beach Marina. ☎ **843/671-2233.**

Locals used to keep this laid-back place near the beach to themselves, but now more and more visitors are showing up. Soft guitar music or Jimmy Buffett is often played. Dress is casual. Sit under one of the sycamores, enjoying your choice of food from an outdoor grill or buffet. Daily until 2am.

Signals. 130 Shipyard Dr., in the Crowne Plaza Resort. ☎ **843/842-2400.**

In this upscale resort, you can enjoy live bands (often, 1940s golden oldies), along with R&B, blues, and jazz. The dance floor is generally crowded. Live bands perform Tuesday to Sunday from 9pm to 1am, and live jazz is presented on Monday from 6pm to 9:30pm. A Sunday jazz brunch is held from 11am to 1:30pm.

6 A Side Trip to Beaufort

Some 30 miles north of Hilton Head Island, ✪ **Beaufort** (Low Country pronunciation *Bew*-fort) is an old seaport with narrow streets shaded by huge live oaks and lined with 18th-century homes. The oldest house (at Port Republic and New streets) was built in 1717. This was the second area in North America to be discovered by the Spanish (1520), the site of the first fort on the continent (1525), and the first attempted settlement (1562). Several forts have been excavated, dating from 1566 and 1577.

Beaufort has been used as a setting for several films, including *The Big Chill.* Scenes from the Paramount blockbuster *Forrest Gump,* starring Tom Hanks, and *The Prince of Tides* were also shot here.

If you're traveling from the north, take I-95 to Exit 33; then follow the signs to the center of Beaufort. From the south, take I-95 to Exit 8 and follow the signs. From

Hilton Head, go on U.S. 278 west, and after N.C. 170 North joins U.S. 278, follow N.C. 170 into Beaufort.

The **Beaufort Chamber of Commerce,** 1006 Bay St. (P.O. Box 910), Beaufort, SC 29901 (☎ **843/524-3163**), has information and self-guided tours of this historic town. It's open daily 9:30am to 5:30pm. If your plans are for early to mid-October, write the **Historic Beaufort Foundation,** P.O. Box 11, Beaufort, SC 29901 (☎ **843/ 524-6334**), for specific dates and detailed information about its 3 days of antebellum house and garden tours.

A tour called **The Spirit of Old Beaufort,** 210 Scott's St. (☎ **843/525-0459**), takes you on a journey through the old town, exploring local history, architecture, horticulture, and Low Country life. You'll see houses that are not accessible on other tours. Your host, clad in period costume, will guide you for 2 hours from Tuesday to Saturday at 10am, 11:30am, 1:15pm, and 3:30pm. The cost is $15 for adults, $7 for children 12 and under. Tours depart from just behind the John Market Verdier House Museum.

John Market Verdier House Museum, 801 Bay St. (☎ **843/524-6334**), is a restored 1802 house partially furnished to depict the life of a merchant planter during the period 1800–25. It's one of the best examples of the Federal period and was once known as the Lafayette Building, because the Marquis de Lafayette is said to have spoken here in 1825. It's open Monday to Saturday from 11am to 4pm, charging $4 for adults and $2 for children.

St. Helen's Episcopal Church, 501 Church St. (☎ **843/522-1722**), traces its origin back to 1712. Visitors, admitted free Monday to Saturday from 10am to 4pm, can see its classic interior and visit the graveyard, where tombstones served as operating tables during the Civil War.

Beaufort is also the home of the famous **U.S. Marine Corps Recruit Depot.** The visitor center (go to Building 283) is open daily from 10am to 4:30pm. You can take a driving tour or a bus tour (free) around the grounds, where you'll see an Iwo Jima monument; a monument to the Spanish settlement of Santa Elena (1521); and a memorial to Jean Ribaut, the Huguenot who founded Beaufort in 1562.

WHERE TO STAY

✪ **Beaufort Inn.** 809 Port Republic St., Beaufort, SC 29902. ☎ **843/521-9000.** Fax 843/ 521-9500. www.beaufortinn.com. E-mail: bftinn@hargray.com. 12 units. A/C MINIBAR TV TEL. $125–$350 double. Rates include full gourmet breakfast. AE, DISC, MC, V.

This is the most appealing hotel in Beaufort and the place where whatever movie star happens to be shooting a film in town is likely to stay. The woodwork and moldings inside are among the finest in Beaufort, and the circular, four-story staircase has been the subject of numerous photographs and architectural awards. The bedrooms, each decorated in brightly colored individual style, are conversation pieces. A wine bar, grill room, and rose garden are more recent additions.

✪ **Cuthbert House Inn.** 1203 Bay St., Beaufort, SC 29901. ☎ **800/327-9275** or 843/521-1315. Fax 843/521-1314. www.cuthberthouseinn.com. E-mail: cuthbert@hargray. com. 6 units. A/C MINIBAR TV TEL. Mar–Nov $145–$225 double; Dec–Feb $125–$225 double, suites $195–$205 year-round. Rates include full breakfast and afternoon tea or refreshments. AE, DISC, MC, V.

One of the grand old B&Bs of South Carolina, this showcase Southern home was built in 1790 in classic style. The inn was remodeled shortly after the Civil War to take on a more Victorian aura, but its present owner, Sharon Groves, has worked to modernize it without sacrificing its grace or antiquity. Graffiti carved by Union soldiers can still be seen on the fireplace mantel in the Eastlake room. Bedrooms are elegantly furnished in Southern plantation style, and some have four-poster beds. The inn is filled with large parlors and sitting rooms, and has the spacious hallways and 12-foot ceilings that are characteristic of Greek Revival homes. Modern amenities and conveniences such as private baths have been tastefully tucked in. Some bathrooms have the old cast-iron soaking tubs. At breakfast in the conservatory, you can order such delights as Georgia ice cream (cheese grits) and freshly made breads.

Red House Inn. 601 Bay St., Beaufort, SC 29902. ☎ **843/524-9030.** Fax 843/521-4286. 9 units. $125–$225 double. Rates include full breakfast, afternoon tea, and wine and cheese. AE, DISC, MC, V.

One of the most elegant historic homes in town, this B&B is on a quiet road with a view of a saltwater estuary. It was built in 1852 by the owners of a plantation on nearby Dataw Island and was used by Union troops as an officers' club during the Civil War. The house later fell into disrepair; it was transformed into a B&B in the 1980s. Eight of the rooms have working fireplaces, and all have TV sets.

The Rhett House Inn. 1009 Craven St., Beaufort, SC 29902. ☎ **843/524-9030.** Fax 843/524-1310. www.rhetthouseinn.com. E-mail: rhetthse@hargray.com. 17 units. A/C TV TEL. $150–$300 double. Rates include continental breakfast, afternoon tea, and evening hors d'oeuvres. AE, MC, V. Free parking.

This inn is certainly very popular, at least with Hollywood film crews. Because it was a site for *Forrest Gump*, *The Prince of Tides*, and *The Big Chill*, chances are that you've seen it before. It's a Mobil and AAA four-star inn in a restored 1820 Greek Revival plantation-type home. Rooms are furnished with English and American antiques, and ornamented with Oriental rugs; eight contain whirlpools. The veranda makes an ideal place to sit and view the gardens. The inn is open year-round. Children under 5 are not accepted.

Sea Island Inn. 1015 Bay St., Beaufort, SC 29902. ☎ **800/528-1234** or 843/522-2090. Fax 843/521-4858. www.bestwestern.com. 43 units. A/C TV TEL. $89–$105 double. Rates include continental breakfast. AE, DC, DISC, MC, V.

This is a basic two-story motel with very reasonable rates for what you get. Few of the rooms have sea views; most overlook a small swimming pool, separated from the rest of the motel in a brick-sided courtyard. Although the rooms are nothing special, they're comfortable and clean.

Two Suns Inn. 1705 Bay St., Beaufort, SC 29902. ☎ **800/534-4244** or 843/522-1122. Fax 843/522-1122. www.twosunsinn.com. E-mail: twosuns@islc.net. 6 units. TV TEL. $133–$159 double. Rates include full breakfast and afternoon tea. AE, DC MC, V.

When this place was built in 1917, it was one of the grandest homes in its prosperous neighborhood, offering views of the coastal road and the tidal flatlands beyond. Every imaginable modern (at the time) convenience was added, including a baseboard vacuum-cleaning system, an electric call box, and steam heat. Later, when it became housing for unmarried teachers in the public schools, the place ran down. But in 1990, a retired music teacher and band leader, Ron Kay, and his wife, Carroll, saw the inn—"an accident stop along the way to North Carolina," they say—bought it, and transformed it into a cozy B&B. Part of the inn's appeal stems from its lack of pretension, as a glance at the homey bedrooms and uncomplicated furnishings will show you.

WHERE TO DINE

✪ **Beaufort Inn Restaurant.** In the Beaufort Inn, 809 Port Republic St. ☎ **843/521-9000.** Reservations recommended. Main courses $21–$27.50. AE, MC, V. Mon–Sat 6–10pm, Sun 11am–2pm. INTERNATIONAL.

Stylish and urbane, and awash with colonial lowland references, this is the local choice for celebratory or business dinners, amid candlelit surrounds. Meat courses include chicken piccata with artichokes and sun-dried tomatoes, and an excellent grilled filet mignon with herbal Gorgonzola butter and shiitake mushrooms; vegetarian main courses include roasted-pepper-and-eggplant torte. On the menu is a variation on a dish whose invention has been claimed by a string of other restaurants in the South Carolina Low Country: crispy whole flounder with strawberry-watermelon chutney.

Emily's. 906 Port Republic St. ☎ **843/522-1866.** Reservations recommended. Tapas $7; main courses $20–$23. AE, DISC, MC, V. Drinks and tapas Mon–Sat 4–10pm; main courses Mon–Sat 6–10pm. INTERNATIONAL.

This is our favorite restaurant in Beaufort, a spot whose ambience and attitude put us in mind of Scandinavia. That's hardly surprising, because the bearded owner is an emigré from Sweden who feels comfortable in the South Carolina lowlands after years of life at sea. Some folks just go to the bar to sample tapas: miniature portions of tempura shrimp, fried scallops, stuffed peppers, and at least 50 other items. Menu items might include cream of mussel and shrimp soup, rich enough for a main course; fillet "black and white" (fillets of beef and pork served with béarnaise sauce); duck with orange sauce; a meltingly tender Wiener schnitzel; and the catch of the day. Everything is served in stomach-stretching portions.

Olly's By the Bay. 822 Bay St. ☎ **843/524-2500.** Reservations recommended but not necessary. Lunch $5.95–$14.95; main courses $12.95–$19.75;. AE, DC, DISC, MC, V. Mon–Sat 11am–3pm, 6–9pm. SEAFOOD/STEAKHOUSE.

This dead-center restaurant seems to change its stripes every other year or so. Today it's an informal haven, both a bar and restaurant. As management admits, we have "cooks only—no chefs," so you know what to expect. Nonetheless, you get some of the best steaks in the area, cooked to your specifications on the grill. A "shrimp burger" is the house specialty. The catch of the day can be broiled, blackened, or sautéed. Try the oyster sandwich or the golden scallops. To keep the menu a little diverse, a few pasta dishes are also offered.

Myrtle Beach & the Grand Strand

12

One of the top vacation destinations along the East Coast, the Myrtle Beach/Grand Strand area stretches south from the South Carolina state line at Little River to Georgetown. It's 98 miles north of Charleston but a world away in ambience.

On a summer day, the population here exceeds half a million people. The ✪ **Grand Strand** hosts more than twice as many visitors each year as Hawaii. The beach is not the only reason people come—shopping, golfing, sightseeing, and live theater are also draws. In the past few years, Myrtle Beach has grown into a year-round destination, and as a result, South Carolina now ranks second only to Florida as a vacation destination, ahead of California, New Jersey, and North Carolina.

Because of its deeply entrenched tradition of theatrical entertainment, the Grand Strand has become a rival to Branson, Missouri, and Nashville as a site for country-western music and variety theater performances that combine several styles of music with comedy, circus acts, ice skating, and more.

Myrtle Beach is at the center of the Grand Strand, a 60-mile string of beaches. Named for the abundance of myrtle trees in this area, Myrtle Beach is an ideal base for a Grand Strand vacation. As the largest beach resort along the Grand Strand, it has the most facilities, entertainment, and restaurants, and as a result, it attracts the most visitors. But if you're looking for a wild, swinging kind of beach resort, this isn't it. The tone is that of a family resort, with almost as much attention paid to children's needs as to those of adults. Many hotels and motels provide activity programs and playgrounds with supervision, and nearly all have baby-sitter lists for parents who like a little nightlife.

The big attraction in the area is the beach, of course. Sunbathing, swimming, boating, and all the other water sports rank first among things to do. Fishing is first-rate, whether you cast your line from the surf, a public pier, or a charter boat. Surf fishing is permitted all along the beach. Charter boats ("head boats," as the locals say) are available at marinas up and down the Strand, and even at the height of the season, you'll be able to book a trip without much difficulty.

You can swing a golf club at any of 87 courses. Most motels and hotels hold guest-membership privileges, entitling you to reduced greens fees. The season extends from February to November. There are also more than 200 public and private tennis courts in the Grand Strand area.

But although the area's tourist growth may be almost unparalleled in America, there are some clouds on the horizon. Environmentalists are concerned that the rampaging development puts the region's natural beauty at risk. Longtime promoters fear that Myrtle Beach's family-friendly atmosphere may be threatened. (Families make up an important part of the trade, and efforts to keep it that way have meant banning thong bathing suits and relegating topless clubs to an industrial park.) Others bemoan the theme-park atmosphere, likening the Grand Strand to a combination of Disneyland and Las Vegas (without the casinos).

Change is slowly coming to Myrtle Beach. North European tour groups are coming to the Grand Strand in increasing numbers, drawn by advertisements that tout the area as a seaside resort that evokes heartland America at its most authentic, least apologetic, and most unselfconscious. Food and booze are super-cheap. And corporate entrepreneurs are pouring money into less expensive versions of Disney World, where a family can amuse itself at rates much, much lower than those offered in Orlando.

1 Essentials

GETTING THERE **Myrtle Beach International Airport** (☎ **843/448-1589**) has scheduled air service via **Air Canada** (☎ 888/442-7533; www.aircanada.ca), **Delta ASA** (☎ 800/221-1212; www.delta.com), **Midway Airlines** (☎ 800/446-4392; www.midwayair.com), **Spirit Airlines** (☎ 800/772-7117; www.spirit.air.com), **US Airways** (☎ 800/428-4322; www.usairways.com), and **Vanguard Airlines** (☎ 800/826-4827; www.flyvanguard.com). If you're driving, U.S. 17 runs north and south along the Grand Strand, and U.S. 17 Business runs through Myrtle Beach; U.S. 501 runs east from I-95.

VISITOR INFORMATION The **Myrtle Beach Area Chamber of Commerce** is at 1200 N. Oak St. (P.O. Box 2115), Myrtle Beach, SC 29578 (☎ **800/356-3016** or 843/626-7444 to order literature only; www.mbchamber.com), open Monday to Friday from 8:30am to 5pm and on Saturday from 9am to 5pm. One publication jam-packed with specific area information is *Stay & Play* (available from the chamber of commerce).

2 The Beaches, the Links & Beyond

Everybody—and we mean that—heads for the **Myrtle Beach Pavilion Amusement Park,** 9th Avenue North and Ocean Boulevard (☎ **843/448-6456**), which received a much-needed touchup in 1994. This horseshoe-shape entertainment complex offers all the summer fun you may remember from the 1960s and 1970s, with rock 'n' roll blasting away, carnival rides, and a carousel. Along with the kiddie rides, the park has the largest flume in the Carolinas, not to mention sidewalk cafes, video games, and even a teenage nightclub where no alcohol is served. The pavilion covers nearly a dozen acres. One of the newest attractions is the Hurricane roller coaster. An all-day pass costs $21.95 for adults, $10.95 for seniors 55 and up, and $10.95 for children shorter than 42 inches. You can purchase individual tickets for $5 (allows 7 rides). The park is open March to October: March to May and in September and October, Monday to Friday from 6pm to midnight and on Saturday and Sunday from 1pm to midnight; June to September, daily from 1pm to midnight.

Other family fun attractions include the **Ripley's Believe It or Not Museum,** 901 N. Ocean Blvd., next to the pavilion (☎ **843/448-2331**). The museum's typically bizarre collection ranges from a two-headed calf to a replica of Cleopatra's barge

The Grand Strand

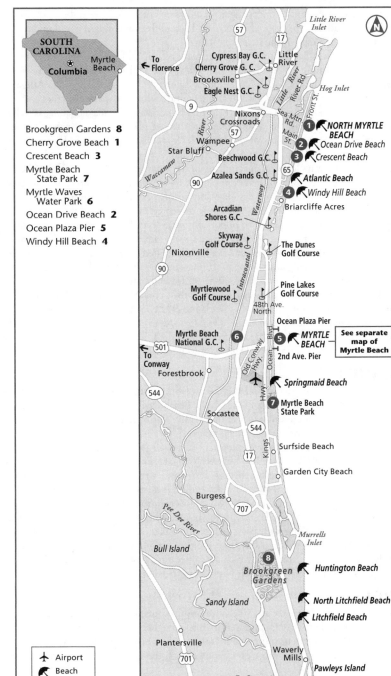

SOUTH CAROLINA
Columbia ★   Myrtle Beach

Brookgreen Gardens **8**
Cherry Grove Beach **1**
Crescent Beach **3**
Myrtle Beach State Park **7**
Myrtle Waves Water Park **6**
Ocean Drive Beach **2**
Ocean Plaza Pier **5**
Windy Hill Beach **4**

To Florence

Little River Inlet

Cypress Bay G.C.
Cherry Grove G. C.
Brooksville
Eagle Nest G.C.
Little River
Hog Inlet

Nixons Crossroads
Wampee
Star Bluff
Beechwood G.C.
Azalea Sands G.C.

❶ NORTH MYRTLE BEACH
❷ Ocean Drive Beach
❸ Crescent Beach
Atlantic Beach
❹ Windy Hill Beach
Briarcliffe Acres

Arcadian Shores G.C.
Skyway Golf Course
Nixonville
The Dunes Golf Course

Myrtlewood Golf Course
Pine Lakes Golf Course
48th Ave. North

Ocean Plaza Pier
Myrtle Beach National G.C.
❻
❺ MYRTLE BEACH
2nd Ave. Pier

See separate map of Myrtle Beach

To Conway
Forestbrook

Springmaid Beach
❼ Myrtle Beach State Park

Socastee

Surfside Beach

Garden City Beach

Burgess

Pee Dee River
Bull Island

Murrells Inlet

❽ Brookgreen Gardens
Sandy Island

Huntington Beach
North Litchfield Beach
Litchfield Beach

Plantersville

Waverly Mills

Pawleys Island

To Georgetown

✈ Airport
☂ Beach

constructed from confectioner's sugar. In all, there are some 750 exhibits. Admission is $9.95 for adults, $6.50 for children 6 to 12, and free for children 5 and under. The museum is open daily from 10am to 10pm.

One of Myrtle Beach's most-visited attractions was built in the mid-1990s on an interconnected series of boardwalks that sprawl over 15 acres of a low-lying saltwater marsh adjacent to the shopping complex known as Barefoot Landing. **Alligator Adventure** is a theme-based natural area teeming with many species of crocs and alligators from throughout the world. You'll find hundreds of Florida alligators, as well as two or three extremely rare albino alligators that are prized by alligator breeders and zoologists and reputed to be worth as much as $1 million each. Behind thick plates of glass is a colony of Komodo dragons, whose bite is so putrid and filled with bacteria that it almost always leads to an agonizing death for anyone unlucky enough to be bit. Also on hand are colonies of snakes, and open-to-view facilities for breeding and keeping endangered species of reptiles alive and healthy. Some kind of show (snake handling, for example, or alligator feeding) is presented every hour on the hour during open hours. You'll have plenty of opportunities to learn how smart and very dangerous many of the croc and alligator species really are, so come here with a healthy respect for the creatures, and never leave the designated observation areas. Year-round, the place is open daily from 9am to 10pm—until 11pm from June to September. Admission costs $11.95 for adults and $7.95 for children ages 4 to 12.

A final attraction, again mainly for the kids, is the **Myrtle Beach National Wax Museum,** 1000 N. Ocean Blvd. (☎ **843/448-9921**), where everybody from Lincoln to Elvis Presley to the participants in *The Last Supper* is re-created. Admission is $5 for adults, $3 for children 6 to 12, and free for children 5 and under. It's open from late February until mid-September. Daily 9am to midnight.

BEACHES

Sand is mostly hard-packed and the color of brown sugar, to which it's often compared. The main action is around the Myrtle Beach Pavilion and Amusement Park (see above) at Ocean Boulevard and Ninth Avenue North. If you'd like more seclusion, head north of 79th Avenue for several miles.

The beach has lifeguards and plenty of fast-food joints. Amazingly, there are no public toilets. South Carolina law, however, obligates hotels to allow beach buffs to use their facilities. (Many male beachgoers don't bother to go inside the hotels but use walls instead—a habit that has provoked endless local-newspaper comment.)

At the southern tier of the beach, **Myrtle Beach State Park** (☎ **843/238-5325**) offers 312 acres of pinewoods and a sandy beach. Admission to the park is $2 per person. It has toilets, along with pavilions, picnic tables, and a swimming pool. Campsites cost $22. It's possible to fish from the pier for $4.50. The park is full of nature trails and offers 350 campsites, which are rented on a first-come, first-served basis for $20 per site. The park is open daily from 6am to 10pm.

GOLF

Golf enthusiasts can tee off at 110 championship courses, making it possible to play a different course every day for almost 3 months straight. Many local courses host major professional and amateur tournaments, such as the DuPont World Amateur Tournament. One of the sport's most prestigious events, the Energizer Senior Tour, is held November 6 to 12.

Variety is a contributing factor to the success and popularity of Grand Strand golf courses, which come in many shapes, sizes, and degrees of difficulty. Courses have

Myrtle Beach

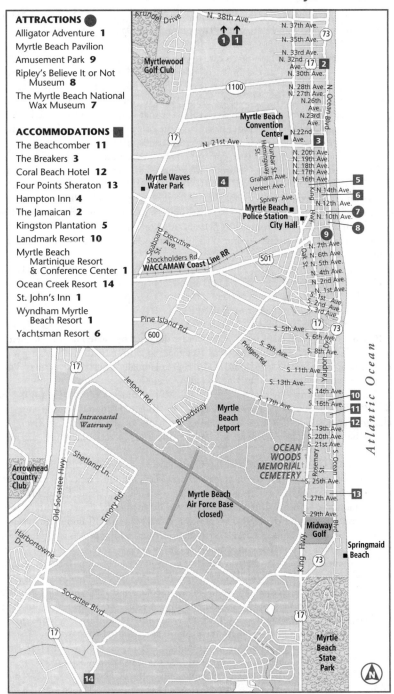

ATTRACTIONS ●

Alligator Adventure **1**

Myrtle Beach Pavilion
Amusement Park **9**

Ripley's Believe It or Not
Museum **8**

The Myrtle Beach National
Wax Museum **7**

ACCOMMODATIONS ■

The Beachcomber **11**

The Breakers **3**

Coral Beach Hotel **12**

Four Points Sheraton **13**

Hampton Inn **4**

The Jamaican **2**

Kingston Plantation **5**

Landmark Resort **10**

Myrtle Beach
Martinique Resort
& Conference Center **1**

Ocean Creek Resort **14**

St. John's Inn **1**

Wyndham Myrtle
Beach Resort **1**

Yachtsman Resort **6**

been designed by some of the best known names in golf: Jack Nicklaus, Arnold Palmer, Rees Jones, Tom Fazio, Gary Player, Don Ross, Dan Maple, Tom Jackson, and Pete and P. B. Dye.

Golf-course architects have taken care to protect the habitats of indigenous wildlife. Players find themselves in the midst of towering Carolina pines or giant live oaks draped in Spanish moss. Some courses overlook huge bluffs with the Atlantic Ocean or Intracoastal Waterway in the background. Some unusual attractions are featured: a private airstrip adjoining a clubhouse, a cable car that crosses the Intracoastal Waterway, and alligators lurking in water hazards. Some courses are built on the grounds of historic rice plantations, which offer Old South atmosphere.

Although golf is played all year, spring and autumn are the busiest seasons. Many golf packages include room, board, and greens fees. For information, call **Golf Holiday** (☎ 800/845-4653).

Arcadian Shores, 701 Hilton Rd., Arcadian Shores (☎ 800/449-5217 or 843/449-5217), an 18-hole, par-72 course, opened in 1974, when it was created by noted golf architect Rees Jones. Just 5 miles north of Myrtle Beach off U.S. 17, the course has bent-grass greens winding through a stately live-oak grove. Electric carts are required, and greens fees are $45 to $52.

Azalea Sands, 2100 U.S. 17, North Myrtle Beach (☎ 800/253-2312 or 843/272-6191), opened in 1972. The 18-hole course features white-sand traps and blue lakes. Designed by architect Gene Hamm, it's a popular course for golfers of all handicaps. Greens fees range from $30 to $35.

Beachwood, 1520 U.S. 17, Crescent Section, North Myrtle Beach (☎ 800/526-4889 or 843/272-6168), is another course designed by Gene Hamm. Opened in 1968, it has 18 holes, charging greens fees ranging from $26 to $42. It's a par-72 course with blue tees of 6,755 yards. The course annually hosts the Carolinas' PGA Senior's Championship and DuPont World Amateur.

Aberdeen Country Club, S.C. 9, North Myrtle Beach (☎ 800/344-0982 or 843/399-2660), is a 27-hole course designed by Tom Jackson and opened in 1990, charging greens fees of $38 to $73. Along the banks of the Waccamaw River, this course has Bermuda greens, along with a pro shop and a practice area with a driving range.

Caledonia Golf Course and Fishing Club, Pawleys Island (☎ 800/483-6800), is set atop what used to be a series of marshy rice paddies, and some of its links are graced with century-old oak trees. This golf course has an intelligent layout favored by pros, and a clubhouse whose architecture was inspired by an antique Low Country plantation house. Its only drawback involves a location that's about a 30-minute drive south of Myrtle Beach. A flotilla of charter boats and deep-sea fishing pros is associated with this place as well. Greens fees range from $45 to $95.

✪ **Legends,** U.S. 501, Myrtle Beach (☎ 800/552-2660 or 843/236-9318), designed by Pete Dye and Tom Doak, opened in 1990. The 54-hole, par-72 course charges greens fees of $39 to $59. Its Mooreland Course was ranked by *Golf Digest* as one of the top five new public courses in America in 1991. Dye's flair for deep bunkers, undulating fairways and greens, and signature bulkheads have transformed this course into one of the strongest challenges along the East Coast. The 42,000-square-foot Scottish-style clubhouse is an impressive entry to the course. Heathland, designed by Doak, has been called "the next best thing to visiting Scotland."

Myrtlewood, 48th Avenue (U.S. 17 Business), North Myrtle Beach (☎ 800/283-3633 or 843/449-5134), a 36-hole, par-72 course, was designed by architects

Ed Ault and George Cobb. Greens fees range from $39 to $50. Bordering the Intra-coastal Waterway, the Pines Course is the fourth-oldest at Myrtle Beach, measuring 6,406 yards. The Palmetto Course is one of the best in the area, with bent-grass putting greens. It stretches for 7,000 yards.

Pine Lakes Country Club, 5603 Woodside Avenue, Myrtle Beach (☎ **800/ 446-6817**), is semi-private, but under some conditions (such as whenever the fairways aren't too crowded), out-of-towners are allowed to play. Established in 1920, it's the oldest golf course in the region, despite a name change that occurred in 1944. Linked to the early days of *Sports Illustrated* magazine, the course is permeated with a more distinctive Scottish flavor than any other golf course in town. It can even get very posh, as when mimosas and/or Low Country stews and chowders are served on the links. Greens fees range from $87 to $135.

OTHER OUTDOOR PURSUITS

✪ **FISHING**   Because of the warming temperature of the Gulf Stream, fishing is good from early spring until around Christmas. You can pursue king mackerel, spade-fish, amberjack, barracuda, sea bass, and Spanish mackerel, along with grouper and red snapper. Great fishing is available aboard any boat of **Captain Dick's,** Business Highway 17, at Myrtle Beach South Strand and Murrells Inlet (☎ **800/344-FISH** or 843/651-3676). Captain Dick offers three charters that go as far as 60 miles offshore. The Sea Bass Fishing Adventure is a half-day trip priced at $84 for adults and $23 per child. The rates include rod and reel, bait, tackle, license. Sightseers can also take this trip for $17 per person.

The Sundown Special Fishing trip is an 8-hour trip that goes slightly farther out than the Sea Bass Adventure, in search of bigger fish. Rates are $49 for adults and $29 for children, including rod and reel, bait, tackle, and license. Electric reels are avail-able for $9. The All Day Gulf Stream trip is an 11-hour jaunt that departs at 7am in search of red snapper, grouper, triggerfish, and amberjack. The rate of $69 per person includes rod and reel, bait, tackle, and license. Electric reels are also available for this trip for an additional $12.

Once a month, between March and November, Captain Dick's hosts the Overnight Gulf Stream fishing expedition for the true fishing enthusiast. The cost of the 21-hour trip, which departs at 8am on Saturday night and returns at 5pm on Sunday, is $135. Rates include rod and reel, bait, tackle, and license; an electric reel is an additional $14. On this trip, the price of the electric reel may well be worth it.

SAILING & WINDSURFING   **Captain Dick's,** Business Highway 17, at Myrtle Beach South Strand and Murrells Inlet (☎ **800/344-FISH** or 843/651-3676), has cruises that offer stunning views of the Grand Strand. The Saltwater Marsh Explorer Adventure is a 2½-hour ecology trip that allows you to see marine life in its true ele-ment. Rates are $16 for adults and $11 for children 12 and under. The "Cruising the Beach" Ocean Sightseeing Cruise along the coast of Myrtle Beach wraps up the trip with a sunset at sea. Rates are $14 for adults and $6 children ages 6 to 12. The Pirate Adventure Voyage recalls the bygone days of swashbuckling. Your guide is the friendly resident pirate who tells stories of the days when Blackbeard and other sea dogs rav-aged the waters. Rates are $11 for adults and $6 for children 6 to 12. Although none of the trips includes refreshments, snacks and soft drinks are available for purchase on the boats.

You can rent windsurfers at **Sail and Ski,** 515 Hwy. 501, Myrtle Beach (☎ **843/626-7245**), from April to September.

Building a Better Bear

One of the most Disneyesque shopping and entertainment malls anywhere is **Broadway at the Beach.** Identified by the neo-Pharonaic pyramid of the Hard Rock Cafe, the complex sprawls between 22nd and 29th boulevards. It's here where you'll find the most unusual shop in Myrtle Beach. **Build a Bear Workshop,** Celebrity Circle, Broadway at the Beach (☎ 843/445-7675), functions more as a family-entertainment attraction than a conventional store. It's part of a national chain established by St. Louis–based Maxine Clark in the late 1980s. Ever since, it has proved amazingly popular with the arts-and-crafts crowd who, with or without their children, come to this place in droves. You'll be confronted with all the raw materials you'll need to make the teddy bear of your dreams, selecting its eyes, clothing, smiles (or lack thereof), and gender. You can choose your bear's "voice" from a prerecorded selection, the houses or caves it inhabits, and any accessories that will communicate very clearly to everyone your bear's unique eccentricities, quirks, and lifestyle. Come here to see how you behave when confronted with the opportunity to play genetic engineer, and also for an insight into the passion with which this creative expression is favored both by conventional-looking families with children and single adults of all ilk— including motorcycle fetishists dressed in highly unconventional ways. By the time the stuffing and compilation of your bear is complete, it will cost anywhere from $20 to $50, depending on the raw materials that went into it. Be prepared to spend at least 90 minutes on-site. An advisory dialogue with an on-site "bear counselor" can be enormously helpful in figuring out the nuances of this place, but the shop is well-equipped with a perky staff ready to indulge you, your kids, or your grandparents in equally cheerful good measure. Open daily 10am to 11pm.

SCUBA DIVING Several wrecks off the coast and a wide variety of tropical fish make scuba diving a popular pastime. One of the best outfitters is **Coastal Scuba,** at 1626 Hwy. 17 S., North Myrtle Beach (☎ 843/361-3323), which has full PADI certification. Charters range from $55 to $85 per person, and boats go out anywhere from 6 to 55 miles offshore. Complete PADI certification costs $200 to $275, with equipment included.

TENNIS The **Myrtle Beach Public Courts,** 3200 Oak St., on Myrtle Beach (no phone), offer a trio of outdoor and asphalt courts next to the Myrtle Beach Recreation Center. A more elegant place to play is the **Kingston Plantation Sport & Health Club,** 9760 Kings Rd., Myrtle Beach (☎ 843/497-2444), home of the annual GTE Tennis Festival. Such greats as Pete Sampras and Jimmy Connors have played these five Har-Tru courts. There are also four outdoor clay courts. Courts cost $17.75 per hour.

Myrtle Beach Tennis & Swim Club, U.S. 17 Business, across from Dixie Stampede, at Myrtle Beach (☎ 843/449-4486), has 10 composition courts, 2 of which are lighted for night play. Courts cost $5 per player per hour for doubles. The cost is $7.50 per person for singles. There's also an on-site pro shop.

WATER SPORTS You can spend a day at the **Myrtle Waves Water Park,** 10th Avenue at U.S. 17 N. bypass (☎ 843/448-1026). Its 20 acres hold a variety of water slides, as well as a wave pool, children's play pool, video arcade, and tanning deck.

Turbo-Twisters is the world's tallest water ride—a 10-story ride that plunges you through one of the three flumes at 50 feet per second, in total darkness. Adults pay $19.95, and children are charged $11.99. Open May 1 to June 4 and August 20 to September 19, daily from 10am to 5pm; June 5 to August 19, daily from 10am to 7pm.

3 Where to Stay

The Grand Strand is lined with hotels, motels, condominiums, and cottages. The highest rates are charged June 15 to Labor Day.

VERY EXPENSIVE

✪ **Kingston Plantation & The Embassy Suites at Kingston Plantation.** 9800 Lake Dr., Myrtle Beach 29572. ☎ **800/876-0010** or 843/449-0006. Fax 843/497-1110. www.kingstonplantation.com. 255 hotel suites, 595 condos and villas. $169–$309 Embassy Suites; $79–$419 condo or villa. Children 17 and under stay free in parents' room. AE, DC, DISC, MC, V. Take Highway 17 to a location near the border of Myrtle Beach and North Myrtle Beach.

This is the most desirable, and one of the best-landscaped, hotel and condominium complexes in Myrtle Beach. Set on 145 rolling acres of intensely manicured gardens, it combines a conventional hotel—the 20-story Embassy Suites—with a labyrinthine collection of individually owned one-, two-, and three-bedroom villas and condos. Be sure to specify your tastes in condo living, either when you reserve or at the time of check-in—some units are in soaring high-rises, others are low-slung townhouse-style accommodations. A few are free-standing, woodsy-looking buildings in their own right. Registration is in the lobby of the above-mentioned Embassy Suites Hotel. Each of the conventional hotel accommodations contains a kitchen, dining area, living room, and at least one bedroom, and is outfitted with a private balcony and a tasteful blend of light-grained woods and pale sand-and-sea colors. Residents of the suites benefit from slightly more intensive service rituals than those in the outlying condos and villas; but all units are extremely comfortable and well maintained.

Dining/Diversions: For such an enormous resort development, it's surprising to find only one restaurant, Azaleas Café and Deli, on the premises. Set on the ground floor of the high-rise Embassy Suites, it segues from breakfast to lunch to dinner without breaking stride, serving a well-prepared but not particularly ambitious menu of American and international specialties.

Amenities: Room service, available only to residents of the Embassy Suites, is offered daily from 6am to 10pm. There's also laundry and valet. The plantation has a $4-million Sports & Health Club that offers a variety of activities; indoor and outdoor pools; tennis, squash, and racquetball courts; a weight and fitness room; a sauna; and a whirlpool bath. Guests also enjoy temporary membership at more than 100 of the region's golf courses.

EXPENSIVE

Wyndham Myrtle Beach Resort. 10000 Beach Club Dr., Myrtle Beach, SC 25972. ☎ **800/996-3426** or 843/449-5000. Fax 843/449-3216. www.wyndham.com. E-mail: msalem@wyndham.com. 391 units. A/C TV TEL. $119–$159 double; $189–$289 suite. AE, DC, DISC, MC, V. Take U.S. 17 for 9 miles north of Myrtle Beach to Arcadian Shores.

This imposing high-rise is shaped like a Y, with accommodations radiating from the central core, where a huge tapestry hangs down 10 floors. It's a more tranquil choice than other hotels right in the bustling heart of Myrtle Beach. The bedrooms open onto the ocean and are furnished in a light, contemporary style, often with rattan pieces. Amenities include personal safes and refrigerators. Some rooms are set aside for nonsmokers.

Dining/Diversions: A formal restaurant offers a continental menu, although you can also patronize the informal coffee shop. Entertainment is featured at the mezzanine-level bar, and light snacks are offered at the poolside cafe in good weather.

Amenities: Room service, laundry, valet, four lighted tennis courts, playground, and small outdoor pool. Privileges at an affiliated golf club next door are available.

MODERATE

In addition to the following listings, a good choice is the **Holiday Inn Oceanfront,** 415 S. Ocean Blvd. (at 6th Avenue S.; ☎ **800/845-0313** or 843/448-4481) in Myrtle Beach.

The Beachcomber. 1705 S. Ocean Blvd., Myrtle Beach, SC 29577. ☎ **800/262-2113** or 843/448-4345. Fax 843/626-8115. www.beachdunes.com. 45 units. $44–$102 double; $51–$114 efficiency. Weekly, monthly, and golf packages available. AE, DC, DISC, MC, V.

These well-furnished oceanfront units, located 2 miles south of the town center, have private balconies. They attract families in summer. Connecting units are available, as are deluxe rooms (with refrigerators) and fully equipped one- and two-bedroom efficiencies. There are two pools (one for children) and a laundry room on the premises. Golf, tennis, shopping, amusement centers, and restaurants are nearby.

The Breakers. 2006 N. Ocean Blvd. (P.O. Box 485), Myrtle Beach, SC 29578. ☎ **800/ 845-0688** or 843/626-5000. Fax 843/626-5001. www.breakers.com. E-mail: info@breakers. com. 400 units. A/C TV TEL. $35–$138 double; $52–$308 suite. Children 15 and under stay free in parents' room. AE, DC, DISC, MC, V.

This longtime family favorite is better than ever. With one of the best north beach-front locations, it occupies both a multistory complex and a 19-floor North Tower seven blocks away. You can book here on any number of plans, so study them carefully. The newer North Tower has its own registration desk and some 140 condos. The accommodations are wide-ranging, from tastefully furnished bedrooms to efficiencies with kitchenettes, and even one- to three-bedroom suites. Extra beds in the form of foldout sofas, Murphy beds, and twin sets of doubles make for flexible family units. Many rooms have balconies and refrigerators.

The Sidewalk Vendor Cafe serves breakfast and dinner, and the Top of the Green rooftop lounge opens onto a panoramic view of the sea, providing entertainment 6 nights weekly under a mirrored ceiling. Amenities include room service, laundry, children's programs (June to Labor Day), two oceanfront pools (both indoor and outdoor), two saunas, a simple health club, and four whirlpools.

Four Points Sheraton. 2701 S. Ocean Blvd., Myrtle Beach, SC 29577. ☎ **800/992-1055** or 843/448-2518. Fax 843/448-1506. www.sheratonresort.com. 226 units. $65–$145 double; $140–$220 suite. AE, DC, DISC, MC, V.

On oceanfront beach property, this 15-floor tower, lined with balconies, is the most southerly at the resort. It's a family favorite and also the darling of the convention crowd. A moderately priced but first-class operation, it has a lobby that suggests the Caribbean, with ceiling fans and nautical colors. Some rooms are efficiencies, and units come with a double bed (or two) or a king-size bed. Extras include refrigerators and private safes. Some of the units open onto spacious balconies overlooking the ocean. American cuisine is offered at the slightly formal restaurant, and entertainment is presented in the lounge. Facilities include a small sauna, whirlpool, fitness room, and outdoor pool.

Landmark Resort. 1501 S. Ocean Blvd., Myrtle Beach, SC 29577. ☎ **800/845-0658** or 843/448-9441. Fax 843/448-6701. www.landmarkresort.com. E-mail: landmark@sccoast.net. 370 units. A/C TV TEL. $55–$99 double; $110–$139 suite. $15 each additional person. AE, DC, DISC, MC, V.

Standing 14 stories tall amid the beach action, the Landmark is one of the Grand Strand's better examples of midpriced accommodations. Its pink-and-green lobby makes a favorable impression, as do the gardenlike restaurant and bar. For more action, try the nightclub or the grill by the outdoor pool. In winter, the same pool is enclosed for year-round use. There is also a sauna. Almost half a dozen floors have small balconies. Rooms are equipped with one king-size or two double beds, tropical colors, refrigerators, and some ocean vistas. The lowest rates are available in December.

Myrtle Beach Martinique Resort & Conference Center. N. Ocean Blvd. (at 71st Ave. N.). ☎ **800/542-0048** or 843/449-4441. Fax 843/497-3041. www.mbmartinique.com. E-mail: martiniq@sccoast.net. 203 units. A/C TV TEL. $43–$152 double; $61–$365 suite. AE, DISC, MC, V.

Lying north of the bustling beach center, this 16-floor oceanfront resort is better than most other moderately priced choices. With a name like Martinique, you expect a tropical ambience, and that's what you get. The bar is Caribbean-style, complete with bamboo, and the restaurant has tall windows opening onto ocean views. (The views, we have to say, are often better than the food.) All the rooms and efficiency units are oceanfront and tropically inspired; most have two double beds, good-size bathrooms, and balconies. Some units contain refrigerators and microwave ovens. The best accommodations are the suites (with whirlpool baths) at the top. The hotel also offers a medium-size pool off the beach, as well as an indoor pool and a small fitness center.

Ocean Creek Resort. 10600 N. Kings Hwy., Myrtle Beach, SC 29572. ☎ **800/845-0353** or 843/272-7724. Fax 843/272-9627. www.oceancreek.com. E-mail: ocreek@btitelecom.net. 385 units. A/C TV TEL. $85–$259 studio or condo. AE, CB, DC, MC, V. Take U.S. 17 north almost to North Myrtle Beach.

One of the finest resorts along the beach, this first-class choice features studios and condos in half a dozen complexes on almost 60 acres. Seven tennis courts accept your serve, and a health center welcomes guests, offering an indoor pool, whirlpool, sauna, and fitness equipment. The Beach Club on the ocean operates in summer. Besides the health-center pool, several outdoor pools are located at the various buildings, which rise as high as 15 stories. Condominiums may be categorized as studios, one-bedrooms, two-bedrooms, three-bedrooms, lodge units, beachside towers, or tennis villas. A restaurant is always open for breakfast.

Yachtsman Resort Hotel. 1400 N. Ocean Blvd., Myrtle Beach, SC 29577. ☎ **800/ 868-8886** or 843/448-1441. Fax 843/626-6261. www.yachtmanhotel.com. 142 units. A/C TV TEL. $45–$200 unit for 4. Minimum stay of 4 days. AE, CB, DC, DISC, MC, V.

Some 8 blocks from the Convention Center, this 20-floor glass tower stands between two more-dated 11-story towers. Rooms in the older towers are timeshare units, available for nightly rentals when the owners aren't in residence. The main tower alone houses 144 well-furnished, albeit somewhat run-of-the-mill, units. Timeshares range from small studios to larger two-bedroom units. Facilities include two outdoor pools, two outdoor whirlpools, an indoor pool, a sauna, and a weight room, along with shuffleboard and miniature golf. Tour groups, golfers, and sometimes honeymooners book accommodations at the hotel.

INEXPENSIVE

Coral Beach Hotel. 1105 S. Ocean Blvd., Myrtle Beach, SC 29577. ☎ **800/843-2684** in the United States or 843/448-8421, 800/682-3138 in Canada. Fax 843/626-0156. E-mail: coralbch@sccoast.net. 301 units. A/C TV TEL. $65–$124 double; $99–$139 efficiency; $62–$185 suite. AE, DC, DISC, MC, V.

As its name implies, the Coral Beach Hotel is decked out in fresh coral paint, with more trendy colors inside. This is an ideal place to take the kids. In case the sun doesn't shine, you can use the indoor pool, fitness room, or game room. There is also an outdoor pool, bowling alley, large outdoor whirlpool, children's pool, sauna, steam room, and Lazy River Tube Ride to keep you busy. For food choices, you have a snack bar, a full-service restaurant, and a grill and food bar. The units are comfortably furnished but basic, with sofa beds or Murphy beds, kitchens with microwave ovens, one or two TVs, and balconies. Rooms that don't have full kitchens have refrigerators.

Hampton Inn. Broadway at the Beach, 1140 Celebrity Circle, Myrtle Beach, SC 29577. ☎ **888/916/2001** or 843/916-0600. Fax 843/946-6308. 141 units. A/C TV TEL. Winter $69–$79 double; high season $129–$149 double. AE, DC, MC, V.

This is the most appealing of the quartet of Hampton Inns in Myrtle Beach. It's clean, affordable, and stylish, with an Iberian-inspired design that emulates a blockbuster version of Spanish-colonial/American Mission. Best of all, it's the only hotel in Myrtle Beach that's within walking distance (across a mammoth parking lot) of the vast nightlife and entertainment complex Broadway at the Beach. Rising eight floors, it contains a seashell-colored, vaguely tropical decor, and an attentive, youthful staff that's well-versed in the facilities at the nearby Broadway complex. Each of the standard-size bedrooms has an iron and a coffeemaker. Amenities include two on-site swimming pools—one seashell shaped, one kidney-shaped. These pools compensate for the hotel's distance from the beach, a 12-minute drive away. There's a sauna and exercise room, plus a fish-shaped Jacuzzi and a bar. Breakfast is the only meal served. The restaurants of Broadway at the Beach are close at hand.

St. John's Inn. 6803 N. Ocean Blvd., Myrtle Beach, SC 29572. ☎ **800/845-0624** or 843/449-5251. Fax 843/449-3306. www.stjohnsinn.com. 88 units. A/C TV TEL. $64–$105 double; $9–$125 efficiency. Golf and entertainment packages available. AE, DISC, MC, V. Pets accepted for $10 per night and $50 refundable deposit.

This three-story motel, north of the town center and across from the beach, is more than just a motel. The fine landscaped grounds and Mediterranean-style building lend themselves to a pleasant stay. The former Caribbean motif has been replaced by more contemporary decor, investing heavily in colors such as hunter green with mauve and gold trim to evoke a rich look. Breakfast is the only meal served, aside from an occasional Friday or Saturday dinner, depending on arbitrary factors such as the number of guests staying at the hotel. An outdoor pool, a whirlpool, and lawn games are available. About one unit in three is an efficiency, and the rooms have one king-size bed or two double beds.

Serendipity Inn. 407 71st Ave. N., North Myrtle Beach, SC 29572. ☎ **800/762-3229** or 843/449-5268. www.serendipityinn.com. 17 units. A/C TV TEL. $89–$119 double; $125–$149 suite. Rates include breakfast. AE, DISC, MC, V. Closed Nov–Jan. Take Kings Hwy. (U.S. 17 N.) to 71st Ave. N.; then turn east toward the ocean.

This is a Spanish-style inn located on a quiet side street, a block and a half from the beach. All the rooms are decorated and furnished individually, and the suites are ideal for honeymooners or for anyone who just wants a little pampering. A breakfast buffet includes fresh fruit, hard-boiled eggs, and hot breads. The heated outdoor pool and whirlpool are good diversions. You can cook your own steaks and chicken on the grill, which is provided for and shared by all guests.

Teakwood Motel. 7201 N. Ocean Blvd., Myrtle Beach, SC 29572. ☎ **800/868-0046** or 843/449-5653. 38 units. A/C TV TEL. $75–$85 double; $80–$90 efficiency; $127 suite up to 4; $85–$130 condo. Weekly rates available. AE, DC, DISC, MC, V.

In the relatively tranquil Dunes area, rooms and efficiencies at the Teakwood are attractively furnished (some in Polynesian decor), with ceramic-tile bathrooms and wall-to-wall carpets. Accommodations open onto private balconies or patios and come with two double beds and a refrigerator. The motel offers free coffee in the lobby, a heated pool, a playground, and a pleasant cookout area with a grill and picnic tables. On the grounds, you can play horseshoes, volleyball, table tennis, badminton, and basketball. Guests gather throughout the day in the Teak social lounge. Airport transportation is offered, along with golf privileges. The motel is 5 miles north of the town center.

CAMPING

You'll find plenty of campsites along the Grand Strand, many on the oceanfront, and rates drop considerably after Labor Day. Most accept families only—no singles. On the ocean, about halfway between Myrtle Beach and North Myrtle Beach, 760 sites are available at **Apache Family Campground,** 9700 Kings Rd., Myrtle Beach (☎ **843/449-7323**). Amenities include a swimming pool and recreation pavilion, water, electricity, shade shelters, modern bathhouses with hot water, sewer hookups, laundry, trading post, playground, public telephones, and ice. You can reserve here year-round, except for the week of July 4. Rates are $35 to $37.

4 Where to Dine

Prices are no measure of quality here; dining costs are unexpectedly moderate at even the better restaurants.

EXPENSIVE

Greg Norman's Australian Grill. 4930 Highway 17 South, North Myrtle Beach. ☎ **843/ 361-0000.** Reservations recommended. Main courses $16–$32. AE, MC, V. Daily 5–10:30pm. INTERNATIONAL/AUSTRALIAN.

This is the most internationally hip, best-designed, and most prestigious restaurant in Myrtle Beach, with enough big-city inspiration to keep out-of-staters comfortable, and enough redneck references to keep locals from getting defensive. It was established in 1999 by one of the most visible pro golfers in the world, Australia-born Greg Norman, across a saltwater estuary from a Greg Norman–endorsed golf course. It occupies what looks like a mock-medieval watchtower on the Rhine, with a soaring, flatteringly lit, woodsy-looking interior designed by Norman's wife. There's a cigar bar on the premises, a somewhat cumbersome emphasis on the establishment's self-image as a citadel of fine dining, an impressive wine list, and a two-fisted, somewhat macho emphasis on Nouvelle Australian cuisine. Its menu promotes itself as "the upper crust of Down-Under dining," although some of the more aggressively promoted items, including an imported Australian crawfish known as "Yabbies" are over-rated. Better choices include any of the succulent cuts of steak or game fish.

Wood-grilled and rotisserie classics are favored, including Australian rib-eye steak or rack of lamb from Down Under. A good-tasting dish is the Aussie pot pie, a classic beef pie baked under puff pastry. You can also opt for Australian lobster tails, tempura fried and served with seared vegetables on sticky rice. The appetizers are some of the best in Myrtle Beach, including fried calamari tossed in a sweet and sour chile glaze, cilantro, and lemon juice and served with a light red curry aïoli.

✪ **The Library.** 1212 N. Kings Hwy. (U.S. 17 Business). ☎ **843/448-4527.** Reservations recommended. Main courses $16.95–$31.95. AE, CB, DC, DISC, MC, V. Mon–Sat 5:30–10:30pm. CONTINENTAL.

In downtown Myrtle Beach, this is the most formal and classic restaurant along the Grand Strand, an area that is not known for its classy food joints. Evoking a library, the walls are lined with old and new volumes. The tables are covered in crisp white linens, and the food service is the best. Serving dinner only, the Library is not innovative in its array of seafood, duck, beef, chicken, and veal dishes, but only first-class ingredients are used. Reserve going here for that special occasion.

MODERATE

Dick's Barefoot Landing. 4700 Highway 17 South, in North Myrtle Beach. ☎ **843/ 272-7794.** Reservations not accepted. Lunch platters and sandwiches $4.99–$7.99; dinner main courses $10.99–$16.99. MC, V. Daily 11:30am–4pm and 4:30–11pm (until midnight Fri–Sat). AMERICAN.

This is the most consistently irreverent restaurant in town, a fact that the owners proudly advertise in a large sign above the entrance. It might remind you of Dante's description of the lettering above the gateway to hell in *Divine Comedy: "Abandon hope all ye who enter here."* Most of the loyal fans of this place seem to revel in the ongoing banter provided by the waitstaff, members of whom compete for the role of sassiest, and/or most abrasive, on site.

You'll enter the equivalent of a wood-trussed airplane hangar with a scattering of motorcycles displayed as cultural icons, and a randomly arranged inventory of bras and panties hanging from rafters above the rough-hewn bar. Table linens are nonexistent—if you don't count the big tear-off sheets of craft paper that soak up the grease from the burgers and ribs that everyone seems to favor. If all of this appeals to you, and if you utterly abandon any ideas about political correctness, you won't be alone, as the cavernous interior of the ample wraparound porches are usually mobbed with everyone from singles who swing to families with young children. How did this place develop into something with a personality so distinct? It was born out of the collapse of a relatively restrained "fine dining" restaurant in Dallas. After its bankruptcy, its owners decided to "go sloppy." They did, literally dipping into aspects of "grunge dining," where spectacularly greasy food is served in huge portions—and sometimes in buckets. Expect pork that's grilled in half-slabs, full slabs, and a genuinely humongous size known as "a full porker." There's also chicken, shrimp, steaks, burgers, and grilled combinations that are evocatively designated as "cluck and moo" (chicken and steak) and "oink and cluck" (pork and chicken). Live music is on offer between 7 and 11pm between June and October.

Hard Rock Cafe. 1322 Celebrity Circle. ☎ **843/946-0007.** Reservations recommended. Main courses $7.79–$16.99. AE, DC, MC, V. Daily 11am–midnight (Fri–Sat until 1am). AMERICAN.

Even if you're a diehard fan of the Hard Rock Cafe chain, you won't be prepared for this nonstandard Hard Rock Cafe. Set a short distance north of Myrtle Beach's center, in the Broadway at the Beach shopping center, it's designed like an ancient Egyptian pyramid, entirely without windows and covered with hieroglyphs. True, there's a vintage motorcycle displayed in front, but no trademark Cadillac is suspended from the ceiling—which appeals to New Agers, who believe that cosmic and psychic forces are amplified beneath any pyramid. This is one of the most successful and popular Hard Rock Cafes in the worldwide chain. You'll find memorabilia associated with the blockbuster cult film, *Rocky Horror Picture Show,* including the silver lamé shorts worn by the sexually ambiguous character played by Peter Hinwood. After a few beers or party-colored cocktails, you might believe that the psychics are right. Proudly displayed is all the rock memorabilia you'd expect; the most prized possession is a guitar used in concert by the late Jerry Garcia (Grateful Dead). Menu items include the usual Americana: French fries, tacos, burgers, barbecued chicken, milkshakes, and banana splits. In midsummer be prepared for waits up to two hours.

Joe's Bar & Grill. 810 Conway Ave., North Myrtle Beach. ☎ **843/272-4666.** Reservations recommended. Main courses $13.95–$24.95. AE, DISC, MC, V. Daily 5–10pm. Drive 15 miles north on U.S. 17. Across from Barefoot landing in North Myrtle Beach. AMERICAN.

It's worth the drive north to sample the fare at this plainly named restaurant with a rustic atmosphere. Joe's is known for its fresh fish and its homemade soups and sauces. With both downstairs and upstairs dining, it has a panoramic view of the saltwater marsh. Beef, veal, and seafood dominate the menu. The roast prime rib of beef is the best in the area, or you may prefer Low Country shrimp sautéed in a peppery butter sauce. Fish specials (look for the board) are from the Carolina coast. Service is excellent.

❂ Nicks and 61st. 503 61st Ave. at U.S. 17. ☎ **843/449-1716.** Reservations recommended. Main courses $12.95–$31.95; lunch $6.95–$10.95. DISC, MC, V. Mon–Sat 11am–3pm, 5–9:30pm. CONTINENTAL.

About a decade ago, this place opened as a French bakery; it has expanded to become one of the finer restaurants along the Grand Strand. Appetizers might include snow-crab-and-lobster cocktail, served over baby greens and yellow tomato, or warm goat cheese baked in a pine-nut crust and served with apricot chutney. For your main course, you may see an open ravioli of seared salmon, marinated grilled fillet of tuna, medallions of beef on sweet onion risotto cakes, or grilled veal chops. Ingredients are exceptionally fresh here and deftly handled by the kitchen staff. Service is formal and polite.

Sea Captain's House. 3000 N. Ocean Blvd. ☎ **843/448-8082.** Reservations recommended in midsummer. Lunch platters, salads, and sandwiches $5.95–$9.95; lunch and dinner main courses $12.95–$28. AE, MC, V. Daily 11:30am–2:30pm and 4:45–10pm. AMERICAN.

Consistently crowded, and evocative of the kind of American-colonial seafood restaurant you might have expected on Cape Cod, this place originated in 1930 as a privately owned beachfront cottage. Today, it retains a few of its original nostalgic touches, including a masonry fireplace that's lit on cold evenings. More prevalent, however, is a sense of decent, well-managed modernity, with glassed-in views overlooking the sea.

The menu is absolutely typical of coastal Carolina—that's no putdown. When regional cuisine is done well, as it is here, it's excellent, especially the fresh coastal crab dishes, either served as an appetizer or in she-crab soup, perhaps a salad or else as sautéed crab cakes. Locals order the Low Country crab casserole served topped with sherry. Other seafood selections include oysters, scallops, and local shrimp. Any dish you order is likely to be decorated with hush puppies. A few poultry and meat dishes such as grilled pork chops are offered, but there's nothing special in that department.

❂ Thoroughbreds. Restaurant Row, U.S. 17 N. ☎ **843/497-2636.** Reservations recommended. Main courses $17.95–$28.95. AE, DC, DISC, MC, V. Sun–Thurs 5–10pm, Fri–Sat 5–11pm. SEAFOOD/CONTINENTAL.

Rivaled only by the Library, Thoroughbreds is one of the few places along the Grand Strand that truly specializes in fine dining. It has been a hit ever since it opened in 1990. Guests select one of four handsomely appointed rooms; it also has a garden terrace and a piano bar. The latest addition is a dining room that seats 30 and features a fireplace. The staff is among the best-trained at the resort, but the food is what keeps people coming back for more. The Caesar salad is prepared tableside by your server; you might begin with a Caribbean seafood chowder instead. The steaks are among the juiciest and most tender along the Strand. You can order blackened prime rib or grilled rib-eye, among other selections. Several excellently prepared veal, duck, and chicken dishes are offered. Call for the entertainment schedule.

INEXPENSIVE

Bojangles Famous Chicken & Biscuits. 2301 S. Kings Hwy. ☎ **843/626-9051.** Main courses 99¢–$9.99. No credit cards. Mon–Fri 6–10pm, Sat–Sun 6–11pm. SOUTHERN.

Sure, it's a chain, but it's also one of the best-value dining choices in town. For the family that likes to feast on Southern cooking but doesn't want to pay much for the privilege, Bojangles is a longtime favorite. Its specialties are (guess what?) fried chicken, homemade biscuits, and Cajun-style dishes. It's one of the most inexpensive ways to eat in town without having to resort to pizza and burgers.

Easyriders Café. Celebrity Square, Broadway at the Beach. ☎ **843/445-2702.** Reservations not accepted. Sandwiches and salads $6.95–$7.95; platters $9.95–$15.95. AE, MC, V. Daily 11am–10pm; bar remains open until 2am. AMERICAN.

Here, no one will mind if you show up in leather, looking as degenerate and scruffy as possible. In fact, you'll probably contribute to a theme that panels of restaurant developers have labored hard to create. The decor, and even the menu, celebrate the lore and legend of the American motorcycle, in a version that's deliberately sanitized for the resort's family-friendly clientele, but not so much that hard-core biking aficionados are driven away. Menu items include "Butt-kicking Chili," "In the Wind Wings," and "Showroom-ready Sandwiches." Main courses feature "Louisiana Voodoo Run" (blackened shrimp and fillet tips) as well as roast pork sandwiches and grilled steaks. There's live music "almost nightly," usually some kind of rock and roll or heavy metal music, for the bar crowd that gathers here beginning around 10pm. In honor of the family trade, the on-site gift shop doesn't stock anything too controversial or too leathery, but the motorcycle-indulgent on-site staff will quickly tell you where in South Carolina you can go if you so wish to equip yourself.

✪ **House of Blues.** Barefoot Landing, 4640 Highway 17 South, North Myrtle Beach. ☎ **843/272-3000.** Reservations not accepted. Main courses $7.95–$13.95 at lunch, $8.95–$22.95 at dinner. AE, DC, MC, V. Daily 11:30am–midnight. AMERICAN/ SOUTHERN.

Many visitors come to this restaurant looking for a burger and a stiff drink, and leave with a newfound appreciation for American folk art. With virtually every inch of its interior plastered over with vernacular art by largely untrained Southern artists, this Grand Strand version of the House of Blues franchise is by far the most aesthetically interesting bar, restaurant, and musical venue in Myrtle Beach. You'll recognize it by a design that emulates a rusted hulk you might have found deep in the Mississippi Delta, the kind of battered venue that might be appropriate for a religious revival and the laying-on-of hands. Redolent of bourbon and live jazz, however, it's more urbanized and hip than the folk-art setting would imply. The best way to gain a respect for this place involves wandering through its labyrinthine interior, sizing up the indoor/outdoor bars and the several dining areas. There's even a rear veranda where a collection of antique hubcaps is elevated to a kitschy, and very charming, art form. Don't be fooled if you think the founders of this place are as naïve as their artworks: Dan Ackroyd, the Belushi family, and members of Aerosmith are all investors, and the organization is used as one of the teaching models at the Harvard Business School.

Culinary fare includes fish, burgers, salads, steaks, ribs, and all the Southern staples you can handle. There's a "Gospel Brunch" ("Have mercy and say yeah") every Sunday from 9am to 2pm, with a buffet that's priced at $16.95 per person. No one will mind if you come here just to drink, mingle, gossip, and flirt. And, if you're interested in music, concerts are scheduled every Thursday, Friday, and Saturday at 10pm, with tickets priced from $15 to $22 each.

NASCAR Cafe. 1808 21st Ave. North. ☎ **843/946-7223.** Reservations not accepted. Sandwiches and platters $6.50–$15. AE,DC,DISC,MC, V. Daily 11am–10pm (until 11pm Fri–Sat). AMERICAN.

This is the most intriguing of the many theme restaurants of Myrtle Beach. It's devoted to the history and memorabilia of the National Association of Stock Car Auto Racing (NASCAR), which, if you didn't already know, includes fans, worldwide, who are almost fanatically devoted to the lore and minutiae of the subculture. Set within a building that vaguely evokes a temple to some exotic high-tech god, the dining room is prefaced with one of the most complete collections of NASCAR memorabilia in the world. Look for Americana that will sometimes make nostalgia buffs weep, including bar stools made from oil barrels, balustrades crafted from the springs of old cars, and the out-of-date logos of spare-parts companies that no longer exist. Food is relentlessly geared to the kind of fare you might have expected at Indy on a super-heated race day. Your waiter (who will identify him- or herself as a member of your "pit crew") will bring you heaping portions of food that includes six kinds of burgers, "supercharged chili," chargrilled shrimp, catch of the day, barbecued ribs, and chicken pot pie.

Rosa Linda's Café. 4635 U.S. 17 N., North Myrtle Beach. ☎ **843/272-6823.** Main courses $8.95–$14.95; lunch $3.95–$8.95. AE, DISC, MC, V. Mon–Thurs 3–10pm, Fri–Sun Noon–10pm. Closed Thanksgiving, Dec 24–25. Drive 6 miles north on U.S. 17. MEXICAN.

With a cantina atmosphere, this is the leading south-of-the-border joint along the Grand Strand. Begin with baked stuffed mussels or Rosa's award-winning seafood stew. Mexican dishes include chiles rellenos; they do it "our way" here. The chef's special is the catch of the day cooked in a bag with peppers, onions, mushrooms, and hot sauce. Paella, burritos, enchiladas, fajitas, tacos, and all that good stuff are served along with a selection of gourmet meals, calzones, and Italian pasta dishes.

5 The Grand Strand After Dark

VARIETY SHOWS & THEATERS

✪ **Alabama Theatre.** Barefoot Landing, North Myrtle Beach. ☎ **800/342-2262** or 843/272-1111. Shows, $26.95 adults, $13 children 3–16, free for children 2 and under; "Christmas in Dixie" holiday shows, $26.95 adults, $13 children.

The country-music supergroup Alabama unveiled this $7-million, 2,200-seat theater, located in an expanding waterside shopping complex, on the Fourth of July 1993. The theater features three kinds of shows. Alabama performs at least 10 shows a year; celebrities such as Johnny Cash, Glen Campbell, and Loretta Lynn fill in at about 20 others. Typical shows combine Opryland-style singing, dancing, and music on the other nights. Alabama began by singing for tips around Myrtle Beach before going on to sell millions of records.

Shows are given daily at 8pm, with additional Tuesday matinees at 2pm March to May and September and October, and Thursday matinees at 4pm June to August. The "Christmas in Dixie" holiday show is presented November 16 to December 30, daily at 8pm, with matinees at 2pm on Saturday. Celebrity concerts are booked for some Friday or Saturday nights, as announced.

○ The Carolina Opry. N. Kings Hwy., at U.S. 17, Myrtle Beach. ☎ **800/843-6779** or 843/238-8888. Tickets $28.95 adults, $13 children 3–16, free for children 2 and under.

Missouri-born musician/entrepreneur Calvin Gilmore has been called a better businessman than a guitarist. He's credited with starting the incredible entertainment explosion in Myrtle Beach by launching this theater back in 1986 and attracting a host of imitators. In 1992, the original Carolina Opry moved into this new 2,200-seat facility, complete with its own recording studio. Shows offer a variety of music, including country, bluegrass, western swing, big band, patriotic, and show tunes, as well as comedy. The Christmas show is so popular that it's often sold out by June. Performances are daily at 8pm.

Dixie Stampede Dinner and Show. N. Kings Hwy. at U.S. 17, Myrtle Beach. ☎ **800/ 433-4401** or 843/497-9700. Tickets $32.99 adults, $16.99 children 4–11.

Owned by Dolly Parton's Dollywood Productions, this showhouse features a rodeo with a Civil War theme. While you eat a four-course meal with your fingers, you're entertained by some 30 horses, riders, and singing Southern belles. The place's appeal is so hokey that Dolly should be ashamed of herself, but locals flock here to feast on chicken, ribs, and corn on the cob while cheering whichever side they're on—usually, the side of Dixie. Drinks (definitely nonalcoholic) are served in the Dixie Belle Saloon before the show. Shows are given mid-February to May and in September and October, daily at 6pm; June to August, daily at 6 and 8:30pm; in November and December, on Wednesday, Friday, and Saturday at 6pm.

○ Legends in Concert. 301 U.S. 17, Surfside Beach. ☎ **800/843-6779** or 843/ 238-8888. Tickets $26.75 adults, $13 children 3–16, free for children 2 and under.

Calvin Gilmore also brought another venture to the town, a show that features impersonations of the biggest stars in the business, including Cher, Dolly, Reba, the Blues Brothers, and (inevitably) Elvis and Marilyn Monroe—the latter two being perhaps the easiest to imitate. Michael Jackson, the Beatles, Nat King Cole, Elton John, Judy Garland, John Lennon, and even Liberace get into the act. Singers, dancers, and a live band are featured.

The Palace at Myrtle Beach. 1420 Celebrity Circle ☎ **800/905-4228** or 843/448-0588. Tickets $32–$46 adults, $24–$35 children.

The newest and largest blockbuster theater in Myrtle Beach was built in 1995, and has been richly popular ever since. This is partially because of a 2,700-seat theater in a red, black, and gold design that's grander than many of its competitors, and partly because of the big-name acts that are usually booked in it. Past luminaries have included The Four Tops, The Beach Boys, The Moody Blues, The Radio City Rockettes, The Tommy Dorsey Orchestra, the (New Orleans–based) Preservation Hall Jazz Band, Bill Cosby, Kenny Rogers, Patti LaBelle, and road-show versions of the Broadway hit *Riverdance.* Be warned in advance that acts here are presented on a schedule that includes many evenings where nothing is booked.

Fantasy Harbour Entertainment Complex. U.S. 501, near Waccamaw Pottery. ☎ **800/ 681-5209** or 843/236-8500.

This is an entertainment complex of five different theaters under different managements, and each offering different family entertainment. Since shows are likely to change, check locally to see what is playing at the time of your visit.

The glossiest theater here is **Crook & Chase,** (☎ **800/681-5209,** or 843/ 236-8500), seating 2,000. Its shows in general are inspired by extravaganzas presented on Broadway. Sometimes the audience is invited to participate, as in competitions for the hula-hoop of the 50s. Tickets cost adults $26, ages 13 to 18 $13, but are free for children 12 and under.

Medieval Times & Dinner Complex (☎ 800/436-4386, or 843/236-8080) is a family-entertainment spectacle that provides a sanitized look at the Middle Ages in its 1,300-seat Grand Ceremonial Arena. Before going into the arena, guests inspect the Hall of Banners & Flags and a Museum of Torture. Falconry, sorcery, and swordplay, along with some horsemen who are "gallant knights," add to guests' amusement. Guests consume a four-course banquet (without utensils) while watching the show. The highlight of the evening is a joust. Tickets go for $37.75 for adults or $19.75 for children under 18.

Ice Castle, formerly the Savoy Theatre, is entirely devoted to skating spectacles, changing its program five times a year. Expect to see shows starring Nancy Kerrigan, the former U.S. Olympic contender, "Halloween on Ice," or even a Jack Frost Christmas version of *The Nutcracker Suite.* Tickets cost adults $26; children 13 to 18 $13; and children 3 to 12 $10. The Ice Castle also handles **The Cercle Theater,** which is sometimes used as a public ice-skating rink.

The final theater includes **The Forum** (☎ 843/903-5100), usually devoted to light comedies and drama. Call for information on what's on offer at the time of your visit.

THE CLUB & MUSIC SCENE

Barefoot Landing, Highway 17 South, straddling the civic boundary between Myrtle Beach and North Myrtle Beach, offers 14 restaurants; a variety and rock-music venue known as the Alabama Theater; an endlessly popular nightlife venue—the House of Blues—and a reptilian theme park known as Alligator Adventure. Everything about this place, frankly, is well-orchestrated except for parking, which during peak seasons, or during weekends, is very, very hard to come by.

Broadway at the Beach, Lying between 22nd and 29th boulevards is the most appealing nightlife, shopping, dining, and entertainment venue in South Carolina. It's a less glossy, and much less expensive, version of Disney World, but with very few of the rides, and less of an emphasis on myths and legends. It sprawls across a vast acreage bisected with saltwater estuaries and lakes in the heart of town. Some of its most visible features include the most famous chain restaurant in town, the pyramid-shaped Hard Rock Cafe, as well as Planet Hollywood, an Aquarium (Ripley's) where schools of fish swim in translucent turquoise waters behind a thick layer of plexiglass. There are shops, a free-standing IMAX theater, a 16-screen conventional movie theater, a gaggle of theme-oriented bars, many with big-screen TVs for sports-watching, and a collection of late-night bars and dance clubs—each within a cluster known as Celebrity Circle—that includes everything from country-western line dancing to Latino salsa. Additional theme restaurants within the complex feature burger joints outfitted like enclaves of the Hell's Angels (the Easy Riders Cafe), or something transplanted directly from the plains of Texas.

Studebaker's. 21st Ave. N. and Hwy. 17, Myrtle Beach. ☎ 843/448-9747. Cover $5–$10.

The 1950s live on at this club, the site of the National Shag Dance Championship in March. The bartenders and service staff are called The Stude-a-Boppers, and there's more entertainment by the "world's oldest living brain donor," DJ Jumpin' Jack Flash. Line dances and a floor show add to the amusement. It's not all 1950s music; you might also hear blasts from the 1960s and 1970s.

2001. 920 Lake Arrowhead Rd., Myrtle Beach. ☎ **843/449-9434.** Cover $8–$10.

With a sing-along piano bar and two dance floors, this is a major stop on the Grand Strand's nightlife circuit. Yakety Yak's Piano Bar is the best in town, providing good, bawdy fun, with the audience getting into the act. Pulsations Dance Club plays top-40 music on a high-tech sound system; live bands alternate with DJs. Adjoining is Razzies Beach Club, where patrons dance the Shag and listen to golden oldies played by the in-house band.

6 Murrells Inlet: The Seafood Capital of South Carolina

11 miles S of Myrtle Beach; 11 miles N of Pawleys Island

Murrells Inlet is often invaded by Myrtle Beach hordes who want a seafood dinner. Just take U.S. 17 (Business) south from Myrtle Beach, and prepare to dig in.

This centuries-old fishing village has witnessed a parade of humanity, from Confederate blockade runners to Federal gunboats, from bootleggers to today's pleasure craft. The island was also visited by Edward Teach, better known as Blackbeard.

Drunken Jack Island lies off Murrells Inlet. During the 1600s, Blackbeard's ship allegedly left a sailor on the island by accident; when the ship returned 2 years later, the crew discovered the abandoned sailor's bones bleaching in the sun, along with 32 empty casks of rum.

In addition to its seafood restaurants (only a few are recommended in this chapter), Murrells Inlet is the setting of Brookgreen Gardens, one of the most-visited attractions along the Grand Strand (see below).

Some people visit Murrells Inlet for its good diving on many offshore wrecks. Some ships sank as far back as the Civil War, although many more date from World War II. The best full-service center for scuba diving is **Mermaid Diving Adventures,** 4123 Hwy. 17 Business in Murrells Inlet (☎ **843/357-3483**), lying between Captain Dick's and Voyager's View Marinas. It is open Monday to Saturday 10am to 5pm.

BROOKGREEN GARDENS

Halfway between Myrtle Beach and Georgetown on U.S. 17 (near Litchfield Beach), Brookgreen Gardens (☎ **843/237-4218**) is a unique sculpture garden and wildlife park on the grounds of a colonial rice plantation. It was laid out in 1931 as a setting for a collection of American garden sculptures from the mid–19th century to the present. Archer Milton and Anna Hyatt Huntington planned the garden walks in the shape of a butterfly with outspread wings. All walks lead back to the central space, which was the site of the plantation house. On opposite sides of this space are the Small Sculpture Gallery and the original plantation kitchen. In the wildlife park, an outstanding feature is the Cypress Bird Sanctuary, a 90-foot-tall aviary housing species of wading birds within half an acre of cypress swamp.

Admission is $8.50 adults, $4 ages 6 to 12. Open daily 9:30am to 5pm. From June 15 through August 31 it stays open until 9pm.

WHERE TO DINE

✪ **Bovines.** Hwy. 17 Business. ☎ **843/651-2888.** Reservations not accepted. Main courses $14.95–$21.95. AE, CB, DC, DISC, MC, V. Daily 5–10pm. SOUTHWESTERN.

On the waterfront, with large windows opening onto marshland, the restaurant evokes the Southwest with its use of cowhide and mounted bulls' heads. In the heart of Seafood Row, the restaurant has made a name for itself with its wood-fired specialties.

You can order honey-crust pizza from the wood-fired brick oven, along with grilled or blackened rib-eye steak. You can also have a choice filet mignon or a New York sirloin strip with sun-dried-tomato butter. Barbecued baby back ribs are roasted with bourbon, honey, and aged balsamic vinegar. Appetizers include crab gazpacho (a refreshing change) and Cajun oyster stew.

✪ **Channel Marker.** Hwy. 17 Business. ☎ **843/651-6440.** Reservations recommended. Seafood buffet $14.95; all-you-can-eat crab legs $17.95. AE, DISC, MC, V. Daily 4:30–9pm. LOW COUNTRY.

A family favorite, Channel Marker is known for its all-you-can-eat seafood buffet, including not only broiled or fried fish, but also steamed or fried shrimp, along with sautéed crabmeat, fried oysters, clam strips, fried scallops, deviled crabs, and shrimp Creole. Oysters are a specialty, served as oyster roast, oyster stew, or oyster cocktails. Hush puppies come with everything, and a salad bar accompanies a festive meal.

Oliver's Lodge. Hwy. 17 Business. ☎ **843/651-2963.** Reservations accepted for parties of 6 or more. Main courses $8.95–$28.95. MC, V. Mon–Sat 5–9pm. SEAFOOD.

Since 1910, this rustic choice on the inlet has been serving fresh local seafood. It's the oldest restaurant in the area; to survive that long on the Grand Strand, it's been doing something right. The setting is one of marsh and wildlife, and the folks are friendly, congenial, and casual. A large selection of broiled, blackened, or grilled seafood is served, although you can also order steaks according to your liking—even barbecue ribs or roast prime rib. Homemade soups and freshly made salads are also featured, and a children's menu is offered.

7 Pawleys Island/Litchfield

25 miles S of Myrtle Beach; 12 miles N of Georgetown

One of the oldest resorts in the South, Pawleys Island has been a popular hideaway for vacationers for more than 3 centuries. Over the years, everybody from George Washington to Franklin Roosevelt and Winston Churchill has arrived. During the 18th century, rice planters made the island their summer home so that they could escape the heat and humidity of the Low Country and enjoy ocean breezes. Storms have battered the island, but many of the weather-beaten old properties remain, earning for the island the appellation of "arrogantly shabby."

This area of South Carolina is sometimes called Waccamaw Neck, a reference to a strip of land 30 miles long and 3 miles wide that extends from the Waccamaw River to the Atlantic Ocean. Both North Litchfield and Litchfield Beach lie between Murrells Inlet and Pawleys Island. (To get here from Myrtle Beach, take Highway 17 S.)

The beaches here are among the best-maintained, least-polluted, and widest along coastal South Carolina. Because so much of the land is private, however, access to public beach areas is severely limited.

Many visitors from Myrtle Beach come to Pawleys Island to shop for handcrafts, such as the famous Pawleys Island rope hammock. The best place to purchase one is at **The Original Pawleys Island Rope Hammock** (☎ 843/237-9122), on Highway 17 at Pawleys Island. It's open year-round Monday to Saturday from 9:30am to 8pm and on Sunday from noon to 5pm. At various plantation stores (known as the hammock shops), you'll find wicker, pewter, miniature doll furniture, clothing, candles, Christmas items, brass, and china.

The **Pawleys Island Visitors Center,** Highway 17 at the Planter's Exchange (☎ 843/237-1921), provides complete information about the area. Hours are Monday through Saturday from 9am to 5pm, and Sunday 10am to 2pm.

ENJOYING THE OUTDOORS

✪ **Huntington Beach State Park,** along Highway 17, 3 miles south of Murrells Inlet, across from Brookgreen Gardens (☎ 843/237-4440), offers one of the best beaches along the Grand Strand. Entrance is $4 adults, $2 children 6 to 12, free 5 and under. The 2,500-acre park has a wide, firm beach, which is slightly orange. Anna Hyatt Huntington and her husband, Archer, the creators of Brookgreen Gardens, once owned this coastal wilderness. The park is the site of their Iberian-style castle, Atalaya. In the park are nearly 130 campsites, along with picnic shelters and a boardwalk. There's terrific birding, as well as bike rentals and toilets. Swimming in specially marked sections is excellent, as is fishing from the jetty at the north side of the beach. Crabbing along the boardwalk is another popular pastime. Campsites are rented on a first-come, first-served basis, at a cost of $23.75 to $26.45 per day. The park is open April through September daily from 6am to 10pm; off-season daily from 6am to 6pm.

The **Caledonia Golf & Fish Club,** King River Road, Pawleys Island (☎ 800/483-6800 or 843/237-3675), opened in 1993. Each tee is marked by replicas of native waterfowl that inhabit the old rice fields. The centerpiece of the course is a clubhouse, a replica of a colonial plantation house from the 1700s. Architect Mike Strantz, a former assistant to Tom Fazio, took care to highlight the natural beauty of the area: huge, centuries-old live oaks; pristine natural lakes; scenic views of the old rice fields; and glimpses of native wildlife. Greens fees are $65 to $120.

WHERE TO STAY

Litchfield Beach and Golf Resort. Hwy. 17, Pawleys Island, SC 29585. ☎ 800/845-1897 or 843/237-3000. Fax 843/237-3282. www.litchfieldbeach.com. 298 units. A/C TV. $89–$159 suite/condo; $139–$255 2–4 bedroom cottage. AE, DC, DISC, MC, V.

One of the largest developments along coastal South Carolina, this complex sprawls across 4,500 acres, with 7 miles of private beach and the best tennis courts in the area. Often catering to groups, it offers a wide range of accommodations, including suites, condos, and cottages. Furnishings are hit-or-miss, described by one returning guest as being "residential beach stuff." The property, however, is well maintained and forms its own private enclave away from the crowds of the Grand Strand.

Facilities include an indoor pool, a total of 10 outdoor pools, an exercise room, aerobics, whirlpools, a steam room, and a sauna. Many of the units have lake, ocean, and marshland views, complete with waterfowl. A restaurant on-site serves standard American food, and there's a grill at the golf club.

Litchfield Inn. 1 Norris Dr., Litchfield, SC 29585. ☎ 800/637-4211 or 843/237-4211. Fax 843/237-4549. www.litchfieldinn.com. 142 units. A/C TV TEL. $104–$195 double. AE, MC, V.

East of Hwy. 17 and north of Litchfield Beach, this understated inn is a tranquil escape from the overblown Grand Strand. A seven-floor inn with shingled two- and three-story buildings, it invites you to sit in a high-backed rocking chair on a screened-in porch in a setting of residential cottages, tidal boundaries, inlets, and sand dunes. Three golf courses are nearby. The inn has 19 tennis courts and walkways over the dunes to the ocean. There is a pool for adults and another one for children, and boating and fishing are easily arranged. Accommodations are in very standardized rooms and efficiencies. Cooking spaces in the efficiencies are limited.

✪ **Litchfield Plantation.** River Rd. (P.O. Box 290), Pawleys Island, SC 29585. ☎ 800/869-1410 or 843/237-9121. Fax 843/237-8558. www.litchfieldplantation.com. 28 units. Summer $210–$540 suite, off-season $160–$490 suite; summer $230 cottage, off-season $170 cottage. Rates include continental breakfast. AE, DISC, MC, V.

Along the banks of the Waccamaw River, Litchfield Plantation is at the end of a quarter-mile avenue of live oaks. There, a stately manor house, circa 1750, overlooks former rice fields. A fine country inn, fully restored, it offers four suites. The Ballroom Suite, for example, occupies the north wing of the second floor. This suite includes a bedroom and fireplace, a bathroom with whirlpool, and a large living room (formerly the ballroom) with a Pullman-type kitchen area and a veranda overlooking the grounds. Rates include the use of a private pool, a cabana, and a private beach club at Pawleys Island. There are on-site tennis courts, plus numerous championship golf courses in the area. There's also a 31-acre equestrian center nearby.

WHERE TO DINE

☼ **Frank's Restaurant & Bar and Out Back at Frank's.** 10434 Ocean Hwy., Pawleys Island. ☎ **843/237-1581.** Reservations recommended. Main courses $14.95–$26.95. DISC, MC, V. Daily 11:30am–3pm and 6–10pm. INTERNATIONAL.

Frank's has been a Grand Strand tradition since 1988. Its fans think that it's the best restaurant along the beach strip. Chef Pierce Culliton borrows inspiration wherever he finds it, from Arizona to Provence, from China to Thailand. Your grilled yellowfin tuna might arrive with a Moroccan-inspired barbecue sauce. The rack of lamb with garlic-laced mashed potatoes is better than many versions of this dish we've sampled in France. With its painted tin ceilings and wood floors, Frank's is an intimate, cozy place. The menu changes every day, based on the chef's inspiration. The Out Back part offers lighter food, such as soups, salads, and sandwiches. You can eat inside or out on the deck when the weather is right, enjoying the towering oak trees.

Tyler's Cove. Hammock Shops, Hwy. 17, Pawleys Island. ☎ **843/237-4848.** Reservations recommended. Main courses $21.95–$19.95. AE, DISC, MC, V. Mon–Sun 11:30am–3pm and 5:30–9pm (10pm on Sat). LOW COUNTRY.

Dine inside or out; live music is played on the deck on Thursday, Friday, and Saturday. The deck's mesquite grill turns out some of the best dishes this place has to offer. The atmosphere inside is warm and inviting, with beamed ceilings, brass lanterns, and brick floors. If you go for lunch, sample the she-crab soup or Low Country shrimp salad. For dinner, the steak teriyaki is excellent, but the Maryland crab cakes won our hearts.

8 Georgetown

28 miles S of Myrtle Beach

The lifestyle of pre-Revolutionary War days comes alive here. Named after George II, this enclave of only 11,000 people boasts more than 50 historic homes and buildings dating back as far as 1737. Masted ships sailed from this riverfront, bound for England with their cargoes of indigo, rice, timber, and "king cotton." You can take a leisurely stroll along the Harbor Walk, tour the antebellum homes, or dine at some of our favorite spots. ☼ Georgetown is rarely crowded with visitors. Located 12 miles from the Atlantic, this community is South Carolina's third-oldest city, and it was recently rated among the 100 best small towns in America. When Elisha Screven laid out the town in 1729, he couldn't know that it was to become a lively shopping enclave.

ESSENTIALS

GETTING THERE   From Myrtle Beach, take U.S. 17 S. From I-95, take U.S. 521 into Georgetown. From Charleston, take U.S. 17/701.

VISITOR INFORMATION   Providing information about sights, accommodations, and tours, the **Georgetown Chamber of Commerce,** 1001 Front St. (P.O. Box 1776),

Georgetown, SC 29442 (☎ 800/777-7705 or 843/546-8436; www.georgetownsc.com), is most helpful. The staff will also provide you with maps and brochures. It's open Monday to Saturday from 8:30am to 5pm and on Sunday from 10am to 2pm.

SEEING THE SIGHTS

Kaminski House Museum. 1003 Front St. ☎ **843/546-7706.** Admission $5 adults, $2 children 6–12, free for children 5 and under. Mon–Sat 9am–5pm, Sun 1–4pm. Closed holidays.

A pre-Revolutionary War home (ca. 1760), this house is visited mainly for its collection of antiques, including a 15th-century Spanish wedding chest, a Chippendale dining table, and some excellent pieces from Charleston in the 1700s. Many of the interior architectural details, including moldings and the original floors, have been left intact. At one time, the house was occupied by Thomas Daggett, a Confederate sea captain. There's also a museum shop selling items related to the decorative arts and the history of Georgetown.

Prince George Winyah Episcopal Church. Broad and Highmarket sts. ☎ **843/546-4358.** Free admission, but donations welcome. Sanctuary tours, Mar–Nov Mon–Fri 11:30am–4:30pm.

Built around 1750 with brick from English ships' ballast, this church was occupied by British troops during the Revolutionary War and by Union troops during the Civil War. The latter occupation resulted in a great deal of damage. The stained glass behind the rebuilt altar was once part of a slaves' chapel on a nearby plantation. In the churchyard is one of the state's oldest cemeteries, the most ancient marker dating back to 1767.

Rice Museum. 1842 Old Market Building, Front and Screven sts. ☎ **843/546-7423.** Admission $5 adults, $4 seniors, $2 ages 12–21, free for children under 12 with an adult. Mon–Sat 10am–4:30pm.

This museum is easy to locate. It's in the Old Market Building, which local residents call "The Town Clock"—Georgetown's answer to Big Ben. The first building in town to be listed on the National Register of Historic Places, it houses a museum devoted to the once-flourishing rice trade. The museum is a repository of maps, artifacts, dioramas, and other exhibits, tracing the development of rice cultivation (which was long Georgetown's primary economic base) from 1700 to 1900. There's also a scale model of a rice mill.

ORGANIZED TOURS

A standard 1-hour tour is offered by the **Georgetown Tour Company,** leaving from 1001 Front St. (☎ 843/546-9485). You can make a reservation. Tours depart Monday to Saturday every 30 minutes from 10am to 4pm. Two stops at historic properties are included; the cost is $8.50 for adults, $7.50 for seniors, and $5.50 for children 11 and under. Another option is the "Ghostbusting Tour," a 2-hour visit to selected haunts. It's given on Tuesday and Wednesday from 2:30 to 4:30pm, and costs $17 for adults and $8 for children 11 and under.

Miss Nell's Tours are more personalized. Nell Morris Cribb, a Georgetown native who conducts tours wearing period dress, complete with a bonnet, provides personalized walking tours of the downtown historic district. The tour takes in about 12 history-rich blocks, lasts about 1¼ hours, and costs $8 for adults (free for children 11 and under). Tours begin at the Mark Twain Bookstore, 723 Front St. (☎ 843/546-3975). The tour is given Tuesday to Thursday at 10:30am and 2:30pm, and on Saturday and Sunday at 2:30pm.

OUTDOOR PURSUITS

CANOEING & KAYAKING   Black River Expeditions can be arranged at Kensington Gardens, U.S. 701, 3 miles north of Georgetown (☎ **803/546-4840**). Kayak, tandem kayak, and canoe excursions cost $20 for a half-day excursion or $45 adults; $25 children, for the whole day. It takes about 1¼ hours to paddle the Black River.

Black Water Adventures (☎ **800/761-1850** for reservations), headed by local Louis Nexsen, offers an "Adventure by Kayak" trip on Lake Moultrie and the Cooper River. The 5-hour canoe trip is available daily for $45 per person.

GOLF   One of the popular Georgetown championship courses, ♦ **Wedgefield Plantation,** just north of Georgetown (☎ **843/546-8587**), is on the site of a former Black River rice plantation and has wildlife in abundance. It was designed by Porter Gibson, and *Golf Week*'s "America's Best" honored it as one of the top 50 golf courses in South Carolina in 1994. Greens fees are $35 to $55, including cart. The signature hole is the par-4 14th, with both tee and approach shots over water.

RIVER CRUISES   The *Carolina Rover* and the *Jolly Rover* (☎ 843/546-8822) set sail from Georgetown Harbor. The *Carolina Rover* offers a 3-hour trip aboard a 40-foot pontoon boat, including a docked stop on North Island. The 45-minute excursion includes a nature walk and an opportunity to go shelling on this rather remote island. Trips leave at 10am and 2pm Monday to Saturday. The *Jolly Rover* is a 3-hour tour of Winyah Bay aboard an 80-foot topsail schooner. On board is a storyteller in a pirate's costume, who relates tales about pirates and ghosts who have prowled (and continue to prowl) the Carolina coast. Trips depart Monday to Saturday at 10am, 1 and 6pm. The cost of each trip is $20 for adults and $10 for children under 12. Reservations are strongly recommended.

WHERE TO STAY

♦ **DuPre House.** 921 Prince St., Georgetown, SC 29440. ☎ **877/519-9499** or 843/546-0298. Fax 843/520-0771. www.duprehouse.com. E-mail: richard.barnett@gte.net. 5 units. A/C. $95–$125 double. Rates include full breakfast. No credit cards.

Missouri-born Marshall Wile has transformed this 1740 New England–style house into a highly appealing bed-and-breakfast hotel where the owner takes a personal interest in the well-being of his guests. Only a 2-minute walk from Georgetown's center and 1 block from the waterfront, it features a working fireplace near the entrance, glowing oaken floors, durable but tasteful furnishings, and five bedrooms that are interconnected via steeply sloping colonial-style staircases. An outdoor swimming pool and a hot tub are on the premises. The good-size bedrooms are conservatively but tastefully decorated with contemporary furnishings. The daily social and gastronomic highlight is breakfast, when the host prepares his personalized version of French toast and makes conversation from a state-of-the-art kitchen.

1790 House. 630 Highmarket St., Georgetown, SC 29440. ☎ **800/890-7432** or 843/546-4821. www.1790house.com. E-mail:jwiley1212@cs.com. 6 units. A/C TEL. $95–$145 double. Rates include full breakfast. AE, DISC, MC, V.

In the heart of the Georgetown National Register Historic District, this B&B has spacious, individual accommodations with colonial furnishings; some rooms include such special features as fireplaces, writing desks, and TVs. A favorite with guests is the Dependency Cottage, featuring a queen-size Windsor bed, a sitting area, a refrigerator, a spacious bathroom with a separate shower and whirlpool tub, and a private entrance enhanced by a patio overlooking the garden. Breakfast includes fresh fruit, homemade muffins and breads, and hot specialties that change daily. The hotel also operates the Angel's Touch Tea Room, serving an English high tea or a "cream tea."

The Shaw House Bed and Breakfast. 613 Cypress Court, Georgetown, SC 29440. ☎ and fax **843/546-9663.** www.bbonline.com/sc/shawhouse. E-mail: jeshaw@sccoast.net. 3 units. A/C TV TEL. $65–$75 double. Each additional person $15. Rates include full breakfast. No credit cards.

Nestled among pine trees overlooking miles of marshland, this colonial B&B has spacious rooms with impressive antiques that evoke the grandeur and culture of the Old South. Mary and Joe Shaw, your gracious hosts, are more-than-adequate innkeepers; their knowledge of the area is encyclopedic. Golf courses, tennis courts, the beach, and two marinas are nearby, as well as the many specialty shops and restaurants of Georgetown. Your day begins with a full Southern breakfast that's probably more than you can eat. Historic walking tours and boat tours can be arranged.

WHERE TO DINE

Daniel's Waterfront Eatery. 713 Front St. ☎ **843/546-4377.** Main courses $10–$16. AE, MC, V. Mon 11am–3pm, Tues–Sat 11am–3pm and 5–9pm. AMERICAN.

A longtime local favorite, this restaurant, located on Georgetown's most historic street, honors the town's nautical past with a boat hanging from the ceiling. The decor is rustic indeed—century-old brick walls made from ships' ballast. Upstairs is a lounge with water views and an outdoor deck. Don't come here for gourmet fare; rather, order such kid-pleasing selections as burgers and hot dogs or even Philly steaks on a bun. Specialties include Cajun shrimp, shrimp- and crabmeat-salad platters, grilled chicken, grilled grouper, salmon cakes, and the standard steaks. Prices are reasonable, so no wonder this restaurant is a family favorite.

✪ **The Rice Paddy.** 819 Front St. ☎ **843/546-2021.** Reservations recommended. Main courses $16.95–$22.95. AE, DISC, MC, V. Mon–Sat 11:30am–2:30pm and 6–10pm. SEAFOOD/AMERICAN.

The Rice Paddy continues the Georgetown tradition of everything historic. This early-20th-century structure has a minimalist decor that relies on the effectiveness of its exposed-brick walls. The river side of the restaurant offers views of the Sampit River, and if you want to sit even closer to the river, an outdoor dining patio with awnings and ceiling fans seats up to 40 patrons comfortably. Cookery has flair and flavor, with a finesse and consistency that keep the most discriminating palates of Georgetown returning again and again. Main-course choices range from lump crab cakes to fillet of beef with shiitake mushrooms to pan-fried quail with grits. The menu changes seasonally to take advantage of the freshest ingredients.

River Room. 801 Front St. ☎ **843/527-4110.** Reservations recommended. Main courses $9.95–$19.95. AE, MC, V. Mon–Sat 11am–2:30pm and 5–10pm. SEAFOOD.

This is about the best Georgetown gets in terms of seafood dining. Some dishes are a bit overcooked, but locals seem to prefer them that way. Guests are rewarded by waterfront views from cozy precincts; an equally inviting bar is decked out in wood and exposed brick. Diners are smartly dressed in a casual way. Daily specials might include seafood fettuccine or a soft-shell-crab sandwich. Main dishes tend to be more elaborate; we fared well with the McClellanville crab balls dressed with spices and herbs. Shrimp Creole is regularly featured, and you can order such Low Country dishes as yellow grits sautéed with shrimp and sausage. Blackened grouper and tuna with basil cream sauce are other favorites.

Thomas Cafe. 703 Front St. ☎ **843/546-7776.** Reservations not accepted. Breakfast $4–$6; plate lunches $4.75–$6.75; sandwiches $3.50–$4.50. DISC, MC, V. Mon–Sat 7am–2pm. Sun 11am–3pm. LOW COUNTRY.

This is the kind of cafe where Charles Kuralt might have come to talk with the locals. With only five tables, a few booths, and a handful of counter stools, it's real Americana. Your waitress might be a spry 80-year-old. Breakfast is a very filling event: grits or hash browns served with eggs, omelets, or pancakes. At lunch, you can have a selection of soups and salads or sandwiches. Regulars like the barbecue with coleslaw. Plate lunches, including fried flounder, are also an item. We've fared better sticking to the plate lunch that includes one meat, a choice of three vegetables, and the inevitable cornbread or biscuit. This is the Old South—with hospitality but no nonsense.

13 Columbia & the Heartland

Moving inland, today's visitor comes face to face with vivid reminders of South Carolina's past, as well as with the New South. Industries such as textiles, chemicals, precision-tool making, and metalworks thrive alongside large farms producing dairy products, tobacco, soybeans, peaches, wheat, and cotton, plus large pine forests for an ever-growing paper industry.

Since the days of George Washington, who once visited Columbia, this area of South Carolina has been known for its equestrian tradition. Horses are ranked No. 3 on the state's commodities list. Camden and Aiken are centers for training racehorses that compete on racetracks around the country. Camden's Springdale Race Course plays host to two major steeplechases each year: the Carolina Cup and the Colonial Cup. The latter event is run in November, with a purse of $100,000. Aiken stages its yearly Aiken Triple Crown on three consecutive Saturdays in the spring.

Most outdoor recreation is in Santee Cooper Country, which offers fishing, golf, camping, hunting, and boating, among other diversions. Lake Marion and Lake Moultrie draw anglers in search of catfish, striped bream, crappie, and above all, bass—white, largemouth, and striped. There's no closed season for fishing.

The center is Columbia, the state capital, 3 miles from the geographic center of the state. It not only has its own attractions, but it's also is a good base for exploring several historic Piedmont towns, including Camden and York.

1 Columbia

120 miles NW of Charleston; 131 miles W of Myrtle Beach

Columbia, unlike many of America's older cities, has the orderly look of a planned community, with streets laid out like an almost-unbroken checkerboard and wide boulevards giving it a graceful beauty. The city was created in 1786 as a compromise capital, located just 3 miles from the exact geographical center of the state, to satisfy both Low and Up Country factions. George Washington paid a visit to Columbia in 1791, just a year after the first General Assembly convened in the brand-new city.

It was here that a convention, held in the First Baptist Church, passed the first Ordinance of Secession in the Southern states on December 17, 1860. (Because of a local smallpox epidemic, however, it was actually signed in Charleston.) Columbia itself was little touched by battle until General Sherman arrived with his Union troops on February 17, 1865, and virtually wiped out the town by fire: An 84-block area and some 1,386 buildings were left in ashes.

Although recovery during Reconstruction was slow, the city that emerged from almost-complete devastation is one of stately homes and public buildings, with government and education (seven colleges are located here) playing leading roles in its economy, followed closely by a wide diversity of industry. Fort Jackson, a U.S. Army basic-training post on the southeastern edge of town, adds another element to the economic mix.

ESSENTIALS

GETTING THERE   I-20 reaches Columbia from the northeast (connecting with I-95 running north and south) and southwest, I-26 from the southeast from Charleston (crossing I-95) and northwest, and I-77 from the north.

If you're flying, the Columbia Metropolitan Airport (☎ **803/822-5000**) is served by **Continental Airlines** (☎ **800/525-0820;** www.flycontinental.com), **Delta Air Lines** (☎ **800/221-1212;** www.delta.com), **Midway Airlines** (☎ **800/446-4392;** www.midwayair.com), and **US Airways** (☎ **800/428-4322;** www.usairways.com).

For information on **Amtrak** service, call ☎ **800/USA-RAIL.**

VISITOR INFORMATION   The **Columbia Metropolitan Convention and Visitors Bureau** is at 1012 Gervais St., Columbia, SC 29201 (☎ **800/264-4884** or 803/254-0479; www.columbiasc.net). Its visitor center is open Monday to Friday from 8:30am to 5pm and Saturday from 10am to 4pm (in summer), dispensing maps and data on the area's attractions.

EXPLORING THE AREA
THE STATE CAPITOL

The State House, at Main and Gervais streets (☎ **803/734-2430**), begun in 1855, was only half-finished when General Sherman bombarded Columbia in 1865. Today, the west and south walls are marked with bronze stars where the shells struck. In the fire that wiped out so much of the city, the State House escaped destruction, but the architect's plans were burned. As a result, the dome is not the one that was originally envisioned. Despite that fact, the building, with its Corinthian granite columns, is one of the most beautiful state capitols in the U.S. The landscaped grounds hold memorial tablets and monuments; inside are portraits and statues of South Carolina's greats. The State House is open Monday to Friday from 9am to 5pm; Saturday 10am to 5pm.

FOUR HISTORIC HOMES

At the ✪ **Historic Columbia Foundation,** 1616 Blanding St. (☎ **803/252-1770**), you can purchase tickets and get a tour map of the capital's most historic homes. Tickets for each property cost $4 for adults and $2.50 for children; a combination ticket to all four properties is $12 for adults, $7 for students and children.

Those 5 and under go free. Hourly tours are conducted Tuesday to Saturday from 10:15am to 3:15pm and on Sunday from 1:15 to 4:15pm, with tours starting on the quarter-hour.

Woodrow Wilson's Boyhood Home, 1705 Hampton St., was built by the president's father in 1872. Much Wilson memorabilia remains, including the family's heirloom furnishings. The red-velvet music room and the plush parlor evoke the Victorian age. The 28th president lived here until 1875, leaving at age 14 when his family decided to move out of state.

Hampton-Preston Mansion, 1615 Blanding St., was purchased by Wade Hampton and occupied by his family until 1865, when Union Gen. J.A. Logan took it over. Much memorabilia of the antebellum period remains, including furnishings and decorative arts. The house dates from 1818. The Hamptons were once called "the Kennedys of the Old South," having grown rich from cotton instead of liquor.

Manns-Simons Cottage, 1403 Richmond St., is a small house from the early 1850s. It was the former abode of Celia Mann, an African-American slave who bought her freedom and walked from Charleston to Columbia. She'd earned money by working on the side as a midwife and started a church for blacks in her basement at the end of the Civil War. Today, her former home houses a museum of African-American culture and an art gallery.

Robert Mills Historic House & Park is at 1616 Blanding St. Mills served seven presidents as the first federal architect, designing such landmarks as the Washington Monument, the U.S. Treasury Building, and the Old Patent Office in Washington, D.C. This is one of the few residences that he actually designed. It's rich in art and furnishings of the Regency and neoclassical periods.

MORE ATTRACTIONS

Columbia Museum of Art. Corner of Main and Hampton sts. ☎ **803/799-2810.** Admission $4 adults, $2 senior citizens and children. Tues–Sat 10am–5pm, Sun 1–5pm.

The museum's plaza has four quadrants: one containing an amphitheater; another, a dining terrace; and two others designed to feature plants and sculptures. The dining section's fountains and pools create an ambience matched nowhere in Columbia. The museum entry is at the rear of the plaza. The museum houses a permanent collection of more than 5,000 items, including paintings; furniture; baroque and Renaissance sculptures; and work by native South Carolinians, including turn-of-the-century photos. Temporary exhibitions (films, lectures, concerts, and special events) draw big crowds. Call the museum for a schedule of events.

Governor's Mansion. 800 Richland St. (at Lincoln St.). ☎ **803/737-1710.** Free admission. 20-minute guided tours Tues–Thurs 10–11:30am, by appointment only.

This house was built in 1855 as an officers' quarters for Arsenal Academy. When General Sherman swept through town, this was the only building on the academy grounds left standing. South Carolina governors have lived here since 1868.

✪ **South Carolina State Museum.** 301 Gervais St. ☎ **803/898-4921;** www.museum.state.sc.us. Admission $4 adults, $3 senior citizens, $1.50 children 6–17. Mon–Sat 10am–5pm, Sun 1–5pm.

The State Museum is housed in what was once the world's first all-electric textile mill. Each of the four floors is dedicated to one of four important areas: art, history, natural history, and science and technology. Hands-on exhibits, realistic dioramas, and laser displays make for exciting browsing through South Carolina's past, from prehistory through the present. Some of the decorative pottery on display was made by slaves. Look for the 1904 Oldsmobile "horseless carriage." Other exhibits focus on "king cotton" and slavery. One exhibit honors African-American astronauts, including Dr. Ronald McNair, a South Carolina native who was killed on the *Challenger.*

University of South Carolina. Gregg, Pendleton, and Main sts. ☎ **803/777-7000.** Free admission. Museum Mon–Fri 9am–4pm, Sat–Sun 1–5pm.

The scenic 218-acre campus is covered with buildings dating from the early 1800s. The campus is filled with ancient oaks and magnolias. Note especially the historic Horseshoe, at the corner of Pendleton and Bull streets. While you're here, it's worth half an hour or so to go by the **McKissick Museum** (☎ 803/777-7251), located in a fine old building at the head of the Horseshoe. The museum features changing exhibitions on regional folk art, history, natural science, and fine art, and contains the university's collection of historic 20th-Century Fox Movietone newsreels.

✪ **Riverbanks Zoo and Garden.** 500 Wildlife Pkwy. ☎ **803/779-8717.** Admission $6.75 adults, $4.25 children 3–12. Mon–Fri 9am–4pm, Sat–Sun 9am–5pm.

Known for its worldwide conservation work, this zoo is a refuge for many endangered species, including the American bald eagle. Animals live in natural habitats, and botanically significant trees and plants are labeled throughout the park. All kinds of domestic animals live at the Farm, which also has an automated milking parlor in action for the education of city-bred folk. The **Aquarium Reptile Complex** introduces the aquatic and reptilian creatures of South Carolina (the last tickets are sold 1 hour before closing). A 70-acre botanical garden opened in 1993. One of the zoo's real treats is actually not inside, but behind it—a place where you can picnic, swim, and revel in the mild rapids along the Saluda River. Wear your swimming trunks, and look for the rope that swings from a tree out over the river à la Tarzan.

NEARBY ATTRACTIONS
✪ EDISTO MEMORIAL GARDENS

To reach the gardens, drive 45 miles southeast of Columbia on I-26 and take U.S. 601 S. to Orangeburg. The 165-acre park, on U.S. 301, is located along the banks of the Edisto River, the world's longest blackwater river. The garden is one of three test gardens in the United States and is known especially for its experimentations in roses. Some 5,000 varieties bloom from mid-April until October. Other vegetation and trees include camellias, dogwood, cherry trees, and thousands of azaleas that bloom from mid-March to mid-April. South Carolina's Festival of Roses, one of the 20 top festivals in the Southeast, is held here annually during the last weekend in April. The gardens are open daily from dawn to dusk, charging no admission.

✪ THE SANTEE COOPER LAKES

From Orangeburg, it's a short drive on U.S. 301 to I-95 N. to Lake Marion and Lake Moultrie, known collectively as the Santee Cooper Lakes, which cover more than 171,000 acres. Anglers, note: Three world-record and eight state-record catches have been recorded here. Anglers flock to try their luck with the striped, largemouth, hybrid, and white bass; catfish; and other panfish stocked in these waters. The lakes are ringed with fish camps, marinas, campgrounds, and modern motels.

You don't have to be an angler to enjoy this scenic region, however; you'll find numerous golf courses, tennis courts, and wildlife sanctuaries. The best place for camping is Santee State Park, which offers 150 sites at two lakefront campgrounds on Lake Marion. Amenities include swimming, tennis, a boat ramp, fishing boats, a tackle shop, and nature programs (including a nature trail).

The **Santee-Cooper Counties Promotion Commission,** P.O. Drawer 40, Santee, SC 29142 (☎ **800/227-8510,** or 803/854-2131 within South Carolina; www. santeecoopercountry.org), can furnish full details on recreational facilities and accommodations. For more on lakefront vacation cabins on Lake Marion, contact the Superintendent, **Santee State Park,** 251 State Park Rd., Box 79, Santee, SC 29142 (☎ **803/854-2408;** www.southcarolinaparks.com). In all cases, be sure to inquire about fishing and golf package deals. To reach the state park from Columbia, take I-26 east to U.S. 301 north to I-95 north; take Exit 98 to Santee and head 3 miles northwest.

Columbia residents also go to **Santee Cooper Country** for 270 holes of golf. For a complete golf kit, contact Santee Cooper Country, P.O. Box 40, Santee, SC 29142 (☎ **800/227-8510,** or 803/854-2131 within South Carolina).

WHERE TO STAY
EXPENSIVE

✪ **Adam's Mark.** 1200 Hampton St., Columbia, SC 29201. ☎ **800/444-ADAM** or 803/771-7000. Fax 803/254-8307. www.adamsmark.com. 305 units. A/C MINIBAR TV TEL. $104–$113 double; $350–$450 suite. Children 17 and under stay free in parents' room. AE, CB, DC, DISC, MC, V. Parking $7.

Near state offices and the University of South Carolina, this upscale, 14-story downtown landmark was known for years as the Columbia Marriott. With its atrium design, Adam's Mark is clearly far superior to its major competitor, the Embassy Suites at 200 Stoneridge Dr. But it lacks the traditional charm of Claussen's Inn at Five Points (recommended later in this chapter). The accommodations have subtle color schemes and either a king-size bed or two double beds. Thoughtful extras include mirrored closets, irons, and ironing boards.

Dining/Diversions: The hotel dining room serves up American cuisine, including fresh fish, in a family-style atmosphere. The entertainment in the lounge is nothing special: taped music and TV.

Amenities: Room service, laundry, baby-sitting, second-floor health club, whirlpool, and indoor pool.

Richland Street B&B. 1425 Richland St., Columbia, SC 29201. ☎ **800/779-7011** or 803/779-7001. Fax 803/256-3725. A/C TV TEL. 8 units. $89–$145 double; $159 suite. Rates include deluxe continental breakfast. AE, MC, V. Free parking.

This 1992-vintage building was built in the Victorian style in the historic-preservation district, within walking distance of the major homes for touring. It's a rival of Claussen's Inn (recommended later in this chapter) in every way. This no-smoking establishment allows visitors to bring children on occasion, but only at the discretion of management. The rooms are tastefully furnished and well maintained, and the suite has a whirlpool.

Dining: The inn serves a deluxe continental breakfast, afternoon tea, and complimentary coffee is available to guests.

Amenities: Hair dryers (all rooms), balconies (two rooms), and whirlpool (one suite).

Whitney Hotel. 700 Woodrow St. (at Devine St.), Columbia, SC 29205. ☎ **800/637-4008** or 803/252-0845. Fax 803/771-0495. www.whitneyhotel.com. 74 suites. A/C MINIBAR TV TEL. $119 1-bedroom suite; $139 2-bedroom suite. Rates include continental breakfast. AE, CB, DC, DISC, MC, V. Free parking.

Southeast of the center, this all-suite hotel is the premier motor hotel in the capital. It's about a 20-minute walk from the University of South Carolina and a mile from Five Points. It's an eight-floor stucco building, traditional in style from its classic marble lobby to its wood-trimmed lounge. All suites are tastefully furnished, with ample bathrooms and complete kitchens with stoves, microwaves, and refrigerators. The suites also have washers and dryers, butler's tables, and balconies. The small staff is congenial, but the hotel is not quite as luxurious as it appears to be in its promotional material.

Amenities: Free airport transportation, valet, pool, bicycles, and free access to nearby health club.

MODERATE

✪ **Claussen's Inn.** 2003 Greene St., Columbia, SC 29205. ☎ **800/622-3382** or 803/765-0440. Fax 803/799-7924. E-mail: claussensinn@columbiasc.com 29 units. A/C TV TEL. $125–$135 double; $149 suite. Rates include deluxe continental breakfast. AE, CB, DC, DISC, MC, V. Free parking.

Just 2 miles southeast of downtown, this is the premier inn of Columbia. It's in the fashionable Five Points district, near the University of South Carolina, and it offers far more charm than any other in the local landscape. The tastefully decorated rooms may have watermelon-color walls, pine armoires, Windsor chairs, and small patios; some have four-poster beds. Sherry and wine are offered in the lobby.

INEXPENSIVE

Red Roof Inn East. 7580 Two Notch Rd., Columbia, SC 29223. ☎ **800/843-7663** or 803/736-0850. Fax 803/736-4270. www.redroof.com. 1098 units. A/C TV TEL. $51–$61 double. Senior discounts available. Rates include complimentary coffee and daily newspaper. AE, DC, DISC, MC, V. Free parking.

This budget choice isn't special, but it's one of the best buys among a lackluster lot of motels on Columbia's outskirts. The bedrooms are routinely furnished, but the housekeeping is good. The inn also has facilities for the disabled.

There's another **Red Roof Inn West** at 10 Berryhill Rd., Columbia, SC 29210 (☎ **800/843-7663** or 803/798-9220; fax 803/798-9065). It offers the same types of rooms and amenities, but it charges only $42.99 to $52.99 for a double.

WHERE TO DINE

Columbia has a host of restaurants, many with chain affiliations. The area around Five Points, close to the USC campus, is ideal for snacks, coffee, or something more substantial.

EXPENSIVE

✪ **Hennessy's.** 1649 Main St. ☎ **803/799-8280.** Reservations recommended. Main courses $12.95–$23.95. AE, DC, MC, V. Mon–Fri 11:30am–2:30pm and 6–10pm, Sat 6–11pm. CONTINENTAL.

This converted hardware store provided us our finest meal on our latest rounds in Columbia. It's the most intriguing in town, and we like it even better than Garibaldi's. The kitchen may not be particularly daring, but it's in capable hands, and the service staff is ready for the big time; it's that good. The food is nicely prepared and fresh-tasting. Virtually all the dishes on the menu—from beef Stroganoff to oysters Rockefeller, from Maryland crab cakes to grouper almondine—are the kind that were served to President and Mrs. Coolidge back in the 1920s. Yet if these dishes have endured all these years, why not? Rack of lamb is accented by cabernet sauce. Some heart-healthy selections are also available.

MODERATE

California Dreaming. 401 S. Main St. (2 blocks south of Blossom St.). ☎ **803/254-6767.** Main courses $7–$20. AE, MC, V. Sun–Thurs 11am–10pm, Fri–Sat 11am–11pm. AMERICAN.

This large and popular restaurant, in a restored 1902 depot, is usually filled with both students and the uptown crowd. You just show up and wait for a seat, because you won't have much luck trying to reserve a table. The freshly made salads are quite good, and the food is prime rib or seafood—typical fare such as that. Barbecued ribs, homemade pasta, and Tex-Mex dishes are also featured. This place is renowned for its large portions.

Garibaldi's. 2013 Greene St. ☎ **803/771-8888.** Reservations recommended. Main courses $6.95–$22.95. AE, MC, V. Sun–Thurs 5:30–10:30pm, Fri–Sat 5:30–11pm. ITALIAN/ SEAFOOD.

Near the university campus, with an inviting ambience, Garibaldi's is the first name that comes to mind when a local wants to eat Italian. Art Deco furnishings add a traditional note, and the helpful staff provides service with a smile. The menu is familiar—the usual array of seafood, beef, and chicken—but ingredients tend to be fresh and are deftly handled by the kitchen, even if Granddad would recognize the recipes. Try the shrimp marinara over angel-hair pasta. Gourmet pizzas are available. Every dish is so generously apportioned that you may not have room for dessert, but that would be no great loss here. Jazz pours forth from the speakers.

Motor Supply Company Bistro. 920 Gervais St. (at Congaree Vista, behind Carol Saunders Gallery). ☎ **803/256-6687.** Reservations recommended. Main courses $10–$23. AE, DC, MC, V. Daily 11:30am–2:30pm and Tues–Sat 6–11pm. INTERNATIONAL.

Despite its unappetizing name, this restaurant serves decent food. It's in an 1890s building, now listed on the National Register of Historic Places, that was once a motor-supply-parts warehouse and has been completely restored. You'd never suspect the building's former role as you sit at the oak German bar or a marble-topped English table. Outside is a sculpture garden, and diners can browse through the gift shop or art gallery inside. At night, the kitchen works harder than at lunch, turning out such well-prepared appetizers as grilled quail with balsamic barbecue and chicken satay with peanut sauce (definitely Thai-influenced). Main dishes might include peppercorn-encrusted pink salmon with champagne *beurre blanc* (white butter) or fillet of beef with crabmeat and hollandaise. The menu changes daily.

INEXPENSIVE

Adriana's. 721 Saluda Ave. ☎ **803/799-7595.** Reservations not accepted. Coffee $1.25–$3.25; desserts $2.35–$4.50; food $4–$10. MC, V. Mon–Sat 9:00am–midnight, Sun 11am–11pm. COFFEES/DESSERT.

This most quintessentially appealing coffeehouse in the area is frequented by university students who drop in either to chill out or warm up. Black-and-white art decorates the walls, and you sit at marble-topped tables on ice-cream-parlor chairs. The homemade desserts are delectable. Try the cheesecake, the velvety ice cream, the yogurt, or one of the flavorful coffees.

Gourmet Shop Cafe. 724 Saluda Ave. ☎ **803/799-3705.** Reservations not accepted. Sandwiches $5.50–$8.50; salads $5.95–$7.95. AE, MC, V. Mon–Sat 9am–7pm; Sun 10am–5pm. BAKERY/WINE SHOP.

Bright and airy, this place is a combination wine shop/coffeehouse/bakery. It's a favorite among students, who come for the convivial atmosphere as much as for the food. The tables on the sidewalk are particularly inviting (except on hot summer days). Sample the wine, the cheese, the fresh French bread, or the "perfect" bottle of wine, or munch down on a deli sandwich. The gourmet cooking shop next door sells kitchen gadgets, many of which you didn't know existed.

✪ Maurice Gourmet Barbecue—Piggie Park. 1600 Charleston Hwy. ☎ **803/ 796-0220.** www.mauricebbq.com. Main courses $4.95–$10.99. MC, V. Sun–Thurs 10am– 11pm, Fri–Sat 10am–midnight. BARBECUE.

Some say this place serves the best barbecue in the South. Because we haven't sampled all the barbecue in the South, we don't know. But this is certainly the first name on the tongues of barbecue fans in Columbia. Maurice Bessinger, king of barbecue, is the

CEO, and the empire-building barbecue-sauce recipe is the legacy of his late father, Big Joe Bessinger. The sauce is mustard-based (the other ingredients are secret), and it's spread (liberally) over pork, ribs, and chicken. Patrons who eschew barbecue aren't kicked out of the joint, but are given other choices, like cheeseburgers and chicken strips. The desserts are homemade, like Mama used to make, including banana pudding, lemon pie, and strawberry shortcake. Don't live in the neighborhood? Simply have the barbecue shipped to you on the Flying Pig Express.

COLUMBIA AFTER DARK
PERFORMING ARTS

The **South Carolina Philharmonic** and the **Chamber Orchestra Association,** 1237 Gadsden St. (☎ 803/771-7937; www.scphilharmonic.com), perform concerts at various venues throughout Columbia and the surrounding area. The music runs from classical music to pop and jazz. The season lasts from October to May. Call for information about performances and tickets.

Columbia Music Festival Association, 914 Pulaski St. (☎ 803/771-6303), puts on a variety of concerts, ranging from classical and opera to Broadway scores, pop, and jazz. Its season runs from late October until late May.

The **Workshop Theater of South Carolina,** 1136 Bull St. (☎ 803/799-4876), which has a season lasting from October to March, produces musicals, comedies, and dramas. You can obtain ticket information from the box office from noon to 6pm on performance days only. For announcements of presentations, look in the local newspapers or call the theater.

Columbians drive over to Abbeville to attend performances at the ✪ **Abbeville Opera House,** Town Square (☎ 864/459-2157). It's known for the high caliber of its productions—everything from plays to musicals. Built in 1908, and one of the most famous opera houses in the South, it used to feature headliners on the vaudeville circuit, including Fanny Brice (the inspiration for *Funny Girl*) and Jimmy Durante. Its summer opera season runs from early June to late August or mid-September, with performances on Friday and Saturday at 8pm, plus a Saturday matinee at 3pm. The winter season begins in early October, running until the end of April. In winter, shows are offered only on Friday and Saturday at 8pm, with a Saturday matinee at 3pm. Tickets cost $15 for adults, $14 for seniors (65 or older) and children 11 and under. The box office is open Monday to Friday from 1 to 5pm. Abbeville lies 90 miles west of Columbia. To reach it from Columbia, go along U.S. 378 to Saluda; then follow the signs into Abbeville.

THE CLUB & BAR SCENE

The Capitol Club. 1002 Gervais St. (between Assembly and Park sts.). ☎ **803/256-6464.**

This is the classiest and most dignified gay bar in South Carolina, modeled on London gentlemen's clubs. Located about a block west of the gold dome of the South Carolina capitol building, it's outfitted with leather sofas, unusual artwork, and a very long bar where many of the regulars sit. No food is served, and almost no one ever opts to dance. Because the place defines itself as a private club, an advance phone call is usually a good idea. In a state widely publicized for its homophobia, don't expect a prominent sign out front—just a discreet plaque.

Metropolis. 1800 Blanding St. ☎ **803/799-8727.**

Every night beginning at 7pm, and lasting until the final guest departs, Metropolis is a major entertainment venue in the capital, attracting a mostly young clientele. Ten 25-inch color TV sets, a booming sound system, and a giant projection TV, fill the room with digital videos and music from the '80s and '90s. The bartenders specialize in frozen drinks, many enjoyed in the courtyard setting. Every night something new is happening, ranging from Margarita Mondays to pool tournament Tuesdays. Entertainment is often provided. The place even serves virgin frozen drinks for all its Shirley Temple patrons.

2 Side Trips from Columbia

North-central South Carolina was the scene of several significant battles of the American Revolution. Camden was actually an important garrison for British general Lord Cornwallis, and the battle of Kings Mountain, many people believe, was the turning point of the Revolutionary War. Battles of another sort are regularly waged these days on Darlington's raceway here, as stock cars engage in fierce competition.

CAMDEN

The 24-mile drive northeast to Camden, via I-20 and U.S. 521, takes you straight back to this nation's beginnings. Founded by Irish Quakers in 1751, it's the state's oldest inland town. During the Revolutionary War, 14 battles raged within a 30-mile radius here. Cornwallis held Camden until the British retreated in 1781, burning the town behind them. During the Civil War, another invader, General Sherman, brought his Union troops to burn the town once more, because it had served the Confederates as a storehouse and as a hospital. Historic relics are everywhere you look.

Camden is equally well known for the training of fine Thoroughbred horses; the internationally known **Colonial Cup** steeplechase, held at the nearby Springdale Course, draws huge crowds.

Make your first stop the **Kershaw County Chamber of Commerce,** 724 S. Broad (P.O. Box 605), Camden, SC 29020 (☎ **803/432-2525;** www.camden-sc.org). Pick up a guidebook and a self-guided driving tour to point you to 63 historic sites in the area. The chamber is open Monday to Friday from 9am to 5pm.

Historic Camden, South Broad Street (☎ **803/432-9841**), is a Revolutionary War park affiliated with the National Park Service. There are restored log houses with museum exhibits, fortifications, the Cornwallis House, a powder magazine, an 80-building model of the original town, and miniature dioramas depicting military actions between 1780 and 1781. The guided tour includes a narrated slide presentation and access to all museums. The park is open Tuesday to Saturday from 10am to 5pm and on Sunday from 1 to 5pm. Adults pay $5, students are charged $2, and children 5 and under enter free. Self-guided tours are free.

At nearby **Goodale State Park,** 2 miles north of Camden on Old Wire Road (off U.S. 1), you'll find lake swimming and fishing, with pedal and fishing boats for rent. Bring along a picnic, and wander the nature trail.

WHERE TO STAY

✪ **The Greenleaf Inn at Camden.** 1308–1310 Broad St., Camden SC 29020. ☎ **800/437-5874** or 803/425-1806. Fax 803/425-5853. www.greenleafinncamden.com. 12 units. A/C TV TEL. $75–$95 double; $150 cottage. Rates include breakfast. AE, MC, V.

This inn, located in Camden's historic district, consists of two separate houses and includes the Reynolds House, which dates from 1805. There are seven rooms in the Reynolds House, the main house of a plantation that once stood here. There are also four rooms to rent on the second floor. The inn is owned by Alice Boykin, of the famous Columbia family. The entire inn is decorated with Victorian furnishings appropriate to its era. Two of the rooms are virtual minisuites, each with a small sitting area. It also has a two-bedroom cottage with two bathrooms and a kitchenette, suitable for up to five guests. The opening of a restaurant on-site was slated for the end of 2000.

WHERE TO DINE

☼ The Mill Pond Restaurant. 84 Boykin Mill Rd., Boykin. ☎ **803/424-0261.** Reservations required. Main courses $18.95–$28. MC, V. Tues–Thurs 5–9:30pm, Fri–Sat 5–11pm. Take U.S. 521 S. to S.C. 261 to Boykin, 10 miles south of Camden. INTERNATIONAL.

Recognized as being one of the finest heartland restaurants, this establishment attracts diners from miles away, often from as far as Columbia. Constructed in the 1890s, it's listed on the National Register of Historic Places. It has Early American decor and offers a view overlooking the mill pond. The chef chooses prime, rigorously fresh ingredients and, with the help of a skillful staff, fashions dishes that are often sublime. The menu typically includes potato-crusted grouper with Calabash shrimp or marinated quail on mixed greens (a local favorite).

DARLINGTON

Stock-car fans in the thousands invade Darlington (70 miles northeast of Columbia via I-20 and U.S. 52/401) in early April for NASCAR's **TransSouth 400** race and again on Labor Day weekend for the **Southern 500.** The **Darlington County Chamber of Commerce,** 38 Public Sq., P.O. Box 274, Darlington, SC 29540 (☎ 843/393-2641), can furnish detailed information on racing, as well as sightseeing in this area. Hours are Monday to Friday from 9am to 5pm.

If you arrive between the year's two main races, hike over to the **NMPA Stock Car Hall of Fame/Joe Weatherly Museum** (☎ 843/395-8821) at the Darlington Raceway, 1 mile west of town on SC 34. It holds the world's largest collection of stock cars, including those of such racing greats as Richard Petty and Fireball Roberts. Hours are 8:30am to 5pm daily, and admission is $3 (free for kids 12 and under).

LOOKING FOR LOCAL FISH CAMPS

This is fish-camp country. Very often, you'll find down-home fish dinners (all you can eat for practically nothing) in rustic cafes on unpaved side roads. Stop at a gas station, grocery store, or some other local shop, and just ask; everybody has a favorite, and it's often worth a detour.

A good place to begin your search is Route 6 (Porter Road). The best time to show up is on a Friday or Saturday night. The operators of these dives are likely to have gone fishin' the rest of the week.

YORK

York is at the heart of South Carolina's northern Piedmont. To get here from Columbia, take I-77 north to Rock Hill, then S.C. 5 about 15 miles northwest to York.

The Department of the Interior has granted York one of the largest historic districts in the United States. The restored downtown area is filled with specialty shops—in all, 180 historical structures and landmarks. Arm yourself with a detailed map from the **Greater York Chamber of Commerce,** 23 E. Liberty St. (P.O. Box 97), York, SC 29745 (☎ 803/684-2590), open Monday to Friday from 9am to 4pm.

Nearby **Historic Brattonsville,** 1444 Brattonsville Rd., McConnells (☎ 803/684-2327), is a restored Southern village of 18th- and 19th-century buildings. To reach it, take U.S. 321 south from York or S.C. 322 from Rock Hill. Restorations include a dirt-floor backwoodsman's cabin, a 1750s frontier home, an authentic antebellum plantation home, hand-hewn log storage buildings, and a brick slave cabin. It's open Tuesday to Saturday from 10am to 4pm and on Sunday from 1 to 5pm. Admission is $5 for adults, $3 for children 5 to 17 and seniors.

KINGS MOUNTAIN

Just across the border from North Carolina, **Kings Mountain Military Park** (☎ 864/936-7921) marks the site of the Revolutionary War battle that was crucial to the eventual colonial victory. The park is on I-85, 20 miles northeast of Gaffney; from York, take S.C. 5 northwest for about 20 miles.

The southern Appalachians were virtually undisturbed by the war until 1780, when British Maj. Patrick Ferguson, who had threatened to "lay the country waste with fire and sword," set up camp here with a large loyalist force. The local backwoodsmen recruited Whigs from Virginia and North Carolina to form a largely untrained, but very determined, army to throw the invaders out. In spite of wave after wave of British bayonet charges, the ill-trained and outnumbered colonists converged on Kings Mountain and kept advancing on Ferguson's men until they took the summit. Ferguson was killed in the battle, and the Appalachians were once more under colonial control. You can see relics and a diorama of the battle at the visitor center. It's open every day of the year except Thanksgiving Day, Christmas Day, and New Year's Day, from 9am to 5pm; admission is free.

3 Aiken: Thoroughbred Country

60 miles SW of Columbia; 17 miles E of Augusta

The international horse set hangs out in the country around Aiken at the Georgia–South Carolina border, where horse training and racing are major preoccupations. When you're driving, you might find yourself sharing the road with a horse and its mount. There's even a stoplight just for horses on Whiskey Road. Nearly a thousand horses winter and train in this area, and Aiken has two racetracks, as well as polo grounds.

The fame of Aiken began in the 1890s, when rich Northerners flocked here in winter, often erecting lavish mansions. It was a rival of Thomasville, Georgia, which also attracted the wintering wealthy. The horsey set amused themselves with horse shows, fox hunts, and lavish parties.

ESSENTIALS

GETTING THERE   From Columbia, take I-20 west for 55 miles to either Exit 22 (Hwy. 1) or Exit 18 (Hwy. 19). Both routes lead into downtown Aiken. From Augusta (Georgia), take I-20 east, getting off at either Exit 18 or 22.

VISITOR INFORMATION   The **Aiken Chamber of Commerce,** 121 Richland Ave. E. (☎ 803/641-1111), offers a 90-minute tour of the historic district every Saturday at 10am, at a cost of $6 per person. A 25-passenger bus takes visitors throughout the historic core to view the old Southern homes. The chamber is open Monday to Friday from 8:30am to 5pm, Saturday from 9am to noon.

SEEING THE SIGHTS

The three weekends of horse racing in March that make up the **Aiken Triple Crown** are the highlight of the year. By contacting **Thoroughbred Country** (☎ 803/649-7981) or 800/542-4536 before you come, you can find out about the many sporting activities that are available.

Even nonhorsey folks, however, will delight in the lovely old homes in the town's historic district. The **Aiken County Historical Museum,** 433 Newberry St. SW

(☎ 803/642-2015), occupies part of a former millionaire's estate. Of special interest are Native American artifacts, a 1930s drugstore from a little South Carolina town that no longer exists, a 19th-century schoolhouse, and a full miniature circus. Admission is by donation. Open Tuesday to Friday 9:30am to 4:30pm, Saturday and Sunday 2 to 5pm.

Hopeland Gardens, 149 Dupree Place (at the corner of Whiskey Road; ☎ 803/ 642-7630), are the pride of Aiken, graced with weeping willows, fountains, and shimmering ponds. The grounds hold the **Thoroughbred Racing Hall of Fame** in a restored carriage house. The gardens' touch-and-scent trail has plaques in both standard type and in braille to identify plants and to lead visitors, blind or sighted, to a performing-arts stage. Here, open-air concerts are given Monday evenings in summer, and theatrical productions are offered periodically. Admission is free. The gardens are open daily from 10am to dusk; the Hall of Fame is open October 15 to May 15, daily 2 to 5pm.

WHERE TO STAY

Aiken is an easy day trip from Columbia, but this part of the state is so beguiling that you may want to settle in here for a day or so. Note that when special events are on (horse races, the Masters Golf Tournament in neighboring Augusta, Georgia, and so on), rates in the Aiken area often go up.

The Briar Patch Bed & Breakfast. 544 Magnolia Lane SE, Aiken, SC 29801. ☎ 803/ 649-2010. E-mail: briarfox@prodigy.net. 2 units. TV. $60 double. Rates include continental breakfast. No credit cards.

Listed on the National Register of Historic Places, this is Aiken's finest B&B. It's very small, however, so reservations are important. Lying a couple of blocks from the polo grounds and 2 miles from the racetracks, it attracts the horse set. The rooms were created from a horse stable, and the bedrooms were once a tack room. The rooms are separated from the main house and furnished with early-American antiques. Both have fireplaces and private bathrooms. Tennis is available, and golfers enjoy privileges nearby. A coffeemaker and refrigerator are available for guest use.

Holly Inn & Holly House Motel. 235 Richland Ave., Aiken, SC 29801. ☎ or fax **803/ 648-4265.** 51 units. Hotel $69.95 double, $89.95 suite; motel $59.95 double. Rates include continental breakfast. AE, DISC, MC, V.

The main part of the inn dates from 1929 and offers tastefully decorated and spa-cious rooms with high ceilings typical of the era. More modern but less interesting standard-size rooms are in the motel, offering modest comfort. Maintenance is excellent. There's also a bar on-site, and several restaurants are within walking distance.

✪ **Willcox Inn.** 100 Colleton Ave. (at the corner of Whiskey Rd.), Aiken, SC 29801. ☎ **803/649-1377.** Fax 803/643-0971. www.willcoxinn.com. 30 units. A/C TV TEL. $99– $125 double; $150 suite. AE, DC, DISC, MC, V.

Washington didn't sleep here, but Winston Churchill and Franklin D. Roosevelt did. So did the Astors, the Duke of Windsor, and an array of other glittering names. This 1897 inn, with its English country-house decor and antique furnishings, is one of the premier inns of South Carolina. It's booked solid during the Masters Golf Tournament at nearby Augusta, Georgia.

The lobby is graced with rosewood and pine woodwork, oak floors, stone fireplaces, and Oriental carpets. Guest rooms are individually decorated, with ornamental fireplaces and a liberal use of Second Empire furnishings.

Now under new ownership, the Willcox is expected to undergo major restoration and refurbishment work sometime in the near future, so call ahead to make sure the hotel will be fully operating when you plan your trip.

Dining/Diversions: The inn's Pheasant Room is also the top restaurant in Aiken. The dining room is lovely, with fresh flowers and sparkling goblets. Well-prepared dishes are drawn from a continually changing repertoire of creative continental fare based on seasonally fresh produce. Have a drink in the Polo Pub, which displays artifacts such as fly rods, cricket bats, and polo mallets. The Pheasant Room is open for breakfast, lunch, and dinner.

WHERE TO DINE

No. 10 Downing Street. 241 Laurens St. ☎ **803/642-9062.** Reservations recommended. Main courses $14–$22. AE, DC, DISC, MC, V. Tues–Sat 6–9:30pm. INTERNATIONAL.

This 1835 Southern colonial house was once the home of the artist, poet, and sculptor James Mathews Legare. Some of his work is still displayed in his former studio, the Legare Room. Today, the house serves some of the best food in town, ranking right up there with the Willcox Inn (recommended above). Six fireplaces, rose-colored walls, and heart-pine floors add a traditional touch. The menu is forever changing, focusing one month on Italy and another month on provincial French cuisine. We've enjoyed candied salmon with wine and garlic, crowned with caramelized onions; and beef tenderloin flavored with garlic and oregano, and given added zest by the use of fresh tomatoes. A bakery on the premises turns out home-baked breads, pies, and cookies. Try the No. 10 Downing Street "werk bread," made with Guinness stout, molasses, and three kinds of flour (including rye).

The Upstate 14

The northwestern region of South Carolina in the foothills of the Blue Ridge Mountains was originally known as the "back country" because it was "in back" of Charleston. Over the years, this land of scenic wonders, with miles of peaks, waterfalls, mountain hamlets, and unspoiled forests, became known as the Up Country (also Upcountry). Here, American patriots trounced vastly superior British forces at the Cowpens, one of the decisive battles of the southern campaign during the Revolutionary War.

Today the region generally referred to as the Upstate offers a wide variety of attractions and outdoor activities: 90 festivals throughout the year, more than 500 historic sites, 12 state parks, and numerous recreational opportunities.

The nation's second-largest hot-air-balloon festival, Freedom Weekend Aloft, is held July 4th weekend at Donaldson Center in Greenville. Another favorite is the Collectors' Market on the Green (antiques and pottery), staged in Pendleton in mid-September. For the history buff, the Cowpens National Battlefield Weekend, featuring 18th-century living-history and tactical demonstrations, is held in mid-January on the anniversary of the battle.

Plantations, parks, churches, and homes of former notables abound. The entire Pendleton District is on the National Register of Historic Places. One of the first separate African-American congregations established in South Carolina after the Civil War is in Greenville. Spartanburg is the site of historic 1765 Walnut Grove Plantation. But the region doesn't sleep in the past; it's also a center of international business, especially in Greenville and Spartanburg.

1 The Upstate's Great Outdoors

The landscape is scenic, with more than 50 waterfalls and countless forested hills, and the moderate climate is ideal for a wide range of activities. There are numerous campgrounds, 12 state parks, golf courses, lakes, and hiking trails. You can even do a little ice skating, although it's indoors at The Pavilion in Greenville.

The best places to enjoy unspoiled nature are the state parks and the areas surrounding the region's lakes, which offer lush vegetation and abundant wildlife. One of the most popular spots is Lake Hartwell, where you can fish, camp, picnic, boat, hike, or swim. Another excellent choice is Oconee State Park, where a mountain lake offers cool swimming on a hot day.

Golf courses range from the Verdae Greens Golf Club in Greenville to the Cotton Creek Golf Club in Spartanburg. Campgrounds vary from primitive to RV sites with hookups and all amenities. Several are located along the Cherokee Scenic Highway, including the campsites at Caesars Head, Keowee-Toxaway, and Lake Hartwell State Parks.

Anglers can do their fishing free at state parks on reservoir lakes, park lakes, and rivers. Savvy locals prefer to head for the larger lakes, such as Jocasse and Hartwell.

Hikers flock to the Foothills Trail, which offers some of the most rugged and scenic territory in the Southeast. The 85-mile trail begins at Table Rock State Park and concludes at Oconee State Park. There are many lonesome trails for equestrians, especially Rocky Gap Trail in the Sumter National Forest, which joins up with the Willis Knob Horse Trail in Georgia. The Rocky Gap portion is 12½ miles, but if you continue into Georgia, the total length is 26 miles.

2 Pendleton

130 NW of Columbia; 68 miles W of Spartanburg; 35 miles W of Greenville

If you can choose only one destination, make it ✪ **Pendleton,** the Upstate's most historic town. The whole town is on the National Register of Historic Places—it's one of America's largest such designated districts—and Pendleton offers nearly 50 buildings that are worth looking at, many of which are open to the public. The town is also an important shopping center for antiques.

The Cherokee Indians occupied this land until September 1776, when the South Carolina militia forces demolished their towns and property to quell an uprising. After this carnage, the Cherokees were forced to sue for peace and ended up surrendering their land to the state. Originally known as Pendleton County, the area was later designated the Pendleton District. In April 1790, land was purchased to establish the courthouse town of Pendleton. It was named after Judge Henry Pendleton for his efforts in fighting for Upstate rights. Although the village began with predominantly Scots-Irish immigrants, it soon became a summer retreat for wealthy Low Country families trying to escape the mosquitoes and humidity of the coast. It's just a stone's throw from Clemson University, which in 2000 was named *Time* magazine's "Public College of the Year."

ESSENTIALS

GETTING THERE   By Train   The nearest rail station is in Clemson, 5 miles north of Pendleton. For **Amtrak** schedules, call the terminal at ☎ **864/653-3410** or 800/872-7245.

By Bus   The closest bus transit is in Anderson, 15 miles south of Pendleton. Call the **Anderson Bus Station** for schedules and fares (☎ **864/224-4381**). After arrival, passengers have to take a taxi to Pendleton.

By Car   From Greenville, head west on I-85 to exit 19B (Highway 76/28). Take Highway 28 7 miles into Pendleton. From Spartanburg, follow I-85 west also to exit 19B. From Columbia, take 26 west to 385 west. Continue westbound on 385 to Greenville and follow the directions above.

VISITOR INFORMATION   Hunter's Store, 125 E. Queen St. (☎ **800/862-1795** or 864/646-3782), is the home of the tri-county **Pendleton District Historical, Recreational, and Tourism Commission.** Here, you will find cassette-tape tours, maps and information on the entire district, locally handmade arts and crafts, and books on the area. The audio tours cost $4 for the tape rental, which includes the use of a tape player and a map. The tour lasts 1½ hours and is offered from 9am to 3pm Monday to Friday. The commission is open Monday to Friday from 9am to 4:30pm (closed holidays).

SEEING THE SIGHTS

Agricultural Museum. U.S. Hwy. 76 (across from Tri-County Tech). ☎ **800/862-1795** or 864/646-3782. Free admission. Open by appointment only Mon–Fri 9am–4:30pm.

Developed by the Pendleton District Commission in conjunction with the Farmers Society, the museum displays pre-1925 farm tools and equipment in a structure resembling a horse barn. Plows, manure spreaders, cream separators, churns, and irons re-create this world of mountain folk. Called Scots-Irish, they came by the hundreds of thousands to the Blue Ridge Mountains throughout the 1700s. This museum gives you an insight into how they made their living by hunting, raising livestock, and "plantin' taters." Some made "white lightning," or moonshine, untaxed whiskey that they tried to keep out of sight of "revenuers"—the dreaded agents of the Internal Revenue Service office.

Ashtabula Plantation. S.C. Hwy. 88 (P.O. Box 444). ☎ **864/646-7249.** Admission $5 adults; $2 children 2–14. Apr–Oct Sun 2–6pm; Nov–Mar by appointment only.

Lewis Ladson Gibbes of Charleston built this house in the late 1820s. *Ashtabula* is the Indian word for "fish river." When the Gibbes family sold the property, it was advertised as "the most beautiful farm in the Upstate." The property eventually fell into the hands of the Mead Corporation, which turned it into a tree farm. In 1961, Mead gave the house and 10 acres to the Foundation for Historic Restoration. The house has been restored and furnished with antiques dating back to the early to mid-19th century. A scrapbook about life at Ashtabula, kept by Mrs. O. A. Bowen in the 1860s, is on display.

Woodburn Plantation. U.S. Hwy. 76 (P.O. Box 37). ☎ **864/646-7249.** Admission $5 adults; $2 children 2–14. Apr–Oct Sun 2–6pm; Nov–Mar by appointment only.

West of town, this four-story house was built in the early 1830s by Charles Cotesworth Pinckney, lieutenant governor of South Carolina in 1833. One of the plantation's other notable owners was Dr. John Bailey Adger, a Presbyterian minister who translated the Bible into modern Armenian. He expanded the house to its current form. In 1966, the plantation was given to the Historic Foundation to be restored and operated as a museum. The four-story structure includes antiques from the 19th century, high ceilings, and columned porches.

SHOPPING

Antiquing is the favorite activity in Pendleton. In addition to the following shops, a famous antiques-and-pottery show, the Collectors' Market on the Green, is held in the fall, sometime between mid-September and mid-October. Dealers from the Carolinas and Georgia gather on the village green to sell their antiques, collectibles, and hand-made pottery. Dates depend on the Clemson University football schedule; the market is scheduled for when there is no home game.

Grandma's Antiques. 204 E. Queen St. ☎ **864/646-9435.**

At the corner of Broad and Queen streets, this shop offers a wide range of antiques, excluding furniture. The inventory includes crystal, china, toys, kitchenware, silver, tools, and jewelry. Hours are Monday to Saturday 10am to 5pm.

Pendleton Antique Co. 134 E. Main St. ☎ **864/646-7725.**

Richard and Shelby Quattlebaum, owners of this store off the town square, specialize in period furniture. Their inventory includes lamps and a limited selection of glassware. Repairing and refinishing services are also offered. Hours are Monday to Friday 10am to 4pm, Saturday 10am to 3pm.

Pendleton Place Antiques. 651 S. Mechanic St. ☎ **864/646-7673.**

This shop offers a selection of primitive antiques, furniture, crystal, glassware, dolls, and collectibles, including Hummel pieces. The owner, Jim Pruitt, is often out doing estate appraisals, so you should call ahead to see whether the store is open. Hours are Thursday to Saturday 9am to 5pm.

WHERE TO STAY

✪ **Liberty Hall Inn.** 621 S. Mechanic St., Pendleton, SC 29670. ☎ **800/643-7944.** Fax 864/646-7500. www.bbonline.com/sc/liberty. E-mail: libertyhallinn@aol.com. 10 units. A/C TV TEL. $89–$94 double. Rates are higher on football weekends. AE, DISC, MC, V.

This inn, which began as a five-room summer home, was enlarged when the property became a boardinghouse. Susan and Tom Jonas renovated the house and opened the inn in 1985, offering Southern hospitality in a relaxed atmosphere. The individually decorated rooms feature high ceilings, armoires, heart-pine floors, ceiling fans, and antique furnishings. A few rooms have individual porches. Smoking is not allowed in the guest rooms. The establishment includes a restaurant serving a delectable contemporary Southern cuisine in its two dining rooms. The menu items include sweet-potato-crusted bobwhite quail; praline trout; and Bourbon Street pasta, which features crawfish, alligator, and andouille sausage in a Creole sauce. Dinner is served Thursday to Saturday from 5:30 to 9pm. Reservations are recommended.

WHERE TO DINE

✪ **Farmer's Hall Restaurant.** 105 Exchange St. ☎ **864/646-7024.** Reservations recommended. Lunch main courses $4.95–$6.95; dinner main courses $10.95–$22.95. AE, DISC, MC, V. Mon–Sat 11am–9pm. INTERNATIONAL.

Constructed as the courthouse for the district in 1826, the building was taken over by the Pendleton Farmers Society, which gives it the historical distinction of being the oldest society hall in the United States. The restaurant is owned and operated by Alex Fraser and Chef Walter "Wink" Waldlaw. The outside gives no hint of what's inside: an inviting interior, with an English-pub/old-inn motif. Lunch features sandwiches and salads, as well as heartier fare such as the chef's special pork tenderloin Bequia. House specialties include fresh fish with innovative sauces, such as halibut in parchment on a bed of leeks and potatoes with vinaigrette, or roast Chilean sea bass. The food is fresh and well prepared, the ingredients are well chosen, and the service is polite and efficient.

Pendleton House. 203 E. Main St. ☎ **864/646-7795.** Reservations recommended. Main courses $14.95–$23.95. AE, DC, DISC, MC, V. Tues–Sat 5–11pm. INTERNATIONAL.

The 1880 Pendleton House is now the site of a restaurant and pub owned by Jinny Morgan. She offers a mix of international flavors in a rustic setting of heart-pine floors and pinewood walls. With a sense of whimsy, you can enjoy a drink in the pub while sitting on a church pew near the fireplace. The menu, which is presented orally with a touch of humor, includes beef, fish, grilled lamb, pork, and poultry. Chef Paul Morgan, Jinny's son, is skilled but never daringly experimental, so as not to offend conservative Upstate palates. If it's on the menu, try the rich Bristol cream sherry cake, a recipe passed down from Jinny's mother.

3 Greenville

102 miles NW of Columbia

Lying halfway between Charlotte and Atlanta, Greenville is an inviting upstate city with tree-lined streets in the foothills of the Blue Ridge Mountains. It's been called the textile center of the world and is known for turning out not only clothing nylon, but also chemicals. It makes a good hub for exploring the Upstate and the forested parks in the area.

Greenville began as a trading post in the 1700s. During the antebellum era, the area was a resort for plantation owners from the Low Country, but it later moved on to textiles. The textile industry began in the 1820s, but mills were not built here until the 1870s. The Huguenot Mill, constructed in 1882, was advertised as being "an electric plant that makes plaid cloth," but the textile connection is long gone. Today, the town is the home of the Metropolitan Arts Council, Upstate Visual Arts, and Historic Greenville Foundation, and the 2,100-seat Peace Center for the Performing Arts.

ESSENTIALS

GETTING THERE   By Plane   The nearest airport is Spartanburg. See "Getting There," in the "Spartanburg" section of this chapter.

By Train   Amtrak stops daily at 1120 W. Washington St. Call ☎ **800/ USA-RAIL** for schedules and fares.

By Bus   For local Greyhound and Trailways information, call ☎ **864/235-4741.**

By Car   I-26 runs from Columbia to Spartanburg; I-85 reaches the city from the northeast and southwest.

VISITOR INFORMATION   The **Greater Greenville Convention and Visitors Center,** 206 N. Main St. (P.O. Box 10527), Greenville, SC 29601 (☎ **800/ 351-7180** or 864/233-0461; fax 864/421-0005; www.greatergreenville.com) is located in the lobby of the city-hall office building. You'll find a selection of more than 200 brochures on area attractions, facilities, and events, along with maps and souvenirs.

SEEING THE SIGHTS

Greenville is enjoying an active downtown revitalization. In addition to the Peace Center (which has been around for at least 10 years, but is the city centerpiece), several festivals draw people downtown on a regular basis all year round. **Fall for Greenville** in October; **First Night,** the alcohol-free New Year's Eve celebration; and **Riverplace Art Festival** every May.

Beattie House. 8 Bennett St. ☎ **864/233-9977.** Free admission. Mon–Thurs 9:30am–4:30pm.

Listed on the National Register of Historic Places, this Italianate-style house was built in 1834 by Mr. and Mrs. Fountain Fox Beattie. The features include Victorian furnishings and architectural details such as the delicate turnings and brackets. The house not only has had two wings added on, but it also has been moved twice. The house is now the center of the Greenville Women's Club.

Bob Jones University Museum & Gallery. 1700 Wade Hampton Blvd. ☎ **864/ 242-5100,** ext. 1050; www.bju.edu/gallery. Admission $5 adults, $4 seniors, $3 students, free for children 6–12. Museum and art gallery Tues–Sun 2–5pm.

This is a nondenominational Christian liberal-arts institution, often denounced in the national media as a center of right-wing extremism. Remember those headlines when George W. Bush was seeking the nomination of his party for president and spoke at this forum? Founded in 1927 by Dr. Bob Jones, Sr., the school emphasizes "Christianity with culture." The Gallery of Sacred Art, begun in 1951, contains 30 rooms displaying representative works of European religious painting from the 14th through 19th centuries, including works by such masters as Botticelli, Titian, Tintoretto, Veronese, Murillo, Gerard David, Rubens, Van Dyck, Rembrandt, and Cranach. The museum also houses collections of Russian icons, Renaissance furniture, and vestments made for the Imperial Chapel in Vienna, as well as the Bowen Bible Lands Collection of items that are relevant to biblical times.

Christ Episcopal Church. 10 N. Church St. ☎ **864/422-2980.** Free admission. Open by appointment only Mon–Fri 8am–5pm.

The church is a Gothic-Revival structure with a cruciform shape and a 130-foot brick spire. Home of the oldest congregation in the city, this church was organized in 1820 by summer people from Charleston. The cornerstone was laid in 1852. The site of the original sanctuary is where the circular fountain and flower bed now lie.

Greenville County Museum of Art. 420 College St. ☎ **864/271-7570.** Free admission. Tues–Sat 10am–5pm and Sun 1–5pm.

Begun in the 1930s as a small regional art gallery, this museum is now recognized as having one of the best collections of regional art in the country. The collection surveys the highlights of American art, primarily through works created in the South or by Southern natives. Among the artists represented are Washington Allston, John Gadsby Chapman, Martin Johnson Heade, George P. A. Healy, John Ross Key, Georgia O'Keefe, William Tylee Ranney, Helen Turner, and Catherine Wiley. In addition, the museum has an impressive collection of contemporary art that includes works by such artists as Ronmare Bearden, Hans Hoffmann, Jasper Johns, Lee Krasner, and Andy Warhol.

Kilgore-Lewis House. 560 N. Academy St. ☎ **864/232-3020.** Free admission. Mon–Fri 10am–2pm.

Situated on 5 acres of gardens and grounds, this house is the headquarters of the Greenville Council of Garden Clubs. On the property is one of the original springs that supplied water for Greenville. There is also a sensory garden for the blind. The house, which has wooden-peg construction, copper roofing, and hand-blown glass windows, is listed on the National Register of Historic Places.

Roper Mountain Science Center. 504 Roper Mountain Rd. ☎ **864/281-1188.** Admission for second Sat $4 adults, $2 students and senior citizens; Fri shows $3 adults, $2 students and senior citizens. Children 5 and under free.

On 62 acres at the intersection of I-385 and Roper Mountain Road, this property includes several attractions and activities. The T.C. Hooper Planetarium/Sciencesphere and the Daniel Observatory are open Friday at 7:30pm. The entire center is open on the second Saturday each month. Attractions include the Living History Farm, the Life Science Education Center, the Sea-Life Room, and Symmes Hall. The nature trails and picnic areas are available Monday to Friday 8:30am to 5pm.

TOURING GREENVILLE

A Glimpse of Greenville, 103 Pebble Stone Lane (☎ **864/987-5572**), is a volunteer tourism program that has won several awards. It offers a wide variety of tours, including customized ones such as the Greenville Sampler, an overview tour of the city that's ideal for people who are relocating to Greenville or for curious travelers. The 2-hour historic tour uses car caravans and costs $5 for adults, $3 for children. Call for appointment at least 24 hours in advance.

The program also offers 90-minute walking tours of historic Greenville, priced at $5 for adults and $3 for students and children. Self-guided tours are available, and a map is also provided.

SPORTS & OUTDOOR PURSUITS

GOLF   C.P. Willimon owns and designed **Bonnie Brae Golf Club,** 1316 Fork Shoals Rd. (☎ 864/277-9838). The 6,484-yard course is a par-72, offering Bermuda greens and fairways. The greens fees are $16 Monday to Thursday, $24 on Friday, and $18 on Saturday and Sunday. Carts rent for $10 for 18 holes. Hours are daily from sunrise to sunset.

A nine-hole option is the **Donaldson Golf Club,** 1074 Perimeter Rd. (☎ 864/ 277-8414). Originally part of Donaldson Air Force Base, this public facility offers three par-36 courses: the 3,197-yard Blue course, the 3,050-yard White course, and the 2,799-yard Red course. Greens fees are $7 Monday to Friday and $10 Saturday and Sunday. Hours are daily dawn to dusk. Cart rentals are $9 per nine holes.

Verdae Green Golf Course, 650 Verdae Blvd. (☎ 803/676-1500), is an 18-hole, 6,757-yard, par-72 course. Set in a pine forest, the Penncross Bentgrass greens and Bermuda fairway were designed by Willard C. Byrd and Associates. Greens fees are $29 (without cart) Sunday to Friday and $37 on Saturdays. Carts rent for an additional $13, and are mandatory on Saturday and Sunday to speed play. Hours are daily 7am to 7pm.

SPECTATOR SPORTS   Clemson and Furman universities offer a plethora of sporting events, including football, baseball, basketball, and soccer. For **Clemson Tigers** information, call ☎ 888/253-6766. For the **Furman Paladins,** dial ☎ 864/ 294-2061 for sports information and ☎ 864/294-3097 for tickets.

Baseball fans can enjoy the **Greenville Braves,** an AA affiliate club of the Atlanta Braves that plays at Greenville Municipal Stadium on Mauldin Road (Exit 46 from I-85). Tickets cost $3.50-$6.50. For schedules and ticket information, call ☎ 864/ 299-3456.

SWIMMING   For swimmers, there are outdoor pools at **Southside Park and East-side Park.** Public sessions go for $3 per person. Hours are Monday to Friday 1 to 4pm for the first session and 4 to 6pm for the second session; Saturday and Sunday 1 to 5pm. The pools are usually open from June to August unless the water temperature is below 70°F. For information, call ☎ 864/288-6470.

TENNIS   More than 50 outdoor public courts are scattered throughout the county, costing $4 per hour. For information, call the **Greenville County Recreation District** (☎ 864/288-6470). **The Pavilion** offers four indoor and six outdoor courts. The use of an indoor or outdoor court goes for $4 per hour. Hours are daily 7am to 10pm.

WHERE TO STAY

At press time, the whole town was talking about the $20-million renovation and restoration of the historic 1925 **Poinsett Hotel.** It was projected that the 200 or so rooms in the stately downtown hotel would be open for business by the end of 2000.

EXPENSIVE

✪ **Embassy Suites Resort Hotel Golf and Conference Center.** 670 Verdae Blvd., Greenville, SC 29607. ☎ **800/EMBASSY** or 864/676-9090. Fax 864/676-0669. www.embassysuites.com. 268 units. A/C MINIBAR TV TEL. Sun–Thurs $99–$129 suite, Fri–Sat $129–$189 suite. Rates include cooked-to-order breakfast and nightly manager's reception. AE, DC, DISC, MC, V. Take I-385 to the Roper Mountain Rd. Exit 37 or the North Laurens Rd. Exit of I-85.

As you walk into the atrium of this all-suite hotel on the Verdae Greens Golf Course, you'll feel that you have stepped into a mini-park featuring plant-lined walkways and bubbling pools and fountains. The nine-story hotel offers comfortably furnished two-room suites decorated with a contemporary flair. Each suite contains two phones, two TVs, a coffeemaker, refrigerator, microwave oven, and wet bar.

Dining/Diversions: At the Cafe Verdae, American cuisine such as baked Gulf snapper and prime rib is served in a casual, relaxed atmosphere. As sunlight turns into moonlight in the atrium, you can unwind with a drink at the 19th Green.

Amenities: Indoor and outdoor pools, sauna, sundeck, whirlpool, and fitness center with cycles, treadmills, and rowing machines. Set in a lush pine forest, the par-72 golf course offers Penncross Bentgrass greens and Bermuda fairways, as well as a driving range and practice green.

Greenville Hilton and Towers. 45 W. Orchard Park Dr., Greenville, SC 29615. ☎ **800/ HILTONS** or 864/232-4747. Fax 864/233-2861. 256 units. A/C TV TEL. $89–$189 double; $285–$360 suite. Children stay free in parents' room. AE, CB, DC, DISC, MC, V. From I-85, take I-385 to Haywood Rd. Exit 39.

In a commercial area on the east side, $3\frac{1}{2}$ miles north of town, this nine-story concrete-and-green-glass hotel offers bright and airy rooms appointed with brass and floral accents, as well as cozy furnishings such as chaise lounges and loveseats. The concierge level features added amenities such as complimentary continental breakfast; evening hors d'oeuvres with honor-bar service; the morning paper delivered to your room Monday to Friday; and bathrooms containing telephones, TVs, and hair dryers.

Dining/Diversions: The Market Place Restaurant offers specialties such as steak au poivre, lobster tacos, and fried catfish. The hotel includes two lounges: the Lobby Lounge, where you can enjoy a quiet evening with a pianist playing in the background, and the Matrix, featuring Top 40 music for dancing.

Amenities: Glass-enclosed pool with adjacent sundeck; health club with whirlpool, sauna, and free weights; room service; laundry and dry-cleaning service; and concierge.

Hyatt Regency Greenville. 220 N. Main St., Greenville, SC 29601. ☎ **800/233-1234** or 864/235-1234. Fax 864/232-7584. www.hyatt.com. 327 units. A/C TV TEL. Mon–Thurs $135–$195 double; Fri–Sun $80–$119 double; daily $225–$610 suite. AE, CB, DC, DISC, MC, V. Parking $5–$10.

In the heart of Greenville's entertainment and commercial district, this eight-story hotel caters to a predominantly business clientele and is the prime choice in town; we prefer it to the Hilton (see above). Patrons enter through a parklike setting created in the eight-story atrium lobby with lush plants and trees, lampposts, and a cascading waterfall. Rooms are comfortably furnished with a rather standardized decor. Several are equipped with workstations, fax machines, and personal amenities, including a printer and a copier on the same floor. The most-desired accommodation is the Brooks Suite, featuring such amenities as a whirlpool with stereo system, walk-in wet bar, grand piano, and full entertainment center.

Dining/Diversions: For dining and entertainment, the Provencia restaurant offers Italian cuisine. A recent addition is the Commons Bar, a cigar lounge with piano music, open until 1am.

Amenities: Full-service business center, whirlpool, and outdoor pool. A fully equipped exercise facility with golf and tennis is nearby.

MODERATE

Courtyard by Marriott. 70 Orchard Park Dr., Greenville, SC 29615. ☎ **800/321-2211** or 864/234-0300. Fax 864/234-0296. www.courtyard.com. 70 units. A/C TV TEL. Sun–Thurs $87–$99 double; $99–$110 suite; Fri–Sat $59–$69 double; $84 suite. AE, DC, DISC, MC, V.

Designed for the business traveler, this hotel offers standard but well-maintained and comfortable accommodations. The rooms include "reach-anywhere" phones, in-room coffee and tea service, TVs, desks, and shower massages. The suites have added amenities such as refrigerators and TVs in both the bedroom and the parlor. The property includes an outdoor pool, whirlpool, and exercise room.

○ **Hunter House Antiques & Bed & Breakfast.** 201 E. College St., Simpsonville, SC 29681. ☎ **800/815-4561** or 864/967-2827. 2 units (none with bathroom). A/C TV TEL. $75–$95 double. Rates include breakfast. MC, V.

With the opening of this inn, Earl and Dianne Neely created the first B&B in the area, offering two rooms individually decorated with a mixture of antique and modern furnishings. Features of this Victorian house include stained-glass windows, 10-foot ceilings, and a hand-carved pine staircase. The bedrooms share a bathroom that offers a claw-foot tub. Breakfast is served in the dining room buffet-style, featuring items such as fresh fruits, croissants, muffins, homemade breads, and quiche. Several rooms are open to guests, including the parlor, which has a piano and a pump organ, and the antique "mall," a back room that's stuffed with period clothing and furnishings that are for sale to the public Monday to Saturday from 10am to 5pm.

Pettigru Place. 302 Pettigru St., Greenville, SC 29601. ☎ **864/242-4529.** Fax 864/ 242-1231; www.pettigru.com. E-mail: info@pettigruplace.com. 5 units. A/C TV TEL. $95– $180 double; $190 suite. Rates include breakfast. AE, DISC, MC, V.

Gloria Hendershot and Janice Beatty own this B&B, which is listed on the National Register of Historic Places. It's on a tree-lined street in the Pettigru Historic District near downtown Greenville. You enter through a small garden into the Georgian Federalist-design house, built in the 1920s. Each of the rooms is individually decorated, ranging from the Chantilly, with its Victorian decor, to a tribute to *Out of Africa* in the Brass Giraffe, which features a 12-inch brass shower head for that rain-forest effect. The most desirable is the Carolinian, appointed with Charlestonian decor in shades of blue and green, a king-size sleigh bed, whirlpool bathroom with hand shower, and private porch. Breakfast is served communally in the dining room, and includes home-baked breads and muffins and a daily chef's special from the oven.

INEXPENSIVE

Hampton Inn. 246 Congaree Rd., Greenville, SC 29607. ☎ **800/HAMPTON** or 864/ 288-1200. Fax 864/288-5667. www.hampton-inn.com. 123 units. A/C TV TEL. $69–$79 double. Children under 19 stay free in parents' room. Rates include continental breakfast. AE, CB, DC, DISC, MC, V.

Conveniently located near many restaurants and entertainment facilities, this hotel provides rooms that are clean and comfortably furnished, although mostly standard-size. The "king study" bedrooms are slightly larger, with king beds and sleeper sofas. The inn has an outdoor pool but no restaurant.

Super A Motel. 27 S. Pleasantburg Dr., Greenville, SC 29607. ☎ **864/232-3339.** 74 units. A/C TV TEL. $47 double; $55 suite. Children under 19 stay free in parents' room. Rates include buffet breakfast. MC, V.

Centrally located, with easy access to shopping and restaurants, the basic but standard-size accommodations are clean and comfortably furnished. Two-room suites offer additional features such as microwaves and small refrigerators. The facilities include a fitness center and an outdoor pool. Although a breakfast bar is included in the rates, there is no restaurant. Vince's Restaurant, adjacent to the hotel, offers continental specialties.

WHERE TO DINE

Locals swear by Sunday brunch at the **Embassy Suites,** 670 Verdae Blvd. (☎ 864/
676-9090), where $20 a person will get you shrimp on ice, Belgian waffles, carving
stations of prime rib and ham, and more. The best Chinese takeout in town is at the
obviously named **China,** 2117 Old Spartanburg Rd., on the east side of town
(☎ 864/322-0405), a family-run spot that serves up deliciously fresh standards like
dumplings, General Tso's chicken, and shrimp with garlic sauce. And for a drive-by
caffeine fix, head over to **Liquid Highway,** 14 Halton Rd., at Congaree Road
(☎ 864/281-9130), a drive-through coffee bar serving excellent coffee, muffins, and
smoothies (the beans are for sale, too). Don't forget to check out **Barley's Taproom &
Pizzeria** and **Blue Ridge Brewing Company,** two downtown bars that serve great
food as well (see "Greenville After Dark," below).

Bistro Europa. 219 N. Main St. ☎ **864/467-9975.** Main courses $6–$10 at lunch, $9–$21
at dinner. AE, DC, DISC, MC, V. Mon–Sat 11:30am–2pm and 5:30–10:30pm. CONTINENTAL.

Kelly and Andrew Baird are the owners of this downtown place, where good service is
stressed and the decor is simple. The European-style bistro offers daily specials, locally
grown produce, a specialty martini list, and its own blend of South and Central
American house coffees. Pastas, salads, and pizzas are featured at lunch. Dinner is
more elaborate, including hand-harvested jumbo scallops and prawns Napoléon,
grilled barbecue double pork chops, and roasted baby vegetables with wild-mushroom
risotto. The cookery has flair and imagination, and the couple has done a lot to wake
up some sleepy local tastebuds.

✪ **City Range Steakhouse Grill.** 615 Haywood Rd. (in front of Baby Superstore).
☎ **864/268-9018.** Reservations not accepted. Main courses $12–$21. Mon–Thurs
11am–10pm, Fri–Sat 11am–11pm. AE, DISC, MC, V. STEAKHOUSE.

This lodgelike building looks out of place (and at least a few time zones too far east)
in the parking lot of a strip mall. But many believe this is the best steakhouse in town.
A large stone fireplace sits in the center of this rustic, open restaurant; the decor runs
to wood beams, earth tones and framed antique photos. Not surprisingly, steaks,
chops and other grilled items dominate the menu—though you might not have room
for the meat after filling up on the killer garlic rolls and house-special Dusty Martinis,
augmented with olive juice and blue-cheese stuffed olives. If you take a shine to the
tangy house steak sauce, buy a bottle on your way out the door.

Coffee Underground. 1 E. Coffee St., at Main Street. ☎ **864/298-0494.** Reservations
not necessary. Main courses $3.25–$5.95. AE DISC MC V. Mon–Wed 8am–11pm, Thurs
8am–11:30pm, Fri 8am–12:30am, Sat 10am–12:30am, Sun noon–7pm. COFFEEHOUSE/
SANDWICHES.

Owners Dana Lowie and Stephen Taylor gave birth to Greenville's only alternative
coffeehouse after a trip to Seattle left them pining for a similar java experience at
home. This cozy basement space in the heart of downtown is a great spot to relax any
time of day or night. In addition to a diverse selection of coffee drinks, teas, and chais
(Asian-style spiced teas), Coffee Underground serves muffins and pastries (breakfast),
a selection of salads, sandwiches and quiche (lunch and dinner), and homemade
desserts (anytime). It's also the place to come for evening entertainment (see
"Greenville After Dark," below).

Johanns at West End. 1 Augusta St. (just south of downtown). ☎ **864/235-2774.** Reservations recommended. Main courses $14.95–$21.95. MC V. Tues–Wed 11am–2pm, Thurs–Fri
11am–2pm and 5–10pm, Sat 5–10pm, Sun brunch 10:30am–2pm. CONTEMPORARY
CONTINENTAL.

Housed in a restored brick mill building, Johanns is an elegant, welcoming place. Most of its charm comes from Johann himself. The affable owner/chef is a regular presence in the dining room, toque and all; he chats up the patrons, cracks jokes, and occasionally assumes busboy duties. While the menu only lists six or eight entrees tops, there's always a long list of daily specials. Fresh seafood is always in evidence. Other popular choices include grilled lamb chops with rosemary essence, Wiener schnitzel and *züricher gschnetzels* (sliced veal in a mushroom cream sauce), the latter two indicative of a decided German presence in the Upstate (BMW constructed its first North American plant just outside of town). Sunday brunch is an impressive spread of meats, quiches, fresh fruit, pastry, and cheeses—a far cry from the usual "meat and three" Sunday dinners to be found in these parts.

Nippon Center Yagoto. 500 Congaree Rd. ☎ **864/288-8471.** Reservations recommended. Collared shirt and pants required for men. Main courses $15–$42. AE, DC, DISC, MC, V. Mon–Sat 6–9:30pm. Closed July 4. JAPANESE.

Housed in a Shoin Zukuri–style building (interiors constructed without nails), this combination restaurant and cultural center features fine Japanese dining, along with celebrations of Japanese festivals and holidays that are open to the public. There are four dining areas, including one where you remove your shoes and sit on the tatami-mat floors while enjoying the Teppanyaki-inspired menu. Specialties include sashimi and sushi. An authentic Japanese tea ceremony is also offered, at a cost of $7 per person.

✪ Pita House. 495 S. Pleasantburg Dr. (directly behind Catherine's Stout Shoppe, at the intersection of East Faris Rd.). ☎ **864/271-9895.** Reservations not accepted. Main courses $5–$10. No credit cards. Mon–Sat 11am–9pm. MIDDLE EASTERN.

Look fast to find the tiny, popular Pita House—its unassuming facade recedes slightly from a generic stretch of local highway dominated by strip malls and super-size gas stations—but it's well worth the search. A gregarious Lebanese family runs this simple diner (a few yellowed posters of the Holy Land and piped-in Arabic pop qualify as the only atmosphere). They serve a full range of pan-Mediterranean dishes—falafel, gyro, souvlaki, lamb kebabs, stuffed grape leaves, beef and chicken *schwarma* (sort of a less-spicy souvlaki) and more. Save room for a wedge of dainty, flaky-sweet pastry (the baklava with pistachios is a favorite). The dozen or so tables spill over into a corner of the restaurant that doubles as a grocery store. You wouldn't think to come across exotic Medjool dates, at least five kinds of olives, and fresh spices galore in this buckle of the Bible Belt.

✪ Seven Oaks. 104 Broadus Ave. ☎ **864/232-1895.** Reservations recommended. Main courses $16.50–$27. AE, MC, V. Mon–Sat 6–10pm. AMERICAN/SOUTHERN.

This restaurant has won numerous awards and was ranked among the top 10 restaurants in the country by the American Academy of Restaurants and Hospitality Services. Located in an 1895 house that has been painstakingly restored, the restaurant features original fireplaces, 14-foot curved ceilings, hand-cut and hand-laid rock-maple parquet floors, and stained-glass windows. In the elegant dining rooms, the tantalizing dishes of Chef Liz Minetta are creative, tasteful, and healthy, and often garnished with herbs and edible flowers from the garden. A recent import to Greenville from Atlanta, Minetta changes her menu quarterly. You may start with the crawfish or mushroom bisque, the Sonoma seared foie gras, or the Gulf shrimp ravioli. For dinner, you may be tempted by the roast halibut with yellow-tomato-and-lobster salad, served with Israeli couscous; grilled quail and smoked wild-boar sausage with sage grits; or the filet mignon with Yukon gold potatoes. For dessert, try the Cookie, a cookie baked when you order and covered with two types of Belgian chocolate. The restaurant has two verandas: a first-floor wraparound veranda, and a smaller second-floor porch that's large enough to host live jazz and beach music on Thursday nights.

Soby's. 207 S. Main St. ☎ **864/232-7007.** Reservations accepted only for parties of 8 or more. Main courses $13–$22. AE DC DISC MC V. Mon–Thurs 5–10pm, Fri–Sat 5–11pm. MODERN SOUTHERN.

Back in 1997, owners David Williams (a chef) and Carl Sobocinsky (an architect) bought and gutted this building, a down-at-the-heels shoe store, and transformed it into a stylish, award-winning restaurant. Restored wide-plank blond floors and brick walls complement a curving, hand-tooled bar and an airy, minimalist mezzanine to create a fusion of old and new. The menu, similarly stylistic, puts a new spin on old favorites: Spinach salad is tossed with dried cranberries, shaved Smithfield ham, and bleu cheese; fried green tomatoes are layered with jalapeño-pimento cheese; and earthy shrimp 'n' grits is dressed up with haricots verts and roasted peppers. Wine is serious business here; the cellar holds over 5,000 bottles, and the restaurant hosts a regular schedule of wine-themed dinners. In addition to this location, Soby's will open a branch in the newly restored Poinsett Hotel, just up the street (see "Where to Stay," above).

GREENVILLE AFTER DARK
PERFORMING ARTS

Bi-Lo Center. 650 N. Academy St. ☎ **864/241-3800.** www.bilocenter.com.

This $63-million facility replaced the older Greenville Memorial Auditorium as the city's venue for Broadway touring shows, rock concerts, rodeos, basketball, ice shows, and art exhibits. It's also the home of the city's new minor-league hockey team, the Greenville Grrrowls. Carrying the corporate name of a local grocery chain, the arena opened in September 1998, with Janet Jackson and Pearl Jam filling the 16,000-seat arena to capacity.

Peace Center for the Performing Arts. 300 S. Main St. ☎ **800/888-7768** or 864/467-3000.

This complex includes a 2,100-seat concert hall, a 400-seat theater, a 200-seat cabaret, a 1,500-seat amphitheater, and a full-service restaurant. Performances include Broadway shows, international dance companies, chamber music, local performing groups, and star entertainers. Call ahead for tickets and times, which vary.

The Warehouse Theatre. 37 Augusta St. ☎ **864/235-6948.**

At Greenville's professional resident theater, the intimate setting is arranged so that all seats are within five rows of the stage. Performances include classical as well as new and innovative theater. Dress is casual. Call ahead for prices and times.

BARS & CLUBS

The number of bars, restaurants and pubs that have sprung up in downtown Greenville is a firm testament to the neighborhood's revitalization. **Soby's** (see "Where to Dine," above) has a thriving bar scene. **Coffee Underground** (see "Where to Dine," above) serves beer, wine and cordials in addition to coffee and tea, and offers a regular schedule of comedy acts, live folk music, and alternative films in its 60-seat theater; log on to www.cucafe.com to see what's playing.

Barley's Taproom & Pizzeria. 23 W. Washington St. ☎ **864/232-3706.**

As if the 27 beers on tap (including a few unusual microbrews) weren't enough of a reason to come to Barley's, they also serve excellent pizzas, with toppings both nouveau (sun-dried tomato, artichoke) and traditional (pepperoni, sausage, and such). There's never a cover to hear live music, which ranges from rock to bluegrass to blues. They've recently expanded into the upstairs space, adding pool tables and several dartboards.

Blue Ridge Brewing Company. 217 N. Main St. (next to Fuddrucker's). ☎ **864/ 232-4677.**

The large copper tanks nested in the picture window out front should be your first indication that this place is all about the beer. Five house brews are standard; a roster of others changes seasonally. The food's not bad, if a little pricey for a brewpub, with a menu heavy on wild game, steak, and a few fresh seafood choices thrown in. Tables are large enough to accommodate big groups, and live bands perform several times a week.

Bubba Annie's. 3101 S. Hwy. 14, at Pelham Rd. ☎ **864/297-0007.**

This beer joint—and that's the best way to describe Bubba Annie's—has the best wings in town. The decor can only be described as *all things Bulldog.* This reflects both the owner's interest in the breed and his collegial affiliation (he went to the University of Georgia, where the Dawg is the offical mascot).

4 Spartanburg

93 miles NW of Columbia

Named after the Spartan Rifles, a Revolutionary War militia unit that served at the crucial Battle of Cowpens, heavily industrialized Spartanburg was incorporated and founded in 1831. Today, this growing community is the headquarters of more than 40 corporations, including Milliken, the world's largest privately owned company. Textiles are the foundation here, but diversification has come over the past 2 decades, with the influx of nearly 90 firms representing 15 foreign countries.

The area is also known for its peaches; some publications tout it as being the "Fresh Peach Capital of the South."

ESSENTIALS

GETTING THERE   By Plane   The Greenville-Spartanburg Airport is served by **American Airlines** (☎ 800/433-7300; www.aa.com); **Continental Airlines** (☎ 800/525-0280; www.flycontinental.com); **Delta Air Lines** and **Delta Connection** (☎ 800/221-1212; www.delta.com); **Northwest Airlink** (☎ 800/225-2525; www.nwa.com); **United Express** (☎ 800/241-6522; www.ual.com); and **US Airways** (☎ 800/428-4322; www.usairways.com).

By Train   For **Amtrak** information, call ☎ **800/USA-RAIL.**

By Bus   For local **Greyhound** and **Trailways** information, call ☎ **864/ 583-3669.**

By Car   I-26 runs from Columbia to Spartanburg; I-85 reaches the city from the northeast and southwest. AAA services are available through **Carolina Motor Club,** 817 E. Main St., Spartanburg 29301 (☎ **864/583-2766**).

VISITOR INFORMATION   The **Spartanburg Tourism and Convention Bureau,** 105 N. Pine St. (P.O. Box 1636), Spartanburg, SC 29304 (☎ **864/ 594-5050**; www.spartanburgsc.com) can furnish detailed brochures on sightseeing, accommodations, and dining.

SEEING THE SIGHTS

BMW Zentrum. Off I-85. ☎ **888/864-7269.** www.bmwzentrum.com. Free admission. Tues–Sat 10am–5:30pm.

This welcome center for BMW visitors includes a museum, an informational and educational center, a BMW souvenir shop, a state-of-the-art video-production theater with surround sound, and a cafe. Displays include technological exhibits, as well as vintage BMW cars, motorcycles, aircraft engines, and concept automobiles. Allow 1 to 2 hours for the tour. Reservations are not required. You can also tour the factory, but children under 12 are not allowed; call for reservations.

Spartanburg County Regional Museum of History. 100 E. Main St. (corner of Main St. and Church St.). ☎ **864/596-3501.** Admission $2 adults, $1 students, children 5 and under free. Tues–Sat 10am–5pm.

Established in 1961 by private citizens, this museum exhibits a permanent collection of more than 100 antique dolls, as well as artifacts from the Battle of Cowpens and the founding of Spartanburg. Five temporary exhibits concerning the Upstate are shown each year.

SIGHTS NEARBY

Hollywild Animal Park. 2325 Hampton Rd., Inman. ☎ **864/472-2038.** Admission $8 adults, $6 children. Apr 1–Labor Day daily 9am–6pm.

The park is the home of more than 500 exotic and native animals, some of which roam freely inside large natural enclosures or on manmade islands. You can feed and have close contact with dozens of the inhabitants. A safari ride is offered through the Outback area—70 acres filled with herds of free-roaming animals. You will see turtles sunning on logs by the pond or babies hidden in the woods. Many of the residents are famous in their own right, having been featured in numerous movies and television shows.

✪ **Walnut Grove Plantation.** 1200 Otts Shoals Rd. (1½ miles SE intersection of I-26 and Hwy. 221), Roebuck. ☎ **864/576-6546.** Admission $4.50 adults, $2 children. Apr 1–Nov Tues–Sat 11am–5pm; year-round Sun 2–5pm. By appointment only all other times.

A short drive south from Spartanburg is this excellent example of a colonial plantation house—not the stately columned style typical of the Low Country, but a large, simple farmhouse typical of landowners' homes in this region. Built in 1765 on a land grant to Charles Moore from King George III, the house has been restored and authentically furnished with pieces from before 1830. The property also features a smokehouse, doctor's office, family cemetery, schoolhouse, herb and flower garden, and nature trail.

SPORTS & OUTDOOR PURSUITS

Most locals head for the state parks and lake just a short drive away, off the Cherokee Scenic Highway. **Croft State Park,** 450 Croft State Park Rd. (☎ **864/585-1283**), offers hiking and horseback-riding trails, swimming, fishing, campgrounds, and picnic areas.

GOLF   Cotton Creek Golf Club, 640 Keltner Ave. (☎ **864/583-7084**), is a 6,653-yard, 18-hole, par-72 championship course with Bermuda fairways and greens. The greens fees are $20 Monday to Friday and $28 Saturday and Sunday. Hours are daily 7am to 7pm. All skill levels will find a challenge on the two bentgrass courses at **Oak Ridge Country Club,** 5451 S. Pine St. (☎ **864/582-7579**). The 6,156-yard blue-tee and 5,487-yard white-tee courses both have a par of 72. Hours are daily from sunrise to sunset. Designed by Gary Player, **River Falls Plantation,** 100 Player Blvd., Duncan (☎ 864/433-9192), features rounds of play in a resortlike atmosphere. The 18-hole, 6,697-yard, par-72 course offers a mixture of Bermuda and bentgrass greens and fairways. Greens fees are $38 Monday to Friday, $48 Saturday and Sunday. Hours are daily 7am to 7pm.

SWIMMING   The **Spartanburg Swim Center,** 447 S. Church St. (☎ 864/596-3900), offers a heated indoor pool with eight lanes for lap swimming and a separate shallow section for water aerobics, water-therapy classes, and water walking. Lap sessions cost $1 per person. Adult swims are Monday to Thursday 7:30am to 8pm and Friday 7:30am to 3pm. Children's sessions are Monday to Thursday 6:30am to 8pm and Saturday 3 to 5pm. Water aerobics are $2.50 per person. Times vary, so call ahead. The center hours are 7:30am to 8:30pm Monday to Thursday, 2:30 to 5pm Saturday, and Sunday April to September 3 to 5pm.

WHERE TO STAY

Hampton Inn. 4930 College Dr., Spartanburg, SC 29301. ☎ **800/HAMPTON** or 864/576-6080. Fax 864/587-8901. www.hampton-inn.com. 110 units. A/C TV TEL. $69 double. Rates include continental breakfast. AE, CB, DC, DISC, MC, V. Junction of I-85 and I-26.

This hotel offers basic rooms at affordable prices but is a less attractive choice than the Ramada Inn (see below). Rooms are decorated in shades of blue and green; some rooms contain king-size beds double beds, or sleeper sofas, as well as desks and tables. Continental breakfast is served from 6 to 10am daily. The inn offers a pool and complimentary passes to Gold's Gym.

Ramada Inn. 200 International Dr., Spartanburg, SC 29303. ☎ **864/576-5220.** Fax 864/574-1243. 222 units. A/C TV TEL. $59–$69 double; $159 suite. AE, DISC, MC, V. Junction of I-85 and I-26.

These are the best motel accommodations in town, with double and king-size beds in the rooms. The suite includes a whirlpool and wet bar. The hotel has an indoor recreation center, which contains a fitness room, whirlpool, sauna, heated pool, and Ping-Pong and pool tables. J.D. Peaches serves a variety of steak and seafood dishes, as well as daily breakfast and dinner buffets. A pianist plays in Fuzzy's Lounge.

Residence Inn by Marriott. 9011 Fairforest Rd. (I-85 at I-26), Spartanburg, SC 29301. ☎ **800/331-3131** or 864/576-3333. Fax 864/574-4888. www.marriott.com. 88 units. A/C TV TEL. $99–$109 1-bedroom suite; $110–$119 2-bedroom suite. Rates include continental breakfast. AE, CB, DC, DISC, MC, V.

This hotel offers well-appointed one- and two-bedroom suites with fully equipped kitchens and living rooms. Most suites have wood-burning fireplaces, and those on the lower level open onto porches with sliding-door access. Facilities include an outdoor pool, hot tub, weight room and health club, and racquetball and tennis courts. Monday to Thursday, a complimentary hospitality hour is held.

Wilson World Hotel & Suites. 9027 Fairforest Rd., Spartanburg, S.C. 29301. ☎ **800/WILSONS** or 864/574-2111. Fax 864/576-7602. 200 units. $79 double; $89 suite. AE, CB, DC, DISC, MC, V.

You enter through a five-story garden-atrium lobby with a bar as the centerpiece. The well-furnished rooms contain small refrigerators, coffeemakers, and hair dryers; suites also offer microwaves, two TVs, and wet bars. Facilities feature an indoor heated pool, putting green, weight room, lounge, and game room. The Blueridge Restaurant serves a mixture of American and international cuisine. Special items include a weeknight prime-rib buffet and a Sunday brunch.

WHERE TO DINE

✪ **Beacon Drive In.** 255 Reidville Rd. ☎ **864/585-9387.** Main courses $3–$10. No credit cards. Mon–Sat 6:30am–10pm. AMERICAN.

This local landmark is the second-largest drive-in restaurant in the country, and as one local put it, "If you visit Spartanburg without coming here, it's like going to New York City and not seeing the Statue of Liberty." The Beacon is one of the few drive-ins that still use carhops, several of whom have been here for more than 40 years. One, Ezell Jackson, is almost 91 years old and was just written up in *Gourmet* magazine. He's been a carhop here since 1950 and gives the Beacon fried chicken plenty of credit for his longevity. Though your own cholesterol count may go through the roof, the food is worth it. The menu offers more that 100 options, including chili cheeseburgers and barbecue plates.

The Maryland Tea Room. East Main and Mills Ave. (in the Galleria). ☎ **864/585-0606.** Reservations recommended. Main courses $4.95–$8.99. AE, DISC, MC, V. Mon–Fri 11am–2pm. SANDWICHES/SALADS.

For a light lunch, head for the Galleria, where you'll find a little tearoom reminiscent of days gone by. The downstairs dining room is decorated in a floral motif, with wicker hanging baskets, and the upstairs room features antiques and whatnots. The menu is comprised of homemade options made fresh daily, including wedding soup, a concoction of meatballs, spinach, and cheese. The favorite of locals is the tea-sandwich platter: a frozen date soufflé surrounded by tiny tea sandwiches. The restaurant offers a good selection of teas, including strawberry and a hot spiced brew for those cold days of winter.

5 Along the Cherokee Foothills Scenic Highway

S.C. 11, the ✪ **Cherokee Foothills Scenic Highway,** curves 130 miles through the heart of South Carolina's Blue Ridge Mountain foothills. It stretches in an arc from I-85 at Gaffney, near the North Carolina border, almost to the Georgia border at Lake Hartwell State Park, where it links up once more with I-85. The "scenic" in this highway's name is best justified at spring-blossom time or when autumn leaves are coloring, but it can't compare with the more dramatic Blue Ridge Parkway of Virginia and North Carolina. Once, the highway was known as the Keowee Path or Cherokee Path. The highway offers access to 10 state parks and several historic sites. For information and a detailed route map, contact the **South Carolina State Park System,** 1205 Pendleton St., Columbia, SC 29201 (☎ **864/734-0156**).

The route begins in Gaffney at the **Peachoid,** the town's water tower (painted to resemble a peach), at Exit 92 off I-85. After you turn onto the highway, you begin a journey through peach country. Peach orchards and stands line the road, selling peaches, tomatoes, cucumbers, and other produce in season. Many of the stands have been in operation for a good number of years, including one that was started more than 30 years ago.

Soon after entering the highway, you come to **Cowpens National Battlefield,** 11 miles west of I-85 near the Highway 11/Highway 10 intersection, Chesnee (☎ **864/461-2828**). On January 17, 1781, Daniel Morgan led his army of tough Continentals and backwoods militia to a brilliant victory over a larger and better-equipped force of British regulars under the command of the much-hated dragoon, Banastre Tarleton. This crucial battle contributed to the eventual defeat of the British at Yorktown. The battle took place over an area of 150 acres; 845 of these acres comprise today's park. In the park, a 3-mile loop takes you around the battlefield and its historical markers. The park also offers a 1¼-mile walking trail. In the visitor center are exhibits and memorabilia such as weapons and survival gear of the period. A 22-minute audiovisual program, *Daybreak at the Cowpens,* is presented every half-hour, at a cost of $1. The park and visitor center are open daily from 9am to 5pm, except for major holidays.

Detours off the route lead to various points of interest. The last covered bridge in South Carolina is **Campbell's Bridge,** built in 1909. To reach it, head 4 miles down Route 14 at Gowensville; then go west half a mile on Route 414. The oldest bridge in the state is believed to be the **Poinsett Bridge,** built in 1820. The stone-arched structure crosses the Middle Saluda River where it overlooks the clear, running water and kudzu-covered countryside. To reach this spot, take Route 25 north until you come to the signposted turnoff.

Other points of interest include **Glassy Mountain,** with its 1,000-foot sheer rock face; **Symmes Chapel** (better known as "Pretty Place"), atop Standing Stone Mountain and offering one of the most scenic overlooks; **Raven Cliff Falls,** where a wooden deck has been built to allow visitors to view a waterfall that plunges 800 feet into a gorge; **Sassafras Mountain,** the state's highest peak, at 3,548 feet; and **Stumphouse Mountain Tunnel,** begun in the 1850s to link Charleston to the Midwest but abandoned at the onset of the Civil War. All these sites are signposted on the highway.

15 Planning a Trip to Georgia

This chapter tackles the practical details of organizing your trip to Georgia. Also look at chapter 3, "For Foreign Visitors"—some of the information you need may have already been discussed there.

1 The Regions in Brief

THE ATLANTA AREA Gateway to the Deep South, Atlanta is one of the most progressive cities in America. The hometown of Martin Luther King, Jr., bears no relationship to the city that Scarlett O'Hara and Aunt Pittypat fled in the wake of Sherman's armies. It's a fast-paced capital city that, while still sporting a few magnolia blossoms and mint juleps, is mostly concerned with marching forward in commerce and culture.

Fortune magazine has called Atlanta "America's Best City for Business," and the title still holds into the 21st century. Approximately 1,400 businesses based in about 40 countries are represented in Atlanta. The city supports 38 colleges and universities. Atlanta is also the shopping mecca of the South and a major sports city. The newest game in town is hockey, with the arrival of the Atlanta Thrashers, a National Hockey League expansion team. The Thrashers join the Atlanta Braves and the Atlanta Hawks as the crown jewels in mogul Ted Turner's sports empire.

NORTHERN GEORGIA Probably the best-kept travel secret in the South, northern Georgia, within 70 to 120 miles of Atlanta, is a virtual national or state park. Still rugged outback, this country stands in sharp contrast to the Blue Ridge Mountains in the northeastern part of the state. The northwest has many Native American sites, as well as the Chickamauga and Chattanooga National Military Park, where the critical Civil War battles for the control of Atlanta and Chattanooga were staged. Lookout Mountain rises like a 100-mile linear barrier from the valleys below.

The southern Appalachians contain a mountain culture that hasn't been completely wiped out, and many of the old ways prevail. **Dahlonega** makes a great base for exploring Georgia's Blue Ridge Mountains, much of which lie within 727,000-acre **Chattahoochee National Forest.**

SAVANNAH The very name evokes a romantic antebellum aura. Savannah is the city that General Sherman gave President Lincoln as

Georgia

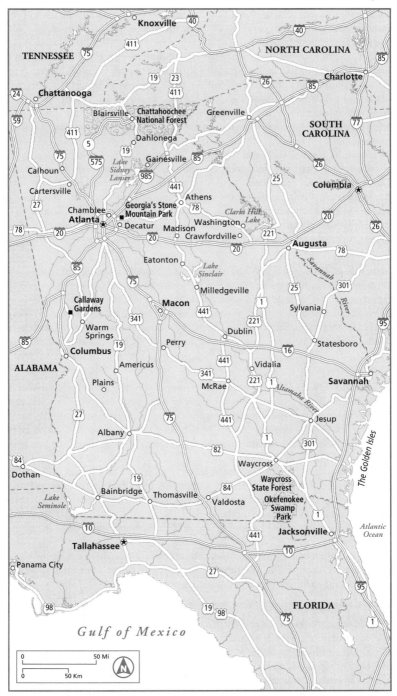

a Christmas present. Crowds flock here to search for Forrest Gump's bench and other nonhistorical monuments, as well as to visit the Juliette Gordon Low House, where the Girl Scouts were born.

The city, founded in 1733 by James Oglethorpe as Georgia's first settlement, is located 18 miles inland on the Savannah River at the South Carolina border. A deep channel connects Savannah to the ocean, attracting massive freighters to the terminals at the Georgia Ports Authority. Visitors can almost touch the ships as they slowly make their way up the river. Lined with classy nightspots and upscale restaurants, as well as a few rough pubs and artsy boutiques, cobblestoned River Street has become a hub for tourists.

Savannah's historic sites rival those of Charleston, but paramount on the list are characters and dwellings from John Berendt's scandalous bestseller, *Midnight in the Garden of Good and Evil.* Ironically, a city that built its claim on historical prominence has become a gathering place for the curious, who flock to Club One, a popular gay nightspot that hosts a nightly transvestite show featuring the Lady Chablis, one of Berendt's main characters. Visitors also dine at Clary's Cafe and gawk at Mercer House, where the shooting described in Berendt's book took place. Oglethorpe would be appalled.

MACON & THE SOUTHWEST   Macon is best seen in March during the Cherry Blossom Festival, but this historic town has year-round attractions, too. It once grew fat on the cotton trade and still boasts some antebellum homes that Sherman's armies didn't completely destroy. Today, it's one of the most rewarding destinations in Georgia. The two other major attractions in the state's southwest are **Callaway Gardens** and **Warm Springs** (where Franklin Delano Roosevelt died). You can visit both towns on a day trip from Atlanta, or you can find plenty of old inns in the area if you want to spend the night.

THE GOLDEN ISLES   Try not to leave Georgia without exploring the Golden Isles area. Start at U.S. 17 about 17 miles south of Darien (or exit off I-95 south at the Golden Isles Parkway), head toward Brunswick, and then travel to St. Simons and Sea Islands. The drive is approximately 72 miles long and culminates in **Jekyll Island,** once the private enclave of wintering wealthy like the Rockefellers and the Vanderbilts but now open to all.

If you can afford it, plan to spend at least one night at **The Cloister** on Sea Island, the grandest resort in the tri-state area. Otherwise, you'll find more reasonably priced choices on St. Simons Island and on Jekyll Island. For escapists, there are also Little St. Simons Island and Cumberland Island, the idyllic island wilderness where John Kennedy, Jr., married Caroline Bessette three years before their tragic plane crash.

Based at a hotel on the Golden Isles, you can make a day trip to one of the greatest attractions in Georgia: the **Okefenokee Swamp,** the largest freshwater swamp still preserved in the United States.

2 Visitor Information

For advance reading and planning, contact the **Division of Tourism,** Georgia Department of Industry, Trade & Tourism, P.O. Box 1776, Atlanta, GA 30301-1776 (☎ **800/VISIT-GA** or 404/656-3590; www.gomm.com). Ask for information on your specific interests, as well as a calendar of events (January to June or July to December).

State Information Centers are located near Atlanta, Augusta, Columbus, Kingsland, Lavonia, Plains, Ringgold, Savannah, Sylvania, Tallapoosa, Valdosta, and

What Things Cost in Atlanta	U.S. $
Taxi from Atlanta airport to downtown (for one passenger)	18.00
Fare between any two MARTA stops	1.50
Local telephone call	.35
Four Seasons Hotel Atlanta (very expensive)	245.00–305.00
Ritz Carlton Atlanta (expensive)	139.00–235.00
Ansley Inn (moderate)	99.00–159.00
Four Points Sheraton Buckhead (inexpensive)	79.00–139.00
Lunch for one at the Atlanta Fish Market (moderate)	24.00
Lunch for one at Mary Mac's Tea Room (inexpensive)	9.00
Dinner for one, without wine, in the Dining Room of the Ritz-Carlton Buckhead (expensive)	70.00
Dinner for one, without wine, at the Buckhead Diner (moderate)	28.00
Dinner for one, without wine, at Mick's (inexpensive)	12.00
Bottle of beer	4.50
Coca-Cola	1.50
Cup of coffee in a cafe	1.50
Roll of 35mm Kodak film, 36 exposures	7.25
Admission to Fernbank Museum of Natural History	8.95
Movie ticket	4.50-7.00
Theater ticket to the Alliance	17.00-36.00

West Point. They're open Monday to Saturday from 9am to 6pm and on Sunday from noon to 6pm. Information sources for specific destinations in the state are listed in the Georgia chapters that follow.

A particularly useful Web resource for travel information is **CityNet** (www.city.net), which provides links organized by location, then by category, to hundreds of other sites throughout the Internet.

3 When to Go

CLIMATE

The average high and low temperatures at coastal Savannah and central Atlanta show Low Country coastal areas to be warmer year round than those farther inland. Winter temperatures seldom drop below freezing anywhere in the state. Spring and fall are the longest seasons, and the wettest months are December to April.

As in the Carolinas, spring is a spectacular time to visit. Many areas become a riot of color, as the azaleas, dogwoods, and camellias are bursting into bloom.

Savannah Average Temperatures & Rainfall

	Jan	Feb	Mar	Apr	May	June	July	Aug	Sept	Oct	Nov	Dec
High (°F)	60	62	70	78	84	89	91	90	85	78	70	62
Low (°F)	38	41	48	55	63	69	72	72	68	57	57	41
Rain (in.)	3.6	3.2	3.8	3.0	4.1	5.7	6.4	7.5	4.5	2.4	2.2	3.0

Atlanta Average Temperatures & Rainfall

	Jan	Feb	Mar	Apr	May	June	July	Aug	Sept	Oct	Nov	Dec
High (°F)	51	55	61	71	79	85	87	86	81	73	62	53
Low (°F)	33	36	41	51	59	67	69	69	63	52	41	34
Rain (in.)	4.8	4.8	5.8	4.3	4.3	3.6	5.0	3.7	3.4	3.1	3.9	4.3

Georgia Calendar of Events

January

- **Martin Luther King Celebration,** Atlanta. This event, occurring over the King Holiday weekend, honors one of Atlanta's native sons in a celebration of the life and accomplishments of the civil rights leader. The program includes a "Salute to Greatness" dinner on Saturday, and a commemorative at Ebenezer Baptist Church on the Monday holiday, with speeches by notables from the Reverend King's former pulpit. Tickets for the dinner cost $200; the commemorative is free; however, seating is limited. For more information, contact the King Center for Nonviolent Social Change at ☎ 404/526-8900. Second week in January.
- **Cultural Film Festival,** Cartersville. This festival of film offers interpretations of Native American culture at one of the most intact cultural centers—Etowah Indian Mounds State Historic Site. Call ☎ 770/387-3747. Mid- to late January.
- **Rattlesnake Roundup,** Whigham. This event, held at 84 East Whigham Rattlesnake Grounds, features arts, crafts, food, entertainment, and snake handling that includes a milking demonstration. Call ☎ 912/762-4066. Last Saturday in January.
- **Augusta Cutting Horse Futurity,** Augusta. This prestigious annual event attracts cowboys and cowgirls from all over the country and the world. Held in the Augusta-Richmond County Civic Center, this event marks the first big date on any equestrian lover's calendar. Call ☎ 706/823-3417 for more information. Late January.

February

- **Wormsloe Celebrates the Founding of Georgia,** Savannah. Wormsloe was the colonial fortified home of Noble Jones, one of Georgia's first colonists. Costumed demonstrators portray skills used by those early settlers. Tickets cost $2 for adults, an $1 for children. Call ☎ 912/353-3023. Early February.
- **Savannah Irish Festival,** Savannah. This Irish heritage celebration promises fun for the entire family, with music, dancing, and food. There's both a children's stage and a main stage. Contact the Irish Committee of Savannah at ☎ 912/234-8444. Mid-February.

March

- **St. Patrick's Day Celebration on the River,** Savannah. The river flows green and so does the beer in one of the largest celebrations held on River Street each year. Enjoy live entertainment, lots of food, and tons of fun. Contact the Savannah Waterfront Association at ☎ 912/234-0295. St. Patrick's Day weekend.
- **Cracker Barrel Old Country Store 500,** Hampton. This suburb outside Atlanta is the site of the Atlanta International Raceway and home to this first of two annual NASCAR Winston Cup events. Tickets to the races range from $20 to $95. For more information and tickets, call ☎ 770/946-4211. Mid-March.

✪ **Cherry Blossom Festival,** Macon. You'll find everything from hot-air ballooning to a giant parade with 100 bands. The entire city is ablaze with thousands of blooming cherry trees. For more information, contact the Macon Cherry Blossom Festival at ☎ **912/751-7429.** Mid to late March.

• **Antebellum Jubilee,** Stone Mountain. This event presents a unique look at the nation's past as living-history events revive an era gone with the wind. Contact Stone Mountain Park at ☎ **770/498-5702** or 770/413-5086. Late March to early April.

April

✪ **Masters Golf Tournament,** Augusta. The first of professional golf's four "major" tournaments, this event was conceived by golf legend Bobby Jones, an Atlantan, who mastered the links as an amateur in the 1920s. Tickets ("badges," as the Augusta National "patrons" call them) are sold out years in advance. However, those who plan well in advance are able to enter a lottery to obtain tickets to practice rounds, which allows you to walk the grounds. "Ike's Tree," along the 18th fairway, was named for former President Dwight D. Eisenhower. Call ☎ **706/667-6700** for additional information. The deadline for lottery registration is usually the middle of July for the following year's event. Hotel rooms are generally at a premium during the Masters, so unless you're attending the tournament, remember that at this time Augusta will be overcrowded. First weekend in April.

• **Georgia Renaissance Festival,** Fairburn. Of the more than 100 shows every day, see the King's Joust and the Birds of Prey Show. There are also games, rides, and unique craft items for all ages, not to mention giant stilt-walkers, minstrels, jousters, and magicians in the re-creation of a 16th-century English county fair. Buy tickets at the gate. Adults $12.95, children $5.75. Contact the Georgia Renaissance Festival at ☎ **770/964-8575.** Weekends April to October, with an autumn complement for five weekends in October and early November.

✪ **Atlanta Dogwood Festival.** Georgia celebrates the coming of spring with garden and house tours, bicycle tours of exclusive Buckhead, concerts, and tons of azaleas and dogwoods in full bloom. On the final weekend, food booths, children's activities, and musical performances are among the events. Piedmont Park events are free, but there are admission charges to many other activities. Call ☎ **404/329-0501.** Three days in mid-April.

• **Riverfest Weekend,** Columbus. This family-oriented festival offers an art show and sale, a custom and classic automobile show, a 5km road race, an orchid show and sale, parades, river events, and lots of food and music. Contact Riverfest at ☎ **706/323-7979.** Late April.

May

• **The Cotton Pickin' Fair,** Gay. Active for more than half a century, this award-winning festival is a family affair, filled with antiques, arts, and crafts. You can make a day of it. There's plenty of food and entertainment too. Admission is $5 for adults or $2 for children. For more information, call ☎ **706/538-6814.** Held semi-annually, first weekend in May and October.

• **Savannah Symphony Duck Race,** Savannah. Each year the Savannah Symphony Women's Guild plays host as a flock of rubber ducks hits the water to go with the flow of the tides along Savannah's historic River Street. There's a $5,000 grand prize for the winning ducky. All proceeds benefit the Savannah Symphony. Call ☎ **912/236-9536.** Early May.

- **Springfest,** Stone Mountain. Cooks from all over the South create mouth-watering samples at this springtime jamboree to compete in the Annual BBQ Pork Cook-off and Great Grill-off. Shop at one of the South's largest garage sales while you enjoy live entertainment. Contact Stone Mountain Park at ☎ 770/498-5702. Early May.
- **Mayfest on the Rivers,** Rome. This spring extravaganza celebrates the three rivers of Rome with canoeing, fishing, running, and cycling competitions; the Mad River Run Corrugated Cardboard Boat Race (where part of the fun is seeing how long each of the flimsy craft can stay afloat); and lots of food, entertainment, and riverboat rides. Call ☎ 800/444-1834. Early to mid-May.
- **Memorial Day at Old Fort Jackson,** Savannah. The ceremonies have a flag-raising ceremony and a memorial service featuring "Taps." Contact the Coastal Heritage Society at ☎ 912/232-3945. Late May.
- **Andersonville Spring Fair,** Andersonville. History comes alive in Andersonville, near the site of the Andersonville Prison, of Civil War infamy. Reenactments of scenes from the war and various demonstrations take you back to the time of the War Between the States. Contact ☎ 912/924-2558, or write to the festival at P.O. Box 6, Andersonville, GA, for more information. For 2 days the last of May.

June

- **Arts Festival of Atlanta,** Atlanta. One of the nation's oldest and largest outdoor art events, this contemporary visual and performing arts festival features regional, national, and international artists. Call ☎ 404/589-8777 for more information. June 11 to 20.
- **Juneteenth,** Savannah. This event highlights the contributions of more than 200,000 African Americans who fought for their freedom and that of future generations. This event is a celebration of the Emancipation Proclamation. Although this promise of freedom was announced in January, it was not until the middle of June (actual date unknown) that the news reached Savannah, thus prompting the remembrance of "Juneteenth." For more information, contact the **Coastal Heritage Society** at ☎ 912/651-6840. Mid-June.
- **The Atlanta Film and Video Festival,** Atlanta. This 7- to 10-day festival celebrates the rising independent movie scene in Atlanta. More than 80 films, videos, shorts, and documentaries are screened to the public throughout the city. Steven Spielberg, arguably the most famous filmmaker in the world, credits this festival with giving his work its first major boost. Call ☎ 404/352-4225 for more information. Late June to early July.
- **Bavarian Summer Nights,** Helen. This is basically the summer version of Helen's Oktoberfest. For further information, contact the Helen Welcome Center at ☎ 706/787-2181. Late June through July.

July

- **Fourth of July Fireworks and Laser Show,** Stone Mountain. Stone Mountain makes for a picturesque canvas for the artistry of the laser show that has been a popular fixture at the park for many years. You need not enter the park to enjoy the show—you can join the thousands who simply pull off to the shoulder of the road to witness the spectacle. Call ☎ 770/498-5600 for more information. July 4.
- **Augusta Southern National Dragboat Races,** Augusta. The stretch of the Savannah River that runs along the Augusta Riverwalk makes for an ideal setting for this annual thunderous event. High speeds and danger fuel these races as boats "fly" by with engines larger than what can be found in most automobiles.

Tickets range from $15 to $50. For more information, call ☎ **706/724-2452.** Mid- to late July.

August

- **Georgia Mountain Fair,** Hiawassee. Enjoy fun-filled days and nights of activities on the shores of Lake Chatuge. There will be country, bluegrass, or gospel music along with clogging, a parade, a midway, a Pioneer Village, and arts and crafts shows. Call ☎ **706/896-4191.** Twelve days in early to mid-August.

September

- **Savannah Jazz Festival,** Savannah. This festival features national and local jazz and blues legends. A jazz brunch and music at different venues throughout the city are among the highlights. Contact Host South at ☎ **912/232-2222.** Mid-September.

- **Yellow Daisy Festival,** Stone Mountain. Every year Georgians gather at Stone Mountain Park to celebrate the blooming of the yellow daisy. Enjoy the arts and crafts, but please don't eat the daisies—they're rare. Call ☎ **770/498-5702.** Mid-September.

- **The 99X Big Day Out,** Conyers. This outdoor music festival at Georgia International Horse Park, a 1996 Olympic Games site in metropolitan Atlanta, is sponsored by the local radio station, 99.7 FM. Benefiting an appointed charity, Big Day Out occurs on three different stages with more than 20 bands. Past bands have included Beck, the Foo Fighters, and the Ramones. For more information, contact 99X at ☎ **404/266-0997.** Mid- to late September.

- **Helen's Oktoberfest,** Helen. Alpine Helen celebrates the South's longest Oktoberfest with live Bavarian music, German food and beverages, and dancing, plus all the other mountain area attractions and activities. Tickets cost $4 to $5. Contact the Helen Welcome Center at ☎ **706/878-2181.** September and October.

October

- **The Cotton Pickin' Fair,** Gay. Active for more than half a century, this award-winning festival is a family affair, filled with antiques, arts, and crafts. You can make a day of it. There's plenty of food and entertainment too. Admission is $5 for adults or $2 for children. For more information, call ☎ **706/538-6814.** Held semi-annually, first weekend in October and May.

- ○ **Big Pig Jig,** Vienna. Hailed by *Travel Agent* magazine as one of the "Top 20 Events in the Southeast," the state's barbecue-cooking championship was born in 1982 when a group of people competed to see who could cook the most succulent pig. The festival has expanded today to include a parade, sidewalk art contest, a "Hog Jog" race, and the naming of Miss BQW City, along with entertainment such as carnival rides. For information, contact www.bigpigjig.com. Mid-October.

- **Fitzgerald Folk Art Festival,** Fitzgerald. Folk Art is expressed in a hundred different media and displayed on brick streets among blooming plaza parks in this historic downtown. Call ☎ **800/FUN-IN-GA.** Third weekend in October.

November

- **NAPA 500,** Hampton. This Atlanta suburb roars again as NASCAR Winston Cup makes its second seasonal stop at this superspeedway. This event is the season finale, and usually the most exciting, as the NASCAR Winston Cup points title is decided by the end of the afternoon. Tickets to the races range from $20 to $95. For more information and tickets, call ☎ **770/946-4211.** Early November.

- **Crafts Festival and Cane Grinding,** Savannah. More than 75 craft artists from four states sell and demonstrate their art. Music is provided by the Savannah Folk Music Society. Contact Oatland Island at ☎ **912/897-3773.** Mid-November.
- **Candlelight Tours,** Atlanta. These evening tours of historic homes and gardens feature music and storytelling in the spirit of the holidays. Contact the Atlanta History Center at ☎ **404/814-4000.** Late November.

December

- **Candles and Carols of Christmases Past,** Mount Berry. This is a Victorian Christmas in the best tradition of the Old South, with candlelight tours and seasonal music and drama. Contact Oak Hill and the Martha Berry Museum at ☎ **800/220-5504.** First Friday and Saturday in December.
- **Christmas 1864,** Savannah. Fort Jackson hosts the dramatic re-creation of its evacuation on December 20, 1864. More than 60 Civil War re-enactors play the part of Fort Jackson's Confederate defenders, who were preparing to evacuate ahead of Union Gen. William Tecumseh Sherman. Contact Old Fort Jackson at ☎ **912/232-3945.** Early December.
- **Annual Holiday Tour of Homes,** Savannah. The doors of Savannah's historic homes are opened to the public in the holiday season. Each home is decorated, and a different group of homes is shown every day. Contact the Downtown Neighborhood Association at ☎ **912/236-8362.** Mid-December.

4 The Active Vacation Planner

The 2000 Super Bowl and the 1996 Olympics brought attention to Atlanta and helped to show the rest of the world that Georgia offers a variety of outdoor experiences. From the beauties of the Golden Isles to the North Georgia uplands, the Peach State offers fishing, golf, sailing, and everything in between.

BEACHES   Georgia's beaches don't offer the lights and entertainment or enjoy the fame of those in the Carolinas. But at one time, the Georgia coast was frequented by the likes of Rockefellers and Vanderbilts, and even though this grand life has faded, the coast remains a quiet retreat for those seeking a true getaway. The Georgia coast is dotted with what are known as the Golden Isles: Historic Jekyll Island, luxurious Sea Island, and secluded Cumberland Island are the Eastern Seaboard's best-kept secrets. For information, call ☎ **800/VISIT-GA,** or write the **Division of Tourism,** Georgia Department of Industry, Trade, and Tourism, P.O. Box 1776, Atlanta, GA 30301.

CAMPING   For information on Georgia's state parks and their camping facilities, contact the **Georgia Department of Natural Resources,** Office of Information, 205 Butler St. SE, Suite 1352, Atlanta, GA 30334. Forty of the state parks in Georgia welcome campers to sites that rent for $8 to $17 per night. Some 25 parks have vacation cottages that rent for $45 to $125 per night. These rates are for the summer and are reduced during other months. Reservations may be made by calling ☎ **800/ 864-PARK.** Be aware that some of the Georgia state parks have become privatized. Site and cabin rentals could be higher at these parks. **Georgia State Parks & Historic Sites** (☎ **404/656-3530**) can provide additional information, including details on hiking.

GOLF   Golf is big in Georgia. Augusta is home to the venerable Augusta National Golf Club, where the Masters Golf Tournament is played (the club's course is not open to the public). Lake Oconee is the golf capital of Georgia, boasting more than seven championship courses by designers like Jack Nicklaus and Ben Crenshaw. Mickey Mantle loved it so much that he spent most of his last days at the Harbor Club golf resort. Its neighbor, Reynolds Plantation, is host to the American qualifications for the World Championship. For information on private and public golf courses across the state of Georgia, call ☎ **800/3-GOLF-GA** to receive your free guide, *Georgia Golf on My Mind.*

FISHING & HUNTING   No license is needed for saltwater fishing, but fishing in Georgia's lakes, streams, and ponds does require a license. Hunting is a sport used to curtail the annual exponential growth of the white-tailed-deer population. Wild turkey and quail also abound. To obtain information about hunting and fishing regulations, contact the **Georgia Department of Natural Resources,** 205 Butler St., Atlanta GA 30334 (☎ **800/241-4113;** www.ganet.org/dnr). Many hunting clubs will allow you to join provided that you have references or can be sponsored by a local friend or family member.

HIKING   The Appalachian Trail begins in North Georgia. For those who want easier hikes, some 40 state parks in Georgia offer trails of varying difficulty. Call ☎ **800/ 864-PARKS** for more information.

LAKES   Georgia is a virtual land of lakes, providing water, electricity, and recreation. East Georgia's Clarks Hill Lake (the Georgia side of South Carolina's Thurmond Lake), northeast Georgia's Lake Hartwell, and middle Georgia's lakes Oconee, Sinclair, and Lanier are the premier spots for boating and fishing. For more information, contact the **Georgia Department of Natural Resources,** Office of Information, 205 Butler St. SE, Atlanta, GA 30334, or call ☎ **404/347-6153.**

PANNING FOR GOLD   Believe it or not, the San Francisco gold rush fever actually started in Dahlonega, Georgia. For a trip back in time, contact the **Lumpkin County Chamber of Commerce** at ☎ **800/231-5543** for information on vacations and day trips to the gold mines, 250 feet below the surface. You get to keep the gold you find, but don't expect a king's ransom.

WHITE-WATER CANOEING & RAFTING   The Amicalola River (pronounced "am-e-cola") is one of the state's more stunning sites, with the towering Amicalola Falls. **Appalachian Outfitters** (☎ **800/426-7117**) is the leading outfitter, offering trips for beginners through experienced rafters.

5 Tips for Travelers with Special Needs

FOR TRAVELERS WITH DISABILITIES   Many hotels and restaurants in Georgia provide easy access for persons with disabilities, and some display the international wheelchair symbol in their brochures. However, it's always a good idea to call ahead.

The **Georgia Governor's Developmental Disabilities Council** (☎ **404/ 657-2126**) may also be of help. The Georgia Department of Industry, Trade & Tourism publishes a guide, *Georgia on My Mind,* that lists attractions and accommodations with access for persons with disabilities. To receive a copy, contact **Tour Georgia,** P.O. Box 1776, Atlanta, GA 30301 (☎ **800/VISIT-GA,** ext. 1903).

For information on associations for persons with disabilities, see "Tips for Travelers with Special Needs," in chapter 3.

For transportation within Atlanta, disabled individuals can call **Rent-A-Van of Atlanta** (☎ **770/422-9025**) or **Wheelchair Getaways, Inc.** (☎ **770/457-9851**).

FOR GAY & LESBIAN TRAVELERS   Atlanta is famous for its thriving gay community. You can access its gay offerings through the listings and articles in a free magazine called *Etcetera,* offered in virtually every gay-owned or gay-friendly bar, bookstore, and restaurant in the Deep South. It boasts a bona-fide circulation of 22,000 readers a week, a figure qualifying it as the largest gay and lesbian publication in the Southeast. If you'd like a copy in advance of your trip, send $2 for a current issue to 151 Renaissance Pkwy., Atlanta, GA 30308.

Another gay publication is *Southern Voice.* Call ☎ **404/876-1819** for information about distribution points throughout the South, as well as information on gay resources and activities in Atlanta.

For more information before you go, refer to "Tips for Travelers with Special Needs," in chapter 3.

FOR FAMILIES   All Georgia visitor centers offer discount coupons for families as well as the *Atlanta Street Map & Visitors Guide.* Families might also pick up the book *A Guide for Family Activities,* by Denise Black, with a host of ideas and activities for children in the Metro Atlanta area. Another local guide is called *Fun Family Vacations—Southeast.*

6 Getting There

BY PLANE   Virtually every major national airline flies through Atlanta's **Hartsfield International Airport,** 13 miles south of downtown off I-85 and I-285. From Atlanta, there are connecting flights to points around the state, including Augusta, Columbus, and Savannah.

Delta Air Lines (☎ **800/221-1212** for reservations and flight information; www.delta.com), which is based at Hartsfield, is the major carrier to Atlanta, connecting it to pretty much the entire country as well as 32 countries internationally. Other major carriers include **America West** (☎ 800/235-9292; www.americawest. com), **American** (☎ 800/433-7300; www.aa.com), **British Airways** (☎ 800/AIRWAYS; www.british-airways.com), **Continental** (☎ 800/732-6887; www.flycontinental.com), **Japan Airlines** (☎ 800/525-3663; www.japanair.com), **KLM** (☎ 800/374-7747; www.klm.nl), **Lufthansa** (☎ 800/645-3880; www.lufthansa-usa. com), **Northwest** (☎ 800/225-2525; www.nwa.com), **Swissair** (☎ 800/221-4750; www.swissair.com), **TWA** (☎ 800/221-2000; www.twa.com), **United** (☎ 800/241-6522; www.ual.com), and **US Airways** (☎ 800/428-4322; www.usairways.com). American, Delta, United, and US Airways all serve Savannah's airport.

BY CAR   Georgia is crisscrossed by major Interstate highways: I-75 bisects the state from Dalton in the north to Valdosta in the south; I-95 runs north-south along the eastern seaboard. The major east-west routes are I-16, running between Macon and Savannah; and I-20, running from Augusta through Atlanta and into Alabama. I-85 runs northeast-southwest in the northern half of the state. The state-run welcome centers at all major points of entry are staffed with knowledgeable, helpful Georgians who can often advise you as to timesaving routes. The speed limit of 55 miles per hour and the seat-belt law are strictly enforced.

Here's a list of approximate mileages to Atlanta from other major cities in the region: Birmingham, AL: 148; Charleston, SC: 320; Charlotte, NC: 240; Jacksonville, FL: 346; Louisville, KY: 417; Nashville, TN: 244; New Orleans, LA: 473; Norfolk, VA: 555; Orlando, FL: 441; Tampa, FL: 458.

BY TRAIN   Amtrak (☎ **800/USA-RAIL**) has stops in Atlanta, Savannah, Jesup, Gainesville, and Toccoa. Bargain fares are sometimes in effect for limited periods; you should always check for the most economical way to schedule your trip. Be sure to ask about Amtrak's money-saving "All Aboard America" regional fares or any other current

Georgia Driving Times & Distances

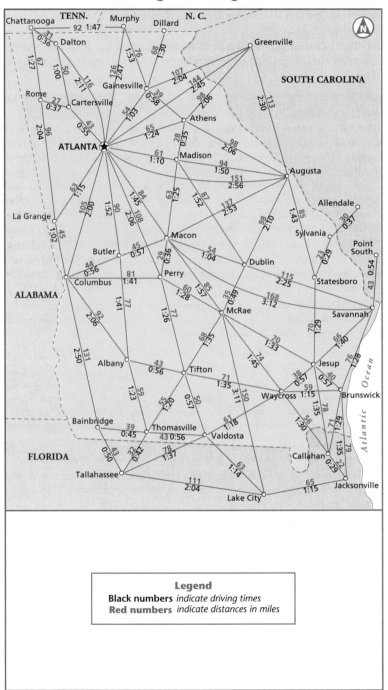

fare specials. Amtrak also offers attractively priced rail-drive packages in the Carolinas and Georgia.

BY BUS   Greyhound/Trailways (☎ **800/231-2222**) has good direct service to major cities in Georgia from out of state, with connections to almost any destination wanted.

7 Getting Around

BY CAR   In addition to the Interstates, U.S. 84 cuts across the southern part of the state from the Alabama state line through Valdosta and Waycross, and eventually connects to I-95 south of Savannah. U.S. 441 runs from the North Carolina border south to Athens, Dublin, and the Florida state line.

For 24-hour road conditions, call ☎ **404/656-5267. AAA** services are available in Atlanta, Augusta, Columbus, Macon, Savannah, Smyrna, and Tucker (see the following chapters for addresses and telephone numbers in Atlanta and Savannah; consult the local telephone directories in other locations).

BY PLANE   From Atlanta, there are connecting flights into Albany, Augusta, Brunswick (for the Golden Isles), Savannah, and (by commuter line) several smaller cities. For information, check with your travel agent. See also "Getting There," earlier in this chapter.

BY TRAIN   Amtrak (see "Getting There," earlier in this chapter) runs from Toccoa to Gainesville and Atlanta, as well as from Savannah to Jesup, and the **Georgia Railroad** operates between Atlanta and Augusta.

Fast Facts: Georgia

American Express   American Express services are available in Georgia through agencies in Albany, Atlanta (five locations; see "Fast Facts: Atlanta," in chapter 16), Augusta (two locations), Columbus, Dalton, Duluth, Macon, and Valdosta.

Emergencies   Dial ☎ **911** for police, ambulance, paramedics, and fire department. Travelers Aid can also be helpful—check local telephone directories.

Liquor Laws   If you're 21 or over, you can buy alcoholic beverages in package stores between 8am and midnight (except on Sunday, election days, Thanksgiving, and Christmas).

Newspapers/Magazines   The *Atlanta Journal-Constitution* is the state's leading daily newspaper.

Police   In an emergency, call ☎ **911** (no coin required).

Taxes   Georgia has a 6% sales tax.

Time Zone   Georgia is in the eastern time zone, and goes on daylight saving time in summer.

Weather   Phone ☎ **900/932-8437** (95¢ per minute) for an update.

Atlanta 16

Atlanta is the gateway to the New South. Bustling and ever-growing—not always attractively—Georgia's capital is the 13th-largest metropolitan area in the United States. If only Rhett and Scarlett could see it now—or, better yet, if only General Sherman could rise from the grave to witness the phenomenal growth of a city that he was able to burn to the ground but whose spirit he couldn't destroy.

Atlanta has enlarged its rail transportation system, brought in six Interstate highways, and acquired an airport to rival Chicago's O'Hare. Some 450 of the Fortune 500 corporations have offices or home offices here.

Perversely (though predictably), it seems that the more progress Atlanta makes, the more serious its problems become. Yet, in spite of overcrowding, unemployment, traffic-clogged streets, and a high crime rate, Atlanta remains the showcase of the New South. It's filled with the homes of the rich and famous (everybody from Ted Turner to Elton John) and is also the Promised Land to immigrants from as far away as Vietnam and as close as the Caribbean and (especially) Mexico.

Ever since Atlanta was selected as the site of the 2000 Super Bowl and the 1996 Summer Olympic Games, the city's face has changed. Massive construction began in the early 1990s with the $215-million, 70,500-seat Georgia Dome, and continued in 1994 and 1995 with the creation of a $50-million, 60-acre Centennial Park, the heart of the public area for the Games. The hard work and construction was not wasted when the Olympics left town. Centennial Park is used for leisure by Atlantans today; the $169-million Olympic Village became housing for Georgia Tech and Georgia State University; the $170-million Olympic Stadium, scaled down to become Turner Field, is the home of the Atlanta Braves; and the Olympic Cauldron still stands in remembrance of the Games. The city's newest sports and entertainment facility, the Philips Arena, opened in late 1999 and hosts the Atlanta Hawks NBA team and the newest professional-sports team in town, the NHL expansion team Atlanta Thrashers.

All this commerce with the outside world has energized the city's cultural life. More than ever before, there are concerts and cabarets, art galleries and avant-garde "happenings," and the many late-night diversions of "Hotlanta." The influx of restaurants featuring international cuisine has put Atlanta on the gastronomic map, but has made it harder and harder to find fried chicken, country ham, hot biscuits, and grits. Locals like to boast that Atlanta has arrived—and they'll be happy to take you by the hand and prove it. You won't have to convince Elton John. The rock star, who owns homes of varying degrees of pomp and elegance all over the world, is said to favor living Southern style in his Atlanta home best of all.

1 Orientation

GETTING THERE

BY PLANE   Atlanta's **Hartsfield International Airport** is the home of **Delta Air Lines** (☎ 800/221-1212; www.delta.com) and served by dozens of other international and domestic carriers, including **American** (☎ 800/433-7300; www.aa.com), **Continental** (☎ 800/221-2000; www.flycontinental.com), **United** (☎ 800/241-6522; www.ual.com), and **US Airways** (☎ 800/428-4322; www.usairways.com).

The **Atlanta Airport shuttle** (☎ 800/842-2770 or 404/524-3400) connects the airport with downtown and major hotels between 7am and 11pm, for a $12 fare ($18 to Lenox Square and Emory University). **MARTA**'s (Metropolitan Atlanta Rapid Transit Authority; ☎ **404/848-4711**) rapid-rail trains run from approximately 4am to 2am, with a downtown fare of $1.50. Taxi fare to downtown is $18 for one passenger, $20 for two passengers, and $28 for three. *Warning:* Be sure the taxi driver knows how to get to where you want to go before you leave the airport.

BY CAR   Atlanta is accessible by car via three Interstate highways: I-75, which runs north-south between Tennessee and Florida; I-85, which runs northeast-southwest between South Carolina and Alabama; and I-20, which runs east-west between South Carolina and Alabama. I-285, more commonly known as the Perimeter Highway, circles the Atlanta metropolitan area.

BY TRAIN   Amtrak trains arrive at the **Brookwood Railway Station,** 1688 Peachtree St. (☎ **800/USA-RAIL**), providing daily service to and from Washington, New York, Boston, and intermediate points to the northeast, and New Orleans and intermediate points to the southwest. This is a very central location, within easy reach of most downtown or Midtown hotels.

VISITOR INFORMATION

Atlanta Convention and Visitors Bureau (ACVB), 233 Peachtree St. NE, Suite 100, Atlanta, GA 30303 (☎ **404/521-6600;** www.atlanta.com), can supply a wealth of information on sightseeing, accommodations, dining, cultural happenings, and special interests. The ACVB also offers the *Atlanta Passport,* a vacation packet filled with coupons, discounts, and an events calendar.

After your arrival, stop by one of the helpful **ACVB visitor information centers,** at Hartsfield International Airport, in the Lenox Square Shopping Center (Buckhead), at 3393 Peachtree Rd., and in Underground Atlanta, 65 Upper Alabama St.

For a more in-depth exploration of the city, Frommer's Atlanta (Macmillan Travel) is available at many bookstores.

Neighborhoods in Brief

Downtown   Atlanta's commercial center is home to numerous gleaming skyscrapers, the most outstanding of which is Peachtree Center. Underground Atlanta, the Georgia World Congress Center, department stores (Macy's, etc.), the downtown branch of the High Museum of Art (in the Georgia-Pacific Center), Grant Park (with its zoo and Cyclorama), and the state capitol are all here. Adjacent to central downtown is the

Atlanta at a Glance

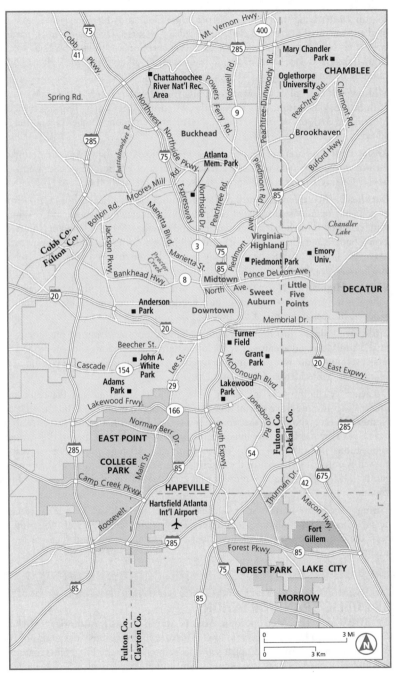

Mt. Vernon Hwy.
400
285
41 Cobb Pkwy
75
Cobb Pkwy
Mary Chandler Park ■
CHAMBLEE
Chattahoochee River Nat'l Rec. Area ■
Oglethorpe University ■
Peachtree Rd.
Clairmont Rd.
Spring Rd.
Powers Ferry Rd.
Roswell Rd.
Peachtree-Dunwoody Rd.
9
285
Northwest
Northside Pkwy.
Buckhead
Brookhaven ○
Buford Hwy.
75
Atlanta Mem. Park ■
Chattahoochee R.
Moores Mill
Northside Dr.
Piedmont Rd.
85
Chandler Lake
Cobb Co. Fulton Co.
Bolton Rd.
Marietta Blvd
Marietta St.
3
Virginia Highland
Emory Univ. ■
Jackson Pkwy.
Proctor Creek
75
Piedmont Park ■
Bankhead Hwy.
8
85
Midtown
Ponce DeLeon Ave.
Little Five Points
DECATUR
20
North Ave.
Sweet Auburn
Anderson Park ■
Downtown
Memorial Dr.
20
Beecher St.
Turner Field ■
Grant Park
20 East Expwy.
Cascade
154
John A. White Park ■
Lee St.
McDonough Blvd
Adams Park ■
29
Lakewood Park ■
Jonesboro Rd.
Lakewood Frwy.
166
Norman Berr Dr.
South Expwy
Fulton Co.
Dekalb Co.
285
EAST POINT
54
COLLEGE PARK
285
Main St
85
675
42
Camp Creek Pkwy.
HAPEVILLE
Thurman Dr.
Macon Hwy.
Roosevelt
Hartsfield Atlanta Int'l Airport ✈
Fort Gillem
285
Forest Pkwy.
85
85
FOREST PARK
LAKE CITY
75
85
85
MORROW

Fulton Co.
Clayton Co.

0 ————— 3 Mi
0 ————— 3 Km

N

315

Martin Luther King, Jr. Historic District, a predominantly black neighborhood that bred and nurtured the revered civil rights leader. The safest downtown streets (particularly after dark) are in the well-traveled "hotel corridor"—bordered by Ellis, Courtland, Baker, and Peachtree streets. Private security officers and the Atlanta Police carefully patrol this area.

Midtown   North of downtown, extending roughly from Ponce de Leon Avenue to 26th Street. Major attractions include the Woodruff Arts Center (housing the High Museum of Art), the Alliance Theatre, the Atlanta Symphony Orchestra, and the Fox Theatre.

Ansley Park   Adjacent to Midtown. Designed by Frederick Law Olmsted around the turn of the century, this is chiefly a residential area of landscaped greenery, and also houses Colony Square, a complex of shops, restaurants, and offices.

Buckhead   About 6 miles north of downtown is Atlanta's affluent district, the setting of gorgeous mansions surrounded by landscaped gardens, posh shops and boutiques, some of the city's top hotels and restaurants, and two top-of-the-line shopping centers—Lenox Square and Phipps Plaza. It's also well known for its bar and restaurant scene. Even the "border" of Buckhead is easily marked by the first of a long stretch of bars you'll see as you drive through.

Virginia-Highland   Northeast of downtown, this is to Atlanta what Greenwich Village is to New York—an area of quirky little shops, bookstores, sidewalk cafes, art galleries, bistros, and some of the liveliest bars in the city.

Little Five Points   Just beyond Virginia-Highland, centered around the junction of Euclid and Moreland avenues. The Victorian homes here became the renovation craze of city residents and now shine in their original glory. This is also where you'll find the Jimmy Carter Presidential Center and Library.

Decatur   A charming village dating from 1823, clustered around the courthouse square, a 15-minute drive east of downtown. Decatur has the huge, bustling Dekalb Farmer's Market, and is also the setting for a variety of cultural events and festivals. In recent years, it has been a popular destination for immigrants, prompting national publications such as *USA Today* to recognize that Atlanta's immigrant population growth is outpacing the rest of the country, especially in the number of Asian immigrants. The neighboring community of Chamblee has been referred to as "Little Hanoi."

Vining   Set to the northwest of Buckhead, inside the Beltway, it's a leafy, pleasant neighborhood whose buildings and homes mostly date from the 1950s. Recently, it's been the site of a residential and commercial building, boom, and focus of lots of attention.

2 Getting Around

BY PUBLIC TRANSPORTATION

BY SUBWAY   The **Metropolitan Atlanta Rapid Transit Authority (MARTA;** ☎ **404/848-4711)** is Atlanta's rapid-rail system, with 36 stations. It extends north to the airport, and east-west and north-south lines intersect at the Five Points Station in downtown. It operates daily from 4am to 2am, and the regular fare is $1.50. There are token vending machines at all stations, and transfers are free. For schedule and route information, call ☎ **404/848-4711** Monday to Friday from 6am to 10pm, and on Saturday, Sunday, and holidays from 8am to 4pm.

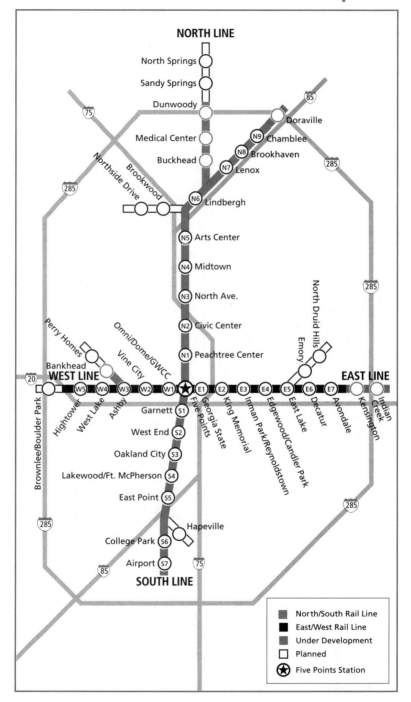

Marta Rapid Rail

BY BUS   MARTA also operates some 150 bus routes, which connect with all rapid-rail stations. You must have exact change for the $1.50 fare, and transfers are free. For route and schedule information, call the MARTA number listed above. They can also tell you when special shuttle buses run from downtown to major sports events.

MARTA provides transportation services for persons with disabilities. Call ☎ **404/848-5389** for details.

BY CAR

It's possible to reach most major Atlanta sites by transit system (MARTA), but a car is preferable, with a few caveats.

Parking isn't usually a problem (though it can be expensive downtown during conventions and sporting events), but traffic often is. (There's even a column in the local newspaper devoted to traffic information and difficulties.) Rush hour—roughly 7 to 9am and 4:30 to 6:30pm—can be vicious, especially when traveling into town in the morning or out of town in the afternoon on any of the interstates. Besides the commuter traffic, there are travelers passing through Atlanta on their way to points north, south, east, and west. Atlanta drivers are generally courteous, but they tend to travel at breakneck speeds well above the posted limit, so it's wise to avoid the interstates—especially I-285, which supports a lot of truck traffic—during peak hours.

All of the major car-rental companies are, of course, represented here and are reachable via toll-free numbers. These include the following: **Avis** (☎ 800/331-1212), **Budget** (☎ 800/527-0700), **Dollar** (☎ 800/800-4000), **Hertz** (☎ 800/654-3131), and **Thrifty** (☎ 800/367-2277). There's also **Atlanta Rent-A-Car** (☎ 404/763-1160), a local, independently owned company, which also has good rates.

AAA services are available through **AAA Auto Club South,** 4540B Roswell Rd., Atlanta, GA 30342 (☎ **404/843-4500**).

BY TAXI

Atlanta's taxis can be a major problem. Many are dirty, mechanically suspect, and manned by drivers not familiar with the city. Be sure the fare is settled before setting off. Fares operate on a set schedule downtown and in Buckhead: $5 to $6 for one passenger, $1 to $2 each for additional passengers. For all other destinations, a single passenger pays $2.90 for the first mile, and $1.40 for each additional mile. You pay $15 per hour for waiting time, and $5 for use of additional space for luggage. Vans or station wagons cost an additional $5. Taxis usually cannot be flagged down on the streets, but must be called, or met at major hotels or the airport. One of the most reliable companies is **Yellow Cab Company** (☎ **404/521-0200**). If you have a complaint about taxi service, call ☎ **404/658-7600.**

Fast Facts: Atlanta

American Express   There are five American Express Travel Service locations: 2184 Henderson Mill Rd., Suite 12-A (☎ **770/723-9488**); Lenox Plaza, 3393 Peachtree Rd. NE (☎ **404/262-7561**); 1052 Perimeter Mall, 4400 Ashford-Dunwoody Rd. (☎ **404/395-1305**); 690 Holcomb Bridge Rd., Suite 160 in Roswell (☎ **770/641-1700**). Offices are open Monday to Friday from 9am to 5pm.

Baby-sitters   Friend of the Family (☎ **770/643-3000**) is a reliable firm with carefully screened, 21-and-over sitters, some of whom speak foreign languages. Twenty-four-hour advance notice is recommended, and you may interview a sitter before making a commitment.

Camera Repair   Try Consumer Tech, 293 14th St. NW (☎ 404/872-5306), open Monday to Friday from 9am to 6pm and on Saturday 10am to 2pm. Go north on Peachtree to 14th Street, then turn left and cross over the Interstate traveling one-half mile. The shop will be on your right.

Currency Exchange   There's a currency exchange service at the airport. In the city, downtown major banks provide the service. Try Bank of America, 35 Broad St. NW (☎ 404/893-8282); and SunTrust, 25 Park Place (☎ 404/588-7694).

Dentists   A free referral service is operated by the Georgia Dental Association of Atlanta (☎ 404/636-7553).

Doctors   For physician referrals, contact the Georgia State Medical Association (☎ 404/752-1564). See also "Hospitals," below.

Drugstores   They're plentiful around the city. Drug Emporium, 2625 Piedmont Rd. (☎ 404/233-1201), is one to choose from, and is open 24 hours.

Emergencies   Call ☎ 911.

Eyeglasses   LensCrafters, in the Lenox Square Mall, 3400 Woodlake Dr. in Buckhead (☎ 404/239-0784), is open Monday to Saturday from 10am to 8pm and on Sunday from 1 to 5pm.

Hospitals   There are 24-hour emergency rooms at the Georgia Baptist Medical Center, 303 Parkway NE (☎ 404/265-4000), and Grady Memorial Hospital, 80 Butler St. (☎ 404/616-4307).

Newspapers/Magazines   The *Atlanta Journal-Constitution* is the major daily newspaper. Others include the *Atlanta Business Chronicle* and the *Atlanta Daily World*. *Atlanta* magazine is an excellent reference for information on current cultural, entertainment, and sightseeing activities. Other periodicals include *Atlanta Now*, and *Where* magazine. The *Southern Voice* serves the gay, lesbian, and transsexual community; and *Creative Loafing* is to Atlanta what the *Village Voice* is to New York, with concert, movie, and theater listings—an insider's guide to what is going on in the city.

Post Office   The main post office is Atlanta Post Office, 3900 Crown Rd., Atlanta, GA 30321 (☎ 404/765-7476, or 800/275-8777 for general information).

Rest Rooms   In addition to bus, rail, and air terminals, public toilets are at Underground Atlanta and Peachtree Center.

Safety   More than 80% of its crimes are property crimes, including thefts from parked cars. Purse-snatchings and muggings are commonplace, especially after dark. After the business clients leave the Downtown and Midtown areas, it becomes a venue for drug dealers and hookers. But there is improvement. Since the end of the Olympics, crime in Atlanta has dropped off thanks to a program that features a battalion of Atlanta Ambassadors. These are unarmed corps of security guards—clad in pith helmets and white uniforms—that act as the eyes and ears of the Atlanta police force. Concentrated in the downtown area, and paid for by a cooperative association of local business owners—they've gone a long way to discourse crime in downtown Atlanta.

Taxes   In addition to the 7% state sales tax, there is a 7% hotel and motel tax. Combined, they make a significant difference in your final hotel bill.

Transit Information   Dial ☎ 404/848-4711.

Weather   Call ☎ 770/603-3333.

3 Accommodations

B&Bs are available in Atlanta in grand style or in modest houses, and are located all over the city. Contact **Bed & Breakfast Atlanta,** 1608 Briarclift Rd., Suite 5, Atlanta, GA 30306 (☎ **800/96-PEACH** or 404/875-0525; fax 404/875-9672). Rates run $75 to $100 including a continental breakfast, with some exceptional lodgings in the $100 to $200 range. There's no booking fee, and major credit cards are accepted.

DOWNTOWN ATLANTA
VERY EXPENSIVE

Hyatt Regency Atlanta. 265 Peachtree St. NE (between Baker and Harris sts.), Atlanta, GA 30303. ☎ **800/233-1234** or 404/577-1234. Fax 404/588-4137. www.atlanta-hyatt.com. E-mail: hrapa@bellsouth.net. 1,264 units. A/C MINIBAR TV TEL. $295–$320 double; from $550 suite. Children 18 and under stay free in parents' room. AE, CB, DC, DISC, MC, V. Parking $17. MARTA: Peachtree Center.

The first of Atlanta's super-hotels, the Hyatt—flanked by two 22-story towers and standing near the Atlanta Mart—launched the chain's atrium look in 1967 when it was first designed by noted architect John Portman. The lobby is somewhat subdued, although striking, with a sculpture extending from the 2nd level to the 12th, much greenery, and bubble-glass elevators. The most desirable rooms are the executive rooms on the 21st and 22nd floors of the main building—they are definitely posh. Expense-account junkies like the rooms in the International Tower overlooking the atrium and opening onto panoramic views of Atlanta.

   Dining/Diversions: The lobby coffee shop is nothing special, but the blue-domed Polaris rooftop revolving restaurant and cocktail lounge is almost reason enough to check in. At lobby level is an Italian restaurant with a 1,800-gallon saltwater aquarium, and an additional lounge.

   Amenities: Room service (19 hours), laundry/valet, airport shuttle, in-room safe; beauty salon, barbershop, full health club, indoor pool (with hot tub), business center, fitness room (with sauna, steam room, and whirlpool).

   ✪ **Ritz-Carlton Atlanta.** 181 Peachtree St. NE (at Ellis St.), Atlanta, GA 30303. ☎ **800/241-3333** or 404/659-0400. Fax 404/221-6578. www.ritzcarlton.com. 444 units. A/C MINIBAR TV TEL. $139–$235 double; from $299 suite. AE, CB, DC, DISC, MC, V. Valet parking $17. MARTA: Peachtree Center.

A premier state-of-the-art hotel in the heart of the business district, this is downtown Atlanta's finest. It has more personal style and glamour than the Atlanta Hilton or Hyatt Regency. Less ostentatious than its Buckhead counterpart, this hotel is more intimately geared to the day-to-day bustle of business-oriented Atlanta. It's richly decorated with silks, tapestries, Persian carpeting, and 18th- and 19th-century paintings. Even the elevator exudes elegance. The guest rooms are restful refuges in tra-ditional style, with bay windows, fresh flowers, and luxurious marble bathrooms. Both the 24th and 25th floors have been set apart as "The Club," where guests enjoy a private lounge with complimentary refreshments and the services of a concierge.

   Dining/Diversions: Beyond the clublike, intimate lounge is an elegant dining room, the Atlantic Grill, where gourmet lunches and dinners, with a special fitness cuisine menu, are accompanied by piano music. Just off the lobby, the Café serves lighter fare.

   Amenities: Room service (24 hours), baby-sitting, laundry/valet, business center, airport shuttle, steam room, fitness center, sauna.

Downtown Atlanta Accommodations & Dining

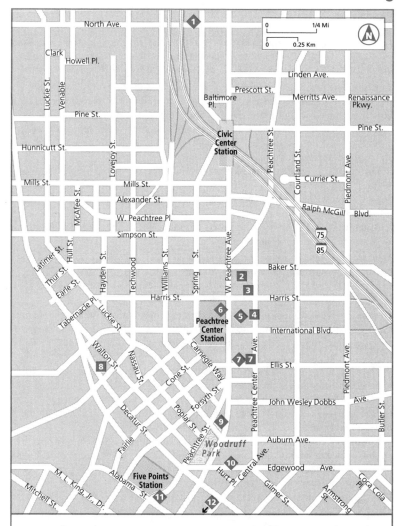

ACCOMMODATIONS ■
Atlanta Marriott Marquis **3**
Hyatt Regency Atlanta **2**
Omni Hotel at CNN Center **8**
Ritz-Carlton Atlanta **7**
Westin Peachtree Plaza **4**

DINING ◆
The Atlanta Grill **7**
City Grill **10**
Hard Rock Cafe **6**
Mick's **11**
Mumbo Jumbo **9**
Planet Hollywood **5**
Sylvia's **12**
The Varsity **1**

EXPENSIVE

Atlanta Marriott Marquis. 265 Peachtree Center Ave. (between Baker and Harris sts.), Atlanta, GA 30303. ☎ **800/228-9290** or 404/521-0000. Fax 404/586-6299. www.marriott. com. 1,672 units. A/C TV TEL. $89–$260 double; from $400 suite. Children 11 and under stay free in parents' room. AE, CB, DC, DISC, MC, V. Parking $12. MARTA: Peachtree Center.

The futuristic design of this Marriott is evident the moment you walk into the seemingly infinite atrium, softened with greenery and sculpture. Some 46 stories tall, this hotel rises dramatically toward the sky, more luxurious than the Hyatt. Reached by bullet elevators, the guest rooms are in shades of rose, mauve, and burgundy, each with a king-size bed or two doubles. Two of the six club levels feature upgraded rooms, although all of them have club-level privileges.

Dining: At the garden level is a bevy of restaurants, including a sidewalk cafe. The Marquis Steakhouse is casual, with steak and seafood, and the Atrium Express offers gourmet sandwiches, salads, and soups. There's also a piano bar on this floor, plus a noisy sports-theme bar.

Amenities: Room service (24 hours), airport shuttle, laundry/valet; health club, large swimming pool, business center.

Omni Hotel at CNN Center. 100 CNN Center (at Techwood Dr. and Marietta St.), Atlanta, GA 30335. ☎ **800/843-6664** or 404/659-0000. Fax 404/525-5050. www.omnihotels.com. 470 units. $139–$314 double; from $775 suite. AE, DC, DISC, MC, V. Parking $5–$17. MARTA: Omni.

Next to the World Congress Center and the brand-new Philips Arena, sports home of the NBA Atlanta Hawks and the NHL Atlanta Thrashers, this 15-story modernistic megastructure houses CNN headquarters. In its way, it's the most anonymous hotel in Atlanta, designed as part of a huge commercial complex that in some ways disguises the fact it is a hotel at all. Its soaring, marble-covered, split-level lobby and tastefully luxurious guest rooms send a contemporary message. Glass elevators climb to the top floors, where some rooms have balconies overlooking the lobby. The well-furnished bedrooms have such extras as irons and ironing boards. There's a VIP floor for the ultimate in luxury and service, attracting CNN news-hounds.

Dining: A coffee shop and two restaurants include one with a northern Italian cuisine. A new restaurant and bar, Prime Meridian, overlooking Centennial Olympic Park, is part of a $9-million hotel renovation.

Amenities: Room service, laundry/valet; three-floor health club in CNN Center (independent of the hotel), where you're likely to see Pat Buchanan in the sauna.

Westin Peachtree Plaza. 210 Peachtree St. NE (at International Blvd.), Atlanta, GA 30303. ☎ **800/228-3000** or 404/659-1400. Fax 404/589-7424. www.westin.com. E-mail: peach@westin.com. 1,068 units. A/C MINIBAR TV TEL. $125–$310 double; from $350 suite. Children 17 and under stay free in parents' room. AE, CB, DC, DISC, MC, V. Valet parking $18; self-parking $16. MARTA: Peachtree Center.

Atlanta's most famous contemporary hotel is also the tallest, with 73 soaring floors. A bank of 18 elevators will carry you to the roof with its revolving restaurant, a grand spectacle for a special evening on the town. If you're not afraid of heights, you'll reach your room in a glass elevator that goes up the side of the building. Try to get a room high up, as the view becomes panoramic. Executive Club rooms are the most desirable; color-coordinated fabrics, light-wood furniture, and well-designed contemporary bathrooms add to the lavish ambience. The hotel is undergoing a $25-million guest-room refurbishment project.

Dining/Diversions: At the Sun Dial Restaurant a 360-degree cityscape comes into view. A refined American cuisine is served here. There are also three ground-level bars dispensing potent libations, plus the Savannah Fish Company, where you can skip the pricey appetizers and go right for the delectable main courses.

Amenities: Room service (24 hours), high-speed Internet connection, laundry/valet, airport shuttle; indoor pool on the 11th floor with a retractable roof, fitness center, sauna.

MIDTOWN ATLANTA
VERY EXPENSIVE

Four Seasons Hotel Atlanta. 75 14th St. (between Peachtree and West Peachtree sts.), Atlanta, GA 30309. ☎ **800/332-3443** or 404/881-9898. Fax 404/873-4692. www. fourseasons.com. 244 units. A/C MINIBAR TV TEL. $260–$370 double; from $550 suite. Reductions granted, depending on occupancy, especially on weekends. AE, DC, DISC, MC, V. Parking $18. MARTA: Arts Center.

It's as opulent and plush as its nearest rival, the Buckhead branch of the Ritz-Carlton, but to its growing legion of fans, it's even better, with a midtown location that's increasingly favored as a venue for hip Atlantans. It occupies the bottom 19 floors of a granite-sheathed tower that soars 53 floors above midtown Atlanta—the upper floors contain private, and very upscale, condominiums. Developed by a Spain-based investment group in the late 1980s, and now managed by the world-class Four Seasons chain, it has the most attentive and sophisticated staff, and the most impressive and dramatic lobby, of any hotel in Georgia. You'll register in a stately looking three-story atrium that vaguely evokes the imperial days of ancient Rome. It's sheathed in thousands of slabs of russet-colored marble, studded with masses of fresh flowers, and ringed with the kind of modern art you want to take time to savor. Accommodations are as plush as you'd expect from this topnotch chain, each room with marble trim, ultra-comfortable chaise longues and deep mattresses, a safe, in-house movies, a TV set that allows direct access to the Internet, and all the electronic extras you'll need to conduct business or enjoy a holiday away from home. Phase two of a multimillion-dollar renovation was completed in 2000.

Dining/Diversions: At the Park 75 Restaurant (see "Where to Dine," below), some of the finest cuisine in the Southeast is dished up with verve by a staff that fully understands its culinary nuances. Nearby, in a setting that evokes a mahogany-sheathed private club in London, you'll find the most urbane and appealing hotel bar in Atlanta.

Amenities: Room service (24 hours a day), a hard-working concierge staff that can arrange virtually anything, complimentary limousine service, within reason and on demand, to most points within central Atlanta, a full-service business center, an Olympic-sized swimming pool, and one of the finest gyms/health clubs in the city.

MODERATE

✪ **Ansley Inn.** 253 15th St. NE (at Lafayette), Atlanta, GA 30309. ☎ **800/446-5416** or 404/872-9000. Fax 404/892-2318. www.ansleyinn.com. E-mail: reservations@ansleyinn.com. 22 units. A/C TV TEL. $109–$189 double. Rates include full breakfast. AE, MC, V. Free parking. MARTA: Arts Center.

Unique in Atlanta, this former stately home in a prestigious neighborhood (Ansley Park) mimics many of the trappings of an exclusive, small-scale European inn. It occupies a yellow-brick Tudor mansion. In 1995, nine additional rooms were added to the back of the house in distinguished style. Those in the front of the house retain a semi-antique flair. All but two of the rooms have Jacuzzis. Breakfast is served in a formal dining room outfitted with English Chippendale, carpets, and Italian crystal chandeliers. Classical music or quiet jazz reverberates softly through the carefully furnished public rooms throughout most of the day.

Midtown Atlanta Accommodations & Dining

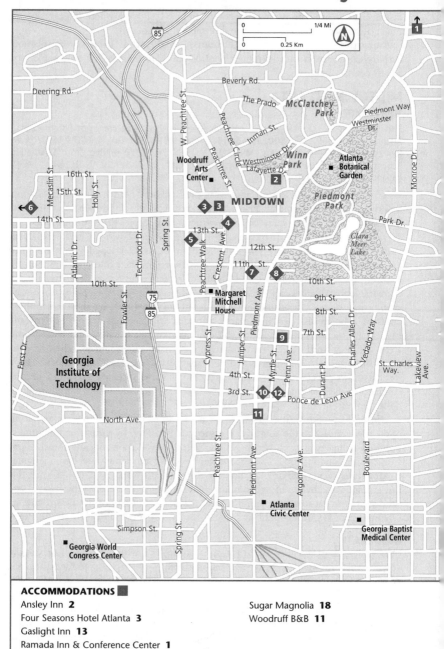

0 ——— 1/4 Mi
0 ——— 0.25 Km

85

Deering Rd.

Beverly Rd.

The Prado

McClatchey Park

Piedmont Way

Westminster Dr.

Inman St.

W. Peachtree St.

Peachtree Circle

Woodruff Arts Center

Westminster Dr.

Winn Park

Lafayette Dr.

Atlanta Botanical Garden

Monroe Dr.

Mecaslin St.

16th St.

15th St.

Holly St.

Peachtree St.

2

14th St.

6

3 3

MIDTOWN

Piedmont Park

Park Dr.

Atlantic Dr.

Techwood Dr.

Spring St.

Peachtree Walk

13th St.

Crescent Ave.

4

5

12th St.

11th St.

7

8

Clara Meer Lake

10th St.

10th St.

9th St.

Fowler St.

75

85

Margaret Mitchell House

Piedmont Ave.

8th St.

Charles Allen Dr.

Vedado Way

St. Charles Way.

Lakeview Ave.

Georgia Institute of Technology

Cypress St.

Juniper St.

7th St.

9

Penn Ave.

Myrtle St.

4th St.

3rd St.

10 12

Ponce de Leon Ave

Durant Pl.

Fern Dr.

North Ave.

11

Peachtree St.

Piedmont Ave.

Argonne Ave.

Boulevard

Atlanta Civic Center

Simpson St.

Spring St.

Georgia Baptist Medical Center

Georgia World Congress Center

ACCOMMODATIONS

Ansley Inn **2**
Four Seasons Hotel Atlanta **3**
Gaslight Inn **13**
Ramada Inn & Conference Center **1**
Shellmont Bed and Breakfast Lodge **9**

Sugar Magnolia **18**
Woodruff B&B **11**

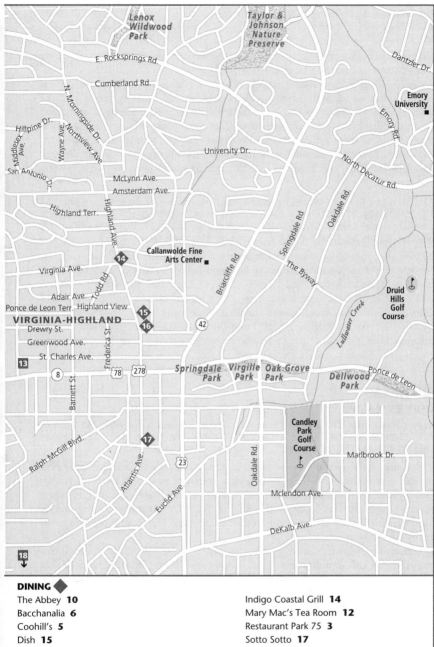

DINING ◆

The Abbey **10**
Bacchanalia **6**
Coohill's **5**
Dish **15**
Einstein's **7**
Harvest Restaurant **16**

Indigo Coastal Grill **14**
Mary Mac's Tea Room **12**
Restaurant Park 75 **3**
Sotto Sotto **17**
South City Kitchen **4**
Zocalo's **8**

Ramada Inn & Conference Center. 418 Armour Dr., Atlanta, GA 30324. ☎ **800/ 282-8222** or 404/873-4661. 370 units. A/C TV TEL. $129 double; $250–$300 suite. AE, DC, MC, V.

Situated in a pocket of greenery that's tucked between the roaring traffic of Route 85 and a commercial neighborhood of Midtown Atlanta, this is a comfortable and well-designed, albeit somewhat anonymous, hotel that's favored by convention partici-pants. Rooms are relatively large, completely standardized, well engineered and well maintained, set within sprawling wings that are designed around a series of landscaped courtyards that provide easy access to an outdoor swimming pool, a bar, and a buffet-style restaurant noted for its generous breakfasts. The guest list is varied and might include families, corporate workers, or members of a leather/motorcycle club. Regard-less of the situation, this hotel and its staff treat any and all guests with graciousness and courtesy.

○ **Shellmont Bed and Breakfast Lodge.** 821 Piedmont Ave. NE (at 6th St.), Atlanta, GA 30308. ☎ **404/872-9290.** Fax 404/872-5379. www.shellmont.com. E-mail: innkeeper@ shellmont.com. 5 units. A/C TV TEL. $100–$150 double; $130–$240 suite. Rates include full breakfast. AE, CB, DC, DISC, MC, V. Free parking. MARTA: North Avenue or Midtown.

Named after the carved seashell adorning the front of this elaborate Victorian, the Shellmont is a stylish and historically authentic period home for overnight guests. Elaborate restoration has filled it with discreetly concealed modern amenities as well as a historically appropriate collection of Oriental carpets, wall coverings and draperies, furnishings, fresh flowers, and 1890s accessories. Only breakfast is served, featuring frittatas or Belgian waffles. From the front, you'll be fully aware of your urban location. From the back garden, however, where there are verandas and a fish-pond, you'll swear you're in a small town in the Georgia countryside. The largest accommodation is the suite, originally conceived as the servants' quarters.

BUCKHEAD
Very Expensive

Grand Hyatt Atlanta. 3300 Peachtree Rd., Atlanta, GA 30305. ☎ **800/233-1234** or 404/365-8100. Fax 404/233-3888. 439 units. A/C MINIBAR TV TEL. $159–$250 double; $525–$1,500 suite. AE, DC, DISC, MC, V. Parking $5–$12. MARTA: Lenox.

This is one of the most distinctive hotels in Atlanta, an award-winning combination of bold postmodern and Chippendale, with attention paid to aesthetic detailing. Grand Hyatt is a striking 24-story monolith with a massive motor entrance that some visitors compare to a set design for *The Wizard of Oz*. Register in the striking rotunda faced with marble and accented with massive chandeliers. The accommodations are in earthy color schemes.

Dining/Diversions: Atlanta's premier Japanese restaurant, Kamogawa, is well rec-ommended. Cassis is more international in scope, specializing in a range of food that covers all shores of the Mediterranean. English-style afternoon teas are served in the lobby, and a jazz trio sometimes entertains in the bar.

Amenities: Room service (24 hours), concierge, baby-sitting, business center, fully equipped health club (with TVs and VCRs on exercise bikes, outdoor pool, and sundeck).

○ **Ritz-Carlton Buckhead.** 3434 Peachtree Rd., Atlanta, GA 30326. ☎ **800/241-3333** or 404/237-2700. Fax 404/239-0078. 553 units. A/C MINIBAR TV TEL. $185–$270 double; from $285 suite. AE, CB, DC, DISC, MC, V. Valet parking $18; self-parking $8. MARTA: Lenox.

The Ritz-Carlton is the most sumptuous and elegant hotel in Atlanta. A 22-story tower soaring above Buckhead, it's awash in oiled paneling, tapestries, marble and hardwood, theatrical bouquets of spotlighted flowers, antiques, and a museum's worth of valuable paintings. It's been likened to Claridge's in London. The staff is artful, polite, soft-spoken, and efficient.

Dining/Diversions: The Dining Room is one of the most sought-after restaurants in Atlanta (see "Dining," later in this chapter). There's also a deli with an attendant espresso bar, and both a cafe and a bar-lounge whose fireplace is frequently blazing. In-room dining is available.

Amenities: Everything you can think of, including 24-hour room service, a full-time concierge, and beauty shop; an opulent health club, meeting space for 750 conventioneers, a private lounge on the 18th-floor reserved exclusively for residents of the club floors, business center, gift shop.

EXPENSIVE

Swissôtel Atlanta. 3391 Peachtree Rd. NE (between Lenox and Piedmont rds.), Atlanta, GA 30326. ☎ **888/737-9477** or 404/365-0065. Fax 404/233-8786. www.swissotel.com. E-mail: kimberley.lowthers@swissotel.com. 365 units. A/C MINIBAR TV TEL. $150–$320 double; $475–$2,000 suite. Children 11 and under stay free in parents' room. AE, CB, DC, DISC, MC, V. Valet parking $17, self-parking $12. MARTA: Lenox.

Here's a hotel that would ordinarily stand head and shoulders above others. But in Buckhead, the Swissôtel is hard-pressed to keep up with the Joneses—in this case, the Ritz-Carlton. Still, it's first class all the way and has a European flavor to it. The guest rooms and suites are the largest in Buckhead, with Biedermeier-style furnishings. The rooms have three dual-line phones with call waiting and voice mail. The marble bathrooms feature oversize tubs, hair dryers, and makeup and shaving mirrors. The suites are especially luxurious, with VCRs and glass-block bathing areas; the Presidential suite houses a fireplace and a terrace with a Jacuzzi.

Dining: The Palm restaurant (see "Dining," later in this chapter) is patterned after the famous Palm Restaurant launched in New York in 1926. The menu is that of an all-American steakhouse.

Amenities: Room service (24 hours), Cybercafe, laundry/dry cleaning, complimentary shoeshine, complimentary shuttle within a 2-mile radius, health and fitness center, gift shop, day spa and salon, business center.

MODERATE

✪ **Beverly Hills Inn.** 65 Sheridan Dr. NE (off Peachtree Rd.), Atlanta, GA 30305. ☎ **800/331-8520** or 404/233-8520. Fax 404/233-8659. www.beverlyhillsinn.com. E-mail: info@beverlyhillsinn.com. 18 units. A/C TV TEL. $99–$120 1-bedroom suite; $140–$160 2-bedroom suite. Rates include continental breakfast. Children stay free in parents' room. AE, DC, DISC, MC, V. Free parking. MARTA: Lindbergh.

Cozy and a bit eccentric, this English-style B&B occupies an immensely desirable plot of land in Buckhead, about 2 blocks from most of this neighborhood's restaurants and shops. Behind the green shutters and awnings of a building that looks as if it might have been transplanted from California, you'll find lots of English Victoriana, a small back garden with a fountain and sitting area, potted plants, and a vaguely bohemian atmosphere. Each unit has its own kitchen. You'll find a half bottle of burgundy in your room along with mementos from other times and places. Port wine is served each evening. Local phone calls are free; there's an in-house washer/dryer and a lounge with photocopy and fax machines.

INEXPENSIVE

✪ **Buckhead Bed & Breakfast Inn.** 70 Lenox Pointe, Atlanta, GA 30324. ☎ **888/224-8797** or 404/261-8284. Fax 404/237-9224. www.insiders.com/atlanta/main-bnb.htm. E-mail: bandb@mindspring.com. 19 units. A/C TV TEL. $85–$105 double. Children under 12 free. Rates include a continental breakfast. AE, MC, V. Free parking. MARTA: bus 39 from Lindbergh Station, about a mile away.

Buckhead Accommodations & Dining

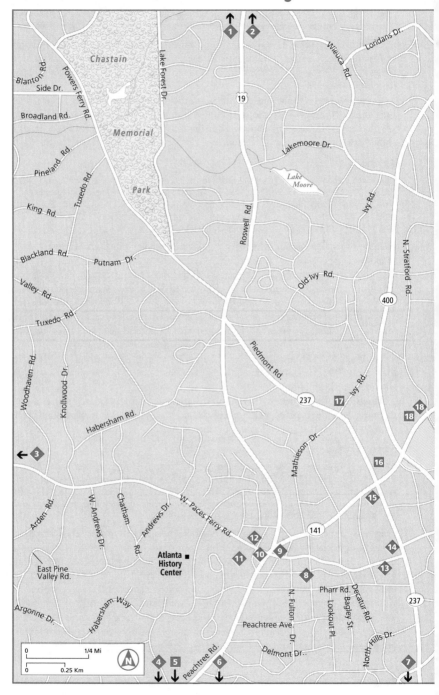

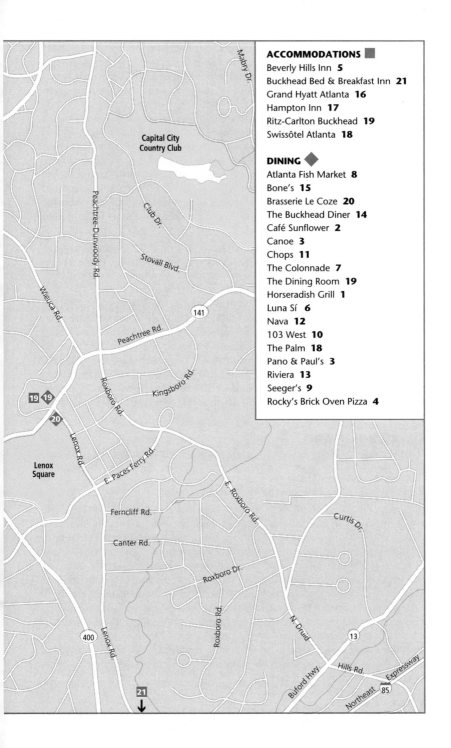

ACCOMMODATIONS ■
Beverly Hills Inn **5**
Buckhead Bed & Breakfast Inn **21**
Grand Hyatt Atlanta **16**
Hampton Inn **17**
Ritz-Carlton Buckhead **19**
Swissôtel Atlanta **18**

DINING ◆
Atlanta Fish Market **8**
Bone's **15**
Brasserie Le Coze **20**
The Buckhead Diner **14**
Café Sunflower **2**
Canoe **3**
Chops **11**
The Colonnade **7**
The Dining Room **19**
Horseradish Grill **1**
Luna Sí **6**
Nava **12**
103 West **10**
The Palm **18**
Pano & Paul's **3**
Riviera **13**
Seeger's **9**
Rocky's Brick Oven Pizza **4**

Capital City
Country Club

Peachtree-Dunwoody Rd.

Mabry Dr.

Club Dr.

Stovall Blvd.

Wieuca Rd.

141

Peachtree Rd.

Roxboro Rd.

Kingsboro Rd.

19 19

20

Lenox Rd.

Lenox
Square

E. Paces Ferry Rd.

Ferncliff Rd.

Canter Rd.

E. Roxboro Rd.

Curtis Dr.

Roxboro Dr.

Roxboro Rd.

N. Druid

400

Lenox Rd.

13

21
↓

Buford Hwy.

Hills Rd.

Northeast
Expressway

85

B&Bs aren't something you associate with upmarket Buckhead, but there is one, lying 4 miles northeast on I-85 (exit 28), at the corner of Lenox Road and Sidney Marcus Boulevard, a busy intersection in a new building enveloped by offices. In this incongruous setting for a B&B, you'll be housed elegantly at an affordable price in superexpensive Buckhead. The building itself is columned with two wide porches, in stark contrast to the neighboring office structures. Rooms are moderate in size, each suggesting their motif by the name on the door—Holly Room, for example, or Oak Room. Each accommodation comes with a private bathroom, four-poster bed, writing desk, armoire, and computer modem lines. Most requested is the Peachtree Room, a spacious accommodation with two queen-size four-posters, dormers, and a vaulted ceiling. The breakfast of pastries and fruit salads is one of the better ones in the area and often includes homemade breads and sausage or ham biscuits. You can relax in the bar with its Windsor chairs and wood-burning fireplace. Unlike most B&Bs, rooms here are linked by an elevator.

Hampton Inn. 3398 Piedmont Rd., NE, Atlanta, GA 30305. ☎ **800/426-7866** or 404/233-5656. Fax 404/237-4688. 154 units. A/C TV TEL. $85–$92 double. Children under 18 free in parents' room. Rates include continental breakfast. AE, DC, DISC, MC, V. MARTA: Lindbergh station.

This hotel is no better than most standard Hampton Inns—it's strictly chain format. But what makes it special is its price and location in upscale Buckhead. Staying in this neighborhood and living well for a reasonable tab brightens the glow of this place. Bedrooms are medium in size and come with all the usual Hampton Inn equipment such as data ports, hair dryers, cable TV, free newspapers, free local calls, and a private safe along with coffeemakers. Some of the rooms are suitable for persons with disabilities, and units are also no-smoking. The hotel has a pool and can arrange temporary visits to a nearby health club. An adjacent restaurant is open daily from 11am to 11pm.

VIRGINIA-HIGHLAND

✪ **Gaslight Inn.** 1001 St. Charles Ave., Atlanta, GA 30306. ☎ **404/875-1001.** Fax 404/876-1001. www.gaslightinn.com. E-mail: innkeeper@gaslightinn.com. 6 units. A/C MINIBAR TV TEL. $95–$145 double; $149–$295 suite. Rates include breakfast. AE, DC, DISC, MC, V. Free parking. MARTA: Bus 2 ("Ponce") or 16 ("Noble").

One of the most appealing B&Bs in Virginia-Highland is this 1913 Craftsman-style house that's set above a steeply sloping front garden, behind a commodious front porch. In the 1990s, it was enlarged and renovated, and a well-proportioned annex was added, separated from the main house by a garden illuminated by flickering gas-fired lanterns. The inn's owners, Jim Moss and Stephen Pararo, also run a successful antiques and decorating business, and part of the inn's allure comes from the antiques in the public areas that span most of the 19th century. Accommodations, especially the suites, are outfitted like private apartments. Four of the six contain working kitchens; the remaining two have access to a kitchen right outside their doors. Breakfast is a high point of the day here: An informal and affable affair, it's served in an early-20th-century dining room accented with a Craftsman-style fireplace and fine paintings. Morning coffee and afternoon wine are offered by the staff, as well as information about attractions and diversions.

INMAN PARK

✪ **Sugar Magnolia.** 804 Edgewood Ave. NE, Atlanta, GA 30307. ☎ **404/222-0226.** Fax 404/681-1067. www.sugarmagnoliabb.com. E-mail: DSTAR37866@aol.com. 4 units. A/C TV. $90–$105 double; $120–$135 suite. Rates include continental breakfast. MARTA: Five Points.

Located in a historic district of Atlanta, this 1892 Victorian house was originally constructed by a southern colonel but turned into a B&B of charm and beauty by its owners, Jim Emshoff and Debi Starnes. They have created an oasis that lives up to its name, with a three-story turret, six fireplaces, oval beveled windows, hand-painted plasterwork, and a grand staircase fit for an entrance by Scarlett O'Hara. A no-smoking house, the inn rents individually styled and commodious bedrooms, including one called the royal suite with a king-size brass bed in a curtain alcove and a rooftop deck with a waterfall garden. The cottage suite has a fully equipped galley kitchen and a vaulted ceiling with skylight, along with a Jacuzzi and open-loft bedroom with a double bed. The delightful Aviary is furnished with antiques and a fireplace; but best of all, this seven-sided room has a painted ceiling of clouds and birds.

STONE MOUNTAIN

Stone Mountain Park Inn. Jefferson Davis Rd. (U.S. 78 E.) (P.O. Box 775), Stone Mountain Park, Stone Mountain, GA 30086. ☎ **800/722-1000** or 770/469-3311. Fax 770/498-5691. 92 units. A/C TV TEL. $99–$149 double. AE, DC, DISC, MC, V. $6 fee into park; otherwise, free parking.

This low-rise, neocolonial hotel was originally built in 1965 for visitors interested in staying as close as possible to the massive bas-reliefs of Stone Mountain's northern face. Set inside the park boundaries, about 16 miles east of the city, it offers bedrooms outfitted in reproductions of 18th-century country furniture. Don't expect a mountain view: Many bedrooms overlook the forest or the hotel's inner courtyard, and you must stand on the plantation-style front porch to catch a glimpse of the laser-light show illuminating the mountain. Views are even better from the hotel's lawns, and even better across the highway, than from the bedrooms themselves. The in-house restaurant, the Mountain View, features a revolving series of all-you-can-eat buffets.

4 Dining

Underground Atlanta, bounded by Peachtree, Wall, Alabama, Pryor, and Central streets and Martin Luther King, Jr., Drive (☎ **404/523-2311;** see "Attractions," later in this chapter), is home to a dozen "food courts" and nightclubs centered around its Kenny's Alley; most are open nightly until around midnight.

DOWNTOWN
EXPENSIVE

The Atlanta Grill. In the Ritz-Carlton, 181 Peachtree St., Atlanta. ☎ **404/221-6550.** Reservations recommended. Main courses $18–$36. AE, DC, MC, V. Daily 11:30am–1am; only light fare 2:30–5pm and 11pm–1am. MARTA: Peachtree Center. STEAKS.

Stylish, well organized, and urbane, this downtown Atlanta steakhouse evokes some of the southern charm of New Orleans, thanks to an elaborate iron balcony that juts out over the sidewalk of one of the busiest sections of Peachtree Street. Inside, flickering gas lanterns and photos of Old Atlanta's political and debutante parties usually evoke dialogues from the most taciturn of local residents. Although meals here are impeccable, this is not a fine dining enclave. Instead, the hotel that contains it refers to it as a steakhouse with extremely refined service rituals, leaving the culinary finesse to the restaurant within the Ritz-Carlton in Buckhead instead. Also, it's the kind of place where the rich-grained bartop doubles as a dining table for the many single, usually business-related travelers who come here. Menu items include many cuts of juicy steak, prime beef, lobster macaroni with cheese, and buttermilk-marinated fried green tomatoes. For lunch you might begin with a mint julep soup made with chilled Georgia peaches or else a seared crab cake. Sandwiches, such as "pulled pork," are available. At night, the menu expands with such Southern-influenced dishes as molasses-grilled pork tenderloin, or tomato stone-ground grits cake with baby summer squash. Most guests finish with a piece of pecan pie and caramel ice cream covered with a vanilla bourbon syrup.

✪ **City Grill.** 50 Hurt Plaza (at Edgewood Ave.). ☎ **404/524-2489.** Reservations recommended. Main courses $14–$38. AE, DC, DISC, MC, V. Mon–Fri 11:30am–2:30pm and 6–10pm, Sat 6–10pm. MARTA: Peachtree Center. CONTEMPORARY AMERICAN.

One of Atlanta's most elegant restaurants is still going strong; it remains a venue for movers and shakers at lunch and for Atlanta's social elite at dinner. The setting for this opulent showcase for creative cookery is the 1912 Hurt Building, long known as the Deep South's most spectacular office building, with its rotunda lined in marble with a gold-leaf dome. You'll be impressed by the boneless quail with creamy gravy or even the crab cakes with pasta or pancake with fennel. Chef David Gross arrived in 1997 and was careful not to upset the clientele with a menu makeover. Among the new items he added, we recommend the barbecue shrimp and a wonderful sautéed trout. The duck is succulent and moist, having been slowly smoked over wood chips. The selection of French and California wines is about as good as Atlanta gets.

Mumbo Jumbo. 89 Park Place. ☎ **404/523-0330.** Reservations recommended. Main courses $9–$18 at lunch, $18–$30 at dinner. AE, DISC, DC, MC, V. Mon–Fri 11:30am–2:30pm, Mon–Sat 5–11pm. SOUTHERN.

The antique, squat-looking warehouse that contains this busy restaurant stands in a parking lot that's surrounded by some of the most futuristic-looking skyscrapers in downtown Atlanta. The nostalgia it evokes of Atlanta when it was a slow-moving Southern backwater makes locals appreciate it even more. Inside, there's a sprawling bar area favored by local office workers, a forest of masonry columns that are whimsically sheathed in glazed pottery shards, and an intriguing mix of iron cutout sculptures and op art. Food is distinctively rooted in the kinds of fare many Southerners remember from their childhood. Examples include a "Mumbo Gumbo" with crayfish, shrimp, okra, and sausage, or field greens with dates, spiced pecans, and bleu cheese. For a main course, a pork shank with grilled asparagus tempts you, as does roast hen with Carolina grits, country ham, and turnip greens. An Angus filet mignon is perfectly roasted with Vidalia onions and wild mushrooms, or else you might be tempted by the sautéed halibut with a fennel salad, red wine lentils, and smoked eel butter. Desserts are rich and excellent, especially the rhubarb tart with strawberry ice cream.

MODERATE

Hard Rock Cafe. 215 Peachtree St. NE (at International Blvd.). ☎ **404/688-7625.** Reservations not accepted. Main courses $6.79–$17.99. AE, DC, MC, V. Sun–Thurs 11am–midnight, Fri–Sat 11am–1am. MARTA: Peachtree Center. AMERICAN.

Now largely eclipsed by Planet Hollywood (see below), the Hard Rock can still pack 'em in on a good night. The music is loud and raucous, the hamburgers aren't bad, and the banana splits evoke those halcyon days of James Dean and Marilyn Monroe.

Mick's. 557 Peachtree St. ☎ **404/875-6425.** Main courses $5.99–$13.99; children's menu $1.99. AE, DC, MC, V. Daily 11am–midnight. MARTA: North Avenue. AMERICAN.

The tile floors, leather booths, and counter stools here are straight out of a 1950s movie set or an Edward Hopper painting. In a renovated building with high tin ceilings, this is one of the most popular members of an Atlanta chain. The menu still gives you those nostalgic soggy pastas with their watery sauces—better stick to chicken pot pie or the meatloaf, the famous blue-plate specials of those long-gone years. Or, better yet, go for the sandwiches, salads, and such down-home dishes as hickory-smoked pork chops that can be quite a taste treat. Remember banana splits? They're still served here, along with cherry Cokes.

Planet Hollywood. 218 Peachtree St. NW. ☎ **404/523-7300.** Reservations not for lesser mortals. Main courses $7.50–$18.95. AE, DC, MC, V. Daily 11am–midnight. (Bar, daily 11am–2am.) MARTA: Peachtree Center. AMERICAN.

Across from the Hard Rock Cafe, this Planet Hollywood became the 24th restaurant in the chain when it opened in Atlanta during the summer of 1995. In a "Hollywood meets Las Vegas" type of decor, props include the green drapery hat worn by Vivien Leigh in *Gone With the Wind,* Debbie Reynolds' dresses from *Singin' in the Rain,* and Rhett's white suit from the burning of Atlanta. Even Tom Hanks's football uniform from *Forrest Gump* is here. The menu is numbingly standard—burgers, pizzas, salads, and a Gardenburger that isn't bad. But skip those soggy French fries. We've had better strip steaks at a roadside pit stop. But that doesn't keep the long lines from forming outside. Who goes here for food anyway?

INEXPENSIVE

✪ **Sylvia's.** 241 Central Ave. ☎ **404/529-9692.** Main courses $8.95–$17.95. AE, DC, DISC, MC, V. Mon–Thurs 11am–10pm, Fri–Sat 11am–11pm, and Sun noon–8pm. MARTA: Five Points or Garnett Station. SOUL FOOD.

From the heart of Harlem where she reigns as the queen of soul food, Sylvia Woods has branched out to entice Atlanta with her brand of finger-lickin' food—yes, chicken and ribs, greens and beans, plus a bit of Southern hospitality. She's come a long way for a woman who in 1962 borrowed money to purchase a small one-room restaurant in Harlem in which she'd worked as a waitress.

She's quickly established herself and her place in Atlanta as a soul food haven, attracting down-home cooking devotees, celebrities, and politicians. Sylvia's is an Art Deco–style, split-level restaurant; a baby grand piano is used nightly for live jazz. Her collard greens are authentically Southern, with just enough sugar added to sweeten the pot. Her BBQ ribs are saucy and spicy, and her Southern fried chicken has made her a legend. Naturally, you get all of Sylvia's favorite vegetables—not just collards, but sassy rice, tomato and okra gumbo, black-eyed peas, and candied yams. Her desserts are made from recipes from Grandma's attic, everything from peach cobbler to red velvet cake, from sweet potato pie to chocolate cake. Look for the daily specials, and we're talking turkey wings "with the right kind of dressing."

The Varsity. 61 North Ave. (at Spring St.). ☎ **404/881-1706.** Reservations not accepted. Main courses 99¢–$4.85. No credit cards. Sun–Thurs 9am–11:30pm, Fri–Sat 9am–midnight. MARTA: North Avenue. AMERICAN.

This local legend offers enough "Grease" for the Broadway show and 80 roadside versions. The world's largest drive-in restaurant, opened in 1928 by Frank Gordy, is run nowadays by his daughter, Nancy Simms and her children. Some 16,000 people a day dine at this Atlanta institution—on hot dogs, hamburgers, French fries, and 300 gallons of chili. Service is fast both carside and inside, with seats and stand-up eating counters; and prices are definitely low. Yes, the orange freezes are just like the ones you had after the senior prom. Ordering can be an adventure. For example, you may be greeted with "whadda ya have? whadda ya have?" Hot dogs are called "dawgs," and hamburgers are "steaks." If you order them plain, just add "naked" to the front of the name—"nekkid dawg" or "nekkid steak," and so on. *Insider's Tip:* If you want a cheeseburger, be sure to ask for pimento cheese. True, it's a mess, but you've never had anything like it.

MIDTOWN
EXPENSIVE

The Abbey. 163 Ponce de Leon. ☎ **404/876-8532.** Reservations recommended. Main courses $18–$29.50. AE, DC, DISC, MC, V. Daily 6–10pm. MARTA: North Marta Station. CONTINENTAL.

The most lavish and charming ecclesiastical setting in Atlanta doesn't function as a church, but as an always-popular restaurant. It was originally built in 1915 as a Methodist-Episcopal sanctuary by a well-funded Atlanta congregation that gradually disbanded and moved to the suburbs. In 1968, the building was deconsecrated and transformed into a theme restaurant that's devoted to earthly pleasures—including an unapologetic emphasis on drinking and fine dining. The waitstaff wears monks' robes in a soaring, high-church setting of English-Gothic design, complete with elaborate stained-glass depictions of the saints in all their humility and majesty. Be warned in advance that every few months or so, a religious fundamentalist manages to become deeply offended by the tongue-in-cheek piety of this place, and storms out in a huff. Most diners, however, interpret the adaptation as charming, a bit bizarre, and a catalyst for some interesting dialogue. Of special interest is the former vestry, once used for the storage of uniforms and communion vessels, which now functions as the Abbot's Cup Bar and Lounge. Because of its location near many of downtown Atlanta's biggest hotels, the place does a roaring business on the corporate convention circuit. A live pianist performs every evening, near a stained-glass depiction of Christ in Majesty, from 7 to 10pm. The cooking is good without being great. Especially satisfying first courses include a foie gras and lobster terrine in a champagne vinaigrette or mussels delectably steamed in a spicy Thai curry broth. Proceed from there to the main dishes, especially pan-seared red snapper with a potato mousseline and white truffle oil or the grilled veal strip in a white Balsamic vinegar and rosemary sauce. The char-grilled New York strip steak is especially good, served in a Gorgonzola and port wine sauce with caramelized onions.

Bacchanalia. 1198 Howell Mill Rd. ☎ **404/365-0410.** Reservations recommended. Set-price 3-course lunch $35; set-price 4-course dinner $58. AE, DC, MC, V. Tues–Sat 11:30am–1:30pm and 6–10pm. MARTA: 10th Street Station. INTERNATIONAL.

Posh, upscale, and artfully contrived to appeal to the entertainment needs of Atlanta's thousands of upscale consumers, this establishment combines a stylish and sought-after restaurant with a series of boutique-style food shops. The setting is in what was built in the 1920s as a meat-packing plant, in an unlikely looking drab stretch of commercial real estate at the edge of midtown. Inside is a dining room that's considerably improved from its old days, but still sheathed in the pale yellow tiles of its original construction.

The team of Anne S. Quatrano and Clifford R. Harrison has brought fine dining all the way from the California Culinary Academy. Portions are small in size but big on flavor. Some recipes have been criticized as "pretentiously experimental," but try the Kumamoto oysters on the half shell from Washington State or sautéed veal sweetbreads with braised baby artichokes. Full-flavored main courses, inspired by what looks good at the market and the whims of the chef, include sautéed turbot with baby red kale, pan-seared breast of duck with caramelized apples and turnips, and braised short ribs of Kobe beef with a potato purée. Save room for desserts, especially the blood orange and rosemary soup with a sheep's milk yogurt sorbet or the ginger soufflé given added zest by a lemon sauce.

✪ **Restaurant Park 75.** In the Four Seasons Hotel Atlanta, 75 14th Street (between Peachtree and West Peachtreet sts.). ☎ **404/881-9898.** Reservations recommended.

Main courses $9–$15 at lunch, $17–$25 at dinner; 4-course set-price dinners $38–$42. AE, DC, DISC, MC, V. MARTA: Arts Center. NEW AMERICAN.

It's chic, it's sexy, and the food that's dished up by the international staff is among the very best in the Southeast. Come here for an insight into the New American cuisine that the Four Seasons chain is promoting with verve, and for a meal you're likely to remember long after it's finished. The setting evokes a dignified-looking pavilion where subtle depictions of lattices and garden ornaments don't interfere with the visual appeal of absolutely superb cuisine. Master chef Brooke Vosika has been described as brilliant by some of the most respected critics in Atlanta, with special praise for his savory versions of upscale vegetarian dishes. Examples include an unusual version of stuffed peppers whose flavors are derived from reducing herbs and root vegetables into stocks that resemble meat-based bouillons. Fish and meats are combined into artful and unexpected combinations that, while sophisticated, never dip into the purely experimental. Menus and wines change frequently and seasonally. Depending on when you arrive, offerings might include a carpaccio of Kobe beef with juniper-flavored foie gras and braised arugula, a succulent version of loin of lamb with cèpe mushrooms and golden tomatoes, and roasted free-range chicken baked with Oregon truffles. Undecided about what to order? Consider one of the set-price menus, which come in both vegetarian and meat-based versions. This restaurant is at its best and most confident at dinner, when your dining experience should probably begin or end within the plush confines of the opulent-looking hotel bar.

MODERATE

Coohill's. 1100 Peachtree St. NE (at 12th St.). ☎ **404/724-0901.** Reservations recommended. Main courses $18.95–$32.95. AE, DC, DISC, MC, V. Mon–Fri 11:30am–2pm; Mon–Thurs 5:30–10pm, Fri–Sat 5:30–11pm. Closed for lunch during summer. MARTA: 10th St. Then walk 5 mins. north on Peachtree St. STEAK/SEAFOOD.

At last Chef Tom Coohill has opened a restaurant under his own name. He's certainly famous enough. So Bistango is gone and Coohill is in. The chef's credentials range from a three-star Michelin restaurant in France to the tony Ma Maison in Los Angeles. This fashionable place draws a lot of theatergoers, as it's only 2 blocks south of the Woodruff Arts Center. Offering Southern flair in a contemporary but lush setting, Coohill's modestly bills itself as a steakhouse and bar, but it is so very much more. Georgia is filled with steakhouses and bars, but there is only one Coohill's.

The starters alone are wildly impressive, with one of the finest appetizers you're likely to be served in Atlanta—blue crab and rock shrimp cake with a lemon-fennel sauce. The potato, corn, and crab chowder would shame the best cooks in New England, and even the salads are delectable, especially the beefsteak tomato and Vidalia onion one with a Clemson bleu cheese dressing.

Some of the city's finest prime steaks are served here—all the favorites from New York strip to porterhouse. Steaks are amazingly tender and perfectly grilled and flavored. But the choice of main dishes extends far beyond that with a succulent array of offerings, ranging from baked Alaskan halibut on stewed tomatoes and a Valencia orange reduction with chive oil and fresh basil to a wood-grilled pork chop with baked Rome beauty apples and a bourbon glaze.

Indigo Coastal Grill. 1397 N. Highland Ave. NE. ☎ **404/876-0676.** Reservations recommended. Main courses $12.95–$18.95; Sun brunch platters $6.95–$11.95. AE, DC, MC, V. Mon–Thurs 5:30–10pm, Fri–Sat 5:30–11pm, Sun 11am–2:30pm (brunch) and 5:30–10pm. MARTA: Lanier University. AMERICAN/INTERNATIONAL.

The Indigo combines the aspect of a lobster shack in Maine with a wharfside restaurant in Key West. Deliberately cheesy replicas of fish hang above an artfully battered bar top that might have nurtured the drinker's elbow of Ernest Hemingway. Main courses include ingredients you may not immediately recognize, but that's part of the fun. Examples include seared ahi tuna edged in sesame seeds, served on a bed of field greens with daikon sprouts and marinated shiitake mushrooms; sesame-flavored catfish with jalapeño tartar sauce and jicama pepper slaw; and free-range chicken with chipotle cream, corn cakes, beans, and rice.

INEXPENSIVE

Einstein's. 1077 Juniper St. ☎ **404/876-7925.** Reservations recommended. Sandwiches and burgers $6.95–$7.95; platters $9.95–$15.95. AE, DC, DISC, MC, V. Sun–Thurs 11am–11pm, Fri–Sat 11am–midnight. MARTA: Midtown. AMERICAN.

The setting of this place is a circa 1904 clapboard-sided bungalow on a quiet street of midtown, very close to some of the neighborhood's tallest towers. Partly because the owner is the godson of the late physicist and partly because lots of scientists appreciate their nuances, you're likely to see several of Einstein's equations decorating blackboards near the bar, sometimes misstated in ways that, during our visit, provoked lots of arguments among this restaurant's clients. You can dine inside, in a woodsy-looking bar, or outside, on an open-air front terrace, elbow-to-elbow with many other residents of this rather liberal neighborhood. The food is well prepared and tasty without being spectacular. Try the grilled pork chop with a pepper and cream sauce or freshly prepared fillet of salmon with a savory barbecue pepper sauce. A signature dish is Einstein's shrimp with a mustard sauce enhanced by mango and orange.

Mary Mac's Tea Room. 224 Ponce de Leon Ave. NE (at Myrtle St.). ☎ **404/876-1800.** Reservations required only for groups of 10 or more. Dinner $8–$15. No credit cards. Mon–Sat 11am–8:30pm, Sun 11am–3pm. MARTA: North Avenue. SOUTHERN.

This landmark follows the tradition of "Southern hospitality with damn Yankee efficiency," a slogan launched in 1945. In a midtown storefront, some 2,000 hungry diners are served daily, including local politicos. Since Jimmy Carter used to drop in for lunch, it's always been a tradition that governors visit for meals. The food is fine if you like the slightly overcooked down-home Southern style. The fried chicken and country ham are really good here, as are the fresh but long-cooked vegetables and the straight-from-the-oven breads. Your best bet might be a sautéed rainbow trout from the North Georgia mountains. For dessert, who would dare order anything but the fresh peach cobbler? Those are Georgia peaches, of course.

South City Kitchen. 1144 Crescent Ave. NE (between 13th and 14th sts.). ☎ **404/873-7358.** Reservations recommended after 6pm. Main courses $12.25–$21.95; Sun brunch $6.95–$12.95. AE, DC, MC, V. Sun–Thurs 11am–11pm, Fri–Sat 11am–midnight. MARTA: Arts Center. NEW SOUTHERN.

Although many critics have found its new-style Southern cookery inconsistent, most Atlantans salute this choice. It's in a renovated two-story building with dining both up and down the stairs. Fireplaces on both floors burn on nippy nights to make the place cozy and inviting. If the weather's fair, patio dining is possible. Try the buttermilk-fried chicken or the sautéed scallops and shrimp over creamy, stone-ground grits. The secret of South City's pork chops is that they're apple-smoked, making them a real winner. Also good are the shredded barbecued pork on jalapeño bread or cornbread with creamy lump crab. The grilled swordfish on a bed of homemade grits with Monterey Jack cheese left us cold, but a taste of pork porterhouse with grilled apples, parsnips, and pepper jelly warmed our souls again.

Zocalo's. 187 10th St. at corner of Piedmont. ☎ **404/249-7576.** Reservations recommended on Fri–Sat nights. Main courses $8.50–$22.95. AE, DC, DISC, MC, V. Sun 10:30am–10pm,

Mon–Thurs 11:30am–2:30pm and 5:30–11pm, Fri 11:30am–2:30pm and 5:30pm–midnight, Sat 11:30am–midnight. MARTA: Midtown. MEXICAN.

This is one of the most charming and authentic Mexican restaurants in Atlanta, with a growing reputation as a meeting place for the young and the restless of this very hip midtown neighborhood. The venue evokes an open-aired *cantina* on the Gulf of Mexico, in a dining room that's little more than a folklorically decorated veranda that's protected from the winter's cold with fold-down plastic flaps. No one will mind if you come only for a fiesta-colored cocktail instead of a full-fledged meal. The bar stocks at least 200 kinds of tequila, priced at from $4.50 to $75 a glass, and their margaritas are, in the words of a local fan, *magnifico*. Menu items do not include any of the Tex-Mex hybrids (burritos, chips with salsa) that you might find in most Mexican-American restaurants. Instead, you'll be treated to authentic, and often creative, Mexican dishes that include *crema de chile poblano* (a creamy soup of stuffed chiles); *molcajete carmelita,* served on a grinding stone and composed of steak, braised cactus leaves, Serrano peppers, and asadero cheese; and *chile en Nogada* (chili peppers stuffed with minced veal, pork, and beef).

BUCKHEAD
VERY EXPENSIVE

Bone's. 3130 Piedmont Rd. NE (half a block below Peachtree Rd.). ☎ **404/237-2663.** Reservations required. Main courses $19.95–$36. AE, CB, DC, DISC, MC, V. Mon–Fri 11:30am–2:30pm and 5:30–10:30pm, Sat–Sun 5:30–11pm. Closed major holidays. MARTA: Buckhead. STEAK/SEAFOOD.

Yes, that's Ted Turner at the next table, and where else would former President George Bush eat when he's in Atlanta? In an atmosphere one food critic called "boardroom frat house," this is just the type of place to get that juicy rib-eye steak weighing in at 16 ounces. Fresh Maine lobster is flown in daily, and the corn-fed beef is butchered and cut into steaks on the premises. Grits fritters are favored by locals, who invariably end their meal with Georgia pecan pie and vanilla-bean ice cream. A cigar humidor can be brought to your table at your request after dinner, but one female CEO from New York found the service by the waiters "sexist."

✪ **The Dining Room.** In the Ritz-Carlton Buckhead, 3434 Peachtree Rd. NE. ☎ **404/237-2700.** Reservations required. Jacket required for men. Fixed-price menu $68 for 3 courses; $82–$130 tasting menu. AE, CB, DC, MC, V. Tues–Sat 6–10pm. MARTA: Lenox. CONTEMPORARY AMERICAN/CONTINENTAL.

Atlanta's most fashionable hotel boasts one of its stateliest dining rooms, where the food, decor, and service are unequaled in the city. The cuisine of award-winning chef Joel Antunes is inventive and relentlessly perfect, and you dine luxuriously here while enjoying peerless service. Against a backdrop of fresh flowers, English hunt pictures, and an overall romantic ambience, you're served small portions on exquisitely arranged platters, backed up by an exceptional wine list. From the Oriental Hotel in Bangkok and Savuer in London, Antunes's menu continues to receive the accolades that seem almost a given for this restaurant; it's been a consistent winner of the AAA five-diamond award and Mobil's five-star rating. Antunes's meshing of French cuisine with Southern flair is definitely a testament to his abilities. The menu changes daily based on his inspiration. Hopefully the selections will include his Jamison Farm lamb loin with risotto and Swiss chard, or his roast turbot with bok choy and peach in tarragon sauce. Game dishes may include pigeon with mango chutney and bok choy in hazelnut sauce, or fillet of duck with rhubarb and turnips in mustard sauce. A dessert of dreams? Persimmon mousse with Georgia golden raspberries and a muscadine sorbet.

☉ The Palm. In Swissôtel, 3391 Peachtree Rd. (between Lenox and Piedmont rds., just south of Lenox Square). ☎ **404/814-1955.** Reservations recommended. Main courses $7.50–$35 at lunch, $14–$35 at dinner; lobsters from $54–$200, depending on their weight. AE, DC, MC, V. MARTA: Lenox. STEAK.

The emphasis in this two-fisted, upscale tavern is macho friendliness, macho portions, and a kind of bustling unpretentiousness. Its namesake in Manhattan was established in 1926 by two Italian immigrants who wanted to name a restaurant after their home town (Parma), and the result was a trattoria whose mistranslated name was "The Palm," which was transformed into an all-American steakhouse. Despite a sense that the place is a bit less glamorous than it was a few years ago, the Palm survives and thrives. There's a long and busy bar where you might be asked to wait for your table, comfortable banquettes within two separate dining rooms (one for smokers); and hundreds of cartoonlike caricatures of former diners, à la Sardi's in New York. (Both Coretta Scott King and Ted Turner have sampled the steaks here.) The Palm's menu is deceptively simple—six different preparations of veal, massive steaks and chops, pastas and salads that would appeal to a vegetarian; and shellfish (including succulent 3-pound lobsters and four preparations of clams). Lunchtime choices are supplemented with some less expensive, less filling items that include sirloin burgers, grilled chicken sandwiches, broiled crab cakes, and Caesar salads with chicken strips.

☉ Seeger's. 111 W. Paces Ferry Rd. ☎ **404/846-9779.** Reservations required. Fixed-price menus $58–$80. AE, DC, MC, V. Mon–Sat 6–10pm. MARTA: Buckhead. CONTINENTAL.

Our trendy foodie friends that we rely on for insider dining tips gave us a mixed reaction to this one—from "the best food in Atlanta" to a "cramped overpriced wannabe with a disastrous staff." You must judge for yourself, although we were treated regally and had our palates uplifted in praise many times on our inaugural and subsequent visits. Opened in 1997, it's Chef Guenter Seeger's own restaurant following the media blitz he created at the swank Ritz-Carlton in Buckhead. Before his move to Atlanta, Seeger received a Michelin star for his restaurant in Germany's Black Forest. The restaurant is in a redecorated 19th-century house, an evocative setting for serving continental fare in the European tradition. Dining options are limited to daily fixed-price menus, but there is much variety and temptation here. Any chef who serves such amusing whimsies as crab salad on quince gelée must be doing something right. You can opt for the more limited three-course menu or else the virtual feast featured on a six-course repast.

Seeger possesses one of the most fertile and creative culinary minds in Atlanta. Who else is offering you octopus carpaccio with chanterelles these days? An artful touch is the grilled lamb chops on a turnip gratin with eggplant "caviar." The mesclun salad with fresh goat cheese, glazed apples, and pecan oil is the perfect way to glide into a meal that might continue with roasted squab with sweetbreads, or fillet of halibut with a cèpe crust, served on a spaghetti squash salad. Desserts are among the most imaginative in the city. After the cherry soup with goat yogurt sorbet, you may want to kidnap the chef and take him home.

EXPENSIVE

☉ Brasserie Le Coze. Lenox Sq., 3393 Peachtree Rd. NE. ☎ **404/266-1440.** Reservations required. Main courses $13–$32. AE, DC, MC, V. Mon–Thurs 11:30am–2:30pm and 5:30–10pm, Fri 11:30am–3pm and 5:30–11pm, Sat 11:30am–3:30pm and 5:30–11pm. MARTA: Lenox. SEAFOOD.

Authentic French food, mainly seafood, is served in what has been called "the most sophisticated of French restaurants," in spite of its location in a shopping mall.

Between Neiman Marcus and Cartier, this Paris bistro was founded by the owners of Le Bernardin in New York: Maguy Le Coze and her late brother, Gilbert. The restaurant's signature dish is fish, whisked from the fire and served at the precise point between being overcooked and undercooked, a startling development when it was first introduced in Atlanta, land of the fried-to-death catfish. The service staff in long white aprons appear with mussels marinière in an aromatic bowl of broth flavored with white wine and flecks of shallots. Sautéed grouper follows, served over a melange of vegetables flavored with curry oil. Believe it or not, some foodies come here for the roast chicken with its crisp skin, a perfectly done dish served with herbed gravy and the best mashed potatoes in Atlanta—creamy and laced with butter and chives. Other dishes include a beautifully seasoned and prepared rack of lamb and even such long-time bistro favorites as *coq au vin* (chicken in wine).

Chops. 70 W. Paces Ferry Rd. (at Peachtree Rd.). ☎ **404/262-2675.** Reservations strongly recommended for dinner. Main courses $9.75–$13.95 at lunch, $13.95–$35.95 at dinner. AE, DC, MC, V. Mon–Thurs 11:30am–2:30pm and 5:30–11pm, Fri 11:30am–2pm and 5:30pm–midnight, Sat 5:30pm–midnight, Sun 5:30–10pm. MARTA: Buckhead. STEAK/ SEAFOOD.

Leave your vegetarian palate at home while dining at this 1930s-era macho enclave of good steaks, another jewel in the crown of restaurateur Pano Karatassos. Chops is the most informal restaurant in his chain, which includes the Atlanta Fish Market and Veni Vidi Vici. Business types, media stars, and locals flock to this handsome, clubby place, with low lighting, roomy banquettes, and tri-level seating.

Their Lobster Bar is one of the best in Atlanta, and large live Maine lobsters are flown in daily. Their seared yellowfin tuna with a pepper crust, a shiitake mushroom and scallion potato mash, and a port wine glaze are worth the trip across town. But the fame of the kitchen rests on its chops and steaks, specially aged and selected from corn-fed beef. Chops Porterhouse for two (weighing in at 3 pounds) is enough to satisfy two gargantuan appetites. Mega-steaks aside, save room for some of Chops' homemade ice cream: The banana white chocolate fudge is to die for, as is the chocolate black-bottom pie. Most of the wines are reasonable in price unless you're tempted by the odd $3,000 bottle.

Nava. 3060 Peachtree Rd. ☎ **404/240-1984.** Reservations required. Main courses $14.50–$27.95. AE, DC, DISC, MC, V. Mon–Fri 11:30am–2:30pm and 5:30–11pm, Sat 5:30pm–midnight, Sun 5:30–10pm. MARTA: Buckhead. SOUTHWESTERN.

It's Atlanta's most sophisticated Southwestern restaurant, with a colorful theme directly inspired by the pueblos, cactus branches, and adobe houses of the Painted Desert. The decor includes beams carved into zigzag patterns, massive lintels resembling a Franciscan mission, sculptures apparently used by once-powerful medicine men, and bold, native paintings you may actually be tempted to buy after your meal. Appetizers include a fire-roasted adobe quail with citrus honey that perfectly captures the flavor of Arizona, as does a tortilla-crusted shrimp rellenos. Main courses have flair and are spicy, especially the wood-roasted pork tenderloin with a tamarind-bean glaze that seems in perfect harmony, as does the giant shrimp with a mango glaze and white-bean enchiladas. Save room for the pumpkin-gingerbread tart with butterscotch. The service here is first rate.

○ Pano & Paul's. 1232 W. Paces Ferry Rd. ☎ **404/261-3662.** Reservations required. Jackets required for men. Main courses $18–$39. AE, CB, DC, DISC, MC, V. Mon–Fri 6–10:30pm, Sat 5:30–11pm. MARTA: Buckhead. CONTINENTAL/AMERICAN.

When this place opened in 1979, it created a dining sensation. Peter Kaiser, the chef de cuisine, continues to earn for this restaurant its position in the nation's "Fine Dining

Hall of Fame." The setting is one of Victorian opulence. Impeccable service, refined cuisine, and an extensive wine list still drown out complaints that the place is snobby and overpriced. The broiled dry-aged sirloin steak or the roast double beef fillet is about the best you'll get in Atlanta. Try white asparagus with smoked salmon and foie gras with an artichoke heart. Some of the Pacific Rim dishes such as limpid wontons are to be avoided, but not any of the potato dishes, including soufflé potatoes. Yes, potatoes are a signature dish. Another tempter is the fried baby lobster tail with waffle fries and a Chinese mustard sauce.

✪ **103 West.** 103 W. Paces Ferry Rd. (off Peachtree Rd.). ☎ **404/233-5993.** Reservations recommended. Jacket and tie required for men. Main courses $17–$34.50. AE, CB, DC, DISC, MC, V. Mon–Sat 6–11pm. MARTA: Buckhead. CONTINENTAL.

Old Atlanta turns out to enjoy the cuisine and opulence of this winning place, one of Buckhead's staples for those who like to flash diamonds when they go out at night. The restaurant, with its watered silks and antique tapestries, has been called palatial. After entering through the porte-cochère, with its coach lights from the 1800s, you find yourself in a gilt world of expensive oil paintings and mirrors. As the piano player wows you with "As Time Goes By," you can peruse the menu to choose among such succulent hot and cold appetizers as country pâtés or champagne, glazed oysters, and French vineyard escargots. The wine list is one of the finest, but no one here complains of the high prices. For a main course, try the Dover sole in garlic butter, the venison with wild mushrooms and mustard fruit, or veal any way it comes.

MODERATE

✪ **Atlanta Fish Market.** 265 Pharr Rd. (between Peachtree Rd. and N. Fulton Dr.). ☎ **404/262-3165.** Main courses $12–$32. AE, DC, DISC, MC, V. Mon–Thurs 11:30am– 2:30pm and 5:30–11pm, Fri 11:30am–2:30pm and 5pm–midnight, Sat 11:30am–midnight, Sun 4–10pm. MARTA: Buckhead. SEAFOOD.

This is the best seafood place in Atlanta, and we don't want to have an argument about that. Even Madonna and Senator Zell Miller agree (probably the only thing they do agree on) that the pecan-crusted catfish and the Carolina mountain trout are the best. The jazzy, 475-seat dining room has been compared to an old Southern train station. It's the creation of Pano Karatassos, sometimes known as "Kingfish." Some locals may be taken aback by the grilled halibut over creamy grits, garnished with shards of apple-smoked bacon, but they're quickly won over. Also try the New Orleans seafood gumbo to start—with crabmeat, spicy sausage, shrimp, and a peppery oceanic stock. For dessert, a wise choice is the pineapple-macadamia upside-down cake. The extensive menu is changed daily.

✪ **The Buckhead Diner.** 3073 Piedmont Rd. (at E. Paces Ferry Rd.). ☎ **404/262-3336.** Reservations not accepted. Main courses $11.95–$15.95 at lunch, $14.95–$22.95 at dinner. AE, DC, DISC, MC, V. Mon–Sat 11am–midnight, Sun 10am–10pm. MARTA: Buckhead. AMERICAN.

Since reservations aren't accepted, you may find yourself waiting in line with Elton John. Even though the place sounds like a hash house for truckers, it's one of the hottest spots in Atlanta. A highly theatrical venture, it has a gleaming stainless-steel exterior adorned with neon. Inside, try the crisp, spicy barbecued oysters served over creamy succotash with a Cajun rémoulade on the side, or butternut squash soup— the city's best. The veal and wild-mushroom meat loaf is a bit overrated, but not the seared calamari with a hot red sauce. For dessert, the coconut sorbet or the chocolate chip crème brûlée will convince you that you've visited no meat-and-taters roadside diner.

ℹ️ Family-Friendly Restaurants

The Varsity *(see p. 333)* It's straight from that old movie *American Graffiti.* Singing car hops never died but live on here, serving the great American hot dog or the great American hamburger, plus 300 gallons of chili daily.

Mary Mac's Tea Room *(see p. 336)* At this Atlanta institution, you can introduce your kid to the delights of a classic Southern cuisine—and perhaps introduce him or her to a former president, Jimmy Carter, who might be found dining at a nearby table. Corn bread and pot likker, fried catfish and turnip greens, it's the kind of fare that Granny on the Beverly Hillbillies knows how to cook.

Rocky's Brick Oven Pizza *(see p. 342)* For that pizza fix, Rocky (not Stallone) will serve you Atlanta's best and most bubbling pie with various delicious toppings, including one with a sweet onion sauce topped with roasted potatoes and rosemary.

Horseradish Grill. 4320 Powers Ferry Rd. ☎ **404/255-7277.** Reservations recommended. Main courses $17–$27. Mon–Fri 11:30am–2:30pm and 5:30–10pm, Fri–Sat 5–11pm, Sun 5–9pm. MARTA: Buckhead. SOUTHERN CUISINE.

Overhyped but satisfying seems to be the consensus about this brash restaurant named for its equestrian art, not the root vegetable. David Berry, a former sous chef who studied at New York's Culinary Institute, took over in 1997. Try the fresh grouper fritters wrapped in bibb lettuce and garnished with ginger-flavored red onions and cabbage slaw. Those inevitable pork chops are moist and made even more delectable with a cheddar-cheese macaroni side dish and cucumber salad. Grilled lamb chops also appear on the menu, as does the catch of the day. Naturally, turnip greens are served, as is cornmeal-battered catfish with home fries. If Aunt Pittypat were to return to Atlanta, she couldn't make a better banana pudding than this chef.

Luna Sí. 1931 Peachtree Rd. NE (between Collier and Brighton Rd.). ☎ **404/355-5993.** Reservations recommended. Main courses $10–$20; 4-course tasting menu $35. AE, DC, DISC, MC, V. Mon–Thurs 5:30–10:30pm; Fri–Sat 5:30–11pm. MARTA: Buckhead. ITALIAN CONTINENTAL.

Diners will no longer be insulted, kicked out, or "mooned" by the chef at this famous Atlanta restaurant. The customer is king once again, following the departure of renegade Paul Luna, its temperamental former chef. Left in charge are his more polite brothers, Juan and Albert, both from the Dominican Republic. They not only give you a warm welcome, but also offer some of the best food at Buckhead in a storefront across from the Piedmont Hospital, where guests are encouraged to scrawl graffiti on the bare walls. To begin your meal, try the cold scallops in a spicy avocado-and-tomato sauce, or the pistachio-flecked duck pâté. A plate of soft-shell crabs may appear, flavored with pepper seasonings, including habañero peppers. They come in a stuffed pepper filled with cheese and chopped vegetables. For dessert, try the smooth, warm chocolate soufflé.

INEXPENSIVE

Café Sunflower. 5975 Roswell Rd. (at Hammond Dr.). ☎ **404/256-1675.** Reservations recommended. Main courses $8.95–$13.95. AE, DC, MC, V. Daily 11:30am–2:30pm and 5–9pm. MARTA: Sandy Springs. CONTINENTAL/VEGETARIAN.

This upscale vegetarian restaurant lies on the Sandy Springs strip. The kitchen takes its inspiration from Mexican, Asian, and Mediterranean cuisine. Against a decor described as Williams-Sonoma, the service is more polite than efficient. The spring rolls are stuffed with shredded vegetables, rice noodles, and tofu, and a red-pepper hummus is served with pita triangles and a medley of crunchy raw vegetables. The quesadilla arrives stuffed with black beans, brown rice, tomato, cheese, and corn, a taste sensation in spite of the too-watery salsa. Eggplant and wood-ear mushrooms are delectable in a garlic-ginger sauce, but forget the house salad. Another good choice is curried vegetables on a bed of couscous spiked with raisins and cashews. Instead of wine or beer, you can order freshly squeezed carrot juice.

The Colonnade. 1879 Cheshire Bridge Rd. NE (near Piedmont Rd.). ☎ **404/874-5642.** Reservations not accepted. Main courses $6.95–$16.95. No credit cards. Mon–Tues 5–9pm, Wed–Sun 11:30am–2:30pm and 5–9pm. MARTA: Lindbergh; then bus no. 27. SOUTHERN.

An Atlanta favorite since 1927, and just as drab as ever, this friendly joint lies between Wellborne Drive and Manchester Street. Like a cheerful American restaurant of the 1950s, it offers great value and attracts the family trade with its down-home cookery and gargantuan portions. Inexpensively priced steaks, chops, seafood, and the inevitable Southern fried chicken round out the menu, along with vegetables boiled all day long. One regular comes here every day to order sugar-cured ham with redeye gravy. Some of the menu items might lead to arterial overload, but fans of the Colonnade love this one.

Rocky's Brick Oven Pizza. 1770 Peachtree St. NW (at 26th St.). ☎ **404/876-1111.** Reservations not accepted. Salads and calzones $3.50–$9.99; pastas $12.99–$14.99; pizzas $5.99–$18.99. AE, DC, DISC, MC, V. Mon–Thurs 11:30am–10:30pm, Fri 11:30am–11pm, Sat 5–11pm, Sun 5–10:30pm. MARTA: Buckhead. PIZZA/ITALIAN.

No, in spite of the name, this is not one of Stallone's restaurant ventures. "Rocky" is ex-Brooklynite Bob Russo (actually his father was named Rocky) who came here to the heart of Dixie in the mid-70s. Everybody shows up here, from locals to movie stars, for the best pies in town, baked in a wood-burning oven shipped from Milan. Russo even grows his own herbs and tomatoes to flavor his pies, and the salad ingredients are organically grown, so this is no typical pizza joint. One pizza honors Rudolph Valentino—made with a sweet onion sauce topped with roasted potatoes and rosemary. The kitchen is strong on Neapolitan pizzas, including the famous white pizza made with fresh garlic and virgin olive oil, roasted potatoes, sun-dried tomatoes, and the house's homemade mozzarella cheese. The calzones—those half-moon shaped stuffed pizzas created by Napoléon as a signature ration for his armies—are also delectable. Each comes with a side of marinara sauce. House pastas are some of the best in Atlanta, even one honoring (of all people) Gorbachev (tricolored tortellini smothered in a Russian vodka-cream sauce with fresh shrimp and scallops). One expatriate confided to us that Rocky's is the best refuge in Atlanta for ex-New Yorkers.

VIRGINIA-HIGHLAND

Dish. 870 North Highland Ave. ☎ **404/897-3463.** Reservations recommended. Main courses $15–$22. AE, DC, MC, V. Sun–Thurs 5:30–10pm, Fri–Sat 5:30–11pm. Bus: 2, 16. CONTEMPORARY GLOBAL & AMERICAN.

More self-consciously trendy, and more deliberately cutting edge than its nearby competitor, the also-recommended Harvest Restaurant, this is an enduringly popular spot with a postmodern design that includes lots of copper—both polished and oxidized—in a mostly green decor. Between April and November, its relatively small (55 seats) interior is doubled, thanks to a sought-after outdoor terrace. Don't overlook the merits of this place as a bar, as local hipsters tend to gravitate here to "dish" whatever local or national icon deserves, in their eyes, deflating. Menu items change, sometimes radically, about four times a year, but at the time of our visit, they included such delights as steamed Penn Cove mussels roasted with garlic and saffron in a tomato broth, or shrimp and seaweed roll with a peanut chili dipping sauce. The main courses have robust flavors and reflect the chef's imagination as evoked by seared scallops and shrimp with a basil fettuccine; sautéed five-spice duck breast with shiitake mushrooms and Chinese cabbage (served with a rhubarb and ginger coulis); and the sautéed halibut with grilled salsify and asparagus served with a lemon and shallot vinaigrette.

Harvest Restaurant. 853 North Highland Ave. ☎ **404/876-8244.** Reservations recommended. Main courses $9.50–$11.95 at lunch, $13.95–$24.95 at dinner. AE, DC, MC, V. Mon–Fri 11:30am–2:30pm, Sun brunch 11am–2:30pm, Sun–Thurs 5:30–10pm, Fri–Sat 5:30–11pm. Bus: 2, 16. AMERICAN.

One of the neighborhood's most enduringly popular restaurants is set in one of the few Arts and Crafts–style bungalows that remain within the increasingly commercialized main drag of Virginia-Highlands. Built in 1905, and painted an appropriate tone of harvest gold, it offers a two-story interior that might have been inspired by a disciple of Frank Lloyd Wright, with lots of turn-of-the-century stained glass and varnished hardwoods, Stickley-style furnishings, a sextet of gas-fired fireplaces, and unusual sculptures and mobiles hanging from the high, sloping ceilings. (Tip: Most romantics and architecture buffs gravitate to a table upstairs.)

Raw ingredients come from several small purveyors, both farmers and fishers, who haul in very fresh components, many of them organic, from Georgia, the Carolinas, and Florida. At lunch you can begin with a prosciutto and arugula salad or else fried calamari with olive relish and a particularly zesty lemon and thyme aïoli. Among the light and beautifully prepared specialties are the pecan-crusted rainbow trout with sweet potatoes and spaghetti squash, or the linguine tossed with Parma prosciutto and served with teardrop tomatoes and fresh spinach whipped with a lemon and oregano oil. The night menu is far more elaborate; start with banana-and-coconut-crusted jumbo Gulf shrimp or an Argentine fillet carpaccio with shaved fennel. The eggless Caesar salad, as a change of pace, is made with sun-dried tomatoes served with griddled shallot croutons and shaved Parmesan cheese. Main dishes have full flavor and imagination, especially the pumpkin seed–crusted halibut with ancho chili mashed potatoes, or the jerk pork tenderloin with a mango salsa and raspberry mayonnaise.

INMAN PARK

✪ **Sotto Sotto.** 313 North Highland Ave. ☎ **404/523-6678.** Reservations recommended. Main courses $11–$22. AE, DC, MC, V. Mon–Thurs 5:30–11pm, Fri–Sat 5:30pm–midnight. TUSCAN/PIEMONTESE/EMILIA-ROMAGNOLA.

The best and most appealing restaurant in Inman Park occupies the unpretentious premises of what was built around 1900 as a low-slung row of brick-fronted stores. In 1999, Stefano Volpi and a team of culinary entrepreneurs from Turin and Milan inserted a stylish minimalist decor of glowing hardwoods and immaculate napery, and added a high-tech, open-to-view kitchen where a team of chefs supervises batteries of bubbling pastas and sauces. Today, the Northern Italian ambience is as authentic and accurate to the European motif as anything you're likely to find in Atlanta, a fact that's appreciated by the residents of increasingly upscale Inman Park. Superbly prepared menu specialties include wood-roasted whole fish (either pompano, trout, or snapper) flown in ultra fresh from Florida; risotto with seafood; and a succulent version of scallops braised with arugula, white beans, and truffle oil. A favorite pasta is tortelli di Michelangelo, stuffed with a mixture of minced veal, pork, and chicken, served with brown butter and sage sauce. Most wines here are Italian, including goodly numbers of Barolos, Brunellos di Montalcino, and Barbarescos.

NEARBY DINING

✪ **Canoe.** 4199 Paces Ferry Rd. NW. ☎ **770/43-CANOE.** Reservations strongly recommended. Main courses $15.95–$23.50. AE, CB, DC, DISC, MC, V. Mon–Thurs 11:30am–2:30pm and 5:30–10pm, Fri 11:30am–2:30pm and 5:30–11pm, Sat 5:30–11:30pm, Sun 10:30am–2:30pm and 5:30–9pm. CONTEMPORARY AMERICAN GRILL.

It's located right at the city's outskirts in Cobb County—of Newt Gingrich fame. Tables at this hip and fashionable restaurant open onto the Chattahoochee River. After World War II the locale was famous as a dance hall for "big dresses, big hair, senior proms, and *East of Eden* scenes." Today the much-gentrified pair of connected Quonset huts housing the restaurant have been upgraded with burnished wood, exposed brick, and a service staff fetchingly clad in patterned vests.

Canoe's appetizers are among the most sophisticated in the city. Sure, they serve catfish, but it comes with a toasted-pistachio green-curry sauce. The chef is known for his light pastas and risottos, one an outstanding pumpkin tortellini with roasted pine nuts and a spicy lamb ragout. The standing menu includes crispy duck with spicy greens and caramel-ginger sauce; slow-roasted pork with Gorgonzola polenta and a spicy escarole; and bacon-wrapped sturgeon with whipped potatoes and sage butter. The waiters warn you to save room for dessert.

5 Attractions

Sit in the tourist office in Atlanta and within an hour at least three visitors will come by and ask for directions to "Tara" or "Twelve Oaks." Regrettably, these places never existed in real life, only in Margaret Mitchell's imagination. Even the movie theater where *Gone With the Wind* premiered in 1939 was gutted by fire in the early 1980s. A marble skyscraper sits on the site where Clark Gable and Vivien Leigh launched the film. But even with no Tara, Atlanta has a great deal to offer.

The Carter Presidential Center. One Copenhill, 453 Freedom Pkwy. ☎ **404/331-3942.** Admission $5 adults, $4 seniors, free for children 16 and under. Mon–Sat 9am–4:45pm, Sun noon–4:45pm.

This center, opened in 1986, is the site from which former U.S. President Jimmy Carter works to advance peace and human rights. Its work in democratization and development, global health, and urban revitalization has touched the lives of people in some 65 countries. The center is 2 miles east of the center of downtown Atlanta, with the skyline as a dramatic backdrop. On the same grounds is the Jimmy Carter Library and Museum, housing millions of documents, photos, gifts, and memorabilia of Carter's career and his years in the White House. You can even view a full-scale reproduction of the Oval Office and use interactive video geared to both children and adults. Displays of gifts received by President and Mrs. Carter range from silver, ivory, and crystal from heads of state, to paintings and peanut carvings from around the world. *Presidents,* a 30-minute film, looks at the crises and triumphs that marked his administration.

✪ **CNN Center.** One CNN Center (at Marietta St. and Techwood Dr.). ☎ **404/827-2300.** Admission $8 adults, $6 senior citizens 65 and over, $5 children 11 and under; $24.50 VIP tour. Tours given every 35 minutes daily 9am–6pm; Turner Store and Studio, daily 9:30am–7pm. Closed major holidays. MARTA: Omni, Dome, or GWCC, reservation required 1 day in advance.

Located in the heart of Atlanta, the CNN Center anchors the city's dynamic entertainment, news, sports, and business core and is adjacent to the Georgia Dome and the Georgia World Congress Center. It houses CNN, Headline News, and CNN International studios and offers guided tours of these facilities daily. Reservations must

Downtown Atlanta Sights

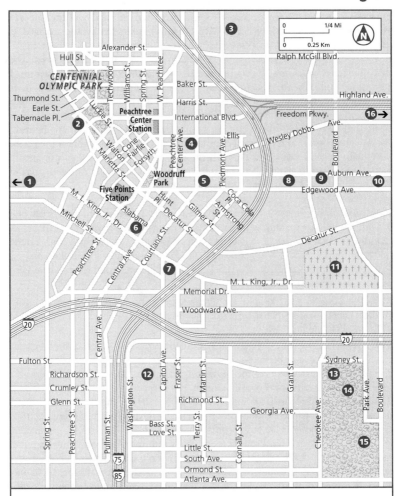

Alonzo F. Herndon Home **1**
APEX Museum **5**
Atlanta Heritage Row **6**
Birth Home of
    Martin Luther King, Jr. **10**
The Carter Presidential Center **16**
CNN Center **2**
Cyclorama **14**
Ebenezer Baptist Church **8**
Georgia State Capitol **7**
Grant Park **13**

High Museum of Art Folk Art
    and Photography Galleries **4**
Martin Luther King, Jr.,
    Center for Nonviolent
    Social Change **9**
Oakland Cemetery **11**
Turner Field **12**
SciTrek **3**
Underground Atlanta **6**
The World of Coca-Cola **6**
Zoo Atlanta **15**

be made 1 day in advance, or tickets can be purchased on the day of the tour at the ticket desk on the ground level of the Atrium. Group tours can also be arranged. Call for tour information and reservations.

Visitors can also reserve seating in the studio audience of **TalkBack Live,** CNN's first interactive talk show, broadcast weekdays from the CNN Center Atrium. For show times and audience ticket information, call ☎ **800/410-4CNN;** tickets are free. The center also features more than 40 one-of-a-kind retail stores. The **Turner Store,** on the ground level in the Atrium, features merchandise from all of broadcasting's networks and properties. Visitors can also create their own CNN news tape by reading the day's top stories in the **Turner Studio** from a TelePrompTer while sitting behind an actual CNN anchor desk. Through the magic of chroma-key, you can also have your photo taken on the pitcher's mound with your favorite Braves players, relax with Scarlett O'Hara and Rhett Butler in a scene from *Gone With the Wind,* or choose from more than 40 other backgrounds.

Visitors can continue their Turner adventure at the **Braves Clubhouse Store** on the ground level in the Atrium, which holds the largest collection of official Braves merchandise in Atlanta. The store is open 7 days a week 9:30am to 7pm, with extended hours on Braves' and Hawks' game days, and for Georgia Dome special events.

The **Atrium** has a variety of eateries in its international food court where visitors can sit down for a quick meal.

✪ **Fox Theatre.** 660 Peachtree St. NE. ☎ **404/881-2100.** Tours $5 adults, $4 seniors, $3 children. Tours given Feb–Nov Mon, Wed, Thurs 10am, Sat 10am and 11am; Dec–Jan Mon and Thurs 10am. MARTA: North Avenue.

This Moorish-Egyptian extravaganza, with its minarets and onion domes, began life as a Shriners' temple. It became a movie theater when movie mogul William Fox, after 2 years of extensive work on the block-long structure, threw open its doors to the public. Its exotic lobby was decorated with lush carpeting; in the auditorium itself, a skyscape was transformed to sunrise, sunset, or starry night skies as the occasion demanded, and a striped Bedouin canopy overhung the balcony. The Great Depression came hot on the heels of the Fox's opening, however, and in 1932 bankruptcy forced its closing. In the 1940s it was brought to life again with installation of a huge panoramic movie screen, but decline closed its doors once more in the 1970s. The Fox was slated for demolition, but Atlantans raised $1.8 million to save their treasured, old movie palace. Restored to its former glory, it now thrives as a venue for live entertainment.

Georgia State Capitol. Capitol Sq. ☎ **404/656-2844.** Free admission. Mon–Fri 8am–5pm. Tours at 10, 11am, 1, and 2pm. Closed major holidays. MARTA: Georgia State.

Writer Colin Campbell saw the 1884 capitol building as "weird, colorful, relentlessly Southern; a super attic of flags, paintings, two-headed snakes, scale models, stuffed animals, and weapons." Its gold-topped dome rises 237 feet above the city. Besides a Hall of Fame (with busts of famous Georgians), and a Hall of Flags (U.S., state, and Confederate), it houses the **Georgia State Museum of Science and Industry** with collections of Georgia minerals and Indian artifacts, dioramas of famous places, and fish and wildlife exhibits. Visit in late January and February to hear Georgia legislators at work. Georgia is a great state, but sometimes these members aren't very up on things—for example, we were treated to a legislator who condemned the 1996 Olympic games out of fear "that it will give all of us AIDS."

Underground Atlanta. Bounded by Peachtree, Wall, Alabama, Pryor, and Central sts. and Martin Luther King, Jr., Dr. ☎ **404/523-2311.** Free admission. Mon–Sat 10am–9:30pm, Sun noon–6pm (clubs and restaurants stay open until midnight or beyond). MARTA: Five Points, with a pedestrian tunnel linking it directly to the underground.

Right in town, 4 blocks of Atlanta's history lie beneath newer city streets. Underground Atlanta is the city's birthplace, where the Zero Milepost of the Western & Atlantic Railroad was planted in 1837. In post–Civil War days, railroad viaducts were built over its rococo buildings, and they lay deserted for the better part of a century. Restoration of the crumbling area has resulted in an authentic picture of Atlanta in the 1800s. During the mid-1980s the historic city beneath a city was closed for massive redevelopment, and in 1989 it reopened with more than 100 establishments, including shops, restaurants, and nightspots. Regrettably, it is looking a bit seedy these days as souvenir shops and fast-food joints have taken over.

The World of Coca-Cola. 55 Martin Luther King Dr. SW (at Central Ave., adjacent to Underground Atlanta). ☎ **404/676-5151.** Admission $6 adults, $4 seniors, $4 children 12–18, $3 children 6–11, free for children 5 and under. Mon–Sat 9am–6pm, Sun 11–6pm. Closed major holidays. MARTA: Five Points.

It has been called "the world's most popular product." It's been called a lot of other things too, including "the Devil's Drink." But Coca-Cola—its recipe still a secret—has been consumed by people all over the world and has endured, even surviving Shirley Temple singing "Sweet Coca-Cola Bush." A three-floor pavilion exhibits memorabilia of the world's most famous drink, from endorsements by fabled stars of yesterday (including those *It Happened One Night* actors Clark Gable and Claudette Colbert) to campy commercials by the Supremes. The pavilion boasts the most innovative outdoor neon sign ever created for a company—an 11-ton extravaganza hanging 18 feet above the entrance. In all, there are more than 1,000 exhibits, including a 1930s vintage soda fountain, complete with a soda jerk.

Georgia's Stone Mountain Park. Hwy. 78 East, Stone Mountain (16 miles east of downtown on U.S. 78). ☎ **800/317-2006.** Major attractions each $5.35 adults, children under 11 free. A ticket for all major attractions is $16 adults, $13 children. Year-round gates open 6am–midnight. Major attractions open fall and winter 10am–5pm, spring and summer 10am–8pm. Parking charge $6 a day, $30 annually (one-time-only charge if you stay on the grounds). Attractions only are closed Christmas Day; park is open. MARTA: to Avondale Station, transfer to a bus to Stone Mountain Village.

A monolithic gray granite outcropping (the world's largest), carved with a massive Confederate memorial, Stone Mountain is a distinctive landmark on Atlanta's horizon and the focal point of its major outdoor recreation area—3,200 acres of lakes and beautiful wooded parkland.

Over half a century in the making, Stone Mountain's neoclassic carving—90 feet high and 190 feet wide—is the world's largest piece of sculpture. Originally conceived by Gutzon Borglum, it depicts Confederate leaders Jefferson Davis, Robert E. Lee, and Stonewall Jackson galloping on horseback throughout eternity. Borglum started work on the mountain sculpture in 1923; after 10 years he abandoned it, because of insurmountable technical problems and rifts with its sponsors. (He went on to South Dakota, where he gained fame carving Mount Rushmore.) It wasn't until 1963, when the state purchased the mountain and its surroundings for a park, that work resumed under Walter Kirtland Hancock and Roy Faulkner. The memorial was completed in 1970.

The best view of the mountain is from below, but you can ascend a walking trail up its moss-covered slopes, especially lovely in spring when they're blanketed in wildflowers, or take the narrated tram ride to the top. Trams run about every 20 minutes in both directions.

A highlight at Stone Mountain is **Lasershow,** a spectacular display of laser lights and fireworks with animation and music. It begins in April, weekends only (Friday to Sunday at 9pm); from early May to Labor Day it can be seen nightly at 9:30pm; in

Georgia's Stone Mountain Park

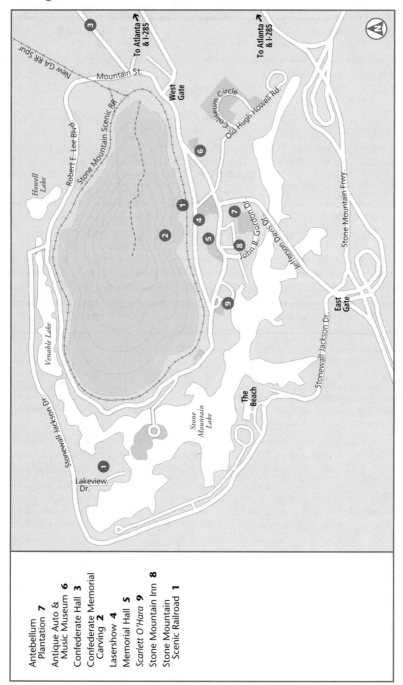

To Atlanta & I-285

To Atlanta & I-285

New GA RR Spur

Mountain St.

West Gate

Coliseum Circle

Old Hugh Howell Rd.

Robert E. Lee Blvd.

Stone Mountain Scenic RR

Howell Lake

Stone Mountain Frwy.

6

1

4

7

2

5

8

John B. Gordon Dr.

Jefferson Davis Dr.

9

East Gate

Venable Lake

Stonewall Jackson Dr.

Stonewall Jackson Dr.

The Beach

Stone Mountain Lake

1

Lakeview Dr.

Antebellum Plantation **7**
Antique Auto & Music Museum **6**
Confederate Hall **3**
Confederate Memorial Carving **2**
Lasershow **4**
Memorial Hall **5**
Scarlett O'Hara **9**
Stone Mountain Inn **8**
Stone Mountain Scenic Railroad **1**

September the weekend schedule is resumed; and in October, it is Friday and Saturday only, at 9pm. Don't miss it.

Other major park attractions include the **Stone Mountain Scenic Railroad,** which chugs around the 5-mile base of Stone Mountain. The ride takes 25 minutes. Trains depart from Railroad Depot, an old-fashioned train station with an attractive restaurant on the premises.

The *Scarlett O'Hara,* a paddlewheel riverboat, cruises the 363-acre Stone Mountain Lake. The **Antique Auto & Music Museum** is a jumble of old radios, jukeboxes, working nickelodeons, Lionel trains, and carousel horses, along with classic cars.

The 19-building **Antebellum Plantation** is a major sightseeing attraction in itself. Self-guided tours are assisted by hosts in period dress. Highlights include an authentic 1830s country store; the 1845 Kingston House; clapboard slave cabins; the 1790s Thornton House, elegant home of a large landowner; the smokehouse and well; a doctor's office; and the 1850 neoclassical Tara-like Dickey House, formal gardens, and a kitchen garden. It takes at least an hour to tour the entire complex (a map is provided at the entrance). Often there are crafts and cooking demonstrations, medicine shows, storytellers, or balladeers on the premises. You can even take a 20-minute horse-drawn carriage ride around the area ($5 for adults, $3 for children 3 to 11; free for children under 3).

Confederate Hall, an information center, houses a large narrated exhibit called "The War in Georgia," a chronological picture story of the Civil War.

Additional activities are golf (on a top-rated 36-hole course designed by Robert Trent Jones and John LaFoy), miniature golf, 15 hard-surface tennis courts (the site of the tennis competition for the 1996 Summer Olympic Games), a sizable lakefront beach with wonderful water slides, 20 acres of wildlife trails with natural animal habitats and a petting zoo, boating, bicycle rentals, fishing, and more. Also located in the park is the **Evergreen Conference Resort,** a 249-room state-of-the-art conference facility.

MARTIN LUTHER KING, JR., NATIONAL HISTORIC SITE

Under the auspices of the National Park Service is an area of about 10 blocks around Auburn Avenue, established in 1980 to "preserve the birthplace and boyhood surroundings of the nation's foremost civil rights leader." It includes King's boyhood home and the Ebenezer Baptist Church, of which King, his father, and his grandfather were ministers. Other Auburn Avenue attractions, not under NPS auspices, include the Martin Luther King, Jr., Center for Nonviolent Social Change (where King is buried) and the APEX Museum. There is a new visitor center at 450 Auburn Ave., across from the King Center. It provides a complete orientation to area attractions and includes a theater for audiovisual and interpretive programs, exhibits, and a bookstore. Guided tours of the area (including those of the Birth Home) originate here. The visitor center is fronted by a beautifully landscaped plaza with a reflecting pool and outdoor amphitheater for Park Service programs.

Martin Luther King, Jr., Center for Nonviolent Social Change. 449 Auburn Ave. (between Boulevard and Jackson sts.). ☎ **404/524-1956.** Free admission. Daily 8:30am–5pm. Closed Thanksgiving, Christmas, and New Year's Day. Bus: 3 from the Five Points MARTA station.

Martin Luther King, Jr.'s commitment to nonviolent social change lives on at this memorial and educational center under the direction of his son, Dexter Scott King. On the premises is an information counter where you can find out about all Auburn Avenue attractions.

The center works with government agencies and the private sector to reduce violence within the community and among nations. It provides day care for low-income families, assists students in developing leadership skills in nonviolence, and holds workshops on topics such as hunger and illiteracy. Its library and archives house the world's largest collection of books and other materials documenting the civil rights movement, including Dr. King's personal papers and a rare 87-volume edition of *The Collected Works of Mahatma Gandhi,* a gift from the government of India. Equally important, it is Martin Luther King's final resting place, a living memorial to an inspiring leader, which is visited by tens of thousands each year, including heads of foreign governments.

Visitors are given a self-guided tour brochure. The tour begins in the Exhibition Hall, where memorabilia of King and the civil rights movement are displayed. Here you can see his Bible and clerical robe, a hand-written sermon, a photographic essay on his life and work, and, on a grim note, the suit he was wearing when a deranged woman stabbed him in New York City, as well as the key to his room at the Lorraine Motel in Memphis, Tennessee, where he was assassinated. In an alcove off the main exhibit area is a video display on Martin Luther King's life and works. Additional exhibits—including a room honoring Rosa Parks and another honoring Gandhi—are in Freedom Hall.

Outside in Freedom Plaza, Dr. King's white marble crypt rests, surrounded by a five-tiered Reflecting Pool, a symbol of the life-giving nature of water. An eternal flame burns in a small circular pavilion directly fronting the crypt.

An important part of a visit is the Screening Room, where four excellent half-hour videos play continuously throughout the day. They show many of Dr. King's most stirring sermons and speeches, including "I've Been to the Mountaintop" and "I Have a Dream"—speeches that are as much a part of America's heritage as the Gettysburg Address.

Ebenezer Baptist Church. 407–413 Auburn Ave. ☎ **404/688-7263.** Free admission, but donations welcomed. Mon–Sat 9am–6pm; Sun only for services, at 7:45am and 11am. MARTA: King Memorial Station; then a long 8-block walk. Bus: 3 from stops on Peachtree St.

From 1960 to 1968 this gothic revival–style church, founded in 1886 and completed in 1922, became a center of world attention. Martin Luther King, Jr., served as co-pastor of the church during the civil rights struggle. Martin Luther King, Sr., a civil rights leader before his son, was also a pastor here. In early 1999, the U.S. Park Service assumed a 99-year lease on the church and will oversee it as a living museum, with guided weekday tours, periodic church services, and a monthly choir performance.

Birth Home of Martin Luther King, Jr. 501 Auburn Ave. (at Hogue St.). ☎ **404/331-3920.** Free admission (obtain tickets at 449 Auburn Ave.). Daily 9am–5pm. Closed major holidays. MARTA: Five Points; then bus 3.

This Queen Anne–style house is where Martin Luther King, Jr., was born on January 15, 1929. He was the oldest son of a Baptist minister and a music teacher. The future leader lived at this modest house until he was 12. It has been restored to its appearance when young Martin lived here. Even the linoleum is an authentic reproduction, and a great deal of King memorabilia is displayed. Be warned that in summer, tickets to the house often run out because of the crowds.

MUSEUMS

Atlanta History Center. 130 W. Paces Ferry Rd. (at Slaton Dr.). ☎ **404/814-4000.** Admission $10 adults, $8 seniors and students 18 or older, $4 children 6–17, free for children 5 and under; Swan House, $1 extra and Tullie Smith Farm, $1 extra. Mon–Sat 10am–5:30pm, Sun noon–5:30pm. MARTA: Lenox; then bus 23 to Peachtree St. and West Paces Ferry Rd., then a 3-block walk.

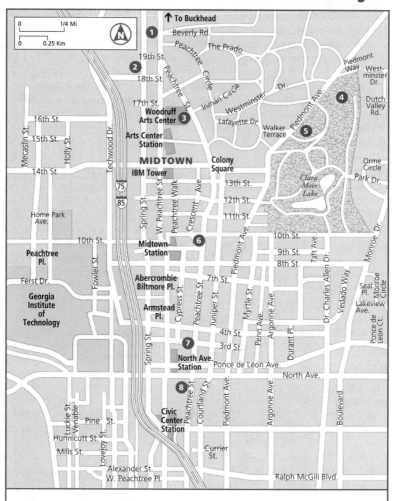

Atlanta Botanical Garden **4**

Atlanta College of Art Gallery **3**

Atlanta Museum **8**

Center for Puppetry Arts **2**

Fox Theatre **7**

High Museum of Art **3**

Margaret Mitchell House **6**

Piedmont Park **5**

Rhodes Memorial Hall **1**

From the Civil War and the burning of Atlanta to the civil rights movement of Martin Luther King, Jr., it's all here in vivid display in this vast museum. There's even a collection of memorabilia from Margaret Mitchell. There are frequently changing exhibits as well—everything from *Gone With the Wind* to Atlanta's first black millionaire.

On the grounds is **Swan House and Gardens,** the finest residential design of architect Philip Trammell Schutze. This classical home was constructed in 1928 by the Edward H. Inman family, heirs to a cotton fortune. It's listed on the National Register of Historic Places. Also on the grounds is a "plantation plain" home, circa 1840, the **Tullie Smith Farm.** Here you can see how Georgia farmers lived in the mid-1800s right before the Civil War.

✪ **Cyclorama.** 800 Cherokee Ave., in Grant Park. ☎ **404/624-1071.** Admission $5 adults, $4 seniors, $3 children 6–12, free for children 5 and under. May–Sept daily 9:20am–5:30pm; Oct–April daily 9:20am–4:30pm. Closed major holidays. MARTA: Five Points; then bus 97 (Georgia Ave.).

For a panorama of the Battle of Atlanta, go to see this 42-foot-high, 356-foot-circumference, 1880s painting with a three-dimensional foreground and special lighting, music, and sound effects. When you see the monumental work, you'll know why Sherman said, "War is hell." One of only three cycloramas in the United States, it has recently been fully restored—an artistic and historical treasure that many visitors to Atlanta miss, erroneously thinking it "strictly for kids." There are 15 shows daily.

✪ **High Museum of Art.** In the Woodruff Arts Center, 1280 Peachtree St. NE. ☎ **404/733-4200** or 404/733-HIGH for 24-hour information. Admission $6 adults, $4 seniors and students, $2 children 6–17, free for children 5 and under, free on Sun. Tues–Sat 10am–5pm, 4th Fri of each month 10am–9pm, Sun noon–5pm. Closed major holidays. MARTA: Arts Center.

This little gem of a museum is one of the finest in Georgia, but sensitive Atlantans warn that it shouldn't be oversold to visitors. It's not the Louvre, the Prado, or the Metropolitan. The building itself, designed in 1983 by Richard Meier at a cost of $20 million, has been called an "architectural masterpiece." Its exterior is coated with white enamel tiles, and the central atrium is flooded with natural light. You'll find first-rate traveling exhibitions along with the museum's permanent collection. Part of the Woodruff Arts Complex, the museum houses some 10,000 works, including one of our favorites, John Singer Sargent. Many are by artists like Mattie Lou O'Kelley and Howard Finster, with roots in Georgia. There's also an extensive sub-Saharan African art collection. We visit at times just to view the Virginia Carroll Crawford Collection of American Decorative Arts, covering changing tastes from 1825 to 1917.

The museum's downtown branch, the **High Museum of Art Folk Art and Photography Galleries,** is located at 133 Peachtree St. in the Georgia-Pacific Center. It's open Monday through Saturday from 10am to 5pm (☎ **404/577-6940**; admission free).

Margaret Mitchell House (birthplace of *Gone With the Wind*). 99 Peachtree St. (at 10th St.). ☎ **404/249-7015.** Admission $10 adults, $8 students and seniors and ages 7–17, free for children 6 and under. Public tours daily 9am–4pm (last tour begins at 4pm). MARTA: Midtown.

Margaret Mitchell was the author of *Gone With the Wind,* the best-selling book in the world next to the Bible, and this is her former home. A suspicious fire damaged the house in 1994, and on May 12, 1996, just 40 days before its scheduled reopening, arson struck again. Daimler-Benz, Germany's largest industrial group, came to the rescue and the property was rebuilt and opened to the public. Although Margaret Mitchell hated the place and called it "The Dump," her turn-of-the-century house is once again a major tourist attraction, even though the author would probably have been horrified to see millions of people traipsing through the place where she lived and wrote and created characters like Scarlett O'Hara and Rhett Butler.

Atlanta's first city landmark and listed on the National Register of Historic Places, the house was dedicated on May 16, 1997, exactly a year after the second fire on the property. You can experience a 40-minute anecdotal guided tour that shares the life story of this amazing author and the impact her book and the movie made upon the world. A new *Gone With the Wind* Museum opened here in late 1999, exhibiting the Herb Bridges collection of *Gone With the Wind* movie memorabilia, to coincide with the 60th anniversary of the movie's premiere in 1939. You can see props, scripts, posters, and even seats from the Loew's Grand Theatre, the Atlanta theater where the movie premiered. More people have seen *Gone With the Wind* than any other motion picture ever produced, including *Titanic*. The collection will be on display here until 2004.

The house and adjacent visitor center contain exclusive photographs and archival exhibits, including the original typewriter on which she crafted her novel, the 1937 Pulitzer Prize, original movie posters from around the world, and other exhibits. Mitchell lived here in this small apartment from 1925 to 1932.

✪ Michael C. Carlos Museum of Emory University. Kilgo St. (near the junction of Oxford and N. Decatur rds. on the Main Quadrangle of the Emory campus). ☎ **404/ 727-4282.** $3 donation recommended. Mon–Sat 10am–5pm, Sun noon–5pm. Closed major holidays. Bus: 6 or 36.

Only a tenth of its holdings are ever on display, so Atlantans return again and again. As an out-of-towner, you can count on something interesting even if it's only a small piece of the Carlos pie. Beautiful objects from the ancient Mediterranean, stunning art from Africa, and pre-Columbian art are among its rich collections. There are also special shows mounted from the museum's vast holdings, including exquisite drawings— some as old as the 1600s. There's nothing in Georgia to equal this collection. The 1916 beaux arts building housing the museum is listed on the National Register of Historic Places.

SciTrek. 395 Piedmont Ave. NE (adjacent to the Civic Center). ☎ **404/522-5500.** www.scitrek.org. Admission $7.50 adults, $6 children 3–17, college students, and senior citizens, free for children under 3. Mon–Sat 10am–5pm, Sun noon–5pm. Closed major holidays. MARTA: Civic Center Station stop.

This interactive museum provides an entertaining hands-on immersion in the wonders of science for the entire family. Among the permanent exhibits are the Cyber Playground, a display of computer games through the years; the Color Factory, where you literally play with color; and KidSpace, a gallery specially designed to entertain small children with interactive exhibits.

Fernbank Museum of Natural History. 767 Clifton Rd. (off Ponce de Leon Ave.). ☎ **404/378-0127.** Museum, $8.95 adults, $7.95 students and seniors, $6.95 children, free for children 1 and under; IMAX, $6.95 adults, $5.95 seniors and students, $4.95 children; combination museum and IMAX show, $13.95 adults, $11.95 seniors and students, $9.95 children. Mon–Sat 10am–5pm, Sun noon–5pm. MARTA: North Ave.; then bus 2 to Clifton Way.

This is the largest museum of the natural sciences in the Southeast, a $43-million complex that abuts 65 acres of virgin forest. Opened in 1992, it has a permanent exhibition, "A Walk Through Time in Georgia," taking visitors through more than a dozen galleries that explore Georgia's scenic wonders. "Spectrum of the Senses" comprises some 65 displays shown on a rotating basis. Adventures here include stepping inside a life-size kaleidoscope, and an IMAX Theater shows films on a six-story screen.

Fernbank Science Center. 156 Heaton Park Dr. NE (at Artwood Rd., off Ponce de Leon Ave.). ☎ **404/378-4311.** Center, free; planetarium shows, $2 adults, $1 students, free for seniors (children 4 and under not admitted). Museum, Mon 8:30am–5pm, Tues–Fri 8:30am–10pm, Sat 10am–5pm, Sun 1–5pm; planetarium shows, Tues–Fri at 8pm, Wed, Fri, Sat, Sun 3:30 and 8pm; observatory, Thurs–Fri at 8:30 (or dusk–10pm); forest trails, Sun–Fri 2–5pm, Sat 10am–5pm; greenhouse, Sun 1–5pm. Closed major holidays.

This is a planetarium, observatory, and museum all rolled into one. Next to the 65-acre Fernbank Forest, it's a branch of the Fernbank Museum of Natural History (see above). Many visitors who've seen all the exhibits come for the 1½-mile forest trail, showcasing some of the state's most popular trees such as magnolias and dogwoods. Inside, you can see the original Apollo 6 space capsule and a spacesuit, as well as a replica of the Okefenokee Swamp (see chapter 21 for details on the real one). The greenhouse, 2½ miles from the center, is open only on Sunday, and presents changing workshops and lectures.

A FASCINATING CEMETERY

۞ Oakland Cemetery. 248 Oakland Ave. SE (main entrance at Oakland Ave. and Martin Luther King, Jr., Dr.). ☎ **404/688-2107.** Free admission. Summer, daily sunrise–7pm; off-season, daily sunrise–6pm. Visitor center, Mon–Fri 9am–5pm. MARTA: King Memorial.

Margaret Mitchell, the most famous author ever to emerge from the Deep South, is buried here. But many other famous personages are also here, including golfing great Bobby Jones. The cemetery is an 88-acre Victorian site founded 10 years before the Civil War. It later became the burial place for nearly 50,000 soldiers, both Confederate and Union. This is actually an outdoor museum of funerary architecture, including both classic and gothic revival mausoleums. People often bring a picnic lunch and eat ham sandwiches among the dead. The visitor center distributes a self-guided walking-tour map and brochure for $1.25.

A HISTORIC HOME

Alonzo F. Herndon Home. 587 University Place (between Vine and Walnut sts.). ☎ **404/581-9813.** Free admission, but donations welcomed. Tues–Sat 10am–4pm (tours on the hour). Closed major holidays. MARTA: Vine City.

Although born into slavery in 1858, only 2 years before the Civil War, Herndon was an industrious man. By 1895 he was the richest black man in Atlanta and had founded the Atlanta Life Insurance Company, the nation's largest black-owned insurer. With his newly acquired wealth, he built this lavish mansion in the beaux arts neoclassical style, complete with a colonnaded entrance, and furnished it with antiques and art he'd amassed over a lifetime. The building stands at the Vine Street edge of the Morris Brown campus.

PARKS & GARDENS

Encompassing 21 acres of downtown Atlanta real estate, **Centennial Olympic Park** (☎ **404/223-4000**), built for the 1996 Olympics, is at the junction of International Boulevard, Techwood Drive, and Baker and Marietta streets. It was designed as a "landscape quilt," and creates a green "lung" in the center of one of Atlanta's most congested neighborhoods. The energy present during the games has long since subsided, but Atlantans still frequent the park with its outdoor amphitheater, reflecting pool, and the Olympic rings fountain. A marker notes the site of the bomb blast that claimed two lives in July 1996. Undaunted by the bombing, people were waiting in line for the park to reopen after the mishap, and that spirit still holds true today. You can stroll among the gardens or put on your bathing suit and jump into the geyserlike fountains—an activity for which they were designed. Twice daily, the fountains spurt water in synchronized patterns, arching gracefully in time to the marching tunes that were played during the 1996 Olympics. Hours of these water spectaculars vary—call the Georgia World Congress Center number listed above for exact showtimes. Admission to the park is free; it is open from dawn to dusk year-round.

Another highlight is **Atlanta Botanical Garden,** at Piedmont Avenue and the Prado, in Piedmont Park (☎ **404/876-5859**). Sprawling across 30 acres, this garden is Atlanta's most tranquil urban retreat, embracing a 15-acre hardwood forest. A highlight is the glass-walled Dorothy Chapman Fuqua Conservatory, which opened in 1989. Admission is $6 for adults, $7 for seniors, $4 for students, and free for children 5 and under. It's open Tuesday to Sunday from 9am to 7pm (to 6pm off-season).

6 Especially for Kids

The Botanical Garden (see above) has added a children's garden loaded with child friendly instructions about plants and other data.

Zoo Atlanta. 800 Cherokee Ave. (in Grant Park). ☎ **404/624-5600.** Admission $13 adults, $10 seniors, $9 children 3–11, free for children 2 and under. Daily 10am–5:30pm, until 6:30pm during daylight saving time. The admission booth closes an hour before zoo closing. Closed holidays. Bus: 97 from the Five Points rail station. A MARTA bus labeled "Zoo Shuttle" runs from Five Points June–Sept. Take I-75 south to I-20 east. Get off at the Boulevard exit and follow the signs to Grant Park.

This absolutely delightful 40-acre zoo is an exciting and creatively run facility, with animals housed in large, open enclosures that simulate their natural habitats. The zoo gained new prestige in 1999 when it became the home of a pair of giant pandas, Lun Lun and Yang Yang, both of which are on loan from China for the next 10 years. **Flamingo Plaza** is the first habitat you'll see upon entering the zoo. Farther on, **Masai Mara** houses rhinos, lions, and African elephants. The lushly landscaped **Ford African Rain Forest** centers on four vast gorilla habitats separated by moats. Sumatran tigers (a highly endangered species) and orangutans live in the **Ketambe** section, an Indonesian tropical rain forest with clusters of bamboo and a waterfall.

A zoo train travels through the **Children's Zoo** area, a peaceful enclave with a playground and children's petting zoo. There are shops and snack bars throughout the zoo and tree-shaded picnic areas in Grant Park. Free animal shows in the Kroger Wildlife Theater are presented daily at 11:30am and 1:30 and 3:30pm May through September.

Center for Puppetry Arts. 1404 Spring St. NW (at 18th St.). ☎ **404/873-3089** or 404/873-3391 for the box office. Museum $5 adults, $4 children 13 and under, students, and seniors. Show prices $5.75 adults, $4.75 children 2–13, students, and seniors. Workshop $4. Mon–Sat 9am–5pm. Closed holidays. MARTA: Arts Center.

Don't miss this place even if you're not traveling with the kids. It offers puppet shows, workshops, and a museum containing puppets from all around the world. A video with the late Jim Henson as host provides an overview of puppetry and takes visitors around the world to meet masters of the art. The puppet shows are sophisticated and riveting, full-stage productions with elaborate scenery. Some are family-oriented, others, with nighttime showings, are geared to adults. Call ahead to find out what's on; reservations are essential.

Six Flags Over Georgia. 7561 Six Flags Pkwy. ☎ **770/739-3400.** Admission $40 for 1 day, $19 seniors and children 42 in. tall and under; admission covers all rides and all shows except for amphitheater concerts. Late May–Labor Day, Sun–Thurs 10am–10pm, Fri–Sat 10am–midnight; Apr–May and Labor Day–Oct Sat–Sun only. Closed Nov–Mar. Take I-20 West for 12 miles; it's just off the hwy.

This theme park is one of the best of its kind in the country. Set on 88 fun-filled acres, it incorporates more than 100 rides, a multitude of shows, and several restaurants. Hours and prices are subject to change, so it's a good idea to call to check.

7 Organized Tours

American Coach Gray Line of Atlanta, 705 Lively Ave., Norcross (☎ **800/ 965-6665,** 404/767-0594, or 770/449-1806), offers three tours of Atlanta that will take you to most of the sites you want to see in the city. *Atlanta's Past and Present* is a tour of historical attractions, or what's left of them. You'll see Peachtree Street proper, the Woodruff Arts Center, Margaret Mitchell's House, the World of Coca-Cola, Centennial Park and other related Olympic sites, and tours of CNN and the Cyclorama. The 4-hour tour departs at 9am and is priced at $35 for adults, $33 for seniors, and $30 for children 6 to 12. The *All Around Atlanta* tour takes you to many of the same sites, but includes a stop at the Martin Luther King, Jr., sites, the Jimmy Carter Museum, and the Governor's Mansion. Departing at 1:30pm, this 4-hour tour costs $40 for adults, $36 for seniors, and $32 for children 6 to 12. The *Black Heritage Tour* covers "Sweet Auburn" and sites associated with the birthplace of the modern civil rights movement. You'll tour the Atlanta University Complex (Morehouse College, Spelman College, and Clark-Atlanta University) and the home of Alonzo F. Herndon, Atlanta's first black millionaire. The tour lasts 4 hours and is priced at $40 for adults, $36 for seniors, and $32 for children 6 to 12.

The most intriguing tours in Atlanta are those found at the **Atlanta Preservation Center,** 156 7th St. NE, Suite 3 (☎ **404/876-2040**). The center offers 11 1½- to 2-hour guided walking tours, each costing $5 for adults, $4 for seniors and students, $3 for students, and free for children 4 and under. Most tours are offered only from February to November and many are specialized; call for details. For example, the Historic Downtown Tour surveys the city's architecture; the Inman Park Tour visits the city's first garden suburb; the Sweet Auburn Tour surveys the stamping grounds of Martin Luther King, Jr.; Walking Miss Daisy's Druid Hills explores the neighborhood of the film *Driving Miss Daisy;* the West End, Hammonds House, and Wren's Nest Tour focuses on Joel Chandler Harris, author of the Uncle Remus stories; and the Vine City Tour examines the community's African-American heritage.

8 Outdoor Pursuits

BIKING   Although it may be a bit crowded, **Piedmont Park** is best for biking because it's closed to traffic. Enter the park on Piedmont Avenue between 10th and 14th streets. Bikes can be rented at **Skate Escape,** across the park at 1086 Piedmont Ave. (☎ **404/892-1292**). It rents single-speed bikes for $6 per hour or $25 per day, with mountain bikes going for $40 per day or $125 a week, including a helmet. Georgia license or a major credit or charge card is required as deposit. It's open daily from 11am to 7pm.

BOATING   **Lake Lanier Islands Beach and Water Park,** 6950 Holiday Rd., Lake Lanier Islands (☎ **770/932-7200**), includes in its entry fee use of canoes, paddleboats, and sailboats. To reach it from Atlanta, a distance of 45 miles, take I-85 north to I-985 (Exit 45); get off I-985 at Exit 1 and turn left at the end of the ramp, following the signs. This family retreat is part of a larger resort complex with golf courses, homes, campgrounds, and freshwater marinas. It contains more than half a dozen water slides, a wave pool, and a tropical lagoon designed exclusively for children. Open Memorial Day to Labor Day, Sunday to Thursday from 10am to 6pm and on Friday and Saturday from 10am to 7pm. Admission is $21 for adults, $14 for children and seniors 55 and over, and free for children 2 and under.

CAMPING   ❂ **The Family Campground,** P.O. Box 778, at Stone Mountain, GA 30086 (☎ 770/498-5600), about 16 miles from Atlanta, has 400 wooded sites for RVs and tents. There are full hookups for RVs, LP gas, showers, a laundry, a supply store, and a restaurant. There's also minigolf, swimming, boating, fishing and other recreational activities. Rates for two campers at tent sites begin at $20, plus $2 for each additional person. Full hookup costs $30 to $35. Take I-285 to the Stone Mountain Exit, then drive 7½ miles east on Ga. 78 to Stone Mountain Park.

FISHING   The Fish Hawk, 279 Buckhead Ave. NE, between Peachtree and Piedmont roads (☎ 404/237-3473), sells Georgia fishing licenses costing $7 for 7 days. Seasonal trout stamps are $13. After supplying you with quality tackle and other gear, it will direct you to the best places to fish along the Chattahoochee River, in the North Georgia mountains, or at Lake Lanier with its 38,000-acre reservoir. The shop is open Monday to Friday from 9am to 6pm and on Saturday from 9am to 5pm. Other information can be supplied by the **Georgia Department of Natural Resources,** Wildlife Resources Division, 2023 U.S. 278 SE, Social Circle, GA 30025 (☎ 770/918-6418).

GOLF   The best course is Georgia's **Stone Mountain Park Golf Course,** in Stone Mountain Park (☎ 770/498-5690), with its 36-hole greens designed by Robert Trent Jones. This challenging course is 16 miles east of the center of Atlanta. Greens fees are $30 to $40, including use of the cart. Open daily from 7:30am to dusk.

JOGGING   Most joggers prefer Piedmont Park in spite of its overcrowding, although the Chattahoochee National Recreation Area is more scenic. Serious joggers should contact the **Atlanta Track Club,** 3097 Shadowlawn Ave. (☎ 404/231-9064).

❂ **"SHOOTING THE HOOCH"**   This is one of the city's favorite outdoor adventures. At the **Chattahoochee Outdoor Center,** 1990 Island Ford Pkwy., in Dunwoody (☎ 770/395-6851), you can rent an inflated rubber raft holding four, six, or eight passengers. With the rental come lifejackets and paddles. Adventurers set out from Johnson Ferry to Powers Island about 6½ miles away, usually a 3-hour trip, although the water is slower some days. The center is open Memorial Day to Labor Day, Monday to Friday from 10am to 8pm and on Saturday, Sunday, and holidays from 9am to 8pm. A four-person raft costs $45; a six-person raft, $65. Rentals require a deposit of $75 per raft or $100 per canoe.

SWIMMING   Dozens of Atlanta hotels have their own swimming pools. Public swimming is available at **Piedmont Park.** If you'd like to swim in climate-controlled conditions, contact **Martin Luther King Jr. Natatorium,** 70 Boulevard (☎ 404/658-7330), open Monday to Friday from 10am to 7:45pm and on Saturday from 10am to 6:30pm. Admission is $2 for adults, $1 for children.

TENNIS   The best courts are those at the **Bitsy Grant Tennis Center,** 2125 Northside Dr., between I-75 and Peachtree Battle Avenue (☎ 404/609-7193), leased from the Atlanta Parks and Recreation Department. Offered are 13 outdoor clay courts (6 lighted for night games), plus 10 outdoor hard courts (4 lighted). No reservations are accepted—it's strictly first come, first to play. Facilities include a pro shop, showers, and lockers. The cost is $3 per person per hour for the clay courts, or $2 per person per hour for the hard courts. Open Monday to Friday from 9am to 8pm and on Saturday and Sunday from 9am to 6pm.

WHITE-WATER ADVENTURES   Just 20 miles from Atlanta, **White Water,** 250 N. Cobb Pkwy., Marietta (☎ 404/424-9283), is a well-run amusement park.

It offers sliding adventures both fast and slow, straight and curvy. You might elect to go through a tunnel or slide on your back. One-person and two-person tubes and rafts holding five are available. It's open the first 4 weekends in May and daily from Memorial Day to Labor Day, but hours vary. Admission is $24 for adults and $16 for children up to 4 feet tall, but not older than 3 years of age. Adjoining is **American Adventures** (☎ **404/424-9283**), which is geared to families with smaller children. Admission is $15, and children needing assistance pay $2.99. It's open year-round; call for variable hours.

9 Shopping

Think of Atlanta as a great shopping bazaar. There's nothing in the American Southeast to equal it. It consists of mall after endless mall—each packed with goodies.

If you're downtown and looking for a souvenir, head for **Underground Atlanta,** but if your tastes are more refined, it's the mall for you. For high fashion—and high prices too—head for **Buckhead,** 8 miles north of the center. Here the main shopping district centers around Lenox Square Mall and Phipps Plaza, and there are at least 200 specialty stores in the Greater Buckhead area.

If you'd like something a little more imaginative, go to **Virginia-Highland,** which has been referred to as "New York's SoHo a decade ago." The neighborhood, near the junction of Highland Avenue at Virginia Avenue and Ponce de Leon Avenue, offers five different art galleries, at least 30 restaurants, a scattering of artsy cafes, and endless rows of stores devoted to clothing, flea-market junk, antiques, jewelry, and everything from high to low camp.

For "New York's downtown a decade ago" meander your way to **Little Five Points,** Atlanta's resident art community. Discover eclectic items from hard-to-find books to jazz vinyl records you thought were a part of the past, plus clothes and jewelry to adorn any aspiring rock star. Its mythical center is at the junction of North and Moreland avenues, just east of downtown Atlanta.

For the antiques buff, one of the densest concentrations of such stores is near the T-junction of Peachtree Road and Broad Street, in the northern suburb of **Chamblee,** 17 miles from central Atlanta.

ANTIQUES

Atlanta is home to several permanent antiques shop clusters that sell everything from arts and crafts to old and custom furniture. The vendors who peddle here are often from around the country and only appear once or twice a year—the result is a revolving roster of hawkers whose wares are always fresh, however often you shop there. Markets are usually held on weekends, and mostly only once a month, so call ahead for details.

Shopping here should be like any yard, garage, or stoop sale—the early bird gets the steal. Get here first—on Thursday during set-up—for the best finds. However, for the best deals, bargain on Sunday, usually the last day of the sale. Many dealers aren't interested in taking their things back home, so bargain hard, although you may not have to.

Lakewood Antiques Market. At the Lakewood Fairgrounds, between downtown Atlanta and the airport. ☎ **404/622-4488.** Free parking. Take I-75/85 south to Exit 88. Go east to the Fairgrounds.

Held at the Lakewood Fairgrounds on the second weekend of each month, this market is by far the largest and most diverse in the area. With more than 1,500 dealer spaces, you'll find something, ranging from old reproductions to books, cookware, linens, custom furniture, pottery, and sculpture. But this only scratches the surface. Open Thursday to Saturday from 10am to 6pm, and Sunday 10am to 5pm on the second weekend of each month. Admission to the market is $3, except for Thursday ("early buyer day"), which is $5.

Pride of Dixie Antiques Market. At the North Atlanta Trade Center, north of Atlanta. ☎ **770/279-9853.** Free parking. Take I-85 north to the Indian Trail Exit (about 25 min. from downtown), then follow the signs.

Some 600 dealers set up the fourth weekend of each month to peddle their wares. You'll find everything from dealers who make their own wares to vendors who have found things you surely thought extinct—items from grandma's attic and estate sales that can date to the 19th century. And of course, there are many antiques to choose from. Open the 4th weekend of each month Thursday to Saturday from 10am to 6pm, and Sunday from 10am to 5pm. Admission is $4; children admitted free.

Rust & Dust Antiques. 5486 Peachtree Rd., Chamblee. ☎ **770/458-1614.** MARTA: Chamblee; then bus 132 (Tilly Mill).

It's one of the larger (and more interesting) stores along Antiques Row. The owners often volunteer to pick up patrons at the Chamblee MARTA station, which lies about three-quarters of a mile away.

ART GALLERIES
Art Station. 5384 Manor Dr., Stone Mountain. ☎ **770/469-1105.** Bus: 120 to Manor Dr.

Established in 1985, this well-recommended art gallery occupies the premises of what was once a garage for trolley cars. It sells works by regional and some national and international artists.

BOOKS
Barnes & Noble. 2900 Peachtree Rd., Buckhead. ☎ **404/261-7747.** MARTA: Lenox.

This popular flagship of seven Atlanta locations, south of the Lenox Square Mall, has everything. When you've chosen among the wealth of books, the cafe invites you to relax with your book or newspaper. Book signings and other events are frequent.

Borders. 3637 Peachtree Rd., Buckhead. ☎ **404/237-0707.**

This upper-Buckhead location affords you the opportunity to sip a caffè latte while you peruse your next book. One of five Borders locations, the late hours are a hit with the working reader.

Chapter 11 Books. In the Peachtree Battle Shopping Center, 2345 Peachtree Rd. NE, Buckhead. ☎ **404/237-7199.** MARTA: Buckhead.

Located in the upscale residential district of Buckhead, this is the largest independently owned bookstore in the Southeast, site of a staggering number of books of every imaginable description, as well as periodicals from virtually everywhere. There's also sheet and recorded music, and book signings by widely read authors. There's a newer branch of this store at 1544 Piedmont Ave. (☎ **404/872-7986**).

DEPARTMENT STORES
Lord & Taylor. In Phipps Plaza, 3500 Peachtree Rd. NE. ☎ **404/266-0600.** MARTA: Lenox.

Lord & Taylor, along with Saks, its premier competitor, function as the anchors for the most upscale and plush shopping mall in Atlanta, Phipps Plaza.

Macy's Peachtree. 180 Peachtree St. (between International Blvd. and Ellis St.). ☎ **404/221-7221.** MARTA: Peachtree Center.

Opened in 1927, this is one of the longest-established department stores in Atlanta, a marble-floored branch of the New York–based store. Despite the grand and imposing Corinthian columns of its interior, Atlanta insiders cite standards that have fallen below those of Saks and Lord & Taylor in recent years. The store's cellar does a brisk business in housewares and cooking equipment, and other merchandise, covering seven floors, moves quickly, especially during the lunch shopping hour. The street level contains a large and diverse selection of Atlanta souvenirs.

Parisian. In Phipps Plaza, 3500 Peachtree Rd. NE. ☎ **404/814-3305.** MARTA: Lenox.

This is the local branch of an apparel chain that originated in Birmingham, Alabama, decades ago. Its prices are less elevated than those at Saks or Lord & Taylor. Brand-name fashions are available for men, women, and children, as well as a large line of cosmetics.

DISCOUNT SHOPPING
Tanger Factory Outlet. 111 Tanger Dr., at Exit 53 (U.S. 441) off I-85N, in Tanger. ☎ **706/335-4537.**

Located 60 miles north of Atlanta, on the highway leading to Greenville, South Carolina, this mall is a targeted destination for dozens of tour buses of shoppers from as far away as Macon. A destination in its own right, it contains 115 factory outlets for well-established manufacturers from around North America. Most merchandise is discounted at an average of 40%.

FASHION
Polo Ralph Lauren. In the Lenox Mall, Lenox Sq., 3393 Peachtree Rd. ☎ **404/261-2663.** MARTA: Lenox.

This is one of the busiest retail stores in Atlanta. All its merchandise is part of the Ralph Lauren collection for both men and women who appreciate the sporty, casually elegant, impeccably tailored look of this leading designer.

✪ **Susan Lee.** 56 E. Andrews Dr., Buckhead. ☎ **404/365-0693.** MARTA: Buckhead.

Its specialty is women's dresses, suitable for the office, evening wear, or cocktail hour, and no matter how hard you look, you won't find a shred of sportswear.

✪ **Versace.** In Phipps Plaza, 3500 Peachtree Rd. NE. ☎ **404/814-0664.** MARTA: Lenox.

It sells more of the garments by the house of Gianni Versace, for both men and women, than many of that designer's other outlets. It's unusual in enjoying exclusivity for all of Georgia, and for maintaining under one roof every line ever produced by the award-winning house.

FOOD
✪ **Atlanta State Farmer's Market.** 16 Forest Pkwy., Forest Park. ☎ **404/366-7522.** Take I-75 south to Exit 78, a 15-minute drive south of downtown Atlanta.

The largest food outlet in the Southeast, it covers 146 acres. About half the vendors sell wholesale only; the other half sell to the public, purveying meats, poultry, plants, flowers, fruits, vegetables, and a staggering variety of home-canned jams, pickles, and relishes. Most vendors don't accept credit cards. Open 24 hours daily.

✪ **Dekalb Farmer's Market.** 3000 E. Ponce de Leon Ave., Decatur. ☎ **404/377-6400.**

Strictly speaking, because all the stalls are owned by the same entrepreneur, this is not a farmer's market at all. Instead, it's one of the largest, best-stocked, and most atmospheric grocery stores in Atlanta, rustically outfitted like your fantasy version of a country fair.

An Antique in Your Future

If you're yearning for granite countertops in your kitchen, or access to some of the most prestigious designers and antiques dealers in Atlanta, chances are good that you'll find them within the cluster of entrepreneurs at **Miami Circle.** Set in the heart of Buckhead, off Piedmont Avenue, it's a premier resource for anyone buying or building a house in any of Atlanta's affluent neighborhoods. Scattered along its length, you'll find purveyors of the good life as you might imagine it in Buckhead. Foremost among the antique dealers is **Randall Tysinger Antiques,** 761-D Miami Circle NE (☎ **404/261-7170**), where a labyrinth of rooms—at least 14—stocks antiques from all parts of Europe. And if you get hungry, Miami Circle's most happening restaurant is **Eclipse de Luna,** 764 Miami Circle (☎ **404/846-0449**), where tapas are served in a whimsical collection of mobiles and artworks.

Roughly equivalent, and also in Buckhead, is the row of antique dealers along the edges of **Bennett Circle,** adjacent to the intersection of Bennett and Peachtree Streets. An especially good choice is **Nottingham Antiques,** 45 Bennett St. (☎ **404/352-1890**). It specializes in stripped pine, some of it English, along with some unusual reproductions that look almost antique. And if all that shopping gives you hunger pangs, consider an informal supper at **Fratelli di Napoli,** 38 Bennett St. (☎ **404/351-1533**). Prefaced with a collection of antique millstones, it's one of the most visible family Italian restaurants in Buckhead—a neighborhood more usually known for more posh venues.

JEWELRY

Richters. 87 W. Paces Ferry Rd., Buckhead. ☎ **404/355-4462.** MARTA: Lenox.

Specializing in antique jewelry, this is one of the most unusual stores in town, a compendium of grandmother's grandest things—don't expect the baroque jewels worn by the grand duchess of Austria. The owners stress that this is not a museum, and that almost everything displayed was made during the 20th century. Pieces incorporate Edwardian, art deco, and the "retro" styles of the 1950s.

MALLS & SHOPPING CENTERS

Lenox Square Mall. 3393 Peachtree Rd. NE, at Lenox Rd. ☎ **800/344-5222** or 404/233-6767. MARTA: Lenox.

North of Atlanta's commercial core, near the upscale district of Buckhead, this began as a small cluster of merchants in 1959, but has been expanded at least four times since then. Today, it incorporates a modern hotel (the JW Marriott), half a dozen movie theaters, two dozen restaurants, and a bewildering array of at least 200 shops.

✪ **Phipps Plaza.** 3500 Peachtree Rd. NE, at the Buckhead Loop. ☎ **404/262-0992.** MARTA: Lenox.

This is the most upscale shopping mall in Atlanta. A short drive north of downtown in Buckhead, it was enlarged in 1992. Today its two largest tenants (Lord & Taylor and Saks) function as "anchors" at the opposite ends of passageways incorporating some of the most elegant boutiques in the Southeast. There's also a food court, a handful of tony restaurants, and a movie theater with more than a dozen screens.

✪ **Underground Atlanta.** Alabama St., between Peachtree St. and Central Ave. ☎ **404/523-2311.** MARTA: Five Points.

Sunk partly underground, on the site of Atlanta's original antebellum core, this site manages to fulfill the roles of living-history museum, nightlife venue, and shopping mall all rolled into one ongoing carnival. (For more information on Underground Atlanta, refer to "Attractions," earlier in this chapter.)

VINTAGE CLOTHING

Stefan's Vintage Clothing. 1160 Euclid Ave., Little Five Points. ☎ **404/688-4929.** MARTA: Inman Park.

Established in 1977, and set in the heart of Inman Park, this store carries rack after rack of pre-1962 clothing. You'll find a limited number of "novelty pieces" from the 1960s (including the flowered bell-bottoms you shudder to think you ever wore) and a limited array of Victorian lawn dresses and men's formal wear from the Jazz Age. Most of the stock is from the 1940s and 1950s, including women's gabardine skirts and jackets that some shoppers think have great style, 1950s-era swing dresses, poodle skirts, and a collection of men's shirts, trousers, and jackets, some from the U.S. military.

10 Atlanta After Dark

Most hotels and motels distribute free the publications *Where, Key: This Week in Atlanta,* or *After Hours.* The Saturday edition of the *Atlanta Constitution* has a "Weekend" section to fill you in further. Should you *still* be at a loss as to how to spend an evening, take yourself to Kenny's Alley at Underground Atlanta.

THE PERFORMING ARTS

CLASSICAL MUSIC   The **Atlanta Symphony Orchestra,** performing in the Woodruff Arts Center, 1280 Peachtree St. NE, at 15th Street (☎ **404/733-4900,** or 404/733-5000 for the box office), celebrated its 50th anniversary in 1995. Under the musical directorship of Yoel Levi, it's acclaimed especially for the 200-voice Atlanta Symphony Orchestra Chorus, formerly the Robert Shaw Chorus.

The season runs from September to May, and includes the master series and the light classics series. The master series features world-acclaimed guest artists. Light classics are likely to dip into such fun shows as "Broadway's Hottest Tickets." The **Chastain Summer Concerts** are held in the 7,000-acre Chastain Park Amphitheater between June and August. It's the custom to bring an elaborate picnic to the event. Artists such as the Beach Boys perform here. Holiday concerts are also performed at Christmas and other times.

Ticket prices vary but are generally $19 to $48 for the master series, $17.50 to $42 for the light classics series, or $19 to $42 for the Chastain Summer Concerts. To reach the Woodruff Arts Center, take MARTA to Arts Center.

OPERA   The **Atlanta Opera,** performing in the Fox Theatre, 660 Peachtree St. NE, at Ponce de Leon Avenue (☎ **404/817-8700** or 404/881-2000), is under the artistic direction of William Fred Scott. Founded in 1979, the opera company has gone on to win national recognition. It presents a trio of fully staged productions each summer at the Fox Theatre, plus various productions at other venues. Tickets cost $16 to $101, with seniors and students granted 50% discounts on the day of the performance if any tickets are available (tickets are generally extremely difficult to obtain). The season lasts from late May to Labor Day. Take MARTA to North Avenue.

BALLET   The **Atlanta Ballet** performs at the historic Fox Theatre, 660 Peachtree St. NE, at Ponce de Leon Avenue (☎ **404/817-8700** or 404/881-2000). The Atlanta Ballet, under artistic director John McFall, is the oldest in the nation, now into its

70th year. McFall creates excitement with new sets, costumes, and choreography. Ticket prices range from $18 to $50. MARTA: North Avenue.

THEATER   7 Stages, 1105 Euclid Ave. (☎ **404/523-7647**), in the Little Five Points district, is the leading producer of new and contemporary plays in Atlanta. It's also a venue for performances by international touring theater companies. Performances run Wednesday to Sunday in the newly renovated theater. Tickets cost $8 to $15 for most productions, with discounts offered to seniors and students. MARTA: Inman Park.

Alliance Theatre Company, at the Woodruff Arts Center, 1280 Peachtree St. NE (☎ **404/733-5000**), is the largest resident professional theater troupe in the Deep South. It produces about 10 plays a year, ranging from *Angels in America, Part I: Millennium Approaches* to stunning revivals such as William Inge's *The Dark at the Top of the Stairs.* Such famous actors as Jane Alexander often appear with this group. Ticket prices range from $17 to $36. The season runs September to May, with occasional productions staged in summer. MARTA: Arts Center.

THE CLUB & MUSIC SCENE
COMEDY CLUBS

Punchline Comedy Club. 280 Hildebrand Dr. NE. ☎ **404/252-5233.** Cover $8–$30, higher for big-name acts.

Some of the best touring comics in America play here in the Balconies Shopping Center and have been doing so for the past 18 years. Jerry Seinfeld has appeared here. The club is small but most tables have a good view.

Uptown Comedy Corner. 2140 Peachtree Rd. ☎ **404/350-6990.** Cover $5–$15.

The future Richard Pryors often get their start here. The crowd is primarily African-American, as are the often-bawdy comedians. Tables are crammed, so you may have to sit elbow to elbow.

JAZZ & BLUES

✪ **Blind Willie's Live Blues Club.** 828 N. Highland Ave. NE. ☎ **404/873-2583.** Cover $5–$8 Sun–Thurs, $8–$10 Fri–Sat.

This is one of the best live blues clubs in Atlanta. Opened in 1986, it has a simple interior of old brick walls and wooden floors, and is dimly lit. Sometimes nationally known acts are booked here, and Cajun entertainment is often featured.

Café 290. 290 Hildebrand Ave. NE. ☎ **404/256-3942.**

Jazz and blues, along with some R&B, form the background in this club, drawing a crowd that ranges in age from 30 to 50. At the back is a sports bar with televised games and pool tables. But most patrons come here for the music. Reservations are needed on Friday and Saturday. Fine dancing is also a feature here, or you can enjoy intimate, candlelit dining. The cuisine is continental, and a specialty is hand-carved steaks. Only fresh ingredients are used, and meals cost $8.75 to $24.95. Every night a late breakfast is offered from 11pm to 1am (until 2am on Friday and Saturday). The venue is suitable for unescorted women.

✪ **Dante's Down the Hatch.** Across from the Lenox Square Mall, 3380 Peachtree Rd., Buckhead. ☎ **404/266-1600.** Cover $6 after 7pm on the ship deck, none on the wharf.

Dante's design has created the illusion of a pirate ship tied up to an old Mediterranean wharf. In the wharf section there's jazz, classical, and flamenco guitar until 8pm nightly. As for the "crew," most have been aboard for a long time, and all really make you feel cared for. Dante himself is always on hand to see that you have a good time.

COUNTRY & ROCK

Dark Horse Tavern. 816 N. Highland Ave. NE. ☎ **404/873-3607.** Cover $3–$5 for bands, no cover to enter.

Opened in 1989, this Virginia-Highland tavern is a trilevel venue. The top floor is for private parties and in the middle is a restaurant and bar, with the original railing used on the set of *Gone With the Wind.* The club is decorated like a riding club with hunter-green walls and an antique brass bar and grill with saddles and bridles. The music offers everything from jazz to rockabilly and pop; rock predominates. Both Atlanta and national bands perform in the downstairs bar.

DANCE CLUBS

Johnny's Hideaway. 3771 Roswell Rd. ☎ **404/233-8026.** Cover varies, but is imposed only for special entertainment, when there's a 2-drink minimum.

This ballroom, frequented by everybody ages 35 to 65, is just a local tavern during the day. The Big Band sounds of the 1940s, including Glenn Miller, live on here, as do the golden sounds of 1950s rock 'n' roll, including the music of Macon-born Little Richard. This is a good place for the single visitor, either male or female. Chances are, if you're lookin' good, you'll be asked to dance. A silver ball still rotates over the dance floor in the grand old tradition. Two big-screen TVs provide further divertissement, and local legend Johnny Esposito keeps the joint humming.

Masquerade. 695 North Ave. NE. ☎ **404/577-8178.** Cover $3–$10, slightly higher for national acts.

This is primarily a dance club with live dance bands, on occasion a center for internationally known rock groups. The three-level club is housed in what was once the Excelsior paper mill. The bar downstairs is appropriately called Purgatory, complete with exposed pipes and video games. The effect is like a dungeon. Hell is just across the way, complete with hanging chains—an appropriate venue for Wednesday's Club Fetish nights, when patrons can live out their S&M fantasies. Loud dance music fills Hell. Heaven, with a capacity of about 1,000 patrons, is painted blue with fluffy clouds.

DINNER THEATER

Agatha's Mystery Dinner Theater. 693 Peachtree St., at 3rd St. ☎ **404/875-4321.** Tickets $40 Sun–Thurs, $50 Fri–Sat.

For the Agatha Christie in all of us, or even for *Murder, She Wrote* fans, this theater is unique in Atlanta. Between courses, an original murder-mystery/comedy is performed, with audience members being selected at random to participate (you can, of course, decline). Each play is an original.

THE BAR SCENE

Atkin's Park. 749 N. Highland Ave. NE. ☎ **404/876-7249.**

One of the most frequented Virginia-Highland taverns, this is called "the Cheers of the neighborhood." It attracts 25- to 35-year-olds. Photographs of the city's tumultuous history decorate the walls. The patio, with a decor of brick, brass, and wood floors, is a little small for dining, but it's extremely lively on weekends. Music is country, pop, Top-40, and rock—and is it ever loud.

Lulu's Bait Shack. 3057 Peachtree Rd. NE, Buckhead. ☎ **404/262-5220.**

If you ever wanted to go back to college and have that one last frat party, here's your chance to do it. Crowded, loud, and definitely fun, Lulu's serves up alcoholic elixirs to patrons who most likely would be wearing lampshades on their heads at any other party. Upstairs is an outside deck that faces onto Pharr Road, allowing ample opportunity for people-watching and seeing what's going on at other Buckhead bars. Order a fishbowl margarita—if you finish it, it may be the end of your night.

Manuel's Tavern. 602 N. Highland Ave. NE. ☎ **404/525-3447.**

This is the hangout for local politicos. Jimmy Carter shows up every now and then, ordering a Moosehead, whereas his Secret Service boys order Atlanta's favorite hometown drink, Coca-Cola. Since 1956 the tavern has been serving its burgers, steaks, and hot dogs to the local gang. Dress is always casual.

Mo's & Joe's. 1033 North Highland Ave. at the corner of Virginia Ave. ☎ **404/873-6090.**

Offering a cool refuge from the blazing Atlanta heat, this is one of the most nostalgia-packed bars in Atlanta. Set at the street corner that gave Virginia-Highland its name, it has thrived here since 1947, amid a collection of sports memorabilia that grows every year. Lots of liquor has been swilled here since its debut (it sells more Pabst Blue Ribbon than any other bar in the Southeast), and it's so genuinely friendly and indulgent that you might quickly adopt it as your local hang. Menu items include a roster of predictable bar platters, including burgers and barbecued chicken wings.

✪ **Park 75 Lounge.** In the Four Seasons Hotel Atlanta, 75 14th St. (between Peachtree and West Peachtree sts.). ☎ **404/881-9898.**

Sheathed in a zillion dollars worth of russet-colored marble and richly figured mahogany, this is the most appealing and opulent hotel bar in Atlanta. A magnet for a clientele that includes lots of well-heeled residents of nearby homes and condominiums, it offers a staggering array of single malt scotches, rare wines by the glass, vintage ports, and two-fisted cocktails that are poured tableside by a hip, well-trained, and endlessly indulgent staff. Light platters and desserts are served as well, in a setting that evokes the best aspects of a discreet but chic private club in London.

The Raccoon Lodge at East Village Grille. 248 Buckhead Ave. NE. ☎ **404/233-3345.**

The lodge and grille stand side by side, and the essentially young crowd (mostly in their 20s) frequents both. Mainly it's a sports bar, with 15 TV sets (two large-screen). The rooftop patio has seating for 110 patrons who can glance at Atlanta's skyline in the evening while having a drink. Previously the first fire station in Buckhead, it's big and wide open—all in stone and brick with some moose and antelope heads for decoration and a big fireplace. The place is known for its Southern cuisine. A DJ plays disco music and rock 'n' roll.

Three Dollar Cafe. 3002 Peachtree Rd. ☎ **404/266-8667.**

Attracting the under-35 crowd, this Buckhead sports bar is the liveliest in the area. People go here not only to watch games, but to eat and drink, enjoying 300 different kinds of beer along with the usual array of burgers, sandwiches, wings, and desserts. All kinds of beer neon signs decorate the joint, and there's a large patio where bands perform as weather permits. The big feature is an array of 45 TV sets, plus three big-screens, showing all sports programs.

GAY & LESBIAN BARS
The Armory. 836 Juniper St. NE. ☎ **404/881-9280.**

This is the largest gay dance club in town (rivaled only by Backstreet), with what some fans claim is Atlanta's finest sound system. A cavernous enclave with a 25-year history, it sports five different rooms (one of which is devoted to drag shows), an outdoor patio, hundreds of mirrors, and a "Robo-scan" lighting system that turns night into quasi-psychedelic day.

Backstreet. 845 Peachtree St. ☎ **404/873-1986.** Membership $10; cover $5 Fri–Sat.

Within Atlanta's gay subculture, the word is out: No matter where you begin your night of partying, chances are high that you'll end up in the wee hours at Backstreet. You'll find a state-of-the-art sound system in the basement for discoing the night away; a drag theater upstairs where latter-day Scarletts strut their stuff; a gift shop with accessories that range from naughty to unmentionable; and balconies that overlook both the dance floor and the Atlanta skyline.

Bulldog & Co. 893 Peachtree St. NE. ☎ **404/872-3025.** Cover $1–$2 for nonmembers.

It was named after the canine pet of the entrepreneur who founded the place in 1978. Today it's a gay-lifestyle staple for men aged 30 and over who, while not addicted to leather, don't flinch at it, either. Inside, you'll find five or six bars, depending on the season, and a crowd that runs from the Marlboro Man to lookalikes for Denzel Washington and Billy Dee Williams. In fact, Bulldogs has been called the most harmonious and gregarious racially mixed bar in the South, with lots of successful dialogues and pairings between black and white men who enjoy one another's company.

The Eagle. 306 Ponce de Leon. ☎ **404/873-2453.** No cover.

Loosely linked to counterparts in Manhattan, Washington, D.C., and Chicago, The Eagle is Atlanta's premier leather bar for genuinely tough guys and guys who want to look that way. The venue is hyper-masculine, and in many cases, genuinely friendly. Most of the socializing here takes place on the street-level bar, but in the cellar is a boutique hawking the accouterments you might have always wanted to buy, but were never able to find at your local suburban shopping mall.

The Heretic. 2069 Cheshire Bridge Rd. ☎ **404/325-3061.** No cover.

Come here for hot music, a big dance floor, and the close proximity of hundreds of buff, well-muscled, and glistening men and men/boys fresh from the gym and/ or the most recent circuit party. Most of the clients are under 35, and hail from virtually everywhere on the North American mainland. Time spent here will really convince you that Atlanta's populace comes from far, far beyond the borders of Georgia. Depending on the night of your arrival, there might be a high percentage of leather and uniforms, even a bit of latex, especially every Wednesday and Sunday after 10pm.

Hoedowns. 931 Monroe Dr. ☎ **404/876-0001.** No cover.

It's cited as the most fun and most charming gay bar in Atlanta. Here cowboys are dancing with cowboys, and the look is long-legged and lean and evokes home on the range within a very urban and very hip setting. There's virtually no attitude among the crowds of steer-busters who hang out here. Tight jeans, Stetsons, and boots are the preferred dress code, and no one will mind if you opt for some chaps and spurs, too.

My Sister's Room. 222 East Howard Ave. ☎ **404/370-1990.** No cover. MARTA: Decatur.

This lesbian club is in Decatur, about 4 miles east of Midtown. Its appealing setting is an old stable from the 1890s, with a landscaped garden and marble-floored terrace. Sandwiches and simple platters are available every day from 11am to 1am, priced from $4.95 to $10.95; wine costs from $3.50 to $5.50 a glass. The main thing is the bar, where women from all walks of life gather for dialogues and conversation. Well-behaved men who happen to wander in are welcome, or at least are tolerated.

✪ **The Otherside.** 1924 Piedmont Rd. (just north of Cheshire Bridge Rd.). ☎ **404/ 875-5238.** Cover $5 Wed and Fri–Sat. Valet parking $3.

This club recoils at attempts to categorize it. Considering the radical eclecticism of the clientele (married couples, single gay men, lesbians, and a spectrum of all the gender-benders in between), a simple description is well-nigh impossible; that adds, however, to the place's sense of fun. It occupies what was originally built as a Steak & Ale chain franchise in Buckhead. There's also a martini bar and a very large disco/dance floor where country-western line-dancing lessons are given every Thursday night, as well as a pair of indoor/outdoor patios.

11 A Side Trip to Kennesaw Mountain

Located 2 miles north of Marietta, off U.S. 41 (the Cobb Parkway), the **Kennesaw Mountain Battlefield National Park** (☎ **770/427-4686**) honors the sites of two major Civil War battles. These are the Battle of Kolb Farmhouse (June 22, 1864) and the Battle of Kennesaw Mountain (June 27, 1864). Both served as temporary setbacks for the infamous march of Union General William Sherman, who eventually bypassed the site's Confederate strongholds and marched over a different route to capture Atlanta. Today the site is marked as a bloody setback for Union troops (Sherman lost 2,000 members of his 16,000-man army, considerably more than the Confederates) and an icon of Confederate pride.

There are 15 miles of walking trails that follow the 11 miles of once-bloody trench lines and bunkers that defined Yankee and Confederate positions. Energetic visitors can climb the signposted trail leading to the top of **Big Kennesaw Mountain** (1,808 feet), where a view extends out over Marietta to faraway Atlanta.

The park's **visitor center** is open daily from 8:30am to 5pm (until 6pm on mid-summer weekends). The park itself is open daily from 8am to 8:30pm. During week-ends throughout the year, there's a free shuttle between the visitor center and the top of Kennesaw Mountain. From Atlanta, take I-75 north to Exit 116 (Barrett Parkway) and follow the signs to the park. Entrance is free.

The **Kennesaw Civil War Museum,** 2829 Cherokee St. (☎ **770/427-2117**), houses a steam-driven locomotive (*The General*) that was highjacked by Union spies in 1862. Admission is $3 for adults, $2.50 for seniors, $1.50 for children 7 to 15, and free for children 6 and under. It's open March to November, daily from 9:30am to 5:30pm; December to February, Monday to Saturday from 10am to 4pm and on Sunday from noon to 4pm.

17

Athens, the Antebellum Trail & Augusta

If you looked for antebellum Georgia around Atlanta, you were in the right church but the wrong pew. The state's pre–Civil War moonlight-and-magnolias romance lives on, and you'll find it some 60 to 100 miles east of Atlanta in charming old towns with patriotic names like Washington, Madison, and Milledgeville, the three classic antebellum towns that Sherman didn't burn. And although the cities of central Georgia that lie along the Antebellum Trail are cut off from the mountains or the seashore, they are at the doorstep of some of the state's most mammoth lakes.

This area also encompasses two of the most famous cities of Georgia, Athens and Augusta. Athens, called "The Classic City," is the home of the University of Georgia, and lies in a setting beside the Oconee River. Many of its restored and still occupied antebellum houses make it a worthwhile stopover. Augusta, founded in 1736, is today famed as the headquarters of the Masters Golf Tournament the first full week in April.

1 Athens

85 miles NW of Augusta; 58 miles E of Atlanta

Just below the foothills of the Blue Ridge Mountains, near the confluence of the North and Middle Oconee rivers, lies the city of Athens amid the rolling red-clay hills of North Georgia.

Athens' fame grew because of the University of Georgia, which covers 605 acres and includes 313 buildings in the center. The university was incorporated in 1785, making it America's first state-chartered college. Abraham Baldwin, one of Georgia's four signers of the U.S. Constitution, was named president. Today, the University of Georgia is ranked among the nation's top research institutions, and boasts America's 19th largest library and many nationally recognized programs of study, including pharmacy, business, and journalism. More than 28,000 students attend the university.

In the last 2 decades, Athens has gained national attention for its music scene as well. This was where R.E.M., the Indigo Girls, and the B-52s got their start. They occasionally return to Athens to play local clubs, but their presence is felt philanthropically through donations to local homeless shelters and AIDS organizations. The town still has a thriving music scene—the latest buzz is around Elephant 6, a conglomerate of several bands who creatively mix and match members.

ESSENTIALS

GETTING THERE From Atlanta, take I-85 northwest to Highway 316, which leads the rest of the way to Athens. From Augusta, take I-20 west to Atlanta, cutting northwest on Highway 78 into Athens, going via Washington.

US Airways (☎ **800/428-4322** or 706/549-5783; www.usairways.com) offers flights only between Athens and Charlotte, North Carolina. Planes land at Athens-Ben Epps Airport (☎ **706/613-3420**).

VISITOR INFORMATION **Athens Welcome Center,** 280 E. Dougherty St. (☎ **706/353-1820**), is open from 10am to 6pm Monday to Saturday and from noon-6pm on Sunday.

SPECIAL EVENTS The best time to visit is during the **Historic Homes Tour,** the last weekend in April. Sponsored by the Athens-Clarke Heritage Foundation, this is one of the most attended events in East Georgia. For information, call ☎ **706/353-1801.**

SEEING THE SIGHTS

Athens begins Georgia's antebellum trail and showcases several buildings of note, many centered around the University of Georgia.

The **Taylor-Grady House,** 634 Prince Ave. (☎ **706/549-8688**), a Greek revival home constructed in the 1840s by General Robert Taylor, planter and cotton merchant, is open year-round. Filled with period furniture, it has 13 columns said to symbolize the original 13 states. Henry W. Grady, a native of Athens, lived here from 1865 to 1868. As managing editor of the *Atlanta Constitution,* he became a spokesperson for the New South. Admission is $3, and hours are Monday to Friday from 9am to 5pm. Closed 1 to 2:30pm.

Athens' **Double Barreled Cannon** is the only one of its kind in the world, and is among the most unusual relics preserved from the Civil War. It was designed by John Gilleland and built at a local foundry in 1863. The concept was to load the cannon with two balls connected by a chain several feet in length. When fired, the balls and chain would whirl out, bola-style, and cut down the unfortunate enemy soldiers caught in the path of this murderous missile. It stands on the City Hall lawn at College and Hancock avenues.

"The Tree That Owns Itself," at Dearing and Finley streets, is another Athens landmark. William H. Jackson, a professor at the University of Georgia, owned the land on which a large oak stood. He took such delight in the shade of the tree that he willed the tree 8 feet of land surrounding its trunk. The original tree blew down in a windstorm in 1942. The local garden club planted a sapling on the land in 1946, grown from one of the acorns from the original. Locals refer to the tree as "the world's most unusual heir and property owner."

The ✪ **University of Georgia's** main campus extends 2 miles south from "The Arch" at College Avenue and Broad Street. For information, call ☎ **706/542-3000.**

The current campus was established in 1801. John Milledge, late governor of the state, purchased and gave the board of trustees the chosen tract of 633 acres on the banks of the Oconee River. The view from the hill on which the 1832 Chapel now stands reminded Milledge of the Acropolis in Athens, and the hill was named after its Greek forbear, the classical center of learning. The school produced its first graduating class in 1804. Later funds were raised for the first permanent structure on campus, Old College (1806), which still stands today.

The **State Botanical Garden of Georgia,** 2450 S. Milledge Ave. (☎ **706/542-1244**), encompassing 313 acres, is a "living laboratory" in teaching and research.

It's open to the public to enjoy its three-story conservatory featuring a display of tropical and semitropical plants. Along the garden's 5 miles of nature trails are diverse ecosystems, with many plants labeled. There are nearly a dozen specialty gardens. The garden lies a mile from U.S. 441, about 3 miles from the university campus. Admission is free; it's open daily from 8am to sunset. A Visitor Center and the Conservatory are open Tuesday to Saturday from 9am to 4:30pm and on Sunday from 11:30am to 4:30pm. Grounds open daily April to September 8am to 8pm; October to March 8am to 6pm.

The Georgia Museum of Art, Jackson Street (☎ 706/542-3254), is the official state art museum, offering an extensive collection of American paintings, prints, and drawings. It is open Tuesday to Saturday from 10am to 5pm, Wednesday from 10am to 9pm, and Sunday from 1 to 5pm. Closed Monday. Admission is free.

Founders Memorial Garden and Houses, 325 S. Lumpkin St. on the University of Georgia campus (☎ 706/542-8972), became the first garden club in the United States, founded in 1891 by 12 Athens women. Set on 2½ acres, it offers varying landscapes and the seasonal foliage of a Southern garden. Plantings range from the native to the exotic, and the gardens are a particular delight in spring when the azaleas burst into bloom. The boxwood garden evokes the formality of bygone ages, and the camellia walk is notable. Admission is free, and the garden is open during daylight hours.

OUTDOOR PURSUITS

Sandy Creek Nature Center, half a mile north of the Athens bypass, off U.S. 441, offers some 200 acres of woodland and marshland, with a live animal exhibit. It has many nature trails for hikers, and on site is a cabin nearly 2 centuries old. For more information, call ☎ 706/613-3615.

Visitors can enjoy **Sandy Creek Park,** north on U.S. 441 (signposted). It offers a beach, fishing, playgrounds for children, softball, volleyball, and shelters for picnics. Paddleboats and canoes can be rented. Hours from April through September are 7am to 10pm Thursday to Tuesday. Off-season hours are Thursday to Sunday from 7am to 7pm.

Golf can be played at the **Green Hills Country Club** (☎ 706/548-6032), an 18-hole, par-72 course at 4080 Barnett-Shoals Rd. Greens fees are $26 to $34, and hours are daily 7:15am to dusk.

WHERE TO STAY

In addition to the listings below, there's a **Holiday Inn** at 197 E. Broad St. (☎ 800/TO-ATHENS or 706/549-4433).

Magnolia Terrace. 277 Hill St., Athens, GA 30601. ☎ **706/548-3860.** Fax 706/546-8040. 7 units. A/C TV. $95–$135 double. Rates include continental breakfast. AE, DISC, MC, V.

In the Cobbham historic district, close to the center of town, this large 1912 house is one of the best B&Bs in the area. Each tastefully furnished guest room offers a private bathroom with period claw-foot tubs and modern showers or whirlpools. It's a hospitable place, warm and gracious.

Nicholson House. 6295 Jefferson Rd. (5 miles north of the UGA campus), Athens, GA 30607. ☎ **706/353-2200.** Fax 706/353-7799. www.bbonline.com/ga/nicholson. E-mail: chneely@aol.com. 9 units. A/C TV TEL. $89–$119 double. Rates include full breakfast. AE, DISC, MC, V.

On 6 wooded acres of rolling hills, this property, run by Stuart Kelley, is a riot of magnolias and azaleas in the spring. Its history goes back to 1779 when land was granted to William Few, a signer of the U.S. Constitution. Now restored, it offers six large, tastefully furnished bedrooms with feather and down pillows on queen- or king-size beds. Each room is equipped with private bathroom, and a large breakfast is served.

✪ Rivendell. 3581 S. Barnett Shoals Rd. (10 miles SE of Athens), Watkinsville, GA 30677. ☎ **706/769-4522.** Fax 706/769-4393. www.negia.net/~rivendel. 5 units. A/C. $70–$85 double. Rates include full breakfast. MC, V. Drive 8 miles south on U.S. 441, then 5 miles west on Barnett Shoals Rd. No children under 11.

Although it was only built in 1989, this inn contains many architectural features that make you think it's much older. Set on the Oconee River on 11 acres of forested private land, it's the finest inn in the area. It contains lofty beamed ceilings, two fireplaces crafted from large stones, antiques collected from around the world, and big windows opening onto views of the surrounding countryside. There are walking paths for woodland strolls with many nice places to stop for picnicking. Complimentary tea and sherry are provided in the afternoon. No smoking.

WHERE TO DINE

✪ Chef Wolfgang's European Cuisine. 1074 Baxter St. ☎ **706/369-8333.** Reservations recommended. Main courses $9.50–$17.50. Mon–Fri 11:30am–2:30pm. AE, DISC, MC, V. Mon–Sat 4–10pm. CONTINENTAL.

The culinary finesse of owner and resident chef Wolfgang Kluth, a denizen of Düsseldorf, has inspired hundreds of students in places as far away as Saudi Arabia and the Cayman Islands. Head for a modern, not particularly dramatic building on a commercial street and enter a dining room outfitted with the Asian and local art Wolfgang has collected. A cosmopolitan staff will take your order for such specialties as the town's best version of oysters Rockefeller, rouladen of beef (stuffed beef with bacon, onions, dill pickles, and mustard), German sauerbraten, beef tenderloin prepared Wellington-style, Hungarian paprika schnitzel, and rainbow trout amandine. On Friday and Saturday nights a string quartet plays. Wolfgang is in the top tier of Athens' chefs, with a cuisine authentic enough to merit kudos from everyone from Muhammed Ali to the Queen of England, for whom he has prepared lavish banquets.

East West Bistro. 351 E. Broad St. ☎ **706/546-9378.** Reservations recommended. Upstairs main courses $12–$20; downstairs sandwiches and pizzas $5–$8, main courses $10–$13. AE, MC, V. Sun–Thurs 11am–10pm, Fri–Sat 11am–11pm. FUSION.

This place, which opened in 1995 on the main street in Athens, is all the rage. Upstairs, dining is more formal, in a classically styled room where the fare of Northern Italy is sometimes prepared with zest and flavor, though the other dishes are uneven at best. Depending on the night, many dishes merit a rave, whereas others, such as shrimp and mussels tossed with spaghetti in a mild red-curry cream sauce, don't make it. Try fresh grilled yellowfin tuna with a parsley caper butter or chicken breast breaded with shaved ginger and orange instead. Downstairs is the largest selection of tapas in Athens, including carpaccio and a Thai ratatouille crepe. Main dishes range from jerk chicken to salmon in rice paper.

Harry Bissett's New Orleans Café & Oyster Bar. 279 E. Broad St. ☎ **706/353-7065.** Reservations recommended for large parties. Main courses $12.95–$20.95. AE, DC, DISC, MC, V. Tues–Sun 11:30am–3pm, Mon–Sun 5:30–11pm. CAJUN/SEAFOOD.

At the gates to the University of Georgia, this is one of the enduring favorites of locals, both students and faculty. Up front is a bar with tables, although a more formal dining room is found in the rear. This building used to be a bank, and the tin ceiling is still intact. A selection of meat dishes—certified Angus only—includes "carpetbagger steak," which is really filet mignon topped with fried oysters. Cajun dishes include crawfish tails, Louisiana oysters, and blackened fresh catch of the day seasoned liberally and seared in a black-iron skillet. You might also try grilled andouille sausage and Gulf shrimp tossed with pasta Alfredo. Dishes are generally reliable, some zesty and full of flavor.

The Last Resort. 174–184 W. Clayton St. ☎ **706/549-0810.** Reservations not accepted. Main courses $7.95–$21. AE, MC, V. Daily 11am–3pm, Sun–Thurs 5–10pm, Fri–Sat 5–11pm. MODERN SOUTHERN.

This is the most artsy haunt in town, attracting a mostly young college crowd. Although its days as a center for avant-garde music are over, it's still a place to find out what's happening in town. We prefer the booths in the bar area, although others like the courtyard with its open end protected by ornate grillwork. In chilly weather, a gas heater blasts away. The chefs really try hard, and many of their dishes are among the best in town, but it's a hit-or-miss affair. Check out the blackboard specialties, or try your luck and sample grilled salmon with Charlestonian grits, chicken stuffed with cheese and covered with a honey praline sauce, or chipotle pork chops grilled and marinated.

ATHENS AFTER DARK

To find out who's playing and what's on tonight, pick up *Flagpole,* Athens' arts, entertainment, and events weekly, free at many shops, restaurants, bars, and clubs. Another good barometer of what's happening is the UGA student newspaper, the *Red and Black.* Remember that this is a college town, so the nightlife scene is much hotter during the school year. Most of the music clubs and bars present nightly live bands from September through June only, shrinking their offerings to just the weekends in the summer.

You can hit **Boneshakers,** 433 E. Hancock Ave. (☎ 706/543-1555), with recorded techno and retro dance music (mostly disco and '80s). They stop serving drinks at 2am, but the dancing goes on much longer. This is also the gay-friendliest joint in town, and you can show up in anything from jeans and a T-shirt to drag.

If you just want to listen, make a pilgrimage to the famous **40 Watt Club,** 285 W. Washington St. (☎ 706/549-7871), the little joint that launched the B-52s and R.E.M. Although you can still hear up-and-coming local bands, these days the 40 Watt is more geared toward national bands, such as Luscious Jackson or the Lemonheads. They also run a late-night disco several times a week, as does the **Georgia Theatre,** 215 Lumpkin St., at the corner of Clayton Street (☎ 706/549-9918). A former movie theater, it gives local college-rock bands (along with a smattering of blues and Southern rock) the chance to jam long into the night. Oh, that skinny guy standing in the corner may just be Michael Stipe.

Our favorite bar in town by far, however, is **The Globe,** 199 N. Lumpkin St. at Clayton Street (☎ 706/353-4721). The place seems more like a bar in New York's Greenwich Village than a watering hole in Athens. In the mix are students, an occasional filmmaker, and a cross-cultural selection of anyone from hip latter-day rebels to necktie-toting salesmen in town for a fling. It's like an English pub, with the largest selection of exotic beers in Athens, more than 150 brands. It also has a collection of 30 kinds of single-malt whiskies that would gladden the heart of any Scotsman. Try Laphroaig or Macallan. There's also wine, port, and sherry, served by the glass, and nine boutique bourbons. Oh, and that skinny guy reading alone at one of the tables just might be Michael Stipe.

2 Madison

52 miles E of Atlanta; 73 miles W of Augusta; 21 miles N of Eatonton

Madison, off I-20, an hour's drive east from Atlanta, was once populated by wealthy merchants and cotton planters who erected houses that were fine examples of Federal and Greek Revival architecture. Antebellum travelers called it "the wealthiest and most aristocratic village between Charleston and New Orleans." Late in 1864, with Atlanta in flames, Gen. William T. Sherman's Union juggernaut reached Madison's outskirts. Happily for us, they were met by former U.S. Senator Joshua Hill, a secession opponent who'd known Sherman in Washington. Old ties prevailed, and the town was spared.

Today, thousands of visitors come to see the oak-lined streets, the historic homes, the parks, gardens, churches, galleries, and antiques shops. The historic district encompasses most of the town and was recognized by the Department of Interior as one of the finest such districts in the South.

ESSENTIALS

The Chamber of Commerce, P.O. Box 826, 115 E. Jefferson St. (☎ 706/ 342-4454), dispenses information about Madison and the area. It is open Monday to Friday from 8:30am to 5pm, Saturday 10am to 5pm, and Sunday 1 to 4pm.

SEEING THE SIGHTS

Stop first at the **Madison-Morgan Cultural Center,** 434 S. Main St., U.S. 441 (☎ 706/342-4743). The redbrick schoolhouse, circa 1895, features a history museum on the Piedmont region of Georgia, an 1895 classroom museum, art galleries with changing exhibits, and an auditorium for presentations. Programs range from Shakespeare to chamber orchestras to gospel singing. Open Tuesday to Saturday 10am to 5pm, Sunday 2 to 5pm. Adults pay $3, children $2.

Pick up a self-guided walking-tour map and other information at the center and walk past the majestic Greek Revival, Federal, Georgian, neoclassical, and Victorian homes lining Main Street, Academy Street, Old Post Road, and the courthouse square. You'll find plenty of places to purchase antiques and handcrafts.

You can relax outdoors at **Hard Labor Creek State Park** (☎ 706/557-3001), near Madison. Leave town via I-20 West and take Exit 49 into Rutledge, then drive 2 miles on Fairplay Road to the park. *Golf* magazine rates the park's 18-hole course as one of the finest public courses in America. You can also swim at a sand beach, fish for bass and catfish, and hike the 5,000 wooded acres. The park has 51 campsites with electricity, water, rest rooms, and showers for $15 a night, and 20 fully furnished two-bedroom cottages at $75 (Sunday to Thursday) and $85 (Friday and Saturday) a night. A Michael J. Fox movie, *Poison Ivy,* was filmed here in the middle 1980s.

WHERE TO STAY

Brady Inn. 250 N. Second St., Madison, GA 30650. ☎ **706/342-4400.** 8 units. $75 double, $150 suite. Rates include full breakfast. AE, DISC, MC, V.

These restored Victorian cottages lie in the center of the historic district (they were once two private homes linked by a walkway). Rooms are tastefully furnished, often with antiques, and the breakfast is most generous. You get old-fashioned hospitality here, along with a good night's sleep.

WHERE TO DINE

Old Colonial Restaurant. 108 E. Washington St. ☎ **706/342-2211.** Reservations not accepted. Full breakfasts $3.50–$5.75; main lunch and dinner courses $3.75–$4.95. DISC, MC, V. Mon–Sat 5:30am–8:30pm.

This is the busiest restaurant in Madison. The site it occupies, close to the town's main square, comprises an early-18th-century tavern that later functioned as a bank and a storefront. The staff manages to be friendly, helpful, and restrained all at the same time. Don't expect grand cuisine: Breakfast is served by the staff at your table; lunches and dinners are summer-camp cafeteria style, with copious portions of Southern vegetables and meat. The atmosphere's just as old-fashioned as the food. If you like candied yams, pork chops, and collard greens, come on in. Cornbread is served with everything.

3 Eatonton

21 miles S of Madison; 22 miles N of Milledgeville; 47 miles NE of Macon; 75 miles SE of Atlanta

Home of Br'er Rabbit and the Uncle Remus tales, this town, filled with antebellum architecture, is a sleepy old place of tree-lined streets and historic homes. Eatonton is not only the original home of Joel Chandler Harris, who created the Uncle Remus tales, but also of Alice Walker, author and Pulitzer Prize winner for *The Color Purple*.

ESSENTIALS

To get here from Madison, take Highway 441 South.

The **Eatonton-Putnam Chamber of Commerce,** 105 Sumter St. (☎ **706/ 485-7701**), dispenses information Monday to Friday 8:30am to 4:30pm.

SEEING THE SIGHTS

Uncle Remus Museum, Highway 441 South (☎ **706/485-6856**), lies in Turner Park, three blocks south of the courthouse. It has a kid-pleasing collection of memorabilia about Br'er Rabbit, Br'er Fox, and Harris's other storybook critters. The log cabin is the combination of two former slave cabins. In each window are scenes of a Southern plantation during the antebellum days. The museum is open Monday to Saturday 10am to 5pm (except 1 hour for lunch), Sunday 2 to 5pm. Admission is 50¢ for adults, 25¢ for children. Closed Tuesday from September through May.

Bronson House, 114 N. Madison Ave. (☎ **706/485-6442**), is the home of the Eatonton/Putnam Historical Society. Constructed in 1822 by Thomas T. Napier, it was purchased in 1852 by Andrew Reid, who was the first patron of Joel Chandler Harris. The author lived with his mother in a tiny cottage in back of the mansion. Several rooms of the Greek Revival mansion have been restored, displaying local memorabilia. The house can be visited only by appointment.

Two sights in the environs of Eatonton merit a visit, including **Lake Oconee,** east of Ga. 16 and north on Ga. 44. This 19,000-acre lake with 375 miles of shoreline was created when the Oconee River was impounded. You can camp, swim at the beach, fish, and boat (there's a marina). Because of a laissez-faire attitude from Georgia Power about shoreline restrictions, Lake Oconee has also been the site of golf community development. For more information, call ☎ **706/485-8704.**

Rock Eagle Effigy lies 7 miles north on U.S. 441, in the Rock Eagle 4-H Center. Shaped like a gigantic prone bird, the 8-foot-high mound of milky quartz has its head turned to the east with outspread wings. It measures more than 100 feet from wingtip to wingtip, the body rising about 10 feet above the ground. The monument may be 5,000 years old and was used, or so it's believed, by Native Americans as a part of religious rites. The monument may be viewed from an observation tower. For more information, call ☎ **706/484-2800.**

WHERE TO STAY

The Crockett House. 671 Madison Rd. (1¼ miles north of the center of town), Eatonton, GA 31024. ☎ **706/485-2248.** www.bbonline.com/ga/crocketthouse. 6 units. A/C. $85–$95 double. Each additional person $20. Rates include full breakfast. MC, V.

This Victorian house was built in 1895. In 1993 it was fully restored by Christa and Peter Crockett and opened as a B&B. The house is set on 4 acres of forested land, with no other buildings in sight. The exterior is painted in shades of lilac and pink, and contains cozy and tasteful public rooms, working fireplaces (11 in all), pinewood floors, 12-foot ceilings, antiques, and an ambience like that of a private home. A bountiful breakfast, usually featuring baked apples and "Crockett House featherbed eggs," is included in the price and served communally in the dining room.

4 Milledgeville

20 miles S of Eatonville; 30 miles NE of Macon; 90 miles SE of Atlanta

This town ranks along with Washington and Madison in historic sights. Locals will tell you this is, in fact, "the antebellum capital" of Georgia. Carved from Native American territories in 1803, Milledgeville was the capital of Georgia until 1868 when the seat was moved to Atlanta. Like Madison, Milledgeville was miraculously spared by General Sherman, and today remains a treasure trove of antebellum architecture.

ESSENTIALS

From Eatonton, follow U.S. 441 south into Milledgeville.

The Welcome Center of the **Milledgeville-Baldwin County Convention & Visitors Bureau** is at 200 W. Hancock St. (☎ 912/452-4687) and is open Monday to Friday from 8:30am to 5pm and Saturday from 10am to 4pm.

SEEING THE SIGHTS

Old Governors Mansion, 120 S. Clark St. (☎ **912/445-4545**), a pink marble Palladian beauty, has been exquisitely restored and refurbished as the home of the president of Georgia College. You may tour the antiques-rich public rooms. The mansion was the home of Georgia's governors from 1839 to 1868. This National Historic Landmark house is an excellent example of Greek Revival architecture. Guided tours begin on the hour from Tuesday to Saturday from 10am to 4pm and on Sunday from 2 to 4pm. Admission is $5 for adults, $1 for children 12 to 17, and free for children 11 and under.

The mansion is on the campus of **Georgia College & State University,** 231 W. Hancock St. (☎ 912/454-2771), a former women's college that dates from 1889 and today is home to some 5,500 students. The college occupies four 20-acre plots. You may want to stroll about the campus.

At the college's **Ina Dillard Russell Library** on Clark Street (☎ 912/445-4047), you can visit the Flannery O'Connor Room. O'Connor, distinguished author of *The Violent Bear It Away* and *A Good Man Is Hard to Find,* lived in Milledgeville and received a bachelor of arts degree from Georgia College, but her former home is not open to the public. You can, however, visit **Memory Hill Cemetery,** the oldest burial ground in the city, where the author is buried along with state legislators, Wild West outlaws, slaves, soldiers, and patriots.

The easiest way to see the town is to take a Historic Guided Trolley Tour. The 2-hour tour explores the major sights in the town, including the old governor's mansion and the former state capitol building (circa 1807). Tours depart Monday to Friday at 10am from the visitors bureau (see above), Saturdays at 2pm. Cost of the tours is $10 for adults, $5 for children 6 to 16, and free for children 6 and under.

Nearby, you can visit **Lake Sinclair,** north on U.S. 441, a 15,330-acre lake with 417 miles of shoreline. It was created when the Oconee River was impounded, and is today a venue for fishing and boating. There's a marina, and camping is also possible. Phone ☎ **706/485-8704** for more information.

WHERE TO STAY

✪ Antebellum Inn. 200 N. Columbia St., Milledgeville, GA 31061. ☎ **912/453-3993** or 914/454-5400. www.alltel.net/~antebellum/. E-mail:antebellum@alltel.net. 5 units. TV TEL $65–$99 double. AE, DISC, MC, V.

Innkeepers Debbie and Hill Thompson welcome you to their well-restored 1890 Greek Revival home in the heart of the Antebellum Trail in the center of Milledgeville, just a block from the Georgia College & State University campus. The Old Governor's Mansion is just down the street. The inn has two old-fashioned parlors and five spacious bedrooms, each individually furnished. Modern amenities are installed as well, including a private phone line with an answering machine, a computer modem hookup, cable TV, and a writing desk. Several of the bedrooms have antique claw-foot bathtubs, and every bed is covered with tasteful linens and down comforters. The town's best B&B breakfast is served in an elegant dining room. If you'd like to recapture the feel of Georgia's former capital, find a rocking chair on the wraparound porch. The grounds are beautifully landscaped with a full-size swimming pool.

Jameson Inn. 2551 N. Columbia St., Milledgeville, GA 31061. ☎ **800/541-3268** or 912/453-8471. Fax 912/453-8482. 92 units. A/C TV TEL. $59 double; $95–$147 suite. Rates include a continental breakfast. Children under 18 stay free in parents' room. AE, DC, DISC, MC, V.

Part of a little chain known in small towns in East Georgia, the Jameson Inn is preferred over its major competitor, the 169-room Holiday Inn out on U.S. 441 North. The Jameson is a two-story inn filled with Southern comfort. Its bedrooms are strictly functional but they're well maintained, with good beds, spacious bathrooms, and fresh linens every day. Facilities include lighted tennis courts and exercise equipment such as weight machines, bicycles, a whirlpool, and a sauna. There is also a swimming pool.

WHERE TO DINE

The Brick. 136 W. Hancock St. ☎ **912/452-0089.** Main courses $5.75–$6.25; pizzas $5.75–$17.50. AE, DC, DISC, MC, V. Mon–Sat 11am–11pm. PASTAS/PIZZAS/SANDWICHES.

This local favorite was initially opened in 1993 with the object of becoming a bar and pizza joint. But what a difference a few years makes! The bar was successful and the restaurant even more so—so much that it had to move its location two doors down the street. Owners Frank Pendergast and Mitch Brooks have made the "new" Brick one of the more exciting dining experiences in a town not known for its dining. Exposed brick, an oak and walnut bar, and heart pine floors adorn a dining area that is not crowded and is conducive to family dining. The lunch and dinner menus offer a wide choice of pastas, calzones, sandwiches, and authentic brick-oven pizzas, with styles ranging from the all-meat "Cannibal" to the all-veggie "Environmentally Correct." This restaurant is a popular choice with the Milledgeville business community and with college students when parents are visiting.

For a taste of the Milledgeville nightlife, the sibling bar, the **Tavern** (née Brick), 120 W. Hancock St., serves alcoholic drinks and burgers from 4pm to 2am.

Cafe South. 132 Hardwick St., Hardwick. ☎ **912/452-3164.** Platters $5.50. AE, MC, V. Sun–Fri 11am–2pm. SOUTHERN.

About a quarter-mile south of the center in the hamlet of Hardwick, it's in an old brick-fronted building, with an old-time decor. The format is cafeteria-style—but waitresses are on hand to bring drinks and difficult-to-carry items directly to your table. Serving hours are limited, but the place is an introduction to virtually everyone in town. Everybody seems to appreciate the simple Southern menu of creamed corn, turnip greens, fried chicken, roast beef, catfish, and—when available—tuna dumplings. The restaurant also serves dinner on Friday and Saturday evenings, offering steaks, seafood, and pastas in a candlelit setting. Merry Ann Finch is the owner. Her brother, a respected local artist, displays and sells paintings of Milledgeville and the Georgia of yesteryear. This is one authentic Southern meal to truly take in and enjoy.

Nicklina's Italian Restaurant. Old Capitol Square Shopping Center, N. Columbia St. ☎ **912/453-8495.** Reservations recommended. Lunch buffets $5.50–$5.99. Main courses $5.25–11.95. Mon–Thurs 11am–2pm and 5–9pm, Fri 11am–2pm and 5–10pm, Sat noon–10pm, Sun noon–9pm. ITALIAN.

Although the namesake of the restaurant, Nicklina Tribuzio, is long gone, her memory lingers on in the respect for fine food lovingly prepared from family recipes. The best and freshest ingredients are offered here, and the food is simple but delicious. In a candlelit setting, you can feast on basic Italian favorites such as pizza, seafood, veal, and chicken dishes. Notable is the veal piccata with angel-hair pasta or the savory chicken cacciatore. A fresh kettle of soup is offered nightly, and you can order an array of salads as well, including a freshly made antipasti. The good food and low prices bring in many local college students.

5 Washington

42 miles S of Athens; 150 miles E of Atlanta; 60 miles NW of Augusta

Founded in 1773, and the first city incorporated in the name of George Washington, the ✪ city of Washington is one of the three most important antebellum towns in Georgia, ranking along with Madison and Milledgeville. It was not visited by General Sherman on his notorious Grand Tour of Georgia, and, as a result, still contains a wealth of antebellum architecture.

Washington was settled by Southern planters, mainly from Britain, who in time rebelled against British rule. At the nearby Battle of Kettle Creek, 8 miles southwest of town on Kettle Creek, off Ga. 44, the settlers destroyed the British stranglehold on Georgia.

Heard's Fort, later Washington, became the temporary capitol of Georgia in 1780. The cotton gin was perfected by Eli Whitney at Mount Pleasant plantation, just east of Washington.

In the closing hours of the Civil War, Jefferson Davis and members of his cabinet fled here to sign the last official papers to dissolve the Confederacy. The site was the Heard House, which no longer stands, although a marker on the main square in Washington indicates where this historic event took place.

ESSENTIALS

GETTING THERE   Take I-20 East from Atlanta to Exit 59, turning left to Washington; from Augusta, take I-20 West to Exit 59, turning right for Washington.

VISITOR INFORMATION   The **Washington-Wilkes Chamber of Commerce,** 104 Liberty St. (☎ 706/678-2013), is open Monday to Friday from 9am to 5pm.

SEEING THE SIGHTS

✪ **Robert Toombs House State Historic Site.** 216 E. Robert Toombs Ave. ☎ **706/ 678-2226.** Admission $2.50 adults, $1.50 children 5–18, free for children 4 and under. Tues–Fri 9am–5pm, Sat 2–5pm.

This restored home was the residence of that unreconstructed Confederate statesman and soldier, Robert Toombs, former brigadier general in the Confederate army who served briefly under President Jefferson Davis (a man he despised) as Secretary of State of the Confederacy.

On May 11, 1865, Yankee troops arrived at his home with orders to hang the former leader from an oak tree on his front yard. His wife, Julia, stalled the troops until her husband could escape on horseback. He fled into the Georgia mountains and became a fugitive in his own country, eventually escaping to Cuba where he made his way to Paris, there to live a bitter life. He returned home just before Christmas in 1866, upon learning of the death of his last living child, Sallie. He refused a presidential pardon from Andrew Johnson. "A pardon?" Toombs asked. "I have done nothing to ask forgiveness for, and I have not pardoned *them* yet!" He spent his remaining years denouncing the "carpetbag rule" of the Reconstruction South, participated in state politics, and was a major force in rewriting the Georgia Constitution. Twenty years after the end of the Civil War, Toombs died at the age of 75.

The frame Federal-style house with a Greek Revival portico is filled with Toombs memorabilia and antique furniture. The house was originally built in 1797 but went through five architectural face-lifts: Federal, Plantation Plain, Greek Revival, Victorian, and Neoclassical. Relatives of the Toombs family lived here until 1973, when the state purchased the house and hired Edward Neal, a Columbus architect, to restore it as it was at the time of General Toombs' death in 1885. Visitors can view a dramatic film, portraying the elderly Toombs relating his sad story to a young reporter.

Callaway Plantation. 5 miles west on U.S. 78. ☎ **706/678-7060.** Admission $4 adults, $2 children. Tues–Sat 10am–5pm, Sun 2–5pm.

This early-American building outside Washington, across from the town's small airport, is designed to illustrate life in the various periods of history of the area. A working plantation, the complex includes a redbrick Greek Revival mansion from 1869. There's also a gray-framed "Federal plainstyle" house circa 1790, with period furnishings. Exhibits include the old kitchen, a formal parlor, and a dignified but rather bleak series of upstairs bedrooms. Accompanied by a local guide, you can also visit several outbuildings.

Washington-Wilkes Historical Museum. 308 E. Robert Toombs Ave. ☎ **706/ 678-2105.** Admission $2 adults, $1 children 5–12, free for children 4 and under. Tues–Sat 10am–5pm, Sun 2–5pm.

The rich history of Washington comes alive at this museum housed in a white clapboard antebellum house circa 1836. Much Civil War memorabilia is exhibited, along with utensils and agricultural equipment. The house has been splendidly restored and furnished. Look for the Confederate gun collection and artifacts of Native Americans.

WHERE TO STAY

Jameson Inn. 115 Ann Denard Dr., Washington, GA 30673. ☎ **706/678-7925.** Fax 706/ 678-7925. 41 units. A/C TV TEL. $53–$57 double. AE, DC, DISC, MC, V.

This is the leading motel in Washington. Crisply modern and inviting, it is the best-maintained and best-managed inn in the county. Designed in a two-story mall with distinct references to 18th-century colonial architecture, it offers a charming staff, comfortable bedrooms with good beds and adequate-size bathrooms, and a two-story format that emulates a drive-through motel but with considerably more grace. Bedrooms are cozy and clean, outfitted with wood-grained furniture. Rates can go up considerably around the Masters golf tournament.

WHERE TO DINE

Another Thyme. 5 E. Public Sq. ☎ **706/678-1672.** Main courses $8.95–$18. AE, DISC, MC, V. Mon–Sat 11am–2:30pm and 6–9pm. NEW AMERICAN/INTERNATIONAL

It's the first restaurant most locals mention when they're looking for a cozy, well-orchestrated meal. Situated in an antique 19th-century storefront on the town's main square, it's steeped in turn-of-the-century memorabilia. Owner Evelyn Bennett, veteran of several trips to France and author of a well-received cookbook, and her cadre of local helpers prepare a changing array of homemade soups, salads, and platters. Sometimes the place resembles an outing at the local country club, filled with the comings and goings of the local gentry, politicos, and business leaders of this close-knit town. At lunch, you can order sandwiches made with homemade bread. Perhaps grilled salmon will be featured on the menu, or else you might prefer baked ham with a honey-mustard sauce.

6 Crawfordville

45 miles SE of Athens; 90 miles E of Atlanta; 55 miles W of Augusta; 20 miles SE of Washington

The moment you arrive in sleepy Crawfordville, you experience déjà vu. You've been to this town before, or at least you feel you have. If you're a moviegoer, you may have seen the Main Street of Crawfordville many times. Locals have dubbed it the Tinseltown of East Georgia. It's been used in a number of films—*Summer of My German Soldier,* a 1940s tale with Kristy McNichol, *Coward of the County* with Kenny Rogers and Dan Biggers, *Paris Trout* with Dennis Hopper and Barbara Hershey, and *Passion for Justice,* with Jane Seymour portraying a newspaper editor. It's also been used as a backdrop for *Carolina Skeletons,* with Lou Gosset, Jr. and Bruce Dern, and *Neon Bible,* with Gena Rowlands.

Since the days of the Depression, no one could afford to make any improvements on the Main Street, so it exists today as a living monument to the early 1930s.

Crawfordville lies only 2 miles off I-20, about midway between Atlanta and Augusta. Take Exit 55 and go north on Highway 22 for 2 miles. Go east on U.S. 278 1 mile to Crawfordville.

SEEING THE SIGHTS

The town's major attraction is the ✪ **A. H. Stephens State Historic Park** (☎ **706/ 456-2602**), site of **Liberty Hall** (☎ **706/456-2221**). The park is named for A. H. Stephens, vice president of the Confederacy and former governor of Georgia. He lived at Liberty Hall from 1834 until his death in 1883. The home has been restored, and is very much as it was in this Georgia hero's day. Some of the antiques on display were used by the Stephens family, and the former vice president's bedroom is furnished with original pieces. Stephens was imprisoned at Fort Warren for part of 1865, at the end of the Civil War. Small in stature and frail in health, he seldom weighed more than 90 pounds.

Adjacent to Liberty Hall is an impressive **Confederate Museum** (☎ **706/ 456-2221**), housing uniforms of the men in gray, along with a display of muskets, swords, documents, letters, diaries, and more than 300 other items related to the Civil War and Stephens. The exhibit is one of the finest collections of Confederate artifacts in Georgia. The museum is open Tuesday to Saturday from 9am to 5pm and Sunday from 2 to 5pm. Admission is $2.50 for adults and $1.50 for children.

The park, which is open daily from 7am to 10pm and charges no admission, offers boating, fishing, hiking, camping, biking, and walking opportunities. It has two lakes along with outdoor cooking and even dancing facilities. Many area residents hunt here, mainly for deer, although wild turkey and squirrels are targets as well. The park stretches across 1,200 acres, with 25 tent and trailer sites. It has an Olympic-size swimming pool and embraces the 18-acre Lake Buncombe, with public fishing. The lake is stocked with bass and brim. The smaller 2½-acre Lake Liberty—stocked with catfish—also offers public fishing. Historic nature trails cut through the park.

WHERE TO DINE

Do not rush to get the editors of *Bon Appétit* on the phone. One old-timer told us that the food served today in Crawfordville was exactly as he recalls it from when he was young here in 1914. But for good, simple, filling fare that's as American as apple pie, you've come to the right place.

Heavy's Barbecue. 2155 Sparta Rd. SE, 4 miles south of Crawfordville. ☎ **706/456-2445.** Sandwiches $3.25; platters $5.75–$8.25. No credit cards. Fri–Sun 9am–9pm. BARBECUE.

Since 1970, this isolated homestead has ladled up platters of barbecue every weekend to travelers from as far away as Atlanta. During deer-hunting season, you will think you have arrived on the set of a remake of *Deliverance.* It occupies a rustic log-and-plank-sided cabin straight out of summer camp, with a thick stone chimney belching up the smoke that seasons the limited array of menu items. Order as you would at a fast-food store from the battered countertop, then carry your selection to one of the three dining rooms. Each has enough accoutrements to stock a museum of local folklore, including a selection of stuffed animals and antique farm implements. Your host is William Grant ("Heavy"), who is assisted by members of his extended family. Take the chance, especially if you're with children, to wander around the compound, whose buildings include cooped-up chickens, roosters, and peacocks, a pond with its own gazebo, and old-fashioned houses. Some folks will drive hours out of the way for a taste of Heavy's.

Southern Magnolia Restaurant. Monument St., opposite the Historical Society. ☎ **706/456-3333.** All-you-can-eat buffet $6.49 lunch only, $6.95 Sun; main courses $5.99–$15.95 dinner only. AE, MC, V. Sun–Thurs 11am–3pm, Fri–Sat 11am–9pm. SOUTHERN.

Southern Magnolia is the only full-service restaurant in town. Decidedly Southern, the interior is decorated entirely with murals, including paintings by local hero Alexander Stephens, as well as paintings by other artists—*Tara* from *Gone With the Wind*, and local churches and homes. The food is decidedly Southern, too. At lunch there is an all-you-can-eat buffet, with different choices of meats and Southern-style vegetables that are so good you may want to take a nap after your meal. Dinners are in a different setting, with a full menu offering oysters, quail, crab legs, flounder, grilled chicken, liver and onions, and a special plate known as Mrs. Bonner's fried chicken—in honor of the lady who cooked for the legendary but now extinct Bonner's Cafe for more than 70 years. They also serve steaks—here the New York strip is simply known as the "Crawfordville steak," a term designed not to "offend" anyone who might not want to eat anything with a New York label.

7 Augusta

139 miles E of Atlanta; 122 miles N of Savannah

Home to one of the world's most prestigious men's professional golf tournaments, the Masters, Augusta is a Southern city of charm and grace. Lying along the banks of the Savannah River, it stands about halfway between Savannah and Atlanta, but bears little resemblance to either one.

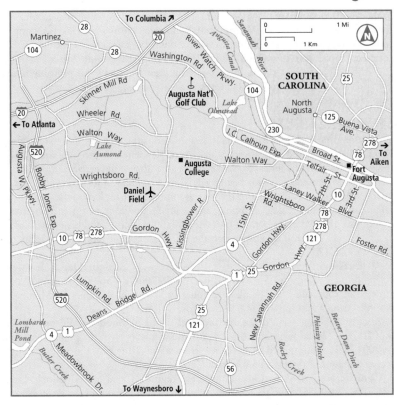

Augusta is the state's second-oldest city, dating from 1736, when it was marked off for settlement by Gen. James E. Oglethorpe, founder of Georgia. Surprisingly, long before Florida became fashionable, it was a major winter resort, attracting the Yankee wealthy seeking to escape their own bitter winters. In time, tycoons such as John D. Rockefeller, who could afford to go anywhere, selected Augusta for extended winter stays on "The Hill," also known as Summerville. Except at the time of the Masters Tournament, Augusta doesn't attract vacationers like it did in its heyday, but that's beginning to change.

ESSENTIALS

GETTING THERE   Augusta lies off I-20, the main route from Atlanta, on the west bank of the Savannah River.

Bush Field Airport lies just a 15-minute drive from the center of Augusta. Fifty commercial flights wing their way into the airport daily. Connections from Atlanta are possible via **Delta** (☎ **800/221-1212;** www.delta.com) or **US Airways** (☎ **800/ 428-4322;** www.usairways.com) from both Atlanta and Charlotte.

VISITOR INFORMATION   The **Augusta-Richmond County Convention & Visitors Bureau,** 32 Eighth St. (☎ **800/726-0243** or 706/823-6600), is open Monday to Friday 8:30am to 5pm.

SPECIAL EVENTS   It seems that half the world—at least the golfing half—focuses on Augusta the first full week in April for the nationally televised ✪ **Masters Golf Tournament,** a tradition since 1934 and now the most prestigious golf tournament in the world. Hotel space is at a premium then, and prices for rooms soar to whatever the market will bear. Call ☎ **706/667-6000** for more information. Tickets are impossible to get, but you might be able to book a multiday package that includes tickets through **Fore International** (☎ **800/798-3673**) or **Best Golf Tours** (☎ **888/817-4653**). They're not cheap, but they're your best shot, and you probably have a better chance of being struck by lightning at that—unless, of course, you're willing to part with several thousand dollars.

SEEING THE SIGHTS

The major attraction is ✪ **Riverwalk,** the tree-lined paths at the edge of the Savannah River, between 5th and 10th streets, which are resplendent with greenery and seasonal flowers. Riverwalk includes 5 blocks of unique development, including a full-service, 67-slip marina. It also boasts a 1,700-seat amphitheater that plays host to various performances throughout the year. It's also perfect for a moonlit stroll, or an afternoon spent picnicking, shopping, and enjoying one of the city's many festivals. You can see the river from both bi-level and tri-level platforms, and historical markers along the way give you an insight into the city's history. For more information, call ☎ **706/821-1754.**

Augusta's most complete antiques mall is **Riverwalk Antique Depot,** Fifth and Reynolds streets, next to St. Paul's Church (☎ **706/724-5648**), which was constructed in 1866 and is today full of antiques and collectibles. Hours are Monday to Saturday from 10am to 6pm and Sunday from 1 to 6pm.

As of this writing, you can see the **Boyhood Home of Woodrow Wilson,** 419 7th St. (☎ **706/724-0436**). It is being restored and will be open to the public some time in 2001. The future president lived here from 1860–70 during the years his father served as pastor of the First Presbyterian Church.

Confederate Powderworks, along the Augusta Canal on Goodrich Street (☎ **706/724-0436**), is a 168-foot-tall chimney, all that remains of the second-largest powder factory in the world, which operated between 1862 and 1865. It is the only permanent structure begun and completed by the Confederate government, and it once consisted of 26 buildings.

Cotton Exchange Museum and Welcome Center. 32 Eighth St. (corner of Reynolds St. and Riverwalk). ☎ **706/724-4067.** Free admission. Mon–Sat 9am–5pm, Sun 1–5pm.

In the restored Cotton Exchange Building, this was the headquarters of the city's booming cotton trade, which made Augusta the second-largest inland cotton market in the world. Many original items from the era remain, including plows, planters, tickertape machines, and a 45-foot wooden blackboard that was uncovered intact and still chalked with cotton currency and commodities' prices dating back to the early 1900s.

Ezekiel Harris House. 1822 Broad St. ☎ **706/724-0436.** Admission $2 adults, $1 seniors, 50¢ children under 18. Tues–Fri 1–4pm, Sat 10am–2pm.

Constructed by Ezekiel Harris, a leading Augusta tobacco merchant, this 1797 house re-creates the heyday of the late 18th century, when locals grew rich trading in tobacco. The planter's house is filled with period furnishings.

Gertrude Herbert Institute of Art. 506 Telfair St. ☎ **706/722-5495.** Free admission, donations accepted. Tues–Fri 8:30am–5pm, Sat 10am–2pm.

This Federal-style house was built in 1818 for Augusta mayor Nicholas Ware at the cost of $40,000—a tidy sum back then. It now serves as an art institute, a center not only for art classes but for changing exhibitions open to the public.

Meadow Garden. 1320 Independence Dr. (near the intersection of 13th St. and Walton Way). ☎ **706/724-4174.** Admission $3 adults, $1.50 seniors and children. Mon–Fri 10am–4pm.

This circa-1791 Sand Hill cottage was the home of George Walton, youngest original signer of the Declaration of Independence and twice Georgia governor. It is the oldest documented house in Augusta and the first historic preservation project in the state.

Morris Museum of Art. Riverwalk and Tenth St. ☎ **706/724-7501.** Admission $3 adults, $2 students and seniors, free for children 6 and under. Tues–Sat 10am–5:30pm, Sun 12:30–5:30pm.

This museum features period galleries that display more than 2,000 works spanning from 1790 to the present. The museum, which hosts changing exhibitions quarterly, also has a museum shop and a visitor orientation gallery. Admission is free on Sunday.

St. Paul's Episcopal Church. 605 Reynolds St. ☎ **706/724-2485.** Free admission. Tours by appointment only. Mon–Fri 9am–5pm, Sat 10am–noon. Regular worship service every Sun.

The fourth structure on the site, the St. Paul's you see today was built after a fire destroyed much of the downtown area in 1915. The first St. Paul's was constructed in 1750 as part of the site of the Fort Augusta constructed by the British in 1739. The Celtic Cross, used to designate the site, still stands. The cemetery next to the church was used during colonial days up through 1819, and many notable Georgians are buried here.

TOURS The best way to introduce yourself to Augusta is to take a 2-hour escorted tour, **Discover Augusta,** to see some of the landmarks and to hear some of the legends. Tours cost $35 for two adults ($5 for each additional participant; children under 12 go free). Call ☎ 706/736-7577 for more information.

   Historic Augusta Tours (☎ 706/724-4067) are conducted every Saturday from 10:30am to noon, leaving from the Cotton Exchange Building at 32 Eighth St. on the Riverwalk. Reservations are required by noon the Friday before. Cost is $10 for adults, $5 for children.

   Garden City Carriage Tours (☎ 706/541-0811) are horse-drawn carriages departing from Riverwalk and Eighth Street by appointment only. Rides take you along the Riverwalk and through the downtown area. Cost is $7.50 for adults, $5 for children.

GOLF & OTHER OUTDOOR PURSUITS

Golf is king in Augusta, and though the famous tournament course at Augusta National isn't open to the public, we recommend **Goshen Plantation,** 1601 Goshen House Club Dr. (☎ 706/793-1168), one of the most beautiful and challenging courses in the CSRA. Ellis Maples designed the course, which offers the largest green in Georgia. It has well-bunkered greens, demanding par threes, fours, and fives and requires you to use every club in your bag. It also has a fully stocked pro shop and an "On the Green" restaurant. Greens fees are $13 to $37, and hours are daily 7:30am to dusk.

   Augusta Canal (☎ 706/722-1071), stretching across two counties from the center of Augusta to Evans-to-Locks Road in Columbia County, is the setting for an array of activities, including bicycling, fishing, canoeing, hiking, running, walks, and picnicking. Visit **Savannah Rapids Park** (☎ 706/868-3349) for easy access to the canal. For canoe rentals, call ☎ 706/738-8500.

   Thurmond Lake, north on Washington Road (about 20 miles from the center of Augusta), offers 1,200 miles of shoreline bordering Georgia and South Carolina. One of the largest inland bodies of water in the South, it has some of the best outdoor sports around, including swimming, sailing, waterskiing, fishing, hunting, or just plain sunbathing. The lake is surrounded by a 70,000-acre park. A Visitor and Information Center is located at the South Carolina end of the dam off Highway 221.

WHERE TO STAY

If you can't get a room in town for the Masters, try for lodgings in Aiken, South Carolina (see chapter 13).

✪ **The Azalea Inn.** 314–316 Greene St., Augusta, GA 30901. ☎ **706/724-3454.** Fax 706/724-3454. www.theazaleainn.com. E-mail: azalea@theazaleainn.com. 21 units. A/C TV TEL. $99–$179 double. Rates include breakfast. AE, MC, V.

Just three blocks from the Riverwalk, on Greene Street, this Victorian inn dates back to 1895. Renovations in 1998 made it all the more desirable. David and Colleen Fogle, your innkeepers, go out of their way to ensure that your stay in Augusta is exactly what you expected. Twenty-one suites, most with 11-foot ceilings, are furnished with Victorian pieces; the Jacuzzis in each room and other present-day amenities tastefully mesh with the past. Several suites offer kitchenettes and glass sun porches. Packages are available for 4 nights year-round, and during the Masters tournament they offer packages where you can rent entire homes for the week with Masters badges or practice-round tickets included in the price. Its location in Old Augusta offers a wealth of antiques shopping, historic sites, and the food and drink of the Riverwalk.

✪ **The Partridge Inn.** 2110 Walton Way, Augusta, GA 30904. ☎ **800/476-6888** or 706/737-8888. Fax 706/731-0826. 156 units. $99–$135 double; $125–$165 suite and studio. Rates include Southern buffet breakfast. AE, DC, DISC, MC, V.

During Augusta's heyday as a winter resort—roughly from 1889 to 1930—The Partridge Inn was known as the city's grande dame. The resort's fame faded when Henry Flagler extended the railroads to Florida and the Great Depression hit, and by the early 1980s the hotel was slated for demolition. Fortunately, it was saved, and in 1988, after a major restoration, it reopened.

Today's accommodations come in an almost dizzying array of combinations, including standard queens, double beds, king-size beds, and some rooms with views or kitchenettes. Furnishings are traditional, with quilted spreads, lots of ruffles, and matching draperies. Room service is provided during operation hours of the restaurant (see "Where to Dine," below), and an outdoor pool with sundeck offers diversion.

Perrin Guest House. 208 Lafayette Dr., Augusta, GA 30909. ☎ **706/731-0920.** Fax 706/731-9009. E-mail: perrinplace@mindspring.com. 10 units. A/C TV TEL. $85–$145 double. Extra person in room $10. Rates include continental breakfast. AE, MC, V. Lies 4 miles from center of Augusta; take Exit 199 off I-20.

This is the finest guesthouse in and around Augusta, lying on 3½ acres of land with an arbor, gazebo, and plenty of trees (including magnolias) for privacy. Its rooms are furnished with antiques from the late 1800s to early 1900s, complete with canopied beds and old-fashioned wardrobes. A two-story building, it offers a bathroom with every bedroom. Jacuzzis are offered in six of the rooms. Evening tea and sherry is served. No smoking.

Radisson Riverfront Hotel. 2 Tenth St., Augusta, GA 30901. ☎ **800/333-3333** or 706/722-8900. Fax 706/823-6513. http://cg.zip2.com/augusta/radisson. 234 units. A/C TV TEL. $109–$125 double, $195 suite. Extra person $15. AE, DC, MC, V.

This chain hotel enjoys the best location in town; its well-furnished but standard rooms open onto the Savannah River and historic Riverwalk. Readers Michael Barnas and Phyllis Feingold-Barnas likened the spacious second-floor concourse of the hotel to a trip back to the "Castle of Versailles, with its sweeping marbled floor length, chandelier after chandelier ceiling, and profusion of flower-filled oversize vases."

Augustino's serves only fair Italian dishes, and an adjoining lounge offers big-screen sports. The staff will direct guests to 19 premium golf courses in the area, a challenge to both novices and pros alike. There are also saunas, a fitness center, and an outdoor heated pool.

✪ **Rosemary Hall and Lookaway Hall.** 804 Carolina Ave., North Augusta, SC 29841. ☎ **800/531-5578** or 803/278-6222. Fax 803/278-4877. 23 units. A/C TV TEL. $75–$195 double. Rates include breakfast and afternoon hors d'oeuvres. AE, DC, DISC, MC, V.

For the ultimate statement in luxury inns in the Greater Augusta area, you have to cross over the border into North Augusta (which is actually in South Carolina, about a 10-minute drive from Highway 20). Rosemary Hall and Lookaway Hall are actually two properties, all with white columns and wraparound porches evoking Tara. Both former private homes were built in the early 1900s by the Jackson brothers, founders of North Augusta, and are located across the street from each other. These restored historic inns represent antebellum living at its best, recapturing the charm of an era gone with the wind. Each guest bedroom has an individual character. Period antiques, fine artwork, and custom-made carpets adorn the rooms. Several have their own Jacuzzis or private verandas. Beautifully furnished public rooms are found on the ground floor of each inn. The entrance hall of Rosemary Hall has a stunning wood staircase, worthy of the one on which Scarlett killed that mean Yankee soldier. Breakfast is served on antique china. If you're considering this inn for Masters accommodations, you'll be disappointed. That week has already been booked for the next several years.

WHERE TO DINE

Le Café du Teau. 1855 Central Ave. ☎ **706/733-3505.** Reservations recommended. Main courses $12.95–$22.95; gourmet pizzas $5.95–$7.95. AE, DISC, DC, MC, V. Tues–Thurs 6–10pm, Fri–Sun 6–10:30pm. FRENCH/CAJUN.

In spite of its hard-to-find location, this place remains one of the most enduring and popular spots with discriminating diners in the Augusta area. Some folks drive all the way from Atlanta. As a very young man, Donn du Teau of Atlanta established this restaurant in what had once been a TV repair shop. The moldy-looking outside is unimpressive, but inside you'll find a long corridorlike room filled with paddlewheel fans, watercolors, hanging plants, and even Gulf Coast driftwood paneling. Live piano entertainment is presented Friday to Sunday. In back is a cocktail lounge.

The waiters in white aprons are quite a hip bunch. Pay close attention to the daily specials, as they are often better than the regular menu. Boudin blanc is a homemade seafood sausage, and you can order such continental favorites as escargot shiitake ragout. Our appetizer, saffron-flavored mussels, was delectable, but the entrée that followed, a crab au gratin, was much too salty. A dinner guest's choice of jambalaya was a mistake (it needed far more spicing). Still, in spite of the uneven fare, some dishes are superb. Renovations to the restaurant added a new bar and kitchen with Augusta's only wood-fired stove, giving a special flavor to an array of gourmet pizzas on the menu. Cheeses used for the pizzas are flown in special delivery from New York. One diner said that their smoky taste "will spoil you."

✪ **French Market Grille.** 425 Highland Ave. ☎ **706/737-4865.** Reservations not accepted. Main courses $12.95–$22.75. AE, DISC, DC, MC, V. Mon–Thurs 11am–10pm, Fri–Sat 11am–11pm. NEW ORLEANS.

In a faux French-market atmosphere located in a shopping center, this restaurant is often hailed as the best in Augusta. It's locally owned and operated by Chuck and Gail Baldwin. Po'boys are featured at lunch, and might be stuffed with everything from spicy chicken to soft-shell crab. A large salad selection is available as well. Recommended is the chef's crab chop à la Charles (crabmeat bound by white sauce, with the added flavor of green onions and other seasonings). Two other guests helped devour our scallops maison, and the etouffée (choice of either shrimp or crawfish) was suitably spicy, Cajun style. The desserts, including pecan praline pie and New Orleans bread pudding, have been voted "best desserts in Augusta" by *Augusta Magazine* several years in a row.

Old McDonald Fish Camp, Inc. Sweetwater Community, North Augusta. ☎ **803/ 279-3305.** Main courses $7.95–$13.95. AE, DISC, MC, V. Thurs 5–9pm, Fri 5–9:30pm, Sat 4–9:30pm. Take I-20 East to Exit 1 in South Carolina, turn left, and go 5 miles. SEAFOOD.

When locals from Augusta hanker for catfish and hush puppies and all those good things, they head right to this old fish camp. It's known for serving the best catfish in the area, although you can also order ocean perch, fried shrimp, scallops, crabs, oysters, and even fried gator. One feature is a Low Country boil, with shrimp, sausage, potatoes, corn, and coleslaw. The Thursday night special is an all-you-can-eat fry of catfish, fish fillet, and perch fillet—a real bargain. It's a family favorite, even if the fish is often overcooked—that's the way the locals like it.

✪ The Partridge Inn. 2110 Walton Way. ☎ **706/737-8888.** Reservations recommended. Main courses $11.95–$19.95. AE, DISC, DC, MC, V. Daily 11:30am–2:30pm and 4–9pm. SOUTHERN.

This historic inn turns out a series of Southern-style dishes with top-quality ingredients, including a wide array of seafood, steaks, and fowl. Its spacious, traditionally furnished dining room also features alfresco dining when the weather's right. Discreet staff members advise on menu choices, which depend whenever possible on local ingredients.

Follow in the footsteps of such former visitors as President Warren G. Harding, and enjoy appetizers ranging from Southern crab cakes to seafood gumbo. Main dish selections we've enjoyed include a perfectly prepared Georgia mountain boneless trout topped with toasted almonds. Summerville shrimp is marinated, then seared on the grill, and herb-crusted rack of lamb is another specialty (reviews are mixed on this one). Desserts are rich and fattening, especially the peanut butter pie with swirls of chocolate sauce.

Guests can dine less expensively in the Bar & Grill next to the main dining room, where a pianist often tickles the ivories. Here you can order the best pesto pasta primavera in Augusta.

North Georgia 18

Within 70 to 120 miles of Atlanta, North Georgia may be one of the Deep South's best-kept travel secrets. City dwellers can hike through national forests, scale Georgia's highest peak, and canoe and swim in mountain lakes and return home at dusk, or stay over in a comfortable lodging or campground.

Tennessee, Alabama, and Georgia meet in the "TAG Corner" on the Cumberland Plateau. "TAG" is a terrain of sheer-walled canyons, limestone caves, boulder-littered fields, steaming waterfalls, and mesa-topped mountains that has been compared to a landscape in the West. The first European visitors claimed they had rediscovered Eden when they first came upon the area. It's amazing how little known these Georgia mountains are—as one visitor said, "I've heard of the Blue Ridge Mountains, but I had no idea they came into Georgia. In fact, I didn't realize Georgia had mountains at all." The mountain chain, occupying some two-thirds of North Georgia, consists of the Blue Ridge Mountain frontal range to the east and the Cohutta Mountains to the west.

Northwest Georgia is also filled with remnants of the Civil War (called "The War of Northern Aggression" in these parts) and with artifacts left over from ancient aboriginal civilizations. Etowah Mounds, off I-75 outside Cartersville, is one of the most significant archaeological sites in North America, offering a view of life as lived some four centuries ago. You'll also be introduced to traditional Appalachian culture, Georgia style. Arts and crafts, including pottery making and basket weaving and quilting, are still practiced in the region. And at all local festivals and even on the front porch on a Saturday night, the sound of bluegrass music still fills the air.

Dahlonega (see below) and its environs are the premier "gateways" to the area. The best parks to visit include Amicalola Falls, Unicoi, and Vogel.

1 The Great Outdoors in North Georgia

As one naturalist said of North Georgia, "Scenic touring is about any road you want to travel." Of course, some trails and scenic highways are more memorable than others. Just north of Helen and within easy reach of Blairsville, the **Richard Russell Scenic Highway** (Ga. 348) is one we always travel, with mountain vistas up to 3,644 feet.

If you don't like to hike, you can see much of the panorama of North Georgia from your car by taking Ga. 52, the highway between Chatsworth and Ellijay (the latter called the apple capital of the state). This road offers scenic previews of **Fort Mountain State Park** (about 5 miles east of Chatsworth) and the **Cohutta Wilderness.**

Much of North Georgia is encompassed by the ✪ **Chattahoochee National Forest,** a vast region of some 750,000 acres, including the Georgia Blue Ridge Mountains to the north. Elevations range from 1,000 to some 5,000 feet. It's a vacationer's paradise, with some two dozen picnic areas, the same number of camp sites, six swimming beaches, and ten protected wilderness areas. The forest takes in such natural attractions as **Anna Ruby Falls,** 6 miles north of Alpine Helen; the **Appalachian National Scenic Trail; Vogel State Park** south of Blairsville; and the **Amicalola Falls State Park,** with the state's highest waterfall, outside Dahlonega.

For information about exploring this vast forest, write to the **U.S. Forest Service,** 508 Oak St. NW, Gainesville, GA 30501 (☎ **770/536-0541**).

In contrast, the **Cohutta Wilderness** alone covers 37,000 acres or some 60 square miles spilling over into Tennessee. When an area called Hemp Top was added in 1986, the region became the third-largest mountain wilderness in the East. Fishers claim that the Cohuttas have the best trout streams in the south. Hikers and anglers alike are seen along the banks of the Conasauga River and Jack's River. Walking trails follow the old logging roads of the 1920s. Hikers and backpackers should take the 16½-mile Jack's River Trail, which virtually crosses the wilderness going northwest to southeast.

For detailed information about this vast wilderness, call ☎ **706/695-6736** and speak to the U.S. Forest Service in advance of your trip. Always check road conditions before venturing into such a wild terrain—roads may be closed in bad weather.

Of course, the most famous trail in the area—in fact, America's most fabled scenic trail—is the "A.T.," or ✪ **Appalachian National Scenic Trail,** beginning at Georgia's Springer Mountain and crossing 14 states until it finally comes to an end some 2,100 exhausting miles later in Katahdin, Maine. Hikers usually leave Georgia in April, arriving in Maine in September or even as late as October, when they earn the right to call themselves a "2,000 Miler." The trail runs across Georgia for 79 miles before reaching the border of North Carolina.

Among our favorite state parks in Georgia is **Cloudland Canyon State Park.** The terrain is rugged, but it has modern outdoor amenities, such as a swimming pool and a tennis court. This is a 2,120-acre scenic park near the village of Rising Fawn, on the west side of Lookout Mountain. Gulch Creek, a deep gorge, slices through the park, with elevations ranging from 800 to 1,800 feet. It has some 75 camping sites and lots of ideal spots for a picnic.

The park lies on Ga. 136, 8 miles east of Trenton and I-59 and 18 miles northwest of La Fayette. It's open daily 7am to 10pm year-round. For additional information, contact the **Cloudland Canyon State Park,** Department of Natural Resources, 122 Cloudland Canyon Rd., Rising Fawn, GA 30738 (☎ **706/657-4050;** fax 706/398-9748).

Lookout Mountain sprawls more than 100 miles, ignoring state lines and spilling into Tennessee, Alabama, and Georgia. The northern end overlooks the city of Chattanooga at the border of Tennessee and Georgia. Two towns—both named Lookout Mountain—lie on both sides of the border. Lookout Mountain is accessible from I-24 from Chattanooga heading toward Georgia.

2 Chickamauga & Chattanooga National Military Park

110 miles N of Atlanta

✪ The country's oldest (1890) and biggest military park stretches across an 8,000-acre site 9 miles south of Chattanooga on U.S. 27. Ranking along with Gettysburg and Vicksburg, the national historic shrine consists of four different parks: Chickamauga, Point Park, Missionary Ridge, and Orchard Knob.

The park is a memorial to both Union and Confederate troops who fought one of the bloodiest battles of the Civil War here in 1862. The casualties were staggering, the battle called "a massive slaughterhouse." It was fought for control of not only Chattanooga but Atlanta.

On September 19 and 20, a Confederate force of 66,000 men met by accident a Union force of 58,000. The two-day battle left 36,000 casualties. It marked the greatest success of Confederate armies in the west, although the advantage was not seized.

Some 1,500 historical markers, tablets, artillery pieces, and monuments mark the movement of troops. At the visitor center (☎ **706/866-9241**), on the northern entrance to the battlefield, self-guided audiotape tours are available. A slide show recounts the battle hour by hour. For those who tire of all the carnage, some 80 miles of hiking trails are cut through the valley. The center is open daily from 8am to 5:45pm from Memorial Day to Labor Day, shutting down for the rest of the year at 4:45pm.

Admission is free to the park, but a multimedia program costs $3 for adults, $1.50 for seniors and children 15 and under. To reach the park, exit I-75 at Ga. 2 and go west for 6 miles to Hwy. 27 (Exit 141), at which point you head south to the park, which is a mile from the town of Fort Oglethorpe.

WHERE TO STAY

Accommodations are available in Chattanooga, or else you can stay at the **Gordon Lee Mansion** (see below) in the town of Chickamauga, 2½ miles south of the battlefield.

✪ **Gordon Lee Mansion.** 217 Cove Rd. (off Hwy. 27), Chickamauga, GA 30707. ☎ **706/ 375-4728.** Fax 706/375-9499. www.fhc.org/gordon-lee. E-mail: glmbb1@aol.com. 5 units. A/C TV (in rooms only). $75–$110 double; $125 cabin. Rates include breakfast. AE, DISC, MC, V.

This restored historic inn lies 2½ miles south of the park. Dating from 1840, it was the headquarters of Union Gen. William Rosecrans during September of 1863. One double offers a four-poster bed, the others queen-size canopied beds. All rooms are furnished with antebellum-style antiques. The lone cabin has one king-size bed and two twin beds, gas and wood fireplaces, an in-room phone, a refrigerator, and a microwave. This is a dry county—no alcohol is sold, so if you want a drink, you must bring your own. There's no restaurant on the premises; most guests drive 15 miles north to Chattanooga for dinner.

3 Calhoun/New Echota

75 miles N of Atlanta

This little town of some 7,000 people was once known as Oothcaloga or "place of the beaver dams" before it was changed to honor John Caldwell Calhoun, secretary of state under President John Tyler. The town itself is of little interest (although it was spared by General Sherman on his way to burn Atlanta), and it's mainly a base to explore New Echota.

ESSENTIALS

GETTING THERE   By Car   From Atlanta, take I-75 North to the Calhoun exit (129). From here go along Hwy. 53 West for 2 miles, turning north on U.S. 41.

VISITOR INFORMATION   The **Gordon County Chamber of Commerce** (Calhoun) is at 300 S. Wall St. (☎ **706/625-3200**), and is open Monday to Friday 9am to 5pm.

SEEING THE SIGHTS

✪ **New Echota Historic Site.** ☎ **706/624-1321.** Fax 706/624-1326. Admission $3 adults, $2.50 seniors, $2 children 6–18. Tues–Sat 9am–5pm and Sun 2–5:30pm. On Ga. 225, ½ mile east of I-75.

This is the restoration of the final Eastern Cherokee capital (1825–38). This community was once a sovereign country within the newly minted United States. To accommodate their new colonial masters, the Cherokees even modeled their new nation on the American government, complete with a supreme court, senate, and house of representatives.

They were the first Native Americans to create their own alphabet, and in 1828 were publishing a newspaper, the *Cherokee Phoenix,* in their own language. But that was the year gold was discovered on their land, and the subsequent gold rush ended all pretense of Cherokee sovereignty. The State of Georgia took over and auctioned off the Cherokee lands to white prospectors.

The Cherokee appealed to the Supreme Court, which ruled in their favor under Chief Justice John Marshall. President Andrew Jackson refused to honor the court's opinion. The president commanded the military to round up the Cherokee in Georgia and North Carolina, and in 1838 they began their infamous 800-mile march along the "Trail of Tears" to Oklahoma, where one-fourth of them died.

Their former capital has been re-created, including a one-room newspaper office and two-story supreme court. The 1805 Vann Tavern was moved to the park, and an 1830s log store is today a museum and orientation center.

WHERE TO STAY

Howard Johnson Inn. 1220 Redbud Rd. (P.O. Box 252), off I-75, Calhoun, GA 30701. ☎ **706/629-9191.** Fax 706/629-0873. 90 units. A/C TV TEL. $40–$65 double. Children 12 and under free in parents' room. Discounts to AAA members. AE, DC,MC, V. 2½ miles from the center of Calhoun off I-75 at Exit 130.

This two-story motel has been completely remodeled and refurbished since it was taken over by Howard Johnson, and now has the distinction of being the largest inn in the area. The hotel is in a typical motel format, yet the rooms are very clean and economical, and the furnishings are fairly new. Families enjoy the pool, which is open during the summer months. The most recent addition to the structure is a new lounge/bar just outside the lobby. The hotel restaurant, the Harbin, offers adequate continental cuisine and is open for breakfast, lunch, and dinner until 9pm nightly.

4 Tate & Jasper

60 miles N of Atlanta

As Georgia towns go, even some state residents draw a blank at the mention of either of these towns that virtually adjoin one another. Tate, in fact, doesn't appear on most maps. Nevertheless, Tate and Jasper contain two of the most famous inns in the northern part of the state. Either town makes an ideal base for exploring the northwest corridor of Georgia, as all the major scenic attractions can easily be reached on day trips.

Jasper is one of the marble centers of Georgia—in fact, marble quarried here was used in the Lincoln Memorial and the Capitol in Washington, D.C. A Marble Festival in early October highlights tours of the quarries, with country music, food, and arts and crafts.

ESSENTIALS

GETTING THERE   By Car   From Atlanta, take I-75 North to I-575, which turns into Hwy. 515 going north. Continue along Hwy. 515 North until you reach Hwy. 53 North, which will take you into the center of Jasper.

VISITOR INFORMATION   Contact the **Pickens Chamber of Commerce,** 500 Stegall Rd., Jasper, GA 30143 (☎ **706/692-5600**). The chamber distributes information about the Tate/Jasper area. Hours are Monday to Friday from 9am to 4pm.

WHERE TO STAY & DINE

✪ **Tate House.** Hwy. 53, P.O. Box 33, Tate, GA 30177. ☎ **800/342-7515** or 770/735-3122. www.tatehouse.com. 14 units. TV. $110 cabin; $132 suite. Suite rates include breakfast. MC, V.

It's the most unusual B&B in northeast Georgia. In 1926, the owner of the Georgia Marble Company, Colonel Sam Tate, ordered a palatial mansion to be built entirely out of a rare vein of rose-colored ("Etonah pink") marble. He died a decade later, but tales of his brutality circulated through the area. After the death of his last surviving relative, the empty house was subject to widespread vandalism and was supposedly haunted by legions of ghosts.

In 1973, against all odds, Arizonan Ann Laird embarked on a restoration project. Today, she and her husband, Joe, and family maintain an inn of aristocratic, European grandeur, richly furnished with taste and style. You can opt for one of the quintet of suites in the main house, which feature both TV and telephone. Less formal, and more woodsy, are the nine log-sided cabins that lie in a grassy meadow, a 5-minute walk from the main house. Cabins, equipped with TV only, carry the added advantage of having large Jacuzzis and overhead sleeping lofts.

The only major drawback to this property is its lack of a restaurant; clients must drive to inconvenient locations (especially on Sunday) for a meal.

✪ **The Woodbridge Inn.** 44 Chambers St., Jasper, GA 30143. ☎ **706/692-6293.** Fax 706/692-9061. www.ngeorgia.com/site/woodbridge.html. 18 units. A/C TV TEL. Sun– Thurs $65 double; Fri–Sat $75 double. AE, CB, DC, DISC, MC, V.

Known for the quality of its food and lodging, this is the most famous inn in Northwest Georgia. It's in an antebellum setting with mountain vistas from all directions. The three-level lodge was designed to take in the views—patios and balconies open off the accommodations. Some of the upper-level rooms have a spiral staircase leading to a sleeping loft. The lodge is completely modern, having been reconstructed after a fire. People drive for miles around, even from Atlanta, to sample the food here. Both European and American dishes are offered, everything from veal Oscar to oysters Rockefeller. All the food is fresh, and dishes are individually prepared. Save room for dessert, especially for the lemon cream pie.

The place has a long history. It was once known as Ed Lenning's Inn. Ed fought as a Confederate soldier and founded the restaurant with money from a gold strike in California. In the old days, when the railroad used to stop out front, people from Florida came here to escape the summer heat.

5 Dahlonega & Environs

70 miles NE of Atlanta

Dahlonega is a Cherokee word meaning "precious yellow." In 1828, according to legend, a trapper named Benjamin Parks stubbed his toe on a rock and uncovered a vein of gold here that quickly brought prospectors streaming into these hills. A town called "Dahlonega" suddenly appeared—America's first mining boomtown. The gold craze changed Cherokee culture forever.

Although prospecting hasn't been a major industry since the Civil War, enough gold is still around to periodically re-leaf the dome of Georgia's State Capitol, and to intrigue visitors who come here to pan for it (see below).

ESSENTIALS

GETTING THERE   By Car   From Atlanta, take Hwy. 19/S.R. 400 North to S.R. 60, which you follow north for another 5 miles to reach Dahlonega.

VISITOR INFORMATION   The **Dahlonega Chamber of Commerce,** 13 S. Park St. (☎ **800/231-5543** or 706/864-3711), is open daily from 9am to 5:30pm. The staff distributes information about scenic attractions, state parks, and gold panning in the area.

SEEING THE SIGHTS

Dahlonega's Public Square sports a rustic look. Old galleried buildings and stores have been turned into shops purveying gold-panning equipment, gold jewelry, mountain handcrafts, antiques, ice cream, and fudge. It's very touristy but still preserves a quaint charm in spite of the hordes who sometimes descend on summer days, mostly families with lots of kids in tow.

Formerly the Lumpkin County Courthouse, the **Dahlonega Courthouse Gold Museum,** Public Square (☎ 706/864-2257), is in the center of the town square. Artifacts, coins, and tools from the nation's first major gold rush are shown, and a 23-minute film chronologically documents the feverish era. Recently, the Gold Museum has added a gold coin exhibit displaying a variety of quarters, half dollars, and whole dollars minted at the Dahlonega Branch Mint from 1838 to 1861. Besides being a gold miners' haven, this old museum is the state's third-oldest standing courthouse. It's also the second-most visited Georgia historical site. The hours of operation are Monday to Saturday 9am to 5pm, and on Sunday 10am to 5pm. Admission is $2.50 for adults, $2 for seniors, $1.50 children 6 to 18 (free for children 5 and under).

In the environs, call at the **Consolidated Gold Mines,** 125 Consolidated Gold Mines Rd. (☎ 706/864-8473). At the turn of the century it boasted the largest and most advanced gold mine east of the Mississippi River, covering more than 7,000 acres, with some 200 tunnels. In one day it recovered about 55 pounds of gold. Tours into illuminated tunnels take about 40 minutes and are conducted by miners. Look for the 250-foot vertical shaft. The mine also offers a chance to pan for gold. It's open daily from 10am to 5pm, charging adults $10; children 4 to 14 $6. The mine isn't really suited for children 5 and under. To reach the mine from the center of Dahlonega, take Hwy. 400 North to Hwy. 60, turn left, and follow the signs.

WHERE TO STAY

The Smith House. 84 S. Chestatee St., Dahlonega, GA 30533. ☎ **800/852-9577** or 706/867-7000. Fax 706/864-7564. www.smithhouse.com. E-mail: info@smithhouse.com. 18 units. A/C TV TEL. $65–$130 double. Rates include continental breakfast. AE,MC, V.

The owners, the Welch family, are known mainly for their restaurant (see below). With the Smith House, they offer plenty of mountain hospitality, if you don't mind staying at a place overrun with visitors. Originally built atop a rich vein of gold ore in 1884, it was turned into an inn in 1922, although the original owners wouldn't recognize today's bustling place. The inaugural $4.50-a-night rooms are long gone, too. Rooms are furnished in a cozy, 19th-century style, and all have been authentically remodeled. One section of the little two-story hotel was originally a carriage house. This is very much a country inn type of place, with rocking chairs on the front porch. A swimming pool was added in the 1980s, and guests can pan for gold on the premises for $3.

STAYING NEARBY

Forest Hills Mountain Hideaway. Wesley Chapel Rd., Rte. 3 (P.O. Box 510), Dahlonega, GA 30533. ☎ **800/654-6313** or 706/864-6456. Fax 706/864-5405. 40 units. $165 double; $208 kitchen cottage. Rooms include breakfast; cottages include breakfast and candlelight dinner. AE, DISC, MC, V. 10 miles west on Ga. 52, then right onto Wesley Chapel Rd. No children.

Surrounded by the mountains of North Georgia, this adults-only retreat is a luxurious hideaway. It offers five B&B rooms in the main lodge, but its special attraction is its rustic 30 cottages, many ideal for a honeymoon with bedroom hot tubs and large canopied beds. A stereo system, color TV, and fireplaces add to the allure. The cottages have a woodland setting best enjoyed from porch swings. The 140 wooded acres border the Chattahoochee National Forest and are about 4 miles from the Amicalola Falls State Park (see below), and have many hiking and bridle trails. There's a swimming pool along with tennis courts, and the food is among the best in the area. Make reservations as far in advance as possible.

Mountain Top Lodge at Dahlonega. 447 Mountaintop Lodge Rd., Dahlonega, GA 30533. ☎ **800/526-9754** or 706/864-5257. Fax 706/864-8265. www.mountaintoplodge.net. E-mail: mountaintop@alltel.net. 13 units. A/C. $85–$150 double. Rates include breakfast. AE, DC, MC, V.

In the early spring you can stand on the grounds of this two-story rustic-style lodge and enjoy a 360-degree view of the Blue Ridge Mountains, reason enough to check in. When the dogwoods burst into bloom is yet another reason. Set on 40 acres of woodland, about 5 miles from Dahlonega, the lodge is made of rough-cut cedar timbering, with tongue-in-groove cathedral ceilings. The effect is barnlike with heavy beams. In the main public room, guests gather around a wood-burning stove on cold days, watching TV. The bedrooms, each with private bathroom, are decorated in an old-fashioned country style, a mixture of antiques and specials from a fire sale. Two rooms have areas to sit, along with whirlpool tubs and fireplaces. Try for a room with a private balcony. The two cabins contain queen-size beds, refrigerators, whirlpool tubs, balconies, and fireplaces. One of the sundecks has a heated outdoor spa. Good country cooking is served in the dining room. The place sometimes takes on the aura of a house party in the mountains.

WHERE TO DINE

✪ **The Smith House.** 84 S. Chestatee St. ☎ **706/867-7000.** Reservations not accepted. All-you-can-eat lunch Tues–Fri $11.19, Sat $14.95, Sun $14.95; all-you-can-eat dinner Tues–Thurs $14.50, Fri–Sun $14.95. AE, MC, V. SOUTHERN.

In North Georgia, this large family-style restaurant—a tradition since 1922—is called "pig-out heaven." A lavish array of Southern food, along with homemade Smith

House rolls, relishes, and desserts, is served at shared tables. Some 2,000 meals are hauled out on Sunday alone. This is true mountain cookin'—and plenty of it, all you can eat. Many dishes are based on recipes 100 years old. Continuously replenished platters arrive, including angel biscuits, sweet-baked country-fried steak, and lots and lots of Southern fried chicken. Barbecue is a feature, and so is fried catfish (is there any other kind?). Everything tastes better with the homemade cornbread, especially the array of Southern-style vegetables, including fried okra, squash casserole, coleslaw, black-eyed peas, rice and gravy, stewed apples, dumplings, and candied yams. No one saves room for dessert, but everyone eats it anyway—banana fritters, strawberry short-cake, fruit cobbler, whatever.

DAY TRIPS FROM DAHLONEGA

From Dahlonega, U.S. 19 winds north into the mountains, toward one of the state's prettiest parks. **The Mountain Crossing/Walasi-Yi Center** (☎ 706/745-6095) at Neel's Gap, is the best "take a break" stop along the Appalachian Trail. The stone and log building is a legacy of the Depression-era Civilian Conservation Corps, and stands as a landmark along the trail. The Center is a hiker's dream, fully stocked with camping gear, travel clothing, and "the best boot selection in the northeast (including special-order and hard-to-fit feet)." You can sip cider at the snack bar while purchasing candy, canned goods, pottery, and crafts; you can't miss one of the largest book selections in northeast Georgia, either. The state maintains about a dozen lean-tos along the 79 miles of the Georgia portion of the trail.

The main attraction in the area is the ✪ **Amicalola Falls State Park** (☎ 706/ 265-8888), lying 20 miles west of Dahlonega, off Ga. 52. Here you'll find the highest waterfalls east of the Mississippi River, dropping 729 feet, called "tumbling waters" by the Cherokees. The falls plunge in seven cascades and are one of the so-called "seven wonders" of Georgia. The upper falls are free falls, but the middle and lower parts cascade through a steep, rocky creek. There are several observation decks.

The state park has a 57-room lodge where doubles range from $79 to $129, 17 tent and trailer sites costing $20 to $22, and 14 cottages going for $95 to $135 for a one-bedroom, $105 to $145 for a two-bedroom, and $115 to $165 for a three-bedroom.

Trout fishing is possible in the park, and it's filled with hiking trails, one of which leads 8 miles to ✪ Springer Mountain, the southern end of the Appalachian Trail.

For more information, write to **Amicalola Falls State Park,** 418 Amicalola Falls Rd., Dawsonville, GA 30534 (☎ **706/265-8888**).

6 Blairsville

105 miles NE of Atlanta

You don't come here to visit this mountain town itself, but you can use it as a center for exploring—including Georgia's highest point, offering a panoramic view of the whole northern part of the state. Blairsville is set in a national forest.

A Sorghum Festival is held the first three weekends in October. Crafts are displayed, canned goods sold, and cane is converted to sweet sorghum syrup before your eyes, with lots of free samples. Square dancing, greased pole climbing, and other contests typical of the mountain folk are followed by country music and dancing.

ESSENTIALS

GETTING THERE   By Car   From Atlanta, take I-75 North to I-575 and con-tinue north on this highway until you reach Hwy. 515. Go north on Hwy. 515 to reach Blairsville.

VISITOR INFORMATION   The **Blairsville Chamber of Commerce,** 385 Welcome

Center Lane, in Blairsville (☎ **706/745-5789**), is open Monday to Friday from 8:30am to 4:30pm, distributing maps and brochures about the area.

EXPLORING THE AREA

✪ **Brasstown Bald,** Georgia's highest mountain, is set in a national forest with an observation tower atop its 4,784-foot summit. Here you'll have a 360-degree view across ridges into four different states. After parking, you can walk up the half-mile paved road or else take a bus to the top. There is no steeper half-mile walk in all of Georgia! At the top you can see a video explaining the legend and lore of the mountain. There's access to four hiking trails ranging from ½-mile to 6 miles in length, and picnic tables are available. The surrounding area is home to a wide variety of plants and animals.

The park is open June through mid-November Monday to Friday from 10am to 6pm and Saturday and Sunday from 10am to 6:30pm. In April and May it is open only Saturday and Sunday. Admission is $2 for parking at the park. The bus ride to the top and back costs $3 for adults, $1 for children 10 and under, and $1.50 for seniors. For more information, write **Brasstown Ranger District,** 1881 Hwy. 515, Blairsville, GA 30512 (☎ **706/745-6928;** fax 706/745-7494). There is also a **Visitor Information Center** at the park (☎ **706/896-2555**).

To reach the mountain from Blairsville, take U.S. 19/129 South for 8 miles. Turn left or east onto Ga. 180 and go 12 miles to Ga. 180 Spur and turn left or north. Another 3 miles leads to the Brasstown Bald parking lot.

✪ **Vogel State Park** is Georgia's second-oldest state park and one of its most frequented. Located in the heart of the North Georgia mountains at the foot of Blood and Slaughter mountains, it sprawls across 240 acres cut through with nature trails. It has a 22-acre lake, Lake Trahlyta, named for a Cherokee Princess. You can swim (there's a bathhouse) or fish for bass, trout, and bream. The park hosts festivals, like Old Timer's Day in August.

Campsites are available with power and water hookups, hot showers, and laundry facilities. The cost ranges from $8 Monday to Friday for a tent, to $15 on weekends. Cottages, 36 in all, are comfortably furnished, with wood-burning fireplaces. Prices range from $55 to $60 for a one-bedroom, $70 to $80 for a two-bedroom, and $80 to $90 for a three-bedroom.

At an elevation of 2,500 feet, park temperatures are cool, even in July and August. The park is open year round daily from 7am to 10pm. It's 11 miles from Blairsville on U.S. 19/129. For more information, write **Vogel State Park,** 7485 Vogel State Park Rd., Blairsville, GA 30512 (☎ **706/745-2628;** fax 706/745-3139).

Richard Russell Scenic Highway is south of Blairsville, via 19/129, and east on Ga. 180. This 14-mile scenic mountain drive, with elevations ranging from 1,600 to 3,000 feet, offers panoramic views at every turn. The drive is especially popular in fall, when hardwoods blaze with colors. At the 3,500-foot Tesnatee Gap, the highway crosses the Appalachian Trail. The road crosses the Blue Ridge and forms the northern perimeter of the eastern half of the Raven Cliffs Wilderness.

WHERE TO STAY

Blood Mountain Cabins and Country Store. U.S. 19/129, Blairsville, GA 30512. ☎ and fax **706/745-9454** or 800/284-6866. www.georgiamagazine.com/bloodmtn. 12 units. A/C TV. $74–$94 cabin for 4. 2-night minimum. DISC, MC, V. Lies 13 miles south of Blairsville along U.S. 19/129.

These cabins stand near the breezy top of Blood Mountain at a 3,000-foot elevation, and the Appalachian Trail crosses U.S. 19/129 only yards away. Summers here are the coolest in Georgia, especially if you're escaping that fiery cauldron known as Atlanta, but winter will send you seeking a seat close to the stove. The owners, Colley and George Case, can be found in their general store, dispensing information on the area and selling freshly brewed coffee.

Cabins are furnished in a rustic style and—at least in spring—don't match up to their natural setting when all the rhododendrons and azaleas burst into flame. Each accommodation has a bedroom and an additional sleeping loft, plus a fireplace, ceiling fan, and a spacious deck with country rockers for taking in that view of Blood Mountain. There's also a fully equipped kitchen and an up-to-date bathroom. Weekly rates range from $369 to $449.

Misty Mountain Inn and Cottages. 4376 Misty Mountain Lane, Blairsville, GA 30512.
☎ **888/647-8966** or 706/745-4786. Fax 706/781-1002. www.jwww.com/misty. E-mail:
mistyinn@whitelion.net. 10 units. A/C TV. $60–$75 B&B room; $79–$89 cottage. Rates
include breakfast in B&B rooms only. MC, V.

This Victorian-style farmhouse in a bucolic setting is both a B&B and an inn, offering rooms with private bathrooms, fireplaces, and balconies, plus a cottage cluster with wood-burning fireplaces and kitchenettes. A pet-friendly environment, it's where you can do nothing more than (at their suggestion) "smell the flowers or listen to the bullfrogs at the pond." Rooms are furnished in a country rustic style, and maintenance is high. Two cabins have whirlpool baths, but no TVs. Queen-size beds, fireplaces, and linens are furnished with each unit. Family cottages sleep five to eight, although two are suitable for only two renters. Hiking trails are found nearby, including the Appalachian Trail, and Brasstown Bald Mountain is less than 10 miles away. White-water rafting is within a short drive, as are trout-filled mountain streams. Boating is possible on two lakes nearby.

7 Alpine Helen

85 miles NE of Atlanta

Once a quiet Appalachian village, Helen has been turned into a bit of Bavaria in the Georgia hills. Main Street buildings have red roofs, flower boxes, balconies, and murals. You can shop for sweaters, porcelains, cuckoo clocks, and Christmas ornaments; enjoy wurst and beer to oompah music at an outdoor beer garden; and in September and October join the revelry of Oktoberfest. Numerous alpine-style hotels, with names that include the Heidi Motel, have comfortable accommodations and restaurants.

ESSENTIALS

GETTING THERE   By Car   From Atlanta, head north on I-85 to Exit 45 near Gainesville. From here take Hwy. 985/365 North for some 20 miles to Hwy. 384. After that, go for another 20 miles to Hwy. 75, then turn right for the final 3 miles into Helen.

VISITOR INFORMATION   Alpine Helen Convention and Visitors Bureau, 726 Brucken St. (½ mile from downtown), right off Main Street (☎ 706/878-2181), dispenses information and provides maps and brochures of attractions in the area. Hours are Monday to Saturday from 9am to 5pm and Sunday from 10am to 4pm.

EXPLORING THE AREA

The best time to be here is for a special event, such as the Hot Air Balloon Festival, which kicks off the race to the Atlantic Ocean in late May (lasting until June), and

Oktoberfest, a pale imitation of the real one in Munich. This beer-drinking fest in alcohol-shy Georgia begins in mid-September and continues to mid-October. German bands from the U.S. and Europe perform nightly, and singalongs and the famous "Chicken Dance" are part of the fun. Show up in an authentic Bavarian costume.

After you've seen all the shows and bought all those beer mugs and lederhosen you don't really need, you can do some serious exploring in the environs of Helen, which many visitors find more alluring than the overly commercialized town itself, with its *faux* Bavarian everything.

Before heading out, you might check out **Museum of the Hills,** Main Street (☎ 706/878-3140), which illustrates Helen's transformation from a pioneer town to its present Heidi madness. The museum is open May through October from 10am to 8:30pm daily. Off-season hours are 9:30am to 7pm daily. Admission is $5 for adults, $4 for senior citizens (62 and up), and $3.50 for students 13 and older. Children 5 to 12 pay $2, and children 4 and younger are admitted free.

Stovall Covered Bridge lies 3 miles north of Helen on Ga. 255. Built in 1895, it's the smallest covered bridge in Georgia—only one span wide.

OUTDOOR PURSUITS

Alpine tubing is the most popular outdoor sport here. If the day is hot, more people can be seen tubing on the Chattahoochee River than buying beer steins. The river runs right through Helen, and tube rental outfits abound all along the banks. Some rapids are here, but they're rather brief, so even small children go tubing. We prefer **Alpine Tubing** (☎ 706/878-8823), which will take you on a 2-hour float and bring you back to your starting point. The cost is $7, or $5 for children 15 and under.

Sunburst Stables, 9 miles east of Helen on Ga. 255 in the Sautee Valley (☎ 706/947-7433), offers 25 miles of scenic wooded trails year round. You can even go riding in winter, perhaps spotting a deer cavorting through the forest. Various types of rides are offered, including a 2-day overnight, or else a 3-hour sunset ride. The stables are set on 60 acres and adjoin the Chattahoochee National Forest. The outfit also offers hayrides.

Advance reservations are required; the hourly rate is $20 per person. No children under 8 are allowed. When making a reservation and agreeing upon the time, give them your height, weight, and experience in riding. A major credit card (American Express, MasterCard, or Visa) is required to hold a reservation. Weight limits of 200 pounds for women and 240 pounds for men are imposed.

SHOPPING

Betty's Country Store. Main St. (Hwy. 75). ☎ **706/878-2943.**

It's the most folkloric large grocery store in Georgia, stocked with all the inventory you'd expect in a modern IGA (of which it's a member), yet permeated with the old-time aura of an early-20th-century general store. Its central core was built in 1937, but even the more recent enlargements feature a decor as rough-hewn as a log cabin in the Georgia mountains, while the completely concealed amenities are as modern as the computer age. Overall, the place is a conversation piece and a bit of a tourist attraction in its own right, a setting right out of the *Old Farmer's Almanac.*

Nora Mill Granary. 7107 S. Main St., Helen. ☎ **800/927-2375** or 706/878-2375.

At first glance, you might bypass this rustic plank-sided building as little more than a battered tourist emporium, on the main road about 2 miles south of Helen. Actually, it's one of the most famous sites in the region, visited by schoolchildren as a slice of Americana, and sought after by engineers eager for a glimpse of its old-time grinding wheels. It was built in 1876 as a water-driven mill powered by the flowing waters of the Chattahoochee River. Today, you can sample grits and oatmeal, which bubble away on a massive antique stove, or buy burlap mini-bags of grits, stone-ground flour (buckwheat, rye, and whole wheat), pancake mix, and bread mix. A gift store next door sells cookbooks, candy, and crafts. Both entities are open daily from 9:30am to 5pm.

The Old Sautee Store. Ga. 17 and 255, Sautee-Nachoochee. ☎ **706/878-2281.**

Four miles from Helen, this 128-year-old country store is as much a museum as it is a store. In fact, an antique museum can be found in a section of the store where the post office used to be. The Old Sautee Store has the largest collection of old-store memorabilia in all of Georgia, including items of merchandise not for sale. It's also a Scandinavian specialty shop: Astrid Fried still remembers her native Norway, and will show you her personally selected imports, including ski sweaters and hand-carved trolls, Scandinavian crystal and dinnerware, as well as Norwegian pewter, gold and enamel jewelry, and gourmet foods. The store is listed on the National Register of Historic Places. Admission is free. Hours are Monday to Saturday from 9:30am to 5:30pm and Sunday from 1 to 6pm.

WHERE TO STAY

Castle Inn. Main Street, Helen, GA 30545. ☎ **877/878-3140** or 706/878-3140. Fax 706/878-2470. www.castleinn-helen.com. 12 units. A/C TV TEL. $120–$150 double. MC, V.

On the Chattahoochee River, overlooking the main square of Helen, the castle inn is a mock castle that conceals a modern and well-appointed hotel. Bedrooms are furnished in a somewhat dull motel style, but are comfortable and immaculately maintained. The most desirable units overlook the river, and each room has its own private balcony. This place is especially popular at Oktoberfest. Located directly below the inn is the Troll Tavern restaurant with indoor and outdoor dining. It features both German and Mexican fare, and even has something for the vegetarian.

Grampa's Room Bed & Breakfast Inn. (P.O. Box 100), Sautee-Nacoochee, GA 30571. ☎ **706/878-2364.** 2 units. $65 double. Children under 12 stay free in parents' room; children 12–18, $12.50. Rates include country breakfast. MC, V. South of Helen, take Hwy. 75/17 for 1½ miles to Hwy. 17. Turn left onto Hwy. 17 and continue for 2 miles.

On the old Unicoi Turnpike, this big old country house was completed in 1872, and is listed on the National Register of Historic Places. It's always been in the same family, and is often filled with grandchildren of the owners, Lib and Mack Tucker. It's still very much a family affair, with lawn tables and chairs and plenty of trees. A few antiques fill the house, but this is no decorator showcase. Bedrooms are large and comfortable, often with antique iron bedsteads that have seen a lot of wear.

Helendorf Inn. P.O. Box 305, Main St., Helen, GA 30545. ☎ **800/445-2271** or 706/878-2271. Fax 706/878-2271. www.helendorf.com. E-mail: helendorf@alltel.net. 98 units. A/C TV TEL. $54–$74 double; $140–$160 suite. MC, V.

Tucked away on a side street, in the Teutonic-looking heart of the village, this hotel sports Bavarian-style frescoes on its stucco surfaces that look oddly incongruous in the Georgia heat. It's one of the town's enduring hotels, with one of the most central locations. Despite its folkloric exterior, it's remarkable for what this hotel doesn't offer: Its lobby is cramped and unimaginative and there's no bar; however, there is a small restaurant, the Wooden Shoe. You'll find an ersatz kind of folklore, a staff with a laconic mountain drawl, and a wide variety of accommodations. The most appealing overlook the Chattahoochee River, which runs against one foundation of the building. Some have hints of alpine coziness, and many have private balconies. Suites contain Jacuzzis and fireplaces.

✪ **The Lodge at Smithgall Woods.** 61 Tsalaki Trail, Helen, GA 30545. ☎ **800/ 318-5248** or 706/878-3087. Fax 706/878-0301. www.smithgallwoods.com. E-mail: sgwoods@stc.net. 14 units. A/C TV TEL. $235–$490 double. Rates include all meals. AE, DC, MC, V.

This elegant mountain retreat stands in the midst of a 5,555-acre conservation area, attracting a well-heeled clientele who enjoy its seclusion and the country charm of a private mountain estate. It also opens onto one of the finest trout streams in Georgia, and, as such, often attracts the movers and shakers of industry who want to get away from it all. In peace and seclusion, the bedrooms are well-furnished and exceedingly comfortable, all with private bathrooms and all spread across five different guest-houses, each opening onto panoramic views. The accommodations are individually decorated, with antiques, well-chosen fabrics, and Oriental rugs, the ambience both rustic yet elegant. The cuisine is another good reason to stay here. Naturally, the chef's specialty is mountain trout, as the nearby river is said to be one of the top 100 trout streams in the United States. You can order the fish smoked, grilled, or pan-sautéed, along with a small but excellent choice of other dishes nightly. In addition to fishing, other activities include hiking, biking, birding, and nature walks.

✪ **Stovall House.** 1526 Hwy. 255 N., Sautee, GA 30571. ☎ **706/878-3355.** www. georgiamagazine.com/stovall. 5 units. A/C. $90 double. Rates include continental breakfast. Discounts of 10% Dec–Mar. AE, MC, V. 5 miles SE of Helen on Hwy. 255.

Nestled amid a copse of trees at the summit of a hill, this veranda-ringed farmhouse was built in 1837 as the centerpiece of a 300-acre plantation. It was converted into a B&B in 1983 by Hamilton (Ham) Schwartz, a hardworking schoolteacher and soccer coach from Philadelphia. Bedrooms are high-ceilinged, outfitted with an eclectic mix of antiques. They include old-fashioned beds, which might not be as comfortable as the ones you're used to, but which compensate with their charm. Top-floor rooms have skylights.

Dinner is a celebration of well-flavored food. Served Thursday to Sunday from 5:30 to 8:30pm, menu items include a "phyllo of the day" (including a version filled with ham, broccoli, and cheddar), chicken stuffed with a mixture of cream cheese and herbs, scaloppini of pork, and at least two different versions of fresh mountain trout. Full dinners are a bargain, tending to range from $9 to $14.50 per person.

Unicoi State Park Lodge. Unicoi State Park (P.O. Box 849), Helen, GA 30545. ☎ **706/ 878-2201.** Fax 706/878-2676. E-mail: dwheeldon@amfacpnr.com. 100 units; 30 cottages. A/C (units and cottages) TV TEL (units only). $89–$139 double; $115–$155 cottages. AE, DC, DISC, MC, V.

Set on a pristine lake in the midst of 1,000 acres of woodland, this state lodge, built in 1972, stands in the heart of the park. Warm and wood-beamed, it offers fully equipped and rather rustic cottages tucked into the wooded hillsides. The guest rooms we inspected needed a refurbishing, but the price was right. Cottages are along the lake and farther up Smith Creek. The lodge has an excellent cafeteria-style dining room serving three meals a day at modest prices. Even if you're not staying here, consider a stopover for an all-you-can-eat buffet, costing $6.25 at lunch and $8.50 at dinner.

WHERE TO DINE

The Hofbrauhaus. 1 Main St. ☎ **706/878-2248.** Reservations recommended. Main courses $9.25–$26. AE, DISC, DC, MC, V. Bar/lounge daily 3pm–midnight; restaurant daily 5–10:30pm. INTERNATIONAL.

By virtue of its name alone, it's the most famous restaurant in Helen, with a Teutonic-derived *schmaltz* that can be endearing in a rather corny way. It sits at the edge of the

Chattahoochee, and caters to a hard-core battalion of serious beer-drinkers, especially during Oktoberfest. Most of the time, however, the place is a family-trade enclave. The menu is divided into six different categories that cover a wide cross section of the cuisine of the world. There's Italian (chicken cacciatore); French (frog legs provençale and steak au poivre), seafood (chargrilled swordfish); German/Bavarian (Wiener schnitzel); and American (fried Georgia mountain trout or prime rib of beef). All main courses include soup, salad, vegetable, roll, and butter. In addition to their dining facilities, the owners maintain a trio of simple single bedrooms upstairs, at a cost of $65 to $85 per night. Because there's no staff here throughout most of the day, don't expect intensely personalized service during the morning and early afternoon.

DAY TRIPS FROM ALPINE HELEN

Unicoi State Park (☎ 706/878-2201) outside Helen (take Ga. 75 North for 1 mile, then right on Hwy. 356) is even more beautiful than Vogel. Visitors can also stay in the park (see "Where to Stay," above) or at least stop by for one of the buffets served at the lodge. The park is one of only five Georgia state parks with lodges and restaurants.

Lake fishing, boating, and swimming are possible, and there are four lighted tennis courts available below the lodge. Four hiking trails are located at Unicoi or nearby Anna Ruby Falls.

Half a mile north of the park is **Anna Ruby Falls,** a double falls created by the junction of the Curtis and York creeks coming off Tray Mountain from underground springs. The Curtis Falls drop 153 feet, the York about 50 feet. From a paved parking area, which charges a $2 fee, it's an easy and scenic half-mile walk through the woods along a rushing white-water stream to an observation platform at the base of the cascades. The falls are open daily from 10am to 6pm.

8 Clarkesville

100 miles NE of Atlanta

Chartered in 1823, this historic old town was named for General John C. Clarke, born a Tarheel from North Carolina in 1776 and the son of General Elijah Clarke, a Revolutionary War hero. Once Clarkesville was a major summer resort, attracting Georgians fleeing the mosquitoes and humidity along the coast. In 1924, the town had the first paved road north of Atlanta, and its fame continues today. Rand-McNally named it among the top retirement and leisure living areas in America.

Clarkesville is the gateway to the famous trout fishing of North Georgia, and is surrounded by thousands of acres of both national and state forest, some 12 public lakes, many golf courses, and private recreation clubs. The hospitality center will supply complete details, depending on your interests.

ESSENTIALS

GETTING THERE   By Car   From Helen (see above), take Hwy. 75 for 1 mile north and turn onto Hwy. 17 East, then turn left onto Hwy. 115 and following it to downtown Clarkesville.

SEEING THE SIGHTS

In the environs of Clarkesville, you can visit **Mark of the Potter,** 9982 Hwy. 197 N. (☎ 706/947-3440). It's at Grandpa Watts' Mill, Ga. 197, Route 3, an old grist mill built over the Soque River 10 miles north of Clarkesville. The mill was built in 1931 for grinding grain and corn into meal, utilizing an intricate system of turbines and the natural flow of water. Mark of the Potter opened in 1969 and is the oldest craft shop in the state of Georgia. The shop offers unique handmade crafts in wood, metal, and ceramic jewelry, plus weaving, handblown glass, and pottery by more than 40 artists and craftspeople. You can even pick up the recipe here for Grandmother's Whiskey Cake. It's open daily from 9am to 5pm.

FISHING IN THE AREA

Some of the most devoted trout fishers from all over the world make the journey to Clarkesville to test their luck. Much of the allure comes from the colonies of brown and rainbow trout that make the Soque River their home. Some anglers insist that the waters of the Soque offer opportunities only slightly less promising than the legendary trout-fishing streams of Scotland, New Zealand, and Chile.

✪ **Brigadoon on the River Soque.** 8137 Hwy. 197 N., Clarkesville, GA 30523. ☎ **706/754-1558.** www.brigadoonlodge.com.

There's no better place for fishing than this area, in a heavily wooded forest 8 miles north of Clarkesville. Brigadoon, which is owned by Travis Stewart, was rated one of the top 10 fly-fishing spots in the U.S. by the sports channel ESPN. In the late 1980s, Stewart's daughter, a hardworking entrepreneur, was able to snatch up a parcel of 1.6 miles of riverbank of the Soque (a major tributary of the Chattahoochee). She also constructed a modern chalet for the use of herself and her father.

Although two rooms within the chalet are available to guests, the building, frankly, lacks comfortable facilities. A better choice would be to check into a local B&B, then pay a rod fee of $300 per person per day to Mr. Stewart. The fee gives you access to unlimited fishing in the river from 9am to 5pm, and includes a simple picnic-style lunch, and daytime use of a bedroom and bathroom in the riverside chalet. In some rare instances, a $50 fishing permit is recommended. Further details are available directly from Mr. Stewart.

WHERE TO STAY

Burns-Sutton House Inn. 855 Washington St., Clarkesville, GA 30523. ☎ **706/754-5565.** Fax 706/754-9698. www.georgiamagazine.com/burns-sutton. 7 units. A/C. $85–$125 double. Rates include breakfast. MC, V.

Built in 1901 and listed on the National Register of Historic Places, this B&B in the historic district lies half a mile south of the main square and just a 15-minute drive to either Helen or Unicoi State Park. It is spacious and filled with touches of Victorian elegance. Wraparound porches, stained glass windows, cutwork in the balustrades, traditional mantels, and picture molding add to its old-fashioned allure. The house has been beautifully restored and decorated with period pieces and a scattering of antiques. It serves an excellent breakfast, and its bedrooms are well maintained.

✪ **Glen-Ella Springs Inn.** 1789 Bear Gap Rd., Clarkesville, GA 30523. ☎ **706/754-7295.** Fax 706/754-1560. www.glenella.com. E-mail: info@glenella.com. 16 units. A/C TEL. $125–$200 double; $145–$200 suite. Rates include breakfast. AE, DISC, MC, V.

Listed on the National Register of Historic Places, this century-old hotel and national historic site was restored in 1987 and given a new lease on life. Rooms are in a rustic yet elegant style, each individually furnished with antiques and locally handcrafted pieces. The inn stands practically inside the Chattahoochee National Forest, set on 17 acres along Panther Creek. Many hiking and walking trails are found in the area. Rocking chairs are on the front porch, and a fire is lit on cool nights in the cozy parlor furnished with antiques. It has a large swimming pool with sundeck. The food is one of the reasons to check in. A classic American cuisine is served, including dishes such as Cajun pasta or pecan-crusted trout. A gardener grows herbs and fresh vegetables in summer. *Atlanta Magazine* recently called it the "best gourmet inn in the north Georgia mountains." Special weekends are scheduled throughout the year, among them winter murder mystery weekends, cooking classes, and theme weeks.

WHERE TO DINE

✪ **LaPrade's Restaurant.** 46 Tradition Circle, Lake Burton, Clarkesville. ☎ **800/ 262-3313** or 706/947-3313. Reservations suggested. Breakfast $6.75; lunch $9.75; dinner $13.75. MC, V. Apr 1–Dec 1, Thurs–Mon 9am–9pm. SOUTHERN.

On Lake Burton, a few miles from the Appalachian Trail, this old-fashioned boarding-house-style restaurant offers good home cooking, and plenty of it. You can even stay around and rent a boat at LaPrade's Marina to try your luck at catching pike, trout, or bass.

Everyone sits shoulder to shoulder at four long tables, where heaping platters of food are passed around family style, and strangers quickly become acquainted. The type of food served here is what made the South famous: red-eye gravy on grits, coleslaw, all kinds of fresh vegetables, sugary hams, cornbread, homemade biscuits, fruit cobblers, and plenty of jams, jellies, and relishes such as chow-chow. Fried chicken, naturally, is the specialty.

If you like the place enough, you may want to stay. Twenty cabins are available, each with gas heat. The cost is $40 per person with a 2-night minimum on weekends. Children 3 to 9 pay half price, and children under 2 are free. Cabins are extremely rustic, like an old 1930s fishing camp with screened-in porches, linoleum floors, and homemade country-crude furnishings.

9 Rabun County

In northeast Georgia, 2 hours north of Atlanta on Hwy. 444, Rabun County is one of the gems of the Deep South. From Atlanta take I-85 North to I-985, then continue to its end at Hwy. 441. Then proceed 30 miles north into the heart of Rabun County, with its Blue Ridge mountain scenery galore.

With cascading waterfalls, lakes, mountain vistas, and fish-filled streams, Rabun is one of the vacation meccas of Georgia. Bordering both Carolinas, it is filled with outdoor adventures—not necessarily those depicted in the famous film *Deliverance* with Burt Reynolds, which was shot here.

A national forest covers more than 60 percent of the county, including wilderness areas like the Chattanooga Wild and Scenic River, which is rated among the top ten white-river runs in America. Attractions range from Tallulah Gorge, called "the Grand Canyon of the South," to Rabun Bald with its panoramic vistas.

✪ TALLULAH FALLS & GORGE

This land of waterfalls and gorges was a fashionable resort with several upmarket hotels until 1913. But the construction of the Georgia Power Hydroelectric Dam changed the fate of the community, and the area became a bit of a ghost town.

At 600 feet, Tallulah Gorge is one of the deepest and most panoramic in the east. The Cherokees believed it was inhabited by a race of "little people," and that those who ventured inside never came out.

Hiking in the gorge is very strenuous. The recreational center is at the 300-acre **Terrora Park and Visitor Center** (☎ 706/754-7970), with picnic areas, 50 campsites with water and electrical hookups, a beach for swimming, a playground, a bathhouse, and tennis courts, along with several nature trails. Office hours are 8am to

5pm. Nightly campsite rentals cost $12 for campers with tents, $14 for those with RVs. **Terrora Park** is immediately north of the bridge over Tallulah Gorge on the west side of U.S. 441 in the town of Tallulah Falls.

LAKE RABUN

About 5 miles from Tallulah Falls and some 20 miles from Alpine Helen, in the Chattahoochee National Forest, **Lake Rabun Recreation Area** has camping sites, a fishing pier, a boat dock, hiking trails, a public beach, and picnic areas. For information about what's there, call the **National Forest Tallulah Ranger District** at ☎ **706/782-3320.** The lake is also the site of one of the area's best-known hotels and many summer homes.

WHERE TO STAY

Lake Rabun Hotel. Lake Rabun Rd. (P.O. Box 10), Lakemont, GA 30552. ☎ **706/782-4946.** 16 units (some with bathroom). $49–$75 double. Rate includes a continental breakfast. DISC, MC, V. Closed Dec–Mar.

This is a real old-fashioned place. First built in 1922, it still has no telephones, air-conditioning, private bathrooms, or TVs. As a getaway it's been called "Georgia's sweetest secret garden." Some of the hotel's original furnishings of rhododendron and twisted laurel are still here, a little worse for wear, but mellow.

Quilts on the beds and tiebacks holding the ruffled curtains add to the old-time charm. Most of the rooms have sinks, but outside bathrooms are shared. Guests gather informally and get to know each other around the big, old fireplace. The food is good and home-cooked. If weather permits, guests have breakfast on the deck by the lake. Try innkeeper Rosa Lee's homemade bread pudding or coffeecake. Canoes are available if you'd like a closer look at the lake. Management warns, "Nobody puts on fancy airs here." They're right!

MOUNTAIN CITY

The mountain is Black Rock Mountain, setting of Black Rock Mountain State Park, so named for its dark granite cliffs. It's the highest state park in Georgia, at 3,640 feet in elevation, embracing some 1,500 acres. On a clear day, views extend for 80 miles. To reach the park, leave Mountain City and go 3 miles north of Clayton via U.S. 441. The park is open daily from 7am to 10pm year-round. It offers 48 tent and trailer sites, 11 walk-in campsites, and 10 rental cottages, plus a playground and a 17-acre lake. There are six scenic overlooks and a 10-mile trail system. For more information, contact **Black Rock Mountain State Park,** Mountain City, GA 30562 (☎ **706/746-2141**).

WHERE TO STAY

York House. P.O. Box 126, Mountain City, GA 30562. ☎ **800/231-YORK** or 706/746-2068. Fax 706/746-0210. www.gamountains.com/yorkhouse. E-mail: yorkhouse@rabun.net. 13 units. A/C TV. $79–$99 double; $99–$129 suite. Rates include country breakfast. MC, V.

This is the oldest B&B in Georgia, once an accommodation for the man who built the Tallulah Railroad. Today, John Hurlburt is the innkeeper with panache, maintaining the collections of oak, cherry, and pinewood furniture that have furnished the place since the early part of the century, and upgrading the accommodations with nostalgic charm and modern style. In 1903, scenes from *The Great Train Robbery* were filmed here, and the building has for many years been listed on the National Register of Historic Places. A kitchen is available in the main house for guest use.

DILLARD

There's one good reason to come here: to eat. Dillard lies along Hwy. 441, 2 miles south of the North Carolina border, about a 2-hour drive north from Atlanta. It's Southern hospitality all the way here, especially at Dillard House.

WHERE TO DINE

✪ **Dillard House.** Old Dillard Rd., U.S. 441/23 (P.O. Box 10), Dillard, GA 30537. ☎ **800/ 541-0671** or 706/746-5348. www.dillardhouse.com. E-mail: reservations@dillardhouse.com. Reservations required for 15 or more. Lunch $11.95–$13.95; dinner $12.95–$16.95. AE, DISC, DC, MC, V. Daily 7–10am, 11:30am–5pm, and 5:30–8pm. SOUTHERN.

The family-style meals served here are famous all over Georgia. More than 5 million hungry eaters have devoured food at the Dillard House since 1915. Country-cured ham, Southern fried chicken, tons of fresh vegetables, old-fashioned cornbread (the yellow kind), pan-fried trout, and all the relishes and desserts you could ever want burden the tables. No one in history has ever left here hungry.

You can also lodge at Dillard House Hotel, which has been restored and furnished in part with antiques. There are 61 rooms, costing $59 to $129. There are also two suites with kitchenettes, costing $99 to $129. Guests have use of a swimming pool and tennis courts, and can also go on horseback rides at the Dillard House Stables.

Macon & the Southwest

Southwest Georgia is the land of peach orchards, pecan groves, and Jimmy Carter. It's also a land of giant textile mills, pulp and paper plants, and manufacturing centers for automobiles, metal, chemicals, and furniture that bear the definite stamp of the New South.

Macon, the cherry tree capital of Georgia, is only 84 miles southeast of Atlanta and might easily be your gateway to the state's southwest. Home of rock legend Little Richard and of Southern poet Sidney Lanier, Macon is filled with white-columned antebellum buildings on the National Register of Historic Places.

After visiting the historic heartland of Georgia, you can cut southwest through two very different tourist districts, which Georgia dubs "Presidential Pathways" and "Plantation Trace." The first honors two presidents: Franklin Roosevelt, who sometimes lived at Warm Springs, and Plains's own Jimmy Carter. Steeped in history, this land is one of rolling hills and green forests. It also encompasses Pine Mountain, the gateway to the 2,500-acre Callaway Gardens—the most beautiful natural setting in Georgia. Along Plantation Trace, Native Americans and frontier soldiers have given way to farmers and timber barons. Its pocket of posh is Thomasville, which in the 1880s became the center for winter sunshine for the wealthy from the North.

1 Macon

84 miles SE of Atlanta

Only Savannah tops ✪ Macon for its striking old buildings. What comes as a huge surprise to visitors, though, is that Macon has 170,000 cherry trees—and they're a remarkable sight in late March when in bloom. Compare Washington, D.C.'s famous Cherry Blossom Festival (with a mere 3,000 trees), and you'll understand how perfumed that time of year is in Macon.

The original city planners designed Macon in 1823 as a "city in a park." Today that heritage has been preserved. Wide avenues are lined with grand, stately mansions, many built before the Civil War during the cotton boom. It's more than a river town today with many cultural offerings—such as the Georgia Music Hall of Fame, the Georgia Sports Hall of Fame, and the Grand Opera House—and educational institutions, such as Macon College, Mercer University, and Wesleyan College, the world's first college for women. And a $36 revitalization project was launched in 1999 to help restore the downtown to its original beauty.

As you'll see below, Macon has a wealth of historic sites, a handful of delightful—in one case, truly grand—places to stay, and the hospitality for which the South is known.

ESSENTIALS

GETTING THERE Take I-75 south from Atlanta, exiting at the signposted exits.

VISITOR INFORMATION If you're traveling south toward Macon on I-75, there's a **welcome center** and rest area north of the city, open daily from 8:30am to 5:30pm. When you get into town, the **Macon-Bibb County Convention and Visitors Bureau,** 200 Cherry St., Macon, GA 31201 (☎ **478/743-3401**), at the foot of Cherry Street in the historic Macon Terminal Station, will provide you with information. It's open Monday to Saturday from 9am to 5:30pm.

SPECIAL EVENTS The ✪ **Cherry Blossom Festival** is traditionally held around the last 10 days in March. During that time, 500 activities are planned around the city. You'll find everything from hot-air ballooning to a giant parade with marching bands and floats. Many events are held in the city parks. The residential areas are filled with thousands of Yoshino cherry trees. For more information, contact the Macon Cherry Blossom Festival, Inc., 749 Cherry St., Macon, GA 31201 (☎ **478/751-7429**).

SEEING THE SIGHTS

You don't have to take an organized tour in Macon. Instead, drive up and down the city's streets to look at the architecture. Be sure to get a map from the welcome center and ask the staff to highlight the historic areas—especially College and Bond streets.

Today the **Macon Terminal Station,** 200 Cherry St. (☎ **478/743-3401**), is home to the convention and visitors bureau, but in its early days, dating back to 1916, it hosted more than 100 trains a day. Tickets are sold from 9am to 5:30pm. At **Central City Park,** a 250-acre recreational area, you can enjoy ongoing events. Dr. Martin Luther King, Jr., made his only major speech in Georgia in 1957 at the **Steward Chapel of the African Methodist Episcopal Church,** 887 Forsyth St. (☎ **478/ 742-4922**). The **Ocmulgee National Monument,** at 1207 Emery Hwy., a memorial to native peoples on the site of an ancient Indian settlement and burial grounds; open daily, free.

✪ **Georgia Music Hall of Fame.** 200 Martin Luther King, Jr. Blvd. ☎ **478/738-0017.** Admission $8 adults, $6 seniors, and $3.50 children 4–16, free for children 3 and under. Mon–Sat 9am–4:30pm, Sun 1–5pm.

When it comes to music, few states can lay claim to the number of influential acts that Georgia has produced. Opened in 1996, the Georgia Music Hall of Fame has since inducted such music greats as Ray Charles, Little Richard, Otis Redding, the Allman Brothers Band, James Brown, Lena Horne, Gladys Knight, Johnny Mercer, Bill Anderson, Ronnie Milsap, The Tams, Curtis Mayfield, Issac Hayes, and Chet Atkins into the hall. The tradition of music continues with more current acts like R.E.M. and the B-52's, two bands who introduced the genre "alternative" to the music industry, forever changing the music landscape like the artists before them. The 12,000-foot exhibit hall includes a virtual Tune Town, re-creating a Georgia village at twilight, with such exhibits as a Gospel Chapel, a Soda Fountain, and the Skillet Licker Café. Music, photos, instruments, and memorabilia can be found at every turn, including the shoes that Otis Redding was wearing the day he died in a plane crash and a classic James Brown costume. A delightful new children's wing, the Billy Watson Music Factory, opened in late 1999, with interactive drums, keyboards, and the like.

Grand Opera House. 651 Mulberry St. ☎ **478/301-5460** or 912/752-5470 for box office information. Tickets $22–$29. Box office Mon–Fri 10am–5pm.

The Academy of Music was constructed in 1884 and later became known as the Grand Opera House. Such old-timers as Sarah Bernhardt, Will Rogers, the Gish sisters, Dorothy Lamour, and Burns and Allen have performed here. With seating for 1,057, it also boasts one of America's largest stages—big enough to accommodate a production of *Ben Hur* with its stage machinery and treadmills for the chariot races. Around Christmas each year, the Allman Brothers Band performs a homecoming concert for a small crowd of friends, family, and fans.

Tubman African American Museum. 340 Walnut St. ☎ **478/743-8544.** Admission $3 adults, $2 children. Mon–Fri 9am–5pm, Sat 10–5pm, Sun 2–5pm.

This offbeat and unusual museum, dedicated to exploring the cultural heritage of African Americans, was named in honor of Harriet Tubman, a former slave who led some 300 people to freedom as a conductor on the Underground Railroad. It includes cultural artifacts, folk and African art, rotating exhibits, and a mural spanning two walls that took decades to complete and depicts African-American culture in the region. The museum will be moving to a new $15 million site in late 2001 or early 2002.

✪ Hay House. 934 Georgia Ave. ☎ **478/742-8155.** Admission $6 adults, $5 senior citizens, $2 students, $1 children 6–12, free for children 5 and under. Daily 10am–5pm. Closed holidays.

If you see nothing else in Macon, see the Hay House. Built between 1855 and 1860 for the then-exorbitant cost of $100,000, this extravagant Italian Renaissance Revival home belonged to William Butler Johnston, the keeper of the Confederate treasury. The restored interiors here are nothing short of spectacular—stained glass, ornate period furnishings, Carerra marble, and trompe l'oeil wall paintings. Its infrastructure was ahead of its time as well, with a cleverly designed ventilation system, hot and cold running water, and central heating. An ongoing restoration is uncovering original hand-painted decorative walls. The house is a registered National Historic Landmark.

✪ Rose Hill Cemetery. Riverside Dr. ☎ **478/751-9119.** Free admission. Open daily until sundown.

This beautiful 68-acre cemetery alongside the Ocmulgee River was landscaped in 1840, making it one of the oldest surviving public cemeteries in the country. Terraced hills and cypress trees give it a grandeur not unlike that of the Forum in Rome. Among those buried here are Confederate generals, Georgia politicians and entrepreneurs, beloved pets, and two members of the Allman Brothers rock band, who died within a year of each other in motorcycle accidents at the same Napier Street intersection.

Sidney Lanier Cottage. 935 High St. ☎ **478/743-3851.** Admission $3 adults, $1 students, 50¢ for children 12 and under, free for children 4 and under. Mon–Fri 9am–1pm and 2–4pm, Sat 9:30am–12:30pm. Closed holidays.

This 1842 Victorian cottage was the birthplace of Sidney Lanier, one of Georgia's most famous citizens, a poet who is best known for "The Marshes of Glynn." The wedding gown of Lanier's wife, Mary Day, is on display; Scarlett O'Hara would have been pea-green with envy over the bride's ultra-tiny waist. The house is outfitted in furnishings of the period and is home to the Middle Georgia Historical Society.

TOURS

Stop at the convention and visitors bureau (see "Essentials," above) for maps of the following self-guided tours: The **Victorian Walking Tour** includes stops at Magnolia Street to see Victorian cottages, the Hill-O'Neal Cottage, the Washington Memorial

Library, and the New Federal Building and Post Office. The **Historic Downtown Walking Tour** includes City Hall, the Municipal Auditorium, Mulberry Street Park, Washington Block where the stagecoach once stopped, the Baber House (1830), and the Grand Opera House. Almost 25 stops are listed in this walking tour. The **White Columns Walking Tour** will highlight the best of Macon's 400 columned buildings and homes, including the Carmichael House, the Edward Dorr Tracy House, the Old Cannonball House, the Hay House, the Woodruff House, the Greek Revival Randolph-Whittle-Davis-Smith House with its round and square portico columns, and the 1842 Inn (see "Where to Stay," below).

Organized tours are offered by the popular **Sidney's Tours of Historic Macon,** Terminal Station Building, 200 Cherry St. (☎ 478/743-3401), which conducts tours of three historic homes. The tour is given Monday to Saturday at 10am and 2pm and costs $15 for adults and $6 for children 12 and under, including admission prices. It's advised that you arrive at least 15 minutes prior to tour departure.

WHERE TO STAY

Along I-75 are many chain hotels and motels, including Howard Johnson, Comfort Inn, Holiday Inn, and Hampton Inn. Off I-475 are Ramada Inn, Travelodge, and a Holiday Inn. The best chain choices are the **Best Western Riverside Inn,** 2400 Riverside Dr. (☎ 478/743-6311), and the **Courtyard by Marriott,** 3990 Sheraton Dr. (☎ 478/477-8899).

✪ **1842 Inn.** 353 College St., Macon, GA 31201. ☎ 800/336-1842 or 478/741-1842. Fax 478/741-1842. www.1842inn.com. 21 units. A/C TV TEL. $215–$255 double. AE, MC, V. Take Exit 52 off I-75, then go 4 blocks to the center of the historic district.

The 1842 Inn is reason enough to come to Macon. It's truly special, and is one of our favorite inns south of the Mason-Dixon Line. This four-diamond, four-star inn is romantic, upscale, and charming. You're likely to find a working fireplace in your room, along with antiques, expensive fabrics, four-poster beds, and maybe even a whirlpool. But what turns this place into something truly memorable is the lovely staff, who have been here for years and who epitomize warm-as-toast Southern hospitality. JoAnne Dillard's specially made mint juleps are fashioned from boiled mint fresh from the kitchen garden, and are served in elegant silver julep cups, along with evening hors d'oeuvres, in one of the parlor rooms. The inn has no restaurant (look for on-site dining facilities in the near future), but travelers arriving late can arrange to have a fine French meal from La Lavandier waiting for them on the candlelit patio. Across the courtyard is a 1900 Victorian cottage with equally elegant rooms. Come to Macon and add your name to the list of celebrities (including Dr. Ruth and Barbara Walters) who have stayed here. Named one of *Country Inn* magazine's Top 10 Inns in 1999.

WHERE TO DINE

Macon has a growing number of upscale restaurants, but if it's down-home Southern cooking you want, you'll find it here. **Len Berg's Restaurant,** in Old Post Alley between Walnut and Mulberry streets (☎ 478/742-9255), is a Macon institution, serving home cooking, pure and simple. Try the fried catfish fillet or the grilled liver with onions, and end with the cream-topped macaroon pie for dessert. Barbecue lovers can opt for **Satterfield's,** on 120 New St. (☎ 478/745-8342), where you can snack on homemade boiled peanuts while you wait for your order of good barbecue, Brunswick stew, and long-cooked vegetables (it even offers an all-you-can-eat-quail night). **Fincher's Barbecue,** 3947 Houston Ave., and three other locations (☎ 478/474-0001), is another local institution, a family-run restaurant with curb service at the Houston Avenue location and good, old-fashioned barbecued pork, ribs, and chicken.

The Back Burner Restaurant. 2242 Ingleside Ave. ☎ **478/746-3336.** Lunch main courses $7.50–$12; dinner main courses $15–$20. Tues–Sat 11:30am–2pm and 6pm–9:30pm. Closed Sun and Mon. NOUVELLE CONTINENTAL.

Chef Christian Losito has brought serious food to Macon at this charming cottage off Ingleside Avenue. The Nice, France, native offers a changing menu that may include a Chilean sea bass in a champagne-and-shallot sauce, rack of lamb in a Dijon-thyme sauce, or grilled shrimp over penne pasta in a mushroom-wine sauce. Lunchtime soups and salads are fresh and innovative. The restaurant is broken into intimate, low-ceilinged rooms, each painted a different, handsome color; white linens and flowers complete the sunny picture.

2 Columbus

109 miles S of Atlanta; 90 miles SW of Macon

Situated on the Chattahoochee River at the foot of a series of falls, Columbus is a former Creek Indian settlement that dates from 1827. Columbus utilized its water supply to become an important manufacturing center, supplying swords, pistols, cannons, gunboats, and other articles of war to the Confederate Army during the Civil War. It fell to Union forces in April of 1865 in one of the last battles of the war. By 1940, Columbus had become a major iron-working center and the second biggest producer of "king cotton" in the South. Today a riverside walkway, the **Columbus Chattahoochee Promenade,** with gazebos and historical displays, stretches from the Columbus Iron Works Trade and Convention Center to Oglethorpe Bridge.

If you anticipate a dreary industrial town, you may be surprised to find a historic district stretching for some 30 blocks. Victorian gardens, antebellum homes, and gazebos maintain the aura of another day, in spite of the industries that are still powered from the Chattahoochee River. Columbus has a 9-foot-deep navigable channel that runs all the way to the Gulf of Mexico.

ESSENTIALS

GETTING THERE   By Plane   The Columbus Airport receives commuter flights daily from Atlanta via **Delta** (☎ 706/327-4397; www.delta.com) and **Northwest Airlines** (☎ 800/225-2525 or 706/323-0790; www.nwa.com). For more specific route information and connections, call the **airport office** at ☎ 706/324-2449.

By Train   There is no service. Train passengers arrive in Atlanta and must continue the rest of the way by bus.

By Bus   Greyhound bus services run between Atlanta and Columbus daily, beginning at 4:20am and lasting until 9pm. Trip time is 3 hours, a one-way fare costing $17.66. Call **Greyhound** at ☎ 706/322-7391 in Columbus for more information about schedules.

By Car   This is the fastest and easiest way to reach Columbus from either Atlanta or Macon. From Atlanta, take I-85 south to I-185, which leads into Columbus. From Macon, take I-80 West into the center of Columbus.

   Historic Columbus Foundation, 700 Broadway (☎ 706/323-7979), distributes self-guided tour brochures outlining walking and/or driving tours. Conducted tours are at 11am and 2pm Monday to Saturday and at 2pm on Saturday and Sunday, costing $5 per person. The foundation is worth a visit on its own, as it dates from 1870 and is furnished with antiques.

VISITOR INFORMATION   The **Columbus Visitors Center,** corner of Bay Avenue and 10th Street (☎ **706/322-1613** or 800/999-1613), offers not only maps and information, but presents a 10-minute video outlining what to see and do in the area. Hours are Monday to Friday from 8am to 5pm, Saturday 11am to 5pm, and Sunday 1 to 5pm.

SEEING THE SIGHTS

Some of history's greatest actors have appeared at the 1871 **Springer Opera House,** 103 10th St. (☎ **706/327-3688**), including Shakespearean actor Edwin Booth. Designated in 1994 by the Georgia Council for the Arts as the first major theater organized in the state, it still presents regular performances. If you're not here when something's on, you can still tour the theater. For guided tours or ticket information, call the number above.

Columbus Museum, 1251 Wynnton Rd. (☎ **706/649-0713**), exhibits prehistoric Native American relics along with artifacts of regional history, works of art from the late 1800s and the early 1900s, decorative art displays, and a restored log cabin. Its Chattahoochee Legacy features a regional history gallery with re-created period settings. It's the most important regional museum of its type in Southwest Georgia. Hours are Tuesday to Saturday from 10am to 5pm, Sunday from 1 to 5pm. Although admission is free, donations are accepted.

Confederate Naval Museum, 202 Fourth St. (☎ **706/327-9798**), should be on the agenda of every Civil War buff, as it displays salvaged remains of the Confederate gunboats *Chattahoochee* and *Jackson.* Uniforms, Civil War paintings, ship models, and various artifacts re-create the War Between the States at sea. Hours are Tuesday to Friday from 10am to 5pm, Saturday and Sunday from 1 to 5pm. Admission is free but donations are accepted.

WHERE TO STAY

Columbus Hilton. 800 Front Ave., Columbus, GA 31901. ☎ **800/HILTONS** or 706/ 324-1800. Fax 706/576-4413. www.hilton.com. 177 units. A/C MINIBAR TV TEL. $99–$149 double; $300–$350 suite. AE, MC, V.

Set adjacent to the river, this is the largest and most unusual large-scale hotel in town. A section of the hotel is an antebellum gristmill that was saved by Hilton in 1982, when it was threatened with demolition. Ironically, in 1865, this same gristmill had been spared by Yankee troops as a humanitarian gesture. Today, an overhead skylight of glass and steel spans a courtyard/lobby where, a century before, wagons and mules hauled away massive quantities of grain, feed, cornmeal, and flour. Only 17 of the hotel's rooms occupy the original three-story historic site: The others lie in a modern, six-story redbrick annex created to imitate as closely as possible the design of the original monument. Bedrooms are comfortably and conservatively decorated in a neutral international style. On the premises is a brick and mahogany-lined bar, Hunter's Lounge, and a restaurant, Pemberton's Cafe.

Sheraton Airport Hotel. 5351 Simons Blvd., Columbus, GA 31904. ☎ **800/325-3535** or 706/327-6868. Fax 706/327-0041. www.sheraton.com. 176 units. A/C TV TEL. $69–$99 double. Occasional Sat–Sun reductions of $10. Children 18 and under free in parents' room. AE, CB, DC, DISC, MC, V. Free parking.

Without the charm and grace of the previously recommended Hilton, this is never-theless a serviceable and good-value hotel, the second best in town. Less than a decade old, the hotel is in good shape, and maintenance is high. Rooms, although standard, are well furnished and comfortable. An outside heated pool adjoins a whirlpool. The Atrium, a middle-bracket restaurant on site, begins breakfast at 6:30am, and also offers a lunch buffet. Dinner features à la carte dining, and there is also a Cheers lounge on site, where entertainment means a DJ playing top-40 music, in addition to occasional live music, karaoke, and the BET Comedy Jam for dancers on the floor. The Sheraton provides transportation to and privileges at the nearby Gold's Gym. Six miles from the center, it is convenient for air travelers.

WHERE TO DINE

Bludau's Goétchius House. 405 Broadway. ☎ **706/324-4863.** Reservations recommended. Main courses $15.95–$45.95. AE, DC, DISC, MC, V. Mon–Thurs 5–9:45pm; Fri–Sat 5–10:45pm. CONTINENTAL.

This is the most upmarket and elegant restaurant in the Columbus area, housed in a restored antebellum mansion from 1839. On the banks of the Chattahoochee River, the house is actually more evocative of New Orleans than southwest Georgia. There are several dining rooms, a darkened downstairs bar, and an outside patio with a fountain in fair weather. Cabbage-rose carpets and gold curtains create a rich, evocative aura. The menu has all those delectable dishes that used to characterize deluxe New York restaurants of the 1950s: clams casino, oysters Rockefeller, frog legs bourguignon, and escargots duxelles. Main courses continue the old-fashioned tradition with such elegant dishes as steak Diane, which is so good it makes you wonder why so many chefs have dropped it from their repertoire.

Olive Branch Cafe. 1032 Broadway. ☎ **706/322-7410.** Reservations recommended. Lunch main courses $5.50–$12.50; dinner main courses $9.95–$25.95. DISC, MC, V. Mon–Fri 11:30am–2:30pm, Mon–Sat 5:30–10pm. MEDITERRANEAN.

This is the liveliest and most ambitious of the independent restaurants in Columbus's downtown. The cafe has dining room dividers, abstract murals in tutti-frutti colors, and the accessories you might expect at Carnival in Venice. Crayons and paper tablecloths amuse children and adults alike. Menu items read like a culinary review of the cuisines of the northern Mediterranean, including manicotti filled with basil and ricotta cheese and topped with mozzarella and marinara; grilled marinated portabello mushroom with fresh vegetables and carrot-ginger oil; or grilled mahimahi served with salsify, potato, roasted garlic, French-style green beans, capers, and a brown-butter sauce.

3 Callaway Gardens

70 miles S of Atlanta

One of the most beautiful spots in the South, Callaway Gardens embraces 14,000 acres of gardens, woodlands, and lakes, with wildlife and outdoor activities. Some 750,000 visitors are attracted to this site annually, especially in spring when its Azalea Trail displays some 700 colorful varieties. But every season brings something new into bloom, from rhododendron and holly trails to the wildflower trail.

Callaway Gardens at Pine Mountain was begun back in the 1930s. Cason Callaway, head of one of Georgia's most prosperous textile mills, once said, "All I've done is try to fix it so that anybody who came here would see something beautiful wherever he might look." He set about rebuilding the soil, nurturing and importing plant life, building the largest man-made inland beach in the world, and providing inn and cottage accommodations—and opened it all to citizens of modest means.

ESSENTIALS

GETTING THERE   From Atlanta, take I-85 South to I-185, continue on I-185 south to Exit 14, and then turn left on U.S. 27 and drive 11 miles to Callaway Gardens.

Driving north on either I-185 or I-85, exit east on Ga. 18 to Pine Mountain, and then turn right on U.S. 27 and enter Callaway Gardens.

SEEING THE GARDENS

✪ **Callaway Gardens,** at Pine Mountain (☎ 706/663-2281), include floral and hiking trails and acres of picnic grounds. Special events abound, particularly the Spring Celebration. In May, Callaway plays host to the Masters Waterski Tournament. July 4 is the occasion of the sunrise-to-sunset Surf and Sand Spectacular, giving way to the PGA Tour's Buick Challenge at the Mountain View Golf Course in the fall. The Fall Festival celebrates the beauty of the chrysanthemums, and Fantasy in Lights at Christmas is a brilliant ride through the gardens with a display of lights and music.

The park has many attractions. The **Cecil B. Day Butterfly Center,** a $5.3-million center, ranks with the world's foremost conservatories in London, Melbourne, and Tokyo. The octagonal conservatory houses more than 1,000 free-flying butterflies and numerous birds. The conservatory includes a 12-foot waterfall and lush tropical foliage.

John A. Sibley Horticultural Center, one of the most advanced garden and green-house complexes in the world, encompasses 5 acres with 20,200 square feet of indoor floral displays, plus 30,675 square feet of greenhouse space. Floral displays integrate indoor and outdoor settings.

Mr. Cason's Vegetable Garden, started in 1960, was the last major project initiated by Mr. Callaway. On 7½ acres, gardeners demonstrate scientific, educational, and practical applications of fruit and vegetable culture. A trio of large terraces in a semi-circular design, the vegetable garden produces more than 400 varieties of crops that range from traditional Southern fruits and vegetables to wildflower test plots. The PBS show *Victory Garden* films its Southern segments from here.

Ida Cason Callaway Memorial Chapel, in the English gothic style, was built to honor Mr. Callaway's mother, Ida Cason. It was dedicated in 1962 by Dr. Norman Vincent Peale. It's patterned much like a rural wayside chapel of the 16th and 17th centuries.

The park is open daily from 9am to 5pm with extended summer hours. Admission is $10 for adults, $5 for children 6 to 11, and free for children 5 and under.

OUTDOOR PURSUITS

BEACH RESORT   Robin Lake Beach, on a 65-acre lake, is the largest inland man-made white-sand beach anywhere in the world. It offers a center for children with a large outdoor playground, as well as miniature golf, badminton, and rides on a river-boat. In summer, a show is presented by Florida State University's Flying High Circus. A trail stretches nearly a mile around the lake with 20 fitness stations. Robin Lake Beach is a virtual mini-resort, with sand, surf, and dozens of other activities. Admission is $10 for adults, $5 for children 6 to 12. The beach is open daily from 9am to 6pm in summer (closes Labor Day until the first of June).

BIKING   Callaway Gardens has 7½ paved miles for bikers who'd like to see the gardens up close instead of from a car. The Discovery Bicycle Trail is a family favorite. It begins at Bike Barn near the beach parking lot at Robin Lake, where you can rent bikes and helmets (some bikes are equipped with child safety seats). A ferry is available near the end of the trail at the boat dock to transport riders across Mountain Creek Lake back to their starting point. The Bike Barn rents daily from 8am to 6pm, charging $10 for 2 hours or $15 per half day.

FISHING   Fishing is available on Mountain Creek Lake, where two persons can rent a boat for $30 per half day or $45 per day.

◐ **GOLF**   Four well-groomed courses, hailed by *Golf Digest* and *Golf* magazine, are set in the midst of clear lakes, lush landscaping, and wooded shores. **Mountain View,** designed by Dick Wilson, is viewed as the best by many golfers. Tight, tree-lined fairways are characteristic of this championship course. At hole no. 15 (par 5), the threat of water looms over both tee and approach shots. This hole is ranked as the fourth most difficult par 5 on the tour by *USA Today.* **Lake View** was the original course, designed only in part by Dick Wilson. Mr. Callaway himself provided the inspiration for this course, whose challenge lies in its nine water holes. The par-70 course is known for its no. 5 with its island tee and serpentine bridge over Mountain Creek Lake to the green in front of the Gardens Restaurant. **Gardens View,** designed by Joe Lee, is a par-72 course, running along a trail of orchards and vineyards. Its hilly terrain, water hazards, and greens-guarding bunkers make this course an excellent test of shot-making ability. **Mountain View** is the most expensive course to play, costing $95 off-season or $110 in summer. The other two courses cost $55 off-season, rising to $75 in summer. Finally, the 9-hole **Sky View,** with its no-cart rule, is a par-31 executive course ideal for an hour or two of fresh air and warm-up for 18 holes. Greens fees here are $22 off-season, going up to $33 in summer.

◐ **TENNIS**   *Tennis* magazine awarded Callaway a "Top 50" national rating. Nine courts are hard surfaced, and eight have Rubico surfaces. Two glass-walled racquetball courts and a pro shop are in the complex.

WHERE TO STAY

Callaway Gardens Resort. U.S. 27, Pine Mountain, GA 31822. ☎ **800/CALLAWAY** or 706/663-2281. Fax 706/663-5080. www.callawaygardens.com. 349 units, 155 1- and 2-bedroom cottages, 49 2- to 4-bedroom villas. A/C TV TEL. $96–$114 double; $136–$300 suite; $171–$333 1- and 2-bedroom cottages; $180–$582 2- to 4-bedroom villas. Honeymoon, sports, and monthly packages available. AE, CB, DC, DISC, MC, V.

In 1951, as the success of Callaway Gardens attracted visitors from around the country, Cason Callaway engaged Holiday Inn to build a motel on gently sloping terrain across the highway from the gardens. Eventually Callaway acquired the property and enlarged it. Despite the complete renovation, some units still evoke the Holiday Inn of old.

Set adjacent to the resort's freshwater beach, rustic two-bedroom cottages contain fireplaces, kitchens, and lots of modern amenities. Popular with families, they're what you'd expect at an outdoor camping retreat, and seem to have endured their share of wear and tear. More stylish are the villas; all have kitchens, relatively formal furnishings, fireplaces, screened-in verandas, and a greater emphasis on style and comfort.

Magnolia Hall B&B. 127 Barnes Mill Rd. (P.O. Box 326) , Hamilton, GA 31811. ☎ **706/628-4566.** Fax 706/628-5802. www.bbonline.com/ga/magnoliahall. E-mail: kgsmag@juno.com. 5 units. A/C TV. $95–$115 double. Extra person $20. Rates include breakfast. No credit cards.

Open year-round, this B&B lies 5 miles from the entrance to Callaway Gardens. An 1890s Victorian home, it's surrounded by an acre of land with azaleas, tea olives, camellias, and the namesake magnolias. Potted ferns and cushioned wicker evoke the Deep South. Antiques-filled rooms, a grand piano in the sitting room, and tall ceilings add grace notes. Bedrooms are spacious. This is not necessarily a place for kids and definitely not a place for smokers.

Valley Inn Resort. 14420 Hwy. 27, Hamilton, GA 31811. ☎ **800/944-9393** or 706/628-4454. 29 units. A/C TV TEL. $50–$79 double; $105 1-bedroom cottage; $120 2-bedroom cottage; $120 mobile home. AE, MC, V.

There's nothing special here, but as motels go, it's one of the best of the lot. Families, especially in summer, like this small resort, set on 52 acres near a lake and with an outdoor pool. Bedrooms are comfortably furnished, some containing kitchens. You can bring your own RV to park in the Travel Trailer Park or rent a two-bedroom mobile home unit that sleeps up to six.

White Columns Motel. Hwy. 27 S. (P.O. Box 531), Pine Mountain, GA 31822. ☎ **706/663-2312.** 13 units. A/C TV. $55 double. AE, MC, V.

Close to Callaway Gardens, this small family-owned and -operated white-columned motel is a favorite budget choice in the area. Rooms are basic, a little worse for wear, but clean and comfortable. Pets are accepted. Within walking distance of the motel are two good and moderately priced restaurants.

WHERE TO DINE

The Country Kitchen. Hwy. 27, near Callaway Gardens. ☎ **706/663-2281.** Reservations not necessary. Breakfast platters $5.50–$5.75; main courses $5–$8.25. AE, DISC, MC, V. Daily 7am–8pm. SOUTHERN.

First things first: Don't come here looking for health food. Despite that, its premises (a stone-built roadside country store about a mile south of the Gardens' entrance, near the top of Pine Mountain) are usually mobbed with families looking for a taste of wholesome country nostalgia. The setting is rustic and woodsy. Menu items include chicken or country ham with biscuits and gravy, an array of vegetables, burgers, and club sandwiches. Dessert might be a portion of muscadine ice cream. If you need grits to get your day started right, have them along with "Mama's pancakes" or a country omelet.

✪ **Georgia Room.** At Callaway Gardens. ☎ **706/663-2281.** Reservations required. Main courses $17.50–$25. AE, DISC, MC, V. Mon–Sat 6–9pm. INTERNATIONAL.

This formal, upscale restaurant in the Gardens' main hotel is complete with candlelight and piano music. Menu items are cultivated and carefully prepared, and served with a reverential hush, and include such dishes as mustard and rosemary-encrusted lamb chops, filet mignon, grilled Atlantic salmon, prime rib, and such specialty salads as spinach and bacon. The restaurant is not suitable for small children.

The Plantation Room. At Callaway Gardens. ☎ **706/663-2281.** Breakfast buffet $8.95; lunch buffet $8.95 Mon–Sat, $15.95 Sun; dinner buffet $16.95 Mon–Sat, $19.95 Fri. AE, DISC, MC, V. Daily 6:30–10:30am, 11:30am–3pm, and 6–10pm. SOUTHERN.

The buffets here celebrate culinary traditions of the Old South. Vegetables are the freshest in summer, when they come to your table just hours after being picked from Mr. Cason's Vegetable Garden. If you've never eaten corn just pulled from the stalk, you'll find how different it is from store-bought corn pulled days before. It can get very crowded here, especially on Friday nights, when the theme is seafood.

The Veranda/The Gardens. Hwy. 27, near Callaway Gardens. ☎ **706/663-2281.** Reservations recommended. Main courses $9–$16 at The Veranda; $9–$19 at The Gardens. The Gardens daily 11am–3pm and Tues–Sat 6:30–9:30pm. The Veranda Wed–Sun 6–10pm. ITALIAN/INTERNATIONAL.

Both of these places occupy a sprawling and immensely atmospheric building whose stout timbers and rambling verandas resemble a grange in Eastern France or Germany. The more formal of the two is The Gardens, where our favorite tables are perched on a balcony overlooking a landscape of golf fairways and a pond that has a serpentine bridge zigzagging across its waters. The menu emphasizes grilled steaks, seafood, and chops. The less expensive of the two is The Veranda, on the building's lower level. There you'll find pastas, salads, shrimp scampi, grouper Florentine, and veal cutlets.

4 Warm Springs & FDR's Little White House

17 miles E of Callaway Gardens; 65 miles S of Atlanta

If you take Ga. 190 east and follow the signs, you'll be directed to Warm Springs, forever associated with the legacy of Franklin D. Roosevelt, who died here on April 12, 1945. Most visitors—some 125,000 a year—come to visit the "Little White House." Warm Springs village is also an attraction. After Roosevelt's death, it became a virtual ghost town, but today the village is alive with 65 shops, selling antiques, crafts, and collectibles.

The **Franklin D. Roosevelt State Park,** off U.S. 27, is one of the largest in Georgia's state system, with many historic buildings, the King's Gap Indian Trail, a swimming pool, and fishing and camping facilities. For more information, contact the Superintendent, 2970 Ga. 190 E. (☎ **706/663-4858**).

ESSENTIALS

GETTING THERE   Take I-85 South from Atlanta to Alt. U.S. 27 South, which you follow into Warm Springs.

To reach Warm Springs from Callaway Gardens, take U.S. 27 North into the town of Pine Mountain. At the intersection of U.S. 27 and Ga. 18, take Ga. 18 east to Ga. 194 and proceed on Ga. 194 east until it joins Alt. U.S. 27. Stay on Alt. U.S. 27/Ga. 194 South into Warm Springs.

VISITOR INFORMATION   Warm Springs Welcome Center, Broad Street (P.O. Box 156), Warm Springs, GA 31830 (☎ **706/655-9096**), is open Monday to Friday, 8am to 4:30pm, dispensing information and maps of the village.

✪ THE "LITTLE WHITE HOUSE"

This home, which came to be called the **"Little White House,"** a quarter of a mile south of Warm Springs on Ga. 85 West (☎ **706/655-5870**), was built in 1932 for $8,738—a modest outlay for a man of Franklin Roosevelt's wealth. This tiny place was once the occasional nerve center of the commander-in-chief of the nation during the greatest war of all time.

FDR discovered Warm Springs in 1924. He contracted polio in 1921, and came here for the beneficial effect of swimming in its healing waters. Two years later he bought the springs, hotel, and some cottages and founded his Georgia Warm Springs Foundation to develop facilities for helping paralytic patients from all over the country. When he became president, this was the retreat he loved most. Today the house is much as he left it when he died here in 1945. At the time he was sitting for a portrait; the *Unfinished Portrait,* his wheelchair, ship models, sea paintings, and Fala's dog chain and the gifts sent him by various citizens are preserved as he last saw them. The house is open daily from 9am to 5pm. Admission is $5 for adults, $4 seniors, and $2 for children 6 to 18. Free 5 and under.

Next door, the **Franklin D. Roosevelt Museum** (☎ **706/655-5870**) holds more memorabilia and shows a 12-minute movie depicting FDR's life. Museum admission is included with entrance to the Little White House.

WHERE TO STAY

Hotel Warm Springs. 47 Broad St., Warm Springs, GA 31830. ☎ **800/366-7616** or 706/655-2114. Fax 706/655-2406. 14 units. A/C TV. $85–$103 double; $120–$175 suite. Rates include breakfast. AE, DISC, MC, V.

This hotel, built in 1907, thrived when the region's economy boomed because of the presence of FDR throughout the war years. Gerrie Thompson, its owner since 1988,

---

The Unfinished Portrait

Although never completed, one of the world's most famous portraits rests in Warm Springs in FDR's "Little White House." He was posing for it shortly before he died on April 12, 1945. In some respects, Elizabeth Shoumatoff's portrait symbolizes Roosevelt's unfinished life, and his unfinished (and unprecedented) fourth term that was to be filled out by Harry S Truman. Roosevelt, plagued by ill health, would have continued to face monumental decisions that year if he'd lived. He would have presided over the defeat of the Nazi armies and been faced with the decision of whether or not to drop the atomic bomb (which he'd ordered built) on Japan. After that fateful spring day, Truman had to make those decisions in FDR's place.

The president's ashen pallor and his tired, drawn face are captured in the unfinished portrait, revealing the stress FDR felt at the end of the most destructive war in history. His wife, Eleanor, arrived in Warm Springs shortly after midnight on the day of his death. When she wrote about that night in *This I Remember,* Mrs. Roosevelt chose not to mention that Lucy Mercer Rutherford, FDR's sweetheart, was with him when he died. However, she later wrote: "All human beings have failings, and all human beings have needs and temptations and stresses." It is Roosevelt's humanity that we remember.

---

can recite a guest list that includes the Queen of Mexico (who came for the cure, and slept on the floor because of an injured spine), the King and Queen of Spain, the President of the Philippines, and armies of journalists, Cabinet members, and Secret Service agents—and a screen legend named Bette Davis.

Despite some half-hearted attempts at redecoration (new curtains, the installation of a heart-shaped Jacuzzi in the honeymoon suite), this artfully dowdy period piece from another age evokes the languor and sultriness of the 1940s in the Deep South. Some of the bedrooms contain old-fashioned oak furniture made in the factory Eleanor Roosevelt established in Val-Kill, New York, to relieve unemployment during the Great Depression. Sitting rooms and a high-ceilinged breakfast room are on the second and third floors. Interestingly, this structure was the home of the first phone system in Warm Springs.

WHERE TO DINE

Set in a 1906 general merchandise store, the **Ashley on Broad Street,** Broad Street (☎ 706/655-2319), is the most popular place in town for lunch.

Bulloch House Restaurant. 47 Bulloch St. ☎ **706/655-9068.** Lunch buffet $5.95; dinner buffet $8.95. AE, DISC, MC, V. Daily 11am–2:30pm and Fri–Sat 5–8:30pm. SOUTHERN.

Set on a leafy hillside, a 10-minute walk from the center of town, the place occupies the genteel premises of a house originally built in 1892. Citizens from virtually every walk of life file by the buffets, plate in hand. There are five different homey, dowdy dining areas. One is a front porch overlooking the road, although most diners remain in the air-conditioned interior. Menu items celebrate deep-fried, local cookery, and always include fried green tomatoes, fried fish, fried chicken, fried okra, butterbeans, turnip greens, potatoes, biscuits, bread, and copious amounts of iced tea. No alcohol of any kind is served. It's very much a family-fry operation.

5 Plains: Jimmy Carter's Hometown

80 miles SE of Callaway Gardens; 85 miles SW of Macon; 10 miles W of Americus

More than any other president in recent years, Jimmy Carter is closely identified with his hometown—Plains, Georgia. The aptly named town of 716 is both plain and sited on the plains.

Humble though it is, Plains is where a young boy grew up to become the 39th president of the United States. If FDR was an American aristocrat, "Jimmy," as he is called locally, was—and still is—a man of the people, the most approachable president in recent history.

You'll know Plains by the little green-and-white train depot, its water tower brightly painted with the Stars and Stripes. Despite the fame of its most outstanding citizen, a small-town charm still clings to Plains and its people. The early-1900s buildings are much as they were before the Depression forced their closing (most were used as warehouses until Jimmy Carter's campaign brought business back to town).

ESSENTIALS

GETTING THERE   From Macon, take I-75 South to Cordele; exit there onto U.S. 280 and head west through Americus to Plains. From Callaway Gardens, take U.S. 27 to Pine Mountain, turn left on Ga. 18 to I-185, and then take I-185 South through Columbus to U.S. 280; head south (or east) on U.S. 280 into Plains.

VISITOR INFORMATION   If you stand in the middle of the street, you can almost see the whole town, including Billy Carter's former service station, which used to sell beer to newspeople when Billy was alive. For a do-it-yourself walking or driving tour to points of interest, stop in at the **Georgia Visitor Center,** east of Plains at 1763 Hwy. 280 (☎ **912/824-7477**), open daily from 8:30am to 5:30pm. The staff there will furnish maps and brochures.

SEEING THE SIGHTS

✪ **Jimmy Carter National Historic Site** (☎ **912/824-3413**) is 77 acres administered by the U.S. Department of the Interior. An old-fashioned railway depot from 1888 is the headquarters of the visitor center—it also served as Carter's campaign headquarters in 1976 and again in 1980 when he lost to Ronald Reagan. The depot is filled with campaign memorabilia, and is open daily (except Thanksgiving, Christmas, and New Year's days) from 9am to 5pm. Admission is free. A cassette auto driving tour of Plains is available for $1, or you can book a guided tour for $5.

The one-story, ranch-style brick **Carter home** is on Woodland Drive; when the Carters are in residence, there are Secret Service booths at this entrance and at the one on Paschal Street (you can get a pretty good look at it by walking and driving west on Church Street). Then there's the **Plains Methodist Church,** at the corner of Church and Thomas streets, where Jimmy asked Rosalynn for their first date. When he's in town, Jimmy teaches Sunday school at **Maranatha Baptist Church.** Visitors are invited—check the notice in the window of Hugh Carter's Antiques on Main Street. **Archery,** a 2½-mile drive west of town on U.S. 280, is where Jimmy Carter lived as a child when his father operated a country store. Anybody in Plains can give you explicit directions.

WHERE TO STAY

✪ **Plains Bed and Breakfast Inn.** Main St., Plains, GA 31780. ☎ **912/824-7252.** 4 units. TEL. $70 double. Rate includes a Southern breakfast. DC, MC, V.

Painted in a stylish shade of dusty rose and built in 1910 by a Baptist preacher, this place provides the only conventional lodgings in Plains. It sits adjacent to the trailerlike building that houses the local sheriff, two doors away from a service station that proclaims its enduring association with Billy Carter. The inn is an odd mixture of small-town virtue and religious revivalism. Its best feature is the spacious veranda for porch-swinging. Most of the inside, however, is old-fashioned. Miss Lillian and her new husband occupied one of the upstairs bedrooms around the time the future president was conceived. A sign in the upstairs hallway obliquely refers to this portentous event in ever-so-polite phrasing. During Carter's term, some of the most visible figures in American media slept here.

WHERE TO DINE

Do as the Carters do and head for nearby Americus—notably the **Grand Dining Room at the Windsor Hotel,** 125 W. Lamar St. (☎ **912/924-1555**). This high-ceilinged, historic restaurant reigns without competition in a town filled with rustic, down-home contenders. Expect the most generous luncheon buffet available. Dinners are more elaborate and showcase upscale versions of Caesar salad garnished with shrimp or chicken; quail stuffed with rice and served with a brandy-cream sauce; and a delectable version of pork Normandy, stuffed with apples and served with an apple-brandy sauce.

A SIDE TRIP TO ANDERSONVILLE

Just 21 miles northeast of Plains (take U.S. 280 to Americus, then Ga. 49 North) is the site of the most infamous of Confederate prison camps, Andersonville. It was built to hold 10,000 but at one time had a prisoner population of more than 32,000, struggling to survive on polluted water and starvation rations. Nearly 15,000 prisoners died here. The commander, Capt. Henry Wirtz, although powerless to help the situation, was tried and hanged after the Civil War on charges of having conspired to murder Union prisoners. Today you can visit the **Drummer Boy Civil War Museum** (☎ **912/ 472-8967**), open Memorial Day to Labor Day, daily from 10am to 5pm; off-season on Saturday from 10am to 5pm and on Sunday from 1 to 5pm. Admission is $1.50 for adults, $1 for children 6 to 12, and free for children 5 and under. You'll see slide shows of the camp's sad history, as well as the remains of wells and escape tunnels. Legend says that **Providence Springs** gushed up in answer to prayers of prisoners during the drought of 1864. **Andersonville National Historic Site** (☎ **912/ 924-0343**) is open daily from 8am to 5pm; admission is free.

After visiting the historic site, browse the antiques shops in the adjacent village of Andersonville. Stop by the **Andersonville Guild Welcome Center** (☎ **912/ 924-2558**) in the old train depot and meet Peggy Sheppard, a gregarious, transplanted New Yorker who spearheaded the village's rejuvenation. The center is open daily from 9am to 5pm.

If you're looking for a bite to eat, try the **Andersonville Restaurant,** 213 W. Church St. (☎ **912/928-8480**)—a real down-home establishment with a buffet groaning under the weight of Southern fried chicken, country ham, and other meats. In summer, fresh vegetables come from the nearby fields, and everybody orders second or even third helpings of biscuits to mop up the juices. Your $5 entitles you to one meat, three vegetables, biscuits, beverage, and dessert—a real bargain. Fresh catfish is fried up for both locals and visitors on Friday night. Its can't-miss location is in the village center.

Andersonville National Historic Site and National Prisoner of War Museum. Ga. 49, Andersonville. ☎ **229/924-0343.** Free admission to museum and site; donations accepted. Museum daily 8:30am–5pm; site daily 8am–5pm. From I-75 North or South, take Exit 127 at Montezuma/Hawkinsville. Travel west along Ga. 26, continuing south on Ga. 49. Park entrance will appear on your left just outside of Andersonville.

This museum was dedicated in April 1998 by a host of senators including John McCain, R-Arizona, a prisoner of war in Vietnam for 5 years, and Georgia Governor Zell Miller. The museum is adjacent to the site of one of the two deadliest Civil War POW encampments, and its 10,000 square feet contain artifacts in tribute to the 800,000 soldiers who have suffered as POWs, from the American Revolution to the Persian Gulf conflict.

Housed within the museum are postcards from soldiers who hoped that their future brides had not assumed they were dead, letters to families who thought they would never see their sons again, pictures, and models of prison cells, including a Vietnamese bamboo cage. The $5.8-million structure was built from private funds raised by POW veterans, with $3.6 million coming from the State of Georgia and the federal government. The first museum of its kind in the United States, it touches a subject long ignored by the American public, in large part due to veterans' reluctance to relive the horrors of imprisonment. There are stories of prisoners in Japanese camps who lost 55 pounds during their stay and tales of brothers who were imprisoned together, with only one surviving.

Adjacent to the museum is the notorious Confederate POW camp Andersonville (see above). When its inmate population was heaviest during the last 14 months of the Civil War, the mortality rate was 29%, partly because of the heat, since Northerners were not acclimated to the Southern weather. The camp's Union counterpart in Elmira, New York (known as "Hellmira") had a mortality rate of 24% during its lifetime, conversely because of the cold; many Southerners froze to death. Visitors are allowed to walk the grounds, and an audiocassette tour of the grounds is available for $1.

6 Thomasville

45 miles W of Valdosta; 35 miles NE of Tallahassee; 25 miles S of Atlanta

From the 1800s to the early 1900s, ✪ Thomasville was one of the world's most fashionable places, hailed by *Harper's Magazine* in 1887 as "The best winter resort on three continents." After the Civil War, when much of the South was embittered and in ruins, a remarkable and progressive group of civil leaders began building resorts that attracted the wintering wealthy. Few other places in the South wanted to encourage the "damn Yankees" at the time. Regrettably, every one of the grand hotels that once flourished here has disappeared, victims of fires, rot, termites, and the opening of nearby Florida as a holiday destination. Many of the Victorian homes of the town, however, remain intact, attracting architectural enthusiasts from around the state.

Considering that the wealth of North America's Gilded Age once disported itself here, Thomasville remains relatively obscure. Even in Georgia, its name sometimes draws a blank. Yet at various times, the world press has descended on the area, notably when President Eisenhower used to play golf here, and when Jacqueline Kennedy was discovered hiding out to recuperate following the assassination of her husband.

Historic Thomasville remains unique in the South today as the centerpiece of a county containing approximately 70 enormous plantations encompassing some 300,000 acres. Only the post–Civil War prosperity of the town's 19th- and early-20th-century tourism allowed these estates to survive intact. Throughout the rest of the South, plantations were broken up, subdivided, sold for back taxes, allowed to fall into decay, and, in a later age, turned into housing developments. Regrettably, of the many that survive, only one is open to the public.

ESSENTIALS

GETTING THERE   By Car   From Tallahassee, head northeast along Hwy. 319. From Atlanta, take I-75 South to the junction with Route 122 to Tifton, exiting onto Hwy. 319 southwest into Thomasville.

VISITOR INFORMATION   Destination Thomasville Tourism Authority at 135 North Broad St. (☎ **229/227-7099**) is one of the most helpful in Georgia, open Monday to Friday from 9am to 5pm and Saturday 9am to 4pm. The center offers a guided tour for groups at $50 per hour, or else will distribute a free self-guided walking and driving guide to the 40 historic homes in the area, covering some 4½ miles. A genealogical library is also maintained by the city.

SEEING THE SIGHTS

The town's mascot is **"The Big Oak,"** at the corner of North Crawford and East Monroe streets, in back of the Federal Courthouse and the Post Office. It's at least three centuries old and has been a respected member of the National Live Oak Society since 1936. If anyone attempted to cut it down or harm it in any way, the townspeople would rise up in revolt. The giant is 68 feet tall with a limb spread of 162 feet and a circumference of 24 feet.

Thomasville Cultural Center, 600 E. Washington St. (☎ **229/226-0588**), is a center for the performing and visual arts, whose art galleries feature both fixed and changing exhibits. It has a children's room and a library; concerts, musicals, art classes, and children's programs are presented here. It's open daily from 9am to 5pm. Admission is free but donations are accepted.

Thomas County Museum of History. 725 N. Dawson St. ☎ **229/226-7664.** Admission $5 adults, $1 children. Daily 10am–noon and 2–5pm.

This is the best place for learning about the extraordinary "Winter Resort Era" that began in Thomasville in the 1880s. Although all the grand Victorian hotels are gone, photographs on display show their remarkable and elaborate architecture. Along with memorabilia of Thomasville from this era are exhibits of historic plantations, restored 19th-century buildings, antique women's dresses, and vintage automobiles. Out back is an antique bowling alley.

۞ Lapham-Patterson House. 626 N. Dawson St. ☎ **229/225-4004.** Admission $4 adults, $2 18 and under. Tues–Sat 9am–5pm, Sun 2–5:30pm.

This example of Victorian architecture, declared a National Historic Landmark in 1975, is known for its fish-scale shingles, Oriental-style porch decorations, long-leaf pine inlaid floors, and a double-flue chimney with a walk-through stairway and cantilevered balcony. Built between 1884 and 1885, it was the winter cottage for a prosperous shoe merchant, C. W. Lapham of Chicago. As a survivor of the Great Chicago Fire, Lapham wanted to make his winter cottage as safe as possible. This explains why, in the 19 rooms in this cottage, there are 45 doors, 26 of them exterior. All of the 53 windows open from the bottom up and the top down.

۞ Pebble Hill Plantation. 5 miles SW of Thomasville via U.S. 319. ☎ **229/226-2344.** Grounds $3 adults, $1.50 children under 12. Main house $7 adults, $2.50 children grades 1–6 (younger children not admitted). Tues–Sat 10am–5pm, Sun 1–5pm.

They called her "Miss Pansy," and she was a local legend, greatly admired by Jimmy Carter. Her name was Elisabeth Ireland Poe (1897–1978), and she was the last of the Hanna dynasty, which owned Pebble Hill. A sportswoman, she was also a patron of the arts, a grand hostess, and a collector, and upon her death she willed that her home should be open to the public for a glimpse into an elegant past. Hers is the only plantation home in Thomas County open to the public.

Established in the 1820s, the house was almost destroyed by fire in the 1930s, but was rebuilt under the direction of architect Abram Garfield, son of the nation's 20th president. Art, furnishings, and lavish decorations, along with antiques, crystal, and porcelain, fill the house. Throughout the house are paintings and prints depicting wildlife and sporting scenes.

WHERE TO STAY

✪ **1884 Paxton House Inn.** 445 Remington Ave., Thomasville, GA 31792. ☎ **800/ 278-0138** or 229/226-5197. Fax 229/226-9905. www.1884paxtonhouseinn.com. E-mail: 1884@rose.net. 12 units. A/C TV TEL. $110–$250 double; $165–$250 suite. Rates include breakfast. AE, MC, V.

This is the finest, best-furnished, and most meticulously clean bed-and-breakfast hotel in Thomasville, the one most often cited as a role model and learning forum for anyone considering going into the B&B trade. It's in a dignified Victorian house within an upper-class neighborhood, four blocks east of the town center. It contains a museum-quality collection of porcelain, acquired over many decades, which decorates virtually every corner of a tasteful and elegant decor, inspired by 18th- and early-19th-century models. Ms. Susie Sherrod is the innkeeper. Breakfasts are lavish and impeccable: Gourmet feasts feature eggs Benedict or orange-flavored French toast, served with meticulous hospitality and Southern charm.

Evans House Bed & Breakfast. 725 S. Hansell St., Thomasville, GA 31792. ☎ **229/ 226-1343.** Fax 229/226-0653. 4 units. $70–$85 double; $125 suite. Rates include breakfast. MC, V.

This is an imposing, socially prominent, clapboard-sided house designed in the colonial revival style in 1898. Its owner, Gladys Veese, has refurbished the inn completely with Victorian pieces. Today, benign ghosts continue to inhabit the building, flushing toilets and pacing the floors at unexpected intervals. Rather than recoiling, many B&B guests enjoy the tales of hauntings, and sleep comfortably in the large bedrooms that are tastefully outfitted with mission oak and turn-of-the-century antiques. The place has an understated, unfussy kind of dignity. Some rooms have TVs; others have phones.

Serendipity Cottage. 339 E. Jefferson St., Thomasville, GA 31792. ☎ **229/226-8111.** www.serendipitycottage.com. E-mail: goodnite@rose.net. 4 units. A/C TV. $80–$120 double. Rates include breakfast. AE, DISC, MC, V.

Partly because of its isolation on a leafy residential street away from city traffic, the Serendipity is in some ways the least obvious B&B inn in town. It's also one of the most charming, a cozy "four-square cottage" that is a perfect example of its architectural style. It was built by a local lumber baron as his private home in 1906. Every board in the building was hand-picked—a source of pride (and an effective marketing tool for his business), until he lost his home and fortune during the stock market crash of 1929. The building's most recent incarnation came about when a couple from Virginia, Ed and Kathy Middleton, tastefully restored the place as a B&B. The house has a cool and airy sense of spaciousness, with many fine interior details inspired by the Arts and Crafts movement. The establishment's signature breakfast usually includes apple-flavored French toast spiked with apple liqueur.

✪ **Susina Plantation.** 1420 Meridian Rd., Thomasville, GA 31792. ☎ **229/377-9644.** 8 units. A/C. $150 double. Rates include dinner and breakfast. No credit cards.

This antebellum gem is 12 miles southwest of Thomasville and 6 miles north of the Florida border. It was originally the showplace of an estate with 102 slaves and 8,000 acres of farm and timberland. Built in 1840, its architect was an English-born clockmaker, John Wind. Notice the sunflower motif carved into the Greek Revival portico—each of his buildings was graced with a different flower poised in an equivalent position on the facade.

The present owner is Swedish-born, California-educated Anne-Marie Walker, whose cuisine, after the architecture, is the building's most addictive lure. Even if you forgo an overnight in one of the nostalgically old-fashioned bedrooms, try to come for dinner. Advance reservations are required for five-course taste treats ($30 per person), where the cuisine is meticulous, elaborate, and steeped in the traditions of Continental Europe. There's a swimming pool on the grounds, plus 115 acres of rolling land for rambling.

WHERE TO DINE

Harrison's. 119 South Broad St. ☎ **229/226-0074.** Reservations recommended. Lunch main courses $4.95–$7.95; dinner main courses $11.95–$22.95. AE, MC, V. Mon–Sat 11am–2pm, Mon–Thurs 5–9pm and Fri–Sat 5–10pm. ITALIAN/FRENCH/AMERICAN.

Behind the landmark Victorian clock in the center of town, this well-established restaurant is the place most recommended when visitors ask the local B&B ladies to name the best place to eat in town. It has an ambitious menu that ranges from America to the continent, and one of the most extensive wine lists in south Georgia. The chefs in the kitchen are skilled, using first-rate produce to turn out such specialties as potato-crusted grouper, topped with a rosemary cream sauce. Milk-fed veal in a vodka cream sauce with basil and fresh tomatoes is another delightful dish, as is cheese ravioli stuffed with pepperoni and sweet sausage, all served with a savory tomato sauce. Guests enjoy the large lists of "decadent" desserts and gourmet coffees. The restaurant is housed in a restored bank, with the vaults used today to store wine.

Terrace by Midnight. 502 Broad St. ☎ **229/228-9844.** Main courses $6.95–$21.95. AE, DISC, DC, MC, V. Mon–Fri 11am–10pm, Sat 4–10pm. CONTINENTAL.

In the cellar downstairs from Simply Delicious—a favorite lunch spot for the local workforce—more formal dining is offered in a less-than-formal setting. Both the lunch and dinner menus feature pasta dishes, salads, burgers, steaks, and seafood. Terrace by Midnight opened in June 1998. Owner Debra Heath tries her hand at creating the best dinner atmosphere in town, and the best food.

Savannah 20

If you have time to visit only one city in the Southeast, make it ✪ **Savannah.** It's that special.

The movie *Forrest Gump* may have put the city squarely on the tourist map, but nothing changed the face of Savannah more than the 1994 publication of John Berendt's *Midnight in the Garden of Good and Evil.* The impact has been unprecedented, bringing in countless millions in revenue as thousands flock to see the sights from the mega-bestseller and the 1997 movie directed by Clint Eastwood. In fact, Savannah tourism has increased some 46% since publication of what's known locally as The Book. Many locals now earn their living off The Book's fallout, hawking postcards, walking tours, T-shirts, and in some cases their own careers, as in the case of the Lady Chablis, the black drag queen depicted in The Book who played herself in the Eastwood film (see below for the Lady's Web sites).

"What's special about Savannah?" we asked an old-timer. "Why, here we even have water fountains for dogs," he said.

The free spirit, the passion, and even the decadence of Savannah resembles that of Key West or New Orleans more than the Bible Belt down-home interior of Georgia. In that sense, it's as different from the rest of the state as New York City is from upstate New York.

Savannah—pronounce it with a drawl—conjures up all the clichéd images of the Deep South: live oaks dripping with Spanish moss, stately antebellum mansions, mint juleps sipped on the veranda, magnolia trees, peaceful marshes, horse-drawn carriages, ships sailing up the river (though no longer laden with cotton), and even General Sherman, no one's favorite military hero here.

Today, the economy and much of the city's day-to-day life still revolve around port activity. For the visitor, however, it's Old Savannah, a beautifully restored and maintained historic area, that's the big draw. For this we can thank seven Savannah ladies who, after watching mansion after mansion demolished in the name of progress, managed in 1954 to raise funds to buy the dilapidated Isaiah Davenport House—just hours before it was slated for demolition to make way for a parking lot. The women banded together as the Historic Savannah Foundation, then went to work buying up architecturally valuable buildings and reselling them to private owners who'd promise to restore them. As a result, more than 800 of Old Savannah's 1,100 historic buildings have been restored, using original paint colors—pinks and reds and blues and greens. This "living museum" is now the largest urban National Historic Landmark District in the country—some 2½ square miles, including 20 1-acre squares that still survive from Gen. James Oglethorpe's dream of a gracious city.

1 Orientation

ARRIVING

BY PLANE   **Savannah International Airport** is about 8 miles west of downtown just off I-16. **American** (☎ 800/433-7300; www.aa.com), **Delta** (☎ 800/221-1212; www.delta.com), **United** (☎ 800/241/6522; www.ual.com), and **US Airways** (☎ 800/428-4322; www.usairways.com) have flights from Atlanta and Charlotte, with connections from other points.

   Limousine service to downtown locations (☎ 912/966-5364) costs $16 one-way. The taxi fare is $20 for one person and $11 for each extra passenger.

BY CAR   From north or south, I-95 passes 10 miles west of Savannah, with several exits to the city, and U.S. 17 runs through the city. From the west, I-16 ends in downtown Savannah and U.S. 80 also runs through the city from east to west. AAA services are available through the **AAA Auto Club South,** 712 Mall Blvd., Savannah, GA 31406 (☎ 912/352-8222; www.aaa.com).

BY TRAIN   The **train station** is at 2611 Seaboard Coastline Dr. (☎ 912/234-2611), some 4 miles southwest of downtown; cab fare into the city is around $4. For **Amtrak** schedule and fare information, call ☎ 800/USA-RAIL.

VISITOR INFORMATION

The **Savannah Visitor Center,** 301 Martin Luther King Jr. Blvd., Savannah, GA 31401 (☎ 912/944-0455), is open Monday to Friday 8:30am to 5pm and Saturday and Sunday 9am to 5pm. The staff is friendly and efficient. Offered here are an audiovisual presentation costing $1.50 for adults and $1 for children, organized tours, and self-guided walking, driving, or bike tours with excellent maps, cassette tapes, and brochures.

   Tourist information is also available from the **Savannah Area Convention & Visitors Bureau,** 101 East Bay St., Savannah, GA 31402 (☎ 800/444-2427 or 912/944-0456; www.savannah-visit.com). For information on current happenings, call ☎ 912/233-ARTS.

   For everything you might want to know about The Book, check out the following Internet site: www.midnightinthegarden.com.

CITY LAYOUT

Every other street—north, south, west, and east—is punctuated by greenery. The grid of **21 scenic squares** was laid out in 1733 by Gen. James Oglethorpe, the founder of Georgia. The design—still in use—has been called "one of the world's most revered city plans." It's said that if Savannah didn't have its history and architecture, it would be worth a visit just to see the city layout.

   Bull Street is the dividing line between east and west. On the south side are odd-numbered buildings, with even street numbers falling on the north side.

Neighborhoods in Brief

Historic District   The Historic District—the real reason to visit Savannah—takes in both the riverfront and the City Market, described below. It's bordered by the

Savannah River and Forsyth Park at Gaston Street and Montgomery and Price streets. Within its borders are more than 2,350 architecturally and historically significant buildings in a 2½-square-mile area. About 75% of these buildings have been restored.

Riverfront   In this most popular tourist district, River Street borders the Savannah River. Once lined with warehouses holding King Cotton, it has been the subject of massive urban renewal, turning this strip into a row of restaurants, art galleries, shops, and bars. The source of the area's growth was the river, which offered a prime shipping avenue for New World goods shipped to European ports. In 1818, about half of Savannah fell under quarantine during a yellow-fever epidemic. River Street never fully recovered and fell into disrepair until its rediscovery in the mid-1970s. The urban-renewal project stabilized the downtown and revitalized the Historic District. Stroll the bluffs along the river on the old passageway of alleys, cobblestone walkways, and bridges known as **Factor's Walk.**

City Market   Two blocks from River Street and bordering the Savannah River, the City Market was the former social and business mecca of Savannah. Since the late 18th century, it has known fires and various devastations, including the threat of demolition. But in a major move, the city of Savannah decided to save the district. Today, former decaying warehouses are filled with restaurants and shops offering everything from antiques to various collectibles, including many Savannah-made products. And everything from seafood and pizza to French and Italian cuisine is served here. Live music often fills the nighttime air. Some of the best jazz in the city is presented here in various clubs. The market lies at Jefferson and West Julian streets, bounded by Franklin Square on its western flank and Ellis Square on its eastern.

Victorian District   The Victorian District, south of the Historic District, holds some of the finest examples of post–Civil War architecture in the Deep South. The district is bounded by Martin Luther King Jr. Blvd. and East Broad, Gwinnett, and Anderson streets. Houses in the district are characterized by gingerbread trim, stained-glass windows, and imaginative architectural details. In all, the district encompasses an area of nearly 50 blocks, spread across some 165 acres. The entire district was listed on the National Register of Historic Places in 1974. Most of the two-story homes are wood frame and were constructed in the late 1800s on brick foundations. The district, overflowing from the historic inner core, became the first suburb of Savannah.

2 Getting Around

The grid-shaped Historic District is best seen on foot—the real point of your visit is to take leisurely strolls with frequent stops in the many squares.

BY CAR   Though you can reach many points of interest outside the Historic District by bus, your own wheels will be much more convenient, and they're absolutely essential for sightseeing outside the city proper.

All major car-rental firms have branches in Savannah and at the airport, including **Hertz** (☎ 800/654-3131, or 912/964-9595 at the airport); **Avis** (☎ 800/831-2847), with locations at 422 Airways Ave. (☎ 912/964-1781) and at 2215 Travis Field Rd. (☎ 912/964-0234); and **Budget** (☎ 800/527-0700), with offices at 7070 Abercorn St. (☎ 912/966-1771).

BY BUS   You'll need exact change for the 75¢ fare, plus 75¢ for a transfer. For route and schedule information, call **Chatham Area Transit (CAT)** at ☎ **912/233-5767.**

BY TAXI   The base rate for taxis is 60¢, with a $1.20 additional charge for each mile. For 24-hour taxi service, call **Adam Cab Co.** at ☎ **912/927-7466.**

Fast Facts: Savannah

American Express The American Express office has closed, but cardholders can obtain assistance by calling ☎ **800/221-7282.**

Dentist Call Abercorn South Side Dental, 11139 Abercorn St., Suite 8 (☎ **912/925-9190**), for complete dental care and emergencies, Monday to Friday 8:30am to 3pm.

Drugstore Drugstores are scattered throughout Savannah. One with longer hours is CVS, 11607 Abercorn St. (☎ **912/925-5568**), open Monday to Saturday 8am to midnight and Sunday 10am to 8pm.

Emergencies Dial ☎ **911** for police, ambulance, or fire emergencies.

Hospitals There are 24-hour emergency-room services at Candler General Hospital, 5353 Reynolds St. (☎ **912/692-6637**), and the Memorial Medical Center, 4800 Waters Ave. (☎ **912/350-8390**).

Newspapers The *Savannah Morning News* is a daily filled with information about local cultural and entertainment events. The *Savannah Tribune* and the *Herald of Savannah* are geared to the African-American community.

Police In an emergency, call ☎ **911.**

Post Office Post offices and sub-post offices are centrally located and open Monday to Friday 7am to 6pm and Saturday 9am to 3pm. The main office is at 2 N. Fahn St. (☎ **912/235-4653**).

Safety Although it's reasonably safe to explore the Historic and Victorian districts during the day, the situation changes at night. The clubs along the riverfront, both bars and restaurants, report very little crime. However, muggings and drug dealing are common in the poorer neighborhoods of Savannah.

Taxes The city of Savannah adds a 2% local option tax to the 4% state tax.

Transit Information Call **Chatham Area Transit** at ☎ **912/233-5767.**

Weather Call ☎ **912/964-1700.**

3 Accommodations

The undisputed stars here are the small inns in the Historic District, most in restored old homes that have been renovated with modern conveniences while retaining every bit of their original charm.

A Note on Rates: Because many of Savannah's historic inns are in converted former residences, price ranges can vary greatly. A very expensive hotel might also have some smaller and more moderately priced units. So it pays to ask. Advance reservations are necessary in most cases, since many of the best properties are quite small.

ALONG THE RIVERFRONT
EXPENSIVE

Hyatt Regency Savannah. 2 W. Bay St., Savannah, GA 31401. ☎ **800/228-1234** or 912/238-1234. Fax 912/944-3678. www.hyatt.com. E-mail: tmunroe@savrspo.hyatt.com. 347 units. A/C TV TEL. $150–$240 double; $234–$900 suite. AE, DC, DISC, MC, V. Parking $13.

There was an outcry from Savannah's historic preservation movement when this place went up in 1981. Boxy and massively bulky, it stands in unpleasant contrast to the restored warehouses flanking it along the legendary banks of the Savannah River.

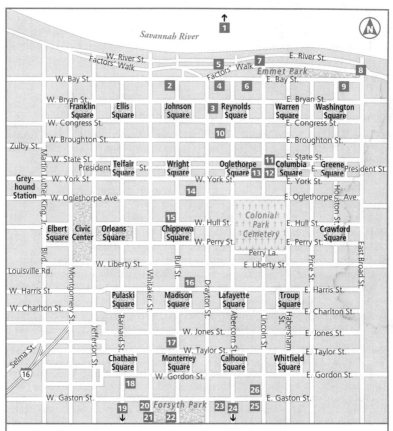

Ballastone Inn **14**

Bed & Breakfast Inn **18**

Catherine Ward House Inn **19**

Courtyard by Marriott **24**

DeSoto Hilton **16**

East Bay Inn **6**

Eliza Thompson House **17**

Fairfield Inn by Marriott **24**

Foley House Inn **15**

The Forsyth Park Inn **21**

Gaston Gallery Bed & Breakfast **25**

The Gastonian **26**

Granite Steps Inn **23**

Hampton Inn **4**

Hyatt Regency Savannah **2**

The Kehoe House **11**

Magnolia Place Inn **20**

Marshall House **10**

The Mulberry-Holiday Inn **9**

Olde Harbour Inn **7**

Park Avenue Manor **22**

Planters Inn **3**

The Presidents' Quarters **13**

River Street Inn **5**

Savannah Marriott Riverfront **8**

17 Hundred 90 **12**

Westin Savannah Harbor Resort **1**

Today it is grudgingly accepted as the biggest and flashiest hotel in town. It has a soaring atrium as well as glass-sided elevators. The comfortable rooms are international and modern in their feel, all with good-size bathrooms and many with balconies overlooking the atrium. Room prices vary according to their views—units without a view are quite a bargain.

Dining: There's a stylish bar and two restaurants with a big-city feel and views over the river.

Amenities: Health club, indoor pool, small fitness room.

Savannah Marriott Riverfront Hotel. 100 General McIntosh Blvd., Savannah, GA 31401. ☎ **800/228-9290** or 912/233-7722. Fax 912/233-3765. www.marriott.com. E-mail: bssmith@ savmarriott.com. 383 units. A/C TV TEL. $149–$225 double; $195–$249 suite. Children 17 and under stay free in parents' room. AE, CB, DC, DISC, MC, V. Parking $7.

At least the massive modern bulk of this place is far enough from the 19th-century restored warehouses of River Street not to clash with them aesthetically. Towering eight stories, with an angular facade sheathed in orange and yellow brick, it doesn't quite succeed at being a top-rated luxury palace but nonetheless attracts lots of corporate business and conventions. We prefer the Hyatt, but this one can be a backup, with comfortable, modern rooms that aren't style-setters but are generous in space, with bathrooms large enough to store your stuff and a generous supply of towels.

Dining: The lobby restaurant, T.G.I. Fridays, suffers from a claustrophobically low ceiling and has faux-Victorian decor with a kaleidoscope of stained-glass lamps.

Amenities: Dry cleaning/laundry service, secretarial services, indoor and outdoor pools, Jacuzzi, health club, business and conference rooms, tour desk, small boutique.

Westin Savannah Harbor Resort. One Resort Drive, PO Box 427, Savannah, GA 31421. ☎ **800/WESTIN-1** or 912/201-2000. Fax 912/201-2001. www.westinsavannah.com. 403 units. A/C MINIBAR TV TEL. $219–$299 double, $275–$800 suite. Water taxis, free for hotel guests, $2 round-trip for everyone else, shuttle across the river to Rousakis Plaza, on River St., at 15-min. intervals. From I-95 and Savannah International Airport: Take Exit 17A to I-16 toward Savannah. Follow sign for Rt. 17-Talmadge Bridge. Take Hutchinson Island Exit onto Resort Drive.

Savannah's largest hotel was opened late in 1999 in a 16-story blockbuster format that dwarfs the city's existing B&Bs. It rises somewhat jarringly from what were until the late 1990s sandy, scrub-covered flatlands on the swampy, rarely visited far side of the river from Savannah's historic core. Conceived as part of a massive resort development project, it derives the bulk of its business from corporate groups who arrive as part of large conventions throughout the year. It's the newest and largest of the four large-scale hotels that dominate the city's convention business, yet despite a worthy collection (more than 250 pieces) of contemporary art that accents the labyrinth of high-ceilinged public rooms here, there's something just a bit sterile, even lifeless, about this relatively anonymous blockbuster hotel. Compounding the problem is its isolated position, both geographically and emotionally, from the bustle, grace, and charm of central Savannah—this in spite of cross-river shuttle ferries that deposit clients into the center of the River Street bar and restaurant frenzy. The most elaborate bedrooms are on the two top floors, and contain extra amenities and comforts designated as Club Level. Otherwise, rooms are comfortable but bland, outfitted in pale colors and conservative furnishings.

Dining/Diversions: On the premises are two not-particularly-exciting restaurants, The Aqua Star, and its less pretentious sibling, The Grill, which lies in the Golf Course Clubhouse. Our favorite is the Midnight Sun Bar, a woodsy-looking bar based on a theme inspired by the musical career of local songwriter Johnny Mercer.

Amenities: 24-hour room service, 4 Har-Tru tennis courts that are illuminated for night play, a 400-foot floating dock for mooring yachts in the nearby river, two outdoor

⊕ Family-Friendly Hotels

The Mulberry/Holiday Inn *(see p. 432)*   Right in the heart of the Historic District is a family hotel that lets kids under 18 stay free if sharing a room with their parents. Children enjoy the pool, and cribs are provided free.

Hampton Inn *(see p. 434)*   One of the most appealing of the city's middle-bracket hotels, this family favorite rises on historic Bay Street. Rooms are spacious, and there's a pool and sundeck on the roof.

River Street Inn *(see p. 429)*   The best bet for families with children along the riverfront is a converted cotton warehouse from 1817. Large rooms make family life easier, and children under 18 stay free. There's also a game room, and many fast-food joints are just outside the front door.

pools. There's an 18-hole golf course designed by Sam Snead and Bob Cupp, and the world's only branch of the Greenbriar (West Virginia) Spa. Set within an ochre-colored annex, and outfitted with the leafy, pale green decor of its namesake, it offers hydrotherapy and massage sessions.

MODERATE

Olde Harbour Inn. 508 E. Factors Walk, Savannah, GA 31401. ☎ **800/553-6533** or 912/234-4100. Fax 912/233-5979. www.oldeharbourinn.com. 24 units. A/C TV TEL. $149–$259 suite. Rates include continental breakfast. AE, DISC, DC, MC, V.

The neighborhood has been gentrified and the interior of this place is well furnished, but you still get a whiff of riverfront seediness as you approach from Factors Walk. It was built in 1892 as a warehouse for oil, and its masonry bulk is camouflaged with shutters, awnings, and touches of wrought iron. Inside, a labyrinth of passages leads to small but comfortable suites, many of which show the building's massive timbers and structural iron brackets and offer views of the river. Some decors feature the original brick, painted white. Each unit contains its own kitchen—useful for anyone in town for an extended stay. Despite the overlay of chintz, you'll have a constant sense of the building's thick-walled bulk. Breakfast is the only meal served.

✪ River Street Inn. 115 E. River St., Savannah, GA 31401. ☎ **800/253-4229** or 912/234-6400. Fax 912/234-1478. www.riverstreetinn.com. E-mail: info@riverstreetinn.com. 86 units. A/C TV TEL. $159–$275 double. Rates include breakfast. Children 16 and under stay free in parents' room. AE, DC, MC, V. Parking $2.50.

When Liverpool-based ships were moored on the nearby river, this building stored massive amounts of cotton produced by upriver plantations. After the boll weevil decimated the cotton industry, it functioned as an icehouse, a storage area for fresh vegetables, and (at its lowest point) the headquarters of an insurance company. Its two lowest floors, built in 1817, were made of ballast stones carried in the holds of ships from faraway England.

In 1986, a group of investors poured millions into its development as one of the linchpins of Savannah's River District, adding a well-upholstered colonial pizzazz to the public areas and converting the building's warren of brick-lined storerooms into some of the most comfortable and well-managed rooms in town. There are many pluses to staying here, including the location, near tons of bars, restaurants, and night-clubs. Breakfast is served in Huey's (see "Dining," below). A wine-and-cheese reception is held Monday to Saturday, and turndown service is offered each evening.

IN THE HISTORIC DISTRICT
VERY EXPENSIVE

✪ **Ballastone Inn.** 14 E. Oglethorpe Ave., Savannah, GA 31401. ☎ **800/822-4553** or 912/236-1484. Fax 912/236-4626. 16 units. A/C TV TEL. $250–$375 double; $375–$420 suite. Rates include full breakfast, afternoon tea, and evening hors d'oeuvres. AE, MC, V. Free parking. No children.

This glamorous inner-city B&B occupies a dignified 1838 building separated from the Juliette Gordon Low House (original home of the founder of the Girl Scouts of America) by a well-tended formal garden; it's richly decorated with all the hardwoods, elaborate draperies, and antique furniture you'd expect. For a brief period (only long enough to add a hint of spiciness), the place functioned as a bordello *and* a branch office for the Girl Scouts (now next door).

There's an elevator, unusual for Savannah B&Bs, but no closets (they were taxed as extra rooms in the old days and so never added); there are many truly unusual furnishings—cachepots filled with scented potpourri, and art objects that would thrill the heart of any decorator. A full-service bar area is tucked into a corner of what was originally a double parlor. The four suites are in a clapboard townhouse a 5-minute walk away and staffed with its own live-in receptionists. A year-long refurbishment project in 1997 resulted in a four-star, four-diamond distinction.

Dining: Though the hotel doesn't serve lunch or dinner, many dining options are nearby. The recent hiring of a chef, however, vastly improved the quality of the breakfast, and the chef also prepares the afternoon tea and evening hors d'oeuvres.

Amenities: 24-hour concierge, laundry, nearby health club with free weights and pool, twice-daily maid service with turndown.

✪ **The Gastonian.** 220 E. Gaston St., Savannah, GA 31401. ☎ **800/322-6603** or 912/232-2869. Fax 912/232-0710. www.gastonian.com. E-mail: gastonian@aol.com. 17 units. A/C TV TEL. $225–$295 double; from 375 suite. Rates include full breakfast. AE, DISC, MC, V. No children under 12.

One of the two or three posh B&Bs in Savannah, the Gastonian incorporates a pair of Italianate Regency buildings constructed in 1868 by the same unknown architect. Hard times began with the 1929 stock market crash—the buildings were divided into apartments for the payment of back taxes. In 1984, the Lineberger family visiting from California saw the place, fell in love with it, and poured $2 million into restoring it. Today everything is a testimonial to Victorian charm, except for a skillfully crafted serpentine bridge connecting the two buildings and curving above a verdant semitropical garden. The rooms are appropriately plush, comfortable, cozy, and beautifully furnished.

Dining: Afternoon tea is served in a formal English-inspired drawing room where Persian carpets and a grand piano add to the luster of the good life from another era; a full breakfast is offered in the dining room with seatings at 8 and 10am.

Amenities: Concierge, tour desk, courtyard and deck with hot tub, meeting rooms.

Granite Steps Inn. 126 E. Gaston St., Savannah, GA 31401. ☎ **912/233-5380.** Fax 912/236-3116. www.granitesteps.com. 5 units. A/C TV TEL. $275 double; $375 suite. AE, MC, V.

This inn is glossier, larger, more opulent, and contains fewer accommodations than most of its other competitors in Savannah. Originally built in 1881 as a showy Italianate residence for a successful cotton merchant, it later belonged to celebrity decorator Jim Williams (the alleged murderer of Danny Hansford in The Book) just before his death. In May 1998, it was lavishly restored by a team of hardworking entrepreneurs associated with George's premier spa, the Chateau Élan, outside Atlanta. Consequently, you'll find more emphasis on hot tubs (most rooms contain one) and somewhat fussy pampering than at any other B&B in town. None of this is lost on such clients as Hollywood producer Nora Ephron (*Sleepless in Seattle; You've Got Mail*) and other West Coast customers who appreciate the inn's striking mixture of Gilded Age glamour, gilded Japanese screens, and free-form modern art decorating the public areas. The midsize-to-spacious bedrooms are endlessly tasteful and very upscale. If you decide to stay here, don't expect down-home Southern folksiness, as the setting is simply too urbane, too discreet, too restrained, and too linked to the European spa motif for hush-puppy, cornpone regionalisms to surface, let alone survive.

✪ **The Kehoe House.** 123 Habersham St., Savannah, GA 31401. ☎ **800/820-1020** or 912/232-1020. Fax 912/231-0208. www.kehoehouse.com. 15 units. A/C TV TEL. $205–$245 double; $275 suite. Rates include full breakfast. AE, DC, DISC, MC, V.

The Kehoe was built in 1892. In the 1950s, after the place had been converted into a funeral parlor, its owners tried to tear down the nearby Davenport House (see "Attractions," later in this chapter) to build a parking lot. The resulting outrage led to the founding of the Historic Savannah Association and the salvation of most of the neighborhood's remaining historic buildings.

Today, the place functions as a spectacularly opulent B&B, with a collection of fabrics and furniture that's almost forbiddingly valuable. However, it lacks the warmth and welcome of the Ballastone. This isn't a place for children—the ideal guest will tread softly on floors that are considered models of historic authenticity and flawless taste. Breakfast and afternoon tea are part of the ritual that has seduced such former clients as Tom Hanks, who stayed in room 301 during the filming of parts of *Forrest Gump*. The rooms are spacious, with the typical 12-foot ceilings, and each is tastefully furnished in English period antiques. Owners Rob and Jane Sales and Kathy Medlock acquired it in 1997 and immediately renovated the back garden, in addition to expanding the guest parking area. Amenities include a concierge and twice-daily maid service with turndown.

Magnolia Place Inn. 503 Whitaker St., Savannah, GA 31401. ☎ **800/238-7674** outside Georgia, or 912/236-7674. Fax 912/236-1145. www.magnoliaplaceinn.com. E-mail: info@ magnoliaplaceinn.com. 13 units. A/C TV TEL. $145–$270 double. Rates include full breakfast, afternoon tea, and evening hors d'oeuvres. AE, DC, DISC, MC, V. Free parking.

This building was begun in 1878 on a desirable plot overlooking Forsyth Square and completed 4 years later by a venerable family who'd been forced off their upriver plantation after the Civil War for nonpayment of taxes. An ancestor had represented South Carolina at the signing of the Declaration of Independence, and so the Second Empire ("steamboat Gothic") house was designed to be as grand as funds would allow. The result includes the most endearing front steps in town (Neiman Marcus asked to display them as a backdrop for one of its catalogs but the negotiations broke down), verandas worthy of a Mississippi steamer, and an oval skylight (an "oculus") that illuminates a graceful staircase ascending to the dignified rooms. Amenities include a 24-hour concierge, a tour desk, meeting spaces, access to a nearby health club, and bicycle rentals.

EXPENSIVE

DeSoto Hilton. 15 E. Liberty St. (P.O. Box 8207), Savannah, GA 31412. ☎ **800/445-8667** or 912/232-9000. Fax 921/232-6018. www.hilton.com. 246 units. A/C TV TEL. $79–$239 double. AE, DC, MC, V.

The name still evokes a bit of glamour—built in 1890, this hotel was for many generations the city's grandest. In 1967, thousands of wedding receptions, Kiwanis meetings, and debutante parties later, the building was demolished and rebuilt in a bland modern format. It's a well-managed commercial hotel, fully renovated by new owners in 1995. The rooms are conservatively modern and reached after registering in a stone-sheathed lobby whose decor was partly inspired by an 18th-century colonial drawing room. Despite the absence of antique charm, many guests like this place for its polite efficiency and modernism.

In the late 1990s, the inn was acquired by one of Georgia's most dedicated and successful innkeepers, Phil Jenkins, a noted musicologist and conductor who was responsible for the revitalization of a historic landmark (the 1842 Inn) in Macon. Emphasizing his new inn's colonial coastal theme, and adding sophisticated touches of *trompe l'oeil* to hallways and salons, he presents a unique afternoon experience every day between 5:30 and 7pm. Then, garnished with glasses of wine and platters of fruit and cheese, Phil or any of his (highly talented) employees will sing and play the piano or guitar as part of a genteel roster of mid-afternoon entertainment. Children under 12 are discouraged.

Dining: On the premises is the Lion's Den bar (formerly a famous club known as Mercers), a coffee shop (Knickerbocker's), and a more formal restaurant, the Pavillion.

Amenities: Concierge, laundry/dry cleaning, pool deck, fitness center with access to the Downtown Athletic Club, golf privileges.

Foley House Inn. 14 W. Hull St., Savannah, GA 31401. ☎ **800/647-3708** or 912/232-6622. Fax 912/231-1218. www.foleyinn.com. E-mail: foleyinn@aol.com. 19 units. A/C TV TEL. $185–$290 double. Rates include full breakfast, afternoon hors d'oeuvres, tea, and cordials. AE, DC, MC, V. No children under 12.

Decorated with all the care of a private home, this small B&B occupies a brick-sided house built in 1896. Its owners doubled its size by acquiring the simpler white-fronted house next door, whose pedigree predates its neighbors by half a century. The staff will regale you with tales of the original residents of both houses—one was the site of a notorious turn-of-the-century suicide.

Dining: Breakfast and afternoon hors d'oeuvres, tea, and cordials are served in a large, verdant space formed by the two houses' connected gardens.

Amenities: Concierge, laundry/dry cleaning.

The Mulberry/Holiday Inn. 601 E. Bay St., Savannah, GA 31401. ☎ **800/465-4329** or 912/238-1200. Fax 912/236-2184. www.savannahhotel.com. E-mail: jrettberg@princebush.com. 145 units. A/C TV TEL. $179–$249 double; $229 suite. Children under 18 stay free in parents' room. AE, DC, DISC, MC, V. Parking $5.

Locals point with pride to the Mulberry as a sophisticated adaptation of what might've been a derelict building into a surprisingly elegant hotel. Built in 1868 as a stable and cotton warehouse, it was converted in 1982 into a simple hotel, and in the 1990s it received a radical upgrade and a dash of decorator-inspired Chippendale glamour. Today, its lobby looks like that of a grand hotel in London, and the rooms, though small, have a formal decor (think English country-house look with a Southern accent). The hotel's brick-covered patio, with fountains, trailing ivy, and wrought-iron furniture, evokes the best aspects of New Orleans.

Dining/Diversions: On the premises is a bar, Sergeant Jasper's Lounge, and two restaurants, the Cafe for breakfast and dinner and the Mulberry for more formal dinners.

Amenities: Pool, sundeck, Jacuzzi, access to nearby health club.

The Presidents' Quarters. 255 E. President St., Savannah, GA 31401. ☎ **800/233-1776** or 912/233-1600. Fax 912/238-0849. www.presidentsquarters.com. E-mail: pqinn@aol.com. 19 units. A/C TV TEL. $147–$235 double. Rates include breakfast. DC, DISC, MC, V. Free parking on premises.

This hotel has many appealing aspects. The rooms and bathrooms are among the largest and most comfortable of any inn in Savannah. It manages simultaneously to combine the charm of a B&B with the efficiency of a much larger place. It has appealed to guests as diverse as the former president of Ireland and numbers of Hollywood actors. Each accommodation is named after a U.S. president who visited Savannah during his term in office.

Dining: A continental breakfast and afternoon tea are served each day on the brick patio off the back of the house.

Amenities: Room service, outdoor whirlpool/Jacuzzi, conference rooms, dry cleaning, access to a nearby health club.

Catherine Ward House Inn. 118 East Waldburg St., Savannah, GA 31401. ☎ **912/ 234-8564.** Fax 912/231-8007. www.catherinewardhouseinn.com. 10 units. A/C TV TEL. $129–$300 double. DISC, MC, V.

The restoration of this house has won several civic awards, and it's so evocative of Savannah's "carpenter Gothic" Victorian revival that Clint Eastwood inserted a long, graceful shot of its exterior in *Midnight in the Garden of Good and Evil.* Built by a sea captain for his wife (Catherine Ward) in 1886 in a location a short walk from Forsyth Park, it offers one of the most lavishly decorated interiors of any B&B in Savannah, but at prices that are significantly less than those offered at better-known B&Bs a few blocks away. Alan Williams, the owner and innkeeper, maintains a policy that discourages children under 16, and that stresses a gay-friendly but even-handed approach to a widely diverse clientele. Breakfast is relatively elaborate, served on fine porcelain in a grandly outfitted dining room. A garden in back encourages languid sun-dappled dialogues. Each midsize bedroom is individually and richly decorated.

MODERATE

East Bay Inn. 225 E. Bay St., Savannah, GA 31401. ☎ **800/500-1225** or 912/238-1225. Fax 912/232-2709. www.eastbayinn.com. 28 units. A/C TV TEL. $159–$210 double. AE, DC, MC, V.

Though the views from its windows might be uninspired, the East Bay is conveniently located near the bars and attractions of the riverfront. It was built in 1853 as a cotton warehouse; green awnings and potted geraniums disguise the building's once-utilitarian design. A cozy lobby contains Chippendale furnishings and elaborate moldings. The rooms have queen-size four-poster beds, reproductions of antiques, and coffeemakers. The hotel frequently houses tour groups from Europe and South America. In the cellar is **Skyler's (☎ 912/232-3955),** an independently managed restaurant specializing in European and Asian cuisine.

Eliza Thompson House. 5 W. Jones St., Savannah, GA 31401. ☎ **800/348-9378** or 912/ 236-3620. Fax 912/238-1920. www.elizathompsonhouse.com. 25 units. A/C TV TEL. $109–$260 double. Rates include continental breakfast. AE, MC, V.

The rooms of this stately home are equally divided between the original 1847 building and a converted carriage house. Both were the domain of Eliza Thompson, a socially conscious matriarch whose husband (a cotton merchant) died shortly after the foundations were laid. After serving as a shop for antiques dealers, it was bought by new owners in 1997. Steve and Carol Day have completely redecorated, using original Savannah colors, beautiful antiques, and Oriental carpets. The heart pine floors have been restored to their original luster, the linens have been replaced, and a program of ironing each sheet and pillowcase has begun. The inn now provides comfortable cotton robes in each room and a *f* service. It's also graced with one of the most beautiful courtyards in the city, featuring three large fountains, sago palms, and camellias. The rooms are comfortable, elegant, and cozy, furnished with tradition and taste. Breakfast is usually a lavish affair, featuring sausage casserole, muffins, and croissants. During nice weather, it's usually served on the brick terrace of the garden patio separating the two components of this historic inn.

The Forsyth Park Inn. 102 W. Hall St., Savannah, GA 31401. ☎ **912/233-6800.** Fax 912/233-6804. www.forsythparkinn.com. 9 units, 1 cottage with kitchenette. A/C TV. $115–$230 double; $220 cottage. AE, DISC, MC, V.

One of the grandest houses on the western flank of Forsyth Park is this yellow frame place built in the 1890s by a sea captain (Aaron Flynt, a.k.a. Rudder Churchill). A richly detailed staircase winds upstairs from a paneled vestibule, and the Queen Anne decor of the formal robin's-egg-blue salon extends through the rest of the house. Guest rooms have oak paneling and oversize doors that are testimonials to turn-of-the-century craftsmanship. The more expensive rooms, including one in what used to be the dining room, are among the largest in town. Home-baked breads and pastries are a staple of the breakfasts. Don't expect frivolity: The inn is just a bit staid.

Gaston Gallery Bed & Breakfast. 211 E. Gaston St., Savannah, GA 31401. ☎ **800/671-0716** or 912/238-3294. Fax 912/238-4064. www.gastongallery.com. 15 units. TV. $90–$200 double. AE, DISC, MC, V.

This major investment in period restoration was built as two separate houses united by a shared Italianate facade. In 1997 a lavish reunification of the two houses was undertaken. Today, the unified building bears the distinction of having the city's longest and most stately front porch (called a gallery in Savannah) and inner ceilings that are almost dizzyingly high. The breakfasts are social events, each featuring a different dish, like curried eggs or Southern grits casserole. Wine and cheese are served every day at 5pm or on your arrival, according to your wishes.

Hampton Inn. 201 E. Bay St., Savannah, GA. ☎ **800/426-7866** or 912/232-9700. Fax 912/231-0440. www.hampton-inn.com. 144 units. A/C TV TEL. Sun–Thurs $129–$159 double; Fr–Sat $139–$169 double. AE, DC, MC, V. Parking $5.

This is the most appealing of the city's middle-bracket large-scale hotels. Opened in 1997, it rises seven redbrick stories above the busy traffic of historic Bay Street, across from Savannah's Riverwalk and some of the city's most animated nightclubs. Its big-windowed lobby was designed to mimic an 18th-century Savannah salon, thanks to the recycling of heart pine flooring from an old sawmill in central Georgia and the use of antique Savannah bricks. Comfortably formal seating arrangements, a blazing fireplace, and an antique bar add cozy touches. The rooms are simple and comfortable, with wall-to-wall carpeting, medium-size tile bathrooms, and flowered upholstery. On the roof is a small pool and sundeck that's supplemented with an exercise room on the seventh floor. There's no restaurant, but many eateries are a short walk away.

Marshall House. 123 E. Broughton St., Savannah, GA 31401. ☎ **800/589-6304** or 912/ 644-7896. www.marshallhouse.com. 68 units. A/C MINIBAR TV TEL. $99–$199 double; $225–$350 suite. AE, MC, V.

Some aspects of this hotel—especially the second-story cast-iron veranda that juts out above the sidewalk—might remind you of a 19th-century hotel in the French Quarter of New Orleans. It originally opened in 1851 as the then-finest hotel in Savannah. In 1864-65, it functioned as a Union Army hospital, before housing such luminaries as Conrad Aiken and Joel Chandler Harris, author of *Stories of Uncle Remus*. After a ratty-looking decline, it closed—some people thought permanently—in 1957. In 1999, it reopened as a "boutique-style" inn. Despite the fact that this place has some of the trappings of an upscale B&B, don't think that it will provide the intimacy or exclusivity of, say, the Foley House. There's something a bit superficial about the glamour here, and some aspects evoke a busy motel, albeit with a more than usual elegant set of colonial-era reproductions in the public areas. Bedrooms succeed at being mass-production-style cozy without being particularly opulent; each sheathed in one of three standardized possibilities: yellow with pinewood furniture, green with wrought-iron furniture, and blue with white-painted furniture. Seven of the largest and most historically evocative rooms in the hotel are on the second floor, overlooking noisy Broughton Street, and are prefaced with wrought-iron verandas with wrought-iron furniture. Room service is daily from 6am to 11pm. Chadwick's is a bar with exposed brick, a very Southern clientele, green leather upholstery, and occasional presentations of live jazz. The Café M, set beneath the glassed-in roof of what used to be the hotel's rear stable yard, is a restaurant serving Southern and international cuisine.

Park Avenue Manor. 107–109 W. Park Ave., Savannah, GA 31402. ☎ **912/233-0352.** www.bbonline.com/ga/parkavenue. E-mail: pkavemanor@aol.com. 5 units. $95–$165 double; $170 suite. AE, MC, V.

Historic and cozy, this is Savannah's premier gay-friendly guesthouse. An 1897 Victorian B&B, it has an old-fashioned charm with antiques, double staircases, two formal parlors, and angel ceiling borders. Many accommodations have four-poster beds with antiques, silk carpets, porcelains, working fireplaces, and period prints. The small-scale inn has a well-rehearsed management style and an emphasis on irreverently offbeat Savannah. Many straight clients also book here, as the place is noted not only for its comfort but its warm welcome and one of the best Southern breakfasts served in town. The guesthouse was created in 1997, when a pair of Victorian houses were "sewn" together into a tasteful whole. A favorite is the Robert E. Lee room with a large bay window.

Planters Inn. 29 Abercorn St., Savannah, GA 31401. ☎ **800/554-1187** or 912/232-5678. Fax 912/232-8893. www.plantersinnsavannah.com. E-mail: plantinn@aol.com. 59 units. A/C TV TEL. $125–$165 double. Rates include continental breakfast. AE, DC, MC, V. Parking $6.75.

This small European-style inn is more businesslike than the average Savannah B&B. Built adjacent to Reynolds Square in 1912 as a seven-story brown brick tower, it boasts a lobby with elaborate millwork, a scattering of Chippendale reproductions, and an honor bar (sign for whatever drink you consume). The rooms are comfortably outfitted with four-poster beds and flowery fabrics; they're rather dignified and formal. The Planters Inn isn't associated with the well-recommended Planters Tavern (which stands next door and is separate).

✪ 17 Hundred 90. 307 E. President St., Savannah, GA 31401. ☎ **800/487-1790** or 912/236-7122. Fax 912/236-7123. www.17hundred90.com. E-mail: 1790inn@msn.com. 14 units. A/C TV TEL. $119–$189 double. AE, MC, V.

A severely dignified brick-and-clapboard structure, this place will remind you of New England's low-ceilinged 18th-century houses. It's the oldest inn in Savannah, permeated with conversation and laughter from the basement-level bar and restaurant (see "Dining," later in this chapter), and by the spirits of its resident ghosts. The most famous is the daughter of the building's first owner, young Anna, who hurled herself over the balcony to her death on the brick walk below as her sailor love sailed away. Accessible via cramped hallways, the rooms are small yet charming, outfitted with the colonial trappings appropriate for an inn of this age and stature. About a dozen contain fireplaces and small refrigerators.

INEXPENSIVE

Bed and Breakfast Inn. 117 W. Gordon St. (at Chatham Sq.), Savannah, GA 31401.
☎ **912/238-0518.** Fax 912/233-2537. www.travelbase.com/destinations/savannah/
bed-breakfast. E-mail: bnbinn@msn.com. 18 units. A/C TV TEL. $79–$150 double. Rates
include full breakfast. AE, DISC, MC, V.

Adjacent to Chatham Square, in the oldest part of historic Savannah, this is a dignified stone-fronted townhouse built in 1853. You climb a gracefully curved front stoop
to reach the cool high-ceilinged interior, outfitted with a combination of antique and
reproduction furniture. Some of the good-size comfortable and tastefully furnished
accommodations contain refrigerators. There's no smoking.

Courtyard by Marriott. 6703 Abercorn St., Savannah, GA 31405. ☎ **800/321-2211** or
912/354-7878. Fax 912/352-1432. www.marriott.com. 144 units. A/C TV TEL. $75–$102
double; from $119–$129 suite. Children 15 and under stay free in parents' room. Senior discounts available. AE, DC, DISC, MC, V. Parking $2.50. From I-16, take Exit 34A to I-516 East
and turn right on Abercorn St.

Built around a landscaped courtyard, this is one of the more recommendable motels
bordering the Historic District. Many Savannah motels, though cheap, are quite tacky,
but this one has renovated rooms with separate seating areas, oversized desks, and private patios or balconies. Family-friendly, the hotel offers a coin laundry, free cribs, and
both a pool and a whirlpool. The restaurant serves à la carte and buffet breakfasts.
Exercise equipment includes weights and bicycles.

Fairfield Inn by Marriott. 2 Lee Blvd. (at Abercorn Rd.), Savannah, GA 31405. ☎ **800/
228-2800** or 912/353-7100. Fax 912/353-7100. www.marriott.com. 135 units. $54–$70
double. Children 17 and under stay free in parents' room. AE, DC, DISC, MC, V. Free parking.
From I-16, take Exit 34A to I-516 East, then turn right on Abercorn St. and go right again on
Lee Blvd.

Not quite as good as Marriott's other recommended motel (above), this reliable budget hotel offers standard but comfortably appointed rooms, with in-room movies and
a large, well-lit desk. The big attraction here is an outdoor pool. Health-club privileges
are available nearby, as are several good moderately priced restaurants.

4 Dining

Savannah is known for the excellence of its seafood restaurants. They're among the
best in Georgia, rivaled only by those in Atlanta. The best dining is in the Historic
District, along River Street, bordering the water. However, locals also like to escape the
city and head for the seafood places on Tybee and other offshore islands.

Some of Savannah's restaurants, like Elizabeth on 37th, are ranked among the finest
in the entire South. And others, like Mrs. Wilkes' Dining Room, are places to go for
real Southern fare—from collard greens and fried okra to fried chicken, cornbread,
and hot biscuits.

ALONG OR NEAR THE WATERFRONT
EXPENSIVE

The Chart House. 202 W. Bay St. ☎ **912/234-6686.** Reservations recommended. Main
courses $14.95–$23.95. AE, CB, DC, DISC, MC, V. Mon–Fri 5–10pm, Sat 5–10:30pm, Sun
5–9pm. STEAK/SEAFOOD.

Overlooking the Savannah River and Riverfront Plaza, "the home of the mud pie" is
part of a nationwide chain—and one of the better ones. It's housed in a building that
predates 1790, reputed to be the oldest masonry structure in Georgia and once a
sugar-and-cotton warehouse. You can enjoy a view of passing ships on the outside

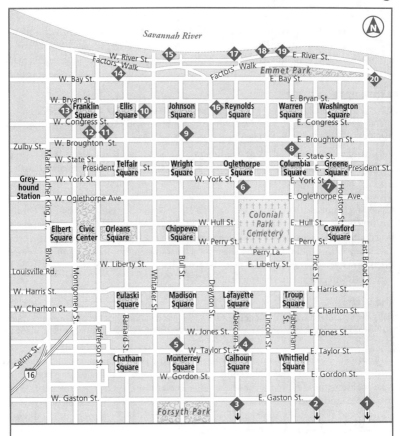

Billy Bob's **15**

The Chart House **14**

Clary's Café **4**

Elizabeth on 37th **3**

The Exchange Tavern **19**

45 South **20**

Garibaldi's **11**

Huey's **17**

Il Pasticcio **9**

Johnny Harris Restaurant **2**

Lady and Sons **13**

Mrs. Wilkes' Boarding House **5**

Nita's Place **6**

The Olde Pink House Restaurant **16**

The River's End **1**

Sapphire Grill **10**

17 Hundred 90 **8**

Shrimp Factory **18**

606 East Café **12**

Wall's **7**

deck, perhaps ordering an appetizer and a drink before dinner. The bar is one of the most atmospheric along the riverfront. As in all Chart Houses, the prime rib is slow-roasted and served au jus. The steaks from corn-fed beef are aged and hand-cut on the premises before being charcoal-grilled. The most expensive item is lobster. You may prefer one of the fresh catches of the day, which can be grilled to your specifications.

MODERATE

✪ **Huey's.** In the River Street Inn, 115 E. River St. ☎ **912/234-7385.** Reservations recommended. Main courses $9.95–$20; sandwiches $6–$10. AE, DISC, MC, V. Mon–Thurs 7am–10pm, Fri–Sat 7am–11pm, Sun 8am–10pm. CAJUN/CREOLE.

At first glance, this casual place overlooking the Savannah River seems little different from the other restored warehouses. But you'll discover it's special when you taste the food, created under the direction of Louisiana-born Mike Jones. He even manages to please visitors from New Orleans—and that's saying a lot. The place is often packed. Breakfast begins with such dishes as a Creole omelet, followed by an oyster "Po' Boy" for lunch. It's at dinner, however, that the kitchen really shines, producing jambalaya with andouille sausage, crayfish étouffée, and crab-and-shrimp au gratin (with Louisiana crabmeat and Georgia shrimp). The soups are homemade and the appetizers distinctive. A jazz brunch is featured Saturday and Sunday 8am to 3pm. The bar next door offers live entertainment.

INEXPENSIVE

Billy Bob's. 21 E. River St. ☎ **912/234-5588.** Reservations not necessary. Main courses $5.95–$21.95. AE, DISC, MC, V. Sun–Thurs 11am–10pm, Fri–Sat 11am–11pm. BARBECUE/SEAFOOD.

Its decor was modeled after a barn somewhere on the panhandle of Texas; the recorded music might remind you of the country-western tunes they play at this place's namesake in Houston. The barbecues here are succulent and tender, having been slowly marinated and spicily flavored. Examples are baby-back ribs, barbecued chicken, shrimp, and beefsteaks. Appetizers feature a warm crab-and-artichoke dip and oysters Rockefeller, and steaks and seafood include grilled swordfish, battered shrimp platters, and at least five kinds of Angus beef.

The Exchange Tavern. 201 E. River St. (east of Bull St.). ☎ **912/232-7088.** Main courses $8.95–$18.95; child's plate $3.99. AE, DC, MC, V. Sun–Thurs 11am–11pm, Fri–Sat 11am–midnight. SEAFOOD/LOW COUNTRY.

A local favorite, it's in a 1790s former cotton warehouse that opens onto the riverfront. The chefs make no pretense about their food. Everything is hale and hearty rather than gourmet. Your best bet is the ocean-fresh seafood, served grilled, broiled, or fried. Hand-cut grilled rib-eye steaks are a specialty, along with Buffalo-style wings, shrimp, oysters, and well-stuffed sandwiches served throughout the day. Since 1971, this place has been dispensing its wares, including shish-kebabs, fresh salads, and homemade soups. It's also a good place for a drink.

✪ **Lady and Sons.** 311 W. Congress St. ☎ **912/233-2600.** Reservations recommended for dinner. Main courses $6–$10 at lunch, $12–$20 at dinner; all-you-can-eat buffet $9.99 at lunch, $14.99 at dinner; $12.99 Sun lunch. AE, DISC, MC, V. Mon–Sat 11:30am–3pm; Mon–Thurs 5–9pm, Fri–Sat 5–10pm, Sun 11am–5pm. SOUTHERN.

Paula Deen started this place in 1989 with $200, the help of her sons, and a 1910 structure. Today she runs one of Savannah's most celebrated restaurants. Her first cookbook, *Lady and Sons Savannah Country Cookbook* (Random House), is in its second printing (John Berendt wrote the introduction), and her second, *Lady and Sons Too,* was published in 2000. One taste of the food and you'll understand the roots of her success. Menu items like crab cakes (one Maryland visitor claimed they were the best he'd ever eaten), crab burgers, and several creative varieties of shrimp best exhibit her style. The locals love her buffets, which are very Southern. With fried chicken, meat loaf, collard greens, beef stew, "creamed" potatoes, or macaroni and cheese, this buffet is more aptly described as "more-than-you-can-eat."

Lunches are busy with a loyal following; dinners are casual and inventive. The aphrodisiac dish has to be the oyster shooters—half a dozen raw oysters, each served in a shot glass ("it's like killing two birds with one stone"). Paula's signature dish, chicken pot pie topped with puff pastry, looks so attractive you'll have reservations about eating it: Maybe that's why *Southern Living* used a picture of it in their magazine. Be careful not to fill up on the cheese biscuits and hoecakes that constantly land on your table. If for some reason you don't want a glorious glass of syrup-sweet tea, you'd better ask for unsweetened. But why rob yourself of the complete experience?

Shrimp Factory. 313 E. River St. (2 blocks east of the Hyatt). ☎ **912/236-4229.** Reservations not accepted. Main courses $7.95–$14.95 at lunch, $10.50–$27.95 at dinner. AE, MC, V. Mon–Thurs 11am–10pm, Fri–Sat 11am–11pm, Sun noon–10pm. SEAFOOD.

The exposed old brick and wooden plank floors form a setting for harborside dining in a circa-1850 cotton warehouse. Lots of folks drop in before dinner to watch the boats pass by, perhaps enjoying a Chatham Artillery punch in a souvenir snifter. Yes, the place is touristy, never more so than when it welcomes tour buses. A salad bar rests next to a miniature shrimp boat, and fresh seafood comes from local waters. A specialty, pine bark stew, is served in a little iron pot with a bottle of sherry on the side; it's a potage of five seafoods simmered with fresh herbs but minus the pine bark. Other dishes include peeled shrimp, shucked oysters, live Maine lobsters, sirloin steaks, and various fish fillets.

IN THE HISTORIC DISTRICT
VERY EXPENSIVE

✪ **45 South.** 20 E. Broad St. ☎ 912/233-1881. Reservations suggested. Jackets advised. Main courses $21.50–$31.50. AE, MC, V. Mon–Thurs 6–9pm, Fri–Sat 6–9:30pm. INTERNATIONAL.

Recommended by such magazines as *Food & Wine, Southern Living,* and even *Playboy,* this ritzy restaurant stands next door to the much more famous Pirates' House (see below). The food has been called "gourmet Southern," and an ever-changing menu is likely to feature smoked North Carolina trout, rack of lamb flavored with crushed sesame seeds, grilled venison with au gratin of sweet potatoes, chicken breast with truffled pâté, or sliced breast of pheasant with foie gras. Appetizers might include everything from South Carolina quail to crab cakes. Among the most expensive restaurants in Savannah, it's softly lit with elegantly set tables and a cozy bar. The service is impeccable.

✪ **Sapphire Grill.** 110 West Congress St. ☎ **912/443-9962.** Reservations recommended. Main courses $19–$34. AE, DC, MC, V. Sun–Thurs 6–10:30pm, Fri–Sat 5:30–11:30pm. AMERICAN/LOW COUNTRY.

One of the city's most consistently stylish restaurants evokes a low-key, counterculture bistro, but its cuisine is grander and more cutting-edge than its industrial-looking decor and its level of hipness would imply. Christopher Nason is the owner and the most talked-about chef of the moment in Savannah, preparing what he defines as a "coastal cuisine" based on seafood hauled in, usually on the day of its preparation, from nearby waters. If you opt for a table here, you won't be alone: Scads of media and cinematic personalities will have preceded you. Collectively, they add an urban gloss of the type you might expect to see in Los Angeles. Launch your repast with a "fire-cracker salad"—that is, roasted red peppers and a red chili and shallot vinaigrette—or crisp fried green tomatoes, perhaps tuna medallions, and even James Island littleneck clams tossed in a foie gras butter, each beginning course a delectable choice. The chef is justifiably proud of such signature dishes as duck served with a roasted tomato can-nelloni or grilled prime tenderloin of beef with Dauphinoise potatoes. The local black grouper is flavored with lemon coriander, and a double-cut pork loin chop is one of the most elegant versions of this dish in Savannah. Each day the chef serves a tasting menu—based on the market price—that includes an appetizer, salad, main course, and confections. Ask about it, as it might be your best dining bet.

EXPENSIVE

✪ **The Olde Pink House Restaurant.** 23 Abercorn St. ☎ **912/232-4286.** Reservations recommended. Main courses $14.95–$24.95. AE, MC, V. Sun–Thurs 6–10:30pm, Fri–Sat 5:30–11pm. SEAFOOD/AMERICAN.

Built in 1771 and glowing pink (its antique bricks show through a protective cover-ing of stucco), this house has functioned as a private home, a bank, a tearoom, and headquarters for one of Sherman's generals. Today, its interior is severe and dignified, with stiff-backed chairs, bare wooden floors, and an 18th-century aura similar to what you'd find in Williamsburg, Virginia. The cuisine is richly steeped in the traditions of the Low Country and includes crispy scored flounder with apricot sauce, steak au poivre, black grouper stuffed with blue crab and drenched in Vidalia onion sauce, and grilled tenderloin of pork crusted with almonds and molasses. You can enjoy your meal in the candlelit dining rooms or in the Planters Tavern.

17 Hundred 90. 307 E. President St. ☎ **912/236-7122.** Reservations recommended. Main courses $17.95–$24.75. AE, MC, V. Mon–Fri noon–2pm and 6–10pm, Sat–Sun 6–10pm. INTERNATIONAL.

In the brick-lined cellar of Savannah's oldest inn (see "Accommodations," earlier in this chapter), this place evokes a seafaring tavern along the coast of New England. Many visitors opt for a drink at the woodsy-looking bar in a separate back room before heading down the slightly claustrophobic corridor to the nautically inspired dining room. Students of paranormal psychology remain alert to the ghost rumored to wan-der through this place, site of Savannah's most famous 18th-century suicide. Lunch might include the quiche of the day with salad, Southern-style blue crab cakes, and a choice of salads and sandwiches. Dinners are more formal, featuring crab bisque, snap-per Parmesan, steaks, and bourbon-flavored chicken. The cooking is of a high standard.

MODERATE

Il Pasticcio. 2 E. Broughton St. (corner of Bull and Broughton sts.). ☎ **912/231-8888.** Main courses $12.95–$22.95. AE, DC, V. Daily 5:30–10pm. ITALIAN.

This restaurant/bakery/gourmet market is one of the city's most popular dining spots. In a postmodern style, with big windows and a high ceiling, it has a definite big-city style. A rotisserie turns out specialties. Many locals come here just for the pasta dishes, all homemade and served with savory sauces. Begin with carpaccio (thinly sliced beef tenderloin) or a tricolor salad of radicchio, endive, and arugula. Main dishes are likely to feature a mixed grilled seafood platter or grilled fish steak with tricolor roasted sweet peppers.

INEXPENSIVE

✪ **Clary's Café.** 404 Abercorn St. (at Jones St.). ☎ **912/233-0402.** Breakfast $4.50–$7.95; main courses $6.95–$10.95. AE, DC, DISC, MC, V. Mon–Fri 7am–4pm, Sat 8am–4:30pm, Sun 8am–4pm. AMERICAN.

⊕ Family-Friendly Restaurants

Mrs. Wilkes' Boarding House *(see p. 441)*   Since your kid didn't grow up in the era of the boardinghouse, here's a chance to experience a long-faded American dining custom. It's an all-you-can-eat type of family-style place. Your kid might balk at the okra and collards, but go for the corn on the cob and barbecued chicken.

Wall's *(see p. 442)*   If your kid is from the North and has never tasted Southern barbecue, take him here. There is no finer introduction. Even the booths are plastic. Spareribs and barbecue sandwiches are the hearty fare, but there's also a vegetable plate for the non-meat eater in the family.

Clary's Café has been a Savannah tradition since 1903, though the ambience today, under the devilish direction of Michael Faber, is decidedly 1950s. The place was famous long before it was featured in *Midnight in the Garden of Good and Evil* in its former role as Clary's drugstore, where regulars like eccentric flea-collar inventor Luther Driggers breakfasted and lunched. John Berendt is still a frequent patron, as is the fabled Lady Chablis. Begin your day with the classic Hoppel Poppel (scrambled eggs with chunks of kosher salami, potatoes, onions, and green peppers) and go on from there. Fresh salads, New York–style sandwiches, and stir-fries, along with grandmother's homemade chicken soup and flame-broiled burgers, are served throughout the day, giving way in the evening to chicken pot pie, stuffed pork loin, or planked fish (a fresh fillet of red snapper—broiled, grilled, or blackened).

✪ **Mrs. Wilkes' Boarding House.** 107 W. Jones St. (west of Bull St.). ☎ **912/232-5997.** Reservations not accepted. Breakfast $6; lunch $12. No credit cards. Mon–Fri 8–9am and 11:30am–3pm. SOUTHERN.

Remember the days of the boardinghouse, when everybody sat together, and belly-busting food was served in big dishes in the center of the table? Mrs. Selma Wilkes has been serving locals and travelers in just that manner since the 1940s. Bruce Willis and Demi Moore and Clint Eastwood are among the long list of celebrities who've dined here. Expect to find a long line of people patiently waiting for a seat at one of the long tables in the basement dining room of this 1870 brick house with curving steps and cast-iron trim.

Mrs. Wilkes believes in freshness and plans her daily menu around the seasons. Your food will be a reflection of the cuisine Savannah residents have enjoyed for generations—fried or barbecued chicken, red rice and sausage, black-eyed peas, corn on the cob, squash and yams, okra, cornbread, and collard greens.

Nita's Place. 140 Abercorn St. ☎ **912/238-8233.** Lunch $6.95–$12.95. Mon–Sat 11:30am–2:30pm. DISC, MC, V. SOUTHERN.

Nita's is a local institution favored by a broad cross section of diners. Outfitted with Formica-clad tables and the kind of chairs you'd expect in the lounge of a bowling alley, it occupies cramped no-frills quarters about a block from Oglethorpe Square. You'll be greeted with a broad smile from Nita Dixon or her designated representative (any of a squadron of loyal friends). Then you follow in line to a steam table where simmering portions of Southern food wait delectably. They'll include crab cakes, crab balls, meat loaf, fried chicken, collards, pork or beef ribs, several preparations of okra, butterbeans, yams, and hoecakes (many recipes were handed down from generation to generation through Nita's long line of maternal forebears). Past guests have included Meg Ryan and *People's Court's* Judge Wapner.

Wall's. 515 E. York Lane (between York St. and Oglethorpe Ave.). ☎ **912/232-9754.** Reservations not accepted. Main courses $5.50–$7.40. No credit cards. Wed 11am–5pm, Thurs–Sat 11am–9pm. BARBECUE.

This is the first choice for anyone seeking the best barbecue in Savannah. Southern barbecue aficionados have built-in radar to find a place like this. Once they see the plastic booths, bibs, Styrofoam cartons, and canned drinks from a fridge, they'll know they've found home. Like all barbecue joints, the place is aggressively casual. Spareribs and barbecue sandwiches star on the menu. Deviled crabs are the only nonbarbecue item, though a vegetable plate of four nonmeat items is also served.

IN & AROUND THE CITY MARKET
MODERATE

Garibaldi's. 315 W. Congress St. ☎ **912/232-7118.** Reservations recommended. Main courses $8.95–$24.95. AE, MC, V. Sun–Thurs 5:30–10:30pm, Fri–Sat 5:30pm–midnight. ITALIAN.

Many of the city's art-conscious students appreciate this Italian cafe because of the fanciful murals adorning its walls. (Painted by the owner's daughter, their theme is defined as "The Jungles of Italy.") If you're looking for a quiet, contemplative evening, we advise you to go elsewhere—the setting is loud and convivial during the early evening and even louder later at night. Designed as a fire station in 1871, it boasts the original pressed-tin ceiling.

Menu items include roasted red peppers with goat-cheese croutons on a bed of wild lettuces, crispy calamari, artichoke hearts with aioli, about a dozen kinds of pasta, and a repertoire of Italian-inspired chicken, veal, and seafood dishes. Daily specials change frequently but sometimes include duck Garibaldi, king-crab fettuccine, and a choice of lusciously fattening desserts.

INEXPENSIVE

606 East Café (Cow Patio). 319 W. Congress St. ☎ **912/233-2887.** Salads, burgers, sandwiches $3–$6.50; platters $6.50–$12.95. AE, MC, V. Mon–Wed 11am–10pm, Thurs–Sat 11am–11pm, Sun noon–10pm. AMERICAN.

This place reigns as the most irreverent and good-natured restaurant in Savannah, the whimsical creation of owner and muralist Sandi Baumer. A self-described "hater of plain white walls," she combined carloads of 1950s kitsch with tongue-in-cheek testimonials to the proud but passé days of psychedelic rock. Food and drinks are served by Cyndi Lauper lookalikes in short crinoline skirts, and live music is usually featured on a side terrace outfitted like a New Orleans courtyard as viewed through a purple haze. Vegetarian lasagna, burgers, pasta primavera, shrimp tempura, and an "amazing" meat loaf sandwich are some choices.

IN THE VICTORIAN DISTRICT
VERY EXPENSIVE

Elizabeth on 37th. 105 E. 37th St. ☎ **912/236-5547.** Reservations required. Main courses $23.50–$31.50. AE, DC, DISC, MC, V. Mon–Thurs and Sun 6–9:30pm, Fri–Sat 6–10:30pm. MODERN SOUTHERN.

This restaurant is frequently cited as the most glamorous and upscale in town. It's housed in a palatial neoclassical-style 1900 villa ringed with semitropical landscaping and cascades of Spanish moss. The menu items change with the season and manage to retain their gutsy originality despite an elegant presentation. They may include roast quail with mustard-and-pepper sauce and apricot-pecan chutney, herb-seasoned rack of lamb, or broiled salmon with mustard-garlic glaze. You might begin with grilled-eggplant soup, a culinary first for many diners. There's also an impressive wine list, and on Thursday all wines are sold by the glass. The desserts are the best in Savannah.

DINING NEARBY

Johnny Harris Restaurant. 1651 Victory Dr. (Hwy. 80). ☎ **912/354-7810.** Reservations recommended. Jackets required Sat night for dancing. Lunch items $4.95–$7.95; dinner main courses $7.95–$18.95. AE, CB, DC, DISC, MC, V. Mon–Thurs 11:30am–10:30pm, Fri–Sat 11:30am–midnight. AMERICAN.

Started as a roadside diner in 1924, Johnny Harris is Savannah's oldest continuously operated restaurant. The place has a lingering aura of the 1950s and features all that great food so beloved back in the days of Elvis and Marilyn: barbecue, charbroiled steaks, and seafood. The barbecue pork is especially savory and the prime rib tender. Colonel Sanders never came anywhere close to equaling the fried chicken here. Guests can dine in the "kitchen" or the main dining room and dance under the "stars" in the main dining room on Friday and Saturday nights, when there's live entertainment. The place will make you nostalgic.

The River's End. 3122 River Dr. ☎ **912/354-2973.** Reservations required on Fri and Sat. Full dinners $11.95–$24.95. AE, DC, MC, V. Mon–Thurs 5–10pm, Fri–Sat 5–11pm. Go 5½ miles east on U.S. 80 to Victory Dr., then ½ mile south on River Dr. SEAFOOD.

At Tassie's Pier next door to the Thunderbolt Marina on the Intracoastal Waterway, this is a great place to relax and watch shrimp boat and pleasure boat traffic. To the sounds of grand piano music, start with either oysters Rockefeller or Savannah she-crab soup. Charbroiled seafood items include salmon, swordfish, grouper, and tuna, but there's more than fish. You can try chicken Alfredo, charbroiled steaks, succulent lamb, or duck a l'orange. Desserts range from fresh Key lime pie to Georgia bourbon pecan pie.

5 Attractions

Most likely, the first sights you'll want to see in Savannah are those mentioned in *Midnight in the Garden of Good and Evil*. So if that's your wish, see "Organized Tours," below.

HISTORIC HOMES

Davenport House Museum. 324 E. State St. ☎ **912/236-8097.** Admission $6 adults, $3 children 6–18, free for children 5 and under. Mon–Sat 10am–4pm, Sun 1–4pm. Closed major holidays.

This is where seven determined women started the whole Savannah restoration movement in 1954. They raised $22,500, a tidy sum back then, and purchased the house, saving it from demolition and a future as a parking lot. They established the Historic Savannah Foundation, and the whole city was spared. Constructed between 1815 and 1820 by master builder Isaiah Davenport, this is one of the truly great Federal-style houses in the United States, with delicate ironwork and a handsome elliptical stairway.

Green-Meldrim Home. 14 W. Macon St. ☎ **912/233-3845.** Admission $5 adults, $3 children. Tues, Thurs and Fri 10am–4pm, Sat 10am–1pm.

This impressive house was built on Madison Square for cotton merchant Charleston Green, but its moment in history came when it became the Savannah headquarters of Gen. William Tecumseh Sherman at the end of his 1864 "March to the Sea." It was from this Gothic-style house that the general sent his now infamous (at least in Savannah) Christmas telegram to President Lincoln, offering him the city as a Christmas gift. Now the Parish House for St. John's Episcopal Church, the house is open to the public. The former kitchen, servants' quarters, and stable are used as a rectory for the church.

Juliette Gordon Low's Birthplace. 142 Bull St. (at Oglethorpe Ave.). ☎ **912/233-4501.** Admission $6 adults, $5 children 18 and under. Mon–Tues and Thurs–Sat 10am–4pm, Sun 12:30–4:30pm. Closed major holidays and some Sun Dec–Jan.

Juliette Gordon Low—the founder of the Girl Scouts—lived in this Regency-style house that's now maintained both as a memorial to her and as a National Program Center. The Victorian additions to the 1818–21 house were made in 1886, just before Juliette Gordon married William Mackay Low.

Andrew Low House. 329 Abercorn St. ☎ **912/233-6854.** Admission $7 adults; $4.50 students, children 6–12, and Girl Scouts; free for children 5 and under. Mon–Wed and Fri–Sat 10:30am–4pm, Sun noon–3:30pm. Closed major holidays.

After her marriage, Juliette Low (see above) lived in this 1848 house, and it was here where she actually founded the Girl Scouts. She died on the premises in 1927. The classic mid-19th-century house facing Lafayette Square is of stucco over brick with elaborate ironwork, shuttered piazzas, carved woodwork, and crystal chandeliers. William Makepeace Thackeray visited here twice (the desk at which he worked is in one bedroom), and Robert E. Lee was entertained at a gala reception in the double parlors in 1870.

Telfair Mansion and Art Museum. 121 Bernard St. ☎ **912/232-1177.** Admission $6 adults, $2 students, $1 children 6–12, free for children 5 and under. Mon noon–5pm, Tues–Sat 10am–5pm, Sun 1–5pm.

The oldest public art museum in the South, housing a collection of both American and European paintings, was designed and built by William Jay in 1818. He was a young English architect noted for introducing the Regency style to America. The house was built for Alexander Telfair, son of Edward Telfair, the governor of Georgia. A sculpture gallery and rotunda were added in 1883, and Jefferson Davis, former president of the Confederacy, attended the formal opening in 1886. William Jay's period rooms have been restored, and the Octagon Room and Dining Room are particularly outstanding.

Owen-Thomas House and Museum. 124 Abercorn St. ☎ **912/233-9743.** Admission $8 adults, $4 students, $2 children 6–12, free for children 5 and under. Mon noon–5pm, Tues–Sat 10am–5pm, Sun 2–5pm.

Famed as a place where Lafayette spent the night in 1825, this house evokes the heyday of Savannah's golden age. It was designed in 1816 by English architect William Jay, who captured the grace of Georgian Bath in England and the splendor of Regency London. The place has been called a "jewel box." You can visit not only the bedchambers and kitchen but also the garden and the drawing and dining rooms. Adapted from the original slave quarters and stable, the Carriage House Visitors' Center opened in 1995.

MUSEUMS

Savannah History Museum. 303 Martin Luther King Jr. Blvd. ☎ **912/238-1779.** Admission $3 adults, $2.50 seniors, $1.75 students. Daily 8:30am–5pm.

Housed in the restored train shed of the old Central Georgia Railway station, this museum is a good introduction to the city. In the theater, *The Siege of Savannah* is replayed. An exhibition hall displays memorabilia from every era of Savannah's history.

Downtown Savannah Sights

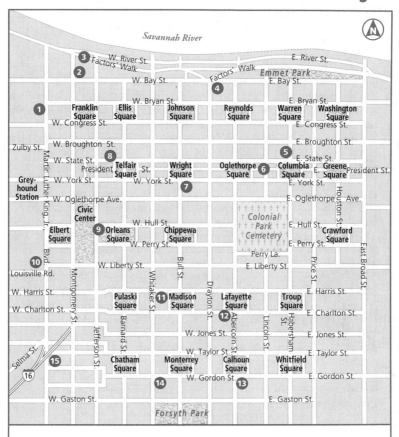

Andrew Low House **12**

Chamber of Commerce **4**

Davenport House Museum **5**

Factors' Walk **3**

First African Baptist Church **2**

Green-Meldrim Home **11**

Juliette Gordon Low's
Birthplace **7**

Massie Heritage
Interpretation Center **13**

Mercer House **14**

Municipal Auditorium **9**

Owen-Thomas House & Museum **6**

Ralph Mark Gilbert
Civil Rights Museum **15**

Savannah History Museum **10**

Ships of the Sea Maritime Museum **1**

Telfair Mansion & Art Museum **8**

Savannah Visitor Center **10**

Martinis in the Cemetery

All fans of *Midnight in the Garden of Good and Evil* must pay a visit to the now world-famous **Bonaventure Cemetery,** filled with obelisks and columns and dense shrubbery and moss-draped trees. Bonaventure is open daily 8am to 5pm. You get there by taking Wheaton Street east out of downtown to Bonaventure Road. (You don't want to approach it by boat like Minerva the "voodoo priest-ess" and John Berendt did—and certainly not anywhere near midnight.)

This cemetery lies on the grounds of what was once a great oak-shaded plan-tation, built by Col. John Mulryne. In the late 1700s, the mansion caught fire during a formal dinner party; reportedly, the host quite calmly led his guests from the dining room and into the garden, where they settled in to finish eating while the house burned to the ground in front of them. At the end, the host and the guests threw their crystal glasses against the trunk of an old oak tree. It's said that on still nights you can still hear the laughter and the crashing of the crystal. In The Book, Mary Harty called the ruins the "scene of the Eternal Party. What better place, in Savannah, to rest in peace for all time—where the party goes on and on."

It was at the cemetery that John Berendt had martinis in silver goblets with Miss Harty, while they sat on the bench-gravestone of poet **Conrad Aiken.** She pointed out to the writer the double gravestone bearing the names of Dr. William F. Aiken and his wife, Anna, parents of Conrad. They both died on February 27, 1901, when Dr. Aiken killed his wife and then himself. The Aikens are buried in plot H-48. Songwriter **Johnny Mercer** is also buried in plot H-48.

But not **Danny Hansford,** the blond hustler of the book. You can find his grave at plot G-19 in the Greenwich Cemetery, next to Bonaventure. After enter-ing Bonaventure, turn left immediately and take the straight path to Greenwich. Eventually you'll see a small granite tile:

DANNY LEW HANSFORD
MARCH 1, 1960
MAY 2, 1981

Incidentally, **Jim Williams** is buried in Gordon, Georgia, a 3½-hour drive northwest of Savannah.

Ships of the Sea Maritime Museum. 41 Martin Luther King Jr. Blvd. ☎ **912/232-1511.** Admission $5 adults, $4 children 7–12, free for children 6 and under. Tues–Sun 10am–5pm. Closed major holidays.

This museum has intricately constructed models of seagoing vessels from Viking war-ships right up to today's nuclear-powered ships. In models ranging from the size of your fist to 8 feet in length, you can see such famous ships as the *Mayflower* and the *Savannah,* the first steamship to cross the Atlantic. More than 75 ships are in the museum's ship-in-a-bottle collection, most of them constructed by Peter Barlow, a retired British Royal Naval commander.

LITERARY LANDMARKS

Long before John Berendt's *Midnight in the Garden of Good and Evil,* there were other writers who were associated with Savannah.

Chief of these was **Flannery O'Connor** (1924–64), one of the South's greatest writ-ers, author of *Wise Blood* (1952) and *The Violent Bear It Away* (1960). She was also known for her short stories, including the collection *A Good Man Is Hard to Find* (1955). She won the O. Henry Award three times. Between October and May, an association dedicated to her holds readings, films, and lectures about her and other Southern writers. You can visit the **Flannery O'Connor Childhood Home,** 207 E. Charlton St. (☎ **912/233-6014**). The house is open only Saturday and Sunday from 1 to 4pm. Admission is free.

Conrad Aiken (1889–1973), the American poet, critic, writer, and Pulitzer Prize winner, was also born in Savannah. He lived at 228 (for the first 11 years of his life) and also at 230 E. Oglethorpe Ave. (for the last 11 years of his life). In *Midnight in the Garden of Good and Evil,* Mary Harty and its author sipped martinis at the bench-shaped tombstone of Aiken in Bonaventure Cemetery (see "Martinis in the Cemetery," above).

Mercer House, 429 Bull St., featured in The Book, is not open to the public. Many of its most elegant contents were auctioned off at Sotheby's in October 2000 for $1 million, including the Anatolian carpet upon which the hapless Danny Hansford is reputed to have fallen after being shot. The house was recently up for sale ($9 million), but failed to snag a buyer and has since been taken off the market. Still, it's been called "the envy of Savannah," and thousands of visitors stop by to photograph it. For more details on the house and the events that took place in it, see the walking tour at the end of this section.

BLACK HISTORY SIGHTS

Savannah boasts the **First African Baptist Church,** 23 Montgomery St., Franklin Sq. (☎ **912/233-6597**), the first such church in North America. It was established by George Leile, a slave whose master allowed him to preach to other slaves when they made visits to plantations along the Savannah River. Leile was granted his freedom in 1777 and later raised some $1,500 to purchase the present church from a white congregation. The black congregation rebuilt the church brick by brick, and it became the first brick building in Georgia to be owned by African Americans. The pews on either side of the organ are the work of African slaves. Morning worship is at 11:30am daily.

Ralph Mark Gilbert Civil Rights Museum, 460 Martin Luther King Jr. Blvd. (☎ **912/231-8900**), close to the Savannah Visitors Center, opened in 1996. It's dedicated to the life and service of African Americans and their contributions to the civil-rights movements in Savannah. Dr. Gilbert died in 1956 but was a leader in early efforts to gain educational, social, and political equity for African Americans in Savannah. Hours are Monday to Saturday 9am to 5pm. Admission is $4 for adults, $3 for seniors, and $2 for children.

NEARBY FORTS

About 2½ miles east of the center of Savannah via the Islands Expressway stands **Old Fort Jackson,** 1 Fort Jackson Rd. (☎ **912/232-3945**), Georgia's oldest standing fort, with a 9-foot-deep tidal moat around its brick walls. In 1775, an earthen battery was built here. The original brick fort was begun in 1808 and manned during the War of 1812. It was enlarged and strengthened between 1845 and 1860 and saw its greatest use as headquarters for the Confederate river defenses during the Civil War. Its arched rooms, designed to support the weight of heavy cannons mounted above, hold 13 exhibit areas. The fort is open daily 9am to 5pm, charging $3.50 for adults and $2.50 for seniors and children 6 to 18; children 5 and under are free.

Fort McAllister, Richmond Hill, 10 miles southwest on U.S. 17 (☎ **912/727-2339**), on the banks of the Great Ogeechee River, was a Confederate earthwork fortification. Constructed in 1861–62, it withstood nearly 2 years of bombardments before it finally fell on December 13, 1864, in a bayonet charge that ended General Sherman's infamous "March to the Sea." There's a visitor center with historic exhibits and also walking trails and campsites. It's open Tuesday to Saturday 9am to 5pm and Sunday 2 to 5pm. Admission is $2.50 for adults, $1.50 for children over 5, and $2 for seniors.

Fort Pulaski (☎ 912/786-5787), a national monument, is 15 miles east of Savannah off U.S. 80 on Cockspur and McQueen islands at the very mouth of the Savannah River. It cost $1 million and took 25 tons of brick and 18 years of toil to finish. Yet it was captured in just 30 hours by Union forces. Completed in 1847 with walls 7½ feet thick, it was taken by Georgia forces at the beginning of the war. However, on April 11, 1862, defense strategy changed worldwide when Union cannons, firing from more than a mile away on Tybee Island, overcame the masonry fortification. The effectiveness of rifled artillery (firing a bullet-shaped projectile with great accuracy at long range) was clearly demonstrated. The new Union weapon marked the end of the era of masonry fortifications. The fort was pentagonally shaped, with galleries and drawbridges crossing the moat. You can still find shells from 1862 imbedded in the walls. There are exhibits of the fort's history in the visitor center. It's open daily (except Christmas) 8:30am to 6:45pm. Admission is $2 for adults and free to those 16 and under, with a $4 maximum per car.

ESPECIALLY FOR KIDS

Massie Heritage Interpretation Center. 207 E. Gordon St. ☎ **912/201-5070.** Admission free, but $2 donation requested. Mon–Fri 9am–4pm.

Here's a stop in the Historic District for the kids. Geared to school-age children, the center features various exhibits about Savannah, including such subjects as the city's Greek, Roman, and Gothic architecture; the Victorian era; and a history of public education. Other exhibits include a period costume room and a 19th-century classroom, where children can experience a classroom environment from days gone by.

6 Organized Tours

If it's a *Midnight in the Garden of Good and Evil* tour you seek, then you've obviously come to the right place. Virtually every tour group in town offers tours of the *Midnight* sites, many of which are included on their regular agenda. Ask any of the tour groups here about their tours. Note that some tour outfits will accommodate only groups, so if you're traveling alone or as a pair, be sure to make that known when you make your tour reservations.

A delightful way to see Savannah is by horse-drawn carriage. An authentic antique carriage carries you over cobblestone streets as the coachman spins a tale of the town's history. The 1-hour tour ($17 for adults, $8 for children) covers 15 of the 20 squares. Reservations are required, so contact **Carriage Tours of Savannah** at ☎ 912/236-6756.

Old Town Trolley Tours (☎ 912/233-0083) operates tours of the Historic District, with pickups at most downtown inns and hotels ($21 for adults, $8 for children 4 to 12), as well as a 1-hour **Haunted History** tour detailing Savannah's ghostly past (and present). Call to reserve for all tours.

Gray Line Savannah Tours (☎ 912/236-9604) has joined forces with **Historic Savannah Foundation Tours** (☎ 912/234-TOUR) to feature narrated bus tours of museums, squares, parks, and homes. Reservations must be made for all tours, and most have starting points at the visitor center and pickup points at various hotels and motels. Tours cost $19 for adults and $8 for children 11 and under.

Negro Heritage Trail Tour, 502 E. Harris St. (☎ **912/234-8000**), offers organized tours ($15 for adults and $7 for children) from the African-American perspective. The trail is sponsored by the King-Tinsdell Cottage Foundation.

Savannah Riverboat Cruises are offered aboard the *Savannah River Queen,* operated by the River Street Riverboat Co., 9 E. River St. (☎ **800/786-6404** or 912/232-6404). You get a glimpse of Savannah as Oglethorpe saw it back in 1733. You'll see the historic cotton warehouses lining River Street and the statue of the *Waving Girl* as the huge modern freighters see it as they arrive daily at Savannah. Lunch and bar service are available. Adults pay $15, and children 12 and under are charged $9.16.

Ghost Talk Ghost Walk takes you through colonial Savannah on a journey filled with stories and legends based on Margaret Debolt's book *Savannah Spectres and Other Strange Tales.* If you're not a believer at the beginning of the guided tour, you may be at the end. The tour starts at Reynolds Square. For information, contact Jack Richards at New Forest Studios, 127 E. Congress St. (☎ **912/233-3896**). Hours for tour departures can vary. The cost is $10 for adults and $5 for children.

Low Country River Excursions, a narrated nature cruise, leaves from the Bull River Marina, 8005 Old Tybee Rd. (U.S. 80 East). Call ☎ **912/898-9222** for information. Passengers are taken on a 1993 38-foot pontoon boat, *Natures Way,* for an encounter with the friendly bottle-nosed dolphin. Both scenery and wildlife unfold during the 90-minute cruise down the Bull River. Trips are possible daily at 2 and 4pm and sunset spring through fall, weather permitting. Adults pay $15, seniors $12, and children 11 and under $10. There's a 30-passenger limit.

7 Outdoor Pursuits

BIKING   Savannah doesn't usually have a lot of heavy traffic except during rush hours, so you can bicycle up and down the streets of the Historic District, visiting as many of the green squares as you wish. There's no greater city bicycle ride in all the state of Georgia.

In lieu of a local bike-rental shop, many inns and hotels will provide bikes for their guests.

CAMPING   The **Bellaire Woods Campground,** 805 Fort Argyle Rd. (☎ 912/748-4000), is 2½ miles west of I-95, 4½ miles west of U.S. 17, and 12 miles from the Savannah Historic District on the banks of the Ogeechee River. Facilities include full hookups, LP gas service, a store, self-service gas and diesel fuel, a dump station, hot showers, a laundry, and a pool. Rates range from $22.50 for tents to $27.50 for RV hookups, and reservations are accepted with a $10 deposit.

Open year-round, **Skidaway Island State Park** (☎ 912/598-2300) offers 88 camping sites with full hookups, costing $17. On arrival, you purchase a $2 parking pass valid for your entire stay. The grounds include 1- and 3-mile nature trails, grills, picnic tables, a pool, a bathhouse, and a laundry. Also open year-round, the **River's End Campground and RV Park,** Polk Street, Tybee Island (☎ 912/786-5518), consists of 128 sites featuring full hookups, with groceries and a beach nearby. Tent sites cost $18 per day and RV sites $24 per day.

DIVING   The **Diving Locker-Ski Chalet,** 74 W. Montgomery Cross Rd. (☎ 912/927-6604), offers a wide selection of equipment and services for various water sports. Scuba classes cost $230 for a series of weekday evening lessons and $245 for a series of lessons beginning on Friday evening. A full scuba-gear package, including buoyancy-control device, tank, and wet suit, goes for $49. You must provide your own snorkel, mask, fins, and booties. It's open Monday to Friday 10am to 6pm and Saturday 10am to 5pm.

Exploring the Savannah National Wildlife Refuge

A 10-minute drive across the river from downtown Savannah delivers you to the wild, even though you can see the city's industrial and port complexes in the background. The ✪ **Savannah National Wildlife Refuge** (☎ 912/652-4415), which overflows into South Carolina, was the site of rice plantations in the 1800s and is today a wide expanse of woodland and marsh, ideal for a scenic drive, a canoe ride, a picnic, and most definitely a look at a variety of animals.

From Savannah, get on U.S. Highway 17A, crossing the Talmadge Bridge. It's about 8 miles to the intersection of hwys. 17 and 17A, where you turn left toward the airport. You'll see the refuge entrance, marked Laurel Hill Wildlife Drive, after going some 2 miles. Inside the gate to the refuge is a visitor center, distributing maps and leaflets.

Laurel Hill Wildlife Drive goes on for 4 miles or so. It's possible to bike along this trail. People come here mainly to spy on the alligators, and sightings are almost guaranteed. However, other creatures in the wild abound, including bald eagles and otters. Hikers can veer off the drive and go along Cistern Trail, leading to Recess Island. Because the trail is marked, there's little danger of getting lost.

Nearly 40 miles of dikes are open to birders and backpackers. Canoeists float along tidal creeks, which are fingers of the Savannah River. Fishing and hunting are allowed in special conditions and in the right season. Deer and squirrel are commonplace; rarer is the feral hog known along coastal Georgia and South Carolina.

Visits are possible daily sunrise to sunset. For more information, write the Savannah National Wildlife Refuge, U.S. Fish & Wildlife Service, Savannah Coastal Refuges, P.O. Box 8487, Savannah, GA 31412.

FISHING   **Amicks Deep Sea Fishing,** 6902 Sand Nettles Dr. (☎ **912/897-6759**), offers daily charters featuring a 41-foot 1993 custom-built boat. The rate is $85 per person and includes rod, reel, bait, and tackle. Bring your own lunch, though beer and soda are sold on board. Reservations are recommended, but if you show up 30 minutes before scheduled departure, there may be space available. Daily departures from the Bull River Marina, 8005 Old Tybee Rd. (U.S. 80 East), are at 7am, with returns at 6pm.

GOLF   **Bacon Park,** Shorty Cooper Drive (☎ **912/354-2625**), is a 27-hole course with greens fees of $18 for an 18-hole round. Carts can be rented for an additional $9.50. Golf facilities include a lighted driving range, putting greens, and a pro shop. It's open daily dawn to dusk.

Henderson Golf Club, 1 Henderson Dr. (☎ **912/920-4653**), includes an 18-hole championship course, a lighted driving range, a PGA professional staff, and golf instruction and schools. The greens fees are $40 Monday to Friday and $42 Saturday and Sunday. It's open daily 7:30am to 10pm.

Another option is the 9-hole **Mary Calder,** West Congress Street (☎ **912/238-7100**), where the greens fees are $13 per day Monday to Friday and $11 per day Saturday and Sunday. It's open daily 7:30am to 7pm (to 5:30pm in winter).

IN-LINE SKATING   At **Diving Locker-Ski Chalet** (see "Diving," above), skate rentals cost $12 for 4 hours and $20 for a full day, with a Friday-to-Monday rental going for $35.

JET SKIING   At **Bull River Marina,** 8005 Old Tybee Rd., Hwy. 80 East (☎ **912/ 897-7300**), you can rent one-, two-, or three-seater jet skis. Prices, regardless of how many seats, rent for $30 per half hour or $60 per hour. It's open daily 9am to 6pm. Reservations are recommended.

JOGGING   "The most beautiful city to jog in"—that's how the president of the Savannah Striders Club characterizes Savannah. He's correct. The historic avenues provide an exceptional setting for your run. The Convention & Visitors Bureau can provide you with a map outlining three of the Striders Club's routes: Heart of Savannah YMCA Course, 3.1 miles; Symphony Race Course, 5 miles; and the Children's Run Course, 5 miles.

NATURE WATCHES   Explore the wetlands with **Palmetto Coast Charters,** Lazaretto Creek Marina, Tybee Island (☎ **912/786-5403**). Charters include trips to the Barrier Islands for shell collecting and watches for otter, mink, birds, and other wildlife. The captain is a naturalist and a professor, so he can answer your questions. Palmetto also features a dolphin watch usually conducted daily 4:30 to 6:30pm, when the shrimp boats come in with dolphins following behind. The cost is $100 for up to six people for a minimum of 2 hours, plus $50 for each extra hour.

RECREATIONAL PARKS   **Bacon Park** (see "Golf," above and "Tennis," below) includes 1,021 acres with archery, golf, tennis, and baseball fields. **Daffin Park,** 1500 E. Victory Dr. (☎ **912/351-3851**), features playgrounds, soccer, tennis, basketball, baseball, a pool, a lake pavilion, and picnic grounds. Both of these parks are open daily: May to September 8am to 11pm and October to April 8am to 10pm.

   Located at Montgomery Cross Road and Sallie Mood Drive, **Lake Mayer Park** (☎ **912/652-6780**) consists of 75 acres featuring a multitude of activities, such as public fishing and boating, lighted jogging and bicycle trails, a playground, and pedal-boat rentals.

SAILING   **Sail Harbor,** 618 Wilmington Island Rd. (☎ **912/897-2896**), features the Catalina 25 boat, costing $100 per half day and $140 per full day, with an extra day costing $80. A Saturday and Sunday outing goes for $200. It's open Tuesday to Saturday 10am to 6pm and Sunday 12:30 to 5:30pm.

TENNIS   **Bacon Park** (see "Golf," above; ☎ **912/351-3850**) offers 14 lighted courts open Monday to Thursday 9am to 9pm, Friday 9am to 4pm and 5 to 8pm, and Saturday 9am to 1am. **Forsyth Park,** at Drayton and Gaston streets (☎ **912/ 351-3850**), has four courts open daily 7am to 9pm. Both parks charge $1.75 per hour during the day and $2.50 per hour after 5pm. The use of the eight lighted courts at **Lake Mayer Park,** Montgomery Cross Road, costs nothing. These courts are open daily 8am to 11pm.

8 Shopping

River Street is a shopper's delight, with some 9 blocks (including Riverfront Plaza) of interesting shops, offering everything from crafts to clothing to souvenirs. The **City Market,** between Ellis and Franklin squares on West St. Julian Street, boasts art galleries, boutiques, and sidewalk cafes along with a horse-and-carriage ride. Bookstores, boutiques, and antiques shops are located between Wright Square and Forsyth Park.

   Oglethorpe Mall, at 7804 Abercorn St., has more than 100 specialty shops and four major department stores, as well as restaurants and fast-food outlets. The **Savannah Mall,** 14045 Abercorn St., is Savannah's newest shopping center, offering two floors of shopping. Included on the premises is a food court with its own carousel. The anchor stores are J. B. White, Montgomery Ward, Parisian, and Belk.

Some 30 manufacturer-owned "factory direct" stores offer savings up to 70% at the **Savannah Festival Factory Stores,** Abercorn Street at I-95 (☎ **912/925-3089**). Shops feature national brand names of shoes, luggage, gifts, cosmetics, household items, toys, and clothing, including T-shirts Plus and the Duckhead Outlet.

ANTIQUES
Alex Raskin Antiques. 441 Bull St. (in the Noble Hardee Mansion), Monterey Sq. ☎ **912/232-8205.**

This shop offers a wide array of antiques of varying ages. The selection includes everything from accessories to furniture, rugs, and paintings.

J. D. Weed & Co. 102 W. Victory Dr. ☎ **912/234-8540.**

This shop prides itself on providing "that wonderful treasure that combines history and personal satisfaction with rarity and value." If you're looking for a particular item, just let the staff know and they'll try to find it for you.

Memory Lane. 230 W. Bay St. ☎ **912/232-0975.**

More than 8,000 square feet of collectibles can be found here. The specialty of the house is a collection of German sleds and wagons. You'll also find glassware, furniture, and pottery.

ART & SCULPTURE
Gallery 209. 209 E. River St. ☎ **912/236-4583.**

Housed in an 1820s cotton warehouse, this gallery displays two floors of original paintings by local artists, sculpture, woodworking, fiber art, gold and silver jewelry, enamels, photography, batiks, pottery, and stained glass. You'll also find a wide selection of limited-edition reproductions and note cards of local scenes.

The Greek Festival. 143 Bull St. ☎ **912/234-8984.**

Many of the clients of this unusual store consider it a valuable resource for the creation of stage or movie sets, fashion displays, or dramatic living spaces. Co-owner Kelli Johnson acquires the molds for pieces of ancient Greek and Roman sculpture, Baroque or Victorian wall brackets, or carved animals (everything from Chinese Foo dogs to giant tortoises bearing tufted cushions for use as coffee tables). Everything is cast in reinforced plaster or concrete, which makes the price a fraction of what it would have been if the objects had been carved individually. The store can arrange shipping to virtually anywhere, and if what you want isn't in stock, you can order from a voluminous catalog.

John Tucker Fine Arts. 5 W. Charlton St. ☎ **800/350-1401** or 912/231-8161.

This gallery offers museum-quality pieces by local artists as well as those from around the world, including Haitian and Mexican craftspeople. In a restored 1800s home, the gallery features 19th- and 20th-century landscapes, marine-art painting, portraits, folk art, and still life.

Morning Star Gallery. 8 E. Liberty St. ☎ **912/233-4307.**

This gallery features the works of more than 80 artists. Pieces include hand-thrown pottery, metalwork, paintings, prints, woodworks, jewelry, and glass (hand-blown and leaded).

Village Craftsmen. 223 W. River St. ☎ **912/236-7280.**

This collection of artisans offers a wide array of handmade crafts, including hand-blown glass, needlework, folk art, limited-edition prints, restored photographs, and hand-thrown pottery.

BLACKSMITH

Walsh Mountain Ironworks. 427 Whitaker St. ☎ **912/239-9818.**

This is the sales outlet of the most successful and high-profile blacksmith in Savannah. Inventories include house, kitchen, and garden ornaments, many of which have modern, but vaguely Gothic, designs. Objects for sale include headboards for beds, garden arbors, trellises, tables, chairs, wine racks, CD racks, and ornamental screens. Prices range from $4 to $1,600, and in some cases require several weeks waiting time.

BOOKS

Book Warehouse. 8705 Abercorn St. ☎ **912/927-0824.**

This store offers more than 75,000 titles, including fiction, cookbooks, children's books, computer manuals, and religious tomes. Prices begin at less than a dollar, and all proceeds are donated to Emory University for cancer research.

E. Shaver, Bookseller. 326 Bull St. ☎ **912/234-7257.**

Housed on the ground floor of a Greek Revival mansion, E. Shaver features 12 rooms of tomes. Specialties include architecture, decorative arts, regional history, and children's books as well as 17th-, 18th-, and 19th-century maps.

CANDY & OTHER FOODS

Plantation Sweets Vidalia Onions. Rte. 2, Cobbtown. ☎ **800/541-2272.**

Outside Savannah, check out the Vidalia onion specialties offered by the Collins family for more than 50 years. Sample one of the relishes, dressings, or gift items as well. Call for directions.

River Street Sweets. 13 E. River St. ☎ **800/627-6175** or 912/234-4608.

Begun more than 20 years ago as part of the River Street restoration project, this store offers a wide selection of candies, including pralines, bearclaws, fudge, and chocolates. Included among the specialties are more than 30 flavors of taffy made on a machine from the early 1900s.

Savannah's Candy Kitchen. 225 E. River St. ☎ **800/242-7919** or 912/233-8411.

Chocolate-dipped Oreos, glazed pecans, pralines, and fudge are only a few of the delectables at this confectionery. While enjoying one of the candies or ice creams, you can watch the taffy machine in action. Staff members are so sure you'll be delighted with their offerings that they offer a full money-back guarantee if not satisfied.

GIFTS & COLLECTIBLES

Candlesticks. 117 E. River St. ☎ **912/231-9041.**

Kalten Bach owns this candle-making place. You can watch a candle being made from beginning to end in about 15 minutes at demonstrations held throughout the day. All personnel train for roughly a year before they can create their own pieces.

Charlotte's Corner. 1 W. Liberty St. (at Bull St.). ☎ **912/233-8061.**

Featuring local items, this shop offers a wide array of gifts and souvenirs. The selection encompasses children's clothing, a few food items, Sheila houses, and Savannah-related books, including guidebooks and Southern cookbooks.

Bothwell Gallery. 422 Whitaker St. ☎ **912/233-5132.**

In the Historic District, this shop features more than 40 artists from throughout the Southeast. You'll find wall hangings, pottery, jewelry, clothing, furniture, and sculptures.

The Christmas Shop. 307 Bull St. ☎ **912/234-5343.**

This shop keeps the Christmas spirit alive all year with a large selection of ornaments, Santas, nutcrackers, and collectibles. Collectors will appreciate the various featured lines, including Dept 56, Polonaise, Christina's World, and Patricia Breen.

Enchantments. 311 Bull St. (at Madison Sq.). ☎ **912/651-9035.**

If you collect bears and dolls, this store has a pet for you. Among its other selections is an array of quality toys and collector's pieces.

JEWELRY & SILVER
Levy Jewelers. 4711 Waters Ave. ☎ **912/238-2125.**

Located downtown, this boutique deals mainly in antique jewelry. It offers a large selection of gold, silver, gems, and watches. Among its other items are crystal, china, and gift items.

Simply Silver. 14-A Bishop Court. ☎ **912/238-3652.**

The specialty here is sterling flatware, ranging from today's designs to discontinued items of yesteryear. The inventory includes new and estate pieces along with a wide array of gift items.

9 Savannah After Dark

River Street, along the Savannah River, is the major after-dark venue. Many night owls stroll the waterfront until they hear the sound of music they like, then follow their ears inside.

In summer, concerts of jazz, Big Band, and Dixieland music fill downtown **Johnson Square** with lots of foot-tapping sounds that thrill both locals and visitors. Some of Savannah's finest musicians perform regularly on this historic site.

THE PERFORMING ARTS
The **Savannah Symphony Orchestra** has city-sponsored concerts in addition to its regular ticketed events. To spread a blanket in Forsyth Park and listen to the symphony perform beneath the stars or be on River Street on the Fourth of July when the group sends rousing strains echoing across the river is to be transported.

The orchestra is one of two fully professional orchestras in the state of Georgia, and its regular nine-concert masterworks series is presented in the Savannah Civic Center's **Johnny Mercer Theater,** Orleans Square (☎ **800/537-7894** or 912/236-9536), which is also home to ballet, musicals, and Broadway shows. Call to find out what's being presented at the time of your visit. Tickets range from $20 to $50.

Savannah Theater, Chippewa Square (☎ **912/233-7764**), presents contemporary plays. Tickets are usually $15 for regular admission and $12 for seniors or students.

September brings the 5-day **Savannah Jazz Festival** (☎ **912/232-2222**), with nationally known musicians appearing around the city.

LIVE-MUSIC CLUBS
Dejà Groove. 301 Williamson St. ☎ **912/644-4566.**

The setting is a severe-looking 19th-century warehouse that's perched on soaring bulwarks on the sloping embankment between River Walk and the busy traffic of Bay Street. Inside, you'll find an intriguing blend of exposed brick and timber, psychedelic artwork, and a youthful (under 35-ish) sense of hip. There's a dance floor featuring dance music from the '70s and '80s, at least two sprawling bar areas, video games, and about a dozen pool tables, priced at $1 per game. Entrance is usually free, but sometimes a $3 cover charge is levied after 10pm. Open Tuesday to Thursday 8:30pm to 3am, Friday and Saturday 8pm to 3am.

✪ **Hannah's East.** At the Pirates' House, 20 E. Broad St. ☎ **912/233-2225.** Cover $3–$5 Fri–Sat after 9pm.

This club, the most popular in Savannah, is the showcase for jazz greats, including Gina Rene and Emma Kelly, "The Lady of 6,000 Songs" who appeared in *Midnight in the Garden of Good and Evil.* Jim Belt is on the scene as the club's new musical director, replacing Ben Tucker (who left for the Lion's Den at the DeSoto Hilton). Emma holds forth Tuesday to Sunday 6 to 9pm. A Monday special features authentic Dixieland and New Orleans–style jazz, beginning at 6pm.

✪ **Planters Tavern.** In the Olde Pink House Restaurant, 23 Abercorn St. ☎ **912/232-4286.** No cover.

This is Savannah's most beloved tavern, graced with a sprawling and convivial bar, a pair of fireplaces, and a decor of antique bricks and carefully polished hardwoods. Because it's in the cellar of the Olde Pink House, many guests ask that platters of food be served at any of the tavern's tables. Otherwise, you can sit, drink in hand, listening to the melodies emanating from the sadder-but-wiser pianist. Foremost among the divas who perform is the endearingly elegant Gail Thurmond, one of Savannah's most legendary songstresses, who weaves her enchantment Tuesday to Sunday night.

Velvet Elvis. 127 W. Congress St. ☎ **912/236-0665.**

For two years in a row, this has been Savannah's number-one live music venue, as noted in Savannah's *Creative Loafing* magazine. It's known as punk-rock heaven to its hundreds of local fans, with a battered but prominent stage for live bands, and a wraparound collection of rock 'n' roll memorabilia and kitsch. Until its current manifestation, it was a hippie-style junk store; now you're likely to find such luminaries as Kevin Spacey, John Cusack, and Tracey Cunningham. There's a cover charge, applicable only when music is playing, of between $3 and $10, depending on the band. Open Monday to Saturday from 5pm to 3am.

The Zoo. 121 W. Congress St. ☎ **912/236-6266.** Cover $5–$10 after 10pm.

In its way, it's wilder, less inhibited, and a bit more insiderish even than Club One, with which it's frequently compared. One thing it isn't—prissy—as you'll quickly realize after a view of its two-fisted clientele (both male and female) and the staggeringly comprehensive array of almost psychedelic cocktails. (One of the house specials, bluntly identified as a Red-Headed Slut, elevated Jagermeister into something mind-bending for between $3 and $4, depending on the size.) If there's a genuine fetishist in Savannah, chances are high that you'll find him, her, or it at this ode to Southern heat. Expect a scattering of military men on weekend furlough, women and men of slightly untidy morality, a dance venue that's devoted to trance and techno music upstairs, and more conservative top-40 hits on the street level. Open Wednesday to Saturday 9pm until 3am.

BARS & PUBS

Churchill's Pub. 9 Drayton St. (1 block south of Bay St.). ☎ **912/232-8501.**

If you like a cigar with your martini (the pub has a large selection), this is the place for you. It's the oldest bar in Savannah, having originally been built in England in 1860, dismantled, and shipped to Savannah in the 1920s. On tap are such imported beers as John Courage, Guinness, Dry Blackthorn, and Bass Ale. You can also order pub grub like fish-and-chips, homemade bangers (English sausage), or shepherd's pie. The pub is open daily Monday to Saturday 11:30am to 2am and Sunday 5pm to 2am. Fans of The Movie will recall this pub; fans of The Book will recall the erroneous placement of this pub in The Movie.

Crystal Beer Parlor. 301 W. Jones St. (west of Bull St.). ☎ **912/232-1153.**

This historic haunt opened its doors in 1933 and sold huge sandwiches for a dime. Prices have gone up since then, but local affection for this unpretentious place has diminished not one whit. Try to go earlier or later than the peak lunch or dinner hours (if you get there at noon, you'll be in for a lengthy wait). Owner Conrad Thomson still serves up fried oysters and shrimp-salad sandwiches, crab stew, and chili. The seafood gumbo is one of the best in the southern Atlantic region. It's open Monday to Saturday 11am to 9pm. Parking is available in the lot off Jones Street.

Kevin Barry's Irish Pub. 117 W. River St. ☎ **912/233-9626.**

The place to be on St. Patrick's Day, this waterfront pub rocks all year. Irish folk music will entertain you as you choose from a menu featuring such Irish fare as beef stew, shepherd's pie, and corned beef and cabbage. Many folks come here just to drink, often making a night of it in the convivial atmosphere. It's open Monday to Friday 4pm to 3am and Saturday and Sunday 11am to 3pm.

Mellow Mushroom. 11 Liberty St. ☎ **912/495-0705.**

Don't expect grandeur here: a member of a Georgia-based restaurant chain, it appeals to a funky, irreverent, and sometimes raucous crowd of college students and faded counterculture aficionados from yesterday. Decor includes rambling murals painted with an individualized—and subjective—iconography that might require an explanation from a member of the cheerful waitstaff. There's the cut-off front end of a VW beetle near the entrance, a limited menu that focuses almost exclusively on pizzas, salads, and calzones, and a die-hard emphasis on cheap beer, especially Pabst, which sells by the pitcher. Expects lots of SCAD students, a battered, dimly lit interior, recorded (not live) music, and a vague allegiance to the hard rock, hard drugs, and hard sex fantasies of the early 1970s.

Mercury Lounge. 125 W. Congress St. ☎ **912/447-6952.**

The venue is as hip, counterculture, and artfully kitsch as anything you might have expected in Manhattan, with the added benefit of a reputation for the biggest martinis (10 ounces) in town. You'll find the most comfortable barstools anywhere (they're covered in *faux* leopard or zebra); a house band (the Mercury Lounge Combo) that cranks out their own version of the latest favorites; and, when the band is not performing, a jukebox. Everything is congenially battered, with enough rock and musical memorabilia to please the curators of a rock 'n' roll hall of fame. It's open from 3pm to 3am Monday to Saturday.

The Rail. 405 W. Congress St. ☎ **912/238-1311.**

Not as aggressively noisy as Club One (see below), the Rail manages to be sophisticated and welcoming of divergent lifestyles. Its name acknowledges the 19th-century day laborers who used to congregate nearby every morning in hopes of being hired for a job on the local railway. Today you can "work the rail" in much more comfortable circumstances among some of Savannah's most engaging writers, artists, and eccentrics. Tavern-meisters Trina Marie Brown (from Los Angeles) and Melissa Swanson (from Connecticut) serve snack-style food, but most folks just drink and chat.

Six Pence Pub. 245 Bull St. ☎ **912/233-3156.**

You can drop into this authentic-looking English pub for a selection of pub grub, including English fare along with homemade soups, salads, and sandwiches. On Sunday an ale-and-mushroom pie is featured. Drinks are discounted during happy hour Monday to Friday 5 to 7pm. On Friday and Saturday, live music is offered, ranging from beach music to contemporary to jazz. It's open Sunday 12:30 to 10pm, Friday and Saturday 11:30am to 1am, and Monday to Thursday 11:30am to midnight.

Wet Willie's. 101 E. River St. ☎ **912/233-5650.**

Few other nightspots in Savannah seem to revel so voluptuously in the effects produced by 190-proof grain alcohol. If you're hoping to get fall-down drunk, in a setting that evokes the more sociable aspects of an ongoing college-level fraternity/sorority bash, this is the place for you. When it's busy, it's loaded with the young, the nubile, and the sexually accessible—a worthy pickup joint if you're straight and not particularly squeamish. If you aren't sure what to order, consider such neon-colored headspinners as a Call-a-Cab, a Polar Cappuccino, a Monkey Shine, or a Shock Treatment. Karaoke is the venue every Monday and Tuesday night; otherwise it's something of a free-for-all with a Southern accent. Open Monday to Thursday 11am to 1am, Friday and Saturday 11am to 2am, and Sunday 12:30pm to 1am.

GAY & LESBIAN BARS

✪ **Club One.** 1 Jefferson St. ☎ **912/232-0200.** Cover (after 9:30pm) $10 for those 18–20, $5 for those 21 and older.

Club One defines itself as the premier gay bar in a town priding itself on a level of decadence that falls somewhere between New Orleans' and Key West's, and it's the hottest and most amusing spot in town. Patrons include lesbians and gays from the coastal islands, visiting urbanites, and cast and crew of whatever film is being shot in Savannah at the time (Demi Moore and Bruce Willis showed up here in happier times). There's also likely to be a healthy helping of voyeurs who've read *Midnight in the Garden of Good and Evil.*

You pay your admission at the door, showing ID if the attendant asks for it. Wander through the street-level dance bar, trek down to the basement-level video bar for a (less noisy) change of venue, and (if your timing is right) climb one floor above street level for a view of the drag shows. There, a bevy of black and white *artistes* lip-synch the hits of Tina Turner, Gladys Knight, and Bette Midler. It's open Monday to Saturday 5pm to 3am and Sunday 5pm to 2am. Shows are nightly at 10:30pm and 1am.

Chuck's Bar. 305 Wet River St. ☎ **912/232-1005.**

Most of the bars along Savannah's River Street are mainstream affairs, attracting goodly numbers of tourists, some of whom drink staggering amounts of booze and who seem almost proud of how rowdy they can get. In deliberate contrast, Chuck's usually attracts local members of Savannah's counterculture, including lots of gay folk, who rub elbows in a tuck-away corner of a neighborhood rarely visited by locals. The setting is a dark and shadowy 19th-century warehouse, lined with bricks, just a few steps from the Jefferson Street ramp leading down to the riverfront. Open Monday to Saturday from 6pm to 3am.

Faces. 17 Lincoln St. ☎ **912/233-3520.**

Regulars sometimes refer to this neighborhood bar as the gay Cheers of Savannah. There's a pool table in back, and the unstudied decor includes battered ceiling beams, semirusted license plates, and an utter lack of concern about decorative fashion. Its provenance goes back to 1817, when it was a tavern. If you detect that the dialogues here might be a bit more insightful than the norm, part of it might be due to ownership by a licensed psychologist. Hours are Monday to Saturday 11am to 3am and Sunday 12:30pm to 2:30am.

DINNER CRUISES

The **Savannah River Queen,** a replica of the boats that once plied this waterway, is a 350-passenger vessel operated by the River Street Riverboat Co., 9 E. River St. (☎ **912/232-6404**). It offers a 2-hour cruise with a prime rib or fish dinner and live entertainment. Reservations are necessary. The fare is $35.95 for adults and $22.95 for children 11 and under. Departures are usually daily at 7pm, but the schedule might be curtailed in the colder months.

10 A Side Trip to Tybee Island

For more than 150 years, **Tybee Island** has lured those who wanted to go swimming, sailing, fishing, and picnicking. Pronounced "Tie-bee," an Euchee Indian word for "salt," the island offers 5 miles of unspoiled sandy beaches, only 14 miles east of Savannah. From Savannah, take U.S. 80 until you reach the ocean.

The **Tybee Island Visitors Center** (☎ **800/868-BEACH** or 912/786-5444) provides complete information if you're planning to spend some time on the island, as opposed to a day trip. If you're interested in daily or weekly rentals of a bedroom condo or beach house (one or two bedrooms), contact **Tybee Beach Rentals,** P.O. Box 1440, Tybee Island, GA 31328 (☎ **800/755-8562** or 912/786-8805).

Consisting of 5 square miles, Tybee was once called the "Playground of the Southeast," hosting millions of beach-loving visitors from across the country. In the 1880s it was a popular dueling spot. In the early 1900s, Tybrisa Pavilion, on the island's south end, became one of the major summer entertainment pavilions in the South. Some of the best-known bands, including those of Benny Goodman, Guy Lombardo, Tommy Dorsey, and Cab Calloway, played here. It burned down in 1967 and was never rebuilt.

Over Tybee's salt marshes and sand dunes have flown the flags of pirates and Spaniards, the English and the French, and the Confederate States of America. A path on the island leads to a clear pasture where John Wesley, founder of the Methodist church, knelt and declared his faith in the new land.

Fort Screven, on the northern strip, began as a coastal artillery station and evolved into a training camp for countless troops in both world wars. Remnants of the wartime installations can still be seen. Also in the area is the **Tybee Museum,** housed in what was one of the fort's batteries. Displayed is a collection of photographs, memorabilia, art, and dioramas depicting Tybee from the time the Native Americans inhabited the island through World War II. Across the street is the **Tybee Lighthouse,** built in 1742 and the third-oldest lighthouse in America. It's 154 feet tall, and if you're fit you can climb 178 steps to the top. From the panoramic deck you get a sense of "the length and breadth of the marshes," as related in the Sidney Lanier poem "The Marshes of Glynn."

For information about the museum and lighthouse, call ☎ **912/786-5801.** Both the museum and the lighthouse are open April to September, daily 9am to 6pm; off-season hours are Monday and Wednesday to Friday 7am to 4pm and Saturday and Sunday 9am to 4pm. Adults pay $4; seniors 62 and older, $2; and children 6 to 15, $3. Kids 5 and under enter free. There are picnic tables here, and access to the beach is easy.

Strolling Around Isle of Hope

About 10 miles south of downtown Savannah is the nostalgic community of **Isle of Hope.** First settled in the 1840s as a summer resort for the wealthy, it's now a showcase of rural antebellum life. To reach Parkersburg (as it was called in those days), citizens traveled by steamer down the Wilmington River or by a network of suburban trains. Today, however, you can reach Isle of Hope by driving east from Savannah along Victory Drive to Skidaway Road. At Skidaway, go right and follow it to LaRoche Avenue. Then take a left and follow LaRoche until it dead-ends on Bluff Drive.

This is the perfect place for a lazy afternoon stroll. The short path is home to authentically restored cottages and beautiful homes, most enshrouded with Spanish moss cascading from the majestic oaks lining the bluff. A favorite of many local landscape artists and Hollywood directors, Bluff Drive affords the best views of the Wilmington River.

As you head back toward Savannah, drive down Skidaway Road. On your left stands **Wormsloe Plantation,** 7601 Skidaway Rd. (☎ **912/353-3023**). Wormsloe, the home of Noble Jones, isn't much more than a ruin. As you enter the gates, you pass down an unpaved oak-lined drive, and the ruins lie less than half a mile off. Dr. Jones, who built Wormsloe as a silk plantation, was one of Georgia's leading colonial citizens and a representative to the Continental Congress. Because of its strategic location, Wormsloe has also been home to forts and garrisons during the Civil and Spanish-American wars. It's open Tuesday to Saturday 9am to 5pm and Sunday 2 to 5:30pm. Admission is $2.50 for adults and $1.50 for students 6 to 18; children 5 and under are admitted free.

When you leave Wormsloe, continue down Skidaway Road. When you hit Victory Drive, head east through Thunderbolt and over the bridge. Take your first left and stop at **Desposito's** (☎ **912/987-9963**). This funky crab shack is the real thing, complete with newspaper on the tables. Here you can sample a variety of fresh seafood straight from the river, listen to oldies by Guy Lombardo or Dean Martin on the jukebox, and wash it all down with a cold Red Dog beer. It's open Tuesday to Thursday and Sunday noon to 10pm, and Friday and Saturday noon to 11pm.

Tybee Marine Center, in the 14th Street parking lot (☎ **912/786-5917**), has aquariums with species indigenous to the coast of southern Georgia. Also on display are the usual cast of marina mammals, sharks, and other creatures. Hours are Monday to Saturday 9am to 4pm and Sunday 1 to 4pm. Admission is $1.

And no trip would be complete without a wonderful seafood lunch or dinner. The **Crab Shack at Chimney Creek,** 40 Estill Hammock Rd. (☎ **912/786-9857**), advertises itself as "where the elite eat in their bare feet." Your lunch or dinner might've arrived just off the boat, having been swimming happily in the sea only an hour or so ago. Fat crab is naturally the specialty. It's most often preferred in cakes or can be blended with cheese and seasonings. Boiled shrimp is another popular item. Kids delight in selecting their crabs from a tank. A Low Country boil (a medley of seafood) is a family favorite, and the jukebox brings back the 1950s.

21 The Golden Isles & the Okefenokee Swamp

Georgia's barrier islands extend along the Atlantic coast from Ossabaw Island near Savannah all the way down to Cumberland Island, near Florida. Although some have been developed, others, such as Cumberland and Little St. Simons, still linger in the 19th century. Some of the islands are accessible only by boat.

This 150-mile-long stretch of Georgia coast is semitropical and richly historic. The scenic Georgia portion of U.S. 17 goes past broad sandy beaches, creeks and rivers, and the ruins of antebellum plantations. The major highlights are the ✪ "Golden Isles"—principally Jekyll Island, Sea Island, and St. Simons Island. Cumberland Island, the newest National Seashore, is still under development.

Brunswick is the gateway to the Golden Isles. Sea Island and St. Simons are just across the F. J. Torras Causeway (which passes over the famous Marshes of Glynn, immortalized by local poet Sidney Lanier). Jekyll Island is south of town, across the Lanier Bridge then south on Ga. 520 (large signs point the way). Together, they form one of the prime resort areas along the Atlantic coast.

The islands became world-famous for their Sea Island cotton, grown on huge plantations supported mainly by slave labor. The last slaver, the *Wanderer,* landed its cargo of Africans on Jekyll Island as late as 1858. The importing of slaves was by that time illegal and the crew was promptly arrested. Without a large labor force, the plantations languished and finally disappeared in the post–Civil War period.

In the late 1880s the Golden Isles got into the resort business when a group of Yankee millionaires discovered Jekyll Island. They bought it for $125,000 and built "cottages" here with anywhere from 15 to 25 rooms and a clubhouse large enough to accommodate up to 100 members. Until 1947, when second-generation members of the Jekyll Island Club sold the property to the state of Georgia for $675,000, the Millionaires' Village was so exclusive that no uninvited guests ever set foot on the place—even invited guests were limited to visits of no more than 2 weeks. Many of the cottages are open to visitors today, and all the attractions that drew the wealthy are now public property.

Sea Island was purchased back in 1927 by Howard Coffin (he already owned another "golden isle," Sapelo Island), who built a causeway from St. Simons to reach the 5-mile-long barrier island. Then he set about developing what has become a world-famous resort, The Cloister, which opened in October 1928.

The Golden Isles

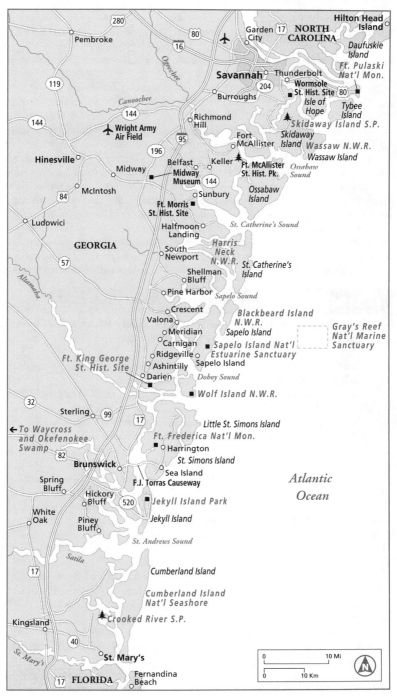

Pembroke

280

80

16

Ogeechee

NORTH
CAROLINA

Garden
City 17

Hilton Head
Island

Daufuskie
Island

119

Canoochee

144

144

Wright Army
Air Field

95

196

Hinesville

Midway

Belfast

Keller

Midway
Museum 144

McIntosh

Sunbury

Ludovici

GEORGIA

84

Halfmoon
Landing

South
Newport

57

Altamaha

Shellman
Bluff

Pine Harbor

Crescent

Valona

Meridian

Carnigan

Ridgeville

Ashintilly

Darien

32

Sterling 99

17

← To Waycross
and Okefenokee
Swamp

82

Brunswick

Spring
Bluff

Hickory
Bluff 520

White
Oak

Piney
Bluff

17

Satila

Kingsland

40

St. Mary's

17 FLORIDA

Fernandina
Beach

Savannah 204

Thunderbolt

Wormsole
St. Hist. Site 80

Burroughs

Isle of
Hope

Tybee
Island

Richmond
Hill

Skidaway Island S.P.

Fort
McAllister

Skidaway
Island

Wassaw N.W.R.

Wassaw Island

Ft. McAllister
St. Hist. Pk.

Ossabaw
Sound

Ossabaw
Island

St. Catherine's Sound

Ft. Morris
St. Hist. Site

Harris
Neck
N.W.R.

St. Catherine's
Island

Sapelo Sound

Blackbeard Island
N.W.R.

Sapelo Island

Gray's Reef
Nat'l Marine
Sanctuary

Sapelo Island Nat'l
Estuarine Sanctuary

Ft. King George
St. Hist. Site

Sapelo Island

Doboy Sound

Wolf Island N.W.R.

Little St. Simons Island

Ft. Frederica Nat'l Mon.

Harrington

St. Simons Island

Sea Island

F.J. Torras Causeway

Jekyll Island Park

Jekyll Island

St. Andrews Sound

Atlantic
Ocean

Cumberland Island

Cumberland Island
Nat'l Seashore

Crooked River S.P.

Ft. Pulaski
Nat'l Mon.

St. Mary's

0   10 Mi

0   10 Km

The Golden Isles are ideal for naturalists, with miles and miles of private secluded beaches plus acres of ancient forests. More than 200 species of birds are sighted locally, so birders flock here, especially to Little St. Simons. Many islands conduct year-round guided nature walks, where locals explain the coastal environment and you can see salt marshes and wildlife.

Temperature and climate make the islands a year-round destination. Spring arrives early in March, with air temperatures ranging from 50° to 80°F and water temperatures at 66°F. Summer is hot, although the heat and humidity are moderated by coastal breezes. Temperatures range from 72° to 90°F, with water temperatures at 80°F—ideal beach weather. Fall arrives in mid-October and is marked by clear days and low humidity, with temperatures averaging 68°F. Winter is brief and mild, with daytime highs in the 60s, lows in the 40s, and water temperatures averaging 50°F.

If all this weren't enticement enough, the Golden Islands are also the gateway to the Okefenokee Swamp Park, an hour's drive to the west. Called the "land of trembling earth," this swamp is one of the most forbidding yet one of the loveliest places in America, covering some 412,000 acres. Boating excursions into the swamp allow close encounters with alligators. The centerpiece is a 111-acre lake that attracts water-skiers, anglers, and boaters. On the west side of the swamp is the Stephen C. Foster State Park, offering cabins and campsites along with signposted nature trails and canoe rentals.

1 Sapelo Island

The fourth largest of Georgia's barrier islands, ✪ **Sapelo Island** is filled with the diverse wildlife of the forested uplands as well as a salt marsh and a complex beach and dunes system. The island is reached from the Sapelo ferry dock, 8 miles northeast of Darien off Ga. 99. Educational tours of this undeveloped barrier island are conducted year-round by the Georgia Department of Natural Resources.

Taking in everything from maritime forests to marshes, the **R. J. Reynolds State Wildlife Refuge** encompasses 8,240 acres. Some 5,900 of these acres have been designated as the **Sapelo Island National Estuarine Research Reserve.**

Guale Indians, Spanish missionaries, English freebooters, and French royalists called this island home before Thomas Spalding purchased the south end of the island in 1802. In the antebellum years, Spalding (1802–51) refined the Georgia Sea Island cotton and sugar industries and designed and constructed an octagonal tabby sugar mill in 1809. (Tabby is a mixture of equal parts of oyster shell, sand, water, and lime.)

In 1912, Howard E. Coffin purchased the island from Spalding's heirs. Coffin undertook a complete rebuilding of **South End House,** Spalding's plantation mansion, which dated from 1810. By 1928 the house was ready to entertain President and Mrs. Coolidge and later President and Mrs. Hoover in 1932. In February 1929, Charles A. Lindbergh landed on the island and visited the Coffins.

The house was purchased in 1934 by the tobacco heir Richard J. Reynolds. Twenty years later Reynolds donated the dairy complex of the farm to the University of Georgia for use as a marine research laboratory. Jimmy Carter used the mansion during his administration in 1980.

Today, there are some 400 acres of private property on the island, concentrated in a hamlet known as Hog Hammock, whose residents are descended from slaves from Spalding's plantation days.

Interpretive programs on the island include marsh and beach walks, bird and wildlife observation, and special historic tours. Salt-marsh vegetation includes needlerush, sea oxeye, salt grass, glasswort, and cordgrass. You'll see osprey feeding in the Duplin River and hear the call of the clapper rail, a marsh bird. The island is inhabited by such species as raccoons, feral cows, white-tailed deer, and a variety of snakes, including the eastern diamondback rattler and the cottonmouth. Chachalacas, a Mexican species of bird introduced to the island as a game bird, might also be spotted.

A 25-minute ferryboat ride from the mainland aboard the **Sapelo Queen** takes visitors to the island. Guides accompany guests on the half-day bus tour, including a marsh walk. The ferry leaves Wednesdays at 8:30am, returning at 12:30pm; Fridays (June 1 to Labor Day only) at 8:30am, returning at 12:30pm and Saturdays at 9am, returning at 1pm. An extended tour is conducted the last Tuesday of each month from March through October from 8:30am to 2:30pm. Reservations are required, costing $10 for adults, children 6 to 18 $6, including the boat ride. To book tours, contact the **Sapelo Visitors Center** (☎ 912/437-3224), Landing Road, in Meridian, Georgia, just outside of Darien, Georgia.

2 Brunswick

75 miles S of Savannah; 15 miles S of Darien

The gateway to the Golden Isles is a sleepy town not quite awake to the tourism potential of its antique houses, palms, flowering shrubs, and moss-draped live oaks.

Brunswick has always been an important port, with a natural harbor that can handle oceangoing ships. In World War II, with Nazi U-boats prowling the Atlantic, Brunswick's shipyard began to construct "Liberty Ships," the name for a stronger, larger cargo vessel. Beginning in 1943, these 447-foot vessels slipped down the ways at the feverish rate of some four a month. Today, instead of Liberty Ships you'll find a large fleet of shrimp boats—the town bills itself as the "shrimp capital of the world."

At some point you'll want to try a Brunswick stew in the town of its origin (although the citizens of Brunswick County, Virginia, would beg to differ). It is made basically with a combination of meats, and flavored with an array of vegetables such as tomatoes, potatoes, okra, lima beans, and corn. In old days cooks would make it with squirrel, rabbit, or what virtually amounted to road kill, all simmering in the same pot—but preparations are less exotic today. A good time to sample the various versions is during the Brunswick Stewbilee, a Brunswick stew cook-off held here the second weekend in October.

ESSENTIALS

GETTING THERE   From Savannah, head west, following the signs to I-95; you'll take the highway south until the Brunswick turnoff.

Six miles north of Brunswick, **Glynco Jetport** (☎ 912/264-9200) is served by **Delta ASA** (☎ 800/221-1212; www.delta.com), an affiliate of Delta. It offers flights to the Brunswick area from Atlanta. At the small airport, car rentals are available, including **Avis** (☎ 912/638-2232 and **Hertz** (☎ 912/265-3645).

VISITOR INFORMATION   The **Brunswick-Golden Isles Welcome Center,** Rte. 10, Box I-95, Brunswick, GA 31520 (☎ 912/264-0202), is on I-95 southbound between exits 8 and 9. The friendly staff can give you area information, and if you come without reservations, can book a room for you at one of more than 20 nearby hotels and motels. Hours are daily 9am to 5pm. There's also a **welcome center** at 2000 Glynn Ave. (☎ 912/264-5337).

SEEING THE SIGHTS

The welcome center will provide you with a free map indicating the main points of interest, which include the waterfront off Bay Street, with its bustling docks and fleet of shrimp boats. Oceangoing freighters are often seen here.

The **Lanier Oak,** along U.S. 17, off Lanier Boulevard, is said to be the tree where the Georgia poet, Sidney Lanier, was inspired to write *The Marshes of Glynn.* Another tree, the nine-centuries-old **Lover's Oak,** at Albany and Prince streets, is also a source of pride for the town.

After dark, the big attractions are the dinner and casino cruises aboard the *Emerald Princess* (☎ 800/842-0115). Bookings can be made at the **Golden Isles Cruise Lines,** 1 St. Andrews Court in Brunswick (☎ 912/265-3558). This 200-foot luxury cruiser offers dining, dancing, and live entertainment on one level, and a full casino with slot machines, poker, blackjack, craps, and roulette on another level. After departure, the ship sails out past the 3-mile limit, where the casino then opens for business. Cruises depart from Golden Isles Cruise Lines docks at the Brunswick Landing Marina (Newcastle and K streets).

Reservations are not required, but you should make them anyway just to be on the safe side. On Tuesday and Thursday, the rate is $25 per person, going up to $35 on Friday, Saturday, and Sunday. On Wednesday a special price of $25 for two is featured. Cruise hours are Tuesday to Thursday from 7pm to midnight, Friday and Saturday 7pm to 1am, and Sunday 1 to 6pm. A special Saturday-morning departure leaves at 11am and returns at 4pm, at a cost of $19.98. There are no sailings on Monday. All cruises offer a full meal at sea, with music, dancing, and games such as scavenger hunts.

WHERE TO STAY

✪ Brunswick Manor. 825 Egmont St., Brunswick, GA 31520. ☎ 912/265-6889. Fax 912/265-7879. E-mail: cjrose@gate.net. 8 units. A/C TV. $65–$90 double; $90–$100 suite. Rates include full breakfast and afternoon tea. MC, V.

This is the most imposing, most impressive, and most elegant B&B in Brunswick. It was built in 1886 by an entrepreneur from Ohio who moved, carpetbagger-style, to manage the local bank and establish a nearby cooperage. The house is an eclectic and rather masculine brick-sided Victorian, with many Eastlake features and the most elaborate Corinthian portico (a later addition) of any house in Brunswick. Inside, a collection of Empire and Federal furniture, a greenhouse-style hot tub, and a collection of miniature electric trains demonstrate the personal flair of the owners, Harry and Claudia Tzucanow. Bedrooms are tastefully outfitted, especially the nautically stylish "Romance of the Seas" room. The least expensive (but still very comfortable) rooms are in the clapboard-sided Victorian house next door.

WatersHill Red & Breakfast. 728 Union St., Brunswick, GA 315210. ☎ 912/264-4262. Fax 912/265-6326. www.watershill.com. 5 units. $85–$115 double. A/C TV TEL. Rates include breakfast. AE, DISC, MC, V.

Some of the most old-fashioned hospitality in Brunswick is found at this restored 1860s Victorian House. It's an exceedingly comfortable place, with guest rooms named after the mothers and grandmothers of the present owners. The B&B is among the most conveniently located in town, right in the center of the historic old section. Each of the bedrooms has had a private bathroom installed, and breakfast is one of the best in the area. Each afternoon, as a quaint old touch, tea or wine with cheese is served in the parlor.

WHERE TO DINE

Mack's Barbecue Place. 2089 Glynn Ave. ☎ 912/264-0605. Sandwiches $2.95–$3.25; main courses $4.95–$7.95. AE, DISC, MC, V. Mon–Sat 10:30am–9pm. BARBECUE.

It occupies a 1960s building of no architectural charm, and lies beside the grimy commercial edges of Highway 17, on the heavily trafficked outskirts of town. Despite its lack of visual appeal, the place serves the best barbecue in the Golden Isles. Notice the neatly arranged cords of oak firewood stacked in the parking lot. The domain is maintained with an iron grip by members of the Wilson family. The interior resembles that of an uninspired steakhouse beside a thruway, enhanced with a smoking chamber that gobbles firewood and looks like a hybrid between a blast furnace and a locomotive. The menu is limited to fabulous sandwiches or platters of barbecued pork, beef, chicken, turkey, ribs, and hamburgers, accompanied with salad, coleslaw, fried mushrooms, onion rings, and corn. And you've got to have Brunswick stew on the side. No alcohol is served.

Spanky's. 1200 Glynn Ave. ☎ **912/267-6100.** Burgers, salads, and sandwiches $5.25–$7.95; platters $7.50–$16.95. AE, DISC, MC, V. Sun–Thurs 11am–9:30pm; Fri–Sat 10:30am–11pm. SEAFOOD/AMERICAN.

Set between the coastal highway and the sea, this place is like a sprawling, clapboard-sided seafood restaurant and saloon in New England. It's rather chaotic, but it's always buzzing with locals. Avoid the place during peak dinner hours on Friday and Saturday, when you might not get a seat. The food is delicious: a wide selection of seafood, burgers, Mexican platters, and steaks, including an especially tasty chicken Reuben sandwich. Seafood platters are served with hush puppies, of course, and there's a superb version of Brunswick stew, which a chef obviously labors over.

3 St. Simons Island

80 miles S of Savannah; 10 miles E of Brunswick

The largest of the Golden Isles, St. Simons is also the most popular for its beaches, golf courses, scenery, and numerous tennis courts.

Through tunnels of ancient oaks, you can bike and drive the length of St. Simons, finding treasures at every turn. It's very much a vacation haven for families.

ESSENTIALS
GETTING THERE   Take I-95 to Ga. 25 (the Island Parkway) or U.S. 17 to Brunswick, where signs direct visitors across the F. J. Torras Causeway (35¢ toll) to St. Simons Island.

VISITOR INFORMATION   The **St. Simons Island Visitors Center & Chamber of Commerce,** 530 Beachview Dr. W. (☎ **912/638-9014**), dispenses maps and helpful information, particularly about beaches. It's open daily from 9am to 5pm.

SEEING THE ISLAND
The best way to introduce yourself to the island is via **St. Simons Trolley Island Tours** (☎ **912/638-8954**), which acquaint you with 400 years of history and folklore, taking 1½ hours and costing $13 for adults and $7 for children 10 and under. Tours depart March 15 to Labor Day, Tuesday to Saturday at 11am and 1pm; off-season, Tuesday to Saturday at 1pm.

The island's chief attraction is **Fort Frederica National Monument** (☎ **912/ 638-3639**), on the northwest end of the island (signposted). Go first to the National Park Service Visitors Center, where a film and displays explain the role of the fort. There isn't much left; about all you'll see of the original construction is a small portion of the king's magazine and the barracks tower, but archaeological excavations have unearthed many foundations. The fort was constructed in 1736 by Gen. James Oglethorpe. On the grounds is a gift shop, and walking tours are also arranged. Admission is $4 per car, and it's open from 9am to 5pm daily.

The second site of interest is the **Museum of Coastal History,** 101 12th St. (☎ 912/638-4666), in a restored lighthouse keeper's house next to St. Simons Light. A gallery dispenses information about the coastal region on the ground floor. Hardy souls will want to climb the lighthouse's 129 steps for a panoramic view of the Golden Isles, which is far more intriguing than any of the museum's exhibits. Adults pay $3 and children 6 to 11 are charged $1 (children 5 and under enter free). It's open Monday to Saturday from 10am to 5pm and on Sunday from 1:30 to 5pm.

Christ Church, 6329 Frederica Rd., at the north end of the island, was built in 1820. It was virtually destroyed when Union troops camped here during the Civil War, burning the pews for firewood and butchering cattle in the chapel. In 1886 Anson Greene Phelps Dodge, Jr., restored the church as a memorial to his first wife, who had died on their honeymoon. It's a serene, white building nestled under huge old oaks. It's open every day from 2 to 5pm during daylight saving time, 1 to 4pm at other times. There's no admission charge.

Scattered from end to end on St. Simons are ruins of the plantation era: the **Hampton Plantation** (where Aaron Burr spent a month after his duel with Alexander Hamilton) and **Cannon's Point** on the north; **West Point, Pines Bluff,** and the **Hamilton Plantations** on the west along the Frederica River; **Harrington Hall** and **Mulberry Grove** in the interior; **Lawrence, St. Clair, Black Banks, The Village,** and **Kelvyn Grove** on the east; and the **Retreat Plantation** on the south end. There's a restored chapel on West Point Plantation made of tabby, with mortar turned pink because of an unusual lichen. Locals say it reflects blood on the hands of Dr. Thomas Hazzard, who killed a neighbor in a land dispute and built the chapel after being so ostracized by island society that he would not attend Christ Church.

Near the airport, the **Coastal Center for the Arts,** 201 Demure Rd. (☎ 912/634-0404), is where local and traveling arts and crafts exhibits are displayed. It's the cultural showcase for St. Simons and is open, free, Monday to Saturday from 9am to 5pm year-round.

BEACHES, GOLF & OTHER OUTDOOR PURSUITS

St. Simons not only attracts families looking for a beach—it's also heaven for golfers, with 99 holes. One golfer we met who's played every hole said that each one presents a worthy challenge. Other sports include boating, inshore and offshore fishing, waterskiing, kayaking, and sailing. Jet skiing, parasailing, charter fishing, scuba diving, and cruising can also be arranged at the **Golden Isles Marina Docks,** 206 Marina Dr. (☎ 912/634-1128), on the F.J. Torras Causeway.

Neptune Park, at the island's south end, provides miniature golf, a playground for children, picnics under the oaks, and pier fishing. There's beach access from the park.

BEACHES　You'll find two white-sand public beaches here, foremost of which is the **Massingale Park Beach,** Ocean Boulevard. It has a county-maintained beach with a picnic area and a bathhouse. It's open with a lifeguard on duty June 1 to Labor Day, daily from 10am to 4pm. Parking is free in designated areas, and drinking is allowed on the beach but only from plastic containers (no glasses). Fishing is free from the beach but allowed only from 4 to 11pm.

Another public beach is the **Coast Guard Station Beach,** East Beach Causeway, again family-oriented, with a bathhouse and showers. Lifeguards are on duty from June 1 to the Labor Day weekend, daily from 10am to 4pm. Parking is free in designated areas, and fishing is permitted during nonswimming hours from 4:30 to 11pm. Drinking is allowed on the beach but from plastic containers only.

Further information about beaches can be obtained from the **Glynn County Recreation Department** (☎ 912/638-2393).

BIKE RENTALS   Ocean Motion, 1300 Ocean Blvd. (☎ **800/669-5215** or 912/638-5225), suggests that you explore St. Simons by bike, and will provide detailed instructions about the best routes. The island is relatively flat, so biking is easy. Beach cruisers are available for men, women, and kids, with infant seats and helmets. Bike rentals cost $8 for 4 hours or $12 for a full day.

BIRDING   Kennedy Charters, 511 Marsh Villa Rd. (☎ **912/638-3214**), arranges tours and marsh-boat rides upon request. Birders can see some of the 200 species of birds inhabiting this region. The marsh boat can accommodate up to six passengers, and the cost is the same regardless of the number of guests: $65 per hour, with the minimum tour lasting 90 minutes.

FISHING   Your best bet is **Golden Isles Charter Fishing,** Golden Isles Marina Village (☎ **912/638-7673**), which offers deep-sea fishing and both offshore and inshore fishing. Captain Mark Noble is your guide.

✪ **GOLF**   It's golf—not tennis—that makes St. Simons Island a star attraction. Foremost among the courses is the ✪ **Sea Island Golf Club,** 100 Retreat Ave. (☎ **912/638-5118**), owned by The Cloister of Sea Island. At the end of the "Avenue of Oaks" at historic Retreat Plantation, the club consists of a number of courses: the Marshside Course (9 holes, 3,260 yards, par 36), the Plantation Course (9 holes, 3,260 yards, par 36), the Retreat Course (9 holes, 3,137 yards, par 36), the Seaside Course (9 holes, 3,185 yards, par 36), and the Ocean Forest (18 holes, 7,011 yards, par 72).

The club opened in 1927, and offers dramatic ocean views adding a measure of excitement to the game. The state-of-the-art Golf Learning Center on the grounds can help improve even an experienced golfer's game. Its greatest fans mention it with the same reverence as St. Andrews, Pebble Beach, or Ballybunion. Former President George Bush liked the courses so much that he played 36 holes a day. Seaside and Retreat are the most requested nines, with Seaside definitely the most famous of all—known for the 414-yard no. 7. *Golf Digest* has called this hole one of the best in golf and among the toughest in Georgia. A drive has to clear a marsh-lined stream and avoid a gaping fairway bunker.

Greens fees for hotel guests only are $125 to $150, with cart included. Clubs rent for $35, and professional instruction is available for $55 to $100 per half hour. Caddies cost $20 to $44 plus tip. On the grounds are a pro shop, clubhouse, and restaurant, and the course is open daily from 7:45am to 7pm.

St. Simons Island Club, 100 Kings Way (☎ **912/638-5130**), is an 18-hole, par-72 course of 6,200 yards. Known for its Low Country architecture, it hosts several popular tournaments every year. The demanding course, designed by Joe Lee, features narrow fairways lined by lagoons and towering pines. Greens fees for Cloister guests are $95.40, cottage guests at Sea Island pay $95.40, and nonguests pay $110, with cart and range balls included. Professional instruction is available at $35 per half hour through arrangements made at the clubhouse and pro shop. There's also a restaurant on the premises. Play is available daily from 8am to 7pm.

Sea Palms Golf & Tennis Resort, 5445 Frederica Rd. (☎ **912/638-3351**), offers outstanding golf on its Tall Pines/Great Oaks (18 holes, 6,500 yards, par 72), Great Oaks/Sea Palms West (18 holes, 6,200 yards, par 72), and Sea Palms West/Tall Pines (18 holes, 6,200 yards, par 72) courses. Some holes nestle alongside scenic marshes and meandering tidal creeks. Reserved tee times are recommended, and cart use is required. The courses are open daily from 7:30am to 7pm, charging greens fees of $58 for hotel guests and $67 for nonguests, with cart rentals included. Professional instruction costs $30 for a 30-minute session, $45 for an hour.

NATURE TOURS   The **Ocean Motion Surf Co.,** 1300 Ocean Blvd. (☎ **800/ 669-5215** or 912/638-5225), offers nature tours by kayak of the island's marsh creeks and secluded beaches. Featured is either a 2-hour dolphin nature tour at $35 or a 4-hour wildlife tour at $60.

SAILBOAT RENTALS   **Barry's Beach Service, Inc.,** at the King and Prince Beach Hotel, 201 Arnold Rd. (☎ **912/638-8053**), arranges hourly, half-day, or full-day sailboat rentals, along with sailing lessons (by experienced instructors) and sailboat rides. Kayak rentals, tours, and instruction are also available.

TENNIS   There are two public tennis courts on the island. The **Mallory Park Courts,** Mallory Street, have two lighted courts open year-round, and admission is free. **Epworth Park,** on Lady Huntington Drive, has two courts open 24 hours but not equipped with lights; it, too, is free.

WHERE TO STAY

In addition to the accommodations listed below, private cottages are available for weekly or monthly rental on St. Simons. You can get an illustrated brochure with rates and availability information from **Parker-Kaufman Realtors,** 1699 Frederica Rd., St. Simons Island, GA 31522 (☎ **912/638-3368**). The office is open Monday to Friday from 9am to 5pm and on Saturday from 9am to noon. Vacation rental cottages can range from two to five bedrooms. Rentals begin at $650 per week in summer, lowered to as little as $550 per week off-season.

Island Inn. 301 Main St., St. Simons Island, GA 31522. ☎ **800/673-6323** or 912/ 638-7805. Fax 912/694-4720. www.stsimonsdestinations.com. E-mail: bwisland@gate.net. 61 units. A/C TV TEL. $78–$88 double; $108–$135 suite. Rates include continental breakfast. AE, DC, DISC, MC, V.

This unassuming, brick-sided motel was built in the late 1980s, about 2½ miles from the nearest beach. The efficiencies have a kitchenette, and the bedrooms are no-nonsense, unfrilly, and economical. About a dozen of them can be connected with adjoining rooms to allow families to create their own live-in arrangements.

King and Prince Beach Resort. 201 Arnold Rd., St. Simons island, GA 31522. ☎ **800/ 342-0212** or 912/638-3631. Fax 912/634-1720. www.kingandprince.com. 187 units. A/C TV TEL. $145–$155 double; $275–395 condo apt. AE, DC, MC, V.

This is an unpretentious, medium-size oceanfront resort founded in 1932 by partners who were evicted from the Jekyll Island Club. Today's reincarnation of five Spanish-style buildings is a venue for frequent corporate conventions. Frankly, it seems devoid of any real pizzazz; Hugh Hefner hasn't visited since the 1950s. Don't expect continuous access to a beach: During high tide, it completely disappears. The resort compensates with four indoor and outdoor pools, four tennis courts, a fitness center, a quasi-formal dining room (the Delegal Room), and a tavern/lounge (the Frederica Tavern). The condo apartments have kitchenettes.

Sea Gate Inn. 1014 Ocean Blvd., St. Simons Island, GA 31522. ☎ **800/562-8812** or 912/638-8661. Fax 912/638-4932. 48 units. $65–$145 double; $85–$120 suite. AE, MC, V.

Its charms and advantages are often underestimated because of its low-rise format, unpretentious entrance, and position near other, much larger hotels. Despite that, this is a clean, respectable hotel whose accommodations are divided into two buildings separated from one another by a quiet road that runs parallel to the sea. The more desirable (and expensive) of the two is the Ocean House, a 1985 annex built on stilts. The less expensive, and less desirable, lodgings are clustered around a swimming pool, roadside-motel style. Some units contain modest kitchenettes. The hotel, incidentally, was named after an old-fashioned ferryboat that used to ply the waters between Brunswick and St. Simons Island.

Sea Palms. 5445 Frederica Rd., St. Simons Island, GA 31522. ☎ **800/841-6268** or 912/ 638-3351. Fax 912/634-8029. 155 units. A/C TV TEL. $124–$149 double; $150–$268 1- or 2-bedroom suite. Children 17 and under stay free in parents' room. Golf, tennis, and honeymoon packages available. AE, DC, MC, V.

This place imitates the older and more upscale resorts nearby. Sprawled over 800 landscaped acres, it combines aspects of a retirement community with a family-friendly resort. Most people stay 3 to 5 days.

After registering in a woodsy bungalow near the entrance, you'll be waved off toward your accommodation to carry your own bags. If you're looking for maximum isolation, this place might be appropriate; otherwise, you might feel it's too anonymous. Each suite contains a kitchenette. There's a golf course on the premises, and views from many of the simply furnished units over some beautiful marshland. The premises contain a dozen tennis courts, two outdoor pools (which are very crowded in summertime), a health club, and a restaurant (the Main Course) with its own lounge. The nearest worthwhile beach is about 4 miles away.

WHERE TO DINE
EXPENSIVE

The Restaurant at the Sea Island Golf Club. 100 Retreat Ave. ☎ **912/638-5154.** Reservations not necessary at lunch, recommended for dinner. Main courses $12–$51. MC, V. Daily 11am–4pm and 6:30–9:30pm. INTERNATIONAL.

Despite the name, this place stands firmly on St. Simons Island. It was built on the ruins of a cow barn of a plantation great house that long ago burned to the ground. The restaurant occupies a simple square dining room in back of the golf course's clubhouse, and has big windows extending out over the landscape of trees and lawns. Uniformed staff members give the impression of being old family retainers while serving a luncheon menu of burgers, salads, club sandwiches, and fresh fish. Dinner is more formal, offering worthy but not particularly experimental dishes including boned and browned Blue Ridge salmon-trout in lemon butter with capers, seafood fettuccine, seafood crepes, and grilled steaks.

The Restaurant at the St. Simons Island Club. 100 Kings Way. ☎ **912/638-5132.** Reservations recommended. Collared shirts required for men. Main courses $15.50–$24. MC, V., Mon–Sat 11:30am–2pm and 6:30–9:30pm, Sun 10:30am–2pm (buffet) and 6:30–9:30pm. LOW COUNTRY/INTERNATIONAL.

Maintained and operated by The Cloister hotel, this is a less formal and slightly less expensive alternative to that resort's main dining room. (It's surrounded by the fairways of the St. Simons Island Club, and is not to be confused with the less formal restaurant at the Sea Island Golf Club; see above.) Expect a high-ceilinged room with exposed rafters, an evening pianist, and an atmosphere like something in the British colonial tropics of the 1960s. The service is attentive and formal, and the cuisine specializes in the Low Country victuals developed here during the early 19th century. Menu items include sautéed swordfish steak with a basil/green-peppercorn sauce, lamb loin with mint-and-rosemary sauce, grilled breast of duck, pastas, and a vegetarian special of the day. In our view, the cuisine needs more spice and flavor.

MODERATE

Blanche's Courtyard. 440 Ocean Blvd. (at Kings Way). ☎ **912/638-3030.** Reservations not accepted. Main courses $12.95–$23.95. AE, DISC, MC, V. Tues–Sun 5:30–10pm. SEAFOOD/SOUTHERN.

This is the island's most popular restaurant. On weekends, diners waiting for a table congregate in a not-very-comfortable brick-floored room. An ersatz Victorian theme dominates what originated as a simple private house that just grew like Topsy. Who inspired all this gaslight-era nostalgia? Blanche La Rouge, a Cajun madam of questionable virtue who plied her trade along the Louisiana coast during the Gay '90s. Frankly, the place would work better if the service staff didn't seem so obviously inexperienced. Mostly college students on summer furlough, they do mean well, despite long delays and an occasional gaffe on our last visit. Don't expect sophisticated creations; think deep-fried.

Chelsea's. 1226 Ocean Blvd. ☎ **912/638-2047.** Reservations recommended. Main courses $10.95–$21.95. AE, DC, MC, V. Daily 5:30–10pm. INTERNATIONAL.

Set close to the road, a few steps from the larger and more visible King and Prince Hotel, this well-known restaurant combines aspects of a singles bar with a relaxed, unpretentious dining room. It's in a long, low-rise building trimmed with ferns, lattices, and wine racks. You never know who you might meet at the bar. The menu includes steaks, salads, pastas, lobster-tail fingers, chicken breasts crusted in Romano cheese, and roast lamb. A menu like that offers few surprises—but few disappointments, either.

INEXPENSIVE

Bennie's Red Barn. 5514 Frederica Rd. ☎ **912/638-2844.** Reservations recommended Sat–Sun. Main courses $9.75–$19.75. DISC, MC, V. Mon–Sun 6–10pm. STEAKS/SEAFOOD.

Established in 1954, the place has a Southern folksiness, almost a hillbilly kind of charm. But the staff can forget their magnolia manners under pressure; try to time your visit to lunch or weekends when it's less hectic here. Menu items include an uncomplicated medley of food to please everyone's Southern grandmother, including fried or broiled fish, chicken, and shrimp. Steaks are sizable slabs, charcoal-grilled and appropriately seasoned. Dinners include house salad, potato, rolls, and tea or coffee. If you're a biscuit-and-gravy kind of diner, you've arrived.

Blue Water Bistro. 115 Mallory St. ☎ **912/638-7007.** Reservations recommended. Main courses $9.95–$19.95. AE, DISC, MC, V. Mon–Thurs 5:30–9:30pm, Fri–Sat 5:30–10pm. AMERICAN.

Set in the island's most congested neighborhood a few steps from the waterfront, this place is New South all the way. It also knows how to throw a good party. Look for the bronze bank-deposit vault piercing its facade, a hint of the building's original role as a commercial landmark. Inside you'll find cozy, nautical decor, an antique Wurlitzer jukebox, and an Atlanta brand of hip. Dishes reflect the region's party ethic with names that include Mardi Gras pasta (with shellfish and andouille sausage). Also available are uptown, urban dishes such as Mediterranean chicken, pescado Veracruzano, and a stew of deep-sea scallops with green-lip mussels. But for dessert, there's Southern-style bread pudding like mother used to make.

The Crab Trap. 1209 Ocean Blvd. ☎ **912/638-3552.** Main courses $8.95–15.95. MC, V. Mon–Thurs 5–10pm, Fri–Sat 5–10:30pm, Sun (summer only) 5–10pm. Closed Thanksgiving and Christmas. SEAFOOD.

For the family trade in pursuit of coleslaw, hush puppies, and fried shrimp, the Crab Trap is the island's most popular seafood restaurant and a good buy. Forget fancy trappings—the place is downright plain. Fresh seafood is offered daily, and you can order it fried, broiled, blackened, or grilled. Appetizers include oysters on the half shell and crab soup. Boiled crab is the chef's specialty, and the seafood platter is big enough for three. For those who aren't turned on by crabs and shrimp, steaks in various cuts are also available. Heaps of battered fries come with most dishes. That hole in the middle of your table is for depositing shrimp shells and corncobs. Dress as if you're going on a summer fishing trip.

Delaney's Bistro. 3415 Frederica Rd. ☎ **912/638-1330.** Reservations recommended. Lunch main courses $5.95–$8.95; dinner main courses $12.95–$20.95. AE, DC, DISC, MC, V. Tues–Sat 11am–2:30pm and 6–10pm. AMERICAN

Local chef Tom Delaney's loyal following includes both islanders and visitors. He aims to appeal to a wide culinary taste, and in general succeeds. In his low-rise building, Delaney offers an array of food ranging from fresh seafood to certified Black Angus beef. The menu at lunch is light, including the usual pastas, sandwiches, and salads and grilled shrimp salad or sautéed crab cakes. Tom is more ambitious at night. You might begin with a pâté of foie gras or baked goat cheese before selecting a main course such as a mixed grill (beef, veal, and lamb chop in a cabernet sauce) or veal Hannah, a scaloppini topped with wild mushrooms and crab). Desserts are made fresh daily.

4 Little St. Simons Island

20-minute boat ride from St. Simons Island

The ideal place to savor the wild beauty of Georgia's coast is still untouched by commercial development. Reached only by boat, Little St. Simons Island—6 miles long and 2 to 3 miles wide—remains one of the last privately owned islands off the Georgia coast. The current owners have welcomed family and friends since the early 1900s, but in 1978 it was opened to the general public, with accommodations limited to 24.

The island is a haven for naturalists and those seeking a secluded getaway. (But be warned that mosquitoes are a serious problem here in summer.) Activities on Little St. Simons include shelling, swimming, and sunbathing along 7 miles of secluded beaches; and hiking (watch out for snakes), exploring, and horseback riding through acres of ancient forest. There are also canoeing and fishing in the island's many rivers and creeks, plus bird watching of at least 200 species. Guests can learn about the local ecosystems by joining naturalists on explorations. In all, 10,000 acres of secluded wilderness have been left virtually untouched for more than a century.

ESSENTIALS

GETTING THERE   Take I-95 to Ga. 25 (the Island Parkway) or U.S. 17 to Brunswick, where signs direct visitors across the F. J. Torras Causeway (pay toll) to St. Simons Island. Once on the island, follow the signs to the Hampton River Club Marina. At the marina, on the north end of St. Simons, a ferryboat departs daily at 10:30am and again at 4:30pm, taking visitors to Little St. Simons. It's privately owned, so unless you're a guest you are not even allowed to ride the ferry and immediately turn around.

VISITOR INFORMATION   All information is supplied directly by the lodge (see below).

WHERE TO STAY & DINE

The Lodge on Little St. Simons Island. P.O. Box 21078, Little St. Simons Island, GA 31522. ☎ **912/638-7472.** 888/733-5774. Fax 912/634-1811. www.littlestsimonsisland. com. E-mail: lssi@mindspring.com. 15 units. A/C. $350–$525 double; 2-, 3-, and 4-bedroom accommodations $600–$2,000 year-round; full island rental for up to 30 persons, $4,700–$6,200 year-round. Rates include full board. Additional person in room $125–$175 extra. AE, DISC, MC, V.

The lodge is for those seeking a Robinson Crusoe type of vacation. It's surprisingly exclusive, but unlike luxury resorts such as Fripp Island, it doesn't have plush upholstery and dramatic architecture. Be prepared for no air-conditioning—even in summer. If you like life summer-camp style, this is for you. Accommodations, in simple bedrooms cooled by ceiling fans, include the 1917 Hunting Lodge in the main house with the dining room, the 1930s Michael Cottage (a two-bedroom cottage at the forest's edge), and the 1980s Cedar Lodge & River Lodge, each a cottage with four private guest rooms sharing a sitting room with a fireplace and screened porch.

You pour your own drinks at a makeshift bar in the corner of a communal living room with hunting trophies from another era. Hearty, homey meals are served family style in the main dining room, and the staff will be happy to prepare a picnic lunch for you. The menu features locally caught seafood and such Southern staples as fried chicken and barbecue.

5 Sea Island

11 miles E of Brunswick

Since 1928 this has been the domain of The Cloister hotel (see below). Today, in addition to the hotel, it's home to some of the most elegant villas and mansions in the Southeast. Most of Sea Island's homes—many in the Spanish-Mediterranean style— are second homes to CEOs and other rich folk. Some can be rented if you can afford it. Call **Sea Island Cottage Rentals** (☎ 912/638-5112) and be prepared for some higher mathematics.

The island was acquired by Ohio-based Howard Earle Coffin, an automobile executive, in 1925. Still owned by Coffin's descendants, The Cloister combines 10,000 acres of forest, lawn, and marshland, plus 5 miles of beachfront. The island has impressed everybody from Margaret Thatcher to Queen Juliana of the Netherlands, plus four U.S. presidents, including George Bush, who honeymooned here with Bar in the 1940s. Many day visitors who can't afford the high prices of The Cloister come over for a scenic drive along Sea Island Drive, called "Millionaire's Row." There's no tollgate.

ESSENTIALS

GETTING THERE   From Brunswick, take the F. J. Torras Causeway (35¢ toll) to St. Simons Island and follow Sea Island Road all the way to Sea Island.

VISITOR INFORMATION   There is no welcome center. Information is provided by The Cloister, but the staff prefers to cater to registered guests.

WHERE TO STAY & DINE

✪ **The Cloister.** Sea Island, GA 31561. ☎ **800/732-4752** or 912/638-3611. Fax 912/ 638-5159. www.seaisland.com. A/C TV TEL. $536–$818 double; $610–$1,234 suite. Rates include all meals (15% service charge and 10% tax extra). Children 18 and under stay free in parents' room. Golf, tennis, or honeymoon packages available. AE, CB, DC, DISC, MC, V.

Georgia's poshest hotel retreat, set amid the most elaborate landscaping on the coast, is a vast compound between the Atlantic Ocean and the Black Banks River. It takes in about 50 carefully maintained buildings, some of them massive and others on neighboring St. Simon's Island. Most replicate the Iberian–Moorish Revival style of the resort's original architect, Addison Mizner.

Everyone from honeymooners to golfers checks in here, with the family trade predominating in July and August. Traditionalists prefer a room in the main building, with twin, double, or king-size beds, often with a private balcony or patio too. These rooms tend to be smaller than the newer units. The secluded cottages and beach houses also contain extra accommodations. The oceanfront rooms are in contemporary buildings with sumptuous modern furnishings, lacking tradition but offering greater comfort (from ironing boards to upholstered chairs) and more room to breathe.

Dining/Diversions: Full American Plan (lodging with three meals included) is required of all guests at The Cloister. The Main Dining Room is the most lavish restaurant in the region, with sumptuous buffets and vestiges of the 1940s apparent in the uniformed service and the hushed, very polite tones of both staff and guests.

Amenities: Room service, child care, laundry/dry cleaning; every imaginable activity is offered at this resort, including 22 tennis courts (4 of which are lighted), 2 swimming pools, 54 holes of golf, lawn games (including croquet), skeet, fishing from hotel docks and on deep-sea cruisers, and cruises along the coastal waterways. Horticultural tours of the gardens, spa-style weight-loss programs, sailing, and a full program of other water sports can be arranged.

6 Jekyll Island

9 miles S of Brunswick

Once a winter playground for the Rockefellers, Pulitzers, Goulds, Morgans, and Cranes, Jekyll Island is the smallest of the state's coastal islands, with 5,600 acres of highlands and 10,000 acres of marshlands. Today it's no longer the exclusive enclave it once was, and is open to all those attracted by its miles of beautiful, white-sand Atlantic beaches and holes of championship golf. It also has far better tennis complexes than St. Simons Island. Families come here for a wealth of outdoor activities.

The word "wealth" had another meaning on the island, at least from 1886 to 1942. The Jekyll Island Club, which owned the then-private island, was reputed to represent more than one-sixth of the world's wealth. A 1904 edition of *Munsey's Magazine* referred to the Jekyll Island Club as the "richest, the most exclusive, and most inaccessible club in the world."

ESSENTIALS

GETTING THERE   From Brunswick, take U.S. 17 South to the turnoff for Jekyll Island. Head east across the Jekyll Island Causeway, paying a daily parking rate of $2 per vehicle to enter the island.

VISITOR INFORMATION   The **Jekyll Island Visitors Center,** 901 Jekyll Island Causeway (☎ **912/635-3636**), is open daily from 9am to 5pm, dispensing maps, brochures, and other helpful information.

SEEING THE SIGHTS

The best way to see the historic district—the former enclave of the millionaires of America's Gilded Age, who built what they called "cottages" here—is to take a guided historic tour departing daily on the hour from 10am to 3pm from the **Museum Orientation Center** (☎ **912/635-2119**) on Stable Road. The tour lasts 1½ hours, costing $10 for adults, $6 for children 6 to 18, and free for children 5 and under. Highlights of the tour include **Indian Mound** (or Rockefeller) **Cottage** from 1892, **du Bignon Cottage** from 1884, and the **Faith Chapel** from 1904, illuminated by Tiffany stained-glass windows.

On your own, you can view the Goodyear Cottage in the district, housing the **Jekyll Island Arts Association** (☎ **912/635-3920**)—with a gift shop and a free monthly exhibition. Admission is free, and it's open daily from 10am to 4pm. Also in the district, **Mistletoe Cottage** (☎ 912/635-2119) showcases the work of the nationally renowned, late Jekyll Island sculptor, Rosario Fiore.

Last, Jekyll Island is also the site of **Horton's Brewery Site,** Georgia's first brewery, signposted on the northwest end of the island. It was started by General Oglethorpe, who evidently knew how to put first things first for his settlers. This two-story ruin, dating from 1742, is one of the oldest standing structures in the state. It was mainly constructed of tabby, a building material made of crushed oyster shells that is native to coastal Georgia. Very near the brewery stands the ruins of a home built in 1738 by William Horton, one of Oglethorpe's captains.

OUTDOOR PURSUITS: BEACHES, GOLF, TENNIS & MORE

If you have a car, take the South Jekyll Loop to survey the scene before concentrating on specifics. Drive south on North Beachview Drive to view some of the island's 10 miles of public beaches with public bathhouses and picnic areas. Your loop around the island's southern end will include the **South Dunes Picnic Area.** Continue around onto South Riverview Drive, passing **Summer Waves** and the **Jekyll Harbor Marina,** until you return to Fortson Parkway.

BEACHES   There are three public beaches on the island, all open daily around the clock and free to the public. Those choosing to swim on Jekyll Island do so at their own risk, as there are no lifeguards on duty. The **St. Andrew Picnic Area,** reached beyond Summer Waves, the water park along South Riverview Drive, is one of the best beaches at the southeastern tip of the island. It has an adjacent picnic area, but no bathhouse or showers available. **South Dunes Beach,** with a picnic area and showers, is north of St. Andrew and is reached along South Beach Drive. Farther along, **Central Dunes** has showers but no picnic area. Saltwater fishing is allowed on the public beaches, and no license is required.

BIKING   Because of its flatness, Jekyll Island is relatively easy to explore by bike. Rentals are available from **Barry's Beach Service** (☎ 912/638-8053), at the Villas by the Sea (see the address below under "Where to Stay"). Bikes rent for $8 for 4 hours or $12 for the full day; $36 for 1 week (includes Lock & Helmet).

FISHING   Freshwater fishing is allowed with a Georgia license, which costs $7 for 5 days and is available at most hardware or sporting-goods stores. No license is required for saltwater fishing.

GOLF   Three championship 18-hole courses await golfers on Jekyll Island, plus one historic 9-hole course. The **Great Dunes Golf Course,** Beach View Drive (☎ 912/635-2170), is a small 9-hole course patterned after the course at St. Andrews, Scotland. It offers some holes that were part of the original course laid out in 1898 when only millionaires played golf here. The course was remodeled as an authentic links course in the 1920s by Walter J. Travis. A 3,023-yard, par-36 course, it's open daily from 8am to 6pm. There are also a small pro shop and clubhouse on the grounds. Greens fees are $21, with electric carts renting for $13.50 to $27. No professional instruction is available.

Jekyll Island Golf Courses, 322 Captain Wylly Dr. (☎ 912/635-2368), consists of three separate courses: the **Oleander** (18 holes, 6,241 yards, par 72), the **Pine Lake** (18 holes, 6,379 yards, par 72), and the **Indian Mound** (18 holes, 6,282 yards, par 72). Dick Wilson's Oleander is consistently ranked among the state's best courses, and the *Atlanta Constitution* called its 12th hole "the most demanding par 4 of any daily fee course in the state." Pine Lakes was also designed by Wilson and is the longest and tightest layout on Jekyll Island. Tree-lined fairways dogleg both left and right as they wind through the island's interior. Indian Mound was designed by Joe Lee with wide fairways and large, sloping greens. All courses prefer you to reserve tee times, and charge $35 for greens fees. Mobile carts can be rented for $14.50 to $29 for 18 holes, and clubs are available for $6. Play is daily from 7:30am to 6pm for all three courses. A clubhouse, restaurant, and pro shop are on the grounds, with professional instruction available at the rate of $40 per hour.

TENNIS   The ✪ **Jekyll Island Tennis Center,** 400 Captain Wylly Dr. (☎ **912/ 635-3154**), was ranked by *Tennis* magazine as one of the nation's top municipal tennis complexes. Its 13 clay courts, 7 of them lit for night play, are favored because of low-impact conditions and cooler court temperatures. The center is open daily from 9am to noon and 2 to 6pm. Ball machines are rented for $14 per hour, and court fees are $14 to $16 per hour. Professional instruction is available for $30 per hour. There's a pro shop on the grounds, plus a restaurant and showers on location.

Only for guests, **Jekyll Island Club Hotel,** 371 Riverview Dr. (☎ **912/ 635-2600**), offers one indoor and eight outdoor courts, three of which are lighted. Open daily from 8am to 6pm, it charges $10 to $20 per hour for court use. You can get professional instruction at $30 per hour. There's a restaurant on the grounds, plus lockers and showers.

WATER SPORTS   **Summer Waves,** 210 S. Riverview Dr. (☎ **912/635-2074**), offers 11 acres of water sports with more than a million gallons of water. Jam-packed with rides, it features attractions ranging from a totally enclosed speed flume that jets riders over three breathtaking humps, to a ride over the rolling waves in the Frantic Atlantic wave pool. You can also hang on around the twisting turns of the Hurricane Tornado and Force 3 slides. For toddlers, there's the Pee Wee Puddle—fun in only a foot of water. Admission is $14.95 for those 48 inches or taller and $12.95 for children. Children 3 and under enter free. Open May 20 to Labor Day, Sunday to Friday from 10am to 6pm and on Saturday from 10am to 8pm.

WHERE TO STAY

Jekyll Island cottage rentals are available through **Parker-Kaufman Realtors,** Beachview Drive (P.O. Box 13126), Jekyll Island, GA 31527 (☎ **888/453-5955** or 912/635-2512), whose staff will mail you a color brochure upon request. The realtor offers 105 individual properties ranging from a small one-bedroom apartment to a six-bedroom home. Rental prices start at $235 per week in winter, rising to $330 per week in the busy summer months. Reservations for summer rentals are accepted as early as December 1. The office is open Monday to Saturday from 9am to 5:30pm.

Motel accommodations are available at the **Comfort Inn Island Suites,** 711 Beachview Dr. (☎ **800/204-0202** or 912/635-2211), and the **Holiday Inn Beach Resort,** 200 S. Beachview Dr. (☎ **800/7-JEKYLL** or 912/635-3311).

Jekyll Island Campground, North Beachview Drive, Jekyll Island, GA 31527 (☎ **912/635-3021**), is managed by the Jekyll Island Authority and is the only island campground in the Golden Isles. On its 18 wooded acres are 220 sites, nestled among live oaks and pines. The facilities include bathhouses, showers, a laundry, camping equipment, pure tap water, a grocery store, garbage pickup, LP gas, and bike rentals. Tent sites cost $12.72; regular sites, $15; full hookup sites, $18.02; full hookup with cable TV $21.20. Stay 6 nights and get your 7th night free.

Jekyll Inn. 975 N. Beachview Dr., Jekyll Island, GA 31527. ☎ **800/736-1046** or 912/635-2531. www.jekyllinn.com. E-mail: lori_strande@meristar.com. 188 units, 76 1- and 2-bedroom townhouses. A/C TV TEL. $59–$119 double; $139–$179 1- or 2-bedroom townhouse. AE, CB, DC, DISC, MC, V.

This is the largest oceanfront hotel on Jekyll Island, set on about 15 flat, sandy acres whose focal point is a rectangular swimming pool. In the early 1990s, it underwent a $2.5-million renovation. It sits near the island's northern tip and is designed in a vaguely Iberian motif of white walls and terra-cotta roofs rising amid pine trees. An expanse of lawn and a breakwater composed of a ribbon of massive boulders separate the compound from the sea. Guests walk over a raised boardwalk to reach the sands. The accommodations are standardized and furnished in a rather bland style. The management rather grandly refers to its units as "villas"; they're more like duplex-style townhouses, each of which abuts similar units to the left and right. On the hotel premises is a bar and a restaurant, the Italian Fisherman.

Clarion Resort Buccaneer. 85 S. Beachview Dr., Jekyll Island, GA 31527. ☎ **888/ 253-5955** or 912/635-2261. Fax 912/635-3230. www.motelproperties.com. E-mail: clarion@ motelproperties.com. 206 units. A/C TV TEL. $75–$175 double; $195–$395 suite. Children 18 and under stay free in parents' room. Golf packages available. AE, CB, DC, DISC, MC, V.

In terms of amenities, this hotel is on a par with the Jekyll Island Club and boasts the added advantage of a location directly on the beach. Set near the island's convention center, it consists of comfortably outfitted units scattered over a compound of half a dozen rather stylish three- and four-story buildings, some of which sport better views of the sea than others. If costs are a factor, ask for a room outfitted with a kitchenette and a view over the forest. The price will be approximately the same as a room without cooking facilities situated closer to the water. The compound, like many of its competitors nearby, is connected to the beach via an elaborate network of raised boardwalks. About a third of the accommodations contain kitchenettes.

There's an island-casual restaurant (the 85 Beach View), a swimming pool, easy access to golf, and an expansive wooden deck for buffets and cocktail parties.

✪ Jekyll Island Club Hotel. 371 Riverview Dr., Jekyll Island, GA 31527. ☎ **800/535-9547** or 912/635-2600. Fax 912/635-2818. www.jekyllclub.com. E-mail: jiclub@technonet.com. 134 units. A/C TV TEL. $99–$139 double; $159–$289 suite. Discounts of around 25% Labor Day to early May. Children 17 and under stay free in parents' room. AE, CB, DC, DISC, MC, V.

This is the undisputed star of Jekyll Island accommodations, steeped in the history of the Gilded Age. A rambling, turreted 1880s monument, it was conceived as a private club for millionaires. In 1987, long after its decline during World War II, the property was restored to its deliberately understated turn-of-the-century grandeur. The bedrooms are high-ceilinged and outfitted in the garnet, sapphire, and emerald tones of the building's original construction. Some are awkwardly shaped, but all are very comfortable and nostalgic. Don't expect easy access to the beach; instead, there's a large swimming pool to enjoy on the grounds, a cellar-level pub, an eight-court tennis complex, a snack bar, and a dining room (see "Where to Dine," below).

Villas by the Sea. 1175 N. Beachview Dr., Jekyll Island, GA 31527. ☎ **800/841-6262** or 912/635-2521. www.villasbythesea.com. 176 apts. A/C TV TEL. $99–$139 1-bedroom apt; $139–$189 2-bedroom apt; $179–$239 3-bedroom apt. Discounts offered for stays of a week or more. AE, MC, V.

This is the most northerly and, after the Jekyll Island Club Hotel, one of the most upscale accommodations on Jekyll Island. Not a conventional hotel, it's a compound of condominium-style apartments scattered among 20 two-story buildings in a 17-acre forest. The 2,000 feet of ocean frontage is longer than that of any other hotel on the island, but you'll have to cross over a raised boardwalk bridging a lawn and a rocky breakwater to reach it. Each accommodation is individually owned by absentee investors and decorated in a taste you may or may not love. Frankly, there are better-built condos and apartments in other parts of the Golden Isles, but still, this place is ideal for vacationers who want lots of space and a working kitchen. The public areas contain a country restaurant-deli (Crackers), plus a video bar.

WHERE TO DINE

Blackbeard's. 200 N. Beachview Dr. ☎ **912/635-3522.** Reservations not necessary. Platters/ main courses $8.95–$17.95. AE, DISC, MC, V. Daily 11am–10pm. Closed Christmas Day. SEAFOOD/AMERICAN.

This restaurant occupies a large, modern building set on a sandy and barren stretch down the island's eastern coast. Its menu items include shrimp, oysters, deviled crabs, scallops, and such fish fillets as flounder. Steak, grilled chicken, and burgers are staples around here, and your sandwich choice might be oysters on a hoagie roll, turkey, or "crabby crabmeat." The food is standard fare but rather tasty and sold at a fair price.

✪ **The Grand Dining Room.** In the Jekyll Island Club Hotel, 371 Riverview Dr. ☎ **912/ 635-2600.** Reservations recommended. Jackets preferred for men. Main courses $19–$27. AE, CB, DC, DISC, MC, V. Mon–Sat 7am–2pm and 6–10pm, Sun 10:45am–2pm (brunch) and 6–10pm; Victorian tea daily 4–5:30pm. INTERNATIONAL.

Graciously formal and steeped in nostalgia, this place reigns as one of the Golden Isles' most elegant. Its design incorporates a double row of columns, soaring windows, and furniture evocative of an English country house. Our preferred spot for a drink is on the cluster of sofas adjacent to a pianist, who performs highly digestible music throughout the dinner hour. Menu items include fresh catch of the day, prepared in any of five different ways; chicken Atlantis (sautéed with crabmeat, shrimp, and cream sauce); scaloppini of veal with sun-dried tomatoes and artichoke hearts; and grilled lamb chops. The cuisine is first rate, using the finest ingredients of any restaurant on island, each dish deftly handled by a well-trained kitchen staff.

Latitude 31. Jekyll Wharf. ☎ **912/635-3800.** Reservations recommended. Main courses $8.95–$21.95. MC, V. Daily 5:30–10pm. SEAFOOD/INTERNATIONAL.

The leading seafood restaurant on Jekyll Island occupies a clapboard-sided house built on stilts above the tidal flats, adjacent to the wharves servicing the Jekyll Island Club Hotel. J. P. Morgan used the site as a mooring for his yacht *The Corsair* ("If you have to ask what it costs, you have no business owning a yacht," he is reported to have said). At the time the building was a warehouse for storing supplies and ice. Today it's evocative of a 19th-century seafront building in Scandinavia, with a pale and airy interior, and·a simple decor that the Shakers would have appreciated. The bar, whose view extends over the mud flats, is appealing. Menu items include prime rib or filet steak, steamed mussels, fried lobster fingers, catch of the day (served grilled, baked, broiled, sautéed, or blackened), soft-shell crabs, seafood crepes, and several preparations of fresh-off-the-boat shrimp.

Morgan's Grill. Golf Clubhouse, Captain Wylly Rd. ☎ **912/635-4103.** Main courses $4.95–$7.50. AE, DISC, MC, V. Open daily 7:30am–5pm. AMERICAN.

Golfers can lunch here daily in a bright, airy room overlooking the greens. Trimmed in oak, the large room with an adjoining bar recalls Florida in its decor. You won't find grand cuisine here, just salads, soups, and sandwiches. From the grill comes a half-pound burger prepared as you like it, and you can also order a grilled chicken-breast sandwich or a super sub served on a hoagie, including ham, turkey, salami, cheese, and other elements. In spite of the plastic plates and spoons, this is one of the most relaxing spots for lunch on the island.

◇ **Zachry's Seafood Restaurant.** 44 Beachview Dr. ☎ **912/635-3128.** Reservations not required. Platters $12.95–$14.95; main courses $10.95–$14.95. DISC, MC, V. Easter to late Aug Sun–Thurs 11am–9pm, Fri–Sat 11am–10pm; late Aug to Easter Sun–Thurs 11am–8pm, Fri–Sat 11am–9pm. Closed 2 weeks at Christmas. SEAFOOD.

This local favorite sits in the midst of a collection of launderettes, convenience stores, and gift shops, in a shopping center across the street from the convention center. Part of its success derives from the Zachry's ownership of their own shrimp boat (the *Miss Angie*), which guarantees an almost-constant supply of fresh seafood. Menu items include stuffed jalapeño peppers served with marinara sauce, deep-fried or boiled shrimp, trout, deviled crab, stuffed broiled flounder, and combination platters. This is real good, finger-lickin' coastal Georgia home cookery, with more authentic flavor than any other place on the island.

7 Cumberland Island

7 miles NE of St. Marys

Nowhere else on the East Coast are peace and unspoiled natural surroundings so perfectly preserved as at ◇ **Cumberland Island.** Since 1972 most of this island has been a National Seashore administered by the National Park Service.

Cumberland Island reached the peak of its prestige in the Gilded Age when Carnegie steel barons used the island as a retreat. Their uninhabited mansion, Plum Orchard, is still standing, although badly deteriorating. Not only the Carnegies wielded power here, but so did the Rockefellers and even the Candlers of Atlanta (founders of Coca-Cola). More recently, the island was the top-secret site of the 1996 wedding of John Kennedy, Jr., and Caroline Bessette.

To visit Cumberland Island, just 16 miles long and 3 miles across at its widest point, is to step into a wilderness of maritime forest (with tunnel-like roads canopied by live oaks, cabbage palms, magnolia, holly, red cedar, and pine), salt marshes alive with waving grasses, sand dunes arranged by wind and tide into a double line of defense against erosion, and gleaming sand beaches that measure a few hundred yards in width at low tide. It is to enter a world teeming with animal life, where alligators wallow in marshes, white-tailed deer bound through the trees, wild pigs snuffle in the undergrowth, armadillos and wild turkeys roam freely about, more than 300 species of birds wheel overhead, and wild horses canter in herds or pick their way peacefully to watering holes.

ESSENTIALS

GETTING THERE   The only public transportation to the island is via the ferry from St. Marys on the mainland (get to St. Marys on Ga. 40 from I-95 or U.S. 17). You must reserve passage on the ferry; contact the National Park Service, **Cumberland Island National Seashore,** P.O. Box 806, St. Marys, GA 31558 (☎ **912/882-4335**). There are two trips daily from March 1 to September 30 (and currently in the fall until November 30) and every day except Tuesday and Wednesday in winter. In summer, book as far in advance as possible. The fare is $10.17 for adults, $8.03 for seniors, $6.05 for children 6 to 12, and free for children 5 and under. An additional $4 is charged as a user's fee.

If you plan to stay overnight, the best way to reach Cumberland is by the inn's ferry, the *Lucy R. Ferguson,* which maintains a regular schedule to Fermandina Beach, Florida. Reservations are necessary, and must be made through the Greyfield Inn (see below). We strongly urge that you bring your bicycle, since there's no public transportation on the island. You can, however, safely leave your car in the Fernandina Beach parking lot across from the police station.

There's an airstrip for small planes near the Greyfield Inn (see "Where to Stay & Dine," below), and air-taxi arrangements can be made from Jacksonville or St. Simons Island (call the inn for details).

VISITOR INFORMATION Information is available from the Greyfield Inn (see "Where to Stay & Dine," below).

EXPLORING THE ISLAND

Don't look for a swimming pool, tennis courts, or a golf course—Cumberland's attractions are a different sort, straight out of *The Prince of Tides*. The inn is just a short walk from those high sand dunes and a wild, undeveloped beach. Beachcombing, swimming, shelling, fishing, and exploring the island are high on the list of activities.

No signs are left of the Native Americans who lived here beginning some 4,000 years ago, nor of the Franciscan missionaries who came to convert them during the 1500s. No ruins exist of the forts built at each end of the island by Gen. James Oglethorpe in the 1700s, and the only thing that remains of his hunting lodge is its name, Dungeness. What you will find as you poke around this island are the ruins of Andrew Carnegie's own massive mansion, **Dungeness** (which burned in 1959); the **Greene-Miller cemetery,** which still holds inhabitants from Revolutionary times through the Civil War era; the **Stafford plantation house** and, down the lane a bit, **"The Chimneys,"** a melancholy post–Civil War ruin (ask at the inn for the full story); and **Plum Orchard,** another Carnegie mansion, fully furnished but unoccupied and now the property of the National Park Service.

WHERE TO STAY & DINE

✪ **Greyfield Inn.** Cumberland Island, GA. Mailing address: P.O. Box 900, Fernandina Beach, FL 32035. ☎ **904/261-6408.** Fax 904/321-0666. www.greyfieldinn.com. E-mail: seashore@greyfieldinn.com. 17 units, 9 with bathroom. $395 double. Rates include full board. 50% deposit required; 17% service and 7% tax extra. DISC, MC, V. No children under 6.

Cumberland's one hotel is no less enchanting than the island itself. The only commercial building (if you can call it that) in the area is this three-story plantation mansion with a wide, inviting veranda set in a grove of live oaks. Built shortly after the turn of the century as a summer retreat by Thomas Carnegie (Andrew's brother and partner), Greyfield has remained family property ever since. Guests today are treated very much as family visitors were in years past: The extensive and very valuable library is open; the furnishings are those the family has always used; the bar is an open one, operated on an honor system (you simply pour your own and note it on a pad); you dine at the long family table, adorned with heirloom silver candlesticks. You're at liberty to browse through old family photo albums, scrapbooks, and other memorabilia scattered about the large, paneled living room (if the weather is cool, a fire is lit in the oversized fireplace). Soft chimes announce meals (dinnertime means "dress"—informal dresses and jackets, no shorts or jeans). If beachcombing or exploring is what you have in mind for the day, the inn will pack a picnic lunch for you. The guest rooms vary in size; some bathrooms are shared and still hold the original, old-fashioned massive fittings. The rooms are not air-conditioned but are cooled by ceiling fans. Reservations must be made well in advance. You should do your phoning before arrival, as the hotel has only a radio-phone for emergencies.

8 The Okefenokee Swamp
8 miles S of Waycross

This swamp is one of the largest preserved freshwater wetlands in the United States. Naturalists have hailed the wetlands as "the most beautiful and fantastic landscape in the world." It's unique on earth—it was once part of the ocean floor—and encompasses some 650 square miles, measuring 40 miles in length and 20 miles in width. The Creek Indians called it "land of the trembling earth" because of its many floating islands.

Okefenokee is one of the most ecologically intact swamps in North America. It takes in everything from tupelo stands to vast open prairies. A few acres fall within the northeastern corner of Florida. Runoff is discharged into the Suwanee and St. Marys rivers.

The swamp was inhabited as early as 2000 B.C. Many Native Americans, displaced from their homelands, settled here in the 1700s and 1800s. Beginning in 1909, the Hebard Lumber Company harvested some half a billion cubic yards of timber—most of it cypress—from the land before they went out of business in 1927. Virgin tracts of cypress still remain, however. Some trees are 6 centuries old. The swamp's bay trees bloom from May to October, with a distinctive white flower.

Conservation-minded advocates persuaded Franklin Roosevelt to designate the swamp a refuge area in 1937. Further protection came in 1974 when Congress added Okefenokee to the National Wilderness Preservation System. This system occupies some 90% of the swamp, home to such wildlife as alligators, deer, and bobcats.

EXPLORING THE SWAMP

Before heading in, you can visit the **Okefenokee Heritage Center,** 2 miles west of Waycross (birthplace of actor Burt Reynolds) on U.S. 82 (☎ **912/285-4260**). Here you can see a restored 1912 steam locomotive and depot, an "operating" 1890 print shop, and the restored 1840 Gen. Thomas Hilliard House, plus general exhibits on local history. The center is open Monday to Saturday from 10am to 5pm and on Sunday from 1 to 5pm. Admission is $3 for adults, and $1 for children.

At the same site, the **Southern Forest World** (☎ **912/285-4056**) is a museum depicting the development and history of the South's forest industry. The collection includes a logging train, tools and other artifacts, and forestry-related relics, as well as a variety of audio-visuals. Hours are the same as those of the Heritage Center. Admission is $2 for those aged 4 to 54, $1.50 for seniors, and free for children 3 and under.

✪ **Okefenokee Swamp Park.** Waycross, GA 31501. ☎ **912/283-0583.** Admission $10 adults, $9 seniors 62 and over, also $9 children 5–11, free for children 4 and under. Summer, daily 9am–5pm; off-season, daily 9am–5:30pm. Take I-95 to Exit296 at Brunswick and then U.S. 82 West toward Waycross; at the intersection with GA. 177, go left for 11 miles to the park entrance.

The park—at the swamp's northern perimeter, on Cowhouse Island—can occupy a day of your time. It offers boat tours (included with admission), canoe rentals, interpretive programs, an outdoor museum, marked trails, and even a serpentarium with reptile shows. Take a cypress boardwalk into the swamp to a 90-foot-high observation tower. You'll see lots of the swamp's most famous residents, a collection of cruising Georgia alligators. There are no overnight facilities, but food and beverages are sold.

✪ **Stephen C. Foster State Park.** Georgia Department of Natural Resources, Rte. 1, Fargo, GA 31631. ☎ **912/637-5274.** Admission $5 per car. Mar–Labor Day, daily 6:30am–8:30pm; off-season, daily 7am–7pm. Take I-95 to Exit 6 at Brunswick and then U.S. 82 West to Waycross; there, head west on U.S. 84. to Homerville, and turn left onto U.S. 441 South to Fargo; at the intersection with Ga. 177, go left and follow the signs to the park.

On the western edge of Okefenokee, 18 miles from Fargo, this is an 80-acre island park with a sprawling forest of black gum and cypress. As a refuge, it forms one of the thickest terrains of vegetation in the Southeast. In the mirrorlike black waters live some 55 species of reptiles, 37 species of fish, more than 40 species of mammals, and some 225 species of birds. The park has a half-mile nature trail and some 25 miles of day-use waterways. Canoes and motorboats can be rented, or you can take boat tours lasting 1 to 1½ hours. Minnie's Lake and Big Water can also be visited. Picnicking and camping are permitted. Two-bedroom cabins are also available for rentals: $50 a night Sunday to Thursday, going up to $60 on Friday and Saturday. Campsites with running water and electricity, including showers, go for only $10 a night. (For reservations, contact the Superintendent at the address and phone number above.) Park gates close between sunset and sunrise to discourage wildlife poachers. Groceries can be obtained at stores in Fargo.

✪ **Suwanee Canal Recreation Area.** U.S. Fish and Wildlife Service, Okefenokee National Wildlife Refuge, Rte. 2, Box 3330, Folkston, GA 31537. ☎ **912/496-3331.** Admission $5 per car. 1-hour tours $8 adults, $4 children 5–11, $3.25 children 1–4; 2-hour tours $16 adults, $8 children 5–11, $6.50 children 1–4. Mar–Sept 10 daily 7am–7:30pm; off-season daily 8am–6pm. Take I-95 to Exit 2 and go west along Ga. 40 to Folkston; there, turn onto Ga. 23/121 South for 7 miles, then turn right onto Spur Ga. 121 and follow the signs for 4 miles to the recreation area.

Run by the U.S. Fish and Wildlife Service, this recreation area offers some of America's finest birding and freshwater fishing. The area provides entry to the prairies of Mizell, Chase, Grand, and Chesser, the last the site of a century-old farmstead. Small lakes and "gator holes" are sprinkled throughout the area. The visitor information center provides an orientation film and offers exhibits of the swamp's flora and fauna.

Take a boardwalk over the water to a 40-foot observation tower. Several interpretive walking trails and picnic sites are available. The 12-mile-long canal results from a failed attempt in the 1880s to drain the swamp. The U.S. Fish and Wildlife Service provides overnight and 2- to 5-day canoe trips, but reservations are essential. Canoe rentals begin at $12 for day trips, rising to $63 for 5-day jaunts. The Canal Recreation Concession rents everything from canoes to boats, from sleeping bags and Coleman stoves to portable toilets. It also offers bicycles, costing $1.50 per hour.

Laura S. Walker State Park. Georgia Department of Natural Resources, 5653 Laura Walker Rd., Waycross, GA 31501. ☎ **912/287-4900.** Admission $2 per car; Wed free. Daily 7am–10pm. Take I-95 to Exit 6 at Brunswick and then U.S. 82 West toward Waycross; at the intersection with Ga. 177, go south for 2 miles to the park entrance.

Offering activities from water-skiing to camping, this state park dates from the WPA days of the 1930s. It's named after Laura Singleton Walker, a conservationist long before the movement became fashionable. Swimming is permitted when the park's pool is open in summer, and fishing is possible all year. The park is located in the Dixon Memorial Forest, which provides access to the Okefenokee Swamp Park some 9 miles distant. A 1¼-mile nature trail is accessible all year. Canoe rentals are available, as are picnic areas (some sheltered). Campsites cost $10 with electrical and water hookups.

Appendix A: The Carolinas & Georgia in Depth

The Carolinas and Georgia have much in common—a similar historical background, shared social traditions, and cherished culinary customs—and as movers and shakers of the New South, they share a dynamic future. Here is a comprehensive cultural, political, and social history of the tri-state region.

1 History 101

Although they have their own political pasts, the Carolinas and Georgia began life as one British colony, and in many other respects, they have a common history. The way that they were settled by Europeans during the 17th and 18th centuries gave the three states a similar character, which has lasted to this day.

ONE BIG COLONY BECOMES THREE   When the first English settlers arrived, they found the region inhabited by bands of American Indians, many of them part of the greater Iroquois and Sioux families. Some native tribes cooperated with the settlers; others were hostile. Whatever their reactions to the newcomers, Indian tribes were decimated by European diseases, and the whites pushed the survivors off their land, either through trumped-up sales or by force. Only the Cherokees, an Iroquoian people in the foothills and mountains of the southern Appalachians, have survived as an organized Indian nation (see chapter 8).

The tribes in today's South Carolina were the first to encounter the Europeans, beginning in 1520, when a Spanish caravelle explored St. Helena Sound. Six years later, Lucas Vásquez de Ayllón tried to establish a Spanish colony, first near the mouth of the Cape Fear River in North Carolina and later on Winyah Bay, but disease, bad weather, and the Indians put an end to it after only a year.

In search of gold rather than colonies, Spanish conquistador Hernando de Soto explored the area's interior in 1540, crossing from Georgia through South Carolina to the mountains of western North Carolina. French Huguenots arrived in 1563 and built Fort Charles at South Carolina's Port Royal Sound, but they pulled up stakes when fire destroyed their supplies. A Spanish contingent from Florida came to the same site in 1566 and built Fort San Filipe; they stayed 20 years but abandoned the colony when English buccaneer Sir Francis Drake raided St. Augustine. (The Forts Charles/San Filipe site is on the U.S. Marine Corps training center's golf course at Parris Island, South Carolina.)

A COLONY LOST   England fared no better in its first attempt to establish a colony. In 1584, Walter Raleigh, a soldier and courtier to Queen Elizabeth I, sent an expedition to search out a suitable site. The expedition returned with glorious tales of an island named Roanoke—inside what we know as North Carolina's Outer Banks—and with two Indians named Manteo and Wanchese. A year later, Raleigh sent Manteo, Wanchese, and 108 Englishmen (but no women) to colonize Roanoke Island. Rather than planting crops, they spent much of their time searching for gold and a passage to the Pacific Ocean. When Sir Francis Drake fortuitously showed up within the year, they hitched a ride with him back to England.

In June 1587, Raleigh's second attempt at colonization—this time with about 120 men, women, and children—arrived at Roanoke Island under the leadership of John White. It was too late in the year to plant crops, and White left for England at the end of August to secure fresh stores. War was on with Spain, however, preventing White's return. When he did sail back 3 years later, he found only the word *Croatoan*—the name of a nearby Indian tribe—carved on a tree. The settlers had disappeared. Among them was White's granddaughter, Virginia Dare, the first child born in America of English parents. Not a trace of the legendary "Lost Colony" was ever found (see "The Lost Colony," in chapter 4).

THE LORDS PROPRIETORS GET THEIRS   The English had better luck at Jamestown, Virginia, in 1607. By the mid-1600s, tobacco farmers had drifted south into the Albemarle Sound region of northeastern North Carolina, around Elizabeth City and Edenton. They were the first permanent European settlers in the Carolinas and Georgia.

But real colonization began after the restoration of King Charles II in England. In 1663, strapped for funds and owing financial and political debts to those who had supported his return to the throne, King Charles granted to eight Lords Proprietors all of North America between 31° and 36° North latitude—that's all of the Carolinas and Georgia. The grant was later extended north to 36½°, to make sure that the Albemarle Sound area wasn't in Virginia, and south to 29°. This extension infuriated the Spanish, because it encompassed nearly half of their colony in Florida.

Dateline

- **1520–26** Spanish arrive in South Carolina.
- **1540** Spanish conquistador Hernando de Soto crosses Georgia and the Carolinas, bringing disease and death to the Cherokee Indians.
- **1587** Sir Walter Raleigh sends English to settle Roanoke Island; the "Lost Colony" disappears.
- **Mid-1600s** Planters from Virginia settle in the Albemarle Sound region in northeastern North Carolina.
- **1663** King Charles II of England grants land between Virginia and Florida to eight Lords Proprietors, who name the region "Carolina" in his honor.
- **1670** South Carolina's first permanent settlement is established on Ashley River.
- **1710** Proprietors appoint Edward Hyde governor of North Carolina, separating its administration from that of South Carolina.
- **1718** British forces behead buccaneer Edward "Blackbeard" Teach during a bloody fight off Ocracoke Island, North Carolina.
- **1729** Lords Proprietors sell Carolina to the English crown; the colony officially divides into North and South.
- **1730s** Ulster Scots, Quakers, and Germans migrate south from Pennsylvania into the Piedmont regions of the Carolinas and Georgia.
- **1732** James Edward Oglethorpe founds Georgia in the southern part of he Lords Proprietors' grant.
- **1750** Slavery is introduced in Georgia, spurring production of rice, indigo, and cotton on large plantations.
- **1752** Moravians from Pennsylvania settle in northwestern North Carolina and found Salem (now part of Winston-Salem).

continues

- **1774** Women in Edenton, North Carolina protest the British tax on tea by refusing to brew English leaves.
- **1775** Patriots sign the Mecklenburg Declaration in Charlotte, declaring independence from Great Britain.
- **1776** North Carolina revolutionaries pass the Halifax Resolves, authorizing their delegates to the Continental Congress to vote for independence. The British attack Charleston, and are repulsed.
- **1779** Gold is discovered near Charlotte in North Carolina, setting off the nation's first gold rush.
- **1780–81** Lord Cornwallis occupies Charleston and is defeated at the Battle of Kings Mountain near Gaffney, South Carolina.
- **1782** The British evacuate Charleston, the last city that they held south of Canada.
- **1793** Eli Whitney's cotton gin leads to an explosion of cotton production throughout the South.
- **1800** The nation's second federal canal (after the Erie) is dug to move cotton from inland South Carolina to Charleston.
- **1819** Northern opposition to the admission of Missouri as a slave state stirs talk of secession below the Mason-Dixon Line.
- **1822** The slave Denmark Vesey leads an insurrection and attempts to capture Charleston. The revolt is put down, and Vesey and 36 others executed. Southern planters blame "outside agitators" and institute tighter controls on slaves.
- **1830s** The abolitionist movement gains strength in the North. Extremists advocate the secession of the South from the North.

continues

The proprietors named their possession Carolina, in the king's honor. You'll see these men's names on places throughout the Carolinas: George Monck, Duke of Albemarle; Edward Hyde, Earl of Clarendon; William, Earl of Craven; brothers Lord John Berkeley and Sir William Berkeley (the latter was then governor of Virginia); Sir George Carteret; Anthony Ashley-Cooper, later the first Earl of Shaftesbury; and Sir John Colleton.

The proprietors soon recruited rice farmers from Barbados, who arrived on the banks of South Carolina's Ashley River in 1670 and planted their first crops 2 years later. Within a decade, they had established Charles Town on the point where the Ashley and Cooper rivers meet. With slaves producing bumper rice and indigo crops, and with one of the colonies' finest natural harbors at Charles Town, South Carolina soon became the wealthiest of England's American colonies. Indeed, Charles Town (its name was changed to Charleston in 1783) was America's busiest port until well into the 19th century.

The proprietors appointed a colonial governor to sit in Charles Town, with authority to appoint a deputy for northern Carolina. The great distances involved made this plan unworkable, however, so in 1710 Edward Hyde (a cousin of Queen Anne, who was then on the throne) was named governor of the north. This arrangement lasted until the proprietors sold their possession to the British crown in 1729, whereupon North Carolina and South Carolina became separate British crown colonies.

CONVICTS & CATHOLICS NEED NOT APPLY   Partially to create a buffer between the Spanish in Florida and flourishing South Carolina, the British crown in 1731 granted a charter to a group of investors, headed by Gen. James Edward Oglethorpe, to establish a colony in the southern part of the original Lords Proprietors grant.

Oglethorpe's utopian goal was to create a microcosm of England—but without land ownership, slaves, hard liquor, and Catholicism. Contrary to popular belief, he did not recruit convicts for this enterprise; instead, he sought industrious tradesmen, small-business owners, and laborers with promises of free passage, land to farm, and supplies. The first of the settlers arrived in the new colony of Georgia in 1732.

Without slaves (and also without liquor, some wags say), the settlers had a rough go of it initially. Only after Georgia's first African slaves arrived in 1750 did rice, indigo, and cotton make the colony economically viable. As in South Carolina, the owners of the large plantations dotting the coastal plain grew rich, as did their merchant friends in the ports of Charles Town and Savannah.

UP COUNTRY, LOW COUNTRY The rich Easterners of the Carolinas and Georgia looked down on the poor, non-slave-owning farmers who settled the inland hills. In South Carolina, these farmers were called Up Country folk by the Low Country folk. In Georgia, the coastal crowd pejoratively referred to their country cousins as crackers—from the practice of cracking corn to make meal.

The rivers in the Piedmont tend to flow from northwest to southeast. South Carolina and Georgia are laid out in these directions, but the rivers took settlers in the hill country of North Carolina to South Carolina ports instead of east to their own state's coastal plain, further adding to the division between east and west.

Beginning in the 1730s, another type of settler arrived in the Piedmont area of all three colonies: Scots-Irish, Germans, and other Europeans who migrated overland into the Carolina and Georgia hills from Pennsylvania by way of the great valleys of Virginia. Most of them were self-sufficient yeoman farmers who built their houses of stone rather than wood. They had no use for slaves and even less for the rich folks down along the coast who didn't work with their hands. Instead of Anglican churches, they worshipped at Presbyterian, Quaker, and Moravian churches.

Thus developed a cultural, economic, and political schism between the lowlanders and the highlanders in all three colonies. Carolinians built their state capitals at Raleigh and Columbia on the boundary between the two groups— the fall line where the rivers rush out of the hills onto the flat coastal plain. Although Piedmont industrial growth reversed the economic situation beginning in the 1880s, and although more recent migration from other states has changed the equation somewhat, this division has survived to a large extent. Some people in the Charlotte and Atlanta areas still look down their noses at their "hick" kin in rural eastern North Carolina and South Georgia, and the Low

- **1830** The South Carolina legislature adopts the "Doctrine of Nullification" of federal laws by the states and threatens to leave the Union. Congress compromises by lowering the export tariff on cotton.
- **1833** Great Britain emancipates all slaves in its colonies.
- **1835** The federal government orders the Cherokee Indians west to Oklahoma Territory. Thousands die on the Trail of Tears; others hide in the mountains and later form the Eastern Band of the Cherokee Nation.
- **1839** A young slave accidentally overheats a North Carolina tobacco barn, baking the drying leaves golden and creating the smooth-tasting Bright Leaf used in cigarettes.
- **1849** South Carolina objects to the admission of California as a free state. The legislature considers secession but backs off when other Southern states refuse.
- **1854** The Republican Party is formed, nominating John C. Fremont for president and adopting an antislavery platform. Democrat James Buchanan is elected president, however.
- **1858** Republicans gain the majority in Congress on a pro-business, antislavery platform.
- **1859** John Brown's aborted raid at Harpers Ferry (then in Virginia) alarms the South.
- **1860** A split at the Democratic National Convention in Charleston over a pro-slavery platform plank helps elect Republican Abraham Lincoln. South Carolina secedes.
- **1861** Georgia secedes on January 19. North Carolina waits until South Carolina

continues

forces attack Fort Sumter on April 15, launching the Civil War.

- **1864** Union Gen. William Tecumseh Sherman drives to the sea through Georgia, leaving a trail of destruction behind.
- **1865** The blockade-running port of Wilmington, N.C., falls to a Union amphibious assault in January. Sherman burns 80 square blocks of Columbia, South Carolina, in February. Confederate Gen. Joseph Johnston surrenders to Sherman in April at Durham, North Carolina
- **1865–67** White-dominated state legislatures pass "Black Code" laws, giving newly freed slaves some rights, but not the vote.
- **1867** Congress passes the Reconstruction Act, dividing the South into five military districts.
- **1870s** The Ku Klux Klan becomes active in the South.
- **1876** Reconstruction officially ends. Whites return to power and adopt "Jim Crow" laws to keep African Americans from voting.
- **1880s** Cotton, tobacco, and furniture factories in the Piedmont give the three states major industries for the first time.
- **1896** The U.S. Supreme Court's *Plessy v. Ferguson* decision legalizes separate-but-equal segregation laws.
- **1901–04** North Carolina builds 1,100 schools, bringing public education to all Tarheels.
- **1903** The Wright Brothers fly the first airplane at Kill Devil Hills on North Carolina's Outer Banks.
- **1911** A hurricane devastates the South Carolina coastal area, ending large-scale rice production.

continues

Country–Up Country (today, Upstate) split is still very much alive in South Carolina.

GIVING CORNWALLIS FITS People in the Carolinas and Georgia had mixed feelings about independence from Great Britain. Being largely of Scots-Irish or other European origins, the hill folk weren't particularly enamored of the English crown, but they also hesitated to endorse a war. Down in the lowlands, the rich planters and merchants saw themselves as being English, but they also chafed at the British import and export taxes, which hurt their businesses.

There were enough go-for-it patriots around, however, to throw things toward the side of freedom. To protest the English tax on tea, the women of Edenton, North Carolina, held a tea party in 1774 and promised never again to brew leaves from England. In 1775, a group of revolutionaries met in Charlotte and passed the Mecklenburg Resolves, declaring themselves to be independent of Britain. The same year, a group of patriots tarred and feathered British loyalists in Charleston, and shortly after the Battle of Bunker Hill in Massachusetts, patriots captured Fort Charlotte in South Carolina. In 1776, delegates from all three colonies endorsed the Declaration of Independence at Philadelphia.

When the British attacked Charleston in 1776, Revolutionary soldiers quickly built Fort Moultrie at the mouth of Charleston Harbor. They used palmetto logs, which proved to be impervious to cannon fire. The fort held out for 4 years, and the palmetto became the new state's symbol.

Lord Cornwallis, the British commander, decided in 1780 to launch a Southern strategy against George Washington's Continental Army. His plan was to take Charleston; march overland through the Carolinas, picking up Loyalist volunteers as he went; and attack Washington in Virginia. It took him 14 battles to finally capture Charleston, but Francis Marion (nicknamed "The Swamp Fox") escaped into the Low Country marshes and organized a series of successful guerrilla raids on the British forces.

The support of loyalist hill folk, which Cornwallis had counted on, disappeared when his forces massacred a group of rebels who were trying to surrender near Lancaster, South Carolina. The locals then pitched in with the patriots to defeat the British army at the Battle of Kings

Mountain, near Gaffney. As a result, Cornwallis was forced to send half his men back to Charleston, thus weakening his forces and significantly contributing to his decisive defeat at Yorktown, Virginia, the following year.

Despite the defeat, Cornwallis marched north and captured Charlotte. A 14-pound nugget had been discovered near Charlotte a year earlier, setting off America's first gold rush. Cornwallis found more patriots than gold, causing him to describe the town as a "Hornet's Nest."

Cornwallis advanced through North Carolina to meet defeat at Washington's hands at Yorktown in 1781. The troops he had sent back to Charleston held out for a year, but they evacuated when Gen. Nathaniel Greene's army advanced to within 14 miles of the city. Charleston was the last British-held city south of Canada.

KING COTTON & THE "PECULIAR INSTITUTION"
Along with rice, indigo, and tobacco, cotton was also important in the region's early history. But it was a labor-intensive crop. Growing and picking cotton was backbreaking work in itself, and after the fiber balls were harvested, someone had to tediously pick out the multitudinous seeds by hand. Thanks to the South's "peculiar institution," slaves did most of the work.

Slavery not only exploited those who were held in bondage, but it also was an inefficient use of human resources. Granted, labor was relatively cheap for the planters, whose major cost (after buying a human being) was keeping a slave alive. But because slaves had no realistic chance of ever gaining their freedom, they had little incentive to work any harder than was necessary to avoid the overseer's whip.

Most slaves were confined to the large coastal plantations during colonial times. Then, in 1793, Eli Whitney invented the mechanical cotton gin on a Savannah River plantation in Georgia. That meant that a small farmer could buy a slave or two, plant his land with cotton, and not have to worry about extracting the seeds. Life in the South would never be the same.

With people in Great Britain and elsewhere beginning to prefer cotton garments to those made of wool and linen, the price of the fluffy white fibers went through the roof. More and more land was devoted to cotton, and production soared, especially in South Carolina and

- **1915** The Ku Klux Klan is reborn in a huge cross-burning atop Stone Mountain, Georgia. A mob enters a Georgia state penitentiary at Milledgeville and lynches Leo Frank, a northern-born Jew convicted of murdering 14-year-old Mary Phagan, a white girl, in an Atlanta pencil factory.
- **1922** Georgian feminist Rebecca Lattimer Felton, then 87, is appointed as the first female U.S. senator.
- **1934** Georgia Gov. Eugene Talmadge declares martial law and uses National Guard troops to break a statewide textile strike.
- **1940** Great Smoky Mountains National Park is dedicated by President Franklin D. Roosevelt.
- **1942** Military bases in the Carolinas and Georgia make the area one of the nation's primary troop-training centers during World War II.
- **1945** President Roosevelt dies of a cerebral hemorrhage at Warm Springs, Georgia.
- **1954** The U.S. Supreme Court declares segregated schools to be unconstitutional.
- **1960** A lunch-counter sit-in at Greensboro, North Carolina, launches similar civil-rights protests across the South.
- **1964** Georgians cast the majority vote for Barry Goldwater as president—the first time that a Southern state goes Republican since Reconstruction.
- **1965** Congress passes the Voting Rights Act, enfranchising Southern African Americans for the first time since Reconstruction. Blacks are elected to Congress, local offices, and state legislatures.
- **1966** Segregationist restaurateur Lester "Ax Handle"

continues

Maddox is elected governor of Georgia.

- **1968** State police open fire during student protests at a bowling alley in Orangeburg, South Carolina, killing 3 and wounding 27.
- **1970** Courting Maddox voters, peanut farmer Jimmy Carter is elected governor of Georgia, promising to end racial discrimination.
- **1972** North Carolinians elect conservative Republican television commentator Jesse Helms to the U.S. Senate.
- **1973** U.S. Senator Sam J. Ervin, Jr., of North Carolina leads the Senate Watergate hearings.
- **1976** Jimmy Carter becomes the first Southerner to be elected president of the United States since before the Civil War.
- **1989** South Carolina legislators are charged with taking bribes to vote for legalized horse-race betting in the FBI sting "Operation Lost Trust."
- **1994** African-American Ernest Finney is elected chief justice of the South Carolina Supreme Court.
- **1995** A federal court orders The Citadel in Charleston to admit the first female cadets.
- **1996** Atlanta hosts the Summer Olympic Games.
- **2000** The South is experiencing dramatic increases in population, largely in the suburbs. South Carolina's Confederate flag over the State Capitol stirs nationwide protest.

Georgia. (Although it produced substantial amounts of cotton, North Carolina remained primarily a tobacco state, like Virginia.) By 1850, cotton accounted for two-thirds of American exports.

But threatening clouds began to gather during the 1830s, with the growth of the abolitionist movement in the North. Some abolitionists were moderates, advocating that slave owners be compensated for the value of their freed slaves, as Britain did in 1833, when it abolished slavery in its colonies. Others were extremists, such as newspaper editor William Lloyd Garrison, who at one point advocated the secession of the North from the South.

JOHN C. CALHOUN & THE DOCTRINE OF NULLIFICATION Secession wasn't a new idea, and soon its chief proponent would be a brilliant South Carolina lawyer named John C. Calhoun.

A chief spokesman for the Low Country planter class, Calhoun served as a U.S. senator, as secretary of war and secretary of state under President James Monroe, and as U.S. vice president under Andrew Jackson in 1828. He was a nationalist in his early days. As a senator, he joined with Kentuckian Henry Clay to advocate a system of national laws and the building of federal roads and canals to bind the states of the rapidly expanding new nation.

Beginning in 1816, Calhoun supported a series of tariffs designed to protect America's emerging industries from inexpensive manufactured goods imported from overseas. He and other South Carolinians reasoned that their state had both water power and cotton, so they could build textile mills to manufacture cloth rather than import it.

But mills in New England profited from the tariffs, which drove up the price of consumer goods. At the same time, expanding production depressed the price of Southern cotton. Compounding the problem, much of South Carolina's land became worn out from overplanting with a single crop, causing some of its best planters to move to the rich black soil of Alabama and Mississippi. Many South Carolinians believed that textile interests up North were getting rich at their expense, and they started blaming their problems on the federal government (a feeling that persisted right up through the civil-rights movement of the 1960s).

With the tariffs hurting his home state, and with the system of national laws that he had once advocated beginning to threaten slavery, Calhoun came up with the Doctrine of Nullification. According to this doctrine, because the U.S. Constitution was merely a compact among 13 sovereign nations, a single

Two Cuts to Blackbeard's Neck

The British expected their American colonies to produce *profits*—as in having the colonists grow the raw materials that factories in Great Britain would use to produce the goods, which the colonists in turn would buy at inflated prices. To make sure that this happened, Parliament enacted a series of import duties designed to keep cheaper goods made elsewhere out of its colonies. The tax levies, which later fomented revolutionary sentiment, helped bring about the so-called Golden Age of Piracy between 1689 and 1718.

What better way to get duty-free goods than through smuggling? And who better to do it than the pirates who stole the loot in the first place?

Edward "Blackbeard" Teach, "Gentleman" Stede Bonnet, Calico Jack Rackham, Charles Vane, Robert Deal, Israel Hands, Anne Bonney, Mary Reed, and others began by roaming the Caribbean, legally plundering French and Spanish ships during Queen Anne's War from 1701 to 1713. But they kept at their trade after the war, so in 1718, the British navy chased them out of the area.

Blackbeard and Bonnet relocated to the tangled web of islands and shifting shoals along the North Carolina coast. Bonnet hid up the Cape Fear River, and Blackbeard settled in Bath, the first town incorporated in North Carolina. His cheap smuggled goods were welcomed, and some colonial officials—including Gov. Charles Eden, for whom Edenton is named—were suspected of helping him make a little money.

But the folks down in South Carolina felt differently, because they were now the pirates' prime targets. When Blackbeard struck Charleston in June 1718, looting merchant ships at anchor and taking hostages for ransom, and when Bonnet did the same thing 2 months later, the South Carolinians had had enough. An expedition led by Col. William Rhett followed Bonnet to his Cape Fear hideout and captured him during a 5-hour battle. Bonnet and 29 of his men were returned to Charleston, tried, and hanged. Over the next 2 months, South Carolinians caught and hanged another 20 pirates.

Rhett didn't find Blackbeard, but two Royal Navy sloops from Virginia under Lt. Robert Maynard did—off Ocracoke Island at dawn on November 22, 1718. Blackbeard and half his crew of 18 were killed during fierce hand-to-hand combat. The survivors were taken to Virginia and executed.

The incident was reported in the *Boston News-Letter* as follows: "One of Maynard's men, being a Highlander, ingaged [sic] Teach with his broadsword, who gave Teach a cut of the Neck, Teach saying well done, Lad, the Highlander reply'd, if it be not well done, I'll do it better, and with that he gave him a second stroke, which cut off his head, laying it flat on his shoulder."

Maynard sailed back to Virginia with Blackbeard's head hanging from his ship's rigging, as if to warn all pirates that their golden age was over. And it was.

state could nullify laws passed by the federal government. By implication, any state was as free to secede from the Union as it was to join.

When Congress passed another, higher tariff in 1830, the South Carolina legislature declared it to be "null, void, and no law," and promised to secede from the Union if the federal government attempted to use force to collect the money. President Jackson declared that the Union could not be dissolved and threatened to use federal force. South Carolina raised a voluntary military force but backed off when Congress reduced the levy.

Nullification was unpopular up in North Carolina, although the Tarheels didn't like Jackson's threat to use force against a "sovereign" state. Down in Georgia, the state legislature said that it "abhorred" the doctrine, but it also proposed a convention of the Southern states.

SAYING GOOD-BYE TO OLD GLORY The issue of secession next came up in 1849, when South Carolina objected to the admission of California as a nonslave state and called for a Southern convention, which met in Nashville, Tennessee, the following year. Congress prevented a showdown, however, by passing the Compromise of 1850, which admitted California as a free state but also enacted stringent fugitive-slave laws. The latter was a key point for Southerners, who wanted their escaped "property" to be returned, even from free states.

From the Southern slave-owning perspective, events in the North over the next decade were most unsettling—especially the creation of the Republican Party in 1854. Two years later, this new antislavery party nominated John C. Fremont for president, and in 1958, it won a majority in Congress. One of the party's prominent members was Abraham Lincoln, a lanky congressman from Illinois.

The Democrats held their 1860 national convention in Charleston, South Carolina. When the delegates refused to adopt a pro-slavery platform plank, the eight cotton states walked out. The split helped elect Lincoln, the Republican nominee. Although he was running on a platform of leaving slavery alone in the Southern states, Lincoln nevertheless frightened the cotton growers.

South Carolina called a convention that adopted an Ordinance of Secession on December 20, and the convention sent delegations to the other Southern states to beseech them to do likewise.

Georgia wasted little time, seceding on January 19, 1861, but a majority of North Carolina voters rejected the idea in February. Only some 35,000 of the 1 million Tarheels owned slaves, and the rest weren't spoiling for what they saw as a "rich man's war and a poor man's fight." The North Carolinians didn't change their minds until April, when Lincoln requested that they send troops to fight against their neighbors.

THE WAR OF NORTHERN AGGRESSION The American Civil War (which many Southerners still call the War of Northern Aggression) began at 4:30am on April 15, 1861, when South Carolina forces opened fire on Fort Sumter in Charleston's harbor. Lincoln immediately called for volunteers to put down the rebellion. Within a few months, federal troops occupied much of the coastal lowlands of the Carolinas and Georgia, leaving only the port cities of Wilmington, Charleston, and Savannah in Confederate hands, albeit blockaded by the Union navy.

Except for a few skirmishes and the bombardment of Charleston in 1863, the Carolinas and Georgia escaped heavy fighting until May 1864, when Union Gen. Ulysses S. Grant told Gen. William Tecumseh Sherman to "get into the interior of the enemy's country as far as you can, inflicting all the damage you can against their war resources." Thus began Sherman's famous March to the Sea, the world's first modern example of total war waged against a civilian population.

Sherman fought his way south from Chattanooga, Tennessee, to Atlanta, a key railroad junction, which the Confederates evacuated on September 1. Leaving Atlanta burning, he departed for the sea on October 17, cutting a 60-mile path of destruction across central and eastern Georgia. "We have devoured the land, and our animals eat up the wheat and corn fields close," Sherman reported. "All the people retire before us, and desolation is behind. To realize what war is, one should follow our tracks."

Despite his orders to the contrary, looting and pillaging were rampant, especially by hangers-on and newly freed slaves, but there were few attacks on civilians and none against women.

Sherman arrived at Savannah on December 10, in time to make the port city a Christmas present to Lincoln. (Fortunately, he did not burn the city.) In January 1865, he turned his war machine northward into South Carolina. He torched 80 square blocks of Columbia in February. Confederate Gen. Joseph E. Johnston made several attempts to slow Sherman's advance. One such attempt was the Battle of Rivers Bridge, between Allendale and Erhardt, South Carolina, in February; the last was the Battle of Bentonville, near Durham in central North Carolina, in March. On April 26, two weeks after Gen. Robert E. Lee surrendered to Grant at Appomattox Courthouse in Virginia, Johnston met Sherman at Durham and handed over his sword. The war in the Carolinas and Georgia was over.

The conflict was monstrously costly to the region—particularly to North Carolina, which had joined the fray only reluctantly in the first place. Of the 125,000 Tarheels who served, 40,000 died in battle or of disease, more than from any other Southern state. Those who fought earned their "Tarheel" moniker because of their tenacious refusal to yield ground during battle.

SCALAWAGS, CARPETBAGGERS & JIM CROW The Civil War survivors straggled home to face Reconstruction. At first, Confederate war veterans dominated the state legislatures in the Carolinas and Georgia. They enacted so-called Black Code laws, which gave some rights to the newly freed slaves but denied them the vote. This and other actions infuriated the radical Republicans who controlled the U.S. Congress and wanted to see the South punished for its rebellion. In 1867, Congress passed the Reconstruction Act, which gave blacks the right to vote and divided the South into five districts, each under a military governor who had near-dictatorial powers. Approximately 20,000 federal troops were sent South to enforce the act.

Recalcitrant white officials were removed from state office, and with their new vote, the ex-slaves helped elect Republican legislatures in all three states. Many blacks won seats for themselves. Despite doing some good work, these legislatures were corrupt (a free legislators-only restaurant and bar in South Carolina was a minor example). They also enacted high taxes to pay for rebuilding and social programs, further alienating the struggling white population.

White Carolinians and Georgians also complained bitterly about "scalawags" (local whites who joined the Republican Party) and "carpetbaggers" (Northerners who came South carrying all their possessions in bags made of carpet). The animosity led to the formation of two secret white organizations—the Knights of the Camilla and the Knights of the Ku Klux Klan—that undertook by terrorism to keep blacks from voting or exercising their other new rights. The former slaves also were disappointed with the radical Republicans when it became obvious that they wouldn't receive their promised "40 acres and a mule." Those who did vote began to cast them for their former masters. Factions also developed between the local scalawags and the Northern carpetbaggers.

All this set the stage for whites to regain control of North Carolina and Georgia in 1871. By January 1877, only South Carolina still had a carpetbagger regime, and when the new President, Rutherford B. Hayes, a Republican, withdrew federal troops from Charleston in April, former Confederate Gen. Wade Hampton became governor. Reconstruction was over.

During the next 20 years, white governments enacted the Jim Crow laws, which imposed poll taxes, literacy tests, and other requirements intended to prevent African Americans from voting. Whites flocked to the Democratic Party, which restricted its primaries—which were tantamount to elections throughout the South—to white voters. Blacks who did try to vote faced having the Ku Klux Klan burn crosses on their lawns, if not being lynched. Indeed, "strange fruit" hung from many Southern trees during this period.

Racial segregation became a legal fact of life in the region, from public drinking fountains to public schools. The U.S. Supreme Court ratified the scheme in its 1896 *Plessy v. Ferguson* decision, declaring "separate but equal" public schools to be constitutional. Black schools in the South were hardly equal, but they surely were separate.

LINTHEADS & BRIGHT LEAF   Economically, the Carolinas and Georgia changed drastically during the 1880s. With slaves turned into sharecroppers and tenant farmers, the region went back to growing cotton after the Civil War—so much of it that the price dropped drastically. Taking advantage of the cheap raw material and free power provided by rushing rivers, enterprising industrialists soon built cotton mills throughout the Piedmont area. Instead of scratching a living out of their hardscrabble land, the Piedmont's farmers flocked to the new factory jobs. These low-paid workers, who worked long hours and included many women and children, became known pejoratively as "lintheads." But at long last, the region had the textile industry that John C. Calhoun had dreamed of.

The Civil War ended for General Sherman's troops at Durham, the heart of North Carolina's tobacco-producing region. The soldiers took home a taste for the smooth-tasting Bright Leaf (the result of a curing process discovered when a slave accidentally overheated a tobacco barn in 1839). Smokers had to roll their own in those days, but the invention of the cigarette-rolling machine in 1881 changed all that. Cigarette factories soon dotted central North Carolina, making fortunes for men such as James B. Duke and R. J. Reynolds.

The Piedmont rivers also powered new furniture factories, especially in North Carolina and northern Georgia.

SITTING-IN AT LUNCH COUNTERS   For the first half of the 20th century, whites were firmly in control in the Carolinas and Georgia. The Democratic Party reigned supreme, and racial segregation was a way of life. For the most part, politics in the three states followed the old Low Country, Up Country split, but with the Piedmont's wealthy industrialists playing an increasingly important role.

From the beginning, the textile-mill owners fought any effort to unionize their predominately white workers, often threatening to replace them with blacks if they voted to join a union. In 1934, Georgia Gov. Eugene Talmadge went so far as to call out the state's National Guard to put down a strike. To this day, the Carolinas and Georgia are antiunion, "right to work" states.

The state legislatures tended to switch between progressive and conservative Democrats, often following hard-fought primary campaigns. The favorite progressive platform called for increased spending for public education. North

Carolina built some 1,100 public schools between 1901 and 1904. But as late as 1942, conservative Governor Talmadge of Georgia claimed that "education ain't never taught a man to plant cotton" (or to mill it, some would say). Accordingly, the three states lagged far behind the nation in education. (To their credit, however, the industrialists did contribute to the region's institutions of higher learning; tobacco interests turned little Trinity College in Durham, North Carolina, into prestigious Duke University.)

Even after the U.S Supreme Court declared in its 1954 *Brown v. Board of Education* decision that segregated public schools were unconstitutional, division of the races continued. Nearly 10 years went by before the first black student enrolled in a South Carolina public school.

But all that began to change with the advent of the civil-rights movement. In 1960, black college students in Greensboro, North Carolina, held the first sit-in at a Woolworth lunch counter. This action launched similar protests across the region. Unlike the violent scenes that erupted in Alabama and Mississippi, most civil-rights demonstrations in the Carolinas and Georgia were peaceful. One exception was a 1962 rock-throwing incident in Albany, Georgia (a demonstration that set the precedent for the later protests of Dr. Martin Luther King, Jr.). Another exception occurred in 1968, when state police opened fire on black students at a bowling alley in Orangeburg, South Carolina.

Although the law was strenuously opposed by powerful U.S. Senators Richard B. Russell of Georgia, Strom Thurmond of South Carolina, and Sam J. Ervin, Jr. of North Carolina, Congress enacted the Voting Rights Act in 1965. No other result of the civil-rights movement has changed the South more. Today, blacks represent several Carolina and Georgia districts in the U.S. House of Representatives; others hold many seats in the state legislatures; and African-American local officials number in the hundreds.

In 1966, Georgia Democrats nominated for governor a man named Lester Maddox, who had waved an ax handle to keep civil-rights protesters out of his whites-only Atlanta restaurant. His Republican opponent actually won a plurality, but the Democratic legislature put Maddox in office. Four years later, a peanut farmer from Plains, Georgia courted Maddox's segregationist voters, but at his inauguration as governor in 1971, Jimmy Carter promised to end the racial divide. In 1976, Carter became the first Georgian, and the first Southerner since before the Civil War, to be elected president of the United States.

The 1980s and 1990s saw many changes in the region. High-tech and other modern industries set up shop, especially in the Raleigh-Durham area in North Carolina, along the I-85 corridor in South Carolina, and in the burgeoning Atlanta suburbs. With them came a migration of people from the North, many bringing Republican leanings. Today, the Carolinas and Georgia are politically competitive, usually voting Republican in presidential elections but splitting their votes at the statehouse level. The old one-party South is a thing of the past.

As the South has moved into the 21st century, more and more urban planners have noted some astonishing trends. For example, since 1970 the suburbs around Atlanta have expanded dramatically and produced entire centers of population. The city of Atlanta, however, has grown less densely populated. At the end of the 20th century, the 10-county region around Atlanta grew by nearly 100,000 people, the second largest annual population increase in its history. But the city of Atlanta itself grew by only 900 people.

Like many other people around the country who live in burgeoning sub-urbs, some Southerners are embracing the tenets of New Urbanism, asking themselves if they want to continue living in communities built around the automobile. As a result, a small number of people have begun to move back to the center of major cities. Still, the rush to the suburbs in most Southern cities continues unabated. It is estimated, for example, that by the year 2025 another one million people will live in Greater Atlanta. Most of these, it is predicted, will reside in the suburbs and, by necessity, will be driving cars.

2 Southern Living Today

C. Vann Woodward, often called America's greatest living historian, prefers to name the millennium South "the Second Reconstruction." He noted, "Now Yankees are coming South; rural life is diminishing; urbanization—all those things have happened. Let's call it the 'Bulldozer Revolution.' It continues, but I don't think it has demolished the South."

This fast-growing region remains one of the most changing and versatile in the country, and yet it still evokes stereotypes, caricatures, and images, some of them still there to be seen: corrupt potbellied sheriffs, crooked Southern Judges, country politicians, demure belles, and hell-raisin' preachers. But it would be wrong to confuse the South with its caricatures or to fail to understand how rapidly the states of North Carolina, South Carolina, and Georgia are chang-ing. Believe it or not, all Southerners do not eat grits, listen to country music, vote with the religious right, or have a crazy aunt or a football-playing brother with three first names.

The New South is meeting resistance, however. In some respects, the battles of the South no longer center on the age-old conflicts between blacks and whites. As if establishing a last stand in the Old South, the right wing of the Republican Party and the religious right are engaging in a cultural war. Rather bizarrely, homosexuality is often the issue today that provokes the most moral outrage, with Southern preachers ranting against it as a "sin against God," whereas more progressive elements in the South (sometimes from the pulpit but more often from the business world) preach tolerance and understanding, with respect for individual rights regardless of sexual preference.

A dramatic case highlighting this occurred in September 2000 when the Atlanta Gas Light Company, one of the biggest utilities in the South, announced that it would be offering domestic partner benefits as an option for its employees, including same-sex couples. The company said that it was inau-gurating this change in its policy in order to attract the brightest and best employees in the future. Georgia Equality Project, the statewide gay political group, immediately hailed the move as a major breakthrough.

GEP is continuing to target other major companies in the state to offer the same benefits, and some of these companies are responding. But in other cases, the proposal is met with a "wall of silence." For the GEP, it's an uphill fight.

On the other hand, the New South has prevailed in other areas. Witness the recent removal of the Confederate flag from the dome of the South Carolina State Capitol. It had been flying since 1962, when it was raised in honor of the 100-year anniversary of the Civil War; in the ensuing years, repeated calls to remove it were rejected. This time, it was a fight to the finish: Election-year presidential hopefuls and media pundits from all over the globe weighed in, and 50,000 protesters marched in Columbia on Martin Luther King's birthday. In the glare of the national spotlight, the opposition agreed to a compromise solution. On July 1, 2000, the flag went down, only to have a shiny replica—said to be more "accurate" than the one that had flown for 38 years—hoisted on a 30-foot pole in front of the Capitol.

Cultural conflicts seem to be inevitable, given the rate of growth and the population shift. The South can boast the fastest-expanding economy in the industrialized world. Each day, the ever-changing population, attracted to the tri-state region by industry and technology, grows larger, wealthier, and better educated. Today, instead of magnolia-lined plantations or outhouse-dotted backwoods, you see a soccer-mom subculture in the southern suburbs of Atlanta and Charlotte, complete with minivans, malls, glass office towers, well-manicured subdivisions, and traffic jams. You'd think that you were in a suburb of Cleveland. Some tourist areas, such as Hilton Head, are flourishing and are filled with Northern transplants.

By contrast, income and population in "Black Belt" counties are shrinking. Ironically, the South also contains some of America's poorest regions, the home of millions who are mired in ignorance and poverty. The *Tobacco Road* image lingers in remote counties where young people often grow up but don't stick around. Problems are on the horizon, as automation and global trade promise to wipe out many of the remaining rural textile jobs. Welfare reform will eliminate the money needed to keep some small towns alive.

But there is reason for optimism and hope here, too. From elegant ballets to symphonies set in the refurbished concert halls of days gone by, Southern tradition is being redefined. Yes, a slow-paced way of life still holds in many small towns, but the cities of the New South are on the move. People have flocked to the cities from all areas of the world—Northerners seeking a milder climate; rural Southerners bored with small-town life; African Americans overcoming years of segregation; Asian immigrants seeking a new life in America; and gays and lesbians, who finally can taste liberation in a region where they were once shunned or which they once fled to escape the prevailing prejudices. People from all these diverse cultures can be seen sipping espresso in coffee shops, reading the *Wall Street Journal* on street corners, and turning once-lethargic areas into fast-paced international business complexes.

But time simply can't take away from the true Southerner his small pleasures: fresh-picked butter beans in the summer, crisp iced tea in the afternoon, a Saturday-morning golf game, sunset cocktails on the porch, church on Sunday, and a generally prevailing politeness and civility. Scarlett O'Hara would be proud that Atlanta has grown into one of the strongest industrial capitals in the world. As the home of some of the best-known companies in the nation (including Coca-Cola, BellSouth, and Delta Air Lines), the city has become a transportation hub and has been highly praised for its capability to adapt to a rapidly changing environment. Hartsfield International Airport is now the third-largest in the country and is internationally friendly.

From Savannah to Charlotte, Southern cities are sprucing up and replacing eyesores with colorful floral gardens and newly designed roadways. Visitors no longer have to restrict themselves to a strictly Southern cuisine, as world-class food marts and restaurants are springing up all across the tri-state area. The land of hospitality has opened its arms even wider.

BUT IS IT STILL THE BIBLE BELT? Despite the impression that many Northerners have about Bible-thumping Southerners, religion is no longer the powerful force that it was before World War II. Adherence to religion (read *Christianity*) often falls along generational lines, and plenty of church-going Southerners have little in common with the Southern Baptist Bible-thumping faction. Thousands of others prefer to spend Sunday morning in bed, rather than listen to a fire-and-brimstone sermon delivered in a church that's always too cold in winter or too hot in summer.

In the 1990s, politics has also split members of the Christian faith. Some people, ardently opposed to abortion and homosexuality, pursue a right-wing Pat Robertson agenda. Other, more tolerant members feel that Christians should return to their traditional role of caring for the needy and supporting humanitarian causes, not political candidates.

America's greatest female photographer, Margaret Bourke-White, who was once married to Erskine Caldwell (author of *Tobacco Road*), traveled throughout the South in 1936, photographing the land and its people. One of her most memorable photographs (taken in Hull, Georgia) shows a crude sign against a backdrop of weather-beaten, unpainted, rickety wooden buildings. The sign reads LOOK NOW IS THE DAY OF SALVATION. Along the backroads of the Deep South, you can still see signs like that one (or the one that reads GOD'S LAST NAME AIN'T DAMN), but chances are that they've been replaced by advertisements for Dr. Pepper.

3 What's Cookin' in Dixie

A Southern-style breakfast may consist of the following: homemade biscuits, country (very salty) ham, red-eye gravy, and grits swimming in butter. If a fellow were still hungry, he might cook up some Jimmy Dean sausage, toss a few buckwheat pancakes with cane syrup (or molasses), and fry a mess o' eggs with the yolk cooked hard. Healthy? Hardly. But it's also easy to eat very well indeed in the South, given the region's bounty of local vegetables and fruits, farm-raised meats, and fresh-off-the-boat seafood.

Southern cuisine is a blend of the Old World (meaning Europe) and the New World (meaning North America). Necessity forced early settlers to find ways to integrate New World foods, like wild turkey and corn, into their bland diet of dumplings and boiled chicken. Many of the most important elements of the cuisine came from the African slaves, who championed such exotica as okra and peanuts, and who turned the vitamin-rich black-eyed peas used by plantation owners to fertilize fields into a Southern classic. These influences came together to create Southern cuisine, an amalgam that embraces such favorites as sweet-potato pie, pecan pie, buttermilk biscuits, sweetened iced tea, long-cooked greens, creek shrimp, fried green tomatoes, pan gravy, and peanuts (preferably boiled). Eating in the South is as much about community as it is about food: Southerners love their hopping John and grits, but most of all, Southerners love setting a table and breaking bread with friends and family.

Virtual culinary wars have broken out over how to make **Southern fried chicken.** Even Colonel Sanders once denounced the way that his chain franchise fried chicken. In the old days, when company was coming, Ma Kettle would rush out into the backyard, grab a chicken, wring its neck, defeather it, and slice it up, tossing the entrails to the hound dogs. She then fried it in lard, sizzling-hot but not smoking. One old-time cook who had a reputation for serving the best fried chicken in Georgia confided that her secret was bacon grease and a heavy black skillet that was 50 years old. "Somehow, that skillet mysteriously flavors my chicken," she told us. "The skillet was given to me by my mother, who'd gotten it from her mother. None of us ever washed that skillet."

The Real Thing

Some would claim that the drink of the South is Coca-Cola, which one Yankee food critic claimed was "Atlanta's only contribution to world gastronomy." It was created in Atlanta in 1886, in a kettle in the backyard of a local pharmacist, John Pemberton. Although some diehard Southerners prefer Dr. Pepper, Coca-Cola is doing just fine, with 2 billion ounces of the beverage being consumed daily in more than 140 countries.

Five years later, another pharmacist, Asa Candler, purchased the rights to Pemberton's drink for $2,300—rights that his family sold in 1919 for $25 million. That's a lot of money even today, but back in 1919, it was a staggering amount. What helped give the drink an initial boost on the market was the added ingredient of cocaine, which caused some people to want to drink a *lot* of Coke. (After 1905, cocaine disappeared from the recipe.)

Many North Carolinians would argue that Pepsi-Cola is the drink of the South, especially those who grew up in the eastern lowlands around New Bern, where in the 1890s, yet another inventive pharmacist, C. D. Bradham, concocted a sweeter version of cola. Today, old-timers like to swill Pepsi out of a cold bottle with a few fried peanuts thrown into the bottom, for a sweet-and-salty kick.

If you travel the hidden back roads of the tri-state area, you can still find a granny cooking country delicacies. To enjoy these offerings, you have to have been born in Dixie "one frosty morn." The most famous dish she's likely to offer is **chitlins** (chitterlings). This backwoods plate is more for Rhett Butler than for faint-hearted Melanie. These pig intestines are turned inside-out and then braised, boiled, and deep-fried to a crispy brown. **Crackling bread** is cornbread with crispy leftovers from the renderings of pork fat at slaughter time. Granny is also the one smelling up the house cooking **collard greens,** prepared the long-simmered way and seasoned with ham hocks.

Brunswick stew, which is similar to Kentucky burgoo, often accompanies barbecue at down-home eateries in the South. Classic recipes call for squirrel, but chicken is usually used today, along with chunks of pork or fatback and lots of vegetables.

What lobster is to Maine, **catfish** is to the Southern palate. Fried catfish and **hush puppies** reign supreme. With a sweet, mild flavor and a firm texture, catfish (now commercially raised in ponds) is one of the most delectable of freshwater fish, despite its ugly appearance. The traditional way to cook it is in grease—a whole lot of grease. Cooks today, having been warned about the health dangers of eating so much fat, have created entire cookbooks about more delicate ways to cook catfish, serving it with such dainty preparations as lime-and-mustard sauce.

Low Country specialties in the Charleston area include such dishes as **shrimp 'n grits** and **she-crab soup. Oyster roasts** are popular in the late fall, when the bivalves grow big and plump. **Confederate bean soup** is made with onion, celery, bacon, sausage, ham stock, brown sugar, baked beans, and heavy cream. "No wonder our boys in gray lost the war," one diner told us.

In a bow to Southern heritage, **wild game** is featured on many a menu. Around October or November, hunters in the South, dressed in blaze orange, set out in the forests to kill deer. The venison may be eaten right away or frozen for later use in the winter, when a steak might appear on your plate with grits and gravy. In the Carolinas, quail sautéed in butter is a tasty delicacy. More modern cooks season it with wine or sherry. Wild duck—brought down by hunters in blinds on the scenic coastal marshes—may be roasted and stuffed with potato-and-apple dressing (winning such noted gourmands as former President Clinton).

Eventually, all talk of Southern cooking comes down to **barbecue.** People in Georgia, for example, have strong opinions about the barbecue that they're served in North Carolina—and take our word for it, those views are never favorable. On the other hand, what Carolinians think about Georgia barbecue is best left unprinted. Unlike Texans, who prefer beef-based barbecue, Southern barbecue artists prefer a slab of pork ribs or pork shoulders. If you use beef brisket or lamb, members of your dinner party might get up and excuse themselves, never to darken your door again.

Some cooks slow-roast the pork shoulder for 12 hours or so. Traditionalists prefer smoking it with hickory wood, although some use charcoal. No one agrees on the sauce. Will it be a pepper-and-vinegar sauce (eastern North Carolina), a pepper, vinegar, and catsup sauce (western North Carolina), or a sweet mustard sauce (South Carolina)? Surely barbecue—regardless of how it's made—has entered Dixie's Hall of Culinary Fame.

In summer, the fruit pickings are plenty, with local **strawberries, blueberries, cantaloupes,** and **plums** ripening at dusty farm stands. Georgia **peaches** are legendarily sweet and fragrant. The melon of choice is the **watermelon.** You'll find the best ones in your own garden or a farm stand. Test for ripeness by giving the melon the thump test (it should have a hollow reverberation), then take the watermelon out on your back porch and slice it. Southerners bring salt shakers to a melonfest. No utensils should be used in eating the melon—only hands and mouth. Southerners suggest that you merely spit out the seeds that you encounter.

One piece of advice comes from Patsy Winton, who calls herself "South Carolina's literary sweetheart," even though her romantic purple poetry has never been published. She gave us this tip on eating watermelon: "Be sure to remove your shoes before you begin slurping, smacking, and finger-licking. No use to ruin a good pair of shoes. Whatever you do, don't scoop the delicious red flesh out with a melon baller. That will get you kicked out of the best Southern homes and invited never to return. Southern tradition must be maintained at all costs."

The most typical of all Southern dishes—and the hardest to come by these days—is **potlikker,** the tasty water left in the pot after the greens, beans, or whatever have been long-cooked, usually in the company of bacon grease, a ham hock, or fatback. Potlikker sounds like something from an old "Hee Haw" routine, with Grandpa Jones smacking his lips, but it's delicious.

Many Southerners point with pride to the fact that you can get continental dishes, French-influenced cuisine, and sushi throughout the South today. But visitors to the region deliberately seek out down-home Southern food—and, unfortunately, it's harder to come by than ever. You *can* find Old South cooking, however, by visiting a Southern bookstore. Look for any cookbook published by a local civic or church group. Sure, you'll probably find recipes that advise you to pour a can of Campbell's mushroom soup over your chicken, but you'll also discover priceless treasures of Americana. Where else can you find a good recipe for blackbird pie?

Southern food is hard to define, because books here speak in many tongues. The region embraces the Spanish flavors of Florida, the French creations of Louisiana, the African inspirations of the Deep South, the English traditions of the Atlantic seaboard, and even a dash of German in certain communities in North Carolina—and we haven't even mentioned the influence of the Native Americans.

4 Recommended Books

This region is particularly identified with its great writers, especially **Thomas Wolfe** (1900–38) of Asheville, North Carolina, and **(Mary) Flannery O'Connor** (1925–64) of Savannah, Georgia. William Faulkner, the Nobel Prize–winning Mississippi novelist, once said about Wolfe, "He tried the hardest to say the most." Wolfe's four long, hauntingly beautiful novels bespeak his realism, lyricism, and brutal views of family life in the Deep South: *Look Homeward, Angel* (1929), *Of Time and the River* (1935), *The Web and the Rock* (1939), and *You Can't Go Home Again* (1940). O'Connor explored such themes as evil, sin, and the religious outlook of the Old South in *A Good Man Is Hard to Find* (1955), *Everything That Rises Must Converge* (1965), and *The Habit of Being* (1979).

No mention of Southern writers is complete without reference to Georgia's own **Carson McCullers,** whose *The Heart Is a Lonely Hunter* was cited in 1998 by Modern Library as being one of the 100 best novels of the 20th century. Her *Member of the Wedding* became a Broadway play, and Elizabeth Taylor portrayed the heroine in the film version of *Reflections in a Golden Eye.* McCullers wrote a strange, powerful kind of fiction—tender and grotesque at the same time, and peopled by characters who always bore some mark of psychic or environmental deformity. All these titles are still in print.

The late **Charles Kuralt,** another famous North Carolinian, was an Emmy Award–winning journalist known for his insightful yet folksy "On the Road" books and TV reports about America's heritage, and for his nationally broadcast CBS News show *Sunday Morning with Charles Kuralt.* He made the bestseller list in 1996 with *Charles Kuralt's America.*

Need we remind you that there's no better introduction to the story of the antebellum South, the Civil War, and the early years of Reconstruction than **Margaret Mitchell**'s classic *Gone With the Wind?*

OTHER FICTION

Ansa, Tina McElroy. *Ugly Ways* (Orlando: Harcourt Brace, 1995). One of the major breakthroughs in African-American literature was the publication of this novel by a St. Simons Island writer. It was named the *Blackboard* African-American Book of the Year. The novel challenged the stereotypical image of the African-American mother as a superwoman of unlimited compassion and wisdom.

Price, Reynolds. *The Promise of Rest* (New York: Knopf, 1995). Price, one of the most sensitive writers of the South, tells the story of a young man with AIDS who has come home to his parents' house to die. The book concludes a trilogy about the Kendal-Mayfield clan that began 15 years ago. Price himself has been diagnosed with spinal cancer, and this remarkable book shows his continued dedication to writing.

Frazer, Charles. *Cold Mountain* (New York: Atlanta Monthly Press, 1997). Hailed as the best Civil War novel since Michael Shaara's *The Killer Angels,* this novel (after you finally work your way through the long, dull opening) is spare and eloquent. It evokes a portrait of Inman, a soldier returning home from war across a devastated landscape. Based on local history and family stories passed down by the author's great-great grandfather, it is also an evocative love story. Frazer received the National Book Award in 1997.

Allison, Dorothy. *Bastard Out of Carolina* (New York: Penguin/Plume, 1993). Set in Greenville County, South Carolina, this is the tale of an illegitimate girl growing up in the wrong era to be illegitimate. It evokes memories of Southern Gothic writing: hard-hitting, effective, and written in tough, terse prose in the style of Carson McCullers and Truman Capote. Allison's latest work, *Cavedweller* (New York: E.P. Dutton, 1998) details the life of a woman determined to give her children the good life in spite of their deadbeat father. The book is set in Cairo, Georgia.

Sparks, Nicholas. *The Notebook* (New York: WarnerVision, 1996). This novel, which evokes the coastal Carolinas, is a *Great Gatsby*–like tale of post–World War II love set in New Bern, North Carolina, just inland from the Outer Banks.

Dodd, Susan. *The Mourner's Bench* (New York: William Morrow, 1998). It takes place on the Albemarle Sound and is very much in the genre of Reynolds Price of North Carolina. The story of a long-lost love, the book brings together the memories of two women who have different voices, the sharp New England Yankee accent contrasting with the molasses-thick Southern drawl.

BIOGRAPHY

Goldberg, Robert, and Jay Gerald. *Citizen Turner: The Wild Rise of An American Tycoon* (Orlando: Harcourt Brace, 1995). This controversial book was written by a father-and-son team. The title is a takeoff on the Orson Welles movie *Citizen Kane*. In it, we learn that launching Cable News Network almost ruined Ted Turner financially and that he cheated on his first two wives. The book explodes some of Turner's favorite myths about himself—for example, that he was a poor underdog when in fact, he grew up rich.

Stump, Al. *Cobb* (Algonquin Books, 1994). The press hailed this book as being the story of a "psychotic at the bat." Ty Cobb, a good ol' Georgia boy, died of cancer in 1961, at the age of 74. According to this insider's biography, he viewed both his life and baseball as being a "blood sport." Cobb's 24-year major-league career began in 1905.

Wilder, Effie Leland. *Out to Pasture (But Not Over the Hill)* (Atlanta: Peachtree Publishers, 1995). At 85, "Miss Effie" published her first novel, a lighthearted but poignant story of growing old in a Southern retirement home.

COOKBOOKS

Junior League of Charleston. *Charleston Receipts* (Junior League of Charleston, South Carolina, 1950). The Grand Old Lady of Junior League cookbooks, now in its 29th printing, can be found on every Charleston cook's kitchen shelf. Its longevity has as much to do with the time-tested recipes as with its Old South appeal. "Receipts"—or recipes—include creamy she-crab soup, okra pilau, benne brittle, and five different versions of shrimp pie.

Bill Neal. *Southern Cooking* (Chapel Hill: University of North Carolina Press, 1985) and *Biscuits, Spoonbread, and Sweet Potato Pie: 300 recipes that celebrate the glories of Southern baking* (New York: Knopf, 1990). As much a social historian as a celebrated cook, the late Bill Neal elevated such standards as shrimp and grits and fish muddle to culinary heights in his too-short lifetime.

Paula Deen. *Lady and Sons Savannah Country Cookbook* (New York: Random House, 1998). This book is already a standard, having sold more than 200,000 copies in just 2 years. Now, with the newly released *Lady and Sons Too,* Paula Deen is confirming her place as Savannah's most heralded cook. Check out the real thing—savory Southern classics, from cheese biscuits to fried chicken to collards—at Deen's popular Savannah restaurant, Lady and Sons.

GENERAL

Berendt, John. *Midnight in the Garden of Good and Evil* (New York: Random House, 1994). This is the book that put Savannah on the tourist map—with a little help from Forrest Gump. Characters such as the Lady Chablis (a wickedly funny black drag queen) and Danny Hansford (a hustler) are introduced in this brilliantly conceived and seductive story of murder (or was it self-defense?) in the steamy Old South. It has been called both a travel book and a murder mystery. Berendt's book—called "The Book" in Savannah—seems to have acquired squatter's rights on best-seller lists, but the sappy movie of the same title, directed by Clint Eastwood, didn't fare as well with viewers.

White, Baily. *Mama Makes Up Her Mind* (New York: Vintage, 1994). The best-yet depiction of life in a small Georgia town, this book made the best-seller list of the *New York Times Book Review.*

HISTORY

Gragg, Rod. *Covered with Glory: the 26th North Carolina Infantry at Gettysburg* (New York: HarperCollins, 2000). This Carolina infantry marched toward Gettysburg with 843 officers and troops, which were reduced in two days to 156 men. This was the highest casualty of any Civil War regiment, and here is their story. This book puts a human face on a tragic war.

Kennett, Lee. *Marching Through Georgia* (New York: HarperCollins, 1995). Gen. William Tecumseh Sherman pledged "to make a trail that would be visible for 50 years"—250 miles long and 60 miles wide, from Atlanta to Savannah. This carefully researched book, the story of both soldiers and civilians, tells how he did it.

Shaara, Jeff. *Gods and Generals* (New York: Ballantine, 1998). Jeff Shaara has completed the sequel to the 1984 Pulitzer Prize-winning work, *The Killer Angels,* written by his late father, Michael. The younger Shaara's book complements his father's work on the Battle of Gettysburg by turning back the clock and portraying the days leading up to the epic battle. It accurately depicts two sides, both of which felt that they were right and were prepared to die to defend their beliefs. Unfortunately, most of them did.

Butler, Lindley. *Pirates, Privateers, and Rebel Raiders of the North Carolina Coast* (University of North Carolina, 2000). A tale of the region's rascals, this saga paints eight compelling sketches of the rogues and Confederate ship captains who operated in North Carolina's coastal waters. Even Blackbeard springs to life along with 1812 commerce raiders, and most definitely Confederate commerce raiders operating out of the port of Wilmington.

Appendix B:
Useful Toll-Free Numbers & Web Sites

AIRLINES

Air Canada
☎ 800/247-2262
www.aircanada.ca

American Airlines
☎ 800/433-7300
www.aa.com

America West Airlines
☎ 800/23-9292
www.americawest.com

British Airways
☎ 800/247-9297
☎ 0345/222-111 in Britain
www.british-airways.com

Canadian Airlines International
☎ 800/426-7000
www.cdnair.ca

Continental Airlines
☎ 800/525-0280
www.flycontinental.com

Delta Air Lines
☎ 800/221-1212
www.delta.com

Japan Airlines
☎ 800/525-3663
www.japanair.com

KLM
☎ 800/374-7747
www.klm.nl

Lufthansa
☎ 800/645-3880
www.lufthansa-usa.com

Midway Airlines
☎ 800/446-4392
www.midwayair.com

Northwest Airlines
☎ 800/225-2525
www.nwa.com

Swissair
☎ 800/221-4750
www.swissair.com

Trans World Airlines (TWA)
☎ 800/221-2000
www.twa.com

United Airlines
☎ 800/241-6522
www.ual.com

US Airways
☎ 800/428-4322
www.usairways.com

Virgin Atlantic Airways
☎ 800/862-8621 in
  Continental U.S.
☎ 0293/747-747 in Britain
www.fly.virgin.com

CAR RENTAL AGENCIES

Advantage
☎ 800/777-5500
www.arac.com

Alamo
☎ 800/327-9633
www.goalamo.com

Avis
☎ 800/331-1212 in Continental U.S.
☎ 800/TRY-AVIS in Canada
www.avis.com

Budget
☎ 800/527-0700
www.budgetrentacar.com

Dollar
☎ 800/800-4000
www.dollarcar.com

Enterprise
☎ 800/325-8007
www.pickenterprise.com

Hertz
☎ 800/654-3131
www.hertz.com

Kemwel Holiday Auto (KHA)
☎ 800/678-0678
www.kemwel.com

National
☎ 800/CAR-RENT
www.nationalcar.com

Payless
☎ 800/PAYLESS
www.paylesscar.com

Rent-A-Wreck
☎ 800/535-1391
www.rent-a-wreck.com

Thrifty
☎ 800/367-2277
www.thrifty.com

Value
☎ 800/327-2501
www.go-value.com

MAJOR HOTEL & MOTEL CHAINS

Best Western International
☎ 800/528-1234
www.bestwestern.com

Clarion Hotels
☎ 800/CLARION
www.hotelchoice.com/cgi-bin/res/webres?clarion.html

Comfort Inns
☎ 800/228-5150
www.hotelchoice.com/cgi-bin/res/webres?comfort.html

Courtyard by Marriott
☎ 800/321-2211
www.courtyard.com

Days Inn
☎ 800/325-2525
www.daysinn.com

Doubletree Hotels
☎ 800/222-TREE
www.doubletreehotels.com

Econo Lodges
☎ 800/55-ECONO
www.hotelchoice.com/cgi-bin/res/webres?econo.html

Fairfield Inn by Marriott
☎ 800/228-2800
www.fairfieldinn.com

Hampton Inn
☎ 800/HAMPTON
www.hampton-inn.com

Hilton Hotels
☎ 800/HILTONS
www.hilton.com

Holiday Inn
☎ 800/HOLIDAY
www.holiday-inn.com

Howard Johnson
☎ 800/654-2000
www.hojo.com/hojo.html

Hyatt Hotels & Resorts
☎ 800/228-9000
www.hyatt.com

ITT Sheraton
☎ 800/325-3535
www.sheraton.com

La Quinta Motor Inns
☎ 800/531-5900
www.laquinta.com

Marriott Hotels
☎ 800/228-9290
www.marriott.com

Motel 6
☎ 800/4-MOTEL6
(800/466-8536)
www.motel6.com

Quality Inns
☎ 800/228-5151
www.hotelchoice.com/cgi-
   bin/res/webres?quality.html

Radisson Hotels International
☎ 800/333-3333
www.radisson.com

Ramada Inns
☎ 800/2-RAMADA
www.ramada.com

Red Carpet Inns
☎ 800/251-1962

Red Lion Hotels & Inns
☎ 800/547-8010
www.travelweb.com

Red Roof Inns
☎ 800/843-7663
www.redroof.com

Residence Inn by Marriott
☎ 800/331-3131
www.residenceinn.com

Rodeway Inns
☎ 800/228-2000
www.hotelchoice.com/cgi-
   bin/res/webres?rodeway.html

Super 8 Motels
☎ 800/800-8000
www.super8motels.com

Travelodge
☎ 800/255-3050
www.travelodge.com

Vagabond Inns
☎ 800/522-1555
www.vagabondinns.com

Wyndham Hotels and Resorts
☎ 800/822-4200 in Continental
   U.S. and Canada
www.wyndham.com

Index

See also Accommodations index below.

FROMMER'S® COMPLETE TRAVEL GUIDES

Alaska
Amsterdam
Arizona
Atlanta
Australia
Austria
Bahamas
Barcelona, Madrid &
  Seville
Beijing
Belgium, Holland &
  Luxembourg
Bermuda
Boston
British Columbia & the
  Canadian Rockies
Budapest & the Best of
  Hungary
California
Canada
Cancún, Cozumel &
  the Yucatán
Cape Cod, Nantucket &
  Martha's Vineyard
Caribbean
Caribbean Cruises & Ports
  of Call
Caribbean Ports of Call
Carolinas & Georgia
Chicago
China
Colorado
Costa Rica
Denmark
Denver, Boulder & Colorado
  Springs
England
Europe

European Cruises & Ports
  of Call
Florida
France
Germany
Greece
Greek Islands
Hawaii
Hong Kong
Honolulu, Waikiki & Oahu
Ireland
Israel
Italy
Jamaica
Japan
Las Vegas
London
Los Angeles
Maryland & Delaware
Maui
Mexico
Montana & Wyoming
Montréal & Québec City
Munich & the Bavarian
  Alps
Nashville & Memphis
Nepal
New England
New Mexico
New Orleans
New York City
New Zealand
Nova Scotia, New Brunswick
  & Prince Edward Island
Oregon
Paris
Philadelphia & the
  Amish Country

Portugal
Prague & the Best of the
  Czech Republic
Provence & the Riviera
Puerto Rico
Rome
San Antonio & Austin
San Diego
San Francisco
Santa Fe, Taos & Albuquerque
Scandinavia
Scotland
Seattle & Portland
Shanghai
Singapore & Malaysia
South Africa
Southeast Asia
South Florida
South Pacific
Spain
Sweden
Switzerland
Thailand
Tokyo
Toronto
Tuscany & Umbria
USA
Utah
Vancouver & Victoria
Vermont, New Hampshire
  & Maine
Vienna & the Danube Valley
Virgin Islands
Virginia
Walt Disney World &
  Orlando
Washington, D.C.
Washington State

FROMMER'S® DOLLAR-A-DAY GUIDES

Australia from $50 a Day
California from $60 a Day
Caribbean from $70 a Day
England from $70 a Day
Europe from $70 a Day

Florida from $70 a Day
Hawaii from $70 a Day
Ireland from $60 a Day
Italy from $70 a Day
London from $85 a Day

New York from $80 a Day
Paris from $80 a Day
San Francisco from $60 a Day
Washington, D.C.,
  from $70 a Day

FROMMER'S® PORTABLE GUIDES

Acapulco, Ixtapa &
  Zihuatanejo
Alaska Cruises & Ports of Call
Bahamas
Baja & Los Cabos
Berlin
California Wine Country
Charleston & Savannah
Chicago
Dublin

Hawaii: The Big Island
Las Vegas
London
Los Angeles
Maine Coast
Maui
Miami
New Orleans
New York City
Paris

Puerto Vallarta, Manzanillo
  & Guadalajara
San Diego
San Francisco
Sydney
Tampa & St. Petersburg
Venice
Washington, D.C.

FROMMER'S® NATIONAL PARK GUIDES

Family Vacations in the
  National Parks
Grand Canyon

National Parks of the
  American West
Rocky Mountain

Yellowstone & Grand Teton
Yosemite & Sequoia/
  Kings Canyon
Zion & Bryce Canyon

FROMMER'S® MEMORABLE WALKS

Chicago
London

New York
Paris

San Francisco
Washington, D.C.

FROMMER'S® GREAT OUTDOOR GUIDES

New England
Northern California

Southern California & Baja
Southern New England

Washington & Oregon

FROMMER'S® BORN TO SHOP GUIDES

Born to Shop: France
Born to Shop: Italy

Born to Shop: London
Born to Shop: New York

Born to Shop: Paris

FROMMER'S® IRREVERENT GUIDES

Amsterdam
Boston
Chicago
Las Vegas

London
Los Angeles
Manhattan
New Orleans

Paris
San Francisco
Seattle & Portland
Vancouver

Walt Disney World
Washington, D.C.

FROMMER'S® BEST-LOVED DRIVING TOURS

America
Britain
California

Florida
France
Germany

Ireland
Italy
New England

Scotland
Spain
Western Europe

THE UNOFFICIAL GUIDES®

Bed & Breakfasts in
  California
Bed & Breakfasts in
  New England
Bed & Breakfasts in
  the Northwest
Bed & Breakfasts in
  Southeast
Beyond Disney
Branson, Missouri

California with Kids
Chicago
Cruises
Disneyland
Florida with Kids
Golf Vacations in the
  Eastern U.S.
The Great Smoky &
  Blue Ridge
  Mountains

Inside Disney
Hawaii
Las Vegas
London
Miami & the Keys
Mini Las Vegas
Mini-Mickey
New Orleans
New York City
Paris

San Francisco
Skiing in the West
Southeast with Kids
Walt Disney World
Walt Disney World
  for Grown-ups
Walt Disney World
  for Kids
Washington, D.C.

SPECIAL-INTEREST TITLES

Frommer's Britain's Best Bed & Breakfasts and
  Country Inns
Frommer's Britain's Best Bike Rides
The Civil War Trust's Official Guide
  to the Civil War Discovery Trail
Frommer's Caribbean Hideaways
Frommer's Adventure Guide to Central America
Frommer's Adventure Guide to South America
Frommer's Adventure Guide to Southeast Asia
Frommer's Food Lover's Companion to France
Frommer's Gay & Lesbian Europe
Frommer's Exploring America by RV
Hanging Out in Europe

Israel Past & Present
Mad Monks' Guide to California
Mad Monks' Guide to New York City
Frommer's The Moon
Frommer's New York City with Kids
The New York Times' Unforgettable
  Weekends
Places Rated Almanac
Retirement Places Rated
Frommer's Road Atlas Britain
Frommer's Road Atlas Europe
Frommer's Washington, D.C., with Kids
Frommer's What the Airlines Never Tell You